EDUCATING CHILDREN
WITH LEARNING
DISABILITIES

EDITED BY

Edward C. Frierson
George Peabody College
for Teachers

Walter B. Barbe
Editor, *Highlights
for Children*

EDUCATING CHILDREN WITH LEARNING DISABILITIES

Selected Readings

New York: Appleton-Century-Crofts

DIVISION OF MEREDITH CORPORATION

For his early and wide-ranging efforts in behalf of
children with learning problems,
this book is dedicated to

PAUL A. WITTY

Gentleman, Scholar and Friend

PREFACE

THE ESSENTIAL CONCERN of this book is the child who needs special educational attention but does not meet the generally accepted criteria for consideration as mentally retarded, emotionally disturbed, visually handicapped, or severely speech- and hearing-impaired. The selections provide a systematic introduction and guide to a more intensive study of special learning disabilities in children. Often the child with special learning disabilities has learning needs and problems similar to those of children classified in other categories, but just as often he has problems, unique to his special deficit, which may be a perceptual, neurological, biochemical, or other specific disorder.

The organization of this book should appeal to the general educator as well as to the clinical specialist or college instructor. Sections are arranged for sequential study, yet the presentation of each group of articles allows them to be considered individually. Thus, the book could serve equally well as the basis for study of a particular aspect of learning disabilities by a workshop or seminar group, for casual reading by the layman, for professional growth by the experienced teacher, as a basic text in a learning disability course, or as a significant related reading for general teacher education courses. Briefly the plan of the book is as follows:

Part I presents an overview emphasizing the evolution of interest in special learning disabilities, an introduction to neurological, language, and behavior problems, and a review of the significant role attributed to brain dysfunction.

Part II introduces the reader to multidisciplinary thinking by presenting the views of special educators, psychologists, remedial specialists, social workers, neurologists, psychiatrists, and pediatricians. This part prepares the reader for the subsequent sections on diagnosis and remediation.

Part III begins with a consideration of general problems in diagnostic work, and proceeds to diagnostic problems specific to the learning disabilities issue, including linguistic measurement and the validity of tests of brain damage. Diagnostic strategies directed toward learning disorders are discussed, and an entire section is devoted to diagnosis of school learning disabilities.

Part IV analyzes some of the theoretical and empirical models upon which many remedial procedures are based. Special procedures are presented as well as an entire section directed toward remediation in the basic school subjects of reading, spelling, and arithmetic.

A glossary of learning disability terms has been developed for inclusion in this book. Definitions and examples have been drawn from original sources and modified so as to be more easily employed by the nonprofessional reader.

The editors are fully aware of the controversies which prevail in the new field of special learning disabilities. An effort has been made, therefore, to present points of view which are provocative and representative even though these views are contradictory. We hope the result is a stimulating collection that will open the door for further study.

The Author Index includes the names of nearly every person who has helped draw attention to special learning disabilities in children. That these leaders occasionally support conflicting theories and procedures is to be expected. Sincere appreciation is expressed to the authors and publishers who gave us permission to reprint their material in this book. A willingness to have one's views presented in a wide-ranging collection is itself evidence of the importance that leaders attribute to the practice of critique and evaluation of ideas.

Special thanks are due to the people whose assistance in the preparation of this manuscript has been invaluable. Mrs. Margaret Betzhold skillfully handled the many problems of obtaining permissions and channeling correspondence. Mrs. Judith Dzur and Mrs. Marge Hook carefully prepared articles and introductions, while Dr. Barbara Hauck of the University of Washington aided considerably in the collection of original materials. We are deeply grateful for the continuous encouragement and special assistance provided by Bettye Frierson and Marilyn Barbe. Their support insured the successful completion of this project. The final product has been influenced by the constructive judgments of many professional educators, and also by the critical observations of students and laymen whose continuing desire for clarity and validity is exceeded only by our own.

E.C.F.
W.B.B.

CONTENTS

I

INTRODUCTION TO LEARNING DISORDERS

INTRODUCTION

T HE TERM "learning disorders" has become an umbrella term under which hunch-labels and scientific hypotheses have huddled together. So diverse are the applications of the term that it has lost its initial capacity to convey a clear, concise concept. In spite of this definition problem, significant progress is being made toward understanding and teaching children with specific learning problems.

Children with learning problems are called brain-injured, neurologically impaired, emotionally disturbed, or are described as hyperkinetic, educationally retarded, immature, perceptually handicapped, or dyslexic. When faced with a child who has a learning problem, one has a natural inclination to label not only the type of problem, but also the child. In too many instances, hunches, or hypotheses, for all their eloquence and seeming logic, are merely educated guesses, neither supported nor disproved by sound research evidence.

TWO POINTS OF VIEW

Two general approaches toward understanding learning problems are prevalent today. The first approach is cause-oriented. The second is an effect-oriented approach. Those who look at learning disorders from the first perspective attempt to identify the source or etiology of observed behaviors. Those who take the second approach are primarily concerned with analyzing, describing and modifying observed behaviors regardless of underlying causes. A pediatric neurologist might locate damaged or impaired nerve centers by observing carefully specified behaviors, but he may not know how such impairment is affecting the reading ability of his patient. The remedial educator might determine the best way to stimulate reading improvement in a child without knowing which nerve centers, if any, are

3

not functioning properly. Therefore, the pediatric neurologist might refer to a youngster as neurologically impaired whether or not the child had school learning problems. The educator might refer to a youngster as a disabled reader whether or not the child has known neurological impairment.

The distinction between cause and effect orientation is readily apparent. Etiological terms include such phrases as minimal cerebral dysfunction, organic brain damage, and organic behavior disorder. Examples of effect terms are hyperkinetic syndrome, specific reading disability, and perceptual handicap. Clinicians generally prefer the etiological description while school personnel usually favor terms associated with school learning abilities.

DEFINING "LEARNING DISORDERS"

Resolution of the definition problem will come from organizations such as the Council for Exceptional Children (C.E.C.), the American Psychological Association (A.P.A.), and the American Medical Association (A.M.A.). However, it may be anticipated that each organization will initially favor terms related to the organization's emphasis. The C.E.C., for example, might tend to establish a new category of "exceptional" child. The A.P.A. might choose a behavioral syndrome approach, while the A.M.A. would assuredly try to isolate and label a pathological condition in the central nervous system. Each organization in its own way would be right.

Clearer communication among disciplines would result from the adoption of terms having mutually accepted usage. The following suggestion is offered:

> *Learning disorder* might best designate a known impairment in the nervous system. The impairment may be the result of genetic variation, biochemical irregularity, perinatal brain insult, or injury sustained by the nervous system as a result of disease, accident, sensory deprivation, nutritional deficit, or other direct influence. *Learning disability* might best designate a demonstrated inability to perform a specific task normally found within the capability range of individuals of comparable mental ability.

The acceptance of this usage would encourage educators to describe school learning disabilities in precise, descriptive terms rather than in speculative terms. Specialists, on the other hand, could continue to infer the existence of a learning disorder based upon theoretical or experimental findings and could, in addition, demonstrate the empirical relationships which exist between known disorders and observed disabilities.

Until a common terminology is accepted, readers must carefully analyze the labels appearing in the literature. For some, the term *learning disorder* refers to all learning problems, while for others, the term is used exclusively to designate the brain-damaged child. The latter practice is unfortunate in that it leads to the type of oversimplification associated with terms such as *mentally retarded* and *emotionally disturbed*. To define a child with learning disabilities as one with brain damage ignores the many alternatives to the brain-damage hypothesis.

THE BASES OF LEARNING DISABILITIES

All learning disabilities observed in the classroom are not caused by brain damage. Likewise, all brain damage does not result in the same kinds of learning disabilities. Strauss and Lehtinen anticipated the current definition problem when they presented the following definition of a "brain-injured child" in a book about mentally defective or retarded children:

> A brain-injured child is a child who before, during, or after birth has received an injury to or suffered an infection of the brain. As a result of such organic impairment, defects of the neuromotor system may be present or absent; however, such a child may show disturbances in perception, thinking, and emotional behavior, either separately or in combination. These disturbances prevent or impede a normal learning process. (Strauss and Lehtinen, 1957, p. 4.)

In 1955, Strauss and Kephart presented a "clinical syndrome of the brain-injured child who is not mentally defective, but who, in spite of 'normalcy in IQ,' as tested is still 'defective'" (1955, p. ix). Hyperactivity, distractability, perseveration, perceptual and conceptual deficits were noted. These characteristics of "normal" but "damaged" children were seen in children throughout the country. Consequently, the "Strauss syndrome" became a diagnostic category used to explain learning disabilities rather than a behavior profile having many possible causes.

Recent attempts to incorporate the Strauss syndrome in a hierarchy of impairment indicate the continuing etiology-behavior confusion. Children classified on a continuing scale would be grouped in the following categories.

Severely brain-injured: The child is hurt so badly that he cannot move or make a sound; if he were injured one tiny bit more, he would be dead.

Moderately brain-injured: The youngster who cannot walk or talk.

Mildly brain-injured: The child who walks and talks poorly.

Strauss' syndrome: The youngster who is hyperactive, uncoordinated, unable to concentrate, and who has learning problems.

Average, with reading problems: The child who is failing in school, who cannot learn to read.

Average: [The child who achieves as expected for his age and grade.]

Above-average, with reading problems: The child who scores considerably higher in math than in reading, who has used his high intelligence to get by in school and even make good grades without
knowing how to read well.

Superior: Both physically and mentally.

Ideal: Very superior physically with genius mentally (Beck, 1964,
pp. 9-10).

An examination of the bases for learning disabilities necessitates consideration of many possibilities other than brain injury. Some of these are
discussed in the following paragraphs.

Neurological disorganization in the absence of known injury may account for learning and behavior problems. The scale used at the Institutes
for the Achievement of Human Potential presented above implies that
many differences among learners can be attributed to differences in neurological organization. Unlike the child development specialists of the past,
the Philadelphia group advocates elaborate training procedures aimed at
establishing neurological organization. The controversial procedures include
using light filters upon one eye, creeping in a prescribed manner (patterning) periodically, and rebreathing one's own breath.

The *neurological lag* or developmental hypothesis has long been popular among early childhood specialists. In educational jargon, the "immature"
first grader has often become the "late bloomer" of the junior high.

Arguing from a genetic point of view, learning disabilities may be
shown to be related to *structural deviations in the human brain.* Just as
all hands, legs, and stomachs are not alike, neither are all nervous systems.
The genetic dyslexic child (one who cannot read due to inherited traits)
is most often a boy, according to theorists. An elaborate explanation based
upon the concepts of natural selection in species survival includes the
proposition that the men who survived in the earliest human cultures were
blessed with such abilities as psychomotor control (threw spears and used
clubs accurately), spatial relations (judged distance from tiger to fire, decided whether to fight or run), and visual motor skills (dodged arrows,
raised shield). Women, prized for their appearance and child rearing abilities, evolved into more verbally-oriented individuals, developing and maintaining superior skills in fine visual-perceptual and auditory discrimination
abilities as related to gestures, coos, babbling, and later, symbolic writings.

Early in this century, Hinshelwood proposed the possibility of being
born with a *congenital defect or structural deficit* in that area of the cortex
destined to become the center for storage for visual word memories. His
books (1900, 1917) introduced the term *word blindness.* Hollingworth
pointed out that Hinshelwood's suppositions were inconsistent with facts

known to psychology (1923, p. 64). She considered *word blindness* a confusing word since she felt it was a "comparatively common thing to find some who lag considerably behind their fellows . . . in acquiring visual word memories." Hollingworth said, "I regard these slight defects as only physiological variations and not to be regarded as pathological conditions."

Mild sensory impairment contributes to learning disabilities. Poor visual acuity can contribute to slow reading. Eye muscle imbalance and problems of convergence are possible contributors toward reading difficulties. In general, however, these kinds of problems do not cause the reading problem, but rather complicate whatever reading problems are present (Campion, 1965).

Perhaps the most influential and still unclarified hypothesis concerning learning disabilities is that pertaining to *dominance* (the tendency for one hemisphere of the brain to predominate, thus causing an individual to be right-handed, right-eyed, or right-footed). So great is the confusion concerning dominance that some argue logically that being completely ambidextrous (able to do all tasks equally well with right or left hand, foot, or eye) is the highest form of neurological integration and should accompany fully developed mental abilities.

On the contrary, the stronger argument has tended to be that unless dominance is clearly established, confusion and distortion are likely to occur. Orton, a neurologist, "explained" the phenomena of mirror writing, symbol reversal, and word blindness using a confused dominance theory. Said Orton, "The nondominant hemisphere possesses images in reversed form and order." These forms require elision. In reading, for example, one must select from the dominant hemisphere those forms which are correctly oriented and in correct sequence. Thus, according to Orton, confusion or delay in selection of responses results in "twisted symbols." Orton coined the term "strephosymbolia" for this behavior (1925).

A final explanation for the existence of learning disabilities may ultimately prove to be the most precise and remediable. Increasingly, the *electrochemical activity of brain and nerve* is seen to hold the key to behavior and learning. While much is known, a great deal is yet unknown. As Eccles states, we are able to "give an account of the specific events (electrical-chemical) in the brain which are linked with specific states in the mind, but say nothing concerning the how of that linkage" (1953, p. 267). Reading failures have been explained in terms of neurophysiological functioning (Smith and Carrigan, 1959), signaling an era when educators and other specialists must know something of each other's terminology.

LEARNING DISORDERS AND BRAIN DAMAGE

An introduction to learning disorders must necessarily be broad enough in scope to offer the reader many avenues for further study. With this objective in view, the editors have not limited the consideration of learning disorders to the literature on brain damage. Brain damage is merely one of several reasons why children have learning problems. The selections chosen for this overview are likewise broad in scope, yet there is a recognition of the importance of brain damage and an awareness that important publications such as Cruickshank's *The Teacher of Brain-Injured Children* (1966) and Birch's *Brain Damage in Children* (1964) have used the term *brain damage* in a wide context in preference to the term *learning disorder*.

Brain damage and learning disorders cannot be separated any more than creative thinking and intelligence can be used as mutually exclusive terms. Gallagher (1966) has proposed a model that seems to depict accurately the evidence available. The set of children who have brain injury and the set of children with various learning problems (called perceptual problems) are not identical, yet the overlap between the two groups may be considerable.

Considering the effects of (1) developmental lags, (2) neurological impairments, (3) nutritional and chemical imbalance, (4) experiential deficits, (5) genetic variations, (6) sensory losses, (7) metabolic disorders, (8) emotional disturbances, and other potentially harmful influences upon the human system, one can only conclude that brain damage, while a prevalent cause of learning disabilities among children with "normal" measured intelligence, accounts for only a part of the learning disorders encountered. Further, it is accurate to discuss many learning disabilities in terms other than organic impairment. One cannot overlook the fact that some manifest disabilities in learning tasks are related to inappropriate education rather than to impaired learning.

References

Beck, Joan, *Unlocking the secrets of the brain* (Chicago: Chicago Tribune Magazine reprint, 1964).

Birch, H. G. (Editor), *Brain damage in children* (Baltimore: William & Wilkins, 1964).

Campion, G. S., Visual problems and reading disorders. In Flowers, *et al., Reading disorders* (Philadelphia: Davis, 1965), pp. 41-45.

Cruickshank, W. M. (Editor), *The teacher of brain-injured children* (Syracuse: Syracuse University Press, 1966).

Eccles, J. C., *The neurophysiological basis of mind* (Oxford: Clarendon Press, 1953).

Gallagher, J. J., Children with developmental imbalances: a psycho-educational definition. In W. M. Cruickshank (Editor), *The teacher of brain-injured children* (Syracuse: Syracuse University Press, 1966).

Hinshelwood, J., *Letter-, word-, and mind blindness* (London: H. K. Lewis, 1900), and *Congenital word blindness* (London: H. K. Lewis, 1917).

Hollingworth, Leta S., *Special talents and defects* (New York: Macmillan 1923).

Orton, S. T., Word blindness in school children, *Arch. Neurol. Psychiat.*, 1925, 14, 581.

Smith, D. E. P., and Carrigan, Patricia, *The nature of reading disability* (New York: Harcourt, Brace & World, 1959).

Strauss, A. A., and Kephart, N. C., *Psychopathology and education of the brain-injured child*; Vol. II, *Progress in theory and clinic* (New York: Grune & Stratton, 1955).

Strauss, A. A., and Lehtinen, Laura, *Psychopathology and education of the brain-injured child*; Vol. 1, *Fundamentals and treatment of the brain-injured child* (New York: Grune & Stratton, 1957).

SECTION A: Overview

1 LEARNING DISABILITIES—YESTERDAY, TODAY, AND TOMORROW

Barbara Bateman

The child with special learning disabilities has recently become the subject of numerous conferences and conventions, books, and articles. Interest in his problems is shared by the fields of general medicine, psychology, special education, neurology, psychiatry, and education. And above all, his problems concern his teachers, parents, and himself. Who is the child with special learning disabilities? He belongs to a category of exceptional children which, like many other categories, is easier to describe than to define. Unlike other types of exceptional children, however, he is often described in terms of characteristics he does not possess; e.g., his learning problems are not due to mental retardation, deafness, motor impairment, blindness, faulty instruction, etc. The children who do have special learning disabilities might be described by some clinicians as educationally retarded, autistic, dyslexic, perceptually handicapped, minimally brain-injured, emotionally disturbed, neurologically disorganized, dysgraphic, aphasic, interjacent, or word-blind, etc.

Remedial procedures currently recommended by some learning disability specialists include such diverse activities as psychotherapy, drugs, phonic drills, speech correction, tracing, crawling, bead stringing, trampoline exercises, orthoptic training, auditory discrimination drills, and controlled diet.

Regardless of the lack of agreement about etiology, definition, incidence, and treatment of special learning disabilities which is implicit in the various terms given above, the child with learning disabilities is perhaps best described as one who manifests an educationally significant discrep-

Reprinted from *Exceptional Children*, Vol. 31, No. 4 (December, 1964), pp. 167-177. By permission of the author and publisher.

ancy between his apparent capacity for language behavior and his actual level of language functioning.

Within this broad concept of learning disabilities, at least three major subcategories can be delineated, although there is certainly much overlap among them.

Dyslexia, or reading disability, is perhaps the most frequent of all types of learning disabilities or language disorders. Estimates of the incidence of dyslexia vary greatly, primarily as a function of the definition used. Those who distinguish "primary" dyslexia as a specific congenital syndrome find fewer cases than do those whose definition is based on a simple discrepancy between apparent capacity for reading and actual level of reading, regardless of etiological or correlated factors. A conservative estimate is that perhaps five percent to ten percent of the school population has severe enough reading problems to require special educational concern and provisions. Disabilities in other academic subject areas such as arithmetic do occur, but much less frequently.

Verbal communication disorders, or difficulties with the comprehension or expression of spoken language, have been labeled aphasic disorders in the past. But the term aphasia is now felt by many to be inappropriate. The term "verbal communication disorders" is used here to designate those children whose comprehension or expressive language problems involve the spoken word.

Visual-motor integration problems have been widely noted, often in conjunction with reading problems. But there are also children who manifest severe spatial orientation, body image, perceptual, coordination, etc., problems and who are not dyslexic.

The appearance of the medical terms dyslexia and aphasia in the categorization is more than coincidence, as physicians were the first professional group to interest themselves in problems of this nature. A parallel development occurred in mental retardation, where the pioneer educators—e.g., Itard, Seguin, Montessori, and DeCroly—were also physicians. However, as Kirk (1962, p. 30) has stated, "special education as viewed today, begins where medicine stops." Until the time of Orton and his followers, medical interest in learning disabilities had focused almost exclusively on the diagnosis and classification of these problems. Little progress was made in remedial techniques until the focus shifted away from the hereditary and cerebral-pathology correlates of learning problems. The very fact that we cannot exchange parents or repair damaged brains has led to the present-day concern of many with behavioral and symptomatic rather than pathological or etiological factors. Kleffner (1962) suggests that:

> Those who have chosen to concern themselves with the *pathology* underlying language problems have rarely been able to go beyond speculation. From this group come guesses about brain damage, cortical inhibition, hemispheric dominance, cerebral plasticity,

synaptic connections. . . . There is no practical value in guessing and speculating about the anatomic-physiologic bases. . . .

   Etiologic investigations . . . have told us little more than that such problems can occur with various etiologic backgrounds or without any significant etiologic factors being apparent. . . .

   The *behavioral* approach . . . has been more fruitful in a practical sense than approaches through pathology and etiology (pp. 106-107).

Cohn points out that the basic reason for the present lack of success in following the neurological pathology or etiological approach is the "lack of definite correlations of brain pathology with inability to learn readily, to retain the meaning of what has been learned, and to recall that which is stored" (1962, p. 34).

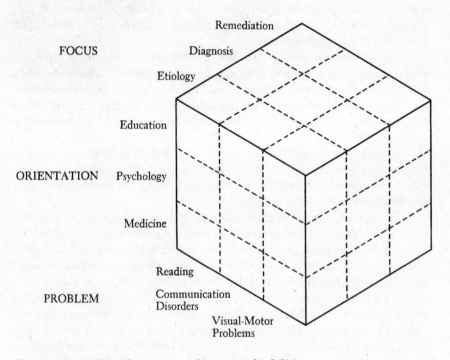

FIGURE 1-1 Three dimensions of learning disabilities.

From a practical viewpoint one might ask how the remedial specialist would proceed even if there were definite correlations between brain pathology and learning disabilities. If it were known that Johnny couldn't read because (etiology) of a lesion in the angular gyrus (pathology), the remedial reading specialist would still have to plan remediation on the basis of behavioral observations.

This is by no means suggesting that learning disability personnel can ignore the medical-neurological contributions presently offered. Drugs, for example, can sometimes facilitate the learning processes of some hyperactive children by the indirect routes of increasing attention span or decreasing distractibility. Rather than ignoring medical-neurological advances, the field of learning disabilities will do well to utilize all the help presently available and to alertly watch for future developments that promise application. In the meantime, it appears that remediation must still be planned on the basis of observed behavior.

A reasonably thorough overview of work to date in the area of learning disabilities would have to include, as an absolute minimum, a discussion of: (a) etiology or correlated factors, (b) diagnostic procedures, and (c) remedial practices in each of the areas of reading, communication disorders, and visual-motor problems. Each of these topics would be further subdivided by professional orientation—medical, psychological, and educational. Figure 1-1 suggests the dimensions that would be involved in such an undertaking. The omnipresent fourth dimension of time (past, present, and future) would also have to be superimposed on this model.

Since a complete overview as shown in Figure 1-1 would require a large volume, some of the terrain of the field today is summarized in the paragraphs that follow.

ETIOLOGY OR CORRELATED FACTORS OF LEARNING DISABILITIES

In all of education it would be difficult to find more voluminous literature than that on causes of reading disability. A large body of literature explores single factors that are believed to cause reading problems. The author wishes to acknowledge reliance on the discussion of single factor etiological theories presented by Corinne Kass (1962). These factors are often physiological and include: (a) damage to or dysfunction of certain localized areas of the brain such as the angular gyrus (Hinshelwood, 1917), second frontal gyrus (Wernicke, 1874) as reported by Penfield and Roberts (1959), connection between the cortical speech mechanism and the brain stem centrencephalic system (Penfield and Roberts, 1959), and the parietal and parietal-occipital areas (Rabinovitch, 1959); (b) hereditary or developmental lag factors such as inherited underdevelopment of directional function (Hermann, 1959), hereditary delayed development of parietal lobes (Drew, 1956), slow tempo of the neuromuscular maturation (Eustis, 1947; Harris, 1957), general development (Olson, 1940); and (c) other factors such as lack of cerebral dominance (Orton, 1928; Delacato, 1963), minimal brain injury (Strauss and Lehtinen, 1947), endocrine disturbance and chemical imbalance (Smith and Carrigan, 1959), and primary emotional factors (Blau, 1946; Gann, 1945; Fabian, 1951; Vorhaus, 1952).

A very different approach to the causes of learning disabilities, reading in particular, is the multiple-factor view which emphasizes the character-istics frequently found in groups of children with learning problems. The multiple-factor symptomatology view is well represented by Malmquist (1958), Monroe (1932), Robinson (1946), and Traxler and Townsend (1955). Prominent among the characteristics mentioned in this literature are visual and auditory defects, inadequate readiness, physical factors such as low vitality, speech problems, personality factors, and social adjustment difficulties.

A third approach to causation of learning disabilities is that referred to earlier as the behavioral or symptomatic view in which correlated (rather than causal) disabilities are assessed. This approach is perhaps the newest and is espoused primarily by those whose basic interest is in remediation of disabilities. Deficits in these areas are among the correlates frequently found in cases of learning disability: visual and auditory perception, per-ceptual speed, strength of closure against distraction, visual and auditory discrimination, phonics skills such as sound blending and visual-auditory association, visual and auditory memory span, kinesthetic recognition, vis-ualization, laterality, verbal opposites, eye-hand coordination, and body image. (e.g., Money, 1962.)

Literature on the etiology of communication disorders has been some-what limited in extent and scope, when contrasted to that in reading prob-lems. Much of the older work has focused on cerebral pathology and language deprivation with a relatively recent upsurge of interest in the processes of language learning. (e.g., Bateman, 1964a.)

Visual-motor disturbances are quite generally agreed to be a manifesta-tion of organic dysfunction and as such the etiology is primarily a medical concern. However, the recent work of Frostig and Horne (1964) and Wit-kin, *et al.* (1962) suggests intriguing relationships between personality and visual-motor functioning.

DIAGNOSIS

General principles of diagnostic procedures for learning disabilities of all types are presented by Gallagher (1962), Haeussermann (1958), Kleffner (1962), Bateman (1964b), Wood (1962), and many others. Recent work emphasizing the diagnosis of reading disability includes Kolson and Kaluger (1963), Roswell and Natchez (1964), and Strang (1964). In general, authorities agree that diagnosis must include assessment of both the level of performance and the manner of performance and that it must seek precise formulation of specific disability. Development of specific diag-nostic tests has enabled diagnosticians to move from global classifications and labels, such as reading retardation or delayed language or poor motor development based only on level of performance, to more precise diagnostic hypotheses such as body image, spatial orientation, and directionality dis-turbances underlying reversals in reading or inability to integrate simul-taneous visual and kinesthetic stimuli.

The specific tests used in the diagnostic process must vary from child to child, but frequently broad coverage tests such as the Binet, WISC, ITPA, or Kephart Perceptual Rating Scale are given first and followed by more specific tests in those areas of difficulty revealed by the comprehensive tests. Among the specific tests frequently used are visual and auditory acuity measures, articulation tests, tests of visual and auditory memory, discrimination and closure, spatial orientation, laterality and directionality, and visual-motor coordination, etc.

A minor cleavage in philosophies of diagnosis is seen in the "standard battery" versus "individually chosen" test approaches. The former is perhaps more useful in screening and in some research, while the latter (discussed below) is most appropriate for clinical purposes.

One view of the relationship between clinical diagnostic and remedial procedures is diagrammed in Figure 1-2. The diagnostic process is conceived here as a successive narrowing of the disability area examined until

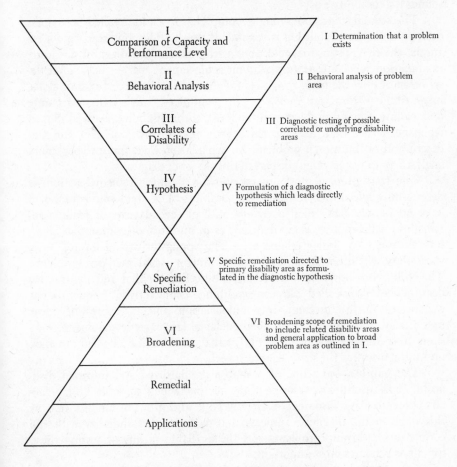

FIGURE 1-2   Schematic representation of the diagnostic-remedial process.

the exact problem can be pinpointed and a diagnostic-remedial hypothesis formulated which is internally consistent and well-supported by objective data. An hypothesis, so stated, leads directly to remedial planning. The remedial process is the inverse of the diagnostic process in that the initial focus is narrowed to the primary area of disability and then gradually broadens.

The first diagnostic step is a comparison of the expected level of functioning with the actual performance of the child. In almost all areas of possible disability, e.g., speech, reading, motor coordination, etc., our estimate of the expected level of functioning is based on some normative combination of mental age, chronological age, and certain experimental factors. Both standardized and informal tests are used in the assessment of the actual level of performance. When a significant discrepancy is found between expected and actual performance (e.g., in reading, a discrepancy between CA and/or MA and the level of difficulty of the misarticulated sounds), a disability exists.

The second step is obtaining as comprehensive and detailed behavioral description of the disability as is possible. If the disability is in reading, for example, the diagnostician would obtain from a standard diagnostic reading examination (in contrast to a reading achievement test) a behavioral description of how the child reads. He might find an absence of phonic skills, inconsistent word attack, lack of sight vocabulary, hurried and inaccurate oral reading, reversal problems, and so forth. If the disability involved spoken language, rather than reading, this step would involve an exact and full description of the speech problem. An articulation inventory or vocabulary analysis, for example, might be part of this aspect of diagnosis.

The third step, a most crucial one for planning remedial action, is determining relevant correlates of the disability. The child who is found to have no phonic skills whatsoever, in spite of several years of reading instruction, will probably show deficiencies in auditory discrimination, auditory closure, or a closely related area. The youngster with a limited sight vocabulary will often show visualization and/or visual memory problems. The child who shows the perseverative, perceptual-spatial and hyperactive disturbances often called "Strauss Syndrome" characteristics frequently has weaknesses in interpreting visual information and in expressing ideas motorically. The child with so-called "delayed language development" may show basic deficiencies in incidental verbal learning, i.e., he fails to pick up "automatically" the intricacies of speech.

The number and scope of available standardized and informal diagnostic tests, useful in exploring these factors which underlie and/or accompany language disorders, is already large and growing rapidly. It is at this stage in the diagnostic process that a thorough familiarity with the correlates of learning problems and the available means of testing these functions becomes most important.

On the basis of the information gathered in the preceding three steps an hypothesis is formulated which must be both precise and comprehensive. It must take into account all the relevant factors and yet be so precise that it leads directly to remedial planning. An example of such an hypothesis is quoted from a case report:

> A thorough review of Casee's test performances, general behavior, classroom functioning, and prior remediation led to formulating a new diagnostic hypothesis: the normal sensory integration processes, by which vision becomes dominant by about age five, had been interrupted. At this time Casee preferred to operate with her intact auditory-vocal skills, and when she was required to use visual-motor skills she was hindered by "interference" or lack of integration between the visual and tactile stimuli. . . .
>
> In summary, Casee showed primary motor encoding and visual decoding disabilities, manifested in these ways:
>
> 1. Visual-motor-spatial disturbances . . . (specifically) (a) gross interferences in response attempts to simultaneous visual and tactile stimuli, and (b) lack of body image and accompanying laterality and spatial orientation confusion.
>
> 2. Overly developed mechanical verbal skills, which were without full comprehension, seen as an overall discrepancy of about four years between the auditory-vocal and the visual-motor subtests of the ITPA.
>
> 3. Difficulty in everyday tasks such as buttoning, putting a lid on a box, getting into cars, etc.—disabilities presumably related to all of the above specific deficits and which involve substantial motor encoding functions.

Remediation was planned to correspond point for point to this diagnostic hypothesis. When the precise disability areas have been remediated, treatment can be broadened to include a more general focus. In the case described, more daily activities were later used in the further development and refinement of motor skills.

Further illustration of broadening remedial focus could be found in a case of reading disability related, for example, to a deficit in auditory closure. After this weakness has been strengthened, remediation could progress to an application of phonics, other word attack skills, and finally perhaps even to speed and comprehension.

REMEDIATION

In order to meaningfully relate the great diversity of remedial techniques abroad in the area of learning disabilities, it is essential to have a schema which shows all the possible areas of behavior in which a disability might occur and shows the relationships among those areas.

Figure 1-3 attempts to schematize language behavior in such a way that all possible remedial foci are included. Language is divided into receptive, intermediate, and expressive processes. Receptive language is further subdivided by the sense modality used in receiving the stimulus; expressive is subdivided into vocal and motor responses; and the intermediate processes are quite arbitrarily called assimilation, storage, and retrieval.

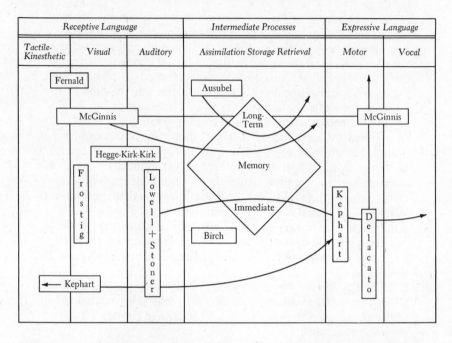

FIGURE 1-3   Schematic model of selected contributors to remediation of learning disabilities.

A further dimension is implicit vertically in that the activities at the top of each column involve a high degree of obtaining or conveying the meaning of language symbols, while those near the bottom involve only the perception or manipulation of the symbol, with little regard for meaning. Memory is divided into immediate (rote), intermediate, and long term storage.

Figure 1-3 indicates only sketchily the areas of primary focus in the work of certain remedial specialists in learning disabilities. Many others could have been chosen—these were selected only to illustrate the diversity of foci which can be encompassed by a schema of this sort. Each of the contributors whose work is represented could quickly and correctly point out that, in fact, he deals with more aspects of language behavior than are shown here.

Some work, such as that of Frostig and Horne, can readily be seen as focusing on remediation of visual perception and assimilation with some attention to certain motor responses. Lowell and Stoner's (1960) work in auditory training, with some focus on certain vocal response characteristics, is somewhat parallel to Frostig's contribution, but on the other primary receptive channel.

In the field of assimilation of stimuli, Birch (1963) has contributed significantly to our knowledge of the integration of nonsymbolic material received on one receptive channel with that received simultaneously on another receptive channel. Ausubel (1960) on the other hand, has done extensive investigations of certain relationships among assimilation, storage, and retrieval of highly complex, meaningful (symbolic) language information.

Fernald's (1939) system of remedial reading can be conceptualized as employing the assimilation of simultaneous visual and kinesthetic symbolic stimuli as an aid to retrieval. The emphases in Fernald's approach are on the meaningfulness of the symbols presented to the child and the facilitation of visual storage and retrieval thereof.

In contrast, the Hegge-Kirk-Kirk (1940) remedial reading system initially emphasizes auditory fusion or sound blending (assimilation with little regard for meaning) and vocal expression in response to the visual stimulus.

And finally, the currently controversial work of Delacato (1963) can be schematized as being centered in neurological (dis)organization and moving through the entire developmental or sequential hierarchy of motor expression. Kephart's (1960) well-established program appears to focus simultaneously on visual, receptive, assimilative (integrative), and motor expressive behaviors at the lower levels, with a gradual ascendance to more symbolic behaviors. Although the remedial programs of both Delacato and Kephart contain a large motor expression or motor activity component, this superficial resemblance reflects quite different theoretical formulations and rationale.

Remedial reading systems per se are legion and still multiplying rapidly. Two of the most helpful ways to categorize them as an aid in selecting the best program for a given youngster are: (a) single versus multisensory approach and, (b) specific, eclectic suggestions for special problems such as improving rate of reading versus tightly integrated, comprehensive programs which are sequentially presented. Fernald's system is primarily visual-kinesthetic and is tightly and systematically organized. Gillingham and Stillman's (1960) program is just as comprehensive and systematic, but is thoroughly multisensory. Monroe (1932) and Harris (1956) offer many specific suggestions for particular problems and are not as concerned with channel or sequence.

Remedial offerings in communication disorders have again been limited, in comparison to those in reading. One of the more comprehensive approaches to communication disorders (aphasia) is presented by Mc-

Ginnis (1963). Interestingly, this system also provides an approach to remedial reading. Further remedial suggestions for children with communication disorders can be found in Agranowitz and McKeown (1964), Myklebust (1954), and Lowell and Stoner (1960). Treatment suggestions for some expressive problems can be found in standard speech correction and pathology texts.

Remedial reading spills over into remediation of visual-motor problems just as it does into communication disorders. Kephart (1960) and Delacato (1963) both offer programs which have an initial primary focus on motor and visual-motor activities followed by a somewhat eclectic reading approach. Teaching methods for children with perceptual disorders are also given by Cruickshank, *et al.* (1961), Strauss and Lehtinen (1947), Gallagher (1960), and Frostig and Horne (1964).

LEARNING DISABILITIES AND THE FUTURE

Within the field of learning disabilities, there is already evident a healthy trend toward early identification of potential cases of learning disabilities. Much, of course, remains to be done in the refinement of both diagnostic and remedial techniques, but it is not too soon to begin intensive work on prevention through appropriate educational experiences. The day may come when such preventive educational treatment at age five or six will be outmoded by medical prevention at a much earlier age. But that day is not as imminent as the day of educational prevention. This focus on early identification and selection of educational remediation is currently being paralleled by at least one pilot effort in the broader field of elementary education (Highland Park, Illinois) to identify the psychological-cognitive learning pattern of normal first-graders and to differentially gear instructional techniques to those patterns.

Another trend which is apparent in special education is that of more and finer categories. In one school system, for example, there is already a special program for culturally deprived gifted which differs from the culturally deprived nongifted program and from the nonculturally deprived gifted program! A glimpse into a rose-tinted crystal ball might suggest some trends not yet so apparent. For example, in the future, this proliferation of programs will perhaps reverse and be replaced by an integrating and unifying application of certain concepts which are now being explored and applied in learning disabilities.

Some of these concepts which the field of learning disabilities will hopefully promulgate are offered here, not as the sole property of this field by any means, but as ideas evolved from many disciplines and belonging to all of education.

The concept of analyzing or evaluating specific patterns has been furthered by the recent work of Guilford (1956) on the structure of intellect. In the same vein, Gallagher and Lucito (1961) have demonstrated, with the cognitive abilities measured by WISC subtests, that retarded children are relatively stronger in tasks requiring perceptual organization than in those demanding verbal comprehension; the gifted show just the reverse or mirror pattern, being relatively stronger in verbal comprehension abilities than in perceptual organization, and that the average group showed patterns of abilities different from both the retarded and the gifted.

Recent work with the ITPA, which yields a profile of nine separate language abilities, has demonstrated identifiable patterns of language strengths and weaknesses among certain groups of children, e.g., retarded, culturally deprived, athetoid and spastic cerebral palsied, receptive and expressive aphasics, partially seeing, etc. But even more importantly, the individual ITPA profile of psycholinguistic strengths and weaknesses points the way for specific planning of educational techniques appropriate for that child. Similarly, Valett (1964) has recently suggested a clinical profile to be used in showing patterns of cognitive strengths and weaknesses as revealed by items passed and failed on the Stanford Binet L-M.

Educators have long discussed the need for recognizing individual differences among children within a group. The application of these new developments in analyzing patterns of cognitive differences within an individual child is a logical and necessary extension of this interest in inter-individual difference. In spite of this widespread acceptance of educational planning for inter- and intra-individual differences, there has been an equally broad dissatisfaction with many of the traditional grouping techniques. Whether one favors homogeneity or heterogeneity of grouping, a crucial consideration is that such grouping be based on relevant variables. Neither chronological nor mental age has proven entirely satisfactory, since each is a highly global measure. Is it too idealistic to suggest that grouping by shape and level of those cognitive patterns most relevant to the subject or content area to be studied is both possible and worthy of exploration? The field of learning disabilities may become a leader in demonstrating the feasibility of such an approach.

Educators have traditionally been concerned with promoting and developing achievement in specific academic areas. There are, however, certain cognitive abilities upon which academic achievement depends. Through a series of historical accidents, American psychologists and educators have belonged to and been primarily influenced by the school of thought which held that intelligence (basic cognitive structures) was innate, hereditary, and unchanged by experience. Only in fairly recent years has the concept of the "educability of educability" become even a little popular or respectable. The field of learning disabilities, and perhaps that of reading readiness, stand as primary contributors at the present time to the area of educating cognitive abilities directly. This type of ability training (focused, e.g., on spatial orientation, visualization, retention, or auditory discrimination) is usually employed in a remedial setting after a youngster has evidenced an inability to achieve in an academic area which requires those underlying cognitive skills in which he is weak. If, in this case, an ounce of prevention is worth a pound of cure, it would follow that a broadening of curriculum to include ability as well as achievement training is in order. The work in early identification of children with potential learning disabilities (e.g., Gillingham, 1960; de Hirsch, 1957) mentioned earlier, is closely related to this concept of ability training.

"Meet the child where he is" is oft heard in educational circles—so oft, in fact, one might suspect that if we were better able to do it we might be less compelled to talk about it. A basic premise of remediation in cases of learning disabilities is that one must determine exactly where the child is functioning and begin instruction at or slightly below that point. Diagnostic teaching is a valuable aid in this determination. Recognition of the fact that a child's presence at a desk in the third grade room does not necessarily insure he is ready for a third grade book is widespread, but the actual doing something about it is not so prevalent. Too often we judge performance level by grade placement or mental age, rather than by actual examination of functioning.

When the teacher and child meet, a major part of the teacher's armament must be a knowledge of principles of learning. Many normal children learn readily in spite of repeated violations of learning principles. However, children with learning disabilities cannot do this. By sharpening our awareness of some of these principles, as applied in teaching children with learning disabilities, we can anticipate broader adherence to them.

Some of these major principles of learning include overlearning, ordering and sizing (programming) of new material, rewarding only desired responses, frequent review, and avoidance of interference and negative transfer.

Analyses of patterns of cognitive abilities, grouping by these patterns, curriculum planning to include the education of underlying abilities as well as achievements, meeting the child where he really is, and teaching him in accord with known principles of learning—all seem worthy of further exploration.

If the promise of maturity now visible in the gawky, uncoordinated, sprawling adolescence of the field of learning disabilities is fulfilled, we will see one more example of special education's contribution to the education of all children, exceptional and not-so-exceptional.

References

Agranowitz, Aleen, and McKeon, M. R., *Aphasia handbook for adults and children* (Springfield, Illinois: Charles C Thomas, 1964).

Ausubel, D. P., The use of advance organizers in the learning and retention of meaningful verbal material, *J. Educ. Psychol.*, 1960, 51, 267-272.

Bateman, Barbara, *The Illinois test of psycholinguistic abilities in current research* (Urbana: University of Illinois Press, 1964a).

Bateman, Barbara, Learning disabilities—an overview. Paper read at CEC 42nd Annual Convention, Chicago, April, 1964b.

Blau, A., *The master hand; a study of the origin and meaning of right and left sidedness and its relation to personality and language* (New York: American Orthopsychiatric Association, 1946).

Birch, G. H., and Lefford, A., Intersensory development in children, *Monogr. Soc. Res. Child Develpm.*, 1963, 28 (5).

Bryant, N. D., Some principles of remedial instruction for dyslexia, *Int. Reading Ass. J.*, 1965.

Cohn, R., Neurological concepts pertaining to the brain-damaged child. In W. T. Daley (Editor), *Speech and language therapy with the brain-damaged child* (Washington, D.C.: Catholic, 1962).

Cruickshank, W. M., Benton, F. A., Ratzeburg, F. H., and Tannhauser, Mirian T., *A teaching method for brain-injured and hyperactive children* (Syracuse: Syracuse University Press, 1961).

de Hirsch, Katrina, Tests designed to discover potential reading difficulties at the six-year-old level, *Amer. J. Orthopsychiat.*, 1957, 27, 566-576.

Delacato, C. H., *The diagnosis and treatment of speech and reading problems* (Springfield, Illinois: Charles C Thomas, 1963).

Drew, A. L., A neurological appraisal of familial congenital word-blindness, *Brain*, 1956, 79, 440-460.

Eustis, R. S., The primary etiology of specific language disabilities, *J. Ped.*, 1947, 31, 448.

Fabian, A. A., Clinical and experimental studies of school children who are retarded in reading, *Quart. J. Child Behav.*, 1951, 3, 15-37.

Fernald, G., *Remedial techniques in basic school subjects* (New York: McGraw-Hill, 1939).

Frostig, Marianne, and Horne, D., *The Frostig program for the development of visual perception* (Chicago: Follett, 1964).

Gann, E., *Reading Difficulty and personality organization* (New York: King's Crown, 1945).

Gallagher, J. J., *The tutoring of brain-injured mentally retarded children* (Springfield, Illinois: Charles C Thomas, 1960).

Gallagher, J. J., Educational methods with brain-damaged children, in J. Masserman (Editor), *Current psychiatric therapies*, vol. II (New York: Grune & Stratton, 1962), pp. 48-55.

Gallagher, J. J., and Lucito, L. J., Intellectual patterns of gifted compared with average and retarded, *Exceptl. Child.*, 1961, 27, 479-483.

Guilford, J. P., The structure of intellect, *Psychol. Bull.*, 1956, 53, 293-297.

Gillingham, Anna, and Stillman, Bessie, *Remedial training for children with specific disability in reading, spelling and penmanship* (Cambridge, Massachusetts: Educators Publishing Service, 1960).

Harris, A. J., *How to increase reading ability* (New York: Longmans, 1956).

Haeussermann, Else, *Developmental potential of preschool children: an evalua-*

tion of intellectual, sensory and emotional functioning (New York: Grune & Stratton, 1958).

Hegge, T. G., Kirk, S. A., and Kirk, Winifred, *Remedial reading drills* (Ann Arbor, Michigan: Wahr, 1940).

Hermann, K., *Reading disability* (Springfield, Illinois: Charles C Thomas, 1959).

Hinshelwood, J., *Congenital word-blindness* (London: H. K. Lewis, 1917).

Kass, Corinne, Some psychological correlates of severe reading disability (dyslexia) (Unpublished doctoral dissertation, University of Illinois, 1962).

Kirk, S. A., *Educating exceptional children* (Boston: Houghton Mifflin, 1962).

Kleffner, F. R., Aphasia and other language deficiencies in children: research and teaching at Central Institute for the Deaf. In W. T. Daley (Editor), *Speech and language therapy with the brain-damaged child* (Washington, D.C. Catholic, 1962).

Kolson, C., and Kaluger, G., *Clinical aspects of remedial reading* (Springfield, Illinois: Charles C Thomas, 1963).

Lowell, E. L., and Stoner, M., *Play it by ear* (Los Angeles: John Tracy Clinic, 1960).

McGinnis, M. A., *Aphasic children: identification and education by the association method* (Washington, D.C.: Alexander Graham Bell Association for the Deaf, 1963).

Malmquist, Eve, *Factors related to reading disabilities in the first grade of the elementary school* (Stockholm: Amquist and Wiksell, 1958).

Money, J. (Editor), *Reading disability: progress in research needs in dyslexia* (Baltimore: Johns Hopkins, 1962).

Monroe, Marion, *Children who cannot read* (Chicago: University of Chicago Press, 1932).

Myklebust, H. R., *Auditory disorders in children* (New York: Grune & Stratton, 1954).

Olson, W. C., Reading as a function of the total growth of the child. In W. S. Gray, *Reading and pupil development* (Chicago: University of Chicago Press, 1940), pp. 233-237.

Orton, S. T., Specific reading disability—Strephosymbolia. *J.A.M.A.*, 1928, 1094-1099.

Penfield, W., and Roberts, L., *Speech and brain-mechanisms* (New York: Princeton University Press, 1959).

Rabinovitch, R. D., Reading and learning disabilities. In S. Arieti (Editor), *American handbook of psychiatry*, vol. 1, Chapter 43 (New York: Basic Books, Inc., 1959).

Robinson, H., *Why pupils fail in reading* (Chicago: University of Chicago Press, 1946).

Roswell, Florence, and Natchez, Gladys, *Reading disability: diagnosis and treatment* (New York: Basic Books, Inc., 1964).

Smith, D. E. P., and Carrigan, P., *The nature of reading disability* (New York: Harcourt, Brace & World, 1959).

Strang, Ruth, *Diagnostic teaching of reading* (New York: McGraw-Hill, 1964).

Strauss, A. A., and Lehtinen, L. E., *Psychopathology and education of the brain-injured child* (New York: Grune & Stratton, 1947).

Traxler, A., and Townsend, Agatha, *Eight more years of research in reading: summary and bibliography* (New York: Educational Records Bureau, 1955).

Valett, R. E., A clinical profile for the Stanford-Binet, *J. Sch. Psychol.*, 1963-1964, 2 (1), 49-54.

Vorhaus, P. G., Rorschach configurations associated with reading disability, *J. proj. Tech.*, 1952, 16, 3-19.

Witkin, H. A., Dyk, R. B., Paterson, H. F., Goodenough, D. R., and Kapp, S. A., *Psychological differentiation: studies of development* (New York: Wiley, 1962).

Wood, Nancy, Evaluation of language disorders in children of school age. In W. T. Daley (Editor), *Speech and language therapy with the brain-damaged child* (Washington, D.C.: Catholic, 1962).

2 PSYCHONEUROLOGICAL LEARNING DISORDERS IN CHILDREN

Helmer R. Myklebust and Benjamin Boshes

Perhaps there is no more important effort in science than the study of learning, inasmuch as it entails all aspects of man's behavior, normal and abnormal. Historically such study was mainly concerned with the relative importance of heredity and environment. Much progress was made in understanding the learning process through this "heredity-environment" controversy. Currently the emphasis is more dynamic, less either-or, with vital interest in the variables and variations which occur. There is a basic curiosity with the ways in which the influences of either heredity or environment might be demonstrated, curtailed, or modified.

Frequently the psychiatrist, neurologist, psychologist, and educator are confronted with a need to understand impositions and deterrents to learning. This need might arise through the case of a child who is not learning to talk, or not learning in other ways according to the demands of the society in which he lives. Perhaps the inquiry arises through an adult who, because of a vascular accident, has lost a specific aspect of his learned behavior, such as the ability to learn to read; now this adult must attempt to relearn that which he lost. Another type of problem, growing in importance, is the need to understand the effects of drugs on learning. Clinically it seems that a drug which is effective in the treatment of a disease such as epilepsy might also be an imposition to learning.

Learning can be affected in many ways. It is advantageous scientifically to classify factors that impair learning into three major categories: those which have a psychological causation, those caused by impairment of the peripheral nervous system, and those due to disorders of the central nervous system. This is shown schematically in Figure 2-1.

Reprinted from *Archives of Pediatrics*, Vol. 77, No. 6 (June, 1960), 247-256. By permission of the senior author and publisher.

FIGURE 2-1

Primary Deterrents to Learning

Affective Disorders	Peripheral Nervous System Disorders	Central Nervous System Disorders
Neuroses	Deafness	Perceptual Defects
Psychoses	Blindness	Language Disorders

Affective disorders have been emphasized a great deal in the past few decades, especially in the United States. Conceivably this emphasis has obscured other significant deterrents to learning. The effects of sensory impairments also have been stressed. More recently other factors which impede learning have come into the foreground. These involve the neurology of learning and can be referred to as *psychoneurological learning disorders*. Such aberrations of the learning process are not explicable on the basis of emotional disturbance, or sensory impairment, although superficially both of these factors often seem to be the etiology.

Psychoneurological learning disorders are those which derive from neurological maladies. It has been recognized that a neurological involvement can cause cerebral palsy and mental deficiency. We are less cognizant that minor motor incoordinations, certain behavior disturbances, disorders in reading, writing, spelling, arithmetic, and speaking might have a neurological causation. The central nervous system involvement may be slight and even inconsequential neurologically, but frequently the effect on learning is marked. It must be emphasized that the term *psychoneurological* includes only those psychological, behavioral deviations which are attributed to neurological causation. While in this paper we are concerned with the psychoneurological disorders in children, this classification might include any psychological deviation resulting from brain disorder. For example, the aphasias, dyslexias, and memory defects which result from brain diseases in middle age, and the deficits of behavior which occur geriatrically, can be viewed as being psychoneurological in nature.

Terms such as "brain-damaged" and "brain-injured" have been used to designate certain children presenting problems of behavior and learning. These terms have marked limitations both clinically and scientifically. The disorder might be due to endogenous, or maldevelopment factors, rather than damage or injury per se. The term *psychoneurological* can be used for all aberrations of behavior which have a neurological basis, irrespective of age of onset and etiology. This term also has the advantage of being less traumatizing and stigmatizing. Psychoneurological disorders may occur in children and adults who otherwise are of average or above intelligence. Moreover, they may be found in individuals who seem to be intact neurologically. It should not be inferred that neurological involvements cannot be demonstrated. On the contrary, research is revealing a high correlation between certain disorders in children and minimal neurological conditions.

Our major purpose here is to accent psychoneurological learning disorders which are congenital in origin. In Blakiston's New Gould Medical Dictionary, *congenital* is defined as "existing at birth." It is in this sense that we use the term. Hence we assume that if the condition is congenital in origin, it was caused either prenatally or during birth. For example, the neurological involvement might have been caused prenatally by maternal rubella, or by anoxia associated with atypical factors at the time of birth. However, although the neurological ailment is congenital, the concomitant learning disorder does not become apparent except through the later development of the child; perhaps at the age when he *should* be talking, dressing himself, or learning to read. The following discussion describes some common learning disorders in children, with case illustrations.

CONGENITAL APRAXIA

Apraxia is the inability to ideationally plan a motor act. It is the inability to relate specific experience to the appropriate motor system when there is no paralysis and when the condition derives from neurological disorder. Although an apraxia may be generalized, perhaps one of the best known apraxic involvements is that which occurs in expressive aphasia. The individual knows the word he wishes to say but cannot relate the *symbol* and the motor system for speaking. Apraxia is a defect in expressive function as contrasted with receptive function; it is an output disorder, not an input disorder. Congenital apraxia, especially in the form of *expressive aphasia*, seems to be more common than has been assumed; it is a common type of psychoneurological learning disorder in children. This condition in children symptomatically often is highly similar to that seen in adults. Another type of apraxia seen less frequently in children is *dysgraphia*; the inability to "think" the motor plan for writing because of neurological disorder, but without paralysis being involved.

CASE ONE: EXPRESSIVE APHASIA

This boy, four years and two months of age, was referred by a pediatrician. The history revealed complications during pregnancy because of "structural" involvements. Etiology is obscure with a possibility of prenatal anoxia.

Psychological study and evaluation of language revealed normal intelligence (IQ 107) with expressive aphasia, dysarthria, visuo-motor disturbance, and a formulation disability. He related to people and used gestures freely in making himself understood.

The neurological examination revealed minimal but definite signs of central nervous system disturbance. Both pyramidal and extra pyramidal systems were involved, the greater evidence on the right side of the body. The EEG was abnormal, a generalized slow record with mild asymmetrical slow waves in the left frontal, left temporal, left parietal, right parietal, and right temporal areas.

He was started on language and educational therapy which continued for two years. He is now six years of age and is in a regular first grade in public school without need for additional specialized training.

CONGENITAL AGNOSIA

An agnosia is an input disorder, not an output disorder. Hence this defect relates to the primary sensory channels in man; visual agnosia, auditory agnosia, and tactual agnosia. Agnosia means a "lack of knowing." It is the inability to interpret, that is, to associate meaning with the sensations being received. Like apraxia, this condition might entail both symbolic and nonsymbolic aspects of behavior. For example, an auditory agnosic might be unable to interpret any sound, or just be unable to interpret the spoken word. Again, it is agnosia for verbal symbols which is most readily recognized and clearly understood clinically. When the auditory agnosia involves the ability to comprehend the spoken word it is referred to as a *receptive aphasia*. If the visual agnosia entails comprehension of the written word it is referred to as *dyslexia*. *Tactual agnosia* is more difficult to determine, especially in children. Interestingly it is more readily recognized in blind children because of their need to use the tactual sense symbolically in learning to read Braille. If the agnosia entails either the auditory or visual aspects of number ability it is referred to as *dyscalculia*.

As the above discussion has inferred, the most commonly recognized psychoneurological learning disorders in children pertain to the acquisition and use of language. This manifests itself frequently through children who do not learn to speak, to read, or to write. In this connection it is helpful to keep in mind that "output" is dependent on "input." Thus, the child will not speak until he has minimal comprehension established, and he will not write until he has established minimal ability to read. As would be expected, it is the receptive disorders which are the most debilitating behaviorally. The child who cannot learn to comprehend the spoken word is more seriously deficient in relation to his environment than the child who cannot get the words out. Another consideration is that the involvements of the brain affecting areas for reception, as contrasted with areas for expression, may be more basic to the total integration of the individual.

A survey which we made of psychoneurological learning problems in children, indicated that the most common language disorder found in public school children is dyslexia. Although there has been some resistance to the term congenital aphasia, the term *congenital dyslexia* has been used widely both in the United States and in Europe. While, like all language disorders, it is a complex problem, usually the child is either unable to learn what the letters look like, or to learn what sounds go with the letters. In other words, dyslexia might result mainly from defects in visual associations or from defects in auditory associations. At times both auditory and visual associations are involved. Often a genetic, endogenous factor is indicated. This has been especially emphasized in Sweden. In our studies, even though endogenous factors are indicated, neurological disturbances usually can be demonstrated.

The concepts of *revisualization* and *reauditorization* are highly useful in the study of learning disorders in children. This is shown most clearly through the child's learning to write. Evidence indicates that the child cannot learn to spell or to write, unless he can simultaneously *revisualize* what the letters look like and *reauditorize* what the letters sound like. The implications of such findings for training and educational therapy are manifold and cannot be discussed here. This criterion is helpful in distinguishing between the child who is truly dysgraphic and the one who cannot write because of defects in revisualization or reauditorization. Furthermore it can be used in differentiating between children who have expressive versus receptive aphasias.

CASE TWO: RECEPTIVE APHASIA

This boy was seen first when he was five years and four months of age. The parents requested a conference because of his inability to comprehend what was said to him. The history disclosed an Rh factor with jaundice after transfusion. Severe convulsions were present for over two years. When first seen he was distractible auditorially. Sounds provoked marked anxiety and hyperactivity. He related to people only to a minor extent, and superficially.

Study revealed a receptive aphasia with echolalia and a marked disturbance of auditory perception. Initially mental capacity could not be established because of extreme scatter of abilities. He was judged clinically to have at least low average mental ability and this has been verified recently when he earned an IQ of 86 on the Performance Section of the Wechsler Intelligence Scale for Children.

Neurological examination disclosed minimal evidence of central nervous system dysfunction. The EEG study showed mild dysrhythmic slowing, mainly in the frontal lobes bilaterally. Drug therapy was inaugurated and has prevented seizures.

Educational language therapy has been in progress for almost three years. He has learned to tolerate stimulation well in a structured environment. As his comprehension has improved, his ability to relate with both children and adults has increased. Progress in learning has been excellent and is continuing. He is now approaching 8 years of age. He is in a regular public school class with a group one year younger than himself, and specialized language therapy is continuing. The outlook is good for self-support and adjustment in society.

CASE THREE: DYSLEXIA

Characteristic of dyslexics, this boy's inability to read and his school failure have been attributed to various causations. When first seen by us he was 15 years and three months of age. The history revealed very difficult labor with possible anoxia at the time of birth. Total evaluation of capacities and learning disorders revealed a dyslexia with difficulties in revisualization and reauditorization, a spelling defect, dysnomia, a deficiency in time-sense and a memory disturbance. Level of mental capacity ranged from average to above average with scores clustering from 96 to 110.

He was referred for neurological examination and found to have minimal neurological signs pointing to a right pyramidal tract lesion. The EEG was mildly abnormal consisting of left occipital scattered slowing, spreading to the right occipital area in the waking state. In this case the psychological findings and the EEG findings are strikingly corroborative.

After 15 months of therapy covering reading, spelling, memory, and other aspects of his learning disorders, he is making good progress. He is in a public high school but receives supplemental educational therapy at the Institute for Language Disorders. At the outset of his training he used many defense mechanisms in attempts to conceal his deficits in learning. He now verbalizes problems which are difficult for him and tries to overcome them. He has excellent motivation and relates well both to his own and peer groups.

CASE FOUR: DYSCALCULIA

This boy was first seen at the age of four years and eight months. He presented problems in behavior, poor speech, and language development. He was studied over a period of time because of the difficulty of obtaining objective evidence of mental capacity. Through language therapy and guidance of the parents behavior improved. Recently on objective tests of mental ability he scored at least 100 IQ. There is now no question about his *ability* to learn.

The only suggestion of etiology from the history is the possibility of anoxia at the time of birth. Inclusive evaluation of behavior and learning revealed a mild expressive aphasia and dysarthria, with dyslexia and a marked dyscalculia.

Neurologically there were mild but definite signs indicating either bilateral cerebral disease involving the pyramidal tracts of both sides, or a lesion in the brain stem in the region of the decussation of the pyramids; the former seemed the most probable. The EEG was mildly abnormal, consisting of slow waves in the biparietal areas, occasionally becoming generalized. Slow waves were observed in the right frontal and right occipital areas more prominently than elsewhere.

This lad has had unusually difficult learning problems. We have now worked with him in educational therapy for approximately six years. He no longer has significant aphasia or dysarthria. Furthermore, dyslexia is no longer a handicap, although the dyscalculia continues to some extent. Interestingly, he can calculate exceedingly well when told to add, multiply, or divide. But he has marked difficulty in ascertaining which of these processes is appropriate when he is confronted with an arithmetic problem.

TOPOGRAPHIC ABILITY, ORIENTATION AND TIME

Psychoneurological learning disorders in children are not limited to language. *Topographic defects* commonly are seen in association with dyslexia. In this condition the inability is one of not being able to associate experience with maps, globes, and other representations of space. *Orientation disturbances* are seen most often as confusions of left and right, and in learning directions. *Time disorders* may include learning to tell time by a clock, learning the days of the week, months and seasons of the year, and many other time relationships.

CASE FIVE: ORIENTATION AND TIME DISORDER

A boy, 7 years of age, was seen because of his inabilities in learning. Study of psychological factors disclosed visual and auditory perceptual problems with minor residual receptive and expressive aphasia. In addition there was a *marked time and left-right disorientation*. Mental capacity fell within the normal range.

Neurological appraisal showed minimal evidences of dysfunction, with the left hemisphere most involved. The EEG was mildly abnormal with slowing in the left-parietal-occipital area in hyperventilation; perhaps some loss of voltage and fusion of waves in the right occipital area in sleep.

Etiology was obscure, with possible anoxia. This child is in the first grade in a public school and presenting serious problems in learning. He is in need of program planning.

IMPLICATIONS OF PSYCHONEUROLOGICAL
LEARNING DISORDERS

A psychoneurological learning disorder in a child has important, sometimes urgent implications. It might be a forewarning of epilepsy. In certain instances there are implications for the presence of progressive diseases such as hydrocephalus, tumors, or Heller's disease.

There are other types of implications. These disorders are found in otherwise bright, even brilliant children. For all children having psychoneurological problems specialized training and therapy are needed if their needs are to be met, if they are to have an opportunity for actualization of their potential. Problems of emotional overlay are common. The parents require assistance in understanding the total needs of the child, the neurological involvements as well as the learning disturbances, which entail a long period of remedial therapy.

Specialized educational training is of critical importance. Because language disorders are encountered so frequently this is an important part of any such program. The area concerned with the scientific study of disturbances of language behavior is referred to as *language pathology*. Knowledge in this area is growing. From research and clinical experience it is increasingly apparent that much can be done to alleviate and modify learning disorders. However, outcomes are related to early diagnosis and therapy. Unfortunately it is common to see children whose psychoneurological problem is recognized only after years of school failure, usually preceded by erroneous diagnosis. We frequently see young adults in high school, and at times even in college, whose learning disorders predated entrance to kindergarten. Proper study often indicates that the onset was prenatal. Through therapy procedures which are firmly based on specific diagnostic findings the child usually can be helped substantially. Each child must be viewed individually, according to his total matrix of disturbances, with a program planned to cover both the medical and learning involvements. When this is done the prognosis is good for independent adjustment in society.

RESEARCH

There is an urgent need for research on psychoneurological problems at all age levels, with children and adults. Our studies covering a period of approximately ten years have pertained principally to children. An extensive research project has been in progress for three years and will continue for the next five years. Children presenting problems in learning are first studied behaviorally to determine that intelligence is normal, that sensory capacities are intact, and to define the type of learning disorders present. Secondly, the child receives neurological and electroencephalographic study. Total time devoted to the examination of each child is from eight to ten hours. All findings, neurologic, electroencephalographic and behavioral are coded and treated statistically through the use of an IBM electronic computer. While it is premature to present statistical findings, some generalizations can be made:

(1) A survey of a public school population indicated that the number of children having psychoneurological learning disorders might exceed five percent.

(2) The incidence of these disorders is at least five times more common in males than in females.

(3) A preponderance of the children who present problems of revisualization have disturbances in the occipital-parietal area.

(4) A highly significant number of children who present problems of reauditorization have disturbances in the temporal-parietal area.

(5) Because there is a relationship between neurological findings and learning disorders, there are indications that in the future the neurologist will be able to predict such disorders from his studies.

(6) Certain psychometric procedures indicate not only the presence of learning disorders, but the area of the brain which is involved.

(7) Educational-language therapy procedures can be planned according to the specific type of psychoneurological problem existing; this provides a scientifically oriented therapy program.

References

Bender, L., Problems in conceptualization and communication in children with developmental alexia. In *Psychopathology of communication* (New York: Grune & Stratton, 1958).

Bender, L., *Psychopathology of children with organic brain disorders* (Springfield, Illinois: Charles C Thomas, 1956).

Cobb, S., *Borderlands of psychiatry* (Cambridge, Massachusetts: Harvard University Press, 1948).

Courville, C., *Cerebral anoxia* (Los Angeles: San Lucas Press, 1953).

Critchley, M., *The parietal lobes* (Baltimore: Williams and Wilkins, 1953).

Eisenson, J., *Examining for aphasia* (New York: Psychological Corporation, 1946).

Ettlinger, G., Warrington, E., and Zangwill, O., A further study of visual-spatial agnosia, *Brain*, 1957, 80, 335-61.

Goldstein, K., *Language and language disturbances* (New York: Grune & Stratton, 1948).

Gooddy, W., Time and the nervous system; the brain as a clock, *The Lancet*, 1958, 1139-44.

Grannick, L., *Aphasia, a guide to retraining* (New York: Grune & Stratton, 1947).

Guttman, E., Aphasia in children, *Brain*, 1942, 65, 205.

Halstead, W., *Brain and intelligence: a quantitative study of the frontal lobes* (Chicago: University of Chicago Press, 1947).

Herman, K., *Om medfdt ordblindhed* (Copenhagen: Munksgaard, 1955).

Lamm, S., *Pediatric neurology* (New York: Lansberger Medical Books, 1959).

Myklebust, H., *Auditory disorders in children; a manual for differential diagnosis* (New York: Grune & Stratton, 1954).

Myklebust, H., Aphasia in children, diagnosis and training, In L. E. Travis (Editor), *Handbook of speech pathology* (New York: Appleton-Century-Crofts, 1957).

Neilsen, J., *Agnosia, apraxia, aphasia* (New York: Hoeber-Harper, 1946).

Orton, S., *Reading, writing and speech disorders in children* (New York: Norton, 1937).

Penfield, W., A consideration of the neurophysiological mechanisms of speech and some educational consequences, *Proc. Amer. Acad. Arts Sci.*, 1953, 82, 5.

Penfield, W., and Roberts, L., *Speech and brain mechanisms* (Princeton: Princeton University Press, 1959).

Reitan, R., *The effects of brain lesions on adaptive abilities in human beings* (Indianapolis: Department of Neurosurgery, Indiana University Medical Center, 1959).

Rheinhold, M., An analysis of agnosia, *Neurol.*, 1954, 4, 128-36.

Subirana, A., Corominas, J., and Oller-Daurella, L., Las afasias congenitas infantiles, *Act. Luso-Espenol. Neurol. Pisquit.*, 1950, 9, 14-25.

Weisenburg, T., A study of aphasia, *Arch. Neurol. Psychiat.*, 1934, 31, 1.

Wepman, J., *Recovery from aphasia* (New York: Ronald, 1951).

3 ON LANGUAGE DISORDERS IN YOUNG CHILDREN. A REORGANIZATION OF THINKING

William G. Hardy ～

Current questions and confusions about the use of the term *aphasia* with reference to young children seem often to reflect semantic problems accruing from professional habits of thinking in terms of etiologic and pathologic labels. It is argued that if the term *aphasia* is generalized simply to refer to inabilities or interferences in the development of language comprehension and use, then it is the task of an evaluating group to describe as well as possible, and in detail, the specific impairments of function in each child. This task commonly requires the use of an extensive period of "diagnostic teaching," wherein care is taken to explore which sensory and motor modalities are working and which are not, and whether integration of various stimuli is taking place.

Some current ideas are discussed with reference to descriptions of impairment, causal factors that are fairly unique in childhood, some thoughts about the neurophysiology of the human "language system," and some psychosocial factors important for language-learning. Special attention is given to various relations, in terms of temporal resolving power, between sensation and sensory integration. A scheme, or model, is suggested which may prove fruitful for experimental design in attacking some of these problems at a prelanguage or premeaning level. It is argued that the proportion of "unknowns" can be reduced by careful study based on information about impaired functions within the sensory-integrative-motor complex, without particular regard for "site and extent of lesion."

From time to time there appears in the literature of various fields a question about applying the term *aphasia* to the problems of language

Reprinted from *Journal of Speech and Hearing Disorders*, Vol. 30, No. 1 (February, 1965), pp. 3-16. By permission of the author and publisher.

disorders in childhood. A typical argument is that children commonly have developmental problems which must be quite different from the language disorders of adults who, after normal development, have sustained some form of cerebral vascular insult. "How," goes the usual question, "can a child be aphasic if he has never developed language comprehension?" It might be of some interest to turn this ordinarily rhetorical question into something like a genuine interrogation. It should be clear, if the argument is sound, that the magic of words has quite as little reality or usefulness in this setting as in any other. It should be clear, as well, that problems of semantics are not simply theoretical in matters that relate directly to interprofessional communication about the status and needs of affected children.

LABELS AND REFERENCES

What we call children whose basic incapacity centers in difficulty in learning and remembering and using verbal symbols probably makes little difference, so long as our definitions and procedures for evaluation are clear. That the problems of many children are fundamentally different from those of language-disordered adults may make considerable difference, both in our theoretical attempts better to understand the human brain in normal and in impaired function, and in our daily practices in trying to deal with the problems of affected persons. What is required is a better understanding of the nature and extent of impairment of each individual, either child or adult.

It seems clear that any abstract term such as *aphasia* can mean to any of us whatever we wish it to mean. Most of us have some of the tendencies characterized by Humpty Dumpty. The meaning is a product of concept and usage, of training, of experience, and of intention. Descriptive reference is a common undertaking of writers of dictionaries and textbooks. From Webster we learn that aphasia involves the "loss or impairment of the power to use or understand speech." Dorland calls it "a defect of the power of expression by speech, writing, or signs, or of comprehending spoken or written language, due to injury or disease of the brain centers." The Oxford reference is more abrupt: "loss of the faculty of speech, as a result of cerebral affection." None of these tells us much more than that the concept is apparently related to difficulties in expression. Yet we all know "affected children and adults" whose articulation during the speech act is quite clear.

Years ago, Town, in a discussion of what she called *congenital aphasia*, offered a definition that seems to be more inclusive: "Aphasia then is an inability, total or partial, to understand or to use language in any one or all of its forms, such inability being independent of any other mental capacity or of deformity or disease affecting the organs of articulation" (1911). What is missing here, however, is some indication of the direction of difference between this inability and "any other mental capacity." The encompassment of both understanding and use is emphasized, as well, by a modern writer who states that aphasia "is an impairment in symbolic formulation and expression" (Eisenson, 1957). This general concept is present in some recently published categories employed in describing *childhood aphasia* as either "sensory" or "expressive" (McGinnis, 1963). The point is that there are important aspects of linguistic lacks or disturbances which involve much more than an expressive modality, or speech act, for both children and adults.

On the other hand, there is a current surge of interest in getting away from an oversimplified, dichotomous description of aphasia. In recent years the literature has included subcategories like "basically a receptive problem with expressive aspects," or "mainly an expressive difficulty with receptive manifestations." Unfortunately, this is comparable to what it must surely be like to try to play patty-cake with an octopus.

More recently still are attempts at reference which seem to be undertaken with a view toward making peace with some classical neurologic descriptions of aphasia. There is "minimal brain damage," only recently discarded by at least some of our colleagues in the United Kingdom. In its place, for the time being, is "minimal cerebral dysfunction" (Mac Keith and Bax, 1963). A cognate form is "chronic minimal brain syndrome." The "brain-injured child" is now a focus of monetary appeal in many communities. His counterpart is the child with a "brain-damage syndrome." In the name of euphemism, perhaps, this is sometimes expressed as the "hyperactivity-distractibility syndrome." One neurologic clinician in particular refers to the "nonmotor brain-damaged child." Another, who specializes in neuropsychology, emphasizes "psychoneurological learning disorders in children." Still another colleague has put forth a cogent argument for a distinction between cerebral injury and agenesis in assessing verbal symbolic disorders in children. This argument was presented at a recent conference on "minimal brain impairment."

Each of these expressions of terminology represents the careful thinking of individuals or groups who daily have to deal with deviant children. A common thread of meaning is the suggestion, at least by implication, that one frequently has to work with children who have small amounts of disturbances or interferences in the central nervous system, rather than large voids in cerebral tissue. Perhaps it must be true that anybody who tries hard to apply reason and logic to problems so confused and confusing as these in reference, feels the need to make converts to his point of view. One way toward freedom from this tendency, which I suspect is common to all of us, is to agree to use the term *aphasia* in broad reference to *an individual's incapacities in language comprehension and use*, and then go on to describe and demonstrate as thoroughly as possible what these incapacities are and what residual, or possibly substitute, capacities are available. In some such terms as these, one may expect to find some genuine differences between children and adults, between adult and adult, and between child and child.

DESCRIPTIONS OF IMPAIRMENT

If one expects to be of much help in habilitation or rehabilitation, in education or special education, he must know fairly well which modalities (for having experiences and for learning from them) are working, and which are not; and whether interferences in the central nervous system involve problems of sensory integration, of language comprehension, of formulation, of spontaneous expression, or of imitation. He would like to know, as well, the shape and nature of the constellation of factors working for and working against the individual's possible ability to learn or to relearn language comprehension and use (compare Schuell, Jenkins, and Carroll, 1962). For years, much of the descriptive work with adult aphasics has been centered on attempts to learn about the capacities and limitations of the subject in all aspects of language. For obvious reasons this is much more difficult to do, if, indeed, it can be done at all, with young children who cannot naturally learn language. Useful descriptions in depth of affected children can ordinarily be elicited only from what is sometimes called "diagnostic teaching," the long procedure of taking each child through careful, ordered, and modality-controlled learning situations, so that one may better know what his capacities and limitations may be.

We can know relatively little about the "premorbid state" of a young child who has never demonstrated any capacity in language comprehension and use. We can only inquire into various genetic possibilities, into the details of prenatal and perinatal events, into developmental and behavioral stages, and into what might be called the psychosocial milieu. Any or all of these may or may not plausibly be contributory to the problem.

Occasionally one hears a professional comment to the effect that the description of aphasia in early childhood involves a circular argument based on negative evidence. A given child is not biologically mentally subnormal to a profound degree; he is not deaf in the sense of a profound peripheral loss of auditory sensitivity; he is not autistic; he is not psychosocially deprived; he is not fundamentally emotionally disturbed: therefore, he must be aphasic. This kind of approach need by no means be a circular argument, however, nor a demonstration after the fact. It is quite logical, particularly if the evaluating group is capable of making some specific determinations of impairment of function with regard to capacities of attention, to foreground-background differentiations in both hearing and seeing, to sensory and sensory-integrative aspects of dealing with rapidly incoming information (that is, what has been called *auding* if the information be acoustic; *vizing*, one supposes, if the information be visual; *tacting*, if tactual, and so forth) and of related capacities of brain storage and recall, both of immediate sensory experience and of long-term general experience. All these aspects of the brain's use of its sensorium contribute to the economy of language in relating the self to its environment.

In practical terms of observing what a child does, many children are apparently baffled by the demands of any communicative situation. With due regard for the fact that each language-deviant child may well compose a class of one, there seem to be at least two quite different groups of involved children. One group commonly reflects basic interferences with mechanisms of attention, which often show as inadvertent shifts between distractibility and perseveration; a child is prone to be stimulus-bound or fleeting, and seems best to learn within very limited boundaries of stimulus and attention. Children in the other group are gregarious enough, but have fundamental difficulties in sensory integration, in memory-storage, and in recall. For most, however, each new communicative experience is a baffling challenge. Children in the first group are quite unpredictable; they may swing rapidly from other-worldly indifference to frenetic drive. Those in the second group are apt to be puzzled and frustrated. Both groups demonstrate a sharp contrast with the deaf three-year-old who has no problems other than a profound loss in auditory sensitivity. He will have learned a fair amount of language through visual input, while the aphasic child probably will not. This is a negative finding with a positive meaning.

CAUSAL CONSIDERATIONS

There is considerable discussion these days about whether the child in the first group, the one with basic disturbances in the mechanisms of attention and control, should not better be thought of as *brain-injured* than *aphasic*. Some of his basic failures show in many other ways than in limitations in the learning and remembering and use of linguistic meanings. Again, I suppose we may call either child whatever we wish. One would suppose, as well, however, that the appellation of *brain injury* would be supported by pertinent evidence of a source of injury with ensuing breakdowns in structure or function, or both. Otherwise, there may be a pseudo-differentiation without a difference, purely a kind of semantic judgment which might well not be helpful as a source of predicting a given child's potentials and needs.

In a recent presentation one of our colleagues suggests a contrast that seems to be in closer track of possible causal relationships (Wepman, 1963). He argues for the distinction between "the minimally brain-injured child and the child with minimally arrested development, or as we have tended to call them, children with mild lags in specific modalities of learning." The one child has been injured; the other shows the effects of agenesis, or aplastic development. The one is "a system which is traumatically open following injury"; the other is an "underdeveloped but closed and unimpaired system." He argues, further, that "arrested or slow development can affect very specific structures in the central nervous system. When it does, behavior subserved by the specific structure will . . . be less available to the child. Learning by the child will be minimal when it requires adaptation, decoding and encoding, motor production and feed-back along the modality or pathway affected by the aplastic development."

Many workers-in-the-field, particularly some of those who are devoted primarily to the study of anatomic structures and their lesions, find it diffi-cult to accept this kind of argument. At what postconceptual moment in time, one might ask, can one clearly distinguish the genetic factor or the developmental accident from an etiologic factor of specific damage—what-ever it may be that can and does affect the foetus and the neonate? The world of knowledge is apparently not yet prepared to answer that defini-tively. On the other hand, if the evaluating group centers attention on a description of impairment of function, a precise answer, although inter-esting, may not be necessary.

It is not a digression at this point in the discussion to wonder about the seemingly ever increasing numbers of these language-deviant children. An oversimplified accounting might go like this: first, there are more chil-dren, therefore the numbers of "different" children would be greater even though the proportion were not; second, perhaps more and better questions are being asked, from which are being derived more careful descriptions and evaluations of dysfunction or impairment than used to occur; and, third, many more children are living who used to succumb to circumstances of prenatal and perinatal distress.

Whichever combination of these things may be close to the truth, without doubt all three forces are active. Current reports outline starkly the obstetrician's accounting of the "hazards of being born" (Barnes, 1963). With an annual birth rate of 25/1,000 population, foetal wastage amounts to approximately 250,000, and in excess of 300,000 babies are known to be damaged or defective by the end of the eight-week perinatal period (four weeks pre- to four weeks postdelivery). These do not include a sizeable pro-portion of the motor-palsied, the communicatively incompetent ones with hearing, language, or speech disorders, many of the so-called retardates, nor many of those with psychosocial problems that interfere with maturation and learning.

The background of even something so specific as deafness sufficient to make imperative very special education is different from former years. Ad-ministrators of schools for the deaf the world over report on the "different-ness" of their children's problems. It used to be that a large proportion of the population of a residential school was composed of the so-called ad-ventitiously deaf, children who had developed language and speech, and then were later stricken with disease or infection which left them with profound hearing impairment. There are many fewer of these children nowadays, apparently because of advances in modern medical diagnosis and treatment. There are no fewer deaf children, but many more are deaf in different ways and, more often, represent prenatal or perinatal causal factors, or simply developmental aplasia (Hardy, 1962a). So, too, is it with children who cannot naturally and well learn language comprehension and use for reasons other than deafness or general biologic incompetence.

THE LANGUAGE-LEARNING SYSTEM

To return to our postulated child with basic difficulties in attention and control, if ways and means can be found to help him learn through or around his distractibility, he can learn language and use it as a tool for other learning. If the child in the other grouping (whose problem is often labelled *sensory aphasia*) cannot learn auditory or visual integration, storage, and recall, he may not have much language as a tool for other learning. Who is to say which is the *true aphasic* in any sense that is useful to the children?

Without doubt, some useful answers lie in our better understanding of the neurophysiology and the neurochemistry of sensory functions and memory. There is clearly a difference in function between the all-or-none activity of the conducting axons of a sensory system and the off-and-on generating transduction of its synaptic terminals. It may well be that the integrity of this relationship, or lack of it, offers the possibility of understanding the difference between a normally developing child and the child with multiple communicative involvements with whom we all have to deal so frequently.

Apparently there are many interactive neural networks in all communicative activities. The afferent inflow of acoustic information, for instance, involves spinal cord, reticular formation, thalamus, cerebral cortex, and cerebellar cortex. Cerebro-cerebellar loops are present in all functions. Involved here, then, is not only the incoming sensory information, but also the complex of perception and almost everything else about the behaving child—particularly attention, storage, and recall—that contributes to the relationship between individual and environment that we call intelligence. One school of thought, in particular, has been concerned with some basic relations between behavior and language in cognition, with no attempt toward a neurologic explanation of observed phenomena (Osgood, 1957). There seems to be some hope from current studies that a neurochemical-neurophysiologic analysis may ultimately account for some of the communicative disturbances, discrepancies, and aberrations, mild or complex, which have often been disguised by the terminology of traditional diagnostic labels. Unfortunately, however, the children with various abstruse problems are here and must be dealt with before these kinds of explanatory analyses are clearly available.

There is much that can be done, presumably, at what might be called the semantogenic level of dealing with communicative disorders of childhood. There is much to be learned from operationally based procedures and clinical descriptions of impairment, all of which can be accomplished without resort to etiologic or pathologic labels. This, in turn, would involve the use of scientific methods in treatment or training, and in follow-up appraisal of the effectiveness of treatment.

Something like this was implied in a previous reference to a status called "the nonmotor brain-damaged child." This is a devious rubric which seems to offer little by way of useful direction, particularly when many of the clinical details are conveyed in terms of motor functions. The more one studies the problems of neurophysiologic and neurochemical interaction and integration, the less important becomes site of lesion in many of these deviant children, and the more important becomes interference with function. Central-nervous-system-interference with function does not necessarily imply locus of damage in classical terms. Rather, it may imply disorganization of function, or some kind of integrative breakdown in communication in the complex of the cerebro-cerebellar feedback systems.

The situation with the *aphasic* adult may be quite different, largely, perhaps, because of his normal pretraumatic experiences. He may be frustrated or euphoric. Short of a global involvement, however, he knows something of what is expected of him in a communicative situation, but cannot meet it. This produces a more or less serious breakdown in relations between self and environment. The young child, on the other hand, can know relatively little of what is expected. He cannot read the signs. In consequence, the aphasic child may seem on occasion profoundly stupid, or deaf, or schizoid, or emotionally disturbed. Indeed, in terms of the demands and confusions in communicative situations day by day, his responses or lack of responses may exhibit symptoms suggestive of all these other conditions. Moreover, because the learning and recall and use of appropriate verbal symbolic behavior depend upon sensory integration, attention, and memory—factors common to all modes of learning—specific disorders of language in childhood may not only be mistaken for, but may also accompany, these other kinds of disorders, particularly problems involving refinements of sensory recognition and integration. This is especially true of deafness and of some kinds of specific reading disability, where the line between sensory and integrative problems is thin, indeed (Hardy, 1962b). In practical terms, our children cannot well be segmented with "Occam's razor"; an obvious recourse is to try to find out what they can and cannot do in controlled circumstances of learning.

The young child with problems of language comprehension and use is quite different from the aphasic adult. His brain is plastic and highly resistant, even after drastic traumatic events. Aside from immediate transitory effects, there has not been a single recorded instance of a child aged three years or less who has been made permanently aphasic by traumatic brain damage of the sort that commonly causes adult aphasia. If he lives, provided that his development was normal up to the time of the traumatic incident, he can be expected to go on to learn language comprehension and use. This is not true of older children.

What of the so-called congenitally aphasic child, who represents some form of developmental aplasia? His brain is presumably equally plastic, albeit interfered with in the sense that various neural networks may not be working in normal ways. The evaluative need remains the same: to delineate the details of successes and failures relative to the brain's tools for learning language comprehension and use. This is commonly a difficult task; thus the need for differentiation from other entities with symptoms similar to those of a disorder of language. Various clinicians have emphasized that these differentiations can usually be made only by ruling out basic factors of mental subnormality, autism, and so forth, and by exposing the young child who does not demonstrate a capacity for language comprehension and use to careful diagnostic study and highly structured diagnostic teaching.

In general, a profoundly mentally subnormal child will have many lags and shortcomings in the development of language comprehension and of speech, but the basic disorder is intellectual lack, not aphasia. So, too, with various psychoses of childhood, which may well involve delays or aberrations in verbal symbolic learning. On the other hand, there is good evidence that many autistic children, sometimes early mistaken as deaf, do, in fact, have serious interferences in language comprehension and formulation as they mature (Eisenberg, 1957, and Eisenberg and Kanner, 1956). Similarly, and obviously, there are children who have both auditory and aphasic disorders, just as there are others who are both deaf and intellectually profoundly subnormal.

Current findings in the laboratory, in the clinic, and in preschool training indicate that the young brain is indeed plastic, and commonly capable of learning through or around many kinds of interference. The multiply involved child requires multiple studies. No aphasic child presents a simple problem. It remains for all of us to learn how better to determine with each child what his interferences are, so that relatively unimpaired modalities may be used for the learning of substantive language.

PSYCHOSOCIAL FACTORS

All this presupposes, perhaps, the fact of a healthful, stimulating psychosocial environment. Unfortunately, this cannot be taken for granted. All children, whether with or without language disorders, seem to react to the various tensions and pressures and attitudes and supports of their environment. The fact of frustration and confusion on the part of many of the children under discussion is not difficult to determine by clinical observation. How much of a fairly obvious emotional disturbance is a fundamental psychosocial aspect of personality and how much is a sequel to a communicative disorder is rather more difficult to determine. And, not infrequently, our habits of thinking in terms of diagnostic entities and labels get in the way of making useful determinations.

Semantic problems of management are apparently reflected, as well, in parental attitudes, hopes, aspirations, discouragement, and blame. This seems particularly true in the management of language-disordered children. Most parents have given little time or thought, through their own childhood and maturity, to the modes and meaning of learning language and speech. The tasks of comprehending the development of language and speech, and of understanding the difference between language and speech, seem almost insurmountable for many parents. Careful, painstaking guidance in these terms, among many others, is a *sine qua non* of both early clinical management and of later education and training. In many ways, the psychosocial involvements between parent and language-disordered child are possibly the most important aspects of the matter, once a reasonably sound evaluation of the child's problems has been accomplished. Here, again, a differentiation between aplasia and brain-injury may amount to much more than a theoretical consideration, at least in terms of prediction about the child's future as a function of parental guidance.

SENSATION AND SENSORY INTEGRATION

Perhaps these ideas can be made more practical if we consider what may happen with the primary sensory system for the development of language in early childhood. It is apparent that *hearing*, in the very broad sense of the principal "receiving function" in ordinary conversational exchange, involves much more than the ears and, indeed, much more than the VIIIth-nerve system.

A considerable amount of work has been done in recent years in studying the implications of motor-speech activities in terms of habitual listening. The listener apparently makes typical, categorical responses. Moreover, these categories seem to be defined in some part by his own speech habits. It is said that "in the course of his long experience with language a speaker learns to connect speech sounds with their appropriate articulation. In time, the articulatory movements become part of the perceiving process, mediating between the acoustic stimulus and its ultimate perception" (Hirsh, 1965, quoting Liberman). We have long been aware that children talk because and as they hear; evidently it is reasonable to think that they also "hear" because and as they talk. Certainly, much more needs to be known about the feedback loop of the speech act, hearing, listening, and linguistic meanings.

In many ways, what we are most concerned about in trying to help children who are language-deviant is to find ways and means for them to do just this—to learn a kind of reflexive relationship within the various aspects of the hearing-language-speech (communicative) act. Auditory self-monitoring, the child's capacity to learn to control what he hears himself say in terms of what he hears others say to him, probably begins early in life. If one is to judge by the emergence of the various phonetic details of dialectal patterns, this capacity does not become a major control-factor until the late third or fourth year of life (compare, Vygotsky's idea about verbal thinking as "egocentric speech gone underground"). The relations between audition (the sensory input) and auding (integrative functions in the brain's management of acoustic information) are a very important part of the developmental process. How all this comes about in the course of normal development has received attention through a variety of studies. Much more information is needed, particularly through the earliest developmental stages.

Our own group has been working on some of these problems for several years, with special attention to the status and needs of various subgroups and language-deviant children. Figure 3-1 suggests some possibilities for studying central-nervous system control of sensory information in relations between acoustic stimuli and psychomotor responses (compare, Chase). The boxes to the left represent functions of the receptor system: first, the mechanical, transducing operations of the external and middle ear, and of the activities of the cochlear duct, probably to the point or level of the sheering action of the inner hair cells, which apparently is directly causal of electrical emission; then, the coding operations whereby the potentials reflect what was originally airborne sound (in the laboratory setting, these are recorded from the round-window membrane as electrical potentials, N^1 and N^2); next is the transmission of potentials through the complex pathways of the afferent tracts, with all the complications of facilitations and inhibition relative to various generative functions at each major synaptic junction; finally, the organizational operations which involve complex loops at the cortico-thalamic level within the multiple connections of the "auditory projection areas."

This is the level of what has been called auditory temporal perception. Among other aspects is the importance of "the recognition of changes in frequency or of intensity with time, or even the recognition of the rate at which such changes occur" (Hirsh, 1965). This is an important function of auditory differentiation upon which much of our receptive communicative fluency depends. Our capacity to know the difference between *lips* and *lisp*, for instance, is a function of the separation of two events in time. It requires several milliseconds to do this. Without this capacity of temporal resolving power any of us would be hard put to try to understand the continuum of the speech we hear.

The rising solid line to the left in Figure 3-1 indicates flow to and from storage functions of the brain relative to the auditory mode, some aspects of which must surely relate in experience to many other capacities of storage of other, relatable experiences.

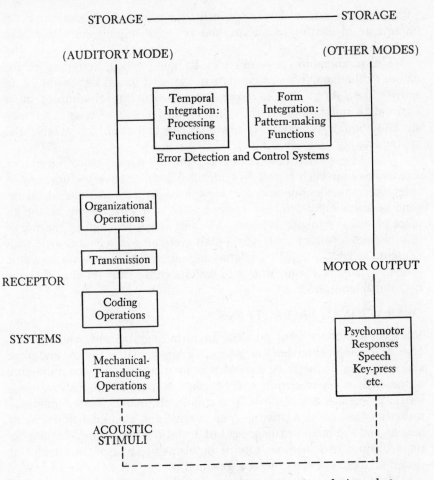

FIGURE 3-1 CNS control of sensory information in relations between acoustic stimuli and psychomotor responses.

Then, to the right, are represented integrative functions of processing bits of information and of forming patterns from them. This is a continuation of the temporal resolving power of the system which begins with an auditory function of recognition. These probably serve, relative to storage and recall, in error detection and control, prior to the selection of an appropriate motor output. This is surely a function of the "grain" of the auditory system relative to past and immediately current auditory experiences. It may well be one form of central programming of response-skills. Implicit here are various efferent controls at a premeaning level, in terms of the functions of the brain in scanning and tracking through states of attention, which may vary from intermittent to fixated. Recent laboratory work with chronic electrodes implanted in the cat has clearly demonstrated the importance of alerting to the size and extent of response-potentials (Galambos, 1960).

The psychomotor responses may be quite varied, according to the nature of the circumstances current. In biosocial terms, one might be an activity like closing a door in response to a particular tonal sequence, or an appropriate imitation of a speech stimulus, or pressing a key as in an operant conditioning procedure, or anything else that might be suitable and appropriate.

It is believed that one can account for any sensory-motor integrative activity in some such terms. Not included here, relative to functions of language comprehension and use, are the mediating functions which depend on meaningful symbolic representation and which comprise the essence of verbal symbolic behavior. Meaning is not required in the use of this scheme. A subject could accomplish everything in reference here with nonsense syllables, or with any array of sounds which have no linguistic content (compare, the use of tapped patterns in the early training of young deaf and aphasic children).

OPERATIONAL PROJECTIONS

We seem to produce many problems from the language with which pathologies or developmental deviations are categorized, relative to time and place and symptoms. It might be somewhat more objective, and certainly more operational, to describe errors or deficits in detection, discrimination, recognition, processing, and so forth. This could well promote better communication professionally, relative to both normal and abnormal functions of hearing and the brain's management of acoustic information. This implies the avoidance of semanto-iatrogenic problems in favor of an attempt at clear descriptions of impairment of function.

Many experts in the management of subjects with aphasia agree that quite commonly there are interferences with the detail of informational intake relative to the usual requirements of a communicative situation. At stake here, in some large part, is a need to distinguish between direct interferences in a sensory modality and breakdowns in the brain's use of this modality. "Sensory aphasia in childhood" is becoming a familiar term these days, and one is not always sure what is meant by it. In several ways this is a peculiar term, for it apparently represents a possible confusion of the sensation with the brain's use of the sensation—the one information-bearing, the other information-using.

The brain's functions in some of these regards can be charted fairly well, regardless of the fact that precise details of tracking and control cannot yet be described. Relative to some important functions of the conveyance of language—reading, writing, and speaking—it seems clear from careful studies of the past hundred years that sufficient damage to the left hemisphere of the cortex can obliterate any of them. This is not true of auding, for this capacity is apparently bi- or trans-cortical. Indeed, if auding is severely damaged, or is profoundly interfered with by some aspect or other of maldevelopment, any or all of the basic language functions may be profoundly impaired or absent. This is one of the reasons, perhaps, why developmental "sensory aphasia" in childhood may be so different from the "sensory aphasia" in adulthood which results from catastrophic trauma. When a severe problem in auding is at stake in childhood, much else may also be affected. Responses to acoustic stimuli, for instance, which may very well have been present in the early preauding months of infancy, are apt to be inhibited and the child may become functionally deaf for the purposes of developing language and speech. This is not so likely to be true of aphasic adults who have developed normally. They may be profoundly impaired in auding, while retaining good abilities in the detection and discrimination of acoustic stimuli.

SYNTHESIS

The meaning of various functions of the nervous system relative to the use of language in behavior has been under intensive study in recent years (compare Osgood, 1963). One can observe, if he wishes, any modality that is available. The principles seem to be quite constant (although the "rules of operation" may change from one "level" to another): a flow from the outside into sensory projection, integration, and verbal-symbolic experience, which constitutes the organism's decoding of current experience; representational functions, solely symbolic in reference, connect present, past, and future behavior, and initiate a flow from the inside to the outside, relative to integration, projection, and, ultimately, a response, which may then become meaningful to an observer or a communicative participant. The medium may be conversation or writing, or, indeed, one must suppose, poetry and the novel. The point is that we cannot very well remove the psyche from psycholinguistics, any more than we can remove it from psychoacoustics. We may know what kinds of signals we introduce to our subjects via a pure-tone audiometer or speech-hearing tests, but the only way we can know about what they perceive is to be able to make a judgment in terms of their behavior.

One may describe children with disorders of language comprehension and use in many different ways. He may wish to differentiate between agenesis and cerebral injury, as has been discussed, or he may prefer to describe differences in terms of contrast between biologic deficiency and suboptimal function. Somewhat different perspectives are involved in the use of this terminology, without necessarily any conflict in view or description of the child. Sooner or later, however, in all evaluations of functions and behavior, one must determine which modalities of input and output are working, and whether integration is taking place. We have come a long way in understanding some of the accomplishments and deviations of children in terms of the presence or absence of learning language comprehension and use. We have still a long way to go to be able infallibly to appraise the capacities and limitations of the next small mind we may have to deal with.

References

Barnes, A. C., The hazards of being born, *Johns Hopkins Magazine*, October 1963.

Chase, R. A., Information system analysis of the organization of motor activity. In P. H. Hoch and J. Zubin (Editors), *Disorders of perception* (New York: Grune & Stratton, 1965).

Eisenberg, L., Course of childhood schizophrenia, *Arch. Neurol. Psychiat.*, 1957, 78.

Eisenberg, L., and Kanner, L., The autistic child in adolescence, *Amer. J. Psychiat.*, 1956, 112.

Eisenson, J., Aphasia in adults—classification and examination procedures; in L. E. Travis (Editor), *Handbook of speech pathology* (New York: Appleton-Century-Crofts, 1957).

Galambos, R., Studies of the auditory system with implanted electrodes. In G. L. Rasmussen and W. F. Windle (Editors), *Neural mechanisms of the auditory and vestibular systems* (Springfield, Illinois: Charles C Thomas, 1960).

Hardy W. G., Human communication—ordered and disordered, *Volta Rev.*, 1962a, 64.

Hardy, W. G., Dyslexia in relation to diagnostic methodology in hearing and speech disorders. In J. Money (Editor), *Reading disability* (Baltimore: Johns Hopkins Press, 1962b).

Hirsh, I. J., Audition in relation to the perception of speech. In V. E. Hall (Editor), *Proceedings of a Conference on Speech, Language, and Communication, UCLA Forum in Medical Sciences*, 1965.

Mac Keith, R., and Bax, M. (Editors), *Minimal Cerebral Dysfunction*—Papers from the International Study Group, Oxford, September, 1962. (London: William Heinemann Medical Books, 1963).

McGinnis, M., *Aphasic Children* (Washington, D.C.: Alexander Graham Bell Association for the Deaf, 1963).

Osgood, C. E., A behavioristic analysis of perception and language as cognitive phenomena. In J. Bruner (Editor), *Contemporary approaches to cognition* (Cambridge, Massachusetts: Harvard University Press, 1957).

Osgood, C. E., On understanding and creating sentences, *Amer. Psychologist*, 1963, 18.

Schuell, H., Jenkins, J. J., and Carroll, J. B., A factor analysis of the Minnesota test for differential diagnosis of aphasia, *J. Speech Hearing Res.*, 1962, 5, 349-369.

Town, C. H., Congenital aphasia, *Psychol. Clin.*, 1911, V, 6.

Wepman, J. M., Cerebral injury or aphasia. In S. A. Kirk and W. Becker (Editors), *Conference on children with minimal brain impairment* (Urbana: University of Illinois, 1963).

Vygotsky, L. S., *Thought and language*. Translated and edited by E. Hanfman and G. Vakar. (New York: M.I.T. Press and Wiley, 1962).

4 BEHAVIOR PROBLEMS OF MIDDLE
CHILDHOOD

Donald R. Peterson

Before the etiology and treatment of children's behavior disorders can be sensibly examined, the disorders themselves must be defined. For the sake of generality and descriptive efficiency, any concepts employed in such definition should be nonarbitrary, unitary, and independent. Factor analytic methods have been employed with salutary effect in the structural definition adult disorders (e.g., Lorr, Jenkins, & O'Connor, 1955; Rubenstein & Lorr, 1957; Wittenborn, 1951; Wittenborn & Holzberg, 1951), but similar work with the disorders of childhood has only begun (Hewitt & Jenkins, 1946; Himmelweit, 1953). The present study extends and refines this earlier research by factorizing uniformly gathered judgments of problem behavior during the kindergarten and elementary school years, and by examining changes in problem expression during that time.

SUBJECTS AND PROCEDURES

In the absence of any accepted theory of structural organization among children's behavior disorders, a sample of problems was chosen by empirical means. The referral problems of 427 representatively chosen cases at a guidance clinic were recorded, and frequencies tabulated for all problems mentioned more than once. Groups of synonymous terms were reduced by eliminating all but the most frequently used expressions, and four concepts were discarded because they were conceptually supraordinate to other terms, and hence redundant. Choice among the remaining variables was determined exclusively by the frequency with which they had occurred, and the 58 most common problems were selected for general investigation.

Reprinted from *Journal of Consulting Psychology*, Vol. 25, No. 3 (June, 1961), pp. 205-209. By permission of the author and publisher.

In use, the variables were ordered randomly, assembled in a format requiring ratings of o (no problem), 1 (mild problem), or 2 (severe problem), and submitted for completion to 28 teachers of 831 kindergarten and elementary school children in six different schools in Illinois. The choice of school children, rather than clients undergoing treatment for judged disorders, was based on the assumption that most such disorders are extremes of continuous "normal" dimensions, and was determined by the desirability of obtaining uniform data on large numbers of subjects within the age range under consideration. The large sample requirement has been met previously (Hewitt & Jenkins, 1946; Himmelweit, 1953) by recourse to case history information, but the dangers of that expedient seemed greater than those in the present course, and the study was begun in the hope that otherwise unselected school children would present sufficiently numerous, severe problems to warrant sensible analysis and yield meaningful results. Distributions of ratings were generally eccentric, but the effects were reduced by excluding some rarely checked problems (dizziness, soiling, and enuresis, which occurred in less than 3 percent of the cases, were eliminated), and by pooling judgments of mild and severe problems (ratings of 1 and 2) for all the remaining variables.

For analysis, the sample was divided into four groups: a kindergarten sample ($N = 126$), a first and second grade sample ($N = 237$), a group from the third and fourth grades ($N = 229$), and a fifth and sixth grade sample ($N = 239$). Two teacher ratings were available for each kindergarten child; the number of actual ratings used in the analysis is thus double the N given above for the kindergarten group. Phi coefficients of intercorrelation were computed separately for the four samples. From each correlation matrix, ten centroid factors were extracted, and from each set of centroid factors two were rotated to conform with Kaiser's varimax criterion (Kaiser, 1958).

Human judgment was involved only once in all that analysis—in deciding how many factors to retain for rotation. The decision to keep only two was based on inspection of plots of variance removed by successive centroid factors, and the application of criteria for factor retention developed elsewhere (Peterson, 1960). Out of personal curiosity, five-factor solutions were also tried for each data set; but these, as expected, were much less stable over age than the two-factor solutions, and only the latter will be reported.

Factor scores were computed for all cases by unweighted summation of pertinent problems checked by the teachers. Interjudge correlations were computed for the kindergarten sample, and further attention directed toward comparing the four age groups. Data for boys and girls were separated in all comparisons, because of well known sex differences in problem expression, and mean factor scores were computed to show trends in the development of behavior problems over the years of middle childhood.

RESULTS

THE FACTORS. All four sets of rotated factor loadings are presented together in Table 4-1, an arrangement permitted only by the marked similarity between results at the four age levels.[1] Factor 1 is obviously a *conduct problem* dimension, closely resembling the like-named factor isolated by Himmelweit (1953) and "unsocialized aggression" as defined by Hewitt and Jenkins (1946). Factor 2 has been labeled *personality problem* in accordance with Himmelweit's designation and common usage. It is much like the "over-inhibited behavior" dimension which Hewitt and Jenkins found. Actually these terms, "personality problem" and "conduct problem," are grossly inappropriate. Both problems are personality expressions, and both affect conduct. But the central meanings seem clear enough. In one case, impulses are expressed and society suffers; in the other case impulses are evidently inhibited and the child suffers.

The generality of these factors appears to be enormous. Not only do they emerge with striking uniformity over the limited age range and the particular variables and subjects examined here; they have appeared in very much the same form with the recorded problems of treatment cases (Hewitt & Jenkins, 1946; Himmelweit, 1953), and remarkably similar factors have appeared in the questionnaire behavior of delinquent boys (Peterson, Quay & Cameron, 1959). Considering all studies together, age has varied from early childhood to adolescence; problem status has varied from none, through clinic attendance, to incarceration for delinquency; data sources have varied from case history records, to standard ratings, to questionnaire responses; methods of factor extraction have varied from cluster inspection to centroid analysis; rotational methods have varied from none, through visual shifts to both orthogonal and oblique solutions, to analytic techniques. Through it all, the factors have stayed the same, and their definition at last seems adequate. The time is ripe for study, particularly experimental study, of dynamics, etiology, and treatment.

FACTOR SCORES AND THEIR RELIABILITY. Such investigations, however, cannot proceed until various properties of the measuring devices have been examined. Factor scores were computed by unweighted summation over the first 15 variables for each factor as listed in Table 4-1. Below that point, many of the variables either have no appreciable loading on either dimension, or approximately equal loadings on both. The former condition holds especially for skin allergy, hay fever, nausea, and stomachaches, which may often be purely somatic and qualitatively distinct from the other variables

---

[1] The rating schedule, correlation matrices, and unrotated centroid factor matrices have been deposited with the American Documentation Institute. Order Document No. 6632 from ADI Auxiliary Publications Project, Photoduplication Service, Library of Congress: Washington 25, D. C., remitting in advance $2.00 for microfilm or $3.75 for photocopies. Make checks payable to: Chief, Photoduplication Service, Library of Congress.

TABLE 4-1: Rotated factor loadings.

Factor	Conduct Problem				Personality Problem			
	K[a]	1–2	3–4	5–6	K[a]	1–2	3–4	5–6
Conduct Problem								
Disobedience	74	77	69	86	03	04	07	11
Disruptiveness	73	67	66	76	—04	19	—03	11
Boisterousness	68	63	67	68	—16	07	—07	—09
Fighting	54	73	61	77	—09	—04	11	07
Attention-seeking	54	67	63	76	—12	10	—07	02
Restlessness	64	58	62	71	04	24	06	20
Negativism	56	64	60	70	12	27	20	15
Impertinence	57	57	53	76	02	—08	00	08
Destructiveness	59	65	51	65	—05	27	19	00
Irritability	53	59	57	69	01	11	04	07
Temper tantrums	54	37	49	64	08	11	22	16
Hyperactivity	51	49	54	49	—06	12	00	03
Profanity	30	42	64	60	—07	11	02	00
Jealousy	23	50	41	56	06	10	12	11
Uncooperativeness	67	67	53	71	09	31	38	21
Distractibility	56	57	61	72	29	42	32	26
Irresponsibility	60	65	49	65	22	18	47	20
Inattentiveness	54	61	36	69	39	30	57	28
Laziness in school	44	59	36	37	29	36	55	31
Shortness of attention span	48	54	31	60	37	34	55	29
Dislike for school	38	40	32	41	06	26	54	13
Nervousness	22	25	46	50	40	44	22	26
Thumb-sucking	29	17	36	05	09	28	—03	15
Skin allergy	—16	02	—20	—05	01	21	05	—20
Personality Problem								
Feelings of inferiority	12	25	13	17	59	56	66	62
Lack of self-confidence	12	26	13	16	60	61	60	58
Social withdrawal	—03	08	04	05	50	64	61	60
Proneness to become flustered	07	28	15	24	54	59	60	58
Self-consciousness	—13	—03	—15	16	55	60	47	63
Shyness	—16	—18	—23	—13	62	57	50	51
Anxiety	01	19	24	10	50	57	55	47
Lethargy	—06	22	01	31	52	47	61	43
Inability to have fun	—15	06	—14	—09	49	48	53	48
Depression	00	20	04	29	47	43	64	42
Reticence	06	20	08	14	45	43	64	41
Hypersensitivity	06	26	18	30	40	53	54	46
Drowsiness	02	09	09	29	39	48	45	41
Aloofness	—16	—03	—04	05	51	32	50	31
Preoccupation	09	12	23	37	47	57	64	41
Lack of interest in environment	24	30	21	51	40	44	67	28
Clumsiness	16	21	36	17	43	54	34	36
Daydreaming	14	26	21	49	53	46	69	47
Tension	21	31	39	39	41	62	27	41
Suggestibility	04	29	31	52	41	42	48	30
Crying	15	14	06	59	27	48	32	19
Preference for younger playmates	28	21	23	14	08	45	37	32
Specific fears	—09	24	—02	—04	24	47	20	20
Stuttering	11	17	08	02	27	35	29	16
Headaches	19	21	00	00	07	46	22	27
Nausea	—10	23	07	—02	01	14	38	37
Truancy from school	27	07	04	22	00	20	39	35
Stomach-aches	10	18	05	—06	—01	30	38	29
Preference for older playmates	—14	05	26	16	01	38	16	01
Masturbation	08	14	26	04	—18	40	04	17
Hay fever or asthma	15	—01	17	—11	05	21	09	03

a Kindergarten.

examined. The latter condition, roughly equal loadings on both factors, holds for crying, nervousness, and certain school attitudes, variables which are either very general in nature or exhibit some kind of developmental change.

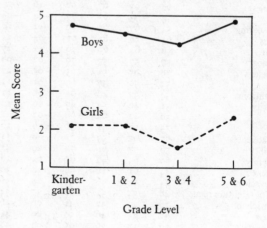

FIGURE 4-1   Mean conduct problem scores.

Reliability and interfactor correlation were examined for the kindergarten group only, since only for that group were dual ratings available. Interjudge r's of .77 and .75 were found for Factors 1 and 2, respectively. These figures are exceptionally good for ratings, and are sufficiently high for most research purposes. The correlation between factors was .18, low enough to meet most requirements for independence.

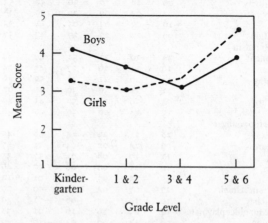

FIGURE 4-2   Mean personality problem scores.

DEVELOPMENTAL CHANGES. Mean factor scores were computed for boys and girls in all age groups, and the results are shown in Figures 4-1 and 4-2. Throughout middle childhood, boys consistently display more severe conduct disturbances than girls, possibly as a function of constitutional differences, but more likely in response to different levels of social expectancy and tolerance for misbehavior. An interesting reversal, however, occurs in the expression of personality problems. Boys evidently start school with more personality problems than girls, but around the seventh or eighth year such problems become more plentiful among girls. Again, social pressures for sex-type conformity seem the likeliest causal agents. Reasons for the apparent upswing in problems at the fifth and sixth grade level are obscure. The increase may arise from the early agitation of adolescence, and the difficulty this can bring about in our society.

SUMMARY

This study was designed to improve structural definition of children's behavior problems and to examine changes in those problems over the years of middle childhood. Teacher ratings of 58 clinically frequent problems were obtained for 831 kindergarten and elementary school children, and four separate factor analyses were conducted, one for the kindergarten subjects and one each for children in grades 1–2, 3–4, and 5–6. Two factors emerged with remarkable invariance in all four analyses. The first implied a tendency to express impulses against society, and was labelled "conduct problem." The second contained a variety of elements suggesting low self-esteem, social withdrawal, and dysphoric mood. It was called "personality problem." Both factors have now appeared in a number of studies despite wide differences in subjects, variables, and analytic procedures.

Comparisons over age showed that boys displayed more severe conduct problems than girls at all age levels examined. Kindergarten and primary school boys also showed more severe personality problems than girls, but at the two highest age levels this trend was reversed, and girls displayed more personality problems than boys.

The definition of both dimensions seems adequate. Reliable, independent measures of the factors can be obtained, and the way toward investigation of dynamics, etiology, and treatment now seems clear.

References

Hewitt, L. E., and Jenkins, R. L., *Fundamental patterns of maladjustment: The dynamics of their origin* (Springfield, Illinois: Green, 1946).

Himmelweit, Hilde T., A factorial study of children's behavior problems. Cited in H. J. Eysenck, *The structure of human personality* (London: Metheun, 1953).

Kaiser, H. F., The varimax criterion for analytic rotation in factor analysis, *Psychometrika*, 1958, 23, 187-200.

Lorr, M., Jenkins, R. L., and O'Connor, J. P., Factors descriptive of psychopathology and behavior of hospitalized psychotics, *J. abnorm. soc. Psychol.*, 1955, 50, 78-86.

Peterson, D. R., The age generality of personality factors derived from ratings, *Educ. psychol. Measmt.*, 1960, 20, 461-474.

Peterson, D. R., Quay, H. C., and Cameron, G. R., Personality and background factors in juvenile delinquency as inferred from questionnaire responses, *J. consult. Psychol.*, 1959, 23, 395-399.

Rubenstein, E. A., and Lorr, M., Patient types in outpatient psychotherapy, *J. clin. Psychol.*, 1957, 13, 356-361.

Wittenborn, J. R., Symptom patterns in a group of mental hospital patients, *J. consult. Psychol.*, 1951, 15, 290-302.

Wittenborn, J. R., and Holzberg, J. D., The generality of psychiatric syndromes, *J. consult. Psychol.*, 1951, 15, 372-380.

5 PERCEPTUALLY HANDICAPPED

Walter B. Barbe

Perhaps the newest arrival in the area of exceptionality, not in existence but in identification, is the brain-injured child who is neither epileptic nor cerebral palsied. For too long this child has been called cerebral palsied, even if no gross motor impairment is evident. For want of another category, the label "cerebral palsy" is applied. It is, of course, true that the brain-injured child may or may not also have cerebral palsy, and that he may or may not be mentally retarded. The same conditions which cause him to be labeled "brain-injured," namely an injury to the central nervous system itself, may also produce cerebral palsy, epilepsy or mental retardation. Alfred Strauss, a pioneer in the study of this type of child, preferred to classify such children as "brain injured with mental retardation, brain injured with motor handicap (cerebral palsy), brain-injured with behavior disturbance, and so on" (1960, p. 137).

Various classifications for this type of child have been made. Referring to the given types of mental deficiency, Strauss set forth the differences between "exogenous" and "inogenous." The term "exogenous" came to be synonymous with the term "brain-injured child." Others preferred to use the expression "brain-damaged, CNS (central nervous system) impairment." The problem is apparently one of terminology. Stevens and Birch suggest the term "Strauss syndrome" (1960, p. 148). Strauss reports that on the basis of his research, these basic deviations in the mental makeup of brain-injured children exist (1960, p. 139):

(1) Disturbances in perception
(2) Disturbances in concept formation (thinking and reading)

Reprinted from *The Exceptional Child*. The Center for Applied Research in Education, Inc., Washington, D. C., 1963, pp. 78-85. By permission of the author and publisher.

(3) Disturbances in language
(4) Disturbances in the emotional behavior

Strauss referred to these as "brain-injured children," but there has been a great deal of controversy about that label. The argument runs that merely because a child behaves in this way does not prove brain damage, and moreover all brain-damaged children are not characterized by this type of behavior. For this reason, Stevens and Birch suggest the term "Strauss syndrome" to describe the brain-injured child displaying the perceptual and conceptual difficulties described by Strauss. Indeed, any label other than "brain-injured" that will provide better understanding for this particular type of child should be adopted. Whether or not one agrees that new terminology is absolutely necessary, the results from accepting a different label which in no way changes either those children who are put into this category or the procedures being developed hopefully to benefit them seems to be the only sensible course of action. One cannot help but wonder why in education, in which there are so many overlapping terms making sweeping generalizations about the types of children to be included, there should have developed such sensitivity about the use of the term "brain-injured." If this is the first sign of more careful diagnosis and delineation of various types of exceptionality, then the trend is indeed a good one. With this understanding in mind, one can refer to those children with no motor involvement he would have formerly called "brain-injured" as "perceptually handicapped" or "Strauss syndrome."

The number of children with brain injury is not known, much less the number of those who would fit into the Strauss syndrome category. It has been estimated that the number of children suffering from brain injuries is 2–5 per 1000. However, it is not unlikely that all individuals suffer some slight brain damage as the result of the perils of everyday living, which consists of falls, bumps on the head, and an almost continuous parade of small accidents.

There is every reason to believe that the number of brain-injured school children reaching school age is on the increase. In times past, most brain-injured children did not survive early infancy because of an inexplicable predisposition to respiratory ailments. With penicillin and antibiotics, what formerly was usually fatal to the brain-injured child is now little more than a normal illness. There are many who feel that the incidence of Strauss syndrome children is much greater than generally suspected. This does not mean that all of these children are in need of special education, but some of the learning difficulties earlier classified as due to poor teaching or lack of readiness may in reality have been cases of the Strauss syndrome.

Information in textbooks about this type of child is conspicuous by its absence. However, the abundance of recent research on children of the

Strauss syndrome type reported in the periodical literature is overwhelming evidence, perhaps, that the Strauss syndrome type of child is coming more to be recognized as another type of exceptionality. The increase in the number of groups concerned with perceptually handicapped persons indicates the increased interest in this area of both lay and professional people.

The diagnosis of brain injury is of course a problem for the neurologist, but the type of child described in the Strauss syndrome can rarely be detected by a gross neurological examination, however. There are cases where examination reveals no positive signs of neurological impairment, but because of many characteristic behavior patterns a diagnosis can still be made with a fair degree of certainty. In instances such as these, supportive psychological examination results are absolutely essential in the diagnostic stage. Whether this comes as a part of the diagnosis or after it makes no great difference, provided that it is not omitted. In any event, thorough psychological examinations of all children suspected of having neurological handicaps is essential for educational planning.

The role the educator plays in the diagnosis of brain injury may be one of referral. Unless suspected brain injury is clearly established by a neurologist's diagnosis, educators refrain from using this emotionally loaded expression. Brain injury is something from which a child never recovers, for brain tissue has been permanently destroyed. Other parts of the brain may be trained so that the damaged areas are perhaps bypassed, but cautious use of the term is nevertheless absolutely essential.

It is important that educators and psychologists be aware of the fact that the child being described is not necessarily mentally retarded. It is true that he manifests many of the characteristics of the retarded; particularly, he does not make normal progress in academic school subjects when taught by regular methods.

For a number of reasons, many children with brain injury are not identified until they enter school. What has until that time been labeled merely a behavioral problem soon becomes a severe learning problem. The school's responsibility in making a referral to the family physician is to describe those behavior patterns and the nature of the child's learning difficulties as clearly as possible. It will probably be the responsibility of the family doctor to refer the child for a neurological examination. If a school psychologist is available, preliminary referral to him will add additional evidence to support the teacher's observations.

Brain injury or damage can occur in the prenatal stage, at the time of, or after birth. The damage may be the result of an actual blow to the head or of any condition which would reduce the supply of oxygen to the brain for a length of time sufficient to cause permanent damage. Excessively high fever is a common cause of brain injury; birth injuries, perhaps, cause the greatest number of brain injuries. When the characteristics revealed by neurological examinations are congruent with those described by Strauss, as opposed to epilepsy or cerebral palsy, the child is said to be of the "Strauss syndrome" type.

The best current definition of brain-injured children is that given by Strauss himself (Strauss and Lehtinen, 1947):

> The brain-injured child is the child who before, during, or after birth, has received an injury to or suffered an infection of the brain. As a result of such an organic impairment, defects of the neuromotor system may be present or absent; however, such a child may show disturbances in perception, thinking, and emotional behavior, either separately or in combination. These disturbances can be demonstrated by specific tests. These disturbances prevent or impede a normal learning process. Special educational methods have been devised to remedy these specific handicaps.

Strauss groups the characteristics of brain-injured children into three categories: perception and perceptual disurbances, thinking disorders, and behavior disorders. He describes perception as "an activity of the mind . . . between sensation and thought," a "means by which the individual organizes and comes to understand the phenomena which constantly descend upon him (Strauss and Lehtinen, 1947). The Strauss syndrome child does not perceive a picture as a whole, each part identified in relationship to it. Rather, he perceives the individual parts separate from the whole. He also has great difficulty separating foreground and background in visual perception. Strauss showed that perception difficulties exist in the visual, tactile, and auditory fields. Perseveration, the inability to shift, is the consistent repetition or continuance of an activity once begun. In thinking disorders it has been found by numerous research studies that the brain-injured child is inclined to give bizarre responses. He is distracted more easily by unessential and accidental details. The child with the Strauss syndrome is inclined to want things in an exact, never-changing order—Strauss refers to this as a "formulistic" arrangement. Behavior disorders in the Strauss syndrome include such things as short attention span, high degree of distractibility, and emotional shallowness. The child's "uncontrollable drive and disinhibition" are perhaps the outstanding characteristics which cause behavior problems in school.

The area of great disagreement over the Strauss syndrome is the fact that there is so much overlapping of classifications. There are those who feel that the Strauss syndrome is not a distinct type of exceptionality, but rather a combination of emotional disturbances, mental retardation, and cerebral palsy. The author's experience with learning difficulties leads him to believe that this is a distinct category greatly in need of further understanding and research.

Strauss found the brain-injured child who was not mentally defective characteristically to have great learning difficulties in school, in spite of proven normal intelligence (Strauss and Kephart, 1955). On such tests the normal brain-injured or Strauss syndrome child scores higher in the verbal area than in the nonverbal. Particular strengths seem to be in vocabulary or word meaning, with decided deficiency in verbal reasoning areas. Eye-hand coordination activities are usually failed as are perception of items involving figure-ground tasks.

An excellent book that explains the "Strauss Syndrome" child is *The Other Child* by Lewis, Strauss and Lehtinen (1960). A section dealing with the education of the brain-injured child in the 1955 edition of the *Psychopathology and Education of the Brain-Injured Child* (Strauss and Lehtinen, 1947, p. 28) is particularly valuable. Special techniques for teaching such children developed at the Cove Schools are carefully outlined. Whether or not the specific techniques are employed, a variety of activities are presented which should be helpful to the classroom teacher in working with any type of child who needs a different approach to learning. A good teacher will, of course, necessarily have to make adaptations to meet each individual case.

The brain-injured child is often placed in a classroom for the mentally retarded if he is unable to score high enough on an intelligence test for enrollment in the regular grades. The danger obvious in this type of placement clearly indicates the need for placement to be made on the basis of more than just an IQ score. Because of their behavior and perception problems, few Strauss syndrome children will be able to score high enough to indicate a potential above that of the retarded classes. But this should not justify assignment to such a class. It has been clearly demonstrated that many such children have potentials higher than previously thought.

Placement in a class for the mentally retarded may not necessarily be harmful, providing the teacher understands this type of child. However, the goal of the teacher in the mentally retarded class is to stimulate the children to the highest level of performance. This is accomplished by providing opportunities for many activities, a wide variety of materials, short periods on individual topics, and much stimulation. The brain-injured child, however, needs to have extraneous stimuli removed. A rather rigid pattern of instruction is strongly recommended, with as little change in the routine as possible. It is possible that the Strauss syndrome child could be educated along with the mentally retarded, but it is this author's opinion that the best instruction for both groups of children is not likely to be achieved in an integrated classroom.

As a result of work in Montgomery County, Maryland, Cruickshank and others recently published a major contribution to the area of teaching brain-injured and hyperactive children that provides much practical information on programming and teaching methodology (Cruickshank, *et al.*, 1962). They placed stress on the regulation of the school environment by means of a rigid time schedule, specific assignments, and follow-through on work expected. The success of the teaching situation was judged in terms of the academic progress of the children.

Residential school placement for the Strauss syndrome child is extremely expensive, and there are only a limited number of places where actual provisions are made for this particular type of child. In those cases where behavioral problems are so great or environmental conditions make remaining in the home inadvisable, residential placement may be necessary. Whenever possible, the child should be provided for in the regular public school, and for the first three grades preferably in special classes. From the fourth grade on the child who is mentally retarded should be directed to the mentally retarded class. The child with normal intelligence might be fitted into the regular classroom. There is an increasing number of school systems recognizing this problem and making special provisions for these otherwise extremely difficult-to-handle children.

In a comparison of brain-injured and non brain-injured mentally retarded children, Gallagher (1957) asks:

> Are the differences that can be seen between these two groups substantial enough to create recognizable differences in the total patterns of the development of children in these groups? The writer believes that this study and previous research direct an affirmative answer to this question. A second crucial question might be: Do these differences imply the need for drastically modified education and training programs or merely slight modifications in existing programs? Here the answer is less clear and depends to a large degree on which brain-injured children you are talking about. The range of different problems and lack of problems within the brain-injured group is large enough to cast considerable doubt on the notion that plans can or should be made for brain-injured children as though they were a homogeneous group.

Gallagher's study and others indicate that when the child with the Strauss syndrome is adequately diagnosed and taught by a teacher who understands his particular learning needs, he may be able to function effectively in classes for the mentally retarded. Placement of a Strauss syndrome child incorrectly diagnosed as mentally retarded in a special class with retarded children can be extremely harmful. But the Strauss syndrome children of normal intelligence will definitely need special educational adaptations. Because the number of these children will not be exceedingly great, the author believes that integrated classes including children of the educable level up to and including those of normal intelligence would be most sensible.

References

Cruickshank, William M., Bentzen, Frances A., Ratzeburg, Frederick H., and Tannhauser, Mirian T., *Teaching methodology for brain-injured and hyperactive children* (Syracuse: Syracuse University Press, 1962).

Gallagher, James J., *A comparison of brain-injured and non brain-injured mentally retarded children on several psychological variables*, Monogr. Soc. Res. Child Develp., 1957, 22 (2), 65.

Lewis, Richard S., Strauss, Alfred A., and Lehtinen, Laura E., *The other child*, 2nd ed. (New York: Grune & Stratton, 1960).

Stevens, Godfrey, and Birch, Jack W., A proposal for classification of the terminology used to describe brain-injured children. In James F. Magary and John R. Eichorn (Editors), *The exceptional child* (New York: Holt, Rinehart and Winston, 1960).

Strauss, Alfred A., The education of the brain-injured child. In James F. Magary and John R. Eichorn (Editors), *The exceptional child* (New York: Holt, Rinehart and Winston, 1960).

Strauss, Alfred A., and Kephart, Newell C., *Psychopathology and education of the brain-injured child*; Vol. II, *Progress in theory and clinic* (New York: Grune & Stratton, 1955).

Strauss, Alfred A., and Lehtinen, Laura E., *Psychopathology and education of the brain-injured child* (New York: Grune & Stratton, 1947).

SECTION B: The Child With Brain Dysfunctions

6 MINIMAL BRAIN DYSFUNCTIONS IN THE SCHOOL-AGE CHILD

Sam D. Clements and John E. Peters

For many years it has been the custom among child guidance workers to attribute the behavioral and learning deviations seen in children almost exclusively to the rearing patterns and interpersonal relationships experienced by such youngsters.We, as well as an increasing number of clinical child workers, feel that when evaluating a disturbed child, we must search as carefully among the myriad possibilities of organic causation as we have in the past among the interpersonal, deprivation, and stress factors; *and certainly without sacrificing the important knowledge which has accumulated in the latter areas.* In many clinics, it has become habitual to assume psychogenicity when no easily recognizable organic deviation can be found in the child. Undoubtedly this has been due, in part, to the difficulty in delineating the contribution to symptomatology and personality structure of subtle organic and central nervous system deviations, and to the relatively greater accessibility of environmental data. Although lip service is often given to "constitutional factors," temperament, heredity, and "possible organicity," the overwhelming tendency has been to weave a complete causative fabric out of the fragile threads of stereotypes such as sibling rivalry, rejecting parents, repressed hostility, oedipal conflict, repressed sexuality, etc., much of which may well be secondary and epiphenomenal rather than primary. It is our contention that an honest blank should be reserved in our thinking for the inclusion of as-yet-unnamed subtle deviations arising from genetic factors, perinatal brain insults, and illnesses and injuries sustained during the years critical for the development and maturation of those parts of the nervous system having to do with perception,

Reprinted from *Archives of General Psychiatry*, Vol. 6, No. 3 (March, 1962), pp. 17-29. By permission of the senior author and publisher.

language, inhibition of impulses, and motor control. Granted the equal and often greater importance of experiential factors, we should not automatically fill the explanatory void with harsh fathers and overprotective mothers and give but cursory consideration to the organism which is reacting to such parents.

In the case of a disturbed child, as one peers in sequence at the presenting symptoms, the precipitating events, the interpersonal experiences, the intellectual and temperamental endowment, the central nervous system deviation and maturational factors, and finally at the brain damage factors, it is like looking through a series of partially transparent curtains of different designs and at different distances from the eye. With experience one gains the feeling that he can focus on each in turn and to some degree evaluate the contribution of each. This approach, however, is not sufficient in view of the additional evaluation methods which are available, but which are not being utilized. It is hoped that future research will make it possible to define and to measure each of the above factors and to relegate to each its proper valence in the determination of a child's behavior.

This article is concerned primarily with a diagnostic evaluation plan for children coming to child guidance and child psychiatric clinics. In addition, treatment and management as practiced in our clinic will be discussed. There have been a number of excellent articles dealing with the core symptom picture with which we are concerned (Burks, 1960; Denhoff, 1961; Eisenberg, 1957; Hanvik, *et al.*, 1953; Laufer, *et al.*, 1957; Lawrence, 1960; Levy, 1959; Illinois Mental Health Center Report, 1957; Thelander, *et al.*, 1958), but few have outlined a diagnostic procedure which includes as part of a *routine* work-up, many of the criteria, tests, and maneuvers which will detect the borderline and equivocal cases of organicity and central nervous system deviation. This symptom picture has been variously referred to as brain-damage behavior syndrome, hyperkinetic syndrome, organic brain syndrome, hyperkinetic-impulse disorder, Strauss syndrome, postencephaletic behavior disorder, and others. This syndrome is also our primary point of reference, but we feel that there are many variations within this symptom complex in which some of the less conspicuous symptoms are the only ones present and which go undetected unless a meticulous diagnostic procedure is carried out. Clear-cut hyperactivity is easily recognized, but solitary dyslexia or dyscalculia may be thought of as a thing apart, and usually blamed on an illusive "learning" or "emotional block."

We have come to rely on the patterns of subtest scores achieved by the child on the Wechsler Intelligence Scale for Children (WISC), and on the "equivocal" neurological signs (Kennard, 1960) as well as on the more easily recognized clinical signs of hyperactivity, short attention span, etc. We feel that the varied and particular tasks undertaken in such a psychological test instrument as the WISC can tell us so much more than a mere overall IQ, and should be respected equally with neurological, clinical, and EEG findings. Many physicians have not been so inclined, and many psychologists have not recognized the diagnostic power of the tools they use every day. We feel great errors are being made in the easy acceptance by psychologists, as well as psychiatrists, pediatricians, and social workers of an over-all IQ score which so often misrepresents the child's potential. Many children have been readily classified as mentally retarded or merely average on the basis of the composite WISC IQ, when either the verbal or performance scores or some isolated subtest scores have been far above this. Our final diagnosis of a brain dysfunction may rest upon either the more obvious symptoms or upon the accumulative weight of several more delicate indicators. Our work is founded upon clinical research and experience and is not yet based on carefully controlled experimentation. At this point in the relative ignorance and knowledge of all of us about the functioning of the brain, there need be no apology for our diagnostic criteria as we and others have developed them. The habitual psychogeneticist, relying on the more easily acquired environmental and interpersonal material, operates ad libitum with his speculations. Our diagnostic efforts are directed toward a balanced consideration of all contributing factors.

It is our viewpoint that most childhood psychoses and aphasoid conditions as well as the variant epilepsies are based upon brain deviations. There is considerable overlapping of symptomatology between the organic behavior and learning syndrome group and the various childhood psychoses. The goal of our diagnostic procedure, using the tools that are available, is to call attention to any central nervous system deviation present and to emphasize the contribution of that deviation to the adjustment problems of the child. There are already many works dealing with the more specialized diagnosis of these children and literally countless works on the intrapsychic and interpersonal aspects of disturbed children.

For the purposes of this paper, the following terms will be used more or less interchangeably depending upon the context: minimal brain dysfunction, organic learning and behavior disorders, minimal brain damage, organic deviation, and central nervous system deviation. Where the word damage is not included, we are allowing for the possibility of deviation on a genetic basis or on the basis of a central nervous system *maturational lag*.

SYMPTOMS

Typical comments made by teachers and parents about a number of these children are:

(1) He seems bright; he is quiet and obedient, but daydreams and can't read.
(2) He is high-strung and nervous; his attention is hard to hold.
(3) He has frequent temper outbursts, sometimes for no apparent reason.

(4) He won't concentrate for more than a few minutes at a time; he jumps from one thing to another, and minds everyone's business but his own.

(5) He lacks self-control; he cannot work with other children; he picks on them constantly; he is very disturbing in the classroom and worse on the playground.

(6) He does not work to capacity; he is not learning to read or work with numbers, but has a good vocabulary and uses words correctly.

(7) He thinks, speaks, and moves so slowly and is a very poor reader; in many ways he seems very intelligent.

Although these remarks represent frequent complaints, the particular behavior which culminated in a referral to the clinic may range from school failure or discipline problem to stealing or other antisocial activity.

Following is a list of the outstanding findings associated with the brain damage behavior syndrome and the broader concept of minimal brain dysfunction, in which only a few symptoms may appear in a particular child.

(1) *Specific Learning Deficits.* Child cannot read at grade or age level; a mildly stressful situation may bring out typical dyslexic errors; spelling poor; difficulty with arithmetic; difficulty with abstractions and whole-part relationships; difficulty in mastering tasks which are dependent on good visual-motor coordination.

(2) *Perceptual-Motor Deficits.* Printing, writing, and drawing poor; poor and erratic performance when copying geometric figures (Bender Visual Motor Gestalt); often the child attempts to compensate for the latter by task-perseverance and/or innumerable and meticulous tiny strokes of the pencil; often has difficulty in reproducing geometric designs with blocks; difficulty with figure-ground and/or whole-part discrimination. (We have wondered if interpersonal communications and the interpretations thereof, might depend on this kind of process at its most abstract level.)

(3) *General Coordination Deficits.* Child often described as awkward or clumsy; this may appear in either fine muscle performance or in overall coordination, or both.

(4) *Hyperkinesis.* Child appears to be in constant motion, flitting from one object or activity to another, or may be merely restless and fidgety; we have considered that the child's "drivenness" may manifest also as voluble, uninhibited speech, or as disorganized thinking, even in the absence of outward hyperkinesis. Some of the children with learning and behavior symptoms and one or more "equivocal" neurological signs do not show hyperkinesis. Such children, because they do not know the typical hyperactivity, are often placed in a purely psychogenic category and treated accordingly.

(5) *Impulsivity.* The child cannot keep from touching and handling objects, particularly in a strange or overstimulating environment; he may

speak without checking himself and even say insulting things; his impulsivity easily leads him into conflict with the demands of conformity as established by family, school, and society. Some of these children may commit striking antisocial acts, even to the point of fire-setting, stealing, and murdering with only a modicum of provocation.

(6) *Emotional Lability.* The child may be "highstrung," irritable, aggressive, or easily moved to tears; he may have quick changes from high temper to easy manageability and remorse; he may be panicked by what would appear to others as a minimally stressful situation; however, some of these children are sweet-tempered, even in the presence of a frustrating inability to read—in such cases, the underlying temperament and benign environmental influences may have made the difference.

(7) *Short Attention Span and/or Distractibility.* Child unable to concentrate on one thing for very long; he especially loses interest when abstract material is being considered; even with this symptom, some of these children show a tendency to become locked in a simple repetitious motor activity or preoccupation with one verbal topic. Some children show good attention span when their interest is aroused, but when not so engaged display marked distractibility to casual stimuli.

(8) *"Equivocal" Neurological Signs.* Among the most frequently seen of such signs are: transient strabismus; dysdiadochokinesia; poor coordination of fingers; mixed and confused laterality (the former refers to the use of hand, foot, or eye, and the latter to ability to distinguish right from left); speech defect (or history of slow speech development or defect); general awkwardness. These and other neurological signs will be discussed in detail later.

(9) *Borderline Abnormal or Abnormal EEG.* In spite of the lack of agreement in this field, the high frequency of borderline records reported is felt to be significant. This is an important area for research (Goldberg, *et al.*, 1960; Hanvik, *et al.*, 1961; Ingram, 1956; Kennard, 1959; Kennard, 1960; Laufer, *et al.*, 1957; Schwade and Geiger, 1956). The 6-and-14-persecond positive spiking pattern has clearly been found to be associated with outbursts of violent behavior (Schwade and Geiger, 1956).

It is important to reemphasize that a given child may not have symptoms in all or even many of these areas; each child has his own particular cluster of symptoms. The level of his intelligence and the nature of his underlying temperament determine the form and the excellence of his maneuvers to compensate for the deficits or deviations.

It is probable that certain general principles underlie the above symptoms. For example, most may be due to perceptual defects having to do with the capacity to receive, hold, scan, and selectively screen out stimuli in a sequential order; to sustain a repertoire of background gestalten as compared with foreground gestalten; to perceive the subtle and often abstract behavior gestalten which allow proper socialization to take place.

Proprioception may be one of the perceptual areas at fault in some of these children, i.e., manifesting as a deficiency in the ability to perceive, discriminate between, and retain images of sequential body movements in space. It may be that there is a deficiency in inhibitory functions having to do with checking and suspending verbal or motor activity until the incoming sensory data are compared with stored information. When the fantastic complexity of the brain is considered, with its myriad interlocking circuits and groupings of circuits, it is not surprising that in the presence of any disordering of stimuli-monitoring, that each child should manifest a unique cluster of symptoms, and that he should be handicapped in learning and in adaptive behavior if the environment is sufficiently trying relative to the magnitude of his defect.

DIAGNOSTIC PROCEDURES

(1) *Physical Examination and History.* Let us assume that the child has been given a conventional physical examination and that gross conditions such as cerebral palsy, frank mental retardation, eye and ear defects, etc., have been detected or ruled out. A careful gestation and developmental history must be taken, and should include virus illnesses during pregnancy, bleeding, premature contractions, rupture of membranes, birth weight, etc. The childhood diseases and other illnesses should be located as to age. The usual interviews with parents and child must be obtained to determine specific interpersonal dynamics, particular emotional stresses and traumata, etc. In addition, behavioral and academic observations by the child's teacher and principal are especially valuable in the overall assessment.

(2) *Psychological Evaluation.* The minimal psychological test battery for any child being evaluated in the child guidance clinic is the complete Wechsler Intelligence Scale for Children, the Bender Visual Motor Gestalt, and a standardized reading test such as Gray's or Gates'. Personality assessment is not considered as a separate and distinct entity, since clues and indicators are constantly being produced by the child, and hence are apt to occur at any time during the work-up. We have not routinely used the *standardized* projective techniques. We feel that in most cases straightforward interviewing and observing during all contacts with the child yields adequate information. A small number of appropriate picture cards, preferably from the Michigan Picture Test (1953), could be used for routine evaluations. We have depended most heavily on the three psychological instruments mentioned above. The final test battery must await further research and applications from the field of perception (Kephart, 1960; Strauss, 1954).

Of great concern to the authors is the prevalent use of relatively unrelated tests and techniques to assess intelligence. Items such as drawings of persons or objects, Rorschach and other projective techniques, or 20-minute interviews are inadequate, even as screening devices, in approximating the intellectual functioning level of children, and in particular, the child with a minimal brain dysfunction.

The complete Wechsler Intelligence Scale for Children (WISC) (Wechsler, 1949), consisting of a minimum of five verbal subtests and five performance subtests, should be administered routinely. There is no combination of three or four WISC subtests which can substitute for the entire scale, since specific deficiencies may go undetected by the omissions. The value of the complete WISC cannot be overstated.

Often other investigators have searched in vain for a single subtest pattern within the WISC which would be diagnostic for brain damage (Beck and Lam, 1955; Ross, 1959). Thus far, we have isolated three principal patterns. The most common pattern is *scatter* in either or both the Verbal and Performance Scales (WISC Pattern I). Low scores (relative to the others) most frequently occur in Arithmetic and Digit Span in the Verbal Scale, and Block Design, Object Assembly, Coding, and Mazes in the Performance Scale. Frequently with WISC Pattern I, the final Verbal and Performance IQ scores turn out nearly equal and the internal variation in subtest scores is ignored by the individual interpreting the results. It is not uncommon in our population of children to find a scale score difference of five to ten points, say between Comprehension and Arithmetic on the Verbal Scale, in favor of Comprehension; or say between Picture Completion and Block Design on the Performance Scale, in favor of Picture Completion. The claim is often made that anxiety will lower certain subtest scores. It is then noteworthy that anxiety can be so selective, and suggests that that particular perceptual system is fragile in such cases. To reduce the achievement variation due to anxiety, we make every effort to place the child at ease and to obtain his confidence both before and during the examination. Subtest presentation order, fatigue, test-motivation, distractibility, and other variables which could affect test performance have all been taken into consideration in our evaluations, with no change in ability on the part of children with minimal brain dysfunctions.

The second most frequent WISC pattern (WISC Pattern II) is that in which the Verbal IQ is 15 to 40 points higher than the Performance IQ. If the Arithmetic subtest score is excluded, the difference is more pronounced (arithmetic being another type of symbol process). In this instance, the child's achievement on the other Verbal tasks is sufficiently high that such a drop in Arithmetic is obscured or compensated for in the total Verbal IQ score. On the other hand, the child experiences difficulty with most of the Performance Scale items, but particularly, the pure visual-motor perceptual tasks, which include Block Design, Object Assembly, Coding, and Mazes. He has less difficulty with Picture Arrangement and Picture Completion. The end-result, however, is that the Performance IQ often falls into the mentally deficient range while the Verbal IQ is in the normal range or above. In such cases, the Full Scale IQ score (the one usually quoted) is virtually meaningless as an indication of overall intelligence, since it is a composite of these two extremely variant dimensions of intellectual functioning. Many of these children are placed with the frankly mentally retarded in the usual hodgepodge special education class or are automatically passed along with their age group, frustrated in their efforts to keep up with the class.

The third and least frequent pattern (WISC Pattern III) is the reverse of WISC Pattern II, i.e., the Performance IQ is 10 to 30 points higher than the Verbal IQ. Such a child has difficulty in expressing himself verbally. He must actively search for the words necessary to express his usually concrete solution to a "thought" problem. On the other hand, he is quite proficient at the subtests which constitute the Performance Scale. In our experience, the child with WISC Pattern III invariably has dyslexia (Rabinovitch, et al., 1954).

The Bender Visual Motor Gestalt (Bender, 1938) is here used as it was intended, that is, as a measure of perception and visual-motor coordination. Others (Byrd, 1956; Fabian, 1945; Hanvik, 1953; Ross, 1959) have noted the common errors made by children with brain damage. Such factors as spatial arrangement, perseveration, "dog-ears," rotations, curvature, closure, etc., are noted since discrepancies commonly occur in these areas. Also, the total test approach and performance must be taken into account. Some children learn (either self-taught or by others) to compensate for poor visual-motor coordination by using many short, light lines when copying designs. Since a change of direction (angles) in drawing is particularly difficult for such children, some learn to make a square by first drawing four spaced dots, then carefully connecting the dots with straight lines. The child who automatically volunteers the information that he "can't draw very well," when asked to copy geometric designs has usually been compared with peers and classmates and is keenly aware of his deficiencies. The overall "organic" Bender Visual Motor Gestalt reproductions stand out strikingly when compared with the norms provided by Bender in her original monograph (1938), which can serve as a frame of reference in lieu of long clinical experience with the instrument. We have found that the failure to obtain a Bender-Gestalt has sometimes led to a wrong diagnosis and treatment plan. Some workers have elected to use it only in those cases where they already suspect brain damage. We believe that it, or an equivalent measure should never be omitted.

Gray's Oral Reading Paragraphs (Gray, 1955) are preferred as a measure of sight reading ability because of their simplicity of administration and content of the paragraphs. Although a formal scoring system is provided, it is not deemed necessary for our purposes. The child is asked to read aloud beginning with the paragraph two grade levels below his present grade placement. The time of the school year must be taken into account when determining reading level. Number and type of errors are noted in the child's reading as well as smoothness, speed, approach (phonetic, or not), and comprehension of the material.

If there develops any doubt about a child's reading under ideal testing conditions, it can be repeated under conditions of at least mild stress, e.g., while being tape recorded, with other persons present, by request for more speed, etc. Under such conditions, a child with a fragile integration of the complex processes involved in reading will very likely begin to show typical dyslexic errors and manifest the behavior which has handicapped him at school. Kanner and Eisenberg (1957; 1959) have provided a simple reading test for screening purposes.

Additional data which should be obtained include a sample of the child's writing, a free-hand drawing, and a spelling test. The words for the latter can be taken from the reading test.

(3) *Neurological Examination.* As usually performed, the conventional neurological examination is reported as "noncontributory" in the type of child under consideration. The physician has his mind set on clear, unequivocal signs and is not sensitive to the value of "equivocal" signs. Complex integrated behavior is rarely observed or specifically tested for by referring physicians or even in the usual child guidance clinic work-up. The physician often does not synthesize in his thinking the fact that these neurological signs, general behavior, and intellectual functioning are all manifestations of the nervous system. Somewhere between the specialties of medicine and psychology, this important synthesis gets lost or neglected.

SPECIAL NEUROLOGICAL EXAMINATION

POSTURAL REFLEXES AND COORDINATION. (1) Extension of arms, eyes closed: Abnormal—wide divergence of arms; convergence of arms; wide difference in arm levels; choreiform movements; lordosis.

(2) Passive rotation of head, eyes closed: Abnormal—wide divergence of arms; convergence till overlap; flexion of occipital arm; drop of chin arm; body rotates at shoulders or hips, or entire body "whirls" to delicate passive turning of head; extreme rigidity or resistance.

(3) Coordination: Heel walk; toe walk; walk a line; hop on one foot; skip; stand on one foot; catch an object. Observe for gait (spastic, ataxic, awkward); tonus (plastic, hypertonic); synkinesia; overshooting; nonspecific awkwardness in movements.

(4) Perceptual-motor tasks: Writing; picture drawing; Bender Visual Motor Gestalt. Note synkinesia.

SELECTED ITEMS FROM "ROUTINE" NEUROLOGICAL. (5) Cranial Nerves: Test for nystagmus; pupillary reflex; equality of pupils; III, IV, and VI— look for slight, transient strabismus and difficulty of convergence (observe for inability to exclude head movements while executing eye movements);

VII, XII—position on extension, fasciculation, speech (describe any deviation in detail).

(6) Deep tendon reflexes: Note symmetry.

(7) Cutaneous reflexes: Abdominal; presence of Oppenheim; plantar —(a) dorsiflexion of great toe with plantar flexion of other toes, (b) dorsiflexion of great toe with fan reflex or fan reflex alone.

(8) Other tests and manifestations: Rhomberg; dysdiadochokinesia (2 hands, then one—observe for synkinesia); finger-nose; fingers-thumb opposition; astereognosis; athetoid or choreiform movements.

MISCELLANEOUS TESTS AND OBSERVATIONS. (9) Reading test: Use a different form from that used in the psychological evaluation.

(10) Right-left confusion (this knowledge normally established by age 7 or 8): (a) Place right hand on left ear, (b) insert diversional test here, e.g., finger agnosia, (c) place left hand on right knee.

(11) Mixed laterality: Hand, foot, eye preference (use peep-hole card—note which eye winks more easily); ambidexterity (by observation and questions regarding writing, throwing, batting, combing, wiping, etc.).

(12) Finger agnosia: Hands placed palms up (doctor touches various fingers and asks patient to name or indicate which one).

(13) Unusual anatomical proportions, asymmetry, other stigmata.

Common "soft" neurological signs are: awkwardness, mixed laterality, confused laterality, stabismus, speech defect, short attention span, and hyperactivity.

The items included in the above special neurological examination have been drawn from the existing literature (Kennard, 1960; Rabinovitch, *et al.,* 1954; Silver, 1952; Strauss and Lehtinen, 1947; Teicher, 1941) to serve as a screening procedure for all child guidance clinic cases. A complete neurological is desirable in many cases. These items do not constitute the final outline for such a neurological examination. Some items may prove less useful than others, and other workers may wish to add items to the list, e.g. the face-hand test of Morris B. Bender (Bender, 1952; Rabinovitch, *et al.,* 1954). Some of these entries have been performed by child psychiatrists when looking for a special condition, e.g. "whirling," or when brain damage is already suspected, but few psychiatrists carry out such procedures routinely. The examination cannot be given in a cursory fashion, but must be done in a leisurely and painstaking manner. The number of children showing various of these signs is considerable, but they can be easily missed if the examiner hurriedly goes through his maneuvers expecting negatives.

The first two items have a long history going back to the work of Magnus, de Kleijn, and Sherrington on postural reflexes. The early work on postural reflexes in humans was done by Homberger, Schilder, and Hoff. The clinical sources used here were Silver (1952) and Teicher (1941). The work of Lauretta Bender in this area is well known. Children under six years of age normally show some of these signs. With experience one learns to recognize the kind of performance appropriate for different ages.

The Bender-Gestalt test mentioned under perceptual-motor tasks is usually given by the psychologist in our clinic, but psychiatrists and neurologists should also familiarize themselves with it and especially should gain experience in its interpretation.

The items from the "routine" neurological were selected by Alfred Strauss (Strauss and Lehtinen, 1947) as being the ones most frequently abnormal in children with the less obvious kind of brain damage. Strauss felt that the solitary appearance of a complete Babinski sign (with due regard for age) or paralysis of cranial nerves III, IV, VI, VII, or XII was of great value in diagnosing brain damage, and that the presence of two or more of the other signs were also "valuable." Kennard (1960) in her study accepted the "equivocal" Babinski and other signs as having the value of true neurological manifestations on the basis of their reproducibility and their correlations with behavioral symptoms and EEG. The examination for nystagmus and extraocular incoordination must be given with extreme care, since the deviation is frequently fleeting and not obvious. It often happens that the eyes depart from parallelness for only a few degrees of the arcs for which they are being tested. We have noted that some children on formal testing show no heterophoria, but are observed to do so momentarily while engaged in other activities. Any speech deviation at all should be noted and described, and questions relative to history of speech irregularities should be asked of the parents. The test for diadochokinesia should be tried several times and for more than the usual few seconds. Synkinesia should be carefully observed for in the opposite hand while the child is performing diadochokinesis with one hand or while performing the fingers-thumb test. Another example of "immature," associated movement is the relative inability to suppress head movements while performing eye movements.

Under miscellaneous tests and observations, most of the items have special reference to dyslexia. In this paper, the term dyslexia is used interchangeably with reading disability and reading retardation. The physician and the psychologist might well evaluate reading with different standardized tests so as to sample the child's reading under different circumstances. At least one of them should evaluate the test results in detail, noting types of errors such as reversals, reading letters or syllables out of sequence, fabricating a word out of minimal cues, difficulties with certain combinations of letters, and relatively greater difficulty with short words as compared to words with more distinctive characteristics. As mentioned previously, it is advisable to compare the child's reading under ideal circumstances with his reading under mildly stressful conditions. Eisenberg (1959) has written a valuable paper on the evaluation of reading disability.

The items on confused laterality (right-left disorientation), mixed laterality, and finger agnosia were drawn from the work of Hermann (1959) on reading disability in children and adults. Thus far, we have not been able to duplicate his findings with finger agnosia, nor was Rabinovitch (1954) able to do so. Hallgren (1950) and Hermann (1959) have convincing evidence that there is an hereditary form of dyslexia which they designate as "specific reading disability." This seems to be the same condition referred to by Rabinovitch as "primary reading retardation." The studies of Hallgren and Hermann show that identical twins are concordant for dyslexia and that fraternal twins have no more concordance than nontwin siblings. Hermann as well as Rabinovitch called attention to the possibility that the pathologic locus of specific reading disability may be related to that of Gerstmann's syndrome (1940).

At this point, we are not in a position to say whether or how much their population of dyslexics (Hermann places the incidence at 10 percent of the general population in Denmark) is different from or overlapping with the kinds of cases we see. We have been able to find the constellation of dyslexia, right-left confusion, ambidexterity, mixed laterality, spelling difficulties, and speech defect in several parent-child pairs, but we have not sought this information routinely. We do find the above symptoms in many children who also have neurological signs and symptoms of organicity. Kawi and Pasamanick (1958) have shown a significant correlation between reading disability and the complications of pregnancy. Pasamanick (Pasamanick, et al., 1956) has postulated a "continuum of reproductive casualty," resulting in a gradation of endpoint manifestations extending from neonatal death through cerebral palsy and to behavior and learning deviations. At present, we can venture no opinion as to the etiology of the central nervous system deviation. There could be a number of causes. It could be that in the case of minimal brain damage, with even slight disorganization of symbol handling, the hereditary trait, or even a "normally" lesser talent (normal curve hypothesis for reading ability) would make inevitable the final symptom of dyslexia. Bender's maturational lag theory is also a plausible explanation. We take the position that pure psychogenic reading disability or "secondary reading retardation" (Rabinovitch, et al., 1954) is an unusual entity. We cannot accept alleged traumatic experiences, methods of teaching, or "emotional blocking" (because of symbolic meanings) as sole causes of reading disability. If the brain substrate essential for reading is intact and sufficiently mature, a child adequately exposed to reading will learn to read normally just as he matures to the point of walking normally. Cunningham (1048) has reported an interesting incidence of an epidemic of reading problems due to forcing large numbers of children to undertake reading before they were sufficiently mature. We have no difficulty in accepting the proposition that mild brain deviation in combination with emotional factors, traumatic experiences, etc., can lead to various degrees of reading problems. The secondary emotional complications in this condition are well known to all and are extremely important.

Thus far, the neurological items most often found to be present in our child guidance population have been: irregularities in gross coordination, perceptual-motor difficulties, defect in fine coordination, strabismus, dysdiadochokinesia, reading difficulties, mixed laterality, some degree of ambidexterity, and the presence of or history of speech defect. Of the behavioral symptoms the most frequent are: short attention span, distractibility, hyperactivity, and impulsiveness.

TREATMENT AND MANAGEMENT

We have found that a surprising and significant number of our minimal brain dysfunction (MBD) cases can be handled by a combination of drugs and infrequent counselling. The drugs we have found most helpful in reducing hyperactivity and irritability, and in increasing attention span are captodiame hydrochloride (Suvren) (Low and Meyers, 1958), thioridazine hydrochloride (Mellaril), and the amphetamines. We have not made extensive use of phenothiazines other than thioridazine. Other clinics have reported favorably on several of them in the treatment of hyperkinesis in children. Captodiame has been given in doses ranging from 200 mg. to 500 mg. daily, either in uniformly distributed doses or more heavily concentrated during that portion of the day when the child has the most difficulty. An average dose would be 100 mg. three times daily. Some authors have noted a metallic taste which it sometimes gives to milk and water. We have not found this to be an important consideration except in about two per cent of our captodiame-treated cases. Taking the drug with meals reduces the likelihood of after-taste.

We have usually given thioridazine in doses of 25 mg. three to four times daily. Though our experience with this medication has been over a shorter period of time, we are entirely satisfied with its effects. In fact, we have not had as many children "escape" from the good effects of thioridazine as we have from captodiame.

We have found that each child responds differently to the various drugs and various dosages. There is often the necessity of a period of experimentation with the different drugs and dosages to reach the best final prescription for a given child.

Although the amphetamines have for many years been used in the treatment of brain damage behavior symptoms (Bradley, 1937; Denholf, 1961; Levy, 1959), we have not found them as helpful as the aforementioned drugs. We have found the amphetamines especially helpful in cases of dyslexia where there is a short attention span or distractibility but no hyperactivity. Teachers report that the child "seems more interested in his work," or "at last he has begun to show some progress in reading." The drug is given at breakfast and at lunch, dextro amphetamine sulfate (Dexedrine) in 5 mg. dosage and racemic amphetamine sulfate (Benzedrine) in 10 mg. dosage. Some authors have maintained that racemic amphetamine sulfate acts differently from dextro amphetamine and is superior in its effects with some children.

After the drug is regulated, the child may then be assigned to one of our "drug management" clinics. These children are seen at two- to three-month intervals for checkups and blood studies.

The parents are given an "organic" interpretation of the learning and/or behavior problems as soon as the diagnosis of minimal brain dysfunction is settled and are then advised as to home and educational management. The relief they feel and the lessening of guilt associated with the possibility of being "bad" parents is obvious. Depending on the parents' attitudes, they are usually advised to administer firm, short, nonnegotiable discipline. In most cases, the organic explanation makes parents more understanding of their children. Because of the difficulty of explaining brain dysfunction or central nervous system deviation, we usually speak of "mild" or "slight" brain damage when informing the parents of "the" cause of their child's condition.

The proper school management of children with minimal brain dysfunction is of extreme importance. These children often require an individualized teaching program (Kephart, 1960; Strauss and Lehtinen, 1947; Strauss and Kephart, 1955) which is geared to their own specific learning deficits and which allows for a slower pace of acquiring knowledge. Some of these children whose grade placement is well beyond their reading level, should have a large part of their lessons read to them so that they will not fall behind in the informational part of their courses. We frequently advise teachers to give oral examinations to such children. Usually, the teacher and the principal should know the child's diagnosis and that a program of treatment has been begun. The greatest difficulty is with those children of normal intelligence (WISC Verbal *or* Performance IQ in the normal range) who have some degree of dyslexia and/or dyscalculia, or sufficient hyperactivity to make them a problem in regular classes. Many of these children fall victim to the very questionable practice of "social passing," or of equal harm, they are placed in a special education class containing frankly mentally retarded children. These children, then, often become educational, social, and emotional casualties. If dyslexia is the major learning problem, the child should have several hours per week of specialized remedial reading instruction in very small groups. In our setting where special education classes of this kind are nonexistent in the public schools, we usually try to arrange for a private tutor or as a last resort, instruct the mother or father in a few basic principles of remedial reading. In a few cases, the special education teacher has such remarkable talents that both MBD children and the mentally retarded children have made enormous gains in spite of the unwieldiness of mixing both groups in the same class. Such a teacher, however, could be much more helpful to both groups if she were able to teach them separately. With the number of retarded readers of average intelligence estimated at ten percent or more of the school population, the time is long overdue for the proper specialized teaching of this group.

There are, of course, a good many of these cases with organic learning and behavior disorders, who in addition to drug therapy and specialized education, also need psychotherapy in the more conventional manner for child or parents or both. Lawrence (1960) in a recent paper and Roman (1957) who was dealing with an older delinquent population, emphasized the importance of psychotherapy. Quite often a gifted tutor is able to provide the needed "relationship" therapy. As mentioned previously it is surprising, however, how many children improve markedly on a regimen of drugs, special teaching, and counselling; this fact is important in answering the complaint often heard that child guidance clinics bog down in a few intensive treatment cases. The community stands to gain by the utilization of any and all methods that are successful.

COMMENT

The diagnosis of a minimal brain dysfunction is made on the basis of clinical behavior, history, psychological evaluation, neurological signs, and EEG findings. The accumulated weight of various signs and symptoms or the singular specificity thereof (e.g., hyperactivity, typical dyslexic errors, large scatter or discrepancy between Verbal and Performance scores on the WISC), guide us in making the diagnosis. These must be evaluated against a background of environmental and interpersonal determinants. At this stage of our knowledge, it is logical to assume that any disorganization of brain function due to injury or naturally occurring constitutional deviations, places a hardship on the developing child. If, in addition, the interpersonal environment is unfavorable, the chances are greater for such a child to experience problems compounded of his original perceptual defects, his reactions to the attitudes of persons surrounding him, and to his own failures. These accidentally or naturally occurring organic deviations must exist in a scale from the gross to the subtle and to different degrees in the various functional and interlocking units within the brain. To deny this premise is to deny that the brain is the organ of the mind and that brains can have important variations from individual to individual.

Our thinking about minimal brain dysfunctions and minimal brain damage was influenced by the following factors: (1) The similarities between the perceptual defects and symptoms of children and adults with known brain damage and children in which a brain damage history cannot be firmly established, yet who have similar symptoms; (2) the fact that the symptoms cluster together to make recognizable entities. This is of course especially true of the hyperactivity syndrome and specific reading disability, but is also true of the subtler variations that do not fit precisely into these categories; (3) the statistical studies (Kawi and Pasamanick, 1958; Pasamanick, *et al.*, 1956) which show a positive correlation between complications of pregnancy and the incidence of later appearing learning and behavioral symptoms. One study (Wagenheim, 1959) indicated such a correlation between the childhood virus diseases occurring under age 3 and reading difficulty; (4) the studies of Hallgren (1950) and Hermann (1959) and Norrie showing that there is a heredity basis for some cases of dyslexia; (5) organicity as a basis for the clinical entities being discussed is lent support by the fact of the high ratio of males to females for hyperactivity, dyslexia, impulsive acts, etc. This could be on the basis of a "normal" developmental lag in males making them more susceptible to the disorganizing effects of brain damage and stresses during the years critical for learning symbol behavior and for acquiring self-inhibiting patterns; (6) the good response of most of these children to drugs and remedial instruction without benefit of psychotherapy, if they are detected early enough; (7) the ever present and oft disparaged fact that innumerable siblings reared under sufficiently equivalent conditions do not show these particular learning and behavior symptoms and that countless children reared under psychopathogenic conditions from the mildest to the most severe do not develop learning and behavior symptoms.

Too often we have seen parents who are good parents and who have a child who cannot learn to read, or who is a behavior problem, or is impulsive and hyperactive, or whose speed of mentation is distinctly different from his siblings, for us to jump to the conclusion that the parents must have mishandled the child. The prevailing climate of opinion in both professional and "magazine" psychiatry is such as to create in these parents the conviction that they are somehow, by some magical, subtle aberration in their attitudes and behavior, to blame for the child's condition.

It is necessary to affirm again that psychiatry must take into account the full spectrum of causality from the unique genetic combination that each individual is, to his gestation and birth experiences, to his interaction with significant persons, and finally to the stresses and emotional traumata of later life after his basic reaction patterns have been laid down. If we cannot at present measure, say, the contribution of the child's genes to his emotional characteristics, then we must leave a large, empty space in the formula of causality until we can. It is all too easy, if one is so committed by bias and habit, to detect in almost any mother or father, attitudes and behavior which can be envisioned as causing the dyslexia, the destructiveness, or the difficulty in concentration on studies.

Perhaps the most distinctive feature of this paper is that we hold that all these areas must be evaluated for each child referred to the child guidance clinic. The psychiatrist or psychologist can no more elect to omit one or more of his basic procedures than the pediatrician can fail to listen to his patient's heart or lungs. The next most distinctive feature is that we point out that there is a prevailing fashion in child psychiatry, psychology, and social work of turning a deaf ear to organic etiology unless it is grossly obvious and of being interested in and attentive only to the intrapsychic and interpersonal factors.

SUMMARY

It was stressed that in the usual child guidance clinic evaluation, subtle organic deviations of brain function are often overlooked and that a wide and false dichotomy has placed most workers in the position of being able to think in terms of only psychogenesis or only organicity. A diagnostic plan for detecting minimal brain dysfunctions in children of school age was outlined which involved careful history taking, a specialized neurological examination, a rigorously defined psychological evaluation, and an EEG. It was stressed that the omission of any one of these procedures makes possible a blatant misdiagnosis, hence makes possible a questionable treatment plan. Also, a plan of treatment was outlined which has been found very helpful with this large but previously neglected group of disturbed children, and which allows for the handling of a larger number of children than is the case with most child guidance clinics.

References

Beck, H. S., and Lam, R. L., Use of the WISC in predicting organicity, *J. clin. Psychol.*, 1955, 11, 154-158.
Bender, L., *A visual motor gestalt test and its clinical use* (New York: American Orthopsychiatric Association, 1938).
Bender, M. B., *Disorders in perception* (Springfield, Illinois: Charles C Thomas, 1952).
Bradley, C., The behavior of children receiving benzedrine, *Amer. J. Psychiat.*, 1937, 94, 577.
Burks, H. F., The hyperkinetic child, *Except. Child.*, 1960, 27, 18-26.
Byrd, E., The clinical validity of the Bender gestalt test with children: A developmental comparison of children in need of psychotherapy and children judged well-adjusted, *J. Proj. Techn.*, 1956, 20, 127-136.
Cunningham J. M., Psychiatric casework as an epidemiological tool, *Amer. J. Orthopsychiat.*, 1948, 18, 659.
Denhoff, E., Emotional and psychological background of the neurologically handicapped child, *Except. Child.*, 1961, 27, 347-349.
Eisenberg, L., Psychiatric implications of brain damage in children, *Psychiat. Quart.*, 1957, 31, 72.
Eisenberg, L., Office evaluation of specific reading disability in children, *Pediatrics*, 1959, 23, 997-1003.

Fabian, A. A., Vertical rotation in visual-motor performance—Its relationship to reading reversals, *J. educ. Psychol.*, 1945, 36, 129.

Gerstmann, J., Syndrome of finger agnosia, disorientation for right and left, agraphia, and acalculia: Local diagnostic value, *Arch. Neurol. Psychiat.*, 1940, 44, 398.

Goldberg H. K., Marshall, C., and Sims, E., The role of brain damage in congenital dyslexia, *Amer. J. Opthal.*, 1960, 50, 586.

Gray, W., *Standardized oral reading paragraphs* (New York: Psychological Corporation and Bobbs-Merrill, 1955).

Hallgren, B., Specific dyslexia: A clinical and genetic study, *Acta Psychiat. Scand., Suppl.*, 1950, 65.

Hanvik, L. J., A note on rotations in the Bender gestalt test as predictors of EEG abnormalities in children, *J. clin. Psychol.*, 1953, 9, 399.

Hanvik, L. J., Nelson, S. E., Hanson, H. B., Anderson, A. S., Dressler, W. H., and Zarling, V. R., Diagnosis of cerebral dysfunction in children, *Amer. J. Dis. Child.*, 1961, 101, 364.

Hermann, K., *Reading disability* (Springfield, Illinois: Charles C Thomas, 1959).

Ingram, T. T. S., A characteristic form of overactive behavior in brain-damaged children, *J. Ment. Sci.*, 1956, 102, 550.

Kanner, L., and Eisenberg, L., Childhood problems in relation to the family, *Pediatrics*, 1957, 20, 155.

Kawi, A. A., and Pasamanick, B., Association of factors of pregnancy with reading disorders in childhood, *J.A.M.A.*, 1958, 166, 1420.

Kennard, M. A., The characteristics of thought disturbances as related to electroencephalographic findings in children and adolescents, *Amer. J. Psychiat.*, 1959, 115, 911.

Kennard, M. A., Value of equivocal signs in neurologic diagnosis, *Neurology* (Minneap.) 1960, 10, 753.

Kephart, N. C., *The slow learner in the classroom* (Columbus, Ohio: Merrill, 1960).

Laufer, M. W., Denhoff, E., and Solomons, G., Hyperkinetic impulse disorder in children's behavior problems, *Psychosom. Med.*, 1957, 19, 38.

Lawrence, M. M., Minimal brain injury in child psychiatry, *Compr. Psychiat.*, 1960, 1, 360.

Levy, S., Post-encephalitic behavior disorder—A forgotten entity: A report of one hundred cases, *Amer. J. Psychiat.* 1959, 115, 1062.

Low, N. L., and Myers, G. G., Suvren in brain-injured children, *J. Pediat.*, 1958, 52, 259.

Michigan Dept. of Mental Health, *Michigan Picture Test (The)* (Chicago: Science Research, 1953).

Pasamanick, B., Rogers, M. E., and Lilienfeld, A. M., Pregnancy experience and the development of behavior disorder in children, *Amer. J. Psychiat.*, 1956, 112, 613.

Rabinovitch, R. D., Drew, A. L., De Jong, R. N., Ingram, W., and Withey, L., A research approach to reading retardation, *Res. Publ. Ass. Res. nerv. ment. Dis.*, 1954, 34, 363.

Roman, M., *Reaching Delinquents through reading* (Springfield, Illinois: Charles C Thomas, 1957).

Ross, A. O., *The practice of clinical child psychology* (New York: Grune & Stratton, 1959), pp. 217-250.

Schwade, E. D., and Geiger, S. G., Abnormal electroencephalographic findings in severe behavior disorders, *Dis. nerv. Syst.*, 1956, 17, 2.

Silver, A. A., Psychologic aspects of pediatrics, postural and righting responses in children, *J. Pediat.*, 1952, 41, 493.

Illinois mental health center report on brain-damaged children (Springfield, Illinois: August, 1957).

Strauss, A. A., Aphasia in children, *Amer. J. phys. Med.*, 1954, 33, 93.

Strauss, A. A., and Kephart, N. C., *Psychopathology and education of the brain-injured child*, Vol. 2 (New York: Grune & Stratton, 1955).

Strauss A. A., and Lehtinen, L. E., *Psychopathology and education of the brain-injured child* (New York: Grune & Stratton, 1947).

Teicher, J. D., Preliminary survey of motility in children, *J. nerv. ment. Dis.*, 1941, 94, 277.

Thelander, H. E., Phelps, J. K., and Kirk, E. W., Learning disabilities associated with lesser brain damage, *J. Pediat.*, 1958, 53, 405.

Wagenheim, L., Learning problems associated with childhood diseases contracted at age two, *Amer. J. Orthopsychiat.*, 1959, 29, 102.

Wechsler, D., *Wechsler intelligence scale for children* (New York: Psychological Corporation, 1949).

7 A PROPOSAL FOR CLARIFICATION OF THE TERMINOLOGY USED TO DESCRIBE BRAIN-INJURED CHILDREN

Godfrey D. Stevens and Jack W. Birch

INTRODUCTION

Educators, psychologists, social workers, psychiatrists, and others concerned with the study of child behavior have become increasingly aware of the existence of certain children with unusual and bizarre behavior who do not fit easily into existing classification schemes. Research in recent years has thrown some light on this problem, and evidence is rapidly accumulating which points to central nervous system impairment as the basis for the problems of many children.

The work of Goldstein (1948), Bender (1949), Doll (1951), and Strauss and Lehtinen (1947), have focused on these problems. The work of Strauss and his associates has come to be synonymous with the term "brain-injured." As is so often the case, certain descriptive terms may prove to be inadequate in light of new developments in philosophic position and the results of research (Anderson, 1952; Goldstein, 1948; Strauss, 1939). It would appear that the term "brain-injured" has become a specific scientific term and is no longer of value in light of what is known about the sequelae of central nervous system impairment.

The term "brain-injured" has been used to describe a wide variety of conditions in the past ten years, and as a consequence the term is rapidly becoming of questionable value as a means of describing the child with disorders of perception and other related central nervous system sequelae. Wortis (1956) points out that "There is . . . no brain-injured child," but only a variety of brain-injured children whose problems are quite varied and whose condition calls for far more refined analysis than some of the current generalizations on the brain-injured child provide."

Reprinted from *Exceptional Children*, Vol. 23, No. 8 (May, 1957), pp. 346-349. By permission of the authors and publisher.

PURPOSE OF THE DISCUSSION

It is the purpose of this discussion to suggest a term that can more accurately describe the phenomena reported by Strauss with a view of clarifying the situation for both scientific purposes and for practical clinical applications. The writers are indebted to Shulamith Kastein for stimulating interest in this problem.

HISTORICAL BACKGROUNDS

The work of Strauss and his associates suggests that there does now exist a child with specific characteristics that have been associated with damage to the brain (Strauss and Lehtinen, 1947; Strauss and Kephart, 1955). There is some controversy on this point (Birch, 1956). The presence of disordered behavior is not always evidence of brain damage, and the existence of brain damage does not necessarily imply the presence of certain kinds of behavior (Birch, 1956; Sarason, 1949).

The term "brain-injured" as used earlier by Strauss (1939) had to do with the problem of children who were defective due to damage to the brain. Later he became interested in what might be thought of as "nonretarded brain-injured" children—children who did not suffer from intellectual limitations as a consequence of a defective brain. Earlier Strauss virtually eliminated the motor handicapped child from his population. However, more recently he has included the motor handicapped child (1947).

THE CONCEPT OF THE BRAIN-INJURED

The term "brain-injured" as used by Strauss in his early writings (1939, 1947) described children with perceptual disturbances, learning disturbances, disturbances in thinking and disturbances in personality. These children had a tendency to perserverate; to be hyperactive; to function with a rigid, stereotyped kind of behavior; to show evidence of motor disinhibition and a tendency to pay attention to details rather than wholes. These conditions have been observed in children (and adults) with verifiable evidence of damage to the central nervous system. This behavior has also been seen in individuals who show no signs of neuropathology.

Historically, early workers associated the disorganized and unpredictable behavior of certain mentally retarded children with similar behavior observed in adult soldiers who sustained brain injuries. The mental retardation and disorganized behavior in the adults was presumed to be caused by the defect in the brain resulting from the wound. Similar behavior in mentally retarded children, even though there was neither clinical nor developmental historical evidence of injury to the brain, was thought to be sufficient reason for attributing the etiology of the retardation to a defective brain. The presence of disordered behavior in individuals without diagnosable lesions made it possible to make an etiological classification on the basis of an inferential diagnosis.

Strauss introduced the term "brain-injured" into this country just before World War II. It was based on some work he had done in Germany (1939). The term "gehirnverletzt" was widely used in Germany and was literally translated into English as "brain-injured." Other substantially synonymous terms used in this country have been "exogenous," "organic," "pathologic," and more recently "neurophrenic" (Doll, 1951).

The term "brain-injured" has certain etiological implications. The term probably came into being because most of the early workers in Europe who were aware of this problem were chiefly medical workers. Since it is common practice to explain the etiology of various pathologies, it became common to refer to this condition from the point of view of the etiology. Reasons for the quick acceptance are suggested by Wortis (1956). The expression was used to explain the basis for the disorders of mentality, behavior, learning, and the other abnormalities in childhood associated with this group of problems. This was an oversimplification with serious and far-reaching consequences. Epilepsy, cerebral palsy, mental retardation, certain kinds of sensory handicaps, the aphasias, and more recently schizophrenia may be attributed to damage to the brain. Thus it becomes apparent that there is a need for avoiding an etiological term in describing behavior which is really part of a condition or a symptom complex in which the actual etiology may be unclear.

WEAKNESSES IN THE CONCEPT

Sarason criticized the endogenous-exogenous concept some years ago when used in relation to problems of mental retardation (1949). More recently, H. Birch has criticized the validity of the concept of "brain damage." He concludes:

(1) That there are individuals with brain damage.
(2) That we have instruments for examining the behavior of these individuals.
(3) That these instruments are often inadequate for the detection of modifications of behavior produced by this damage.
(4) That we have to produce better methods of approaching analysis of behavior. (Birch, 1956)

While he was somewhat pessimistic and negative in his review of the work done until now, he felt that here was a field for fruitful scientific endeavor.

Wortis recently questioned the validity of the use of the term "brain-injured" and suggests that it is inappropriate.

The term "brain-injured" as used in its generic sense in medical nomenclature would mean exactly what it implies, "damage to the brain." This in no way tells what the consequences of such damage to the brain may mean in terms of specific behaviors. The sequelae of brain damage are often disorders such as epilepsy, mental retardation, cerebral palsy, and its related conditions, personality disorders, or combinations of these. The amount of brain tissue involved and the locale of the lesions seems to determine to a large degree the behavioral significance of such damage.

The term "brain-injured" then can only compound confusion if it is used to describe the symptom complex associated with any of the conditions mentioned above, since it is intended to be an etiological concept, which can account for a number of other conditions.

Another weakness in using an etiological concept as a basis for this description grows out of the fact that a therapeutic approach is difficult or impossible to construct when we know only the presumed cause. In general, under present conditions the therapeutic pedagogy which will palliate the problems associated with central nervous system impairment can best be built on a thorough understanding of the overt behaviors making up the symptom complex or syndrome. When children are multiply handicapped it is virtually impossible to develop appropriate teaching procedures based on the presumptive knowledge that the child is "brain-injured." In actual practice, teachers and clinicians tend to utilize their clinical sense in developing suitable procedures built on what they observe in the child, rather than on the notion that the child has an injury to the brain. In light of present knowledge the very nature of the physiology of nerve tissue brings the psychologist and educator to a method of symptom reduction rather than an etiological therapy.

In looking through the literature, we find the term *perception* frequently used to describe the condition associated with learning disturbances in children known or thought to be brain-injured. It has been suggested that the defects in perception tend to account for practically all the behavioral disturbances associated with the problem. That is to say, if an individual does not perceive his environment normally he cannot make an adequate adjustment to his world and, therefore, will tend to react in an unusual manner. Thus he will have difficulty in learning consequently, or difficulty in adjusting. There are several leaps of verbal logic in this analysis which are only vaguely supported by research evidence. Much more work will need to be done before differing kinds of perceptual experience can be firmly linked to variations in everyday life behavior and to central nervous system lesions in anything approaching a cause-and-effect way.

THE "STRAUSS SYNDROME" AS A DESCRIPTIVE TERM

It would seem desirable to clarify the problem for the purposes of scientific integrity and to reduce the confusion growing out of the semantic problems of clinical language. Strauss' notion of the "brain-injured child" describes disturbances in three broad, general groups, i.e., disturbances in thinking;

disturbances in perception; and disturbances in behavior. In detail, the child with central nervous system impairment may show any or most of the following observable characteristics:

(1) Erratic and inappropriate behavior on mild provocation.
(2) Increased motor activity disproportionate to the stimulus.
(3) Poor organization of behavior.
(4) Distractibility of more than ordinary degree under ordinary conditions.
(5) Persistent faulty perceptions.
(6) Persistent hyperactivity.
(7) Awkwardness and consistently poor motor performance.

Any child who presents the above symptom complex can be said to exhibit the Strauss Syndrome. The child may or may not be mentally retarded. There is no implication as to the cause or causes of the child's behavior when he is said to exhibit the Strauss Syndrome. Rather, the way is left open to seek the cause or causes of the symptom complex.

In view of the foregoing discussion, it is therefore suggested that the term "Strauss Syndrome" be used to describe this symptom complex. It is our belief that science would profit by this course. First, it would pay tribute to a man who has devoted his life to the study of the significance of central nervous system impairment and who has tried to develop appropriate procedures to mitigate the impact lesions in the brain on the adjustment of the child. Second, it would be consistent with past scientific practice to isolate a symptom complex or syndrome by attaching to it the name of the man who has done most to identify the problem.

Third, much confusion in scientific thinking would be eliminated by avoiding the unfortunate practice of referring to children as though their behavior were entirely dependent upon lesions in the central nervous system.

SUMMARY

In view of the confusion growing out of the inappropriate use of the term "brain-injured" to describe a group of children with mild-to-severe perceptual disturbances and disorganized behavior, it would appear that a new term would be of value for both clinical practice and theoretical validity. There is still much confusion regarding the existence of a clinical entity and evidence up to this point is drawn from clinical impressions.

In order to clarify this issue, we have attempted to rationalize the present situation. In general, there are at least four objections to the use of the term "brain-injured."

(1) The term is an etiological concept and does not appropriately describe the symptom complex. This is important because the

condition which prevails is viewed in terms of symptoms rather than etiology.

(2) The term is associated with other conditions some of which have no relation to the symptom complex commonly referred to as "brain injury."

(3) The term does not help in the development of a sound therapeutic approach and in practice teachers and clinicians tend to approach the problem in terms of symptom reduction.

(4) The term is not suited for use as a descriptive one since it is essentially a generic expression, the use of which results in oversimplification.

The term "Strauss Syndrome" is therefore suggested to be used to describe the kind of child who does have evidence of defects in perception and related disorders. The recommended term pays tribute to a great worker and more clearly isolates the phenomena in terms of the symptom picture which Strauss has worked with for many years.

References

Anderson, Camille, Organic factors predisposing to schizophrenia, *Nerv. Child*, 1952, 10 (1), 36.

Bender, Loretta, Psychological problems of children with organic brain disease, *Amer. J. Orthopsychiat.*, 1949, 19, 404-15.

Birch, Herbert, Theoretical aspects of psychological behavior in the brain-damaged, *Psychological Services for the Cerebral Palsied*, Morton Goldstein (Editor), (New York: United Cerebral Palsy Association, 1956), p. 56 ff.

Doll, Edgar A., Neurophrenia, *Amer. J. Psychiat.*, 1951, 108, 50-53.

Goldstein, K., *Language and language disturbances* (New York: Grune & Stratton, 1948).

Sarason, Seymour, *Psychological problems in mental deficiency* (New York: Harper & Row, 1949).

Strauss, A. A., Typology in mental deficiency, *Amer. J. ment. Def.*, 1939, 44, 85-90.

Strauss, A. A., and Kephart, N. C., *Psychopathology and education of the brain-injured child*, vol. 2 (New York: Grune & Stratton, 1955).

Strauss, A. A., and Lehtinen, L. E., *Psychopathology and education of the brain-injured child*, vol. 1 (New York: Grune & Stratton, 1947).

Wortis, J., A note on the concept of the "brain-injured child," *Amer. J. ment. Def.*, 1956, 61 (1), 204-6.

8 MINIMAL BRAIN DAMAGE IN CHILDREN

Raymond L. Clemmens

Many processes, both environmental and biological, contribute to an individual's overall development. It is generally accepted that in the child who is without intellectual deficit, most deviations in behavior and performance are determined primarily by psychocultural factors. Less emphasis is apt to be placed on the importance of the integrity of the central nervous system through which behavior and learning are mediated and monitored.

In our clinic, a multidiscipline diagnostic clinic for handicapped children, operated by the University of Maryland in Baltimore, and the Maryland State Department of Health, we have evaluated 525 patients and have encountered a surprisingly high number—19 percent of the total group —in whom, after exhaustive examination and assessment, the final diagnosis was minimal cerebral dysfunction or minimal brain damage without intellectual subnormality.

This clinic population is not by any means a representative segment of handicapped children, but is a highly selected group of children referred to the clinic from various places throughout the State of Maryland over a three-year period. It seems likely, however, that other pediatricians have encountered youngsters with the same perplexing problems.

The subject of minimal brain damage involves considerable controversy as to whether or not this is a diagnosable clinical entity. The dispute is not unexpected, however, for several reasons:

(1) The subject matter deals with inherently complex functions which are difficult to measure.
(2) The clinical techniques available to assess brain function are relatively crude and, in general, not designed to elicit subtle deviations in higher cerebral performance.

Reprinted from *Children*, Vol. 8, No. 5 (Sept.-Oct. 1961), pp. 179-183. By permission of the author and publisher.

(3) In an era in which the importance of environmental stresses in the causation of abnormal activity has been emphasized strongly, it has become somewhat unfashionable to diagnose organic cerebral pathology in the absence of specific neurological signs.

GENERAL CONSIDERATIONS

The brain is an organ of enormous complexity, some of the more delicate functions of which are not readily assessable by the usual neurological examination. Among these functions are perception, cognition, judgment, concentration, impulse control, visual and auditory memory, perceptual motor function, and symbol organization. Injury to or maldevelopment of the cerebrum may interfere with these higher brain functions and contribute to certain behavioral deviations, language disorders, and learning disabilities in the absence of specific neurological signs of mental retardation.

When cerebral dysfunction exists and the clinical neurological examination is normal, the term "minimal brain damage" or "minimal cerebral dysfunction" is used in designation. The conduct disturbances associated with minimal brain damage are termed "organic behavior disorders." The language problems and learning disabilities that are related to neurological impairment are classified as neuropsychiatric learning disorders.

The clinical manifestations of this kind of neurological deficit vary with with the age of the patient and severity and location of the abnormality. Such disorders may not be apparent in infancy. Not uncommonly they present themselves as developmental deviations in the preschool years. Most frequently such disturbances are first noted in the early school years. Characteristically, adjustment and academic problems occur between the ages of five and eleven years.

As components of a continuum, behavior disorders and neuropsychiatric learning disabilities caused by minimal brain damage usually exist together in varying combinations, though they may occasionally appear independently. Characteristic of this impairment is absence of specific neurological signs, although minor degrees of motor incoordination, nonspecific awkwardness, mixed laterality, time and spatial disorientation, or adiadochokinesis (inability to perform rapid alternating movements) can usually be detected. Delayed speech development, mechanical speech imperfections, echolalia (meaningless repetition of others' words), strabismus, visuo-motor impairment, and abnormal electroencephalograms are found in greater numbers than in control subjects.

ORGANIC BEHAVIOR DISORDERS

It has long been known that persistent disturbances in personality may be noted in a child who has suffered epidemic influenzal encephalitis or severe head injury. (Bond and Smith, 1935; Blau, 1936) Behavioral deviations similar to those associated with postencephalitic and posttraumatic states are also found in children in whom no convincing evidence of cerebral insult can be elicited. Frequently noted in the histories of these children are maternal pregnancy complications, prematurity, and perinatal difficulties (Pasamanick, 1954).

The borderline between that which is normally active behavior and that which is pathological is not easy to define. In extreme cases, however, if familiarity with the pathological condition has been established, the difference may be recognized without difficulty.

There are no pathognomic signs for minimal organic impairment of the central nervous system, but it is possible to describe in general terms those characteristics which are frequently noted in children with such impairment and to point out trends which suggest neurological impairment, based on objective but inferential observations. Similar characteristics are at times noted in children who are healthy and normal. However, when they occur in greater frequency, with greater severity, and in combination, and persist through the various stages of development, they can be regarded as related to cerebral dysfunction.

Hyperkinesis (hyperactivity) and distractibility are the two most striking features of organic behavior disorders. The child is constantly in motion. More important, however, than the degree of hyperactivity, is the quality of his overall performance. Because of excess distractibility he cannot ignore the countless inconsequential visual and auditory stimuli which the normal child selectively screens out. As his interest and attention are directed first to one object and then to another with little design or apparent intent, his overall demeanor may assume a bizarre character—disorganized, disruptive, and unpredictable. Cohen (Kahn and Cohen, 1934) described this kind of childhood activity in detail over 20 years ago and used the term "organic driven-ness" to denote the apparent surplus of inner compulsions.

Whatever its causation, this non goal-directed, semivolitional, seemingly irrational deviation from normal patterns is extremely difficult for others to tolerate. The child's classroom adjustment is apt to present a major problem. The task of learning becomes extraordinarily difficult, due, at least partially, to restlessness and the inability to exclude irrelevant sensory impressions.

Impulsiveness, perseveration, emotional lability, lowered frustration tolerance, inappropriate and sometimes overwhelming anxiety further contribute to the child's anomalous adjustment.

It was Strauss (Strauss and Werner, 1942; Strauss and Lehtinen, 1950; Lewis, et al., 1960) who first presented a systematized approach to the psychological assessment of the brain-injured child and stressed the disturbances in perceptual and conceptual functions. He pointed out the importance of the differential diagnosis to determine whether a youngster with bizarre behavior is neurotic, psychotic, brain-injured, or mentally retarded.

Additional and important contributions to our understanding of children with these perplexing symptoms have been made more recently by Bradley (1957), Eisenberg (1957), Laufer (1957), Rogers (Rogers, *et al.*, 1955), Knobloch (Knobloch and Pasamanick, 1959), Bender (1949), and others in this country, and Luria (1961) in the U.S.S.R.

It was Pasamanick (1954) who first presented convincing evidence of the high incidence of pregnancy and perinatal complications in the histories of hyperkinetic children. He postulated that certain organic behavior disorders are reproductive casualties related to cerebral palsy, epilepsy, and mental retardation.

One of the conspicuous characteristics of the child with subclinical neurological impairment is the manner in which he relates to people. This may take one of two extremes: an inappropriate and unselective display of affection to total strangers; or a pronounced and continued disregard of people, similar to the responses of patients with early infantile autism, whose regard for individuals is not unlike their regard for furniture.

However strong the observer's organic orientation might be, he will find it difficult to ignore the strikingly high incidence of psychopathology in the families of these children, although this is not a universal phenomenon among them. While neurological dysfunction, from whatever cause, contributes to only a small fraction of all conduct disturbances in children, in brain-damaged children there seems to exist a lowered emotional threshold as a result of cerebral disorganization and thereby a predisposition to embarrassment by environmental stresses—stresses under which the non brain-injured child might manifest no compromise.

Eisenberg (1957) in his classical paper on the psychiatric implications of minimal brain injury has stressed the psychobiological background of this syndrome and its expression as a physiological disorganization of adaptive behavior.

Cohn (1961) has referred to the syndrome as "social dyspraxia," a splintered, apparently aimless, searching demeanor which is other than merely a reaction to environmental stresses.

IMPORTANCE OF DIAGNOSIS

Differential diagnosis in the child who may be neurotic, schizophrenic, autistic, or brain-injured is of more than academic importance. The usual psychotherapeutic approaches may need modification to assist the child with cerebral dysfunction effectively. Parent counseling, with the object of helping the parent understand why this child has been so hard to rear, might be carried out in a significantly different manner than with parents of a child whose basic difficulty was emotional disturbance.

In the assessment and management of the disturbed parent-child relationship, either as cause or effect of the child's disorder, it seems pertinent to recognize whether the child's environmental needs are excessive because of neurological disturbance. Parents who would be well-equipped to satisfy the needs of a healthy normal child may be incapable of meeting the requirements of a child who is brain-injured, so that the child is left in a state of relative environmental deprivation. For the needs of the brain-injured child are excessive: for understanding, acceptance, affection, guidance, and well-directed, consistent, firm, and early discipline.

Although the organic background of hyperkinetic behavior seems certain, the point of view that this is not amenable to psychological therapeutic intervention cannot be justified. Organic drives can be modified by environmental influences although this may be a difficult undertaking (Bender, 1956).

Drug therapy has been of significant value in decreasing the hyperactivity, distractibility, and extreme anxiety associated with brain injury. Many pharmacologic agents have been used. Encouraging and at times dramatic results have been obtained with dextro-amphetamine, benadryl, and, notably, dilantin.

If secondary emotional complications have been avoided, the long-term outlook of the hyperkinetic child with adequate intellectual endowment is favorable. As he matures, the child often develops the ability to compensate for perceptual distortions. In most such children, hyperactivity and impulsivity can be expected to show significant resolution shortly after puberty, either with or without medication.

LEARNING DISORDERS

The language and learning disorders associated with cerebral dysfunction cannot be ascribed merely to shortened attention span and poor classroom adjustment. They represent specific disabilities which are related to high cortical functions (Ingram, 1959; Myklebust and Boshes, 1960). As such they are extremely difficult to diagnose.

It is well known that the schools contain many children who seem destined to be educational casualties—bright children whose school life is burdened because of inordinate difficulty in mastering the basic academic skills. A characteristic of most of these children is delayed acquisition of reading ability. They may also have a similar difficulty with arithmetic, spelling, and writing. If the child is a nonreader, he eventually encounters difficulty in all academic processes which require comprehension of written language. The usual presenting complaint is overall academic deficiency.

Often when the ordinary investigations reveal no apparent physical cause for such learning difficulties and when psychological testing indicates average ability or better, these children are categorized as lazy, poorly motivated, or emotionally blocked.

In the most severe cases, their disabilities may derive from:

(1) *Auditory agnosia*, a condition in which sound is received by the brain, but not interpreted, and so has no meaning attached.

(2) *Motor aphasia*, in which there is interference with ability to express a meaning in language.

(3) *Dyslexia*, in which there is impairment of the reception, integration, and utilization of visual symbols, and so, an inability to read (Wood, 1960).

The milder forms of psychoneurological learning disorders may be manifested only as inconsistent auditory comprehension, mild articulation defects or difficulties in word finding, or slight delay in the acquisition of reading skills.

Failure to recognize the neurological background of these problems may lead to serious psychic trauma, to which the child is already predisposed because of a coexisting lowered emotional threshold. The constant, and seemingly inevitable, day-to-day failures these children experience produce feelings of inadequacy and eventually lead to anxiety, hostility, rebellion, and school phobia, thus further aggravating their unsatisfactory school adjustment and academic achievement.

It is unlikely that all, or even most, specific language and learning disorders are due to tissue injury. The high incidence of such disabilities in the families of children presenting these difficulties (Hallgren, 1950) and the predominance of males among them suggests the possibility of a genetic inheritance in a significant number. This has evoked the concept of cerebral dysmaturation—or developmental deviation—not related to native intelligence, but involving specific centers or pathways of the brain (Ingram, 1960). However, the exact location and nature of these defects has not been described.

It is necessary to recognize that the constellation of behavior and learning disorders described here represents highly specific if often ill-defined disabilities. They constitute only a small percentage of all adjustment and academic problems among children.

Children with the symptoms described here appeared in our clinic and were studied conscientiously by competent professional workers for many months before a gradual awareness of the complex psychobiological background of these disorders evolved.

AN INTERDISCIPLINARY PROBLEM

Out of our study and experience we have arrived at the following observations:

(1) Some educators, neurologists, psychologists, and audiologists have been aware of the significance and importance of minimal brain dysfunction for many years (Orton, 1928).

(2) The inherently complex nature of the problems of children with this disability crosses many professional boundaries, but the professional workers have not learned to complement each other effectively in their efforts to help. They have not cultivated the interprofessional communications and exchange of ideas which are necessary for our mutual understanding of these complex problems.

(3) Many children, the nature of whose handicaps are not well understood, are being treated in child guidance clinics, remedial reading centers, speech correction classes, and special educational settings, although they have never been adequately studied and have not responded well to long-term and intensive intervention (Hanvik, *et al.*, 1961; Tannhauser, 1959).

(4) Brain-damaged children are being treated for schizophrenia or autism and presumed environmental deprivation without consideration of the fact that their detailed developmental history often reveals that they were never healthy, normally responsive children even in earliest infancy.

(5) Speech therapists are treating children for mechanical speech defects when, in some instances, a profound central language disorder exists.

(6) Known bright children with specific reading disabilities have been managed for long periods of time on the presumption that they were poorly motivated, emotionally blocked, or neglected at home.

(7) Intelligent children with reading disabilities are being considered mentally retarded on the basis of group intelligence tests which presuppose the one skill which is notably impaired.

(8) Hyperactive children have been excluded from schools as anti-social without recognition of the nature of their handicaps and without provision of appropriate educational facilities and techniques to meet their special needs.

(9) The usual neurological examination is sensitive to less than 50 percent of brain function, yet many clinicians have excluded the possibility of any central nervous system pathology on the basis of this type of examination alone.

(10) The skills and techniques of the clinical psychologist, audiologist, and speech pathologist may detect neurological impairment in the absence of classical neurological signs (Taterka and Katz, 1955).

(11) The electroencephalogram can be expected to yield significantly valuable information about central nervous system function even in the absence of clinical seizures. It is abnormal in over 50 percent of children with hyperkinetic behavior, specific reading disabilities, and language problems (Poser and Zeigler, 1958; Rabinovitch, *et al.*, 1954; Kennard *et al.*, 1952).

The current controversy over the implications of minimal cerebral dysfunction does not promise to be resolved in the foreseeable future. The full significance of this type of impairment is not yet known and must await the time when the medical, paramedical, and educational disciplines have learned to communicate with and complement each other.

References

Bender, L., The psychological problems of children with organic brain disorders, *Amer. J. Orthopsychiat.*, 1949, 19, 404.

Bender, L., *Psychopathology of children with organic brain disorders* (Springfield, Illinois: Charles C Thomas, 1956).

Blau, A., Mental changes following head trauma in children, *Arch. Neurol. Psychiat.*, 1936, 35, 723.

Bond, E. D., and Smith, L. H., Post-encephalitic behavior disorders: a ten-year review of the Franklin School, *Amer. J. Psychiat.*, 1935, 92, 17.

Bradley, C., Characteristics and management of children with behavior disorders associated with organic brain damage, *Pediat. Clin. N. Amer.*, 1957, 4, 1049.

Cohn, R., Relayed acquisition of reading and writing abilities in children, *Arch. Neurol.*, 1961, 4, 153.

Eisenberg, L., Psychiatric implications of brain damage in children, *Psychiat. Quart.*, 1957, 31, 72.

Hallgren, B., Specific dyslexia: a clinical and genetic study, *Acta psychiat. neurol.*, *Suppl.*, 1950, 65.

Hanvik, L. J., Nelson, S. E., Hanson, H. B., Anderson, A. S., Dressler, W. H., and Zarling, V. R., Diagnosis of cerebral dysfunction in childhood, *Amer. J. dis. Child.*, 1961, 101, 364.

Ingram, T. T. S., Specific developmental disorders of speech in childhood, *Brain*, 1959, 82, 450.

Ingram, T. T., Pediatric aspects of specific developmental dysphasia, dyslexia, and dysgraphia, *Cerebral Palsy Bull.*, 1960, 2, 248.

Kahn, E., and Cohen, L. H., Organic driveness: A brain stem syndrome and experience, *N. E. J. Med.*, 1934, 210, 748.

Kennard, M. A., Rabinovitch, R. D., and Wexler, D., The abnormal electroencephalogram as related to reading disability in children with disorders of behavior, *Canad. Med. Ass. J.*, 1952, 67, 330.

Knobloch, H., Pasamanick, B., Syndrome of minimal cerebral damage in infancy, *J.A.M.A.*, 1959, 170, 1,384.

Laufer, M. N., Denhoff, E., and Solomons, G., The hyperkinetic impulse disorder in children's behavior problems, *Psychosom. Med.*, 1957, 19, 38.

Lewis, R. S., Strauss, A. A., and Lehtinen, E. L., *The other child*. 2nd ed. (New York: Grune & Stratton, 1960).

Luria, A. R., An objective approach to the study of the abnormal child, *Amer. J. Orthopsychiat.*, 1961, 31, 1.

Myklebust, H. R., and Boshes, B., Psychoneurological learning disorders in children, *Arch. Pediat.*, 1960, 77, 245.

Orton, S. T., Specific reading disability—Strephosymbolia, J.A.M.A., 1928, 90, 1095.

Pasamanick, B., The epidemiology of behavior disorders of childhood, Res. Publ. Ass. Res. nerv. ment. Dis., 1954, 34, 397.

Poser, C. M., and Ziegler, D. K., Clinical significance of fourteen and six per second positive spike complexes, Neurology, 1958, 8, 903.

Rabinovitch, R. D., Drew, A. L., DeJong, R. N., Ingram, W., and Withey, L., A research approach to reading retardation, Res. Publ. Ass. Res. nerv. ment. Dis., 1954, 34, 363.

Rogers, M. E., Lillienfeld, A. M., and Pasamanick, B., Prenatal and paranatal factors in the development of childhood behavior disorders, Acta psychiat. neurol. Scand., Suppl., 1955, 102, 1.

Strauss, A. A., and Lehtinen, E. L., Psychopathology and education of the brain-injured child (New York: Grune & Stratton, 1950).

Strauss, A. A., and Werner, H., Disorders of conceptual thinking in the brain-injured child, J. nerv. men. Dis., 1942, 96, 153.

Tannhauser, H. T., Educational management of children with communication disorders, Proc. Md. Child Growth Develpm. Inst., June 1959. (Available through the Maryland State Department of Health.)

Taterka, J. H., and Katz, J., Study of correlations between electroencephalographic and psychological patterns in emotionally disturbed children, Psychosom. Med., 1955, 17, 63.

Wood, N., Language disorders in children, Monogr. Soc. Res. Child Devel., 1960, 25, 15.

9 A NOTE ON THE CONCEPT OF THE "BRAIN-INJURED" CHILD

Joseph Wortis

The concept of the "brain-injured child," as developed by Strauss and Lehtinen, declares that there is a type of defective child, frequently but not necessarily retarded, whose mental defect, in contrast to the familial or hereditary type of deficiency, is due to actual brain injury and that these children tend to be hyperactive, distractable and awkward individuals, poorly integrated in their motor performance, faulty in their perceptions, poorly organized and unpredictable in their behavior, who go to pieces on relatively slight provocation. Moreover, say Strauss and Lehtinen, it does not matter what the nature of the defect or injury is, whether infectious, traumatic, toxic or embryonic, nor what its localization or extent, the clinical consequences are the same, "since all brain lesions, wherever localized, are followed by a similar kind of disordered behavior" (1947, p. 20).

This concept has been rather widely accepted by workers in the retardation field—especially teachers—for several reasons: first, it relates the disturbance and disability of a certain group of defective or problem children to a known or supposed actual deficiency of the brain; second, it more or less correctly describes a recognizable clinical grouping of children who have had demonstrable brain injury and who display a similar combination of symptoms, and thirdly—and perhaps most important of all—it prescribes a carefully contrived and apparently useful plan of management or education for dealing with these children.

In spite of this, the concept appears to me to be faulty, and perhaps seriously misleading, for several reasons. Although the notion that mental deficiency is often associated with brain injury represents an important ad-

Reprinted from the *American Journal of Mental Deficiency*, Vol. 61, No. 1 (July, 1956), pp. 204-206. By permission of the author and publisher.

vance over the old idea that it is usually merely inherited, nevertheless the scope of familial or hereditary deficiency has been so greatly constricted in recent years that it should no longer play so dominant a role in our thinking about retarded children. If we forget for the moment those milder defectives who are much more likely to have been influenced by social and material deprivations, we have to accept the fact that practically *all* severe mental deficiency is organic in origin. Benda, for example, basing his conclusion on 250 post-mortem examinations, categorically states, "There is no patient with a severe mental inadequacy who could not be classified . . . 'organic brain syndrome'" (1952, p. 9). "An analysis of severe mental defect," he goes on to say, "demonstrates that all cases are characterized by pathology of the central nervous system. There is no condition which cannot be expressed in terms of developmental or metabolic brain pathology."

To illustrate the extraordinary variety of cerebral defects and injuries commonly encountered, I can report that in the past few years in our Retardation Clinic we have diagnosed numerous cases of anoxic birth injury, brain hemorrhage and contusions, hydrocephaly, microcephaly, brain injury secondary to skull deformity, post-encephalitides, Tay-Sachs Disease and other brain lipodystrophies, Hurler's Snydrome, developmental midline defects, endocrinopathies, post-anesthesia cerebral injury, brain injury following erythroblastosis fetalis, tuberosclerosis, neurofibromatosis, hemangiomatosis, toxoplasmosis, Van Gierke's glycogen storage disease, cretinism, mongolism, and phenylpyruvic oligophrenia (both of which latter conditions are associated with extensive and irreversible brain pathology).

Those among you who have worked with even a few of these clinical groups will recognize that only a small proportion of them fit into the clinical picture that has been described as the "brain-injured child." Among our children we actually encounter a great variety of characteristics: placid, passive, bland, empty, tense, peculiar, destructive, anxious, restless, with quite a few who can sit for hours in quiet absorption before a television screen, or who engage in simple repetitive activities, or who sink into long periods of passive torpor until distracted or disturbed. A sizeable number appear quite normal except for their general retardation in all spheres, so that they earn the description of "children" far into adulthood.

Behavior and mental processes in the brain-injured child, as in the normal child, are dependent on at least four separate sets of factors: (1) the anatomical equipment and configuration of the brain, (2) the settled stereotype of learned behavior we call personality or character, (3) the actual situation at the point of observation, and (4) the less substantial something that we can call the condition of the organism: fatigue, sleepiness, good or poor health, the play of nutrients and blood supply or endocrine influence and a host of other subtle variables. . . . If, to develop our argument, we neglect the last three sets of factors or regard them as constant, it still would be difficult on the basis of our present knowledge to ascribe very specific behavior to specific organic defects, and it would be very rash indeed to declare that *any* lesion, diffuse or discrete, regardless of degree or localization, would tend to produce the same pattern of behavior.

Brain function is dependent upon an extraordinarily complicated network of nerve tracts transmitting their impulses across synaptic junctions heaped together and deployed in various nuclear masses. A hierarchy of functional levels exists in which the brain cortex controls, mediates and connects the highest conscious nervous activities. Decortication, whether produced anatomically by ablation or destruction, or pharmacologically by the narcotizing action of alcohol or other agents, in either case induces some loss of cortical efficiency and control, so that as a consequence the finer motor and sensory integration is impaired, inducing motor awkwardness and crude or distorted perception, while at the same time freeing the uncontrolled motor impulses of the lower centers from restraint. It is probably this pattern of partial decortication which characterizes the "brain-injured child" of Strauss or the "neurophrenic" of Doll. The cortex, it must also be remembered, is especially vulnerable to both anoxic and other nutritional lacks (such as hypoglycemia) and to injury from hemorrhage or other external insult. When, however, the damage is diffused throughout the brain, the relationship among the parts may not be so drastically altered, and in a setting of general defectiveness the "driven" behavior may be lacking. Furthermore, selective or disproportionate injury to subcortical centers may induce quite different pictures, while circumscribed small injuries to the motor cortex, speech areas or other sensory analysors may create quite distinctive patterns of deficiency in which the relative loss of cortical tissue may not loom large. Small cortical lesions or scars, for example, may not only produce a defect but may also serve as an irritative focus to induce new symptoms. When to this already complicated pattern of possibilities is added the not infrequent confusions and distortions that arise from a confused or ambivalent lateralization of function, the possibilities for other developmental difficulties become intricate indeed.

Under the circumstances, I think it would be wise for the scientific educator to enlarge his concept of the brain-injured child to include a much greater variety of patterns and possibilities and to make allowance for quite varied handicapping conditions that may impede the educational process. Educators, psychologists, and psychiatrists alike are faced with the necessity of carefully studying, observing, and evaluating the child before them, noting the developmental history, the neurological status, and clinical behavior of the child in detail before estimating the child's potentialities for development or proposing a rehabilitation plan. And in many if not most cases the estimate and plan alike may have to derive from a period of patient observation and active work with the child before an adequate picture of the biological deficits or abilities can be defined.

There is, in short, I believe, no "brain-injured child," but only a variety of brain-injured children whose problems are quite varied and whose condition calls for far more refined analysis than some of the current generalizations on the brain-injured child provide.

References

Benda, C. E., *Developmental disorders of mentation and cerebral palsies* (New York: Grune & Stratton, 1952).

Strauss, A. A., and Lehtinen, L. E., *Psychopathology and education of the brain-injured child* (New York: Grune & Stratton, 1947).

~II~

SPECIALIZED APPROACHES
TO LEARNING DISORDERS

INTRODUCTION

THE EMERGENCE of learning disorders as a major concern in education and special education has been paralleled in other disciplines. Psychology has increased steadily the number of studies dealing with impaired learning. Disorders in central nervous system function are being studied by medical specialists to determine which disabilities are related to chemical imbalance, nutritional deficit, known tissue damage, emotional states, and developmental differences among children. New attempts to understand the nature of learning disorders are reflected in the work of other trained specialists such as biomedical engineers, psycholinguists, and recreational therapists.

As a result of multidisciplinary interest in learning problems, communication among specialists has taken on new importance. Terminology which has found acceptance within a discipline may provoke confusion among other specialists. For this reason, it is necessary that one become familiar with the points of view, language and contributions made by several disciplines.

The educator has a special need to understand the limitations of other disciplines in providing educationally significant information. At the same time, the educator should be sophisticated enough in his knowledge that he can use the contributions of many special disciplines in designing programs for children with learning problems. Conversely, specialists outside the field of education must communicate more clearly the information they gather which is relevant to school learning. This can only be done as specialists understand the relationship between teaching procedures and their special interests.

THE NEED FOR SPECIALIZED APPROACHES

To the uninitiated, it seems obvious that a reading problem ought to be resolved by a "reading specialist." Likewise, a slight coordination problem ought to be improved by a "physical education specialist." In short, the casual observer is confused by multidisciplinary efforts to identify and correct such a "clearcut" condition as "he can't read." No small part of the confusion can be attributed to the confusion among the professions concerning the roles that each trained group can fulfill best.

Fernald (1943, p. 60) made two observations which illustrate the scope of professional involvement required to understand fully a reading disability. She pointed out that "no other animal sits relatively still in front of a sheet of paper and moves the eyes across line after line with periodic stops on each line." Specialists who understand the physiology of the eye may be needed to analyze eye coordination problems among disabled readers.

On the other hand, specialists who work with group dynamics may be required to contribute their skills in a reading disability case. When a child fails to learn to read, his world can become a disturbed one. As Fernald observed, "sometimes a note is sent home, which may result in anything from a prayer meeting to a thrashing (1943, p. 187). A child with a learning disorder may require the skills of the neuropsychiatrist and the social case worker as well as those of other specialists if he is to acquire and maintain reading skills.

SPECIALISTS AND GENERALISTS

Leaders in fields requiring advanced training have been characterized as (a) differentiators of knowledge or (b) integrators of knowledge. Differentiators are those who dig deeply into narrow aspects of their fields until they have uncovered new information. Integrators are those whose contribution does not consist of disclosing new information in a limited field, but rather consists of creating frames of reference which allow new combinations of information from several fields to be made.

Learning disorders are better understood today because of the differentiators. However, the children who have such disorders desperately need the insight and imaginative programming of the integrators. Recent conferences on minimal brain impairment (Kirk and Becker, 1963) and reading disorders (Flower et al., 1965) involved many specialists (differentiators). A list of disciplines represented below highlights the great task which is faced by the generalists (integrators). That all these specialists cooperated is a remarkable assurance that communication among disciplines is improving.

(1) Pediatrics
(2) Ophthamology
(3) Orthoptic Technique
(4) Otolaryngology
(5) Pediatric Mental Health
(6) Psychiatry
(7) Speech Pathology
(8) Psychology
(9) Neurology
(10) Medical Research
(11) Special Education
(12) Education
(13) Physical Therapy
(14) Sociology

Among the conference participants, integrators are noticeably absent. Included were the director of a school for educational therapy, the director of an achievement center for children, and the director of a comprehensive institute for language disorders. The most unfortunate omission from interdisciplinary conference programs is the neglected classroom teacher specialist. A masterful classroom specialist is perhaps the most effective integrator of knowledge.

APPROACHES TO LEARNING DISORDERS IN THE FUTURE

No discipline is an island. Knowledge cannot be compartmentalized and linked by a series of simple bridges. Knowledge about the human learner is being discovered by biochemists as well as brain surgeons. Engineers and electronic technicians are creating circuitry which may eventually simulate cerebral circuits. The influence of the weatherman may even be felt more specifically in the future as recent studies have shown relationships between barometric pressure, relative humidity, and classroom behavior (Brown, 1964). As unrelated as these fields appear, they are, in reality, meshed. Learning involves brain, biochemical change, electrically charged circuitry and bodily response to environment. Yet to study the organism without considering language and culture would be like trying to understand a car without considering gasoline or highways.

The future clearly requires several important changes in approach to learning disorders.

(1) The acceptance of terms which have interdisciplinary applicability, are clearly defined and may be incorporated into a cumulating literature whose goal is clarity and simplicity in scholarly communication.
(2) The accordance of respect to all individuals who employ sound, scientific methods regardless of the field with which they are identified.
(3) The insistence on role definition in interdisciplinary settings with a willingness to modify (and eliminate, if necessary) traditional boundaries in the interest of full cooperation with a minimum duplication of effort.

(4) The creation of administrative frameworks which give unity of purpose, ease of access and coordinated services among disciplines while maintaining the freedom of procedure necessary for the effective fulfillment of role.

(5) The elimination of false promise, both positively and negatively, through the commercialization and publication of findings in forms apt to be misleading to the nonprofessional reader.

(6) The development of interagency training, research and service reducing the proliferation in Methods, Systems, "Prophets," and "Disciples" and thereby maintaining a focus upon essential issues and practices rather than upon names and locations.

The promise of the future is being demonstrated in multidisciplinary centers throughout the country. Unfortunately, the most common pattern at present is not a coordinated effort. School personnel, parents, and doctors are unable to refer children for thorough learning diagnoses because the kinds of diagnostic procedures needed are scattered in many different places in the typical city.

As universities cooperate in training, as community agencies provide a setting for interdisciplinary action and as educators become more sophisticated in screening children with problems, many of the school failures today will be the productive citizens of the future. The need to understand the similarities and differences among specialists leads to a consideration of the selections chosen for Part II.

References

Brown, G. I., The relationship between barometric pressure and relative humidity and classroom behavior, *J. Educ. Res.*, 1964, 57 (7), 368-370.

Fernald, Grace M., *Remedial techniques in basic school subjects* (New York: McGraw-Hill, 1943).

Flower, R. M., Gofman, Helen, and Lawson, Lucie I., *Reading disorders: A multidisciplinary symposium* (Philadelphia: Davis, 1965).

Kirk, S. A., and Becker, W. (Editors), *Conference on children with minimal brain impairment* (Urbana: University of Illinois Press), 1963.

SECTION A: Special Education, Psychology, and Sociology

10   A NEW FRONTIER IN SPECIAL EDUCATION

Donald A. Leton

The purpose of this article is to describe a new problem in the field of special education. It may seem futile to propose a new challenge in a field which is undermanned because of a shortage of trained, qualified teachers, and overburdened with tasks of discovering methods and materials and of providing guidance to children with many types of handicaps. Nevertheless, in behalf of the regular classroom teachers, who are already confronted with a wide range of individual differences among normal children, there seems to be a pressing urgency for special consideration of the atypical children described in this article.

There is a sizable group of exceptional children for whom no adequate educational facilities exist. These are children who have incurred a mild neurological impairment, and, as a result, may have severe learning disabilities, or may exhibit behavior deviations which make adjustment in the regular classroom difficult, even though their intelligence scores are within the range for "normal." The problems which these children present to the regular classroom teacher are manifold. There are, however, no courses or experiences in the teacher-training curriculum which would prepare a teacher to cope with a brain-injured child. To continue these children in regular classrooms would extend the concept of individual differences quite beyond its intended meaning.

CLASSIFICATION OF SYMPTOMS

First, in order to identify these children in a practical way, a description of the symptoms which they display will be helpful. There is one group of related symptoms of physical behavior which is commonly referred to as "organic drivenness." This syndrome includes impulsive behavior, hyperactivity, distractibility, difficulty in maintaining a quiet attitude, difficulty in maintaining attention, manual incoordination, impulsive motor discharge, and sensitivity to extraneous stimuli.

There is a second constellation of traits in the area of social behavior. This group is characterized by asocial behavior, which is of a different quality from the antisocial behavior seen in emotionally disturbed and neurotic children. The latter usually have targets for their aggressive and hostile acts, while the asocial organics show a diffuse aggressiveness. Their asocial behavior is dictated by inner impulsiveness and disinhibition. These children may have difficulty in learning social and cultural norms and group conformity. Many of them show poor social judgment. When there is a cortical dysfunction they may have difficulty in establishing a conscious control over their behavior.

There is a third syndrome in the area of speech and language functions. This may include aphasia or dysphasia; that is, irregular speech development and speech impediments. This syndrome may also include alexia or dyslexia, the inability to recognize printed symbols, and retardation in reading development. It frequently includes dysgraphia, illegible writing, a lack of co-ordination in writing and drawing, and a confusion between letters and sounds. This third syndrome may be related to impairment in the speech and motor areas of the brain and to perceptual retardation.

The foregoing description neatly parcels all of the related symptoms into three syndromes; however, not all brain-injured children display the same symptoms, nor to the same degree. Those with marked neuromuscular involvement will be identified as spastics. Many others, who show only the behavior or learning difficulties, may remain unidentified in regular classrooms.

In view of the importance of reading and writing in the modern curriculum, the learning difficulties which these children encounter present a real problem to the teacher. Even before the learning problem or the perceptual difficulty is recognized, however, parents and kindergarten teachers are faced with a more serious problem of managing the social and physical behavior. Parents and teachers alike find that the usual methods for training and for discipline do not produce the desired results.

THE CAUSES

It is perhaps premature to consider the educational requirements for these children, particularly when there is a lack of adequate diagnostic instruments to identify them. The number of these children in the school population has never been determined. There are some indications, however, that they are increasing. Improvements in obstetrical techniques and in prenatal and nursery care have decreased the incidence of birth mortalities.

Many children are alive today who would not have survived under previous conditions. Some of these may have little or no residual impairment, while others have varying degrees of retardation.

For purposes of illustration, several possible causes for neural damage will be reviewed. It would be difficult to estimate the number of children who suffer mild losses from infectious fevers, whooping cough, chicken pox, measles, and forms of encephalitis and meningitis. Although the incidence of residual damage may be very slight for any one of these illnesses (e.g., measles and whooping cough), since practically all children have common illnesses, the consequent total who are affected represents a sizable number.

For a more specific example of advancement in medicine, consider the condition of Rh (blood type) incompatibility in the mother. In the past the toxic condition which developed from this cause often led to permanent brain injury or death. The possibility of this condition is now determined in prenatal care, and preventive measures are taken to minimize the hazards. If transfusions are administered at the appropriate time, the infant may show no apparent residuals. This is only one of the recent advancements which have decreased infant mortalities and brain damage.

In order to appreciate the problems of diagnosis and the number of children who may be involved, some of the more general causes of neural damage should be considered. Anoxia, or oxygen deprivation at birth, is commonly recognized as one of the prominent causes. Actually, this is not a primary cause, since it often reflects a condition which is present before birth. It can also develop during the birth process. In certain premature births the breathing reflex may be intermittent or shallow because of neural underdevelopment. When there is a birth injury, the nerve tissues may be impaired; consequently, the administration of oxygen is necessary to help establish the breathing reflex. In recent research the need for controlled oxygen supply has also been discovered. Excessive oxygen or irregularities in the oxygen supply, as well as oxygen deprivation, may be conditions of neural impairment. Because congenital asphyxia is frequently associated with premature delivery, it would be difficult to isolate the separate causes of neural damage and their respective influence.

Birth injury may be due to factors involved with the labor or, in a minor percentage of cases, it may arise in the use of obstetrical instruments. If there is an unusual presentation in delivery and prolonged labor, there may be a compression of the infant's skull. The damage to the brain in such a case may stem from a cerebral hemorrhage or from a direct injury to the brain tissues. The probability for injury in post-mature births appears to be higher than for normal-term deliveries. Head injuries in infancy and childhood are not considered to be an important cause of brain injury. These injuries, however, provide convenient explanations for some parents.

The number of children involved in automobile accidents, bicycle accidents, and sidewalk falls is certainly much greater now than three or four decades ago. Although the percentage of children who suffer permanent damage is very slight, accidents do contribute to the total picture. It is not the intent in this paper to include all of the possible causes for brain injury, but rather to indicate the wide variety of causes which contribute to the problem.

RELATION OF CAUSES AND SYMPTOMS

There is a critical problem which all of the behavioral sciences eventually face: that is, relating causes and symptoms. At this point, research is not sufficiently advanced to establish a causal relationship between the symptoms observed in children and the conditions which exist in the central nervous system. It is not so much a problem of defining the symptoms as it is of describing the exact state and condition of the central nervous system. At the present time one can only draw inferences from the coexistence of the behavioral symptoms and the health history, which may indicate the organic conditions.

Since the inferences regarding the relationship between brain injury and behavior symptoms are gradually being supported by research evidence, they are not completely in the realm of theory. So that parents and teachers can understand the probable causes for impulsive behavior and learning difficulties, these relationships will be discussed in further detail. This understanding would serve to prevent the unfortunate situation in which parents blame the teachers for the learning difficulties, and teachers blame the home or the parents. The major causes actually reside within the child.

It is well known that the cortex plays an important role in the control of behavior. In normal behavior there is a dynamic equilibrium between the cortex and the hypothalamus. The cortex has an inhibiting influence over the more primitive and emotional expressions of the hypothalamus. The circuit of this relationship has been established in neurophysiological research. When damage to the cortex disrupts the neural balance, uninhibited behavior may follow.

RESULTS OF DAMAGE

The symptoms are not determined entirely by the nature or the extent of the damage. If the damage is diffuse or extensive, more areas of function may be involved. If the damage is of a severe localized nature, the child may have difficulty in maintaining a state of consciousness. In other circumstances the child may have difficulty in the perception of spatial relationships, in speech development, or in motor coordination. Many times the general level of brain functioning may not be affected. This fact accounts for the appearance of normal intelligence scores for children who may have neuromuscular difficulties or specific learning handicaps.

The sensory association, speech, and motor areas of the brain have been charted for some time. Their importance to sensory perception, speech development and volitional movements has been established. Observations have shown also that inadequate social behavior results from damage to the frontal lobes.

One explanation of the diffuse effects of brain injury in children is that the foci of functions are not well differentiated in the developing brain. There is also a strong likelihood that later neural development may compensate for early damage. How the normal brain accomplishes a synthesis of all of the incoming perceptual experiences is still unknown. How the brain achieves a selective interrelation between thought processes and memory is a further mystery. The most widely accepted theory of mental development at the present time is that there is a progressive differentiation and integration, as concurrent processes, in cerebral organization from prenatal stages through adolescence. Either or both of these processes may be involved in the neurally impaired child.

ERRONEOUS EXPLANATIONS

In many cases the parents of a brain-injured child have been assured by a physician that there is nothing physically wrong with the child. This may be a statement of fact, since a child is considered to be physically healthy when there is no evidence of a disease process. On the other hand, this provides little help to parents who are concerned about problems of development, behavior, and management. This reassurance may even have a negative effect when parents feel that the child's behavior is a reflection of their relationship or their method of training. Parents will naturally develop ambivalent feelings toward a child who does not respond to developmental expectancies in learning how to walk, to talk, or to develop emotional independence. Mothers are unable to understand the prolonged physical and emotional dependence of children who continue to be "lap babies" until six or seven years of age.

Still other parents may be informed that their child will outgrow his difficulty. They wait for growth which may never occur. More practitioners should keep in mind that "time" in and of itself does not heal. There are really only two processes which take place over the course of time that may change the symptom picture. In brain-injured children these are: first, the accumulation of social experience which may help to moderate the organic impulse; second, the physical structural changes which may occur with later neural development. To reassure a parent when there is no promise of improvement is cruel.

Because of the influence of psychoanalysis and psychosomatic medicine, there has been a tendency to rely on the psyche to explain many conditions. In the fields of education and social work there is also a tendency to explain the child's behavior in terms of sociointeractional theories of personality. These explanations do not take adequate account of the constitutional determinants of behavior. A multitude of erroneous emotional causes may be unearthed from the psyche or from the social environment of any child. Some of these errors of diagnosis are then seen as the interrelating of symptoms. For example, the adjustment difficulties which are experienced by brain-injured children may be explained on the basis of the reading disability or the speech handicap. The social difficulty may be blamed on the home, and the learning difficulty blamed on the school. These learning difficulties may suffice to explain away the symptoms, but they do not contribute to a real understanding of the causes.

11 MINIMAL BRAIN DYSFUNCTION:

A DILEMMA FOR EDUCATORS

Lloyd M. Dunn

Children with minimal brain dysfunction have been receiving more attention recently than at any other time in the special education movement. Credit for initiating a focus on this syndrome goes to Strauss who attached the term brain-injured (or exogenous) to this group of children in 1947 (Strauss and Lehtinen, 1947). One can only speculate on the reasons for the heightening concern for this area almost 20 years after it was brought to the attention of the field. Probably three factors are operating: (1) the increased number of such children today, (2) the growing sophistication and outspokenness of parents, and (3) the dissatisfaction of parents and professionals alike over placing such children in either the regular grades or in special classes for the retarded. In any event, parents and teachers are about at their wits' end, and demanding that professional persons increase their efforts to ameliorate the many problems which such children present. And they have hardly begun to make their voices heard. Community pressure is increasing to establish special school programs specifically for this group. New parent groups are becoming organized to the point where they can exert the kind of pressure that other groups have done in the immediate past on legislators, on school board members, and on other elected officials. Even professional persons in addition to educators are beginning to feel the surge of reproach and demand. The critical needs of these children require that we focus our attention on this area with new vigor and imagination. Thus, it is a pleasure to explore this issue with you from the point of view of the educator.

Reprinted from unpublished manuscript, George Peabody College: Institute on Mental Retardation and Intellectual Development, 1965. By permission of the author.

DESCRIBING AND DEFINING THE SYNDROME

Most of us who work with such children believe we have a fairly clear picture in mind of the syndrome. How familiar does this sketch sound to you? "Ed is a ten year old boy without a motor handicap other than clumsiness. His speech is fairly distinct. Ed's intelligence quotient score is 80. His teacher complains that he talks incessantly, constantly interrupts the class with irrelevant remarks. He has a strong need for attention and thus bothers other children who are working by knocking things off their desk, by hiding their pencils, and by hitting them on the head. His learning patterns are very uneven. It is nearly impossible to settle him down to academic work because he cannot concentrate on one thing for any length of time. In fact, he is at the mercy of any idea which occurs to him, or any environmental event which reaches him."

One would think that such children would be easy to define and identify. Such is not the case. For example, rather recently clinical terms of a chain of *Child Study Centers* located across a Southern state were meeting together as a group for the first time. In studying the annual reports of these dozen centers, one discovered that in some clinics, 30 to 40 percent of the children seen during the year were diagnosed as "emotionally disturbed," and 10 to 20 percent were placed in each of the categories "mentally retarded" or "brain injured." In other centers, 30 to 40 percent were labelled "mentally retarded," and relatively few "brain-injured" and "emotionally disturbed." In still other centers, 30 to 40 percent were diagnosed as "brain-injured," with much smaller numbers placed in the categories "mentally retarded" and "emotionally disturbed."* Now how could this be? When presented with these data, the clinicians discussed them at length. They contended that part of the variance could be accounted for by the type of service being initiated in a community, thus leading to selective referral. Another explanation was that most children had all three types of disability and the conflict arose in designating the major one. However, another factor seemed more crucial. The diagnostic category selected depended on the training, professional make-up, philosophy and predisposition of the diagnostic team. Three different groups, depending on their biases, could label the same child *brain-injured, emotionally disturbed,* or *mentally retarded.* A dilemma indeed!

Similar findings are revealed by a review of psychological research literature. Many psychometric tests have been devised to elicit differences among the organically impaired, mentally ill, and mentally retarded. Among the many are the Goldstein-Scheerer sorting tests, memory-for-design tests, the Bender-Gestalt copying of designs test, marble-board tests, Halstead and Reitan batteries of neuropsychological tests, etc. Such critical reviews of the research literature as those by Yates (1954), and by Klebanoff,

---

* Other children seen fell in other areas of exceptionality.

Singer, and Wilensky (1954) point out that such tests usually differentiate any and all groups of the organically impaired, mentally retarded, and mentally ill from the normal. However, their record for differential diagnosis among the three groups is appallingly poor. Too, it is even worse for *individual* cases.

Parenthetically, neurological findings have been equally equivocal. In general, the neurologists, pediatricians, or pediatric neurologists report they can find no abnormal signs in many of these children we are labelling *minimally* brain-damaged. Similarly, many EEG patterns are normal. However, in retrospective studies comparing *groups* of such children with normal controls, the former usually have significantly more abnormal EEG's and neurological signs. But this is of limited value in *individual* diagnosis. A puzzling state of affairs indeed!

At this point in our knowledge, the question arises as to the utility of labelling such children. *On the one hand,* there are those who contend we should get rid of all labels in this area. They base their arguments on such positions as the following: The labels we have devised, to date, are not badges of distinction. Children in this category are so different from one another that no group treatment is known to be effective. Labels are blocks to thinking. *On the other hand,* there are those who contend we must find and agree on a label. Their arguments include: We usually cannot provide special education services, unproven as they may be, until we describe the children we propose to serve. Another is the contention that we cannot advance knowledge in the area until we describe the condition. In any event, there has been no paucity of terms introduced. Enumerated below are some of them:

(1) Agenesis child
(2) Birth damaged child
(3) Chronic brain syndrome
(4) Clumsy child
(5) Exogeneous child
(6) Hyperactive child
(7) Hyperkinetic syndrome
(8) Imperceptive child
(9) Interjacent child
(10) Major learning disordered child
(11) Minimal cerebral injured child
(12) Minimal brain dysfunctioned child
(13) Nervous child
(14) Neurologically handicapped child
(15) Neurophrenic child
(16) Neuropsychological impaired child
(17) Neurosensory disordered child
(18) Organically impaired child
(19) Perceptually impaired child
(20) Perceptual-motor impaired child
(21) Psychomotor disordered child
(22) Psychoneurological disordered child
(23) Strauss syndrome

As one hears these terms, besides being confused and dismayed, you may also tease out four clusters. *One group* presupposes an organic etiology; for example, in the term "minimal brain damage," etc. A *second* group re-sorts to behavioral terms with no attempt to imply causation, such as "hyperactive," "perceptually impaired," "learning disordered," etc. A *third* group utilizes a neutral term, such as the "Strauss syndrome." A *fourth* group straddles the fence on etiology implying an interaction of environmental and biological factors; for example "psychoneurological learning disorders."

Where is the field moving in terms of consensus on terminology? There are two developments.

First, the National Institute on Neurological Diseases and Blindness of the U. S. Public Health Service and the National Society for Crippled Children and Adults have collaborated in sponsoring a task force on "terminology and identification." Clements (1964) has prepared a report on the deliberations of this group who chose the term *"minimal brain dys-function"* to best describe the syndrome. Since this task force was made up primarily of physicians, one can understand the proclivity to choose a term which implies causation, because this has generally been the route to prevention and medical treatment. The term "brain dysfunction" rather than "brain injury" suggests that a fruitful hypothesis on etiology may be a bio-chemical one rather than brain damage, per se. The biological scientists appear to be moving through the progression: from birth-injured, to brain-injured, to biochemically disordered.

Second, the U. S. Office of Education in collaboration with the NEA Council for Exceptional Children has moved in a different direction. These organizations have selected the term *"major learning disorder"* to include the Strauss-syndrome child plus others. More specifically, the term has a wider connotation to include all children with disabilities who do not fit into the usual categories, such as the retarded and disturbed, but are educ-cationally handicapped. As for educators, this term has two advantages: it does not imply causation, and it indicates a need for special education. Thus, while it is a very loose term, it may have utility in providing special education services.

For purposes of behavioral research, a more restrictive term than "major learning disorder," more amenable to an operation definition, would appear to be needed. My personal preference is for the neutral term "Strauss syndrome,' a term advocated by Stevens and Birch (1957). In any event, the movement toward consensus on terminology is a heartening one. Whether one chooses the term "minimal brain dysfunction" or "Strauss syndrome," it is generally agreed we are talking about the child so skillfully described by Strauss in 1947.

What is the body of knowledge on the behavioral correlates of this condition? What procedures have been advocated for the education of these children? Three sections follow dealing with these issues: *First* is summarized the theoretical-clinical literature; *second*, the educational approaches advocated; and *third*, some evidence on their effectiveness.

THEORETICAL-CLINICAL LITERATURE

(1) The initial impetus to the field appears to have come from the classic research by Goldstein & Sheerer (1941) on traumatically brain-injured, World War I soldiers. Their major contributions included the following: (1) They shifted us back from a localization theory of brain injury, to thinking about generalized brain damage. (2) They gave us the terms "abstract" and "concrete" thinking; characterized the brain-injured as "concrete" thinkers. (3) They gave us their four characteristics of the brain-injury syndrome in adults: namely, (a) catastrophic reaction, (b) rigidity, (c) distractibility, and (d) again, the concrete mode of thinking.

(2) The next link in the chain is the contributions of Strauss, Lehtinen, Werner, Kephart, etc. in relating (or probably a better term would be extrapolating) Goldstein's findings on brain injury from adults to children. As leader of this group, Strauss described his subjects as having four *behavioral* characteristics: (1) perceptual disorders, (2) perseveration, (3) thinking and conceptual disorders, and (4) behavioral disorders including especially hyperactivity and disinhibition. He quite clearly noted that his three *biological* signs, namely, (1) slight neurological signs, (2) a history of neurological impairment, and (3) no history of mental retardation in the family, could be all negative, and still the child could be diagnosed as Strauss brain-injured solely in the behavioral characteristics. It is most unfortunate that Strauss named his subjects "brain-injured." People in the field have not read the fine print in the Strauss-Lehtinen work, or talked with persons who worked with Strauss. Thus, too many have equated a Strauss-type child with a neurologically impaired child. Generally, today special educators label a child as fitting the Strauss syndrome when he displays: (1) hyperactivity, (2) incoordination, (3) lack of inhibition, (4) distractibility, and (5) an uneven pattern of learning disabilities, especially in language. Perhaps disturbances of (6) perception and (7) concept formation should also be mentioned but these are more difficult for teachers to observe. Educators recognize these children do not possess these seven characteristics in the same amount. However, if they demonstrate the first five to a considerable degree, the term "Strauss syndrome" is usually attached to them by teachers.

(3) Another thread in the theoretical-clinical literature comes from the Bellevue group in New York City. Schilder (1935), Bender (1956), and others have argued that specific lesions of the brain result jointly in specific disabilities in the motor and psychological areas. *Body image* has a major place in this dual disorganization.

(4) Gellner (1959) and her associates at Columbus (Ohio) State School have identified *four* classifications of *so-called brain-injured* children. Included are: (1) visual somatic, (2) visual autonomic, (3) auditory somatic, and (4) auditory autonomic.

(5) Doman and Delacato (1960) have a theoretical rationale for an

unusual educational treatment. They argue that the organization of the brain progresses from the medulla, to the midbrain, up to the cerebral cortex. Brain injury results in neurological disorganization which can be remedied by taking the child through the progression of neurological organization moving from primitive forms of perception and movement to the more complex.

(6) Benoit (1960) has applied Hebb's neuropsychological theory to the field. Hebb postulates that sensory and motor responses are composed of cell assemblies. Congenital brain damage before the cells have assembled is more serious than adventitious brain injury which occurs after the neutral pathways and higher mental processes have been established. The latter is not so disorganizing because once concepts have been formed they are less dependent on specific nerve pathways. Such brain injury may not irradicate old learnings but will interfere with new learnings.

(7) The Halstead (1947), Reitan (1962), Luria (1961) literature has had a profound effect on the education of so-called brain-injured children. These men have been primarily interested in devising psycholinguistic diagnostic tests to determine the location of brain lesions in adults. Researchers are presently modifying their psychometric measures downward for children. This may yield valuable dividends in providing educators with a profile of behavioral characteristics of individual Strauss-type children. Kirk and McCarthy (1961) have developed the Illinois Test of Psycholinguistic Abilities, yielding a profile of nine measures of oral language with norms for children two and one-half to nine years of age. This is the first major thrust in developing a diagnostic instrument for identifying appropriate remediation instruction.

(8) Frostig and others (1961) have taken the position that neurological damage in children results in severe visual perceptual disturbances which need to be remediated by systematic training.

(9) A final theoretical position about the nature and modification of human behavior bears mentioning. This is the Skinnerian (1953) one. This group would contend that concern for the etiology or behavioral characteristics of the Strauss syndrome is not a major consideration in modifying their behavior. Furthermore, they would advocate an individualized approaching rather than attempts at grouping children with common characteristics into clusters with labels. Finally, they would agree it is possible to teach almost anything to almost any child by programming instruction into small, sequential steps, and reinforcing (rewarding) in a contiguous fashion appropriate behavioral modifications.

EDUCATIONAL APPROACHES

Below are outlined the various educational approaches based on the theoretical-clinical literature just presented. They are pulled together here under a different classification scheme.

(1) One of the educational approaches for the Strauss-type child stresses physical education, *motor development*, motor trainings, mobility, coordination, or psychomotor development. Such an emphasis is a part of at least three approaches, namely the Doman-Delacato, Kephart, and Schilder-Bender positions. The Philadelphia group under Doman and Delacato see the so-called brain-injured child as needing to move through seven stages of mobility: (1) beginning with movements of the arms and legs without bodily movement, (2) through crawling in the prone position, (3) to creeping on hands and knees, (4) to walking with the arms used extensively in balance, (5) to walking with the arms not necessary for balance, (6) to walking and running in different patterns, (7) to using the hands and legs to perform tasks other than those simply involved in mobility. Kephart and his group also stress the need for systematic training to foster motor development among the brain-injured. Since motor development proceeds from the head to the feet, he argues that motor training needs first to involve the muscles of the head, and then proceed downward to the arms and shoulders, to the abdomen, and finally to the legs and feet. Furthermore, he contends that motor development proceeds outward from the central axis of the body toward the periphery. Therefore large movements of the arms and legs should precede fine movements of the wrist, fingers, ankles, and toes. He then proceeds to outline a wide variety of exercises to develop specific movements, arguing that the brain-injured need special attention in the development and coordination of *patterns* of movement needed for complex acts. Kephart of Purdue University (like Doman and Delacato) argues that the brain-injured need to be taken back and brought up through the different stages of motor development to establish these complex motor movements involving balance, coordination, and movement; otherwise, the child is likely to develop *splinter* skills. Kephart stresses the need to develop laterality including an awareness of the difference between the right and left side of the body. Freidus (undated) has outlined a variety of techniques for *developing* body image, based on the Schilder-Bender constructs. For example, included are feeling and naming parts of the body, counting on the body, crawling under bars, etc. Thus we see a remarkable overlap among the recommendations for psychomotor development among the Philadelphia, Purdue, and Bellevue groups. While this emphasis does not constitute a total program of training for the brain-injured child, authorities obviously consider it quite basic. Thus for the young child or the severely handicapped youngster, major attention must be given to this psychomotor—or first stage.

(2) The second area (or stage) of training for the so-called brain-injured child—namely perceptual training—shows up in one form or another in many of the rationales. This may be as narrow as training in visual perception, to as broad as a comprehensive program of sensory-motor training. After a child has developed an adequate level of motor proficiency, Kep-

hart argues the training should shift to the development of perceptual organization. He considers it extremely important to *match* perceptual data with motor activity through developing exercises so that visual and auditory information are integrated with the *tactual* system. Thus he argues that perceptual learnings depend upon prior motor learnings. When a child is ready for it, Kephart recommends pencil and paper exercises to develop visual perception and left to right orientation, so necessary for reading readiness. The Los Angeles group headed up by Frostig (1961) focuses on visual perception for the neurologically handicapped child at the stage where this can be developed through pencil and paper exercises. She has published a visual perceptual test and a pencil and paper training program for remediating specific visual disabilities. It is only because of the need for brevity that additional authorities are not cited here as emphasizing the need for perceptual-motor training. In fact, so many writers focus on this area that it is not surprising that classes established for perceptually impaired children enroll youngsters with very similar characteristics to those classes designated to serve brain-injured children.

(3) A third stage or emphasis in training programs for the brain-injured focuses on concept formation including training in the various school subjects. Here the pioneer work was done by Lehtinen in Part 2, Volume 1, of *Psychopathology and Education of the Brain-Injured Child* by Strauss and Lehtinen (1947). Recommended guide lines for the instruction of the pupil with the Strauss syndrome included the following: (1) An undistracting school environment should be provided. Translucent rather than transparent window panes should be used in the classroom. The teacher's dress should be plain and free from ornaments. The class should be located on the top floor and made free from distracting stimuli. Cubicles and screens should be utilized to reduce distractions. (2) Instruction should be individualized. The class groups should be small with 12 children as a maximum. For individual work, pupils should be removed to the periphery of the group, faced toward a wall, or screened off from the rest of the children by the cubicles. (3) An elemental rather than a global approach to teaching should be emphasized. For example, the teaching of reading should begin with the learning of individual letters; later these should be assembled into words; and finally the words should be used in sentences, paragraphs, and stories. (4) Emphasis should be placed on the use of colored letters, words, and numbers as well as other concrete cues to focus the child's attention on the relevant materials. (5) Motor activity should be involved in academic learning, with emphasis on concrete manipulative materials. (6) Emphasis should be placed on the basic tool subjects. Instruction in social studies, geography, and science should be considered incidental. (7) No use should be made of the project or unit method. (8) Social activities, group learning, and oral language should be de-emphasized. This is but a brief glimpse at the Lehtinen techniques. However, they have had almost universal

acceptance by educators implementing special education programs for the Strauss-type child. In the next section, some research will be presented on the efficacy of these Lehtinen techniques. Kephart, as one of the Strauss-Lehtinen group, utilizes the Lehtinen techniques. He contends that solid concepts rest upon solid percepts which in turn rest upon solid basic motor patterns. However, he de-emphasizes concept and symbolic learnings, arguing that educators are preoccupied with this area and move on to it before the child is adequately trained in the motor and perceptual areas. Epps and others (1958) have roughed out teaching techniques for the four types of so-called brain-injured children described by Gellner (1959). For the visual-somatic type which has movement blindness, a kinaesthetic and auditory approach, combined with a blindfold, is recommended. For the visual-autonomic type which has a visual disability involving close to total blindness, it is necessary for the individual to learn about his environment through tactual and auditory techniques. For the auditory-somatic type who have sound and word deafness, it is necessary to use a visual approach. For the auditory-autonomic type who have meaning deafness, it is important to stress meanings in that these children are often very verbal but the materials are incomprehensible. Very clearly, the Gellner-Epps techniques presented here might have been presented under perceptual training. Similarly the Doman-Delacato approach outlined above under motor development may have been included here. This total training program moves a child from motor, to perceptual, to language development (including reading and writing).

The other approaches to education for the brain-injured child do not fit neatly within the three categories above, but bear mentioning. The Strauss group including Lehtinen were concerned with modifying the unacceptable behavioral characteristics of the Strauss-type child. This group argues that hyperactivity may be reduced by cutting down on environmental stimulation. The catastrophic reaction was to be controlled by keeping the brain-injured child in a standard familiar environment and not placing him in situations of unusual stress. Thus the simplified protective routine environment was aimed at making these children more tractable. Needless to say, there is some evidence on what happens to a hyperactive child in a barren and stimulating environment. Perhaps drug therapy including the use of tranquilizers should be included here as a method of controlling the behavior of the Strauss-type child.

Another approach to training is that of Kirk and Bateman (1962) already alluded to when the Illinois Test of Psycholinguistic Abilities was presented. These scientists believe that each individual child has his own unique profile of abilities and disabilities. They are systematically moving ahead to finding ways of teaching to the weaknesses of children so as to remediate them. The next decade is likely to see a goodly supply of research devoted to answering the question as to whether it is most desirable to teach to strengths, weaknesses, or across the board when dealing with handicapped children including the so-called brain-injured. Dunn and Smith (1965) have developed the Peabody Language Development Kit aimed at an overall approach to oral language development in contrast to the Kirk and Bateman approach of remediating weaknesses.

Finally, under educational approaches, one must return to the Skinnerian position described above. This group would see no need for the psychometric approach involving pre and post tests with a training program intervened. Instead, they would take the individual child forward, through programmed instruction, from the point to which he has developed. Here the *method* takes precedent over the characteristics of the child, classroom organization, or materials. However, it could be argued that the Skinnerian techniques of operant conditioning could be applied to the procedures advocated by all of the other writers mentioned above.

EMPIRICAL EVIDENCE

Fragmented though it is, there is a growing body of knowledge concerning the behavioral correlates of brain injury. Good reviews of the literature have appeared of late in Robinson and Robinson (1965) and in Ellis (1963). No attempt will be made here to review comprehensively the literature on the more psychological aspects of the area. However, before becoming a devotee of any of the theoretical-clinical positions which have been advocated, it would be well to study some of these references since research usually can be found to refute each of the various positions. Three or four examples are cited by way of illustration.

Hyperactivity has been regarded as a very consistent and stable symptomatic characteristic of the Strauss-type child. Lehtinen has argued that hyperactivity is heightened even further by a stimulating environment and reduced by a barren one. Furthermore, it has been argued that the Strauss-type child will learn better in a barren environment than in one of reasonable stimulation. These generalizations cannot be substantiated conclusively from the literature. While there are data to support this position, in a review of this field by Cromwell and others in the Ellis "Handbook of Mental Deficiency," contrasting theories and findings have been uncovered. For example, the Strauss-Lehtinen group tends to argue that incoming stimuli activate the brain and produce increases in body activity. By reducing the external stimulation, one reduces the activity of the brain and the corresponding physical activities. A contrasting theoretical position is that the neural connections of brain-injured children are less developed than those of other subjects. Hyperactivity on the part of brain-injured children is an attempt to induce more stimulation. From this theoretical position, it woud be predicted that increases in visual and auditory stimulation should decrease the activity level of individuals with sensory impairment such as Strauss children have. Cromwell and his associates have conducted a series of studies on the effects of this stimulus variable. Generally they found that visual stimulation did reduce activity level. Furthermore, the activity level of hyperactive retardates decreased significantly with such tactual stimulation as bouncing and handling. Thus there is some support for the theoretical notion that hyperactivity may be a result of a seeking of stimulation because of partially blocked neural pathways. Burnett (1962) has one of the few studies investigating the influences of classroom environment on the school learning of retarded subjects with high and low activity levels. He measured the speed with which retarded subjects learned to read a list of words in a standard and a restricted classroom setting, finding no significant differences, indicating that hyperactive children learn as well in a standard as in a restricted environment. Evidence of this nature should lead us to be cautious in establishing a Lehtinen-type classroom for hyperactive children. Conceivably, it may be the exact opposite situation to the one in which such children can learn best.

In terms of *personality characteristics*, again the research is far from uniform. Strauss and his co-workers have pointed out that most brain-injured children display erratic, uncoordinated, uncontrolled, disinhibited, and generally unacceptable behavior. There are studies to support this contention. However, Semmel (1960) failed to find these personality characteristics more frequently among so-called brain-injured children than among Mongoloid children of similar intellect. Zigler (1962) has argued that brain-injured children may display these personality characteristics, not because of any central nervous system pathology, but because such children usually come from middle and upper class homes where they are exposed to parents who display much more anxiety and who put much more pressure on the child than would be the case with the usual working-class parents of cultural-familial retardates.

Another area of confusion deals with *concept formation*. Brain-injured children are supposed to display greater variability and disabilities. Yet we have a number of studies which do not support this observation. One such was done by Capobianco (1956) who compared the arithmetic processes of cultural-familial and neurologically-impaired subjects, some of which displayed the Strauss syndrome. He found no differences in computation, reasoning, achievement, reversals, or understanding of the concept zero. Capobianco and Miller (1958) analyzed the reading processes of the cultural-familiar and neurologically-impaired, finding little or no difference between the two groups in their reading achievement or in their patterns of reading errors. Gallagher (1957) compared brain-injured and non brain-injured mentally retarded children on several psychological measures. Generally, he found no significant differences between the groups except that children with central nervous system damage were superior in language traits. He concluded that having a physician identify a child as brain injured creates such a heterogeneous group that it is of little use to educators and psychologists. It must be pointed out that in the studies mentioned above, the researchers were dealing with neurologically-impaired children, so identified by a physician. Thus they were studying brain-injured children with biological signs rather than children who displayed behavioral traits characteristic of the Strauss syndrome.

Turning to the effectiveness of special education for the brain-injured, Gallagher (1960) conducted a three-year experiment in a residential school setting on tutoring children of 7 to 9 years of age with neurological impairments. Each pupil was given one hour a day of individualized tutoring based upon that child's own pattern of strengths and weaknesses. There was a crash program of perceptual, conceptual, and language development exercises but there was no attempt to follow the Lehtinen approach per se. As contrasted to a control group, his experimental subjects improved in intellectual development, increased in attention span, and achieved more in verbal than in nonverbal skills. He concluded:

> It is quite likely that history will also record we have been entirely too pessimistic about the possible training potential of the brain-injured, and that this pessimism has prevented us from giving them the intellectual and educational stimulation that we would wish for all our children (p. 168).

Here we have evidence that the Strauss-Lehtinen techniques are not necessary to achieve moderately good results with neurologically-impaired pupils. In a follow up of his subjects to determine the effects of removal of the special tutoring, he discovered that the gains were lost in a year after the tutoring ceased. He claimed that the loss of these gains may have been a result of the unstimulating environment of the residential facility, and that the gains would likely have been more permanent in a more normal community setting. Finally, he pleaded for an intensive, individualized approach to build conceptualization among young, neurologically impaired pupils, rather than almost exclusive devotion or attention to the development of social skills as has been so often the case when such children are enrolled in special classes for the educable mentally retarded. This position would meet with the support of many leaders in the field, including Lehtinen.

Cruickshank and others (1961) conducted a two year demonstration study with 40 subjects, half of whom were diagnosed as brain-injured and half as emotionally disturbed. The brain-injured were not only detected by neurological tests, but were hyperactive-aggressive as well. A typical Lehtinen-type classroom environment was created for at least the experimental groups. The investigators concluded that: "While still further evidence needs to be obtained, it is the opinion of the authors that hyperactive children in an unstimulating environment and a structured program demonstrate sufficient progress to warrant continuance of this approach with such children." However, in light of the methodological problems encountered and the statistical evidence, it is difficult to determine how this statement is justified. One has difficulty in ascertaining whether the subjects were brain-injured, emotionally disturbed, or hyperactive, or all three. The teachers with contrast groups were allowed to set up any type of treatment they wished and many of them chose to adopt the Lehtinen techniques similar to those used in the experimental classes. Thus the treatments were confounded. Finally, there is little statistical evidence in the final report that the experimental groups made greater progress than the controls. However, if one wishes to accept the conclusions of the authors, we have some support for the use of the Lehtinen procedures with the Strauss-type child.

Vance (1956) provided daily, highly structured educational programs in reading readiness over an eight-month period with matched groups of non brain-injured and neurologically-impaired children in a residential school. He found no significant difference between the groups at any time on reading and reading readiness tests indicating both groups learned equally well under the treatment she provided.

Frey (1960) conducted a retrospective study which tested the Lehtinen teaching techniques with Strauss-type children. He selected a group of 20 neurologically-impaired children who, on psychological tests, also exhibited perceptual disorders, and who had been under a special education program utilizing the Lehtinen techniques. These were compared with 20 non brain-injured retarded children of similar age and intellect who had been attending conventional programs in regular and special classes. In his survey of the reading behavior of these two groups, Frey found the Strauss-type group to be superior in silent reading tests and in sound blending ability. Too, he found the Strauss-type child to have a normal profile of reading areas while the non brain-injured group showed excessive errors in faulty vowels, faulty consonants, omissions of sounds, and omissions of words. This study is extremely important because it demonstrates that the Lehtinen techniques appear to work at least in reading for Strauss-type children. Whether these techniques will work equally well in other areas in instruction and with cultural-familial retardates and even with the intellectually normal has yet to be demonstrated. However, until research is accumulated to the contrary, teachers will apparently be on fairly safe grounds in experimenting with the use of the Lehtinen techniques in teaching children who have the Strauss syndrome. Too, school systems cannot be discouraged from experimenting with special classes for the Strauss-type pupil on the basis of the Frey study—but some of the other evidence should lead us to be extremely cautious in advocating the Lehtinen approach uncritically.

Unfortunately, no research evidence was found in the literature on the efficacy of the motor development techniques advocated by the Doman-Delacato, Kephart, or Schilder-Bender-Freidus groups when applied specifically to children with the Strauss syndrome. The same can be said for perceptual development. But Forgnone (1966) has shown that Frostig Visual Perception Exercises are effective in increasing scores on the Frostig Developmental Test of Visual Perception for an undifferentiated group of special-class, educable retardates. Here again, the problem simply is that researchers have not elected to select Strauss-type children specifically for efficacy studies.

CONCLUSION

In light of the foregoing review of the literature, the following conclusions are suggested: (1) Neurologically impaired children so identified by physicians, provide such a heterogeneous group of children behaviorally that they have little utility for educational treatment, yet most of the studies to date have been done with neurologically impaired children rather than with children who display the behavioral characteristics of the Strauss syndrome. Conceivably, the Strauss syndrome is even too much of a catchall. Perhaps we need to identify subgroups within this classification such as those with hyperactivity vs. visual perceptual impairments for study. (2) Except for the Frey retrospective study, there is no empirical evidence to demonstrate the differential effectiveness of the Lehtinen techniques for teaching concepts including academic learnings to the Strauss-type child. What is sorely needed is a well-designed experimental study to determine if the Lehtinen techniques are differentially effective for the Strauss-type child as contrasted with the cultural-familial retardate, if not the normal child. Thus there is little empirical evidence at this time either to justify, or not, special classes for the Strauss-type pupil wherein the Lehtinen techniques would be utilized. Furthermore, efficacy studies in the areas of motor development and perceptual training with Strauss-type children are nonexistent. Research on teaching to weakness on profiles of abilities, and behavior shaping utilizing operant conditioning techniques have, as yet, been case studies. Yet educators must teach children in groups so investigations involving clusters of pupils is imperative.

My sincerest plea would be that psychologists in the South reduce sharply their use of psychometric tests and take leadership roles in solid experimentation with differential techniques of teaching children who display the various behavioral characteristics of the Strauss-type syndrome. It is probable that structured, systematic teaching (applying operant conditioning techniques) will provide us with evidence that Strauss-type children can learn much more than we have assumed. Hopefully, from the South in the next decade, will come research which will lead us to establish sound educational programs for the Strauss-type pupil based on empirical evidence rather than on theoretical and philosophical positions.

References

Bender, L., *Psychopathology of children with organic brain disorders* (Springfield Illinois: Charles C Thomas, 1956).

Benoit, F. P., Application of Hebb's theory to understanding the learning disability of children with mental retardation, *Training Sch. Bull.*, 1960, 57, 18-23.

Burnette, E., *Influences of classroom environment on word learning of retarded with high and low activity levels* (Unpublished doctoral dissertation, Peabody College, 1962).

Capobianco, R. J., Qualitative and quantitative analyses of endogenous and exogenous boys on arithmetic achievement. In Dunn, L. M. and Capobianco, R. J. (Editors), *Studies in reading and arithmetic in mentally retarded boys* (Lafayette, Indiana: Purdue University, *Child Development Publications*, 1956), *Monogr. Soc. Res. Child Develpm.*, 1954, 19.

Capobianco, R. J., and Funk, Ruth A., *A comparative study of intellectual, neurological, and perceptual processes as related to reading achievement of exogenous and endogenous retarded children* (Syracuse, New York: Syracuse University Research Institute, 1958).

Capobianco, R. J., and Miller, D. Y., *Quantitative and qualitative analysis of exogenous and endogenous children in some reading processes* (Syracuse, New York: Syracuse University Research Institute, 1958). (USOE Cooperative Research Project Report).

Clements, Sam D., *Minimal brain dysfunction in children* (Washington, D.C.: National Institute of Neurological Diseases and Blindness, 1964).

Cruickshank, W. M., Bentsen, Frances A., Retzeburg, F. H., and Tannhauser, Mirian T., *A teaching method for brain-injured and hyperactive children* (Syracuse, New York: Syracuse University Press, 1961).

Doman, R. J., and Delacato, C. H., et al., Children with severe brain injuries, *J.A.M.A.*, 1960, 174, 257-262.

Ellis, N. R., *Handbook of mental deficiency* (New York: McGraw-Hill, 1963).

Epps, Helen O., McCammon, Gertrude, and Simmons, Queen D., *Teaching devices for children with impaired learning: A study of the brain-injured child from research project Fifty at the Columbus State School*, 1958.

Forgnone, C., *Effects of group training in visual perception and language development upon the abilities of special class retardates* (Unpublished doctoral dissertation, Peabody College, 1966).

Frey, R. M., *Reading behavior of brain-injured and non brain-injured children of average and retarded mental development* (Unpublished doctoral dissertation, University of Illinois, 1960).

Freidus, E. S., New approaches in special education of the brain-injured child (New Jersey: N.J. Assoc. for Brain-Injured Children, undated).

Frostig, M., et al., A developmental task of visual perception for evaluating normal and neurologically handicapped children, *Percept. motor Skills*, 1961, 12, 383-394.

Gallagher, J. J., Changes in verbal and nonverbal abilty of brain-injured mentally retarded children following removal of special stimulation, *Amer. J. ment. Def.*, 1962, 66, 774-781.

Gallagher, J. J., A comparison of brain-injured and non brain-injured mentally retarded children on several psychological variables, *Monogr. Soc. Res. Child Develpm.*, 1957, 22, 3-79.

Gallagher, J. J., *Tutoring of brain-injured mentally retarded children* (Springfield, Illinois: Charles C Thomas, 1960).

Gellner, Lise, A *neurophysiological concept of mental retardation and its educational implications* (Chicago: J. Levinson Research Foundation, 1959).

Goldstein, K., and Sheerer, M., Abstract and concrete behavior—An experimental study with special tests, *Psychol. Monogr.*, 1941, 53, (2).

Halstead, W. C., *Brain and intelligence* (Chicago: University of Chicago Press, 1947).

Kephart, N. C., *The brain-injured child in the classroom* (Chicago, Illinois: National Society for Crippled Children, 1963).

Kephart, N. C., *The slow learner in the classroom* (Columbus, Ohio: Merrill, 1960).

Kirk, S. A., and Bateman, B., Diagnosis and remediation of learning disabilities, *Except. Child.*, 1962, 29, 73-78.

Kirk, S. A., and McCarthy, J. J., *The Illinois test of psycholinguistic abilities* (Champaign, Illinois: University of Illinois Press, 1961).

Klebanoff, S. G., Singer, J. L., and Wilensky, H., Psychological sequences of brain lesion and ablations, *Psychol. Bull.*, 1954, 51, 1-41.

Luria, A. R., *The role of speech in the regulation of normal and abnormal behavior* (London: Pergamon Press, 1961).

Reitan, R. M., Psychological deficit, *Ann. Rev. Psychol.*, 1962, 13, 415-444.

Robinson, H. B., and Robinson, N. M., *The mentally retarded child* (New York: McGraw-Hill, 1965).

Schilder, P., *The image and appearance of the human body* (New York: International University Press, 1935).

Semmel, M. I., Comparison of teacher ratings of brain-injured and mongoloid severely retarded (trainable) children attending community day-school classes, *Amer. J. ment. Def.*, 1960, 64, 963-971.

Skinner, B. F., *Science and human behavior* (New York: Macmillan, 1953).

Stevens, G. D., and Birch, J. W., A proposal of clarification of the terminology and a description of brain-injured children, *Except. Child.*, 1957, 23, 346-349.

Strauss, A. A., and Kephart, N. C., *Psychopathology and education of the brain-injured child*, vol. II (New York: Grune & Stratton, 1955).

Strauss, A. A., and Lehtinen, Laura E., *Psychopathology and education of the brain-injured child* (New York: Grune & Stratton, 1947).

Vance, Helen S., Psychological and educational study of brain-injured and non brain-damaged mentally retarded children, *Dissert. Abstr.*, 1956, 17, 1033.

Yates, A. J., The validity of some psychological tests of brain damage, *Psychol. Bull.*, 1954, 51, 359-379.

Zigler, E., Social deprivation in familial and organic retardates, *Psychol. Rep.*, 1962, 10, 370.

12 PSYCHOLOGICAL PROBLEMS OF
CHILDREN WITH ORGANIC BRAIN DISEASE

Lauretta Bender

When a child comes to the Children's Service of the Psychiatric Division
of Bellevue Hospital with a behavior problem associated with an organic
brain disorder (Bender, 1942b and 1946; Bender and Yarnell, 1941) there
are always other social and emotional problems in his life situation severe
enough to account for the behavior disorder on a dynamic interpretation
alone. Our follow-up studies on children with inflammatory encephalitis
(Bender, 1942a and 1942b) and traumatic encephalopathy (Bender and
Fabian, 1947 and unpublished) have led us to emphasize the dynamics of
personality development and inadequacies in early childhood emotional
experiences as contributory factors in the subsequent behavior disorder. Also
it has been our experience that some children with acute traumatic or
encephalitic disturbances who were cherished in adequate homes showed
no subsequent behavior disorder (Blau, 1936; Bowman and Blau, 1940;
Schilder, 1945). Consequently we have come to a more favorable and
positive evaluation of the brain-damaged child than the literature has generally advocated, provided the child has not suffered from social and emotional deprivation as well.

This positive evaluation has also depended on a considerable body of
knowledge accumulated from many fields. (1) It must be possible to evaluate the nature of the organic damage from its effects on the functioning
brain and on the developing child in his motor, perceptual, impulsive, and
emotional behavior. (2) It must be possible to determine the special needs
of such a child and how these needs can be met. (3) We must be able to
anticipate from sufficient clinical experience what may be expected ultimately for the brain-damaged child.

Reprinted from *American Journal of Orthopsychiatry*, Vol. 19 (July, 1949), pp. 404-
414. By permission of the author and publisher.

There must be a thorough well-grounded organic neurological approach on the basis of the following neuropathological insights: (1) the epidemiology of childhood diseases and traumas, (2) the observation and evaluation of the patterned neurophysiological reflex behavior, (3) the motor maturation of the child (Gesell, 1945 and 1946, and (4) the meaning of motor play and the pattern of impulsiveness or impulse to action (Schilder, 1931). There must be knowledge gained from the motor-perceptual psychology, patterned as the Gestalt school of psychology teaches (Bender, 1938) with maturation and configuration, including the body image concept of Schilder (1935), as in the drawing of a man (Goodenough, 1926) and in other projected behavior patterns whereby the child makes articulate his responses to the environment and his inner fantasy life. There must be knowledge of the personality maturation, patterned in terms of the relationship with the mother or parent figure and ultimately with society, together with the knowledge of the development of the emotional life and conceptual thinking, and the signs and meaning of anxiety where normal maturation is frustrated.

Children with various biological problems have common psychological problems. These common problems are best described as: (1) difficulties in patterned behavior in motor, perceptual, and emotional-social areas with tendencies to regressed or retarded maturation; (2) a severe anxiety, also poorly patterned (Greenacre, 1941); (3) a greatly increased need for human support in all these areas. This formulation gives us all that we need for diagnostic evaluation, prognostication, and therapeutic approach to the psychological problems. There will not be time to discuss the differential diagnostic techniques, or the analysis of each clinical syndrome, or possible therapeutic regimes or probable life courses for the different kinds of organic brain disorders. The emphasis will be on the common problems.

My own experiences have led me to include the following with the biologically or organically determined behavior disorder: childhood schizophrenia (Bender, 1947), language retardations or lags (including reading disabilities), motor lags (the so-called palsies), the mental defects or congenital deviations, epilepsy, as well as inflammatory encephalitis (with burn encephalopathies (Bender, 1943)) and traumatic encephalopathy (including birth injuries, prematurity, and cerebral anoxia).

Any knowledge gained about children in any of these biologically determined problems will lead to a better understanding of all other biologically determined problems, and incidentally in all problem children and growing children without problems. For example, the relationship between anxiety and the regressive motility patterns and projection of the body image preoccupations in the art work of the schizophrenic child teaches us about the dynamics of the process-determined conflict. It is then easier to understand other children with different pathology who show much of the same clinging, grasping behavior even though combined with focal neurological disorders referred to one or another part of the body. Efforts to express body image problems in art often are frustrated by difficulties in drawing in children with gross encephalopathies, but the drawings will still show some of the same features. The scattered, somewhat infantile patterning in all areas in the maturation curve of the preschool child who later develops a reading disability, with compensation by wild, asocial, clowning behavior and highly articulate drawings, makes it easier to understand the retardation in personality of the motor lags and certain of the early-determined encephalopathies. Some of these problems will be discussed by other speakers today and I have discussed them elsewhere. I am to limit myself to a consideration of the psychology of the traumatic and inflammatory encephalopathies and those congenital motor deviations which are especially closely allied.

It is necessary to emphasize that the examination of the brain-damaged child requires different techniques from those used with adults; this is especially true of the neurological examination. One must really forget about the reflex arc and tendon reflexology, as well as the usual tools of a neurologist, and think in terms of observing neurophysiological patterns as exemplified by the postural reflexes. These must be related closely to the dynamics of the evolution of locomotion and motor and nutritional independence. Grasping, sucking behavior or manual manipulation and oral activity must be evaluated in the same ways. The neurological examiner must also observe the child at play, cognizant at each age level of normal motility, degree of activity, tonic states, ability to relate, or to be independent. Organically damaged children tend to give way to impulses for primitive reflex patterns and to reflex play such as whirling postural response, or motor impulse to action which leads to perseverative and compulsive phenomena, as well as to unusual grasping, touching, pointing, and devouring. Some diffuse organic disorders merely lead to a psychologic clinging or dependency, a tendency to relate too closely and identify with every object and cause.

A neurological examination of a child is not complete which does not include an examination of the way the child relates himself to the adult. Does the child use the adult's body to compensate for his own organic disability and disorganization? Is he clinging, physically dependent, cohesive? Is he plastic or resistive to bodily manipulation, fondling, lap-holding, and to permissive indulgence in reflex motor play, such as whirling, bouncing, tossing, and swinging against gravity? These responses in children more than two years of age are reliable signs of the disorganization of the motor maturation and indicate retardation or regression in motor development. There may also be more or less choreathetotic motor behavior and tonic changes of muscles which can only be evaluated by intimate observation and actual manipulation of the child's body. They will never be detected by any physician whose careful neurological examination is performed on a prone child, covered with a sheet to his chin, and with the physician's hands busily engaged with tuning forks, percussion hammers, ophthalmoscopes, etc. Incidentally, the organic child is a clever deceiver and has more ways of concealing his symptomatology than the unwary physician has of revealing it. This is one reason why the neurological signs in early childhood organic diseases fluctuate from day to day.

The neurological examination is not complete that does not also take into consideration the child's anxiety and his way of dealing with it. All organically disturbed children suffer profoundly from anxiety because of the disorganization, the difficulty in relating themselves to reality, and the frustration in achieving normal maturation. There may also be difficulties in making articulate the anxiety that stems from unknown inner sources rather than a reality situation in the environment. I have come to the formulation that any severe anxiety in a child which cannot be readily accounted for and corrected by a reality situation is invariably pointing toward a threatening and disorganizing illness. I include schizophrenia in this category. I have never seen a conversion hysteria or major anxiety hysteria in childhood which could not be accounted for by an organic illness. A four-year-old girl was sent to me with a diagnosis of an hysterical paralysis on the basis of a castration anxiety. I observed that the profound anxiety of the child could not mobilize her to the use of her limbs. A four-year-old girl might certainly feel herself castrated by the loss of use of her limbs from a severe systemic disease (although undiagnosed) but not by the knowledge of the little brother's unimpressive genitals. Unfortunately, the interpretive psychotherapy which this child nevertheless received did not save her life from the leukemia which was subsequently diagnosed. I do not doubt, however, that the therapist gave the child some supportive help through a trying period, in the warmth of the therapeutic relationship.

My earliest insight into the psychological problems of children with organic brain disorders came with the observation of children with cerebellar disorders (Bender, 1940). Cerebellar disorders often exist in relatively pure form and are not complicated with other perceptual or impulse disorders. They therefore lend themselves especially well to the study of the effect of motor disorders on the personality development. They help us recollect that the mother in the first months of life functions not only to give birth, food, affection, and personal care to the child but also to support the child in all its motor functions. The infantile relationship of the child to the mother is as much determined by the slow development of the motor system as it is, for example, by the dependency on her for nutrition. In a cerebellar disorder it is necessary for the mother to give motor support to the child for a much longer period of time, not only in regard to locomotion, but also in feeding, dressing, and even in speech. Such children tend to cling to the mother or a substitute and as a result are capable of deep emotional attachments and dependency relationships. These children are brought to us because of the difficulties arising out of the dependency on the so-called oversolicitous mother. Often not until the child was actually separated from the mother did it become evident how great was the child's need for the solicitous care of the mother, and that her apparent excessive care was actually only a response to this real need. Similar problems are seen in other motor disabilities including the extrapyramidal disorders, the choreathetotic disorders, the choreas, and the pyramidal tract paralyses. The grasp reflex in these children serves the purpose of obtaining support from the mother's body as well as protection for the child from the pull of gravity. The grasping reflex is related, therefore, both to the feeding responses and motor development. This is especially true when maturation has been impeded. The psychological counterparts are readily seen in the psychological clinging and dependency and the deep attachments. Profound anxiety states are induced by threats to deprive the child of the needed support.

Thus the child with the cerebellar dysfunction is held back to a more primitive stage in the development of equilibrium as well as in its emotional life. Clinging and dependency occur in both fields. This is related to non-specific motor difficulties, lack of equilibrium due to cerebellar asynergias, muscle weakness, and disturbed tone distribution plus tendencies to maintain or regain postures. The effects upon the personality are more profound since cerebellar disorders are usually present from birth and yet are developmental lags which tend to correct themselves. If the infant's greater needs have been recognized and met, and he has not been left helpless or unaided in his efforts to attain and maintain posture and equilibrium, there are usually no subsequent difficulties in giving up the dependency relationship when it is not needed. The clinging does not remain in the motor sphere alone, but becomes a psychosexual clinging which is easily transferred from mother to other love objects. Only the child whose need for help in solving the motor problems has not been met is likely subsequently to show hysterical features.

Schilder, in his study of grossly brain-damaged children in 1931 (Schilder, 1937), and his experience with adult obsessional neurotic problems (Schilder, 1940), concluded that unsolved motor problems in infancy concerning security and equilibrium may well be one factor which leads to an anxiety neurosis later on, and unsolved problems in the patterning of impulses may be connected with compulsive and obsessional neurosis.

Many of the developmental lags classified with the congenital palsies represent more extensive system involvements than the cerebellar diseases and include the pyramidal tract as well as other extrapyramidal systems. Such developmental lags are nearly always more severe on one side than the other and in either the upper or lower part of the body. For this reason the diagnosis of diplegia or monoplegia is often made although careful examination will show that the motor disability is general. The organism is presented with problems similar to those of the child with cerebellar disease. These are problems in maintaining and regaining posture and equilibrium, the control of tonic disorders, relating to supporting agents, and acting out of impulses and experiencing patterns interwoven from all of these factors. Similar problems are often produced by encephalitis and other encephalopathies early in infancy. These problems are quite independent of the specific motor disability which varies in every child, and supportive care is indicated for individual disabilities, in addition to any specific treatment or program for motor retraining.

In 1942 I reviewed the problem of encephalitis in children and came to the conclusion that there were three major problems:

1. The motor or motility disturbance which was mostly extrapyramidal and tended to progress.
2. The specific intellectual defect which was based on difficulties in gaining patterned behavior through perceptual experience.
3. The personality disturbance related mainly to the hyperkinesis and deficiencies in social orientation.

The postencephalitic child shows difficulties in perceptual experience in the psychometric patterning which is fairly typical for most organic brain disorders. There are difficulties in spatial orientation, visual or auditory memory, and baragnostic sense. These are all patterned perceptual-motor functions. Specifically, there are failure to copy a diamond or even a square (especially in younger children), poor memory for digits especially backwards, inability to reproduce designs from memory, and often failure to distinguish weights (IX Stanford-Binet, 1916 revision). The visual motor gestalt test (Bender, 1938) is of diagnostic value because of its specific perceptual motor nature. Most significantly the Goodenough drawing of a man is usually two years or more below the mental age on the Stanford-Binet (Bender, 1940). This indicates a specific imperception for body image which is defined as a performance of total integration of various perceptions of the whole organism. There is no difficulty in perceiving as such, but in integrating perceptions from the various fields into meaningful wholes. The drawing of a man is not the man seen, but a self-portrait or the inner man experienced by integrating all experiences. The specific difficulty in integrative function gives some clue as to the frustration which the organically sick child suffers. The constant drive to make contact with the world and to use one's body in action and perception does not come to a final pattern and does not give satisfaction. This, in turn, leads to an increase in drive to contract and to experience contacts and in itself accounts for the hyperkinesis with the drive to touch, see, hear, feel, and finally to devour and destroy every object which cannot otherwise be appreciated. It also increases the drive to cling which arises from the inadequacy in the motor fields for independent posture and locomotion. This inability to appreciate the perceptual experiences, and the frustration that rises from it, increases the anxiety.

In some organic brain disorders, the ability to draw a man is not impaired, due undoubtedly to different localization of pathology. These children draw compulsively—like some schizophrenic children or those with reading disabilities—and often draw unusually well. However, the drawing of a man nearly always reveals the neurological disorder or motility problem, or expresses the presence of an unsolved problem in motor impulses with compulsive features.

Finally, one may say that the hyperkinesis may be understood as an effort continually to contact the physical and social environment, to reexperience and integrate the perceptual experiences in a continual effort to gain some orientation in the world. The asocial behavior may be understood as the result of a lack of capacity to live out normal psychosexual drives and build up some understanding of one's place in the world in a longitudinal pattern, through learning from past experience and building up concepts for future satisfactions.

One can reconsider these matters from the point of view of unpatterned impulses to perception and to action. The emphasis has been on the hyperkinetic or hypertonic disorders. One sees as many hypokinetic children and hypotonic conditions. One sees children who part of the time are hypokinetic and part of the time are hyperkinetic, depending upon excessive external stimuli and mounting frustration with anxiety. Hypokinetic children show apathy, blocking, and mutism frequently with daydreaming and compulsive behavior. Overtalkativeness with confabulations, swearing, obscenities occur with increased oral impulses together with biting, spitting, kissing, and devouring. Some encephalitic children will show a continuous flow of impulses which cannot be controlled, increased, or diminished. Such a child was Eileen, whose mother complained that she demanded too much attention. Her mother even had to think and act for her. Eileen showed many compulsive features as the only way of organizing her too slow but steady impulse stream. She talked constantly but monotonously and engaged in endless daydreams when she did not have an audience. Her prepuberty daydreams concerned themselves with the awkwardness in her motility, her difficulties in competing with other children, and difficulties in her relationship with her mother. In puberty, they dealt with sexual matters and unrealistic fantasies of building her own family life. She was a compulsive reader and compulsively drew human figures in the complex social situation with which she could not deal. The heads of her drawn figures were always pulled to one side, as Eileen's was in reality by her tonic responses and the impulse to carry out postural reflex patterns. She also had compulsive tendencies to hit, touch, and point while she talked, either aggressively against children or toward genitals—her own or others'. Such acts, however, were never completed.

The training and treatment of such children depend on establishing satisfactory patterns within the flow of impulses. Basic is the relationship with the mother through the infantile periods when the actual needs of the child are being ministered to. Basic also is the relationship with whatever therapist or tutor the child needs in order to correct special disabilities. Ordinarily, special psychotherapy is not indicated. A dynamic interpretation of disordered behavior may indeed be an accurate description of the dynamics involved, but still does not indicate the cause of the disorder (Whitehorn, 1947). Interpretive psychotherapy may be comforting, or it may add to the disturbance and make further difficulties in more basic interpersonal relationship. It will not be curative.

Edward, a seven-year-old Negro boy, was referred to Bellevue because of sluggishness, inability to learn, dullness, and a tendency to go to sleep in class. His parents were of unusual mixed cultural and racial background, and as a result appeared to be in conflict, although they formed a solid, warm, family group who showed high levels of attainment. Edward, because of the school problem, had been sent to a rigid grandmother in the country. He had an IQ of 130 but no educational accomplishments. It was easy to arrive at a dynamic formulation of a conflicted child reacting to anxiety and rejection with blocking and inhibitions in learning. We had already learned that Negro children (Bender, 1939) respond to anxiety with blocking, inhibitions, and sleeping. Some such interpretation was made to the child and parents who were encouraged to keep him in their own family circle. He returned two years later, at nine years, because of increasing attacks of sleeping in school, and still was unable to read.

A more careful study revealed that there was a severe illness with pneumonia at three months and five months of age in which the child was prostrated and after which he remained apathetic for a long period. Repeated neurological examinations showed fluctuating disorders in oculomotor control and postural responses. The electroencephalogram was diagnostic for narcolepsy. Further psychodynamic investigation disproved psychogenic features in the narcolepsy. This was treated with benzedrine. The learning difficulty was recognized as an independent developmental lag or reading disability. He was sent home again when a school was arranged that would provide necessary remedial tutoring.

Two years later, at 11 years of age, he was seen again. He was at this time a happy member in his family, school, and community group. He had learned to read, and in these two years had brought his school work up to a grade placement suitable for his chronological age, though still below his higher mental age. Benzedrine helped to control his sleepiness though a sufficient dose made him mildly toxic. We are now trying to make further adjustments in his pharmacological therapy.

This case is important in demonstrating that a dynamic interrelation may describe the psychological problem but still does not touch the cause. It is also important in indicating that two independent biologically determined processes may be present in one child and still be independent; that each must be evaluated on its own merit and treated specifically; that the prognosis is dependent upon applying the specific treatment and also upon meeting the general need of supporting the child in his own group and emphasizing the worth of the individual.

It is also important in showing that while an organic illness may have its own specific residual symptom due to focal pathology, like Edward's narcolepsy, it also tends to exaggerate the personality problems which belong to the individual because of his heredity, constitution, and cultural background. At first Edward seemed like a very good example of a blocked, inhibited, withdrawn, anxious Negro boy in a conflicted family. The father said, "I was just like him as a boy. I was slow in reading, and stubborn and lazy, and slept, and I've always been the black sheep in the family." It appears that the organic process, because of the increased, poorly patterned flow of impulses and the diffuse, nonspecific anxiety, tends to exaggerate the dynamic problem and make the individual more vulnerable to stress and strains and less able to manipulate his own relationship to reality. There is also the factor that the organic child clings psychologically to the mother or father and other adults. This leads to a close identification, and the parent often responds in kind. Eileen's mother said, "She is a replica of me and I was like her when I was a child; clumsy, slow, daydreaming and lazy." Actually Eileen was a caricature of her mother as well as her mother's concept of herself.

The question of anxiety in the brain-damaged child has been very much misunderstood except for the work of Greenacre (1946). The anxiety is of a diffuse nonspecific type, and the child, too, becomes inured to it and conceals it as he has learned to conceal many of his neurological signs. In my early work with the organic child, I too undervalued it. I have already indicated that the diagnostic evaluation of the child organically sick must include the anxiety and the way the child deals with it. The presence of anxiety not readily related to a reality situation and not responding to an attempt to correct the reality situation is an indication of an organic illness (including schizophrenia). Even though a dynamic interpretation may be made, this is not sufficient evidence of the cause or origin of the anxiety. However, an organic illness which interferes with normal maturation in any field, such as motor function, perceptual integration, or in relating to reality, will give rise to anxiety. The earlier the illness, the more physiological or nonspecific or nondynamic is the anxiety. It increases all the other psychological problems of the brain-damaged child—his clinging to adult figures, the unpatterning of impulses, and the drive to overcome these difficulties with further activity and regression of pattern.

Greenacre postulated the predisposition to anxiety as a physiological tendency to anxiety due to organic suffering at or near the time of birth with a heightened basic anxiety and a secondary anxiety arising from frustration and the inadequacy of the neurotic defense. The concepts of facile identification and of mirroring and weak relationship to reality are all similar to the experiences which we observe directly in the organically brain-damaged child.

This anxiety is best met by a close and continuous stream of well-patterned support in the earliest years with a prolongation of the infantile period. It should be realized, however, that the security gained for the child in support of posture and motility and relationship with the environment is not an end in itself but only a means for subsequent independent action. The impulse for action is as basic as the need for security (Schilder, 1937).

There are many remarkable things about the organic brain-damaged child which also remind us of the miraculous capacity of all children to grow up, to maturate, and to be as normal as they are. The drive for normality and for living through a regular maturation pattern as a global response of the biological unit is much stronger than the disorganizing tendency resulting from other focal or diffuse structural pathology or destructive and depriving influences in the environment. Deviations or pathology in the central nervous system tends to produce a general kind of disorganization of behavior patterns even in the motor activity or personality function with resulting primitive unpatterned responses. Often, therefore, there are none of the usual neurological signs sought by the neurologist. Observation will, however, show immature, retarded, or regressed motor play, locomotion, postural reflexes, or the grasping, sucking reflex pattern. The impulses for action are inadequately patterned for the growing individual. At the same time the total personality is impelled to strive for normal maturation. Because of the need for motor support, as well as related emotional problems, there is a prolongation of the infantile period with a need for dependency on the mother or mother figures and on the total environment for support. Failure to receive such support leads to inadequate patterning of behavior with increased anxiety. This, in turn, leads to the so-called oversolicitous mother who is responding to the special needs of the child often, of course, with resentment because she does not understand either the situation or the criticism it brings upon her. The pathology may also show itself in other areas of disorganization. At the motor level there is an increase in regressed motor play with whirling and other kinds of reflex play. The unpatterned motor impulses meet the compulsive, repetitive, or perseverated tendencies which have been looked upon as the hyperkinesis of brain damage.

SUMMARY

The psychological problems of the organically sick child are dependent on these fundamental factors:

Motor or motility disorders make the child dependent on the mother in a prolonged infantile relationship and promote deep emotional attachments.

Perceptual or intellectual problems are due to difficulties in organizing or interpreting and appreciating the totality of perception, which lead to frustration due to a poor relationship to reality. Drives to contact the world and obtain satisfaction from perception and reality experiences account for the hyperkinesis and asocial behavior.

Further difficulties in organization or patterning of impulses lead to distortion in the action pattern with final compulsive features.

Anxiety is a central problem basic to the physiological disorganization and secondary to the frustration and lack of satisfaction and to the difficulties in the relationship.

The answer to the problem is to give mothering support to the organism from the earliest period and for as long as needed; to avoid isolating experiences; to give specific aids for specific disabilities which will increase the patterning in motility, perceptual fields, or personal relationship, as indicated.

The dominating drive of the organically sick individual like the normal individual's is for normality in development and freedom for independent action; every normal and pathological process will be bent to this goal.

References

Bender, Lauretta, Visual motor gestalt test and its clinical use, *Res. Monogr.*, No. 3 (New York: American Orthopsychiatric Association, 1938).

Bender, Lauretta, Behavior problems in Negro children, *Psychiatry*, 1939, 2, 213-238.

Bender, Lauretta, The Goodenough test (drawing a man) in chronic encephalitis in children, *J. nerv. ment. Dis.*, 1940, 91, 277-286.

Bender, Lauretta, The psychology of children suffering from organic disturbances of the cerebellum, *Amer. J. Orthopsychiat.*, 1940, 10, 287.

Bender, Lauretta, Cerebral sequelae and behavior disorders following pyogenic menengo-encephalitis in children, *Arch. Ped.*, 1942a, LIX, 772-784.

Bender, Lauretta, Neuropsychiatric contributions to mental hygiene problems of the exceptional child, *Ment. Hyg.*, 1942b, 26, 617.

Bender Lauretta, Post-encephalitic behavior disorders, Chapter XIV, 361-385. In *Encephalitis. A clinical study*, Josephine Neal (Editor) (New York: Grune & Stratton, 1942c).

Bender, Lauretta, Burn encephalopathies in children, *Arch. Ped.*, 1943, 60, 75.

Bender, Lauretta, *Organic brain conditions producing behavior disturbances*. In *Recent Trends in Child Psychiatry*, Nolan D. C. Lewis, and B. L. Pacella, (Editors) (New York: International University Press, 1946).

Bender, Lauretta, Childhood schizophrenia, *Amer. J. Orthopsychiat.*, 1947, 17, 1.

Bender, Lauretta, and Fabian, A. A., Head injuries in children: Predisposing Factors, *Amer. J. Orthopsychiat.*, 1947, 17, 1.

Bender, Lauretta, and Fabian, A. A., Personality problems and the head-injured child. (Unpublished.)

Bender, Lauretta, and Yarnell, Helen, An Observation Nursery, *Amer. J. Psychiat.*, 1941, 97, 1159-1174.

Blau, Abraham, Mental changes following head trauma, *Arch. Neurol. Psychol.*, 1936, 35, 273.

Bowman, Karl M., and Blau, A., Psychiatric states following head and brain injuries in adults and children, Chap. XIII in *Injuries of skull, brain and spinal cord*, Samuel Brock (Editor) (Baltimore: Williams & Wilkins, 1940).

Gesell, Arnold, and Ilg, Frances L., *Infant and child in culture of today* (New York: Harper & Row, 1945).

Gesell, Arnold, and Ilg, Frances L., *The child from five to ten* (New York: Harper & Row, 1946).

Goodenough, Florence, *Measurement of intelligence by drawing* (New York: World, 1926).

Greenacre, Phyllis, Predisposition to anxiety, *Psa. Quart.*, X, 1941, 1 and 4.

Schilder, Paul, Brain and personality. Studies in the psychological aspects of cerebral neuropathology, *Nerv. ment. Dis. Monogr.*, No. 53, New York, 1931.

Schilder, Paul, Image and appearance of the human body, *Psyche Monogr.*, No. 4 (London: Routledge & Kegan, Paul, 1935).

Schilder, Paul, *Psychological implications of motor development in children*, Proc. Fourth Institute on the Exceptional Child. Child Research Clinic of the Woods School, October, 1937.

Schilder, Paul, Neurosis following head and brain injuries, Chap. XII in *Injuries of skull, brain and spinal cord*, Samuel Brock (Editor) (Baltimore: Williams & Wilkins, 1940).

Schilder, Paul, Structure of obsessions and compulsions, *Psychiatry*, 1940, 3, 549-560.

Whitehorn, John C., The concept of "meaning" and "cause" in psychodynamics, *Amer. J. Psychiat.*, 1947, 104, 289-293.

13 COUNSELING THE PARENT OF THE BRAIN-DAMAGED CHILD

Ray H. Barsch

The child with brain damage is a complex organism. While some progress has been made in understanding the complexity of this problem, investigative efforts have been largely centered on differentiating this child from others by means of psychological tests or upon his unique learning problems. This child has often been studied out of context. He is a social being and a full understanding of his problem is dependent upon viewing him in his social setting as well as in his test experiences.

The concern of his parents is great. They require as much help as their child. These parents are no less obligated to society than the parents of a normal child to transmit the culture and help the child become a sufficiently acceptable member of his social group, that he may survive socially as well as biologically.

Unfortunately, the parents of the brain-damaged child have been neglected in most research studies to date. The only significant effort in this particular field has been the publication of *The Other Child*, a small book for parents and laymen (A. A. Strauss and Laura E. Lehtinen, New York: Grune & Stratton, 1961).

Too many professional specialists give parents the feeling that they have little time to discuss the problems with them, communicate in a technical jargon that effectively confuses and overwhelms the parents, and generally show little or no interest in the personal problems of the parents.

Those who work with the parents should be able to vicariously experience the strength and nature of their frustrations while at the same time structuring the relationship so as to facilitate change in parent attitudes

Reprinted from *Journal of Rehabilitation*, Vol. XXVII, No. 3 (May-June, 1961), pp. 1-3. By permission of the author and publisher.

and practice. If we feel an obligation to the exceptional child, it is hard to justify the lack of feeling or obligation toward his parents.

There is a great need for a specialized program for parents confronted with the problems of rearing a brain-injured child. This program should help parents solve the day-to-day problems they face, and should not be highly technical in content.

For the past 11 years, the staff of the Child Development Division of the Jewish Vocational Service in Milwaukee has been devoting its major energies to developing an evaluation, training, and counseling program for brain-injured children and their parents.

The evaluation effort has been directed toward (a) development of modifications of various psychological tests; (b) general experimental work with psychological tests to determine their potential use in evaluation; and (c) design of a number of brief tests to supplement the general psychological evaluation. Fifteen hundred children have been evaluated.

The training effort has been directed toward developing a specialized tutorial technique in perceptual and conceptual organization, relying principally on utilization of stimulus-response learning theories. Children are seen for 45-minute periods two or three times weekly, for an average 18-month span. Two hundred fifteen children have received this training.

The counseling effort has been directed toward development of techniques for use with parents of brain-injured children on an individual and group counseling basis. This effort focuses primarily upon the children's needs and the unique day-by-day problems encountered with a "misperceiving" organism. Two hundred ninety-five parents have been seen in groups and 325 for individual counseling.

PROGRAM DEVELOPMENT

Seven years ago, a program of group discussions for mothers of children with organic damage was initiated. During the first three years, four programs were organized annually. Each group was composed of ten mothers; care was taken to match the groups in terms of chronological age and learning level of the child and socioeconomic status of the family. The groups met for 30-36 sessions during the school year from September to June.

Meetings were held at the same time each week, which enabled the mothers to maintain a fixed schedule in terms of baby-sitting and housekeeping arrangements. All mothers were between the ages of 25 and 40. None had a serious emotional problem that would detract from her potential to profit from the group experience.

A fee was charged for the group program on a three-semester basis. Fees were adjusted to the income level of each mother. Individual counseling was continually available for specific problems that could not be discussed in the group.

The past two years have witnessed a gradual expansion of the program. With the development of a preschool and nursery program for children, we have been able to establish a concurrent mothers' discussion group related to each program of group services to children. In this manner seven additional mothers' groups have been organized, with each group meeting weekly while the children are in nursery school. Two couples' groups of six each were also organized to meet on a biweekly basis during evening hours; one group comprised parents of adolescents. Both parents must attend each session.

Subsequent paragraphs describe a general approach that has been utilized with 13 groups of parents during the past two years. All groups were composed of 8-12 participants.

OBJECTIVES

This program was an attempt to provide a comfortable group setting where parents might meet regularly with a sympathetic and understanding professional to discuss their day-to-day problems concerning their children, and to learn from other parents. Additional objectives are:

(1) To constructively alter the parents' perception of the brain-injured child;

(2) To teach parents principles for day-by-day identification, understanding, and guidance of the child's behavior;

(3) To correct misconceptions, folk tales, and mystical beliefs regarding handicapped children;

(4) To acquaint parents with present knowledge in the field of child growth and development;

(5) To teach parents to recognize significant cues in their child's behaviorisms that are indicative of needs;

(6) To teach them a systematic and consistent method of aiding development of organized response patterns in their child.

This counseling seeks to improve the parents' ability to deal effectively with the immediate problems in their lives, particularly in relation to their brain-injured child. The program is not designed to seek basic changes in the personality organizations of the mothers. No effort is made to uncover or probe. No encouragement is given to mothers to present problems that represent conflicts having no direct bearing upon their child.

In a sense, the leader protects the mothers from involving themselves unduly in their intrapsychic conflicts and rewards and reinforces their efforts to stay within the boundaries of the group objectives. If a mother in the group appears on the verge of "exposing" herself, the leader diverts the group tangentially. Although there is some griping among the mothers about the "head-in-the-sand attitudes" of their husbands, the discussion is kept at a level where no real secrets of the marital relationships are divulged. However, the counselor may invite the mother to an individual session to discuss a special problem.

ROLE OF THE COUNSELOR

The same counselor served all groups included in this report. During the early meetings of each group, he functioned on a direct basis, asking mothers to describe specific problem situations that had previously been discussed in individual counseling sessions. This was done to establish the "learning set" for the sessions.

Initially, this was a two-way conversation between the group leader and the mother whose problem had been selected. Within this conversation, the counselor drew in other mothers who were experiencing similar problems with their children. In each situation, he pointed out the misperceptions of the child, specific background-foreground problems, and tendencies to react to such irrelevant reactions as perseverative distractions, etc.

The particular behavioral situation was discussed in the light of normal growth and development, and similarities and dissimilarities pointed out. The counselor asked the mother of the child under discussion and the group to define what they felt might be appropriate behavior in such a situation, and to delineate the specific skills and maturation comprising the elements of the situation. The counselor showed that behavioral configurations are made up of many different elements, and that failures of children in given situations may be traceable to their inability to cope with certain elements or their inability to organize their responses because of undeveloped skills.

After this learning situation, the group (initially, the counselor) worked out a possible approach to the problem that the reporting mother might attempt in improving the problem during the intervening week. The following week's session was devoted in part to this mother's report of her efforts in attempting the approach suggested.

This format became the pattern for all discussion periods with the counselor serving as moderator to move the group through the 5 steps: (1) reporting on a specific problem; (2) labeling the characteristics; (3) comparing to normal development and growth; (4) listing situational elements and skills; and (5) proposing a method to deal with the problem.

The initial directing, controlling, and organizing role of the counselor gradually changed to a more passive role as group interaction improved and as the mothers began to learn the process. This improved interaction permitted the counselor to be more sensitive to the group dynamics.

He injected comments into the group discussion whenever an emphasis or shift of emphasis seemed indicated, whenever a significant relationship needed to be pointed out, whenever a cue needed underlining, or whenever general background information on normal development or the theoretical thinking on brain injury could contribute to the discussion and expand the group's perception potential.

The counselor at all times kept the group at its work—analyzing their behavioral situations in terms of certain fixed principles and developing a solution that they, as parents, might attempt in the home situation. Involvement of the mother as an integrated and necessary part of the therapeutic effort to organize the child was continually pointed out.

During the course of the year, the mothers are taught the following principles:

(1) The brain-injured child misperceives; his erratic and confusing behavior stems from these misperceptions. Recognizing his misperceptions is the first step toward understanding him.

(2) Each failure of the child to conform or to see relationships becomes a challenge. If relationships and standards are made very simple, the child can conform. The problem becomes one of setting standards at such an easy level that the requirements are within the child's potential.

(3) Simplicity becomes the key word in setting up behavior patterns for the child. Complicated routines or response patterns are achieved only gradually and then only when the various elements constituting the whole of a behavior pattern have been learned individually.

(4) Each difficulty faced by the mother in relating to her child, or in her child's relationship to his environment, may be analyzed in terms of components; a plan of development utilizing structured activity may be formulated experimentally to help the child.

(5) The child cannot organize for himself; someone must do it for him. Once his living has been organized, he can gradually assume more and more responsibility for his own organization.

(6) The child offers clues in his behavior that become warning signals of behavioral disorganization; the parents must become alerted to these clues in order to anticipate his needs.

(7) An organized base is necessary before the child can advance to more complicated behaviors.

(8) The parent is the chief organizer for the child because of the intensity of contact. Professional people help, but contact is too brief to effect total organization.

Experience with 38 groups over a seven-year period has brought the following to light:

(1) All parents start the group process at an *information-seeking* level. They want to ask questions and receive direct and specific answers. They want to know what to do, how to do it, and when.

(2) This first stage gradually gives way to a *sharing* process in which

they try to help each other by citing their own successes or failures and discuss each other's specific problems in terms of "Why don't you try this?"

(3) This sharing stage, which operates specifically in the area of technique, gradually gives way to the *feeling* stage in which they help each other to examine their own feelings about their child's behavior, and to see how their own motivations, tensions, and attitudes are reflected in their child's behavior.

(4) From this stage, they move into the *generalization* process in which they begin to consider the dynamics of child development and parental relationships for their other children as well.

(5) The parents finally arrive at a *maturity* stage in which they integrate their brain-injured child into their total family unit and deal effectively with his problems because they understand the complexities of his development, and learn guiding principles to apply to their family relationships.

Through the group discussions, the parents learn how to set limits for their children and learn why limits are necessary. They learn how to prepare their children for new experiences. They learn how to set achievable standards for their children. The parents also learn how to reinforce positive constructive responses and to extinguish negative patterns.

Comparisons between the needs of normal children and brain-injured children are continuously pointed out by the group counselor as the parents discuss their problems.

The general therapeutic process is supportive and educative and aims at covering processes and reinforcing positive defense resources, rather than uncovering dynamics of conflict.

The daily problems of living with the brain-injured child create a stress upon a mother's normal defense structure, and threaten her personality organization. If her defense structure enabled her to cope effectively with her family problems prior to this child, this becomes only a matter of developing her resources to cope with the additional pressure.

CONCLUSIONS

On the basis of this seven-year experiment in group counseling, several conclusions appear to be warranted:

(1) A counseling technique to help parents develop experimental approaches to behavior organization in their brain-injured child is ego-strengthening, supportive, and practically helpful.

(2) These parents experience a homogeneity of anxieties stemming from apprehension regarding the psychological and educational development of their children. Only on a secondary basis do they appear to concern themselves with factors in physical development.

(3) A selection process is necessary to determine whether the needs of a particular parent might best be served in a group or individual counseling setting, or whether referral for psychotherapy might be more profitable.

(4) The parent of the brain-injured child must be considered an integral part of the organization of the child's behavior.

(5) Parents can be taught to perceive their children differently and learn to deal with their children's problems more effectively.

(6) Comments of the mothers consistently reflect changed response patterns in relation to problems represented by their children; they learn to apply a technique. There is some restoration of feelings of competency and self-worth.

(7) The mothers learn to recognize their unique responsibility in developing organized response patterns in their children.

(8) The number of mothers (10) selected for each group on an arbitrary basis has proven an effective and workable figure.

We feel that this technique has potentiality for effective counseling with parents of other types of child problems as well.

14 THE BRAIN-INJURED CHILD:

A CHALLENGE TO SOCIAL WORKERS

George R. Krupp and Bernard Schwartzberg

The brain-injured child has been given little attention as a treatment entity by social workers in the fields of child welfare, family casework, foster care and adoption, and psychiatric casework. In recent years, however, several agencies have discovered that an increasing percentage of children under care or referred for service seem to fall within this category.

The social worker can be of considerable assistance in the recognition of this disability, and in getting the parents to accept the diagnosis. In the agency, the parents can obtain the counseling they need, and also can be directed away from inappropriate casework therapy for the child. When a total therapeutic regime for the child is required, it can be planned and followed through within the casework setting.

In considering the caseworker's role with the parents of a mentally retarded child, Kelman notes, "A particularly crucial function . . . is that of guidance or treatment of parents. . . . They have a right and a responsibility to participate closely in planning for [the child's] care. . . . Some parents have experienced profound difficulties in caring for their . . . child, owing to the nature of the child's condition, to their own subjective difficulties, or, as is usually the case, to a combination of the two." He adds that they should be encouraged to participate in planning, not only for humanitarian reasons but also to ensure that the treatment program instituted may be carried on appropriately in the home. These proposals also are sound in regard to the parents of the brain-injured child.

The social worker's role in helping the brain-injured child is (1) to provide counseling and guidance for the parents, and (2) when desirable, to

Reprinted from *Social Casework*, Vol. 41, No. 2 (February, 1960), pp. 63-69. By permission of the senior author and publisher.

provide the child with direct help, including the necessary therapy when the agency is equipped to give it, or appropriate referral when the agency is unable to provide direct service. The family service agency, whose case-work treatment is family oriented and which can provide a range of services, lends itself well to such a program.

The parents' feeling of bewilderment and confusion concerning the child's behavior is a crucial problem. Special attention should be given to the fact that many of these parents have not been able to accept the diag-nosis of brain injury, despite their having been advised of it—sometimes years before—by various doctors, clinics, and special educational resources. Because of their anxiety and lack of knowledge, the parents frequently fight against the acceptance of this diagnosis. They often mention the child's highest level of performance as proof that the child is not retarded or dam-aged, and ignore other areas in which the child functions poorly. This tendency is not surprising, since the brain-injured child's behavior is almost always erratic or spotty. Hence, the parent rationalizes and cites scores of examples to disprove the previous diagnosis and recommended course of action. Invariably, in the first contact with the caseworker, the parent will deny the child's condition, and complain that the case has been mishandled in the past.

The brain-injured child is frequently brought to the attention of the social worker either by the parents because of his poor school adjustment, or by the school itself because of his poor educational achievements. Some-times the referring school or parent is also concerned about the child's high degree of volatility as well as by his lack of any real social adjustment.

It has been estimated by various authorities that the incidence of chil-dren suffering from this condition is much larger than the public realizes. For example, Weir and Anderson (1958) note that a large proportion of the five percent of failing children in the school system in Rockford, Illinois, was suffering from the results of brain injury. That such a comparatively large proportion can go generally unrecognized may be due, in part, to the fact that the parents see the children primarily in the protected environment of the home. When the child goes to school, he is then observed in relation to his learning ability and in new social situations that create anxiety. His atypi-cal behavior leads to a recognition of his condition. Frequently the school and the family are in conflict because the parents do not accept the school's observations and recommendations. The social worker should not be in-volved in this struggle, but must maintain his focus on the meaning of the child's behavior.

BEHAVIOR CHARACTERISTICS

The particular behavior defect that the brain-injured child manifests de-pends upon the area of the central nervous system that is damaged. If the intracranial centers that initiate and coordinate muscular activity are the areas involved, the consequence may be cerebral palsy. If the areas of the brain that are concerned with intelligence are affected, one consequence may be mental deficiency. The injury of the particular areas that control speech and sight may result in distorted sensory perception. Disorders of other areas may produce epilepsy. If the damage occurred early in life and the involvement is diffuse, the result may show itself in altered behavior in relation to many functions. It is the child who falls within this last category who is of primary concern in this discussion—the child who usually has no gross motor or sensory disturbance and whose intelligence is average or even above average. It is this child whose disability often goes unrecognized. Frequently, such a child is diagnosed as having a severe behavior disorder, as being mentally defective, or as suffering from schizophrenia. Once the clinician is familiar with the clinical picture, brain injury is not difficult to recognize, but proving the diagnosis is often difficult.

No behavioral act is the result of a single preceding or predisposing event; and every act has both conscious and unconscious components. A particular symptom may have both physiologic and psychodynamic determinants. Although the organic factor is one of several factors that influence the child's total adjustment and personality, the behavior patterns of brain-injured children reveal a distinctive similarity. The parents, too, reveal a distinctive similarity in that they are almost always anxious and worried and usually give a confused and contradictory description of the child's history and present functioning.

The common behavior characteristics of the brain-injured child have been described by numerous authors (Bakwin, 1949; Strauss and Lehtinen, 1947; Bender, 1955; Doll, 1953; Bradley, 1955). He is different from others of similar age and development. He tends to be outside, or on the periphery of the group, and presents a strikingly erratic performance. This erratic and inconsistent performance is what causes the parents (and frequently the social worker and the school teacher) to be perplexed. This erratic quality has resulted in their describing the child's behavior as poorly integrated, variable, uncoordinated, inconsistent, strange, queer, and lacking in stability. The child tends to be hyperactive or hyperkinetic. He is often described as overactive, hypermotile, or driveless. His behavior is often characterized by sudden rages, irritability, lability, and uncontrolled impulsivity. The lability in the intellectual sphere is evidence by his poor concentration, distractibility, and short attention span. Frequently such children have difficulties with number concepts and with arithmetic owing to their difficulty in conceptualization. Instead of grasping number concepts as a whole they will count out the number. An example is a five-and-a-half-year-old who, when asked how many coins (4) were shown to him, had to count each coin separately to the total of four; he could not perceive the four as a whole.

Another characteristic usually noted is perseveration or the tendency to repeat behavior whether or not it is appropriate. This tendency is frequently assumed to be a form of negativism, particularly when the child refuses to give up or shift his activity (Bradley, 1955). Because the child's attention may be distractible but also highly perseverative the behavior picture is confused. Another trait frequently found is low tolerance for stress and frustration. The child may be attentive when it pleases him to be so, yet hopelessly inattentive when efforts are made to control him. For example, a ten-year-old child was able to sit and listen to records at home for long stretches of time but was unable to sit still at school for more than five minutes. Moreover, the brain-injured child is almost invariably ostracized by other children. Often, he has poor muscular coordination and finds it difficult to ride a bicycle, tie his shoelaces, or engage in sports.

If the clinician specifically asks about the types of behavior described above, it is astonishing how frequently the child's behavior will then be described in these terms. One of the bewildering aspects of his behavior is its sudden and frequent change. The child will have periods during one day or for days when everything goes well and he appears to be relatively bright; then there will be periods when everything goes wrong and he appears and acts quite stupid. His anxiety readily becomes intensified and disrupts his performance; his conduct is unpredictable and alternates between infantile and more mature behavior. His ability to establish rapport alternates with inaccessibility, and his affectionate acceptance of others alternates with negativistic withdrawal (Doll, 1953).

Authorities have advanced various hypotheses to explain these behavioral phenomena (Strauss and Lehtinen, 1947; Bender, 1955; Doll, 1953; Bradley, 1955) in terms of the basic brain injury. In summary, they all seem to agree that these children have the following defects which the uninjured do not have: (1) Faulty powers of inhibition and control, motor and emotional; the child is forced into actions that are not intended. (2) Disturbances of perception. Perception is more than receiving stimuli; it is an act or a process in which meanings are attributed to the sensed stimuli. (3) Predisposition to anxiety due to impaired organization, confused interpretation of the environment, and early postural reflex disturbance. The child has impaired visual-motor performance, with a corresponding inability to distinguish foreground figures and background details. There is a sort of confusing-the-forest-for-the-trees response. Distortions of body image are also present. (4) Secondary psychological defense mechanisms related to the repeated frustrations (anxiety) encountered by the brain-injured child and his parents. These may be character reactions such as meticulousness, clinging or withdrawal; psychoneurotic reactions such as phobias, obsessions, and compulsions; psychotic reactions such as schizophrenic thinking disturbances and specific disabilities.

DIAGNOSIS

Despite the ease of making a diagnosis in typical cases of brain injury, clinicians frequently fail to make it. One of the reasons for this failure may be the erroneous assumption that this diagnosis implies a hopeless future. The fact is that such a child tends to improve as he grows older and develops greater ego control. An accurate diagnosis can be made if the clinician bears in mind the six following considerations. These are given in what seems to be their order of value to the clinician.

(1) The composite picture described above and the developmental history. These distinctive patterns must be present. They constitute the soundest basis for making a diagnosis of brain injury.

(2) The child's performance on judiciously selected psychological tests. These must be administered by a psychologist *sensitive to the special problems of the brain-injured child*. In our opinion the psychological test is amost always more significant for the diagnosis than the neurological examination. Without positive findings on the psychological tests a definite diagnosis is difficult to make.

(3) Past medical history. Prenatal factors, such as toxemia, abnormal vaginal bleeding, maternal infection. Prenatal factors, including trauma, anoxia, prematurity, Rh incompatibility. Post-natal factors, including trauma, meningitis, encephalitis, convulsions, cerebral hemorrhage.

(4) Neurological investigation. The presence of neurological disabilities strongly supports the diagnosis. Pediatric neurological examination should emphasize postural reflexes, eye convergence, motility, and the manner in which the child relates to other individuals. Such evidence may not be present if organic factors are in operation. Thus, Silver notes, "Fully 20 percent of all children seen in the Bellevue Hospital Mental Hygiene Clinic suffer from organic defects incurred during prenatal, paranatal or neonatal life . . . In them . . . classic neurological examination . . . gives essentially normal results" (Silver, 1958).

(5) Consideration of the family background and of other members of the family. If the child is extremely disturbed, but the family is well-adjusted and the mother in particular is not schizophrenic, rejecting, or controlling, the clinician should consider the possibility of an organic defect.

(6) Electroencephalogram. This is of limited value, since it can be positive when organic findings are absent and negative when they are present. Much too much emphasis has been placed on this diagnostic procedure.

The child who has suffered a severe brain injury in early life, and the child who presents typical schizophrenic symptoms (autism, bizarre thinking, merging with the environment, withdrawal from people) following a period of normal development are not too difficult to distinguish diagnostically. There are, however, many children for whom a differential diagnosis is not easy to make. Some children seem to have both conditions. Many workers in the field feel that the same cerebral defects or dysfunctions associated with mental retardation or brain injury may and do induce certain patterns of disorganized thinking which are termed schizophrenic (Pollak,

1958; Wortis, 1958). The authors agree with this but use the term "schizophrenic" only when no organic factors are revealed in the clinical picture, the psychological tests, and the history.

THE ROLE OF THE SOCIAL WORKER

In working with the brain-injured child and his parents, the social worker should have three main objectives: (1) recognition of the brain-injured child; (2) formulation of a treatment plan for him and his family; (3) offering assistance in carrying out the treatment plan.

RECOGNITION. The social worker needs to acquire a basic understanding of the clinical entity known as the brain-injured child and the meanings of each aspect of the child's behavior. He should recognize not only the individual elements of the syndrome, but also the combination of factors which characterize this diagnosis. He needs to know both the emotional and the physical reasons for the child's behavior and for the lack of impulse control. Above all, he needs to understand the relationship of the organic brain damage to the child's educational and social adjustment. This knowledge enables him to help the parents to understand the child better, and to work out a treatment plan with the school and other community resources.

Paramount in the worker's mind must be the fact that the brain-injured child has specific disabilities in the area of perception, and that his ability to conceptualize is impaired. This child finds it difficult to master two and three dimensions, he responds more to details than to the whole, his motor and emotional controls are poor, and he needs to repeat experiences. When the social worker recognizes that the child's perception is defective and that his learning ability is thus impaired, he will be able to understand better why the parents are so confused in their assessment of the child's intellectual capacities. Many of these children have average and above average IQ's, yet fail miserably in school and in new learning situations. For example, the parents of one child who had been examined by several clinicians could not accept the diagnosis. By making tape recordings of the child's responses to their questions, the parents attempted to prove to the examiners that the child was not so slow and retarded as all the examiners had indicated. When one listened to the tape recording it was quickly apparent that the child had good ability in rote matters and that they had given him indirect clues to the correct answers. Hence, they were overoptimistic in assessing the results. It should be emphasized that in order to understand the child's behavior and his poor learning ability one must recognize his difficulty in abstract thinking and in conceptualization. For example, one child could take measurements of two halves of a table but could not add them together to get the whole.

A social worker alert to this diagnosis will notice the child's gait, posture, and facial expression. He will observe the particular speech characteristics—immaturity, slowness, and an echoing quality. A history of erratic behavior, hyperactivity, impulsivity, and social unacceptability, significant information derived from the genetic history, and the above observations should immediately suggest to the worker the need for psychologic and psychiatric consultation to confirm the diagnosis of brain disorder.

The psychiatrist is in the best position to help the social worker understand the medical and neurological implications of brain injury. He may make his contribution as a member of the staff of the psychiatric clinic, as a consultant in a family or children's agency, or as a teacher of a seminar in which all the members of the casework staff of the agency participate. He may also be used as a diagnostician who sees the child for a diagnostic interview to ensure the validity of the diagnosis made.

FORMULATION OF A TREATMENT PLAN. The worker in a social agency needs to take into consideration the assets and liabilities of the parents, as well as the nature and extent of the injury to the child, and the limitations of the child's functioning because of the damage. In general, however, an appropriate treatment plan includes counseling and guidance for the parents, referral to a medical resource for medical or drug therapy needed by the child, some sort of relationship therapy when indicated, and suggestions for modification of the average educational plan, such as placement in a special class or securing a teacher of the homebound, if this is possible. When the school does not permit any modification of the usual curriculum, or when the parents are unwilling or unable to benefit from a counseling or guidance relationship, it may be necessary to work out plans for the child away from his home—foster care, placement in a treatment institution or in a specially structured educational setting. The psychiatrist usually participates in formulating the plan.

The brain-injured child has a weak ego and a history of repeated failure in handling his own needs and his environmental pressures. Special educational techniques are required to help him develop ego mastery. These are divided into two main groups by Kaliski (1959) and include "experiences in every day living, awareness and interpretation of each other's needs, feelings, forming relationships (adults and peers), getting acquainted with the community, its structure, its resources, its needs, civic responsibilities," and "learning the skills and acquiring the tools necessary to function independently in our culture." An atmosphere in which the child is relaxed and in close contact with the teacher is a most important tool for his educational retraining.

It should never be taken for granted that the child will understand and follow ordinary verbal directions, especially when time and space relationships are involved. The brain-injured child has difficulties in perceiving the relationships and similarities between things in the world around him, which is the basis for abstract thinking. He often perceives things quite differently from the normal person and his attention is distracted by any insignificant or meaningless detail. Therefore, it is important to avoid any unnecessary or distracting stimuli.

At the same time, each task the child is asked to perform must be concretized for him. It must be broken down into its component parts, and each one must be made concrete. For example, the child may be unable to tie his own shoelaces. The special educator, educational therapist, or psychologist who is helping him learn to perform this task can do so only by over-concretizing the material. Each step is broken down into its simplest elements. The child learns each step in minute detail, and gradually learns to put the steps together. Or again, the child may know his multiplication tables and spelling by rote. He may know that two times three is six, but he does not know why it is six. The educator may use diagrams and teach him by adding two threes. What he already knows by rote can be used in developing conceptualization in this way; thus, multiplication and division are spelled out.

The child's attention has to be directed through the use of special techniques, because one of his major limitations is his inability to concentrate on ordinary visual or auditory stimuli. This can be done through specially designed visual stimuli such as lights, color, or forms, or through special auditory stimuli. In addition, certain kinesthetic approaches may be used to increase conceptualization. For example, the special educator may hold the pencil with the child, and go over the letter that is being taught, or the letter may be made out of clay, pinned out flat, and then traced with a stick or the finger. These and other kinesthetic approaches increase the child's comprehension by moving from the concrete to the abstract. Although special techniques have been developed, educators of the brain-injured child by no means have the final answer for educating him. As Strauss and Lehtinen state, "what we present today is only a vague, preliminary 'scouting' in the field of defect and disease and as yet we do not even know to what extent our efforts toward alleviating disease and defect are efforts in the right direction" (1947).

ASSISTANCE IN CARRYING OUT THE TREATMENT PLAN. In establishing a treatment program for the brain-injured child, the social worker must be aware that any plan will involve three groups of people: the school authorities, including the psychologist, principal, and classroom teacher; the family physician or pediatrician; and the parents themselves. Even the child with superior intelligence usually has had a history of failure in school, and the referral to the agency often comes at a point of desperation. Thus, it is vital to secure the cooperation of school personnel in working out a special program, or in securing greater understanding of the child in the regular curriculum if this is possible. Hence, the school psychologist should be included in the plan as early as possible in order to make sure that the other school authorities, including the classroom teacher, understand the child and his problem and work to help him within the school setting.

Second, especially when drug therapy is part of the child's treatment (other than in a psychiatric clinic) the cooperation of the family physician must be secured, since it will be he who administers the drug treatment in conjunction with the consultant psychiatrist of the agency, and relates this treatment to the total physical functioning of the child. His cooperation in the planning should be secured as early as possible.

Finally, the major task of the social worker, that of giving guidance or casework counseling to the parents or parent substitutes, is carried on simultaneously with the other aspects of the treatment plan. The parents or foster parents are thus enabled to accept the diagnosis and plan on a continuing basis and to handle their own personal feelings which may interfere with their seeing the child as in need of special help.

CONCLUSION

The brain-injured child must be understood in terms of his biological damage, his psychological defense mechanisms, and the environmental forces acting on him. The social worker also needs to be aware that the child tends to improve as he grows older.

The social worker, therefore, needs to be alert to the overt signs which point to the existence of this type of damage in order to carry out his function of providing service to the brain-injured child and his parents. He must see his role as one of helping the parents to secure additional direct help for the child when it is needed while providing concurrent counseling. Consultation with or participation by both psychiatrist and psychologist is essential to any social agency considering a program of this nature.

The social worker cannot be expected to assume the responsibility for making the clinical diagnosis of the brain-injured child. He should, however, be able to spot the chief behavioral characteristics and typical history of this type of child, and to understand some of the dynamic implications of the child's psychopathology. Unless he is able to do so, time will be spent needlessly in exploring the possibility of other diagnoses, in interviewing the family members, and often in attempting inappropriate casework treatment of the child. This is not only an inappropriate use of the caseworker's time, but also does the family and child a disservice.

When the social agency clearly sees its responsibility in helping a brain-injured child, and does the job in a professional and competent manner, it can be of considerable assistance to both the child and his parents. In this way, the social worker helps the child, the family, the school, and the community in which the child lives. All benefit from the social worker's efforts, and the child is able to lead a more fruitful and productive life.

References

Bakwin, Harry, Cerebral damage and behavior damage in children, *J. Pediatr.*, 1949, 34 (3), 371.

Bender, Lauretta, *Psychopathology of children with organic brain disorders* (Springfield, Illinois: Charles C Thomas, 1955).

Bradley, Charles, Organic factors in the psychopathology of childhood. In *Psychopathology of childhood*, Paul H. Hoch and Joseph Zubin (Editors) (New York: Grune & Stratton, 1955), pp. 80-104.

Doll, Edgar A., Mental deficiency vs. neurophrenia, *Amer. J. ment. Def.*, 1953, 57 (3), 477.

Kalinski, Lotte, The brain-injured child—Learning by living in a structured setting, *Amer. J. ment. Def.*, 1959, 63 (4), 688.

Pollak, Max, Brain damage, mental retardation, and childhood schizophrenia, *Amer. J. Psychiat.*, 1958, 115 (5), 422.

Silver, Archie A., Behavioral syndrome associated with brain damage in children, *Pediat. Clin. N. Amer.*, Vol. V, No. 3 (Philadelphia: Saunders, 1958), p. 688.

Strauss, A. A., and Lehtinen, Laura E., *Psychopathology and education of the brain-injured child*, Vol. 1 (New York: Grune & Stratton, 1947).

Weir, Homer F., and Anderson, Robert L., Organic and organizational aspects of school adjustment problems, *J.A.M.A.*, 1958, 166 (14), 1708.

Wortis, Joseph, Schizophrenic symptomatology in mentally retarded children, *Amer. J. Psychiat.*, 1958, 115 (5), 429.

15 THE NEUROLOGICAL STUDY OF
CHILDREN WITH LEARNING DISABILITIES

Robert Cohn ✺

When a child in the course of good pedagogical practice fails to achieve grade level work, attempts are generally made to determine the cause of failure. If failure is primarily due to the child's attitudinal posture, or to distracting environmental conditions, these factors are usually amenable to correction and as a consequence the child continues in regular classes and matures in a normal intellectual way. At times, such treatment does not result in improvement in the child's learning ability and the parents, on the advice of teachers, seek further help to determine if the child is incapable of achieving normal rates of learning because of brain damage. This diagnosis is usually hinted to the parents by the experienced teachers and referring psychologists. Under these conditions, the child is ordinarily seen by the neurologist as part of a comprehensive clinical evaluation to determine whether there is definite evidence of a structural lesion of the nervous system. The rationale of this procedure is the general recognition that, in the absence of critical brain tissue capable of normal function, there will be disturbances in the biological integrity of the child. Furthermore, the disclosure of neurological deficits might alter the overall approach, and enhance the effectiveness of training; the prognosis for the individual's eventual competence might be given to the parents with more assurance.

STATEMENT OF THE BASIC PROBLEM

From the recent literature (Anderson, 1963; Boshes and Myklebust, 1964; Kennard, 1960) it is evident that many neurologists believe that there are a number of minimal, or "soft," neurological signs in individuals who have

Reprinted from *Exceptional Children*, Vol. 31, No. 4 (December, 1964) pp. 179-185. By permission of the author and publisher.

difficulty in acquiring verbal language functions necessary for information transfer. It is implied that these minimal neurological findings can be equated with minimal brain damage, and that this minimal brain damage retards the organizational capacity of the child to synthesize and classify incoming data. This writer takes exception to the equating of minimal brain damage with minimal neurological signs on the basis of three major considerations.

(1) It is only by definition that certain clinical findings are described as "minimal." Various neurologists might be impressed differently depending on the basic training and interpretation of what constitutes minimal. For example, under certain conditions a minimal paresis of the right upper limb or a mild headache might be considered of no great moment, but in combination these findings might well indicate the onset of a devastating neurological process. Thus an ensemble of small signs in many instances may point to a major brain lesion.

(2) It has not been demonstrated neuropathologically that minimal clinical signs are in fact related to minimal brain pathology. There are only a very few clinical-pathological reports in the literature relating structural brain lesions with language difficulties in children. Minimal signs may be concomitant with remarkable lesions of the brain. For example in case two of Cohn's paper (1962), it was demonstrated that severe damage to the right cerebral hemisphere had given rise to relatively minimal clinical signs. These consisted of mild weakness to the left side since birth, headaches, fainting spells, and inability to learn to read or write. At autopsy, there was intense atrophy of the frontal and parietal regions of the right cerebral hemisphere. In another reported study of a child with delayed acquired language function (Landau, Goldstein and Kleffner, 1960), the patient showed only a mild diplegic gait, a right sided Babinski sign and an increased amount of slow activity over the right occipital region in the EEG. This individual had large bilateral cerebral defects involving the opercular structures, extending to the occipital region on the left side. From these two cases it is quite evident that minimal neurological findings may be associated with severe brain tissue damage or loss. As a converse phenomenon, this writer observed a child from the age of two years who showed a progressive inability to relate to environmental changes. She was remarkably spastic, never verbalized, but only gurgled; she ground her teeth and tended to stare in forward gaze. At the initial examination she was able to stand with slight support. Over the years she gradually regressed to the level where she was unable to stand or even sit and could only lie in an hyperextended posture. She died at the age of nine years. Although her brain has not yet been studied in minute detail, it certainly has no evidence of gross pathological change. The major point is that only with a large number of brain studies in cases of delayed acquisition of language function can a proper correlation between neuro-

logical signs and neuropathology be established. It is no simple process whereby the relation between the equating of minimal clinical signs with minimal brain damage, either unilateral or bilateral, can be accomplished.

(3) The ensemble of minimal clinical signs is directly dependent on the variety of tests used by the neurologist and on the basic philosophy that underlies his thinking. In a number of reported instances, neurological study consisted only of a standard initial physical examination performed by the neurologist (Boshes and Myklebust, 1964; Dreifuss, 1963; Goldstein, et al., 1959). For the most part, the disturbances in the motor apparatus were considered by the authors to be of greatest significance; eye findings in general were considered minor. In cases one and three, Dreifuss (1963) implied that bilateral hyperactive deep tendon reflexes, bilateral Babinski signs, and increased jaw jerks were evidences of only minimal brain damage. In his presentation, he was attempting to demonstrate that delayed language acquisition of the type seen in school children was the result of lack of cerebral dominance resulting from minimal bilateral brain lesions.

THE NEUROLOGICAL STUDY

This writer believes that the neurological study should encompass the totality of the systematically recognizable receptor activities and the general subsequent responses of the child to these received stimulus patterns; any deviations from the range of normal should not be considered *minimal*. There is, instead, an *ensemble of signs* (the extent of which depends on the ingenuity, repertoire, and competence of the examiner) that help to determine whether the child has the necessary properly functioning nervous system apparatus required to communicate in a manner consistent with the culture in which he is reared. It should be recognized that in interpersonal relationships it is only by responsive movement that one can infer that the child was the recipient of the message from the sender. In the category of movement, the neurologist must include not only the intrinsic patterns of personal action of such parts as the jaw, tongue, face, extremities, etc., but also the movement of the child as a receiver that indicates reception of information. These intrinsic patterns include such movements as gestures, body positioning for graphic presentations, eyeball scanning movements in reading, etc. Thus it becomes important to study the patient's behavior and actions not only for the rates and degrees of development of the function that he has attained, but for the types of reactions in social settings. It is important to assess how the child responds to peers, to authority figures, and to subordinates. Thus knowledge of the home activities and recreational actions of the child become a rightful domain of the neurological study. Formal study of station, gait, and spontaneous activity must be carefully observed, along with postural reflexes, etc. Special attention must be paid to the somatic sensory perceptions, particularly in adaptation and persistence times, to toe and finger positions and to pin prick. By these latter methods sensory function becomes an objective and reliable source of information rather than a purely subjective phenomenon with all of its attendant difficulties. The use of homolateral paired simultaneous tactile stimulation is of inestimable value as an index of general sentiency, and the specific abilities of the child to discriminate and respond to competing stimuli (Cohn, 1953). Obviously the superficial and deep tendon reflexes, clonus, etc., must be tested. The electroencephalogram (EEG) must also be recorded, not as a phenomenon unto itself, but as a single element in the complete neurological study of the child. It is important to recognize that even if seizure activity (clinical and electrical) is evident, this finding alone is hardly sufficient to account for disturbance in language function unless the seizure activity is of an almost continuous type, or if the seizures are only one of the manifestations of gross underlying brain lesions.

Of major importance in all neurological testing is the experience of the neurologist with essentially normal children who have no obvious gross problem in language function. When such controls are systematically obtained in an adequate number of subjects without scholastic difficulties it is recognized that there are many children who have neurological deficits of variable intensity which do not however interfere with their learning abilities (Cohn, 1961). In general, these deficits in the control children are isolated, disparate, and do not cluster. Such phenomena seem to indicate that the organism has sufficient reserve to compensate for certain isolated defects, and that in any biological system, normalcy must have a considerable range.

It must be emphasized that in children with language, and ancillary concomitant behavioral problems, it is improper to conduct the neurological examination according to a standard form or check list. The child must be treated as a biological system with disturbed function. The examination must be obtained in such a way that the input (learning or address) capacities, the consequent necessary relation of these input data with past experience, and the output capacity are capable of relatively precise evaluation. On this basis, to achieve rapport and general cooperation, the time element for address and retrieval of data must not be of major import; the primary object is to put in and extract as much data as possible to the limit of the child's ability. In many instances the entire success of the study depends on the irregular sequences of examination. Under these latter operational conditions the neurological study becomes quite inclusive and as a result can give basic data to which subsequent neuropathological findings can be correlated.

It is important to reiterate that a neurological examination is a study of function and that the role of the neurologist is to determine whether the disturbances disclosed are likely to be associated with central nervous system lesions. When certain well authenticated patterns of disturbance are elicited, such as unilateral increased deep tendon reflexes, ankle clonus and

Babinski signs, the inference of a pyramidal tract lesion is quite likely. But even if such lesions are disclosed, it does not mean that the language function need necessarily be involved to the extent of delayed learning. A case in point is that of a 13-year-old girl who is the only living child in her family. On arrival at the examination room she was quiet and well behaved. In the opening salutations she did not speak very distinctly but this was thought to be the result of heavy orthodontic braces. The mother stated that the girl had had a normal spontaneous delivery, but it was early recognized by the attending physician that she had a remarkable decrease in thyroid function. As a consequence, the patient had been receiving three grains of thyroid extract per day since the age of a few months. Despite such medication the child was unable to roll over until the age of nine months; she sat at 16 months and walked at about two years of age. She produced many unintelligible verbalizations but did not speak recognizable words until the age of six or seven years. The patient was studied at the Johns Hopkins University Hospital in Baltimore just prior to her departure for France; it was predicted by the examiner at that time that this girl would "never learn French." On arrival in France she was enrolled in an elementary school and within three years she became an ostensibly "French girl" —her diction was utterly fluent and her basic knowledge of the language was impeccable. As my examination progressed, the general language repartee became free and it was noted that the patient's voice had a marked nasal quality, and that there was a preponderance of vowel sounds. The lip and tongue movements were decreased in amplitude as the conversation became more fluid. She giggled considerably and showed evident lack of emotional control (which her mother believed indicated immaturity). At this time too, the girl became more restless; she squirmed in the chair and showed many aberrant movements of the extremities. During the ophthalmoscopic examination, there was a low amplitude lateral nystagmus but no abnormal vertical eyeball movements were seen. She was unable to converge; the right eye remained fixed in forward gaze, the left had a minimal inward rotation. In toe and heel walking the associated upper limb movements were overactive and the patient appeared gauche. There was an unsustained ankle clonus on the right. A most remarkable finding was her inability to resolve paired homolaterally applied tactile stimuli; she succeeded in only five out of approximately 30 paired stimuli and this difficulty occurred irrespective of the rates of application of the paired stimuli. There was a moderate amount of tremor in finger to nose to finger tests; as she approached the target, there was a low amplitude oscillation. The extended arms showed a marked angulation at the carpal joints but the fingers were not hyperextended. With the arms extended and the eyelids closed, there were some low amplitude finger movements. But this type of movement did not seem to be much greater than that which is often observed in a large number of normal children. The EEG showed an increased amount of generalized slow activity which was considered as moderately abnormal. Her arithmetic operations were slowly but accurately performed; reading and writing were well executed. It is interesting that in a short visit to Spain she had learned the Spanish language very rapidly. In summary, this girl showed evidence of generalized extrapyramidal motor system dysfunction with slow development of motor abilities including phonetic language, but despite these handicaps she has become an effective linguist with hopes of being an interpreter.

To illustrate the other side of the coin, a child who was six years and nine months of age was referred to the hospital because of dizzy spells in which he walked into the wall; these episodes were preceded by a stomach ache. His speech was mechanically and ideationally normal. He had completed kindergarten. He was friendly, small and had a thin dyplastic, wan face. He threw a ball right handed and, in writing, he spontaneously utilized the right upper extremity. In catching the ball, he used both hands clumsily but the pattern of catching and recovery after the "miss" was very immature and dyscoordinate. In formal gait testing he was quite adequate. All the cranial nerves functioned normally. He resolved all simultaneously applied paired stimuli. He was unable to name or match colors or to even learn the color names in a protracted drill. However he did learn to recognize one and zero when they were written on the palms of his hands; he recognized pictures of common objects when they were drawn for him. Propositional right-left orientation was undeveloped. He indicated that he could write his name, Alvin, but produced the following done from right to left: IVIA. For the requested picture of a boy he drew a lamb standing on its head. He could not spontaneously draw the picture of a person. To dictation however, he could "draw the head," "draw the eyes" etc., by making appropriate marks until the picture was completed. The picture was drawn upsidedown! In a copy of my picture of a person he copied certain elements of the head but finally indicated it was "his brains popping out." He was unable to copy an acute angle; he could neither produce nor copy a birdhouse, particularly the angulated roof. His EEG was within the range of normal variation. In summary this was a moderately clumsy boy who was otherwise neurologically normal except for his visual-verbal and color recognition. In other words, he had a delayed acquisition of, and a distorted, language function; yet he had relatively few neurological abnormalities.

In the writer's experience pure congenital auditory aphasia has been quite uncommon; the great majority of the individuals so classified have presented only varying degrees of difficulty in comprehension of the spoken words. These individuals, in general differ from the deaf child by their active sound productions. Essentially, pure congenital visual aphasia (or word blindness) is met with much more frequently than auditory defects (Worster-Drought and Allen, 1930).

In many children with disturbed language ability there is an associated high degree of latent and overt violence. This has been particularly evident in the individuals with the more idiosyncratic difficulties; the child who does everything reasonably well except read. This appears to be a substitute of unchanneled movement for the more orderly movement patterns generally utilized in interaction speech and in graphic receptions and productions. In the younger hyperactive children, it appears that much of the difficulty resides in the inability to discriminate and orderly classify the patterns of incoming data. This inability is elegantly demonstrated in the large number of children with delayed language abilities who fail to resolve paired, simultaneously applied tactile stimuli.

CLINICAL, NEUROLOGICAL, AND NEUROPATHOLOGICAL CORRELATIONS

As a foundation for the knowledge of the relation between delayed and improper language acquisition and brain pathology, great effort must be exerted to obtain material for study. In such studies the reports must be detailed, and the findings adequately illustrated (Cohn and Neumann, 1946). When the cases are presented in a superficial, short publication, the importance of clinical-neuropathological correlations is endangered. A case in point is that of Landau *et al.* in 1960. They reported on a child who showed signs of congenital auditory aphasia. In the report there was no gross picture of the bilateral cerebral lesions; and the overwhelmingly important point as to the absence or vestigial presence of the medical geniculate bodies was not convincingly demonstrated; furthermore from the accompanying photograph the designated myelin loss of the pyramidal tracts appeared to be in the region of the arcuate nuclei.

Although neurological and neuropathological studies most probably will not result in one to one correlations, such work must form the fundamental basis from which other, more subtle techniques can be rationally applied.

TREATMENT

The basic treatment for the amelioration of language disturbances seen in the child of school age appears to require almost complete individualization. Since the precise cause of language disturbances is not known due to the lack of clinical-pathological correlations, ignorance of chemical determinants etc., all treatment must necessarily be nonspecific. That is, there should be no specific attempt to "develop" dominance (Delacato, 1963), to sedate, or to activate the central nervous system. The child should be neurologically studied in great detail in a manner somewhat as outlined previously to determine what avenues of the address system are open and might allow introduction of information. With these data, information should be administered to the level of tolerance of the particular individual. All emphasis should be taken away from correction and applied to development and growth. The child should be supported, and allowed to progress in general intellectual activities through the relatively intact input channels. In this way, the child, as he matures chronologically, achieves some self-respect and more security in his abilities. Under these conditions the great majority of students with relatively normal brain function can and do overcome their initially overwhelming handicaps. The children who can not develop under these conditions, in the writer's experience, have language difficulties that are secondary to reduced organizational capacity of their central nervous system.

For the children showing relatively isolated delayed visual-verbal abilities, their generally remarkable ability with nonverbal symbols has suggested that planned rebus writing and other basic pictorial forms, as in hieroglyphic writing, should be liberally employed in therapeutic drill sessions.

From the writer's studies, it appears that nearly all children with language difficulties under either formal or informal instruction, progress with varying degrees of success and achieve variable proficiencies in language, but most individuals studied in detail did not acquire a language function sufficient to endow them with any literary facility comparable to the normal. Of the 45 children first studied as part of the Syracuse University project in the Montgomery County Schools in 1957, only three have achieved regular school. Most of these children (on repeated neurological examination studies) remain in special education. All have learned to read and write with some proficiency. Two children have learned to read well, but they have not learned to organize and utilize the information they have acquired. Nearly all are loners; they have few associates and appear isolated. These particular children in special education now are approaching the age where obligate schooling is no longer required. To date only three children of those I have been able to follow have shown any ability to earn money by cutting grass and other unskilled activities. It will be most interesting to see how, and if these children integrate into society.

CONCLUSION

It has been shown that neurological practice at the present time can not determine with precision the correlation between minimal signs and minimal brain damage. Neurological practice by precise examination can point out the channels of relatively normal input systems, and thereby indicate the means whereby language can be introduced and developed in the most fruitful way possible for the individual.

References

Anderson, W. W., The hyperkinetic child: A neurological appraisal, Neurology, 1963, 13, 968-973.
Boshes, B., and Myklebust, H. R., A neurological and behavioral study of children with learning disorders, Neurology, 1964, 14, 7-12.

Cohn, R., Role of "body image concept" in pattern of ipsilateral clinical extinction, A.M.A. Arch. Neurol. Psychiat., 1953, 70, 503-509.
Cohn, R., Neurological concepts pertaining to the brain-damaged child. In W. Daley (Editor), Speech and language therapy with the brain-damaged child (Washington, D.C.: Catholic, 1962).
Cohn, R., Delayed acquisition of reading and writing abilities in children. Arch. Neurol., 1961, 4, 153-164.
Cohn, R., and Neumann, M. A., Porencephaly. A clinico-pathologic study, J. Neuropath. exp. Neurol., 1946, 5, 257-270.
Cowen, D., and Olmstead, E. V., Infantile neuroaxonal dystrophy, J. Neuropath. exp. Neurol., 1963, 22, 175-236.
Delacato, C. H., The diagnosis and treatment of speech and reading problems (Springfield, Illinois: Charles C Thomas, 1963).
Dreifuss, F. E., Delayed development of hemispheric dominance, A.M.A. Arch. Neurol., 1963, 8, 510-514.
Goldstein, R., Landau, W. M., and Kleffner, F. R., Neurologic assessment of some deaf and aphasic children, Amer. J. Otolaryngol., Rhinolaryngol., Laryngol., 1958, 67, 468-479.
Kennard, M. A., Value of equivocal signs in neurologic diagnosis, Neurology, 1960, 10, 753-764.
Landau, W. M., Goldstein, R., and Kleffner, F. R., Congenital aphasia: A clinicopathologic study, Neurology, 1960, 10, 915-921.
Worster-Drought, C., and Allen, J. M., Congenital auditory imperception (congenital word deafness): And its relation to idioglossia and other speech defects, J. Neurol. Psychopath., 1930, 10, 193-236.

16 PSYCHIATRIC IMPLICATIONS OF BRAIN DAMAGE IN CHILDREN

Leon Eisenberg

INTRODUCTION

The disturbances in behavior associated with brain damage provide a particularly striking instance of a psychobiological disorder. At first glance, it might seem as if the problem would be solely neurological. Yet clinical experience soon dispels naïve expectations of a 1:1 correlation between tissue loss and behavior pathology. Children with the lesser tissue destruction may exhibit the more disorganization in behavior. This seeming paradox does not justify the conclusion that brain substance has little to do with psychological function, but suggests a need to re-examine our notions of the relationship between structure and function.

Basic to an understanding of the clinical facts, is the concept that the patient is a psychobiological entity, subject both to biological and to social influences and manifesting a psychological continuity of his own (Eisenberg, 1953). The outcome of brain injury, then, will be determined by factors operating in all these spheres. To begin with, one observes the quantitative and qualitative alterations in brain function produced by damage to its structure. On a second level, the behavior observed is influenced by the reorganization of the previous personality of the patient in the face of his functional deficit. On still a third level, the social environment has a profound influence on the patient's performance—and, under certain conditions, the decisive influence. It is the interaction between these three classes of factors that determines the outcome in each particular case. It need, therefore, not be a surprise that study of intracranial pathology *alone* does not suffice to account for the vicissitudes of clinical behavior.

From this viewpoint, the interest of the psychiatrist in the phenomena

Reprinted from *Psychiatric Quarterly*, Vol. 31, No. 72 (1957) pp. 72-92. By permission of the author and publisher.

associated with brain injury is not merely a question of the "psychogenic" factors that play upon the child or his "adjustment" to his illness. It is rather that brain injury constitutes a compelling demonstration of the complexity of psychophysiological interrelationships—and it is this aspect of the problem that will be the primary concern of the following discussion.

THE CLINICAL PROBLEM

Obviously, there is no single pattern of behavior that is produced by brain injury, for the area or areas damaged, the extent of the damage, and perhaps also the type of damage, are important determinants of the features of each case. Nevertheless, it is possible to describe in general certain signs and symptoms which are frequently found. It must be admitted at the outset that these signs and symptoms per se are *not* pathognomonic for organic impairment of the central nervous system. Similar difficulties may be observed in non brain-damaged children. But the much greater frequency of their occurrence in cases of brain injury, their greater severity, their presence in combination, and their appearance following injury justify us in regarding them as related to brain damage. It will not be possible to consider the features of given syndromes which follow the havoc wrought by specific etiologic agents. The uniqueness of such syndromes suggests a predilection on the part of specific agents for preferential destruction of particular central nervous tissue. This may partially explain such clinical observations as the much greater severity and poorer prognosis of the behavior disorders seen following the epidemic encephalitis of the 1920's (Bond and Smith, 1935) as compared, for instance, with posttraumatic syndromes (Blan, 1936). However, the present concern is with the common features of brain-damaged children (Bakwin and Bakwin, 1953; Kanner, 1948).

In the motor sphere, one of the most outstanding characteristics is *hyperkinesis.* Hyperkinetic children are constantly on the move, unable to sit still, fingering, touching, mouthing objects. They are frequently destructive, at times by design, at others inadvertently, because of impulsive and poorly controlled movements. Their overactivity thrusts them at all times into the center of the group so that they are typically described as attention-seeking. This aspect of their behavior has been vividly described, by Kahn and Cohen (1934) in the term "organic drivenness." These authors ascribe the constant activity to "a surplus of inner impulsions." Whatever its etiology, the hyperkinesis becomes a primary source of conflict with the social environment, which inevitably finds this behavior difficult to tolerate.

A parallel disorder may be seen in the sensory sphere. Brain-injured children tend to display *a very short attention span* and *marked distractibility.* They seem at the mercy of every extraneous sound or sight. Their interest flits from object to object in the environment, resting for only a very brief period on each. This makes for great difficulty in school where the task of learning becomes extraordinarily difficult, because of inability to exclude irrelevant sensory impressions. This factor must, of course, be borne in mind in evaluating the results of intelligence testing. Tasks requiring sustained application are often failed even when, not only each of the individual operations, but also the sequence of the ensemble, would be within the child's grasp except for his inability to stay with the problem until its completion. This inference can be substantiated when either good rapport with the examiner or the judicious use of drugs lowers the pitch of nervous activity.

A third feature that is often present is *marked lability of mood.* Frustration threshold is reduced. When this threshold is exceeded, outbursts of angry behavior result. Mercurial changes of mood from tears to laughter are sometimes seen. Unprovoked frenzies of rage, in which for no apparent reason the child strikes out blindly at all about him, often inflicting harm on others, can be noted. When these attacks terminate, the child may be bewildered by what he has done and genuinely apologetic for it—only to undergo another uncontrollable crisis not long afterward. The lack of adequate provocation and the disproportionate destructiveness suggest the escape of the lower, more primitive rage mechanisms from cortical control.

Antisocial behavior, in the form of lying, stealing, truancy, cruelty, and sexual offenses, may be a prominent feature. Often, though not always, the behavior seems inexplicable in terms of the customary determinants of similar behavior in non brain-damaged children. That is, the behavior lacks understandable motivation and may be discordant with the child's previous social adjustment. Furthermore, the individual episodes may turn on and off abruptly and may appear to be beyond the control of the remorseful child. The lack of adequate motivation, the abruptness, and the lack of integration with the child's total personality suggest an automaticity in the antisocial behavior. It seems to resemble in some respects the complex, highly organized and sustained episodes of dissociated behavior that may be observed in cases of psychomotor (temporal lobe) epilepsy (Livingston, 1954; Jasper, *et al.,* 1938; Gibbs, *et al.,* 1948).

There may be a greater or lesser degree of *intellectual deficit,* depending, in part, upon the extent and location of the damage. The intellectual loss, when present, has a tendency to be patchy in distribution, in that some abilities are more gravely impaired than others (Schaffer and Lazarus, 1952). Thus, the pattern of the test performance may be more indicative of brain damage than the aggregate score, which fails to distinguish between primary development failure and secondary deterioration, unless a preinjury control value is available. Tasks requiring abstract thought are particularly apt to be difficult for these children, whereas concrete problems may be successfully completed (Goldstein, 1954). In sorting tests, such children reveal uncommon responses and tend to group objects by unusual, accidental and insignificant details. They may exhibit perseveration in responses and often display meticulous and pedantic behavior as if they are desperately trying to keep a chaotic inner world in order by limiting outer stimuli (Strauss, 1944; Strauss and Werner, 1942). The distinction between figure and ground appears to be blurred, and tests which require the child to recognize figural outlines on a background of extraneous lines and shapes are useful in bringing this disability to the fore (Strauss and Lehtinen, 1950).

Finally, brain-injured children frequently display manifest *anxiety* (Bender, 1951). Slightly unfamiliar situations, tasks that tax their abilities or disapproving attitudes toward them precipitate sweating, tremor, tachycardia and hyperpnea. Anxiety, which may key the normal child to a higher pitch of adapative alertness, appears to have a destructive effect upon the functioning of the brain-damaged. The anxiety may mount to the proportions of panic—the so-called catastrophic reaction (Goldstein, 1954)—if it is not possible to remove the child from the tension-producing situation or to offer him meaningful emotional support in the midst of it. This constitutes an important problem in management. Learning obviously requires new and necessarily tension-producing experiences; at the same time, if the anxiety generated exceeds the low level of tolerance, learning is not only blocked, but function may be reduced to a lower level than before.

These, then, are some of the signs and symptoms that may be found in the presence of brain injury: hyperkinesis; distractibility; emotional lability; antisocial behavior; intellectual deterioration, particularly in abstract functions; and overwhelming anxiety. To what extent can one account for these clinical manifestations in terms of present conceptions of neurophysiological, psychological, and social function?

NEUROPHYSIOLOGIC CONSIDERATIONS

In evaluating the functional consequences of damage to central nervous system structure, it must first of all be stressed that the brain is a highly complex and delicately-integrated structure, the proper working of each of its parts dependent upon the proper working of most, if not all, of the others. This is by no means an unparalleled situation in biology, though it is the most exquisite example of it, for so much simpler a unit as the chromosome exhibits similar characteristics. Not only will the loss, or modification by mutation, of a given gene alter the expression of the remaining genes, but the mere shift in position of genes on the chromosome (that is, a redistribution of the *same* genic material) may result in alteration of the genotype. At the cortical level, this can be seen, for example, in the fact that isolation of a given area of the cortex, which is otherwise left intact, results in the appearance of "suppression bursts" in the electrocorticogram (Henry and Scoville, 1952) "which may be a factor in the mechanism underlying focal cortical seizures" (Echlin, *et al.*, 1952). This conception of the *interdependence of functional areas and their subordination to total integration* must be borne in mind if the error is to be avoided of regarding the injured brain as merely the same brain minus the functions specific to the area destroyed. This error rests upon the faulty analogy of the brain to a telephone switching center, for, in such a model, the loss of circuits affects only the functions they subserve and does not change the others, except insofar as the alternative routes are eliminated.

As Coghill (1929) so beautifully demonstrated, the development of function in the embryo proceeds, not in the pattern of building individual reflex arcs one upon the other until total function is achieved, but rather in a diametrically opposite fashion. From the first, the organism responds as a whole, wherever a stimulus is applied. Growth is associated with the progressive differentiation of more and more delicately selective and appropriate responses to specific stimuli, both by facilitation of appropriate channels and inhibition of maladaptive ones. Tissue loss, then, is followed by the reorganization of remaining structures on a more primitive level, still attempting to serve the same general biological purposes, but in a less effective manner. This is the conception of "dedifferentiation" in Goldstein's terminology (1939) or of "dissolution of function" in Hughling Jackson's (1932).

The integrative neurological basis of behavior is apparent from other considerations (Lashey, 1950). A square is seen as a square whether it is large or small, light or dark, in the center or at the periphery of the visual field. Thus, there is an equivalence of excitation patterns, irrespective of the anatomic field to which they are projected, a feature incompatible with the trunk-line theory of nervous function. Similarly, in the motor sphere, behavior is organized, not in terms of isolated pathways to particular muscles, but rather in terms of function. Damage to individual motor units will be followed by a more or less successful attempt to achieve the same goal by employing the available alternate muscle groups. *The neural organization of behavior is thus in terms of overall organismic needs.* This both allows us to understand the persistence of adequate function in the presence of tissue destruction in subordinate areas and prepares us to find that damage to the higher integrative mechanism has catastrophic effects for the individual.

A second important—and inadequately appreciated—principle of neural organization is the *vital role played by inhibition.* The simplest reflex pattern, the stretch reflex, which involves only two neurons in the arc between stimulus and response, has built into it simultaneous inhibition of antagonistic muscles (Lloyd, 1941 and 1946). Evocation of the flexion reflex will cause prompt and total cessation of activity in extensor muscles, just as effectively as if the motor nerve had been severed (Fulton, 1949). Inhibition is prominent at successively higher levels of the central nervous system through the brain stem (Magoun and Rhines, 1947) to the "suppressor areas" of the cortex, (Dusser de Barenne and McCullough, 1941; Dusser de Barenne, *et al.*, 1941; Hines, 1937) and to the "centrencephalic" area of Penfield and Jasper (Penfield, 1950; Penfield and Jasper, 1946; Hunter and Jasper, 1949), the excitation of which causes prompt suspension of all ongoing purposive behavior.

Attentiveness to a task, the prerequisite for efficient learning, is associated, first of all, with the sensitization of the specific receptor area by background subthreshold excitation (Lashley, 1950; Jasper, 1952). At the same time, however, there is a decrease in the input to other nonrelevant cortical areas. For example, in straining to hear a distant sound, we become more aware of auditory, and less aware of other, sensations. The decreased awareness may be "passive" (withdrawal of interest) or "active" (inhibition). The latter state of affairs may be observed when we "put out of mind" an unwelcome thought or sensation. Just such tasks are exceedingly difficult for a brain-injured child, who appears to have little ability to focus on stimulus A by excluding stimulus B. It is probable that this deficiency is in part responsible for the blurring of figure-ground discrimination, because the child attends as closely to irrelevant as he does to relevant stimuli.

In the motor sphere, the overactivity displayed by the brain-injured child can be understood as a consequence of his inability to inhibit, or even delay, upsurging inner impulses. Such children have great difficulty in postponing present gratification for future gain and it is this that provides one of the most vexing problems in management. When one considers that it is during the delay between a need and its satisfaction that the most complex human functions appear, one can understand the handicap that this disability constitutes for the brain-injured.

Learning, itself, is as dependent upon inhibition as it is upon facilitation. This can be illustrated by the dog who is conditioned to salivate at the sound of a bell. If a bell of a particular frequency is reinforced by the provision of food and a second bell not reinforced, the dog, after a number of trials, no longer responds to the second bell. What has happened is that the previous general response has become specific for a given frequency by inhibiting responses to other frequencies (Pavlov, 1928). Recent experiments with human subjects have given a clear demonstration of cortical inhibition during such conditional discrimination (Morrell and Ross, 1953).

The task of distinguishing between auditory cues is a limited example of the more general conceptual problem of distinguishing similarity from identity. Brain-injured children, given objects to sort, often classify them—as has been noted—on the basis of the possession of common but irrelevant details. On the other hand, they are unable to recognize general regularities because of their preoccupation with these same details (Strauss and Werner, 1942). These conceptual difficulties once again involve failure of the inhibitory mechanism to function properly. Indeed, it has been demonstrated that "patients with cerebral lesions show striking inability to learn conditioned responses, which normal subjects learn regularly and promptly" (Reese, et al., 1953).

A third and final general consideration is the so-called "mass action" effect of tissue loss. If, for a moment, the problem of localization is ignored there is some indication that the volume of tissue lost, almost without regard to its distribution, is an important determinant of the resulting functional impairment. This mass effect does not appear until after considerable destruction has occurred (Lashley, 1929). The basis for this phenomenon would appear to lie in the following considerations: With the exception of the strictly private sensory pathways from receptors to primary receiving areas in the cortex, most nervous pathways are routes employed in common by impulses originating from many different points. Each path, however, can be employed by only one pattern of impulses at any given time. Under normal operating conditions, the number of available paths is large enough so that the chance of getting a "busy signal" is small enough to permit efficient function. But if a significant number of these common routes are destroyed—or are usurped by pathological trains of impulses—messages originating elsewhere cannot be transmitted to their destinations. (The problem then becomes one that is familiar to communication engineering and can be analyzed statistically) (Weiner, 1948). We would expect, therefore, that the brain-damaged individual would be unable to handle complex tasks or handle multiple single tasks simultaneously, whereas the same problems, broken down and presented singly, could be carried through. It would further follow that the elimination of extraneous stimuli would also facilitate the successful completion of tasks.

These, then, are some of the general effects of brain lesions upon integration, inhibitory mechanisms, and transmission efficiency. Attention will now be turned to the more specific effects of lesions that impinge on the neural mechanisms underlying (a) alertness or wakefulness, (b) emotional responses, and (c) higher intellectual functions.

Fundamental contributions from Magoun's laboratories (Magoun, 1952; Starzl, et al., 1951; Lindsley, et al., 1950; Moruzzi and Magoun, 1949) report isolating an *"activating system" in the brain stem reticular formation which is necessary for the maintenance of the waking state.* Stimulation of this center rouses the sleeping animal and causes a simultaneous desynchronization of the EEG from sleep to waking patterns. The arousal reaction produced by strong sensory stimuli depends on collateral projections to this area, for it can be produced after the classical sensory pathways have been sectioned at the tegmental level, but it disappears after destruction of the activating system. The somnolent and akinetic states observed in human subjects with brain stem lesions can now be understood in terms of damage to this "wakefulness center" (Cairns, et al., 1941; Cairns, 1952; Myer and Hunter, 1952). A second ascending influence on the cortex has been described, the "diffuse thalamocortical projection system," whose function is to enhance or inhibit the elaboration of impulses, once they have reached their primary destination in the cortex (Jasper, 1949).

However, it is evident from mere introspection that wakefulness and alertness are not simply matters determined by subcortical elements, for the normal subject can voluntarily retard or induce sleep in himself and can choose to increase or decrease his attentiveness to peripheral stimuli. The neurophysiological substrate for this voluntary mechanism has recently been clarified by the work of French *et al.* (1955), who have demonstrated projections from ("suppressor") areas of the cerebral cortex extending precisely to the brain stem activating system. Cortical stimulation has now been shown to be capable of interrupting the sleep electroencephalogram and of causing arousal by way of cortico-reticulo-cortical pathways (Segundo, *et al.*, 1955).

Consciousness, from the neurophysiological standpoint, *is now seen to depend upon a reciprocal relation between cortex and brain stem that* (1) maintains the cortex on the *qui vive* for incoming stimuli and (2) differentially alerts it for particular stimuli. Brain stem lesions are apparently implicated in the disturbances in vigilance, alertness, and "set" displayed by brain-damaged patients. The wide variability among patients may result from the fact that the inhibitory and facilitatory mechanisms are so closely interwoven anatomically in this system that small shifts in the site of lesions can produce markedly different effects. An additional experimental finding of clinical significance is the great sensitivity of the brain stem mechanism to drugs (French, *et al.*, 1955). It opens the possibility of selectively altering the dysfunction of this mechanism without impairing cortical functions.

The *affective disturbances* associated with neurologic lesions are currently the focus of much interest (Langworthy, 1955). It has long been known that stimulation of the hypothalamus in animals produces the somatic and visceral components of rage reactions (Bard, 1928). It early became clear that this "sham rage" differs from the physiological state in that it is unmotivated, transient, and cannot be conditioned; it is clearly a reflection of the role of the hypothalamus as a co-ordinating center for the *expression* of rage, but does not justify the conclusion that it is the source of the emotion or the seat of the experience felt (Masserman, 1946). More recently, attention has centered upon the "visceral" or limbic brain, a higher coordinating center for emotional experience, though still not its final integrator (MacLean, 1952 and 1955). Lesions at specific sites within the closed circuit of the visceral brain have been reported variously to produce, depending on the site, hyperactivity, tameness, and changes in sexual behavior in experimental animals (Fulton, 1951; Klüver and Bucy, 1939; Pribram and Fulton, 1954). Stimulation within this anatomical complex can produce the behavioral concomitants of emotional reactions, but these are again unconnected with the conditions that normally incite them (Hess, 1954; Hess and Akert, 1955; Smith, 1945; Ingram, 1952).

Physiological emotional states clearly reflect the role of the neocortex, as the analyzer by which the subtle implications of external events take on meaning to the individual. Emotional experience cannot but be profoundly altered when lower centers are divorced from cortical control (Landis, 1952; Landis, *et al.*, 1950). The changes in emotional state frequently observed in brain-damaged children imply dysfunction in cortical-subcortical relations. The apparently unmotivated emotional outbursts which have been described in those children suggest the presence of a discharging pathological focus in the "visceral" brain. The patient cannot be held responsible for such behavior when it occurs; but it by no means follows that we are helpless to alter the reaction pattern. Reenforcement by means of repetition of the measures that are normally effective for producing inhibition of socially unacceptable behavior may serve to bring the autonomously discharging focus under at least partial cortical control.

When one turns to the problem of the intellectual deficits associated with brain damage, the key question that emerges is that of localization of function. Evolutionary considerations lead to the expectation that higher functions will be most significantly depressed following destruction of the frontal lobes, but clinical verification of this prediction has not been forthcoming (Hebb, 1945). There is, however, good evidence to support the view that the entire cerebral cortex plays the dominant role in intellectual activity. Battersby and his collaborators, studying patients with cerebral neoplasms, have demonstrated a significant loss in "abstract attitude" and figure-ground discriminations in patients with hemispheric lesions, as compared with patients with simple increase in cerebrospinal fluid pressure or cord tumors (Battersby, et al., 1953). They could not distinguish in their tests patients with frontal, from those with temporal or occipital tumors. Teuber (Teuber, 1952 and 1955; Teuber, et al., 1951) suggests that there is a continuum from specificity to "mass effects" in cerebral lesions. Citing his own work on patients with cerebral gunshot wounds, he describes, in occipital lesions, "specific deficits" (scotomata); "diffuse deficits," still confined to their particular system (depression in critical flicker fusion frequency); and "nonspecific deficits" (difficulties in figure-ground discriminations). The first two types of deficits are to be found only in patients with occipital lesions, but the last type appears whenever marked cortical damage is present. This modified notion of localization is in keeping with Harlow's studies on monkeys with experimental cortical lesions. He concludes that "although no specific intellectual function is localized in any single cortical area, the different cortical areas play markedly unequal roles in the mediation of our diverse intellectual processes" (Harlow, 1952).

The intellectual difficulties of the brain-injured child, then, can be related to the loss or malfunction of cortical tissue. In part the deficits may be specific; but the deterioration in "general functions" cannot be ascribed to particular cortical areas. This conclusion brings us back to the considerations which initiated this discussion of the relationship between structure and function. The *central nervous system* is not to be regarded as a network of telephone circuits but rather as *a complex of transient electrical fields whose reciprocal interrelation is the essence of normal function.* This comparison is the more applicable the higher the function is that is studied; and it leads to the anticipation that any distortion in the feltwork of the cortex will alter the social adaptability of the organism. But it is also true that distortions in the social setting, to which the child endeavors to adapt, will, in their turn, produce pathological changes in his behavior and its physiological substrate.

The production of experimental behavior disorders in animals with structurally intact nervous systems illustrates the dramatic effect of input pattern on brain function (Kempf, 1953; Finger, 1944). The multiplicity of methods for inducing experimental "neuroses" share the general feature that the animal is faced with tasks that it cannot solve. It may be required to make discriminations beyond its sensory capacities, or the cues given to it may be made so inconsistent that choice becomes meaningless. The result is an animal whose behavior becomes bizarrely maladaptive and whose visceral physiology is disordered. *Extrinsic influences have produced nervous dysfunction no less total than that which can be caused by intrinsic lesions.* But if this holds true for lower animals, it applies with manifold greater force to man whose *human* characteristics are *social* products. The brain-injured child, handicapped by his organic disorders, is by his handicap that much more subject to deleterious psychosocial influences, since his adaptive flexibility is restricted.

PSYCHOSOCIAL FACTORS

Thus, *knowledge of the relation between nervous structure and function,* however useful it may be, *cannot suffice for an understanding of the problems of the brain-damaged child.* Tissue destruction imposes limits which function cannot transcend, but the degree to which the patient realizes his remaining potential will depend upon the ways in which he is influenced by his environment, including the adequacy of the treatment available to him. It cannot be too strongly stressed that evaluation of the patient's behavior is impossible without psychiatric study of the setting in which it occurs and the meaning of that setting to the patient.

Precisely because of his handicap, the brain-damaged child is in need of emotional support, above and beyond the requirements normal for his age. Unlike the brain-injured adult, who may compensate in part by drawing upon previously developed skills and who may seek an environment that puts minimal stress on his inadequacies, the child has no such choice (Goldstein, 1954; Brown, 1952). He inevitably regresses to a lower functional level; yet he may be expected to face a school situation that makes no allowance for, and is unable to comprehend, his difficulties. His behavior, impulsive, demanding, often antisocial, is particularly apt to provoke rejection. Its very lability and unpredictability make it the more difficult to accept, for the fact that he does so well one day and is so difficult on another leads to the feeling that "he could do better if he would." His failure to do so is regarded as a sign of basic intransigence. An impatient attitude and unjustified blame by the teacher increase the child's anxiety and result both in more disturbed behavior and in less ability to learn. Unless therapeutic intervention occurs, this self-perpetuating cycle is likely to end only with expulsion from school or persistent truancy.

The important role of social factors in governing the manifest behavior of the brain-damaged child is nowhere more clearly evident than at home. The same youngster who is a holy terror in an unsympathetic, rigid, and rejecting home may be transmuted into a friendly and reasonably competent child in a warm, supportive foster home or residential school. In other cases, the feelings induced in parents by their child's affliction may lead to smothering overprotectiveness. The child learns little or no self-sufficiency, because things are done for him before he has a chance to try them on his own. His parents are unable to exert effective and consistent discipline. This, coupled with the organically-induced difficulty in establishing internal controls, keeps the patient perpetually infantilized and prone to tantrums, behavior that may be mistakenly regarded as intrinsic to his disease.

Parental attitudes will help determine the child's own attitude toward his illness. The extent and severity of the problem he faces require that a high level of motivation be sustained if treatment is to achieve its full goals. Yet one sees children, whose organic handicaps are not too great, but who are crushed and defeated by parental perfectionism and who feel that nothing can help them. With such children, the primary task of therapy is to win them over into a relationship of trust and beginning hopefulness, for it is only then that they are willing to try. The child who is strong enough to rebel may release his resentment against unreasonable expectations in antisocial channels; his surface bravado is accompanied by a cynical and fatalistic outlook toward the future. Other children may wallow in self-pity, encouraged by an attitude at home that continually curses the fate that selected them as its victims. In all these situations, *environmental pathology becomes the crucial determinant of the disturbances in behavior.*

DIAGNOSIS

From these considerations it should be evident that a knowledge of the neuro- and psychodynamics of brain damage in children carries important consequences for treatment. It becomes, therefore, all the more important that the clinician be sensitive to the diagnosis. It is an unfortunate, and perhaps somewhat unavoidable, consequence of the rapid expansion of interest in psychogenic behavior disorders that there is a growing tendency to ascribe all difficult behavior to purely psychological factors, often even in the presence of unequivocal evidence of brain injury. Children with cerebral palsy, postencephalitic and postmeningitic states, lead enecphalopathy, and even brain tumors have been appearing at the Harriet Lane Home Clinic (Baltimore) in increasing numbers with the label "emotional block" pinned to them by previous examiners. Differential diagnosis is no mere acadamic issue; the successful resolution of the problem—and in some cases the preservation of the patient's life—depends on diagnostic accuracy.

Correct diagnosis is suggested, in the first instance, by a history of behavior that on careful clinical psychiatric examinations exhibits the characteristics associated with brain damage. In a high percentage of such cases, the taking of a detailed medical history will reveal the presence of etiologic factors. Neurological examination is likely to uncover confirmatory signs precisely in proportion to its detail and refinement. It cannot consist merely of a cursory survey of reflexes but must assess complex motor and sensory activity (Schilder, 1937). Marked "scatter" on standard intelligence tests suggests an organic pattern though, as Strauss and Lehtinen point out, "with few exceptions there does not exist at this moment a pattern or type of response characteristic and specific for the brain-injured child on standardized test of intelligence, academic achievement, or visuomotor performance" (1950). This test must be supplemented by special psychological tests of abstractive and synthetic abilities (Strauss and Werner, 1942; Strauss and Lehtinen, 1950; Bender, 1940). In addition, Rorschach responses may reveal signs of organicity (Fisher, et al., 1955). The EEG, though usually nonspecific for etiology, may give definite evidence of intracranial pathology (Cohn, 1949). In special cases, pneumoencephalography or arteriography may be indicated.

There is obviously a spectrum of cases that extends from those of unquestionable organic etiology to those in which final evaluation must rest upon clinical judgment. But, in all cases, the initial survey must include a thorough-going evaluation of psychodynamic factors in the family unit, for these are not only of importance in assessing the cause of behavior but may actually be the decisive factors in determining outcome. The aim is not only to interrupt pathological trends that may interfere with therapeutic efforts, but also to capitalize upon healthy features of family life that may facilitate therapeutic efforts.

PRINCIPLES OF TREATMENT

With the theoretical considerations previously outlined as a basis, one might now appropriately turn to the general principles of treatment, for the physician's ultimate concern is not with purely contemplative knowledge, but rather with an amelioration of the patient's lot in life.

If the first fundamental notion is borne in mind that *the organism functions as a totality*, it should follow that *particular aspects of treatment must always be seen in the perspective of overall function*. On the motor level, this implies that training should be organized and presented in terms of meaningful tasks. For example, the patient who cannot move his triceps on request may be able to employ this muscle in the act of reaching for a toy or candy. Similarly, an intellectual task that can be related to the child's everyday world is more likely to be attempted than one that he sees as an academic exercise. Furthermore, as Goldstein has stressed, the subjective experience of failure or success will have an important bearing on perform-ance (1954). The anxiety evoked by a difficult task may generalize into panic which renders impossible the solution of problems that are easily within the patient's grasp. A well-regulated, familiar classroom and ordered activities will help minimize extrinsic anxiety. Most important of all, to quote Strauss and Lehtinen, "the relation of the teacher to the brain-injured child is of the greatest influence on the child's behavior and on success in retraining" (1950). The teacher must have an intimate knowledge of the particular psychological set of each patient so that he may choose tasks that will cause the patient to do what he has not done before—and yet tasks that will not overburden his capacities.

The disability in inhibitory function implies a need to supply controls from without. *A routine, ordered existence and consistent discipline are primary virtues.* It cannot be expected of the child that he will be able to constrain his impulsiveness, at least at first, for more than brief periods, so that sustained concentration should be demanded for only brief, but gradu-ally extended, intervals. The social pressure exerted by activities in small groups enchances the child's control of his behavior. It should be noted that this recommendation for firm and consistent discipline in organic behavior disorders runs contrary to the usual approach in psychogenic problems. The writer has seen a number of dismaying examples of brain-injured children, misdiagnosed as "emotional block," whose parents were advised to be per-missive, with disastrous consequences for the child and for the family.

Both the inhibitory dysfunction and the reduction in the number of available channels for impulse transmission have as their therapeutic corol-lary the principle that *the number of stimuli presented to the patient at any one time should be restricted.* Extraneous and distracting influences should be reduced by subduing classroom decorations, and even the teacher's cloth-ing. Furthermore, the more successful one can be, through psychotherapy, in ridding the patient of emotional preoccupations that stem from feelings of inadequacy, sense of rejection, and so on, the more of his nervous struc-ture and energy will be available for growth and learning.

The fluctuations in vigilance and alertness that characterize the brain-injured are, of course, also responsive to general feelings of comfort and security. But there is some evidence that these fluctuations can be modified by pharmacological therapy. The well-known paradoxical responsiveness of brain-damaged children to sedative and stimulant drugs requires a careful search for the proper agent in each case (Lindsley and Henry, 1942). Re-cent experience with Rauwolfia preparations suggests that they may play a useful role. But, whatever the agents of choice, the judicious use of drugs is an important part of the treatment program.

The emotional disorders, whether or not they have organic roots, also have psychogenic ones, and attention to the family setting and the emo-tional atmosphere of the classroom can often produce marked changes in behavior patterns. Particularly in those instances that suggest a discharging focus at a subcortical level, pharmacotherapy should be employed. But even in these cases, since it is usually correct to assume that the connection to the cortex is not entirely severed, the same principles that guide normal development in other children will be applicable here, except that greater reinforcement will be necessary. The wanted child, supported through his difficult moments and exposed to as little unnecessary frustration as possible, will exhibit a minimum of outbursts.

With regard to the intellectual limitations of the child, the primary requirements are the assessment of his potential and the adjustment of expectations for him to reasonable levels. This requires the combined understanding of the physician, the teacher, and, above all, the parents. The educational program must be designed to meet the conceptual difficulties of brain-injured children (Strauss, 1952).

If any one point in treatment should be stressed, it is the need for acceptance of the brain-injured child, who needs more, and not less, love, because of his illness. The task for his parents is not an easy one. They may have to give up fond hopes that were realizable before the child's affliction occurred. They need help in dealing with the feelings aroused in them by his disease and his behavior. A well-designed program of treatment requires that a good deal of effort be directed at the parents, who need support—yes, and acceptance—no less than the child. Parent groups with the opportunity for ventilation, mutual support, and self-help are an extremely useful part of the therapy of the brain-injured child.

SUMMARY

The brain is an instrument of enormous subtlety and complexity that mediates the relationship between the child and his world. Damage to its structure has profound implications for all levels of psychobiological function. Treatment of the disorders associated with brain injury, therefore, requires attention to biological, psychological and social factors and is a challenge to the psychiatrist as a medical specialist. It serves to emphasize his need to comprehend the roots of behavior in the broadest sense if he is to discharge his function adequately. The reward he can hope to achieve is the restoration of a child to his full human rights.

References

Bakwin, H., and Bakwin, R. M., *Clinical management of behavior disorder in children* (Philadelphia: Saunders, 1953), pp. 433-444.
Bard, P., A diencephalic mechanism for the expression of rage with special reference to the sympathetic nervous system, *Am. J. Physiol.*, 1928, 84, 490-513.
Battersby, W. S., Krieger, H. P., Pollack, M., and Bender, M. B., Figureground discriminations and the "abstract attitude" in patients with cerebral neoplasms, *Arch. Neurol. Psychiat.*, 1953, 70, 703-712.

Bender, L., The Goodenough Test (drawing a man) in chronic encephalitis in children, *J.N.M.D.*, 1940, 91, 277-286.

Bender, L., The psychological treatment of the brain-damaged child, *Quart. J. Child Behav.*, 1951, 3, 123-132.

Blan, A., Mental changes following head trauma in children, *Arch. Neurol. Psychiat.*, 1936, 35, 723-769.

Bond, E. D., and Smith, L. H., Post-encephalitic behavior disorders: A ten year review of the Franklin School, *Am. J. Psychiat.*, 1935, 92, 17-31.

Brown, J. R., Management of patients with brain damage, *Neurology*, 1952, 2, 273-283.

Cairns, H., Disturbances of consciousness with lesions of the brain stem and diencephalon, *Brain*, 1952, 75, 109-146.

Cairns, H., Oldfield, R. C., Pennybacker, J. B., and Whitteridge, D., Akinetic mutism with an epidermoid cyst of the third ventricle, *Brain*, 1941, 64, 273-290.

Coghill, G. E., *Anatomy and the problem of behavior* (London: Cambridge University Press, 1929).

Cohn, R., *Clinical electroencephalography* (New York: McGraw-Hill, 1949).

Dusser de Barenne, J. G., Garol, H. W., and McCulloch, W. S., Functional organization of sensory and adjacent cortex of the monkey, *J. Neurophysiol.*, 1941, 4, 324-330.

Dusser de Barenne, J. G., and McCulloch, W. S., Suppression of motor responses obtained from area 4 by stimulation of area 4-S, *J. Neurophysiol.*, 1941, 4, 313-323.

Echlin, F. A., Arnett, V., and Zoll, J., Paroxysmal high voltage discharges from isolated or partially isolated human and animal cerebral cortex, *EEG. Clin. Neurophysiol.*, 1952, 4, 147-164.

Eisenberg, L., Treatment of the emotionally disturbed preadolescent child, *Proc. Child Res. Clin. Woods Schools*, 1953, 35, 30-41.

Finger, F. W., Experimental behavior disorders in the rat. In J. McV. Hunt, (Editor), *Personality and the behavior disorders*, Vol. I (New York: Ronald, 1944), pp. 413-430.

Fisher, J., Gonda, T. A., and Little, K. B., The Rorschach and central nervous system pathology: A cross-validation study, *Am. J. Psychiat.*, 1955, 111, 487-492.

French, J. D., Hernandez-Peon, R., and Livingston, R. B., Projections from cortex to cephalic brain stem (reticular formation) in monkey, *J. Neurophysiol.*, 1955, 18, 74-95.

Fulton, J. F., *Physiology of the nervous system*, 3rd Edition (New York: Oxford University Press, 1949), pp. 93-104.

Fulton, J. F., *Frontal lobotomy and affective behavior* (New York: Norton, 1951).

Gibbs, E. L., Gibbs, F. A., and Fuster, B., Psychomotor epilepsy, *Arch. Neurol. Psychiat.*, 1948, 60, 331-339.

Goldstein, K., *The Organism* (New York: American Book, 1939), pp. 131-156.

Goldstein, K., The brain-injured child. In H. Michal-Smith, (Editor) *Pediatric problems in clinic practice* (New York: Grune & Stratton, 1954), pp. 97-120.

Harlow, H. F., *Functional organization of the brain in relation to mentation and behavior in the biology of mental health and disease* (New York: Hoeber-Harper, 1952), pp. 244-256.

Hebb, D. O., Man's lobes: Critcal review of methods in analysis of cerebral function, *Arch. Neurol. Psychiat.*, 1945, 54, 10-24.

Henry, C. E., and Scoville, W. B., Suppression burst activity from isolated cerebral cortex in man, *EEG Clin. Neurophysiol.*, 1952, 4, 1-22.

Hess, W. R., *Diencephalon: Autonomic and extrapyramidal functions* (New York: Grune & Stratton, 1954).

Hess, W. R., and Akert, K., Experimental data on role of hypothalamus in mechanism of emotional behavior, *Arch. Neurol. Psychiat.*, 1955, 73, 127-129.

Hines, M., The "motor" cortex, *Bull. Johns Hop. Hosp.*, 1937, 40, 313-336.

Hunter, J., and Jasper, H. H., Effects of thalamic stimulation in unanaesthetized animals, *EEG Clin. Neurophysiol.*, 1949, 1, 305-324.

Ingram, W. R., Brain stem mechanisms in behavior, *EEG Clin. Neurophysiol.*, 1952, 4, 397-406.

Jackson, J. H., *Selected writings* edited by J. Taylor, vol. II (London: Holder & Stoughton, 1932), pp. 3-118.

Jasper, H. H., Diffuse projection systems: The integrative action of the thalamic reticular system, *EEG Clin. Neurophysiol.*, 1949, 1, 405-420.

Jasper, H. H., Electrical activity and mechanisms of cerebral integration. In *The biology of mental health and disease* (New York: Hoeber-Harper, 1952), pp. 226-240.

Jasper, H. H., Solomon, P., and Bradley, C., Electroencephalographic analyses of behavior problem children, *Am. J. Psychiat.*, 1938, 95, 641-658.

Kahn, E., and Cohen, L. H., Organic drivenness: A brain stem syndrome and an experience. *N. E. J. Med.*, 1934, 210, 748-756.

Kanner, L., *Child psychiatry*, 2nd Edition (Springfield, Illinois: Charles C Thomas, 1948), pp. 263-306.

Kempf, E. (Editor), Comparative conditioned neuroses, *Ann. N.Y. Acad. Sci.*, 1953, 56, 141-380.

Klüver, H., and Bucy, P. C., Preliminary analysis of functions of the temporal lobes in monkeys, *Arch. Neurol. Psychiat.*, 1939, 42, 979-1000.

Landis, C., Zubin, J., and Mettler, F. A., The functions of the human frontal lobe, *J. Psychol.*, 1950, 30, 123-138.

Landis, C., The frontal lobes and anguish: A new formulation of an old problem, *J.N.M.D.*, 1952, 115, 203-214.

Langworthy, O. R., Newer concepts of the central control of emotions: A review, *Am. J. Psychiat.*, 1955, 111, 481-486.

Lashley, K. S., *Brain mechanisms and intelligence: A quantitative study of injuries to the brain* (Chicago: University of Chicago Press, 1929).

Lashley, K. S., Functional interpretation of anatomic patterns, *Res. Publ. A.R. N.M.D.*, 1950, 30, 529-547.

Lindsley, D., and Henry, C. E., The effects of drugs on behavior and the EEG of children with behavior disorders, *Psychosom. Med.*, 1942, 4, 140-149.

Lindsley, D., Schreiner, L. H., Knowles, W. B., and Magoun, H. W., Behavioral and EEG changes following chronic brain stem lesions in the cat, *EEG Clin. Neurophysiol.*, 1950, 2, 483-498.

Livingston, S., *The diagnosis and treatment of convulsive disorders in children* (Springfield, Illinois: Charles C Thomas, 1954), pp. 111-113.

Lloyd, D. P. C., A direct central inhibitory action of dromically conducted impulses, *J. Neurophysiol.*, 1941, 4, 184-190.

Lloyd, D. P. C., Integrative pattern of excitation and inhibition in two-neuron reflex arcs, *J. Neurophysiol.*, 1946, 9, 439-444.

MacLean, P. D., Some psychiatric implications of physiological studies on frontotemporal portions of limbic system (visceral brain), *EEG Clin. Neurophysiol.*, 1952, 4, 407-418.

MacLean, P. D., The limbic system (visceral brain) and emotional behavior, *Arch. Neurol. Psychiat.*, 1955, 73, 130-134.

Magoun, H. W., An ascending reticular activating system in the brain stem, *Arch. Neurol. Psychiat.*, 1952, 67, 145-154.

Magoun, H. W., and Rhines, R., *Spasticity: The stretch reflex and the extrapyramidal systems* (Springfield, Illinois: Charles C Thomas, 1947).

Masserman, J. H., *Principles of dynamic psychiatry* (Philadelphia: Saunders, 1946), pp. 101-103.

Morrell, F., and Ross, M. H., Central inhibition in cortical conditioned reflexes, *Arch. Neurol. Psychiat.*, 1953, 70, 611-616.

Moruzzi, G., and Magoun, H. W., Brain stem reticular formation and activation of the EEG, *EEG Clin. Neurophysiol.*, 1949, 1, 445-473.

Myer, J. S., and Hunter, J., Behavior deficits following diencephalic lesions, *Neurology*, 1952, 2, 112-129.

Pavlov, I. P., *Lectures on conditioned reflexes*, translated by W. H. Gantt. (New York: International Publishers, 1928), pp. 205-212.

Penfield, W., Epileptic automatisms and the centrencephalic integrating system, *Res. Publ. A.R.N.M.D.*, 1950, 30, 513-528.

Penfield, W., and Jasper, H. H., Highest level seizures. *Res. Publ. A.R.N.M.D.*, 1946, 26, 252-271.

Pribram, K. H., and Fulton, J. F., An experimental critique of the effects of anterior cingulate ablation in monkey brain, *Brain*, 1954, 77, 34-44.

Reese, W. G., Doss, R., and Gantt, W. H., Autonomic responses in differential diagnosis of organic and psychogenic psychosis, *Arch. Neurol. Psychiat.*, 1953, 70, 778-793.

Schilder, P., The psychological implications of motor development in children, *Proc. Child Res. Clin. Woods Schools*, 1937, 4, 38-59.

Segundo, J. P., Naguet, R., and Buser, P., Effects of cortical stimulation on electrocortical activity in monkeys, *J. Neurophysiol.*, 1955, 18, 236-245.

Shaffer, G. W., and Lazarus, R. S., *Fundamental concepts in clinical psychology* (New York: McGraw-Hill, 1952), pp. 136-161.

Smith, W. K., The functional significance of the rostral cingular cortex as revealed by its responses to electrical excitation, *J. Neurophysiol.*, 1945, 8, 241-255.

Starzl, T. E., Taylor, C. W., and Magoun, H. W., Collateral afferent excitation of reticular formation of brain stem, *J. Neurophysiol.*, 1951, 14, 479-496.

Strauss, A. A., Ways of thinking in brain-crippled deficient children, *Am. J. Psychiat.*, 1944, 100, 639-647.

Strauss, A. A., The education of the brain-injured child, *Am. J. ment. Def.*, 1952, 56, 712-718.

Strauss, A. A., and Lehtinen, L., *Psychopathology and education of the brain-injured child* (New York: Grune & Stratton, 1950).

Strauss, A. A., and Werner, H., Disorders of conceptual thinking in the brain-injured child, *J.N.M.D.*, 1942, 96, 153-172.

Teuber, H.-L., Some observations on the organization of higher functions after penetrating brain injury in man. In *The Biology of mental health and disease* (New York: Hoeber-Harper, 1952), pp. 259-262.

Teuber, H.-L., Patterns of cerebral localization. Paper presented at Psychology Colloquium, Johns Hopkins University, March 4, 1955.

Teuber, H.-L., Battersby, W. S., and Bender, M. B., The performance of complex visual tasks after cerebral lesions, *J.N.M.D.*, 1951, 114, 413-429.

Wiener, N. S., *Cybernetics* (New York: Wiley, 1948), pp. 168-180.

17 MEDICAL ASPECTS OF READING
FAILURES IN INTELLIGENT CHILDREN

George E. Park

American educators are becoming increasingly concerned about children who fail in reading. An awareness of the dilemma should stimulate other branches of science, particularly psychology and medicine, to help determine and understand more fully the reasons for the great number of children and adults with reading disabilities. Also, parents must realize the roles they play in this situation. It is through such understanding and multidiscipline cooperation that new ways of dealing with the problem will be developed.

The term dyslexia defines a syndrome which is characterized by an inability to learn to read properly even though the individual's intelligence is normal or superior. Dyslexia cannot be considered as a simple reading disability. There are many ramifications extending into the physical, psychological, and social fields as well. Abnormal factors which are associated with dyslexia are functional, and correctible in approximately 85 percent of the cases, in contradistinction to alexia, which is due to brain injury or lack of intelligence.

DEVELOPMENTAL CONSIDERATIONS

In the entire syndrome one must investigate also the development of personality and emotional maturation and stability, the hereditary traits, and especially the environment in which the child lives. Occasionally dyslexia is found in successive generations of the child's ancestors. This should not be interpreted as an inherited trait, for it is likely that the characteristic environment has been experienced from one generation to the other. Before we ascribe dyslexia to genetic origin per se it is necessary to eliminate all

Reprinted from *Sight Saving Review*, Vol. 29, No. 4 (Winter, 1959), pp. 213-218. By permission of the author and publisher.

peripheral and functional disorders. There is nevertheless a possibility that heredity may occasionally contribute circumstances that predispose to dyslexia. Acceptance of the hereditary concept would be disastrous, for then the parents, teachers and particularly the child would consider the condition hopeless and treatment would be doomed to failure.

Caution should be a paramount consideration in the administration and interpretation of a psychological test. Accepting or implying that because children's IQ's have been reported as such without knowing the qualifications of the examiner is fraught with danger. Experience has shown that if the abilities of a child are rated too high or too low, teachers, parents and especially the child adopt compensatory methods with disastrous effects. Intelligence is not an innately acquired static quotient. It is a dynamic progression influenced by past experiences, motivations and the psychophysiologic needs and stimulations of the individual at any particular time. Actually the psychological determination of the IQ is an estimate of the individual's potential. It is the differential between the potential and the achievement of the dyslexic child which we are now considering.

Reading is a complex achievement. The more intelligent a person is, and the more perceptual experience he has encountered, the more quickly he should learn from abstractions and symbols. The degree to which normal or abnormal functions influence the process of learning as a whole depends upon the individual's ability to maintain homeostasis in response to the psychophysiological stimuli that are imposed upon him. The degree of this homeostasic stability and adaptation depends on the degree of normality in all the diverse functions that are involved in the reading processes, including the central perceptual and conceptual processes as well as the entire peripheral ocular mechanism in all its complexity.

MEDICAL FACTORS

Only brief mention can be made here of some medical factors which we have found associated with dyslexia. First let it be understood that there are many complexly interrelated determinates which make it hazardous to assign a single causative factor to reading disability. All possible factors are involved—physical, psychological, and educational. These do not act separately but as an integral in an environmental field to which, in turn, the individual reacts as a whole.

It is singular that the ratio of failures in reading is approximately four times as many boys as girls. What are some of the factors which may influence such an uneven distribution of cases? This question cannot be answered with finality but it is ripe for speculation. One could suspect an hormonal connection. Furthermore, apparently boys are more aggressive and rebellious than girls. When children enter school reading and learning can become a sublimation of the aggressive drive; and should this sublimation become thwarted, it is possible that dyslexia becomes a corollary.

INFLUENCE OF ENDOCRINES

As reviewed by Ivy and Krasno it is generally conceded that the endocrines, especially the thyroid gland, are influences in the maintenance of the intellectual functions and normal personality.

One of the most remarkable facts which experimental and clinical research determines in humans is that the optimum effects of the thyroid functions or medication upon mental growth occur before eleven or twelve years of age, and that administration of thyroid extract is almost futile after that age as far as mental growth is concerned. On the other hand, individuals who develop a hypothyroid condition subsequent to the full growth and maturation of their nervous systems do not manifest a true mental deficiency although they may become dull and physically sluggish, whereas the hyperthyroid is irritable, jumpy and may be emotionally unstable. Adequate medication may change these states and make the hypothyroid patient more responsive and the hyperthyroid less reactive.

In our study 27 percent of the children had hypothyroidism and four percent had hyperthyroidism, to a degree where therapeutic intervention was indicated. A few showed definite pituitary imbalances.

REACTION TO STIMULI

Reflexes are suggestive of the status of the nerve reactions to stimuli. As ideas and learning are basically the reaction to perceptual experiences arising from sensations, both motor and sensory, abnormal reflexes influence the individual's ability to respond normally to sensations.

A source of confusion is the lack of awareness of our abstractions and projective processes. As an example, use can be made of a stereoscope with a white card viewed by one eye and a black area before the other eye. These are superimposed by fusion. The resulting color is interpreted as silvery gray. In identifying one level of abstraction from another the term silvery gray does not refer to the color on the card, as is so often naïvely assumed. Instead, it refers to the abstract determined by the individual's nervous system. In our cases 15 percent had sluggish reflexes, while 11 percent had exaggerated reflexes. Jerking of head, twitching of face or other choreic symptoms were present in six percent.

ELECTROENCEPHALOGRAM RESULTS

A preliminary analysis of the EEG's seems to indicate a tendency toward certain changes, but precise opinions have not been formed. However, approximately 50 percent of the children had borderline or mildly abnormal EEG records, none severely abnormal. The most commonly observed borderline record was the unusually low build-up of voltage and slow waves during hyperventilation. Although this occasionally occurs in normal children, it occurred in approximately 30 percent of dyslexic children. This is an observation which we shall pursue further. Some mild electrical alterations from normal rate or amplitude occurred in the parietal lobe of the brain in approximately 20 percent of these children. However, once again care must be exercised in the interpretation of these data since parietal asymmetries can occur in normal children.

BONE MATURATION

Using as a criterion the carpal bone growth as standardized by Todd, eight percent of the dyslexic children show retardation in the chronological physical maturation. Some authorities believe that reading failures are due to this slow process. In a limited number of cases this may be the predisposing etiology, associated with other factors.

BLOOD CONDITION

A comparison was made of the blood counts of 200 dyslexic children with the standardized values established by Albritton. By correlating the number of circulating blood cells per cubic millimeter it was found that the erythrocytes were equal in the dyslexic and standardized values. In the differential leukocyte count there was a variance. The number of circulating lymphocytes corresponded with the standardized values, but there was a 27 percent lowering of the normal differential for neutrophils. We are now carrying on a control study of this aberration to eliminate any possibility of an artefact.

EMOTIONAL FACTORS

The influence of a disturbance of interpersonal home and school relationships must be a primary concern of any person involved with the care of a child with reading failures. The incidence of enuresis in our patients has been 18 percent, i.e., they gave a history of having had it, or it was still persistent.

When we consider that emotional factors are implicated as the outstanding cause of this condition, and that such factors are related to the stability or instability of parental figures and home environment we must not overlook them, whether or not the child has enuresis. It should be stated that enuresis is not felt to be a symptom of reading difficulty nor is reading difficulty secondary to enuresis. In many instances they are both symptoms of an emotional conflict which involves interpersonal relations with parents and siblings. The child may be reacting unconsciously to overstrictness, or to inconsistent firmness in the family situation. It has been interesting to observe the correlation between the problem of enuresis and the neuropathic features of nail biting, thumb sucking, feeding difficulties and temper tantrums.

A fear of loss of parental love develops in the child when it fails to measure up to the parents' expectations. That fear is often reflected in overcompensation to be a "good" child and please its parents while awake. However, when the child goes to sleep, confused feelings are released in night terrors, bad dreams, and enuresis. As this condition is usually a corollary to other symptoms of personality disturbances, which are present almost without exception in dyslexic children, it is well to look for excessive goals and standards, undue amount of criticism, or unfavorable competition. The home should be a place of security, serenity, encouragement, and affection. Ideally, from the child's vantage point, the parents must personify all things that are good and wholesome.

HEARING AND SPEECH

Hearing is such an essential factor in language function that a detailed examination is most important. Acute otitis media is usually the cause for diminution of hearing. This may accompany an acute or chronic infection of the nasopharynx as evidenced by hyperplasia and inflammation of the tonsils, adenoids, turbinates or hypertrophied lymphatic nodules on the posterior pharyngeal wall. Furthermore, as evidence of the severity of the early diseases of childhood which our patients had experienced, 14 percent gave a history of having had abscessed ears.

If a child cannot hear properly the influence upon spelling achievement is particularly noticeable, for he misinterprets oral instruction and seems to become willfully heedless. Such a child may appear stubborn, indifferent, "dumb." He eventually becomes an extreme introvert as he withdraws from social contacts. It is necessary that communications and directions, given by parents and teachers to a child with this handicap, be heard and understood. Care should be taken to seat him to best advantage in the schoolroom.

Whereas vocalization is the means by which most of our ideas and instructions are expressed, and since it is so closely related to hearing, one must consider the physical development and flexibility of the vocal organs and the ability to coordinate and control them during the production of speech sounds. Nine percent of our series were late in learning to talk. Many children who are unstable emotionally show a blocking when required to read either silently or orally. Some of our cases have become so emotionally upset and frustrated that their voices were tremulous, their faces pale and nervous, with visible twitching. It is quite evident that no one, however expert, could teach a child in that state of homeostasis.

VISUAL FUNCTION

It is customary to accept the concept that reading is simply seeing words, phrases, and sentences. If it were as simple as that the visual processes would be practically the predominant factor in dyslexia. When a discussion of this problem is begun with most people they remark that "it must be due to eye trouble." Actually only 19 percent of our cases need spectacles. We have removed many pairs of glasses which had been prescribed empirically to aid the patient with his reading. Such prescription should be frowned upon when glasses are not necessary, for some of the children had a high degree of exophoria which was aggravated by the convex lens.

Fifteen years ago the number of investigations and publications dealing with the controversial question of dominance, eyedness, handedness, and footedness was considerably greater than today. In our experience these functions are not significantly related to reading ability.

Weak duction reserve, coincident with convergent insufficiency or accompanying accommodative or convergent spasm, has been present in many patients, causing undue fatigue.

Dyslexia cases were inferior in their ocular function to that of the norms where rate of reading, number of fixations, regressions and span of recognition were considered.

Other erroneous ideas about causes of reading difficulties relate to strephosymbolia and mirror vision. These are apparently self-imposed psychological processes, maybe accidental at first, but with definite significance when analyzed in relation to the aspirations and motives of the child. He may use them as a means of getting attention, or as an escape, believing that if other people think he has a rare malady he will not be required to learn to read.

In our experience we have found no cases of typical mirror reading. Several of the children were using these mental gymnastics when we first saw them. One began to write his name and 3's, 5's and 7's backwards. A presumed authority had spent two hours explaining to the mother how the function of the right hemisphere of her son's brain had been transplanted to the left hemisphere, and vice versa. Naturally, the mother was extremely apprehensive. Our concern was to find the reasons why the boy was using this excuse and technique for not learning in school. We did. He gained one year in reading within six months. Why not? He had an IQ of 136. He also stopped his monkey business.

Another boy had used this type of mental gymnastics in school for five years. Even on his first visit to the Institute he drew a picture of a cat standing on its head on a broomstick. When asked why he had drawn the picture thusly his answer was: "I wanted to show the cat with his feet on the broom handle. Something happens to my brain that no one can explain so I don't know why the feet aren't on the broom handle." He also described seeing things upside down in past years, saying, "I would see spots before my eyes and these would be upside down." He cleared up also with careful educational management.

Now, in brief, it would be erroneous to take the peripheral ocular mechanism habits as the standard and the visual acuity as the determinant of cerebral action or perceptual processes. It is also inconclusive to take mental processes as the sole factor influencing the modus operandi of peripheral ocular performance. Since the roles are probably interchangeable, it would be difficult to determine which acts as the originator and which the compensator. All available faculties plus the desire to achieve the universal concept are probably integrated in the processes of learning.

The final goal in attacking reading difficulty is to get the child to read for himself, for pleasure.

~III~

DIAGNOSING LEARNING DISORDERS

INTRODUCTION

D IAGNOSTIC PROCEDURES may have many purposes, but the ultimate
purpose of educational diagnosis is to determine what specific
learning problems exist. Diagnostic reports are expected to indicate what can be done to reduce or remove both the observed symptoms
(disabilities) and the underlying causes (disorders) of learning problems.
Educational diagnoses are complex. Symptoms and causes are often confused. Theories and facts do not always agree. In many cases, diagnostic
information merely discloses what is not wrong without clarifying what is
wrong.

Educators are unnecessarily apologetic about treating symptoms. It is
pointed out that medical specialists diagnose illness and prescribe treatment on the basis of etiology. However, a clear cut diagnosis is not always
possible; therefore doctors treat symptoms (stop running noses) while continuing to search for ultimate causes (bacteria, viruses, etc.).

In many cases, learning problems and psychological deviations are related to pathology within the nervous system. However, behaviors must
often be modified while exact causes remain a matter of conjecture. The
educator must be aware of the complex diagnostic task which specialists
have and must not expect all information to have educational relevance.
On the other hand, the educator must not delay remediation while awaiting
the perfect diagnosis.

ETIOLOGICAL DIAGNOSIS AND EDUCATION

Attempts to identify the psychological correlates of neuropathology are
rewarding but often not specific to reading, writing, and arithmetic teaching. However, the educator who ignores etiological diagnoses ignores an
opportunity to make a crucial contribution—establishing the successful
teaching procedures that are correlates of neuropathology.

The disclosure of a neuropathological condition as the cause of a specific learning problem may follow a thorough diagnosis. Having identified the cause doesn't necessarily lead one to the removal of the effects, however. Consider the following categories of neuropathology, all of which produce different psychological consequences and behaviors (Burgemeister, 1962):

(1) Developmental defects   (6) Metabolic disease
(2) Infections   (7) Diseases caused by toxins
(3) Vascular lesions   (8) Demyelinating diseases
(4) Tumor   (9) Degenerative and heredodegenerative
(5) Trauma   (10) Unknown etiology

The diagnosis of etiology is essential for an effective interdisciplinary approach to learning disorders. Clearly such diagnosis is beyond the capability of the educator and may not always be useful for prescribing educational therapy. Nevertheless, diagnosis which never reaches beyond symptom description may, in the long view, hamper complete educational therapy.

BEHAVIORAL DIAGNOSIS AND EDUCATION

The most common approach to educational diagnosis is the descriptive-predictive approach. The diagnostician attempts to accurately describe the ability level of the child on the basis of carefully selected tests. Samples of test behavior then enable the examiner to predict which new learning tasks a child will be able to do well. Statistically speaking, this procedure enables one to predict whether a child will reach certain levels in school subjects. Too often, the tests do little more.

Until recently diagnostic reading tests such as the Doren (1956) and the Durrell (1955) provided much more specific information to the teacher than did intelligence tests. The diagnostic reading test directed the teacher's attention to specific skills areas which needed improvement.

More recently, diagnostic tests have been developed which analyze performance on tasks thought to be essential to reading (Frostig, et al., 1961). Rather than describing the reading tasks that the subject cannot perform, tests are being designed to describe those underlying tasks which the subject can perform.

THEORY AND PRACTICE IN DIAGNOSIS

Just as theories are useful in discussing the nature of man and the function of atoms, they are helpful in analyzing language and learning. It is important to remember, however, that we have theories because we do not know the full truth about learning. Diagnosis of learning disabilities rests upon assumptions concerning the nature of learning abilities; therefore each new set of assumptions results in new diagnostic procedures.

The influence of theory is often underestimated by test users. The test designer and the test user may have different purposes in mind. The test user may use test items as behavioral goals toward which remedial teaching is directed. The test designer often selects items on the basis of their "strength" in supporting the designer's theory. Thus test items should not be used as models for training activities. Likewise, users may find tests to be valuable for reasons other than those offered by the designer's rationale.

Understanding the rationale which lies behind the development of diagnostic procedures and specific measures is more difficult when diagnosis is multidisciplinary. Rabinovitch (1962) has pointed out that reading retardation may result from (1) a basic disturbed pattern of neurologic organization, (2) brain injury, or (3) secondary causes such as anxiety, depression and emotional blocking. Unfortunately, the criteria for definite differential diagnosis are still uncertain and the problem is complicated by much overlap in etiology.

In spite of overlapping disability factors and complex etiological problems, general diagnostic patterns are emerging. Increasing emphasis is being placed upon early identification (prenursery and preschool). Combined measures are being used to observe linguistic, neurological, educational, and psychological performance. Test data are being supplemented by other case study materials. Finally, members of various disciplines are talking to each other concerning diagnostic conclusions. A new level of understanding is being brought about as theory, general diagnostic, practical and specific school learning evaluation are united through interdisciplinary activities in clinics, school systems, and training institutions.

References

Burgemeister, Bessie B., *Psychological techniques in neurological diagnosis* (New York: Harper & Row, 1962), pp. 6-8.

Doren, Margaret, *Doren diagnostic reading test of word recognition skills* (Minneapolis: Educational Test Bureau, 1956).

Durrell, D. W., *Durrell analysis of reading difficulty* (New Edition) (New York: Harcourt, Brace & World, 1955).

Frostig, M., Lefever, D. W., and Whittlesey, J. R. B., A developmental test of visual perception for evaluating normal and neurologically handicapped children, *Perceptual and Motor Skills*, 1961, No. 12, 383-394.

McCarthy, J. J., and Kirk, S. A., *The construction, standardization and statistical characteristics of the Illinois test of psycholinguistic abilities* (Urbana: University of Illinois Press, 1963).

Rabinovitch, R. D., and Ingram, Winifred, Neuropsychiatric considerations in reading retardation, *The Reading Teacher*, May, 1962, 15, 433-438.

SECTION A: Rationale for Diagnosis

18 THE ILLINOIS TEST OF PSYCHOLINGUISTIC ABILITIES—AN APPROACH TO DIFFERENTIAL DIAGNOSIS

Samuel A. Kirk and James J. McCarthy

Since the time of Alfred Binet, psychologists have been very busily engaged in the development of instruments for evaluating various aspects of personality and intelligence. One area of interest has been the classification and diagnosis of children with intellectual deficits.

The individual omnibus type test like the Binet or Wechsler Scale has been and is now being used extensively in the assessment of general intellectual levels of children. But psychologists have become increasingly dissatisfied with the use of the general intelligence test as a diagnostic instrument. This dissatisfaction is shown in their tirades against the IQ, their use of a series of verbal and performance tests on the same child, and in their discussions concerning classification, diagnosis, and differential diagnosis.

One source of difficulty which has arisen is in our attempt to use a classification instrument as a diagnostic measure. It is necessary to differentiate between these concepts. *Classification* is for the purpose of labeling a child as belonging to a particular group, type, or category. When we administer a Wechsler or a Binet type test to a child, determine an IQ and/or an M.A., we tend to label the child as average, educable, or trainable mentally retarded; or, in older terminology, average, borderline, moron, imbecile, or idiot. The tests are therefore used for classification—not for diagnosis. *Diagnosis*, on the other hand, can mean that the child is assessed in such a way that an educational or remedial program can be initiated. Unless the examiner can assess a child in a way that leads to specific treatment or remediation, the assessment cannot be considered a diagnosis.

The purpose of the present report is to submit a procedure for diagnosis

Reprinted from *American Journal of Mental Deficiency*, Vol. 66, No. 3 (November, 1961), pp. 399-413. By permission of the senior author and publisher.

—a scheme which extends beyond classification of the Binet or Wechsler type test into an assessment which will suggest the areas needing remediation. This area is not new, since clinical workers have attempted to appraise acquired or developmental defects such as the aphasias, apraxias, agnosias, agraphias, and dyslexias. These appraisals have usually been made by informal diagnostic methods with some assistance from psychometric tests. In the field of reading disabilities, diagnostic instruments leading to remediation have been developed. In the intellectual field, evaluating the primary mental abilities can be considered an attempt at differential diagnosis. The present approach is an attempt at diagnosis in the psycholinguistic field.

During the past five years, we have attempted to develop a psycholinguistic psychometric instrument for young children. We have called this diagnostic test The Illinois Test of Psycholinguistic Abilities (McCarthy and Kirk, 1961). We shall attempt to describe this test and to explain how it can be used for diagnosis—i.e., assessment leading to remediation of psycholinguistic deficits in children.

In its development, the test has gone through numerous stages. The first task was to develop the theoretical structure upon which the differential diagnosis was to be based. The second task was to implement this theory with operationally defined tests. The third task was to adapt these subtests in terms of clinical knowledge. This was followed by the standardization of the tests on a normal population as a reference point. The final task will require the development of remedial procedures for children with specific deficits.

THEORETICAL MODELS

The most comprehensive theoretical model which appeared to have a relationship to our work was a formulation by Osgood (1957) who was generating models in communication theory and particularly in psycholinguistics. This has been an area which psychologists have tended to neglect because of its complexity. Osgood has extended Hull's mediation hypothesis into a behavior model which appeared to us to have potential for the development of a differential diagnostic test.

To quote Osgood (1957a, pp. 76-77) directly:

> It [the model] envisages two stages and three levels of organization between stimulus and response in the complete behavioral act. The first stage is what I shall call *decoding*, the total process whereby physical energies in the environment are interpreted by an organism. The second stage is what I shall call *encoding*, the total process whereby intentions of an organism are expressed and hence turned again into environmental events. The three levels of organization are assumed to apply to both sides of the behavioral equation, to both decoding and encoding: (1) a *projection level* of organization, which relates both receptor and muscle events to

the brain via "wired-in" neural mechanisms; (2) an *integration level*, which organizes and sequences both incoming and outgoing neural events; and (3) a *representation* or *cognitive level*, which is at once the termination of decoding operations and the initiation of encoding operations.

A fuller description of the elements within the model which include evocative and predictive integrations, as well as association, are described in detail by Osgood (1957a and 1957b).

Wepman, Jones, Bock, and Pelt (1960) have postulated a clinical model which has some similarities to Osgood's theoretical model. Wepman describes his language model as involving three levels of function: conceptual, perceptual, and reflexive. It includes integration at all levels as well as imitation and includes the function of memory. In view of the clinical nature of the model, he uses the terms "agnosia and apraxia" instead of decoding and encoding, and distinguishes these from "aphasia." Agnosia and apraxia are considered as "transmissive, nonsymbolic processes of disruption." Aphasia is conceived as a disruption of integration, and neither a sensory nor a motor problem.

Wepman's model is distinguished from Osgood's in that it is *not* assumed to be completely general in its application, but is limited to aphasia. Wepman drew his model to represent the different kinds of people he saw in therapy. It is, therefore, based on clinical observation and reflects the fact that he sees patients who have different kinds of language disturbances affecting the input and output at different levels.

THE CLINICAL MODEL OF THE ITPA

The clinical model of the Illinois Test of Psycholinguistic Abilities (ITPA) is presented in Figure 18-1. This diagram presents the three dimensions of the model; namely, (a) channels of communication (auditory input, vocal output, and visual input, motor output); (b) levels of organization (automatic-sequential and representational); and (c) psycholinguistic processes (decoding, association, encoding). The numbers in the figure (1, 2 . . . 9) correspond to the subtests of the battery and are placed within the model to indicate the channel, level, and organization. For example, test number 1 (auditory decoding) measures decoding through the auditory channel at the representational level, while test number 2 refers to decoding through the visual channel at the representational level.

The model of the ITPA has considerable communality with the Osgood model, except for the tests at the integrative level. Osgood's evocative process does not allow for a memory component, whereas the tests at this level in the ITPA include sequential tests involving auditory and visual memory. In this respect, the tests at this level resemble the concepts in the Wepman model.

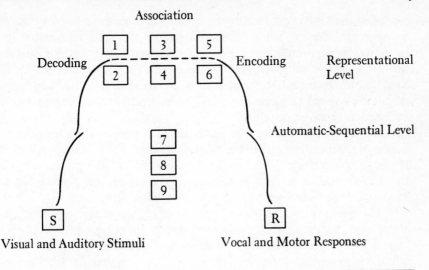

Representational Level

1. Auditory Decoding

2. Visual Decoding

3. Auditory-Vocal Association

4. Visual-Motor Association

5. Vocal Encoding

6. Motor Encoding

Automatic-Sequential Level

7. Auditory-Vocal Automatic

8. Auditory-Vocal Sequential

9. Visual-Motor Sequential

FIGURE 18-1   The clinical model for the Illinois Test of Psycholinguistic Abilities.

The dimensions of the model as well as a description of the subtests of the ITPA are presented below.

The model reflects: (1) modes of input and output, (2) levels of organization, and (3) psycholinguistic processes.

(1) *Modes of Input and Output.* The channels or routes through which communication flows are the modes of language input and output. While it is adequate to state in a generalized behavior model that there exist decoding and encoding processes, in order to build tests to measure these abilities, we were required to construct tests which utilized discrete modes of visual and auditory input and vocal and motor output. On decod-

ing tasks, the visual and auditory modes of input are considered significant to language behavior, while on encoding tasks, the vocal and motor (gesture) modes of output are considered the most important for language usage. On association tasks, the channel (with both input and output utilized) is the significant linguistic avenue. In the model, S (stimulus) represents either visual or auditory stimuli while R represents the response by either vocal or motor reactors.

(2) *Levels of Organization.* In the act of communication the necessary degree of organization within the individual is described by the levels of the language organization. The two levels identified as having been modified by learning and of interest to the language clinician and teacher are the automatic-sequential level and the representational level.

The auditory-vocal automatic aspects of the *automatic-sequential* level correspond to the "predictive" function of the Osgood concept. The auditory-vocal sequential and visual-motor sequential functions of the automatic-sequential level may be more closely related to the Wepman model since they incorporate a memory and imitative factor. Activities requiring the retention of symbol sequences and "automatic" habit chains are mediated at this level. A child repeating "da da da" to his father's urgings without having any established meanings for his utterances is operating at this linguistic level.

The *representational* or meaning level mediates activities requiring the meaning or significance of auditory or vocal symbols. When a child learns to say "da da" to the appropriate father object, he is operating at the representational level. Thus, this level of the model is directly comparable to the representational level of the Osgood model.

(3) *Psycholinguistic Processes.* Language processes constitute learned abilities necessary for language usage. Three main abilities are considered: (a) decoding, (b) association, and (c) encoding. *Decoding* refers to those abilities required to obtain meaning from visual and auditory linguistic stimuli, that is, receptive language ability. *Association* is the ability required to manipulate linguistic symbols internally. It is a central process elicited by decoding and which in turn elicits expressive processes. *Encoding* is the sum of those abilities required to express ideas in words or gestures. All of these processes are interdependent both in their operation and development.

A DESCRIPTION OF THE SUBTESTS OF ITPA

The nine subtests of the battery are described below so that a later discussion of the results will be somewhat clearer. The numbers (1, 2, 3, etc.) correspond to the numbers in Figure 18-1.

TESTS AT THE REPRESENTATIONAL LEVEL. A. *The Decoding Process.* Decoding at this level is measured by the two following subtests:

Test 1. Auditory Decoding. This process is tapped by requiring "yes" or "no" answers to such questions as, "Do airplanes fly?" "Do bicycles drink?" Since decoding, and not encoding is the process being measured, if the child cannot say "Yes" or "No," a gesture response is accepted.

Test 2. Visual Decoding. In this subtest, the child is first presented with a stimulus picture which is then removed and the child is asked to point to one picture from among a set of four pictures. The correct choice is semantically identical to the stimulus picture but is not physically identical; e.g., a silver knife and a jack knife.

B. *The Association Process.* Association is assessed by two tests utilizing different channels.

Test 3. Auditory-Vocal Association. In this subtest, the auditory perception and the vocal expression require minimal ability while the association process is tested by items of increasing difficulty. The analogies test is a "controlled association" test utilizing a sentence completion technique; for example, "Father is big, baby is _____."

Test 4. Visual-Motor Association. This process is tapped by a picture association test. The child is presented with a single stimulus picture and a set of four optional pictures, one of which is associated with the stimulus picture. The child is asked, "Which one of these (pointing to the set of optional pictures) goes with this (pointing to the stimulus picture)?" The child is to choose the one picture from among the set of choices which has a conceptual communality with the stimulus picture.

C. *The Encoding Process.* Encoding at the representational level is assessed by two subtests, one requiring vocal and the other motor responses.

Test 5. Vocal Encoding. In this test, the child is shown a series of familiar objects such as a ball or a block and is asked to "Tell me all about this." The score is the number of discrete concepts enumerated.

Test 6. Motor Encoding. At the representational level, motor encoding is tapped by a gestural manipulation test. An object or picture is shown to the child and he is asked to "Show me what we should do with this." The subject is to supply the appropriate motion, such as drinking from a cup or playing a violin.

TESTS AT THE AUTOMATIC-SEQUENTIAL LEVEL. This level mediates less complex, more automatic, processes than the representational level. This is illustrated by the ability to recite poems and sing songs without conscious effort. Defects at this level interfere with sequential imitation and the ability to retain sequences of visual and/or auditory stimuli. There are three tests at this level: an auditory-vocal automatic test, an auditory-vocal sequential test, and a visual-motor sequential test.

Test 7. The Auditory-Vocal Automatic ability is assessed by a grammar test. The child is shown a picture of a hat and a picture of two hats as ancillary aids to the auditory-vocal task. The examiner says, "Here is a hat. Here are two ————." The child completes the sentence. The test increases in difficulty by requiring the correct use of increasingly less familiar English inflections.

Test 8. The Auditory-Vocal Sequential ability is assessed by a digit repetition test. The test differs from that of the Stanford-Binet in that the digits are presented at the rate of two per second and the child is allowed two trials with each sequence of digits before the task is failed.

Test 9. The Visual-Motor Sequential ability is assessed by a test requiring visual sequential memory. This task requires the child to duplicate the order of a sequence of pictures or geometrical designs which has been presented by the examiner and then removed.

These discrete tests have been constructed to differentiate defects in (a) the three processes of communication, (b) the levels of language organization, and/or (c) the channels of language input and output. Poor performance on specific subtests of this battery should therefore indicate the existence of psycholinguistic defects.

We hesitate to draw parallels between our model and tests, on the one hand, and terminologies in the field of aphasia, on the other hand, since we are dealing with developmental and acquired defects in young children. Nevertheless, a clinician will be able to see some similarities between what we have termed "auditory decoding" and such terms as "word deafness," "sensory or receptive aphasia," "auditory agnosia," and so forth. There may be some similarity between our "visual decoding" and "visual agnosia" or some forms of dyslexia. Likewise, there may be a suggested relationship between what Wepman calls "aphasia" and our concepts of auditory-vocal association, and between "vocal encoding" and expressive aphasia—or in Wepman's term "apraxia." Since the terminologies of aphasia or alexia have been applied primarily to acquired language disorders in adults, we prefer not to use these terms or concepts with children, but rather to rely on operationally defined functions based primarily on behavioral, not neurological, theory. It is believed that remediation of deficits in children can be more easily programmed from learning theory than from neurological speculations.

THE CONSTRUCTION AND STANDARDIZATION OF THE TEST

The major technical problems with which we were faced consisted of creating tests which (a) could be administered to young children, (b) would measure one ability at a time, (c) would have statistical reliability and adequate construct validity, and (d) would be short enough to administer to a young child in one examination period.

Three major test revisions were required to produce the final test. Each revision followed the same pattern. Once the number and type of subtests to be included in the test battery had been determined, items were created to implement each subtest. Materials were constructed; scoring samples, keys, scoring sheets, and test manuals were developed; and examiners were employed and trained to administer the test. For each revision, about 60 children were tested, 20 at each of the following age levels: 2-0 to 3-0, 4-0 to 5-0, and 7-0 to 8-0. Following the completion of testing, subtest and item analyses were performed on the test data.

Each time an item, subtest, or procedure was changed, of course, previous data were invalid. During the preparation of the present form of the test, changes were required because of lack of theoretical validity, poor statistical characteristics, and materials and procedures which proved to be impractical in a standardized testing situation with young children. As a result, three complete revisions were required before arriving at the present version of the test.

The final test was standardized on 700 children between the ages of 2½ and 9, and language age and standard score norms were calculated. A full report of the standardization procedure and the reliability of the subtests will be published later.

THE CLINICAL USE OF THE TEST

The end result of this theory, model construction, and test construction has been a method of differential diagnosis of children which can be presented in the form of a psychodiagnostic profile. Such a profile depicts the abilities and deficits of a particular child. This method of diagnosis should lead to a program of remediation or treatment which will utilize the child's assets to develop the areas in which he is deficient. At present, research is in progress to determine the effects of remedial programs on the removal of specific deficits in children.

The following case studies are presented as examples of the use of the test in diagnosis.

CASE 1. J. P. was examined at the age of 8-9. His Binet IQ was 53, and his mental age as shown in Figure 18-2 was 4-8. On the WISC his total IQ was 53, with little difference between verbal and performance IQ's. On the Peabody Picture Vocabulary Test, his vocabulary age was 5-7. According to these scores, this child could be classified as a trainable mentally retarded child.

J.P. had had convulsions as a child and had been diagnosed as brain-injured.

The psycholinguistic scores, as shown in Figure 18-2, give a rather clear picture of J.P.'s psycholinguistic abilities and deficits which are not evident from the psychometric tests. On decoding, both visual and auditory (Tests 1 and 2), his score is equivalent to an average child of 6-8. This means that J.P. receives and interprets auditory and visual stimuli at a significantly higher level than is shown by his mental age. He is also relatively superior in vocal encoding (Test 5), and in auditory-vocal sequencing at the auto-matic-sequential level.

J.P.'s deficits are shown as the low points on the profile and are labeled in the model (in the upper left hand corner of Figure 18-2) as deficits in visual-motor association at the representational level (4), motor encoding at the representational level (6), and visual motor sequencing at the auto-matic-sequential level (9).

The diagnosis and recommended remediation for this child may be described as follows:

(1) The lowest, and probably the primary deficit in this boy is in motor encoding at the representational level. This does not indicate motor incoordination, but rather the inability to express ideas (at the representa-tional level) in manual rather than in vocal terms. This is the kind of dis-ability which Kephart (1960) has recently described as related to deficits in body image, and for which he has tried to organize a training program. There also appears to be a similarity between this dysfunction and the defi-cit which Seguin (1907) tried to remedy by applying what he called a "physiological method" of training.

(2) The visual-motor association deficit at the representational level (Test 4) may be a secondary deficit associated with and resulting from the deficit of motor encoding. In this kind of task the child is unable to relate visual objects which belong together. One can speculate in this case that the inability to encode manually has inhibited his ability to associate and relate visual objects, even though he is able to interpret discrete visual stimuli as shown by his relative superiority in visual decoding. Training in visual-motor association can be carried on in conjunction with training in the develop-ment of motor encoding abilities.

(3) The deficit in visual sequencing, which involves the reproduction of discrete, unrelated nonmeaningful symbols from memory, may also be a correlate of motor encoding inability in this case. A training program should include activities to develop sequential visual memory.

CASE 2.   Case 2, M.W., was referred for examination because of the inability of the school to understand his lack of progress. M.W. entered

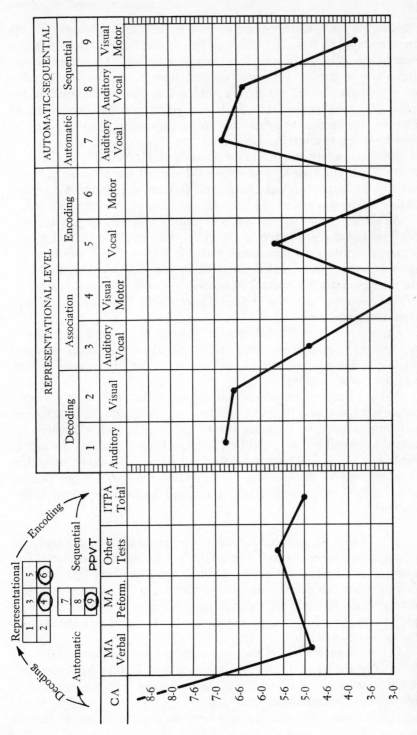

FIGURE 18-2   J.P., Case 1.

school at the age of six. He made no progress in school because of his apparent inability to understand the teacher. It was believed that he had a severe hearing loss and he was placed in a class for hard-of-hearing children. After a year in this class, it was discovered through his speech and audiometric tests that he did not have a hearing loss. He was returned to the regular grades and remained in the second grade until the age of nine. At this time, the teacher reported that he was unable to learn and that he seemed not able to understand directions.

Intelligence tests resulted in an IQ of 66 on the WISC Verbal and 73 on the Binet, although he was within the normal range on performance tests. On the basis of his lack of academic progress in class and the psychometric tests, he was placed in a class for the educable mentally retarded.

At age 10-1, the boy was again examined with various psychometric tests including the test battery of the ITPA. The profile of the test results, all translated into age scores, are presented in Figure 18-3. It will be noted from this profile that on verbal tests (the Binet and WISC Verbal) M.W. is in the classification of mental retardation, but on performance tests (the WISC Performance and the Ontario School Ability Examination) he is in the normal range.

On the profile of Psycholinguistic Abilities, the assets and deficits of this boy appear in a clearer focus. He scored above the norms on visual decoding at the representational level and was relatively superior in both vocal and motor encoding.

Although several examiners had suggested that this boy's responses approached those of a "sensory aphasic," or "aphasoid" child (whatever these terms mean), no examiner was willing to make such a diagnosis because of his verbal encoding ability. The profile, however, shows the various deficits in the boy, and helps to explain why he was unable to respond to the instruction in the classroom. Specifically, this boy's major deficits, charted in the model as deficits in 1, 3, 4, 7, and 8, may be explained further as follows:

(1) The lowest point on the profile is in the automatic-sequential level in the auditory-vocal channel. The auditory-vocal automatic deficit (Test 7) means that he has not learned auditory-vocal responses by contiguity. We know that this deficit is not the result of a deficit in vocal encoding since he scored relatively high in this area. We also found that he has no ability in auditory fusion since he was unable to blend two sounds, like sh-oe, presented auditorily.

(2) Auditory memory at the sequential level was also deficient. He was unable to reproduce a sequence of auditory stimuli such as digit repetition. He was superior in visual memory of discrete visual forms as compared to auditory-vocal sequential memory.

(3) Another major deficit was in auditory decoding. Here he was un-

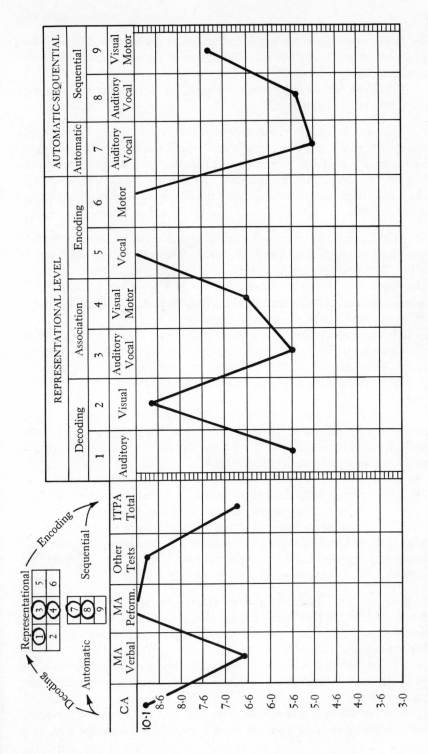

FIGURE 18-3 M.W., Case 2.

able to interpret adequately words and sentences presented auditorily. These results conformed to the teachers' description of the boy as unable to understand directions.

(4) M.W. shows deficiencies in association in both the auditory-vocal and visual-motor channels.

The assets of this boy, together with the deficits shown in the profile, now give us clues to a training program which was not forthcoming from the series of verbal and performance psychometric tests given previously. Programmed instruction for this boy can follow a pattern of instruction which will utilize the assets to develop the deficits. These may be described briefly as follows:

(1) The superiority in visual decoding and visual sequencing indicate, from the few similar cases observed, that this boy will probably learn to read by the "look-and-say" method of teaching reading, i.e., an emphasis on the visual approach. Interestingly, he has learned word recognition by the "whole" method and can read at about the low first grade level. He has no ability to sound words or to recognize unknown words. But he has acquired a limited sight vocabulary. It is possible that this kind of a profile could tell us to emphasize the sight method of teaching reading, while an opposite profile, with basic deficiencies in the visual decoding and visual motor sequencing, would require phonic training. This becomes more evident in Case 3.

(2) Two programs of instruction for the training of deficits are suggested from the diagnosis. The first is to organize a program of instruction for both auditory decoding and auditory-vocal association. Such a program can utilize his visual decoding ability through such tasks as (a) showing him a picture which he can decode visually, then (b) asking him to tell which man in the picture is the biggest, or tallest, or is performing a certain task. In this way he will have a visual clue to aid him in auditory decoding and in auditory-vocal association. The second area of instruction should include training in auditory memory of nonmeaningful materials. Whether such deficits can be ameliorated by specific training is the subject of present ongoing research in the training of psycholinguistic abilities.

CASE 3.   S.N. (Figure 18-4) is an atypical case from the point of view of age, since she is now over 15 years old. Her case, however, is included here because she demonstrates the types of difficulties encountered by such children in a school situation.

S.N. is a cerebral palsied child, diagnosed as quadriplegic, who is at the age of fifteen, confined to a wheelchair. She can walk a little with braces and assistance.

S.N. has never attended school but has had in the past some homebound instruction. After a year or so of homebound instruction with little

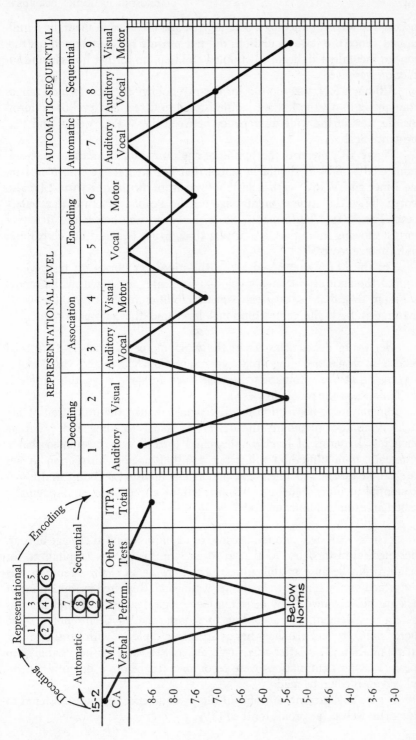

FIGURE 18-4 S.N., Case 3.

success, she was examined by a psychologist and classified as mentally handicapped. Since the state regulations did not provide for homebound instruction for mentally handicapped crippled children, no further homebound instuction was given.

Although S.N. was too old for the psycholinguistic test (which ranges from ages 2 to 9), the test was administered to detect her level of performance in view of the wide discrepancy between the WISC Verbal and Performance Scales.

Figure 18-4 presents the profile of age norms for the various tests administered to S.N. It should be noted that her mental age equivalents on the Binet and WISC Verbal Scale ranged from 8½ to 9½ years. She also scored above the 10 year mental age on the Peabody Picture Vocabulary Test. The WISC Performance Scale, however, was below the five year norms, showing more than a four year discrepancy between her verbal and performance scores.

On the ITPA she scored above the nine year norms on tests which utilized the auditory-vocal channel. This indicates, as shown in the model in Figure 18-4, that her relatively superior abilities are in the auditory-vocal channel at both the representational level and the automatic-sequential level.

Her major deficiencies are in the visual-motor channels, with special deficits in visual decoding at the representational level and visual-motor sequencing at the automatic-sequential level. In some ways, this profile is the opposite of the profile in Case 2.

Programming instruction for S.N. would require the utilization of her auditory abilities to modify the defects in visual decoding and visual sequencing. In terms of teaching this child to read, it is postulated that a systematic phonic method will bring results. Remedial instruction in her case can be directed to ameliorate the deficits in visual decoding and visual sequential memory. Much of this instruction can be given in a systematic remedial reading phonic method.

CASE 4.   S.K. was referred because of inability to talk at the age of four. Her medical history showed that at seven months she was hospitalized for malnutrition because of difficulties in swallowing. A slight operation was performed on the tongue to facilitate swallowing. Repeated examinations of this girl did not reveal any definitive neurological signs of central nervous system involvement, but according to reports, the physicians noted some motor difficulty and classified her as an atonic diplegic, with possible mental retardation. The latter was suggested as the cause of her inability to speak. Further examinations were recommended before a definitive medical diagnosis could be made.

Figure 18-5 presents a profile of the psychometric tests administered to this girl as well as the profile for the ITPA.

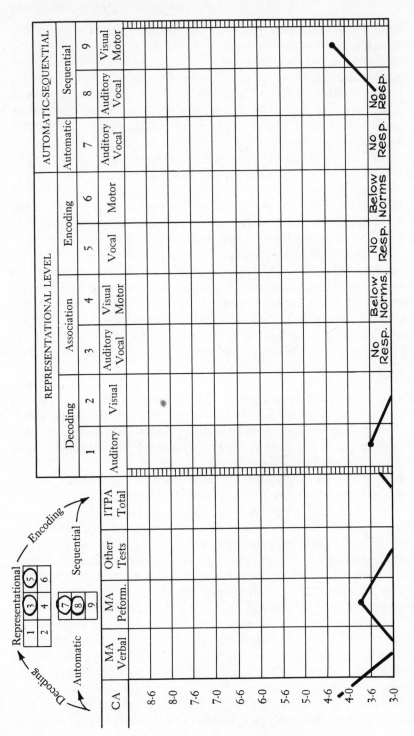

FIGURE 18-5 S.K., Case 4.

Psychometric examinations with young children, especially with those who have little speech, are always questionable. An estimate of intelligence is made on the basis of a number of psychometric examinations over a period of time. On the Kuhlmann Tests of Mental Development, this child's IQ was 52 with an M.A. of 2-4. On the Minnesota Preschool Scale, she scored below the norms for 18 months on the verbal scale, but scored an IQ of 91 on the nonverbal scale. The latter score was inflated because on a visual discrimination item she scored quite high. Eliminating this one item her verbal and nonverbal scores did not differ. She scored an IQ of 90 on the Ontario School Ability Examination and an IQ of 72 on the Peabody Picture Vocabulary Test.

Because of no speech, this child could not score on any tests on the ITPA that involved a vocal response, but scored on auditory decoding at age 3-6, visual decoding at age 3, and visual-motor sequencing at age 4-4.

The history of this child showed no babbling and very little imitation, even in the gestural field. The basic deficit is obviously vocal encoding and a deficit in the auditory-vocal automatic-sequential level. Remedial instruction in her case would necessarily begin by an attempt to develop babbling, imitation of sounds and words, and in auditory-vocal memory. Periodic examinations after each four to five months of remediation may reveal other deficits which might change the emphasis in remediation.

EPILOGUE

A battery of tests of psycholinguistic abilities has been described. The test is presented, not as a classification instrument, but as a diagnostic instrument which leads to clues for remediation of deficits in various psycholinguistic functions found particularly among cerebral palsied, brain-injured, and some emotionally disturbed children.

In the past, there has been a concentration of effort on the part of psychologists in constructing and refining omnibus tests of intelligence which have been useful for classification purposes, but of little use in prescribing remedial education. There have also been numerous studies on discrete tests of visual-motor and other functions for the purpose of differentiating brain-injured from non brain-injured children. This type of study has also concentrated on methods of classification. Diagnosis of children for language disorders has been somewhat clouded by the concepts derived from the study of adult aphasics.

The Illinois Test of Psycholinguistic Abilities does not make any assumptions with respect to neurological or neurophysiological correlates of behavior. Its emphasis is on assessing behavior manifestations in the psycholinguistic field, in relating the assets and deficits to a behavioral (not a neurological) model, and in extending this type of behavior diagnosis to a remedial teaching situation. It is recognized by the authors that there may be more than nine functions and that further clinical and basic research is needed before we arrive at a more complete diagnostic procedure which will lead to definite and prescribed remedial methods. Ultimately, when this stage has been reached and we are able to demonstrate that programmed instructions can ameliorate, if not remove, specific deficits in children, we will have arrived at what Alfred Binet tried to accomplish in his procedures of "mental orthopedics," which he described in his classic report on the "The Educability of Intelligence" (Binet, 1909).

References

Binet, Alfred, *Les ideas modernes des enfants* (Paris: E. Flemmarion, 1909).

Kephart, N., *The slow learner in the classroom* (Columbus, Ohio: Merrill, 1960).

McCarthy, James J., "Qualitative and quantitative differences in language abilities of young cerebral palsied children (Unpublished doctoral dissertation, University of Illinois, 1957).

McCarthy, James J., and Kirk, Samuel A., *Illinois test of psycholinguistic abilities: Experimental edition* (Urbana, Illinois: Institute for Research on Exceptional Children, University of Illinois, 1961).

Olson, James L., A comparison of sensory aphasia, expressive aphasia and deaf children on the Illinois Test of Language Ability (Unpublished doctoral dissertation, University of Illinois, 1960).

Osgood, Charles E., *Contemporary approaches to cognition, a behavioristic analysis* (Cambridge, Massachusetts: Harvard University Press, 1957a).

Osgood, Charles E., Motivational dynamics of language behavior, *Nebraska Symposium on Motivation* (Lincoln: University of Nebraska Press, 1957b).

Seguin, E., *Idiocy: And its treatment by the physiological method* (New York: Teachers College, Columbia University, 1907).

Sievers, Dorothy J., Development and standardization of a test of psycholinguistic growth in preschool children (Unpublished doctoral dissertation, University of Illinois, 1955).

Wepman, J. M., Jones, L. V., Bock, R. D., and Pelt, D. V., Studies in aphasia: Background and theoretical formulations, *J. Speech and Hearing Disorders*, 1960, 25, 323-332.

19 THE VALIDITY OF SOME PSYCHOLOGICAL
TESTS OF BRAIN DAMAGE

Aubrey J. Yates

It is customary to distinguish two main types of validity; these may be named *higher-order* (internal) and *lower-order* (external) validity. Internal validation consists essentially in measuring the correlation between different tests supposed to measure the same variable. Consideration of this method of validation will be reserved until later, since the tests to be evaluated below have not generally been validated in this way, and the use of this method is comparatively rare. Lower-order validity implies the use of an external criterion against which the test is validated. In the development of a test of brain damage, for instance, the external criterion would consist of a number of clinical groups, such as a brain-damaged group of patients, a group of psychiatric (functional) patients without brain damage, and a group of normal controls; a valid test of brain damage would then be expected to distinguish patients in the brain-damaged group from those in the other two groups. The difficulty in using this method of validation lies, of course, in the fact that the criterion itself is in need of validation. It has been shown by Ash (1949) and others that the reliability of psychiatric diagnosis is so low that it is difficult to rely on such classifications in the development of tests. Even when very broad groups are used, the degree of error may be considerable. It seems necessary to use the classification system given above, however, because this is the procedure adopted by the authors of most of the tests to be discussed, because the groups may be more reliably discriminated than in most cases, and because, in the case of the brain-damaged group at least, independent confirmation may be forthcoming in the shape of neurological signs, post-mortem examination, etc.

Reprinted from *Psychological Bulletin*, Vol. 51, No. 4 (1954), pp. 358-379. By permission of the author and publisher.

It is assumed, then, that it is possible to isolate such broad groups for the purposes of research; however, there remain other conditions which must be fulfilled before the validity of a given test can be discussed. In general, these may be summarized as follows:

(a) The test should present data for adequate samples of the above-mentioned three groups (brain-damaged, functional, and normal).

(b) The data should be presented in such a form as to enable the clinician using the test to estimate the degree of possible error when assigning a patient to any one of the groups. Such data may be stated in three different ways. First, the optimum cutoff point may be given; this is the point at which it is possible to identify as many brain-damaged patients as possible and at the same time misclassify as few functionals and normals as possible. (If the distributions are normal, this can be stated simply in terms of the mean and standard deviation.) Second, the point beyond which no normals or functionals of the samples fall should be given. Third, the point beyond which no brain-damaged patient of the sample falls should also be given.

(c) The reliability of the results should be verified by applying the test to new groups that are independent of the original criterion groups. Alternatively (or, preferably, in addition), the findings should be confirmed by another worker in another hospital.

(d) The influence of various factors, such as age, sex, and intelligence, and any special factors (such as visual acuity when perceptual tests are used, and motor coordination when mechanical tests are used) should be controlled.

It will be the purpose of this paper to show that most of the tests purporting to be measures of brain damage do not meet the conditions set out above and that, therefore, their validity either cannot be considered as established or cannot even be evaluated. It may be pointed out, however, that, even if these conditions were adequately met, no general judgment can be made about the validity of a particular test. Whether a given test is considered to be a valid measure of brain damage, or whether it is not, will depend on many factors. The most important of these will be whether or not the test works in practice. Because a test is usually standardized on relatively pure groups, the discriminating power must necessarily drop when the test is used clinically. Again, precise confidence limits are difficult to apply. Thus, a test that identifies only 20 percent of brain-damaged patients admitted to a hospital may be a very useful clinical instrument if these patients are not identifiable at the time of testing by any other means. On the other hand, a test that identifies 60 percent of all brain-damaged patients may not be very useful clinically because most of the patients it identifies are obvious cases of brain damage and can be detected by simpler means. In some instances, it may be possible to use a cutoff point in such a way that a patient falling above it is unequivocally identified as brain-damaged, while, if he falls below it, he (being brain-damaged) is not misclassified; but the question remains an open one, no statement being made about the patient. However, when considering the standardization of a test, one may reasonably demand a low percentage of misclassification, because the groups are carefully chosen for their clinical differences. The various tests of brain damage will now be considered to see how far they fulfill the criteria already laid down.

The tests will be considered under two broad headings—those tests which employ qualitative methods and those which employ quantitative methods. Those tests using quantitative methods will, in turn, be grouped into those utilizing the concept of deterioration and those measuring perceptual or motor functions. Such a division is, of course, quite arbitrary, and is dictated by convenience.

QUALITATIVE TESTS OF BRAIN DAMAGE

The criteria laid down above presuppose adequate statistical treatment of data. However, such treatment is almost entirely lacking in one of the most widely used and reputable batteries of tests of brain damage—the tests of abstract concept formation developed by Goldstein and Scheerer (1941) and their colleagues. These tests are so well known that it is unnecessary to describe them. The basic criticism to be made of these tests is not that they are invalid, but that there is no basis for a discussion of their validity. The tests are unique in diagnostic psychological testing in providing no quantitative data on the subjects used and providing no percentage of incorrect diagnoses, in ignoring the effects of age and intelligence level completely, and in assuming that the performance of normal people of average intelligence will be without error. Under these circumstances, it is clear that the validity of the tests is something private to each individual user. It is possible that, in the hands of a skilled clinician, the tests have a high validity; but, even in the case of Goldstein himself, no information is available about the number of times he has been in error. Two further points may be made: First, there has never been any clear agreement concerning what the tests measure. Goldstein believes that they measure the ability to abstract, and that brain injury leads to a defect in assuming the abstract attitude, which is revealed in test performance; on the other hand, Hutton (1942) believes that failure on the Block Design test is due to overabstraction, not failure of abstraction. Second, it is significant that the Goldstein-Scheerer tests have been used to determine the presence or absence of schizophrenic thought disorder, and that other tests, developed specifically to test for schizophrenia, bear a strong resemblance to the Goldstein tests, e.g., the Hanfmann-Kasanin Test of Concept Formation. Little work has been done to differentiate between the performance of schizophrenics and brain-damaged patients on these tests; hence, they are very difficult to apply clinically.

That the necessary quantification would be possible may be easily inferred from examination of Goldstein's manual, where many possible dimensions of measurement are indicated in qualitative form. A beginning has, in fact, been made. Boyd (1949), using 54 normal hospitalized subjects, set up quantitative norms for the Block Design test by giving weights to the various steps utilized by Goldstein. When he divided his group according to Wechsler IQ, he found that perfect performance would indeed be expected, provided the IQ was 100 or more. As the IQ dropped, however, so did the score on the Block Design test, from a mean score of 120 ($SD = 0$) for IQ 100-109 to a mean score of only 99.5 ($SD = 34.5$) for IQ 66-79. He was able to give limits within which a person of a given IQ level would be expected to fall. He thus demonstrated that intelligence is an important factor in performance on these tests; he also found that psychotics tended to do worse than brain-damaged patients (though his numbers were very small).

Lidz, Gay, and Tietze (1942), using the scoring system developed by Kohs, found that the Kohs test discriminated significantly between 21 organics with deterioration, and 15 nondeteriorated schizophrenics (with a misclassification of only 2/36). However, there was no control for age, the difference between the two groups being certainly significant. Another attempt to quantify the Block Design test was reported by Armitage (1946). Using three groups of subjects—normal, neurotic, and brain-damaged—he calculated the percentage of controls and organics requiring assistance at each of four steps. He concluded that the quantitative results were disappointing from the standpoint of a screening device; so, to determine whether the discriminatory ability of the test could be increased, he made a multiple approach. This involved the computation of such variables as the time taken to complete each design, the number of incorrect moves, the order or sequence of placing the blocks, and the number of correct first block placements. None of these methods proved successful.

Tooth (1947) gave a series of tests, including the Kohs Block test and the Weigl Color Form Sorting Test, to 100 cooperative naval officers and ratings admitted to a naval hospital with a history of an injury to the head and a diagnosis of postconcussional state. As controls, he used 50 convalescent patients in the surgical wards of the same hospital and 50 neurotics carefully chosen from 2,000 cases seen in a naval psychiatric clinic. After careful statistical analysis of the results, he concluded that the method did not give sufficient quantitative discrimination between head injury cases and normals to be of much practical importance in the assessment of the individual case. Furthermore, in these two tests, a difference of as great a magnitude was found between the normal controls on the one hand and a series of neurotic patients in whom no organic condition was known to exist on the other.

With respect to object sorting, Halstead (1940), using groups of cases with lesions in various areas of the brain, compared them with a normal group on an object-sorting test, larger in content and presented under conditions somewhat different from those obtaining in the Goldstein test. The sorting behavior was analyzed according to a number of criteria, including the percentage of objects grouped, the total percentage of objects recalled after five minutes, and the percentage of objects grouped that were recalled after the same interval. With respect to these three variables, for 11 normals and 11 cases of frontal lobe injury there was no overlap in the scores of the two groups on the first and third variables, and only two brain-damaged cases exceeded the lowest normal score on the second variable. On the other hand, cases with lesions in other parts of the brain showed considerable overlap with normals. Halstead's results confirmed to some extent Goldstein's hypothesis that performance as a whole on this test tends to be lowered in cases of frontal lobe lesion. He also offered some evidence for the hypothesis that patients with injury to the frontal lobes cannot sort according to an abstract principle. In terms of the number of abstract groupings produced, there was again no overlap between the normals and the cases of frontal lobe injury.

A rather radical and important departure from the usual procedure in the Block Design test has been made by Grassi (1947; 1953) in his Block Substitution Test for measuring organic brain pathology. Essentially, the main innovations are that the patient copies not a drawing but a set of blocks, and an attempt is made to measure both concrete and abstract reproduction at two levels. The test consists of five designs or models, each of which is reproduced by the patient at four levels of increasing complexity. In the simple concrete task, the patient copies only the top side of the model. In the simple abstract task, he copies the top side again, but this time using different colors from those of the model. In the complex concrete task, the patient has to copy the model correctly with respect to all six sides, while in the complex abstract task, he copies the complete model again, but this time using different colors from those of the model. The scoring system is simple, accuracy and time being rewarded; the maximum score possible is 30. The standardization groups are unusually large for this kind of work, consisting of 86 normals, 86 schizophrenics (equally divided into deteriorated and nondeteriorated cases), 72 organics, and 30 postlobotomy cases. Grassi states that no influence of age, sex, or other factors was found, while test-retest reliability was high (+.85). Means and ranges are given for the four groups and show that (using a cutoff point of 16) there was no overlap between the two organic and the two nonorganic groups. If this finding can be confirmed, it is clearly of great importance. There is some doubt, however, about the accuracy of Grassi's figures. For example, although the ranges of the organic and nonorganic groups do not overlap, Grassi reports in another section that six schizophrenics scored below 16 and were not included in the standardization data; also, that eight organics scored "slightly above" 16 and were correctly identified by qualitative examination. However, the misclassification is sufficiently small to make further research on this test imperative.

Grassi's (1953) attitude toward his own statistics is difficult to understand. He writes: "It cannot be too strongly stressed that test scores taken alone will lead to incorrect conclusions. The score is intended as a *guide*, not as the *sole* criterion for the final conclusion. Behavior cannot be too greatly emphasized and should be, in most cases, the basis for diagnosis. Test score and intellectual level are supporting factors. They must not, *ever*, be the sole basis for final classification" (1953, p. 63, italics his). Two comments are relevant here. In the first place, for the standardization groups at least, since there is no overlap, it is hard to see how a quantitative score could lead to a false diagnosis of brain damage. Second, a subjective statement that the patient's behavior was qualitatively such and such is in fact a preliminary quantitative statement of behavior, albeit in a crude and inaccurate way. The aim of any test constructor must surely be to quantify as soon as possible his initially crude and unrefined observations and thus set up proper control. Why Grassi, having done this, should then turn his back on it, is difficult to see. The consequences, however, are serious. Although Grassi himself states that intelligence can influence performance, no adequate information is given. This would have been especially valuable in view of the relatively large numbers of subjects used. In spite of these criticisms, the Grassi test represents an important advance over the original Goldstein tests.

Clinical use of the Color Form test of the Goldstein battery has suggested that it is too easy to be useful in the detection of brain damage except in severe cases. This was confirmed by McFie and Piercy (1952) who used 55 cases of known brain damage and scored the test simply as "pass" or "fail" on the basis of the patient's ability to sort the pieces both by form and by color. They found that only 9 of the 55 patients failed the test. An important modification of the Color Form test has, however, been published by Scheerer (1949). Three large model figures—a circle, a triangle, and a square—are used, and there are 12 test figures, four being subsumed under the concept of roundness, four under the concept of triangularity, and four under that of squareness. The three large figures lie on the table as model figures. The subject is shown each of the remaining figures in turn and asked to indicate with which model figure it belongs. Each figure is removed from the subject's sight before the next one is presented. A simple, objective system of scoring has been devised, failure being counted when the subject incorrectly assigns a figure. If this happens, a series of three "helps" is given, similar in nature to the successive steps on the Block Design test. The test was standardized on four groups of subjects. The first group consisted of 44 college students; the second group was made up of 20 noncollege students; the third group consisted of 20 brain-damaged patients; and the fourth group included 20 retarded high school pupils who were used as controls for those brain-damaged patients of low intelligence. Scheerer found that the percentage of subjects needing the three "helps" fell rapidly after the first help for the three non brain-damaged groups, but that all the brain-damaged patients needed the third help and 75 percent of them failed all three helps; no subjects in the other three groups failed all three helps.

This study is of importance, not only for its success in identifying brain-damaged patients, but in representing one of the few serious attempts at quantification of the Goldstein-Scheerer tests. However, some criticisms are possible. The instructions contained in the original article are inadequate for clinical use—for instance, it is not made clear what happens if the subject makes more than one error after the first help has been given; the test objects are presented in a fixed, not random, order, so that a pattern of response may be set up which masks inability to do the test. In this connection it may be noted that the figures given by Scheerer indicate that, compared with the noncollege group, fewer of the retarded group needed the third help, and that, compared with the college group, fewer retarded needed the second help. Again, the test has not been given to a group of functional patients, so the degree of overlap between such a group and the brain-damaged group is not known. As far as is known, no subsequent information has been made available on this test, and no critical studies have been published.

Zangwill (in Buros, 1949) has criticized the Goldstein tests on the general grounds that they are qualitative; that some psychotics show impairment; that some brain-damaged patients with traumatic injuries behave essentially normally on the tests; and that gross impairment on the tests, due to a specific lesion, may be present in the absence of any occupational or social difficulties. It may be added that no information is available concerning the factorial composition of the tests.

QUANTITATIVE TESTS OF BRAIN DAMAGE

TESTS EMPLOYING THE CONCEPT OF DETERIORATION. The tests considered under this heading are based on the principle that brain damage leads to deterioration of an irreversible nature. This deterioration usually is contrasted with that found in the functional disorders, wherein deterioration is considered to be more apparent than real, and to be due to inattention, the assumption being that the patient retains normal ability if he could be made to perform at his best level. It is not proposed to discuss the concept of deterioration as such, and these tests will be criticized only in so far as they claim to distinguish brain-damaged patients from other groups.

The Hunt-Minnesota Test for Organic Brain Damage (1943) consists of three major divisions—a vocabulary test, which is relatively insensitive to brain damage; a group of tests sensitive to deterioration; and a group of interpolated tests. The subject's Stanford-Binet vocabulary score, in relation to his age, determines the score level at which he is expected to perform the more sensitive tests. The deterioration tests, consisting of pairs of words and of designs that the subject is expected to associate and later recall and recognize, determine the level at which he is actually functioning. The amount of discrepancy between the subject's expected score and the score he actually makes on the word and design associations (when corrected for age) is the basis for the diagnosis of brain damage. The discrepancies are indicated by T scores; those T scores which fall higher than a certain critical point are considered to be indicative of brain damage. Originally, this critical T score was fixed at 68; later it was reduced to 66. The test may be given in either a short or long form.

Two groups of subjects were used in the development of the test: 33 patients suffering from brain damage (all but three were cases of diffuse damage); and 41 controls, consisting of 15 neurotics, 11 normals, 6 psychotics, and 8 nonpsychiatric patients. All subjects had to be able to read and speak English, had attended school to third grade, were adequately cooperative and attentive, had adequate muscular coordination and sensory acuity, and were between the ages of 16 and 70. For discriminative purposes, 25 persons equated for vocabulary and age were drawn from each group. Using a cutting point of 68, Hunt found that only one of the 50 standardization subjects was misclassified, and that, of the remaining 25 subjects, only three were misclassified. (He ignored three subjects who scored 68.)

Hunt's use of the interpolated tests (tests of concentration and attention) was based on the following assumptions: deteriorated brain-damaged patients would fail the learning tests but not the interpolated tests; functional, "apparently deteriorated" patients would succeed on both learning and interpolated tests; functional, "genuinely deteriorated" patients would fail both learning and interpolated tests. Implicitly, therefore, failure on the interpolated tests was to be utilized as a measure of whether a functional patient was really, or was only apparently, deteriorated. In fact, this ingenious hypothesis was not directly tested by Hunt; his only finding was that both of the groups he used were not differentiated by the interpolated tests.

While, in its construction and standardization, this test fulfills to some extent the first two criteria laid down earlier in this paper, the results reported by Hunt have not been confirmed by other workers, while important reservations in the use of the Hunt-Minnesota vocabulary test are necessary.

The discrimination between normals and organics has not been found by other investigators. Thus, Aita and his associates (1947), using groups already referred to in the study by Armitage (1946), found that 10 percent of their control subjects obtained a T score greater than 90, but that only 2.2 percent of their brain-damaged subjects obtained a score as high as this. On the other hand, 41.3 percent of their brain-damaged subjects obtained a score that was in the normal range, i.e., below 70. Many of the brain-damaged patients actually scored well below the cutoff point used by Hunt, 23.9 percent of them falling within the range 50-54. When the brain-damaged group was divided into three categories—severe, moderate, and mild—only the mean T score of the severe group was significantly different from that of the controls.

A study by Canter (1951) reinforced this finding that the amount of overlap between a brain-damaged group and a normal group may be considerable. For 47 arteriosclerotic patients the mean T score was 69.04 (SD = 12.49)—that is, the group mean fell within normal limits. Malamud (1946), in a preliminary study, found that six out of ten members of the psychology department at her hospital were suffering from brain damage according to results on this test! She therefore administered the test to 64 subjects who satisfied Hunt's basic criteria. She found that 54.7 percent of these normal subjects obtained scores indicating organic brain damage. The exact critical score used did not influence the results appreciably. When all vocabulary scores above 33 words or more were arbitrarily reduced to 32, no less than 42.2 percent of the total group still fell within the pathological range.

In addition to this overlap between organics and normals, it has been shown by Meehl and Jeffery (1946) that some functionals at least may show pathological scores on this test. They gave the test to a group of 15 patients with functional depressions, of whom 9 were psychotic and 6 neurotic. The possibility of brain damage was ruled out in all cases, and 11 of the subjects did not fail any of the interpolated tests. The mean T score of the entire group was 70.2 (SD = 15.41). Using a critical score of 70, they found that one in four functionally depressed patients would obtain an organic score; using a cutoff point of 66, the ratio would be one in three.

We have already seen that Malamud found that a high vocabulary score did not markedly affect the proportion of normals showing a pathological score on this test. However, a study by Juckem and Wold (1948) showed that when the test was given to a group of 50 college students who reached Superior Adult III level on the Binet vocabulary test, they obtained a mean T score of 69.6, whereas Hunt's control-group mean was 50. Only 3 percent of Hunt's control group obtained a score greater than this mean score. Of this college population, no less than 60 percent had scores above Hunt's critical point. Juckem and Wold conclude that the test yields far too many false positives among persons of high vocabulary level. If a normal T score were to be obtained, the vocabulary level would have to be reduced to 21 words.

These studies show that, in practice, the test has not lived up to the claims made for it by its author, and its usefulness as a test of brain damage is very much in doubt.

The Shipley-Hartford Retreat Scale (1940) is a short test of two parts, one consisting of a vocabulary test, which is supposed to hold up with age or illness; the other, of a set of abstract reasoning problems, supposedly sensitive to deterioration. A Conceptual Quotient (CQ) is derived from scores on the two parts of the test and may be defined roughly as Mental Age (Abstractions Test)/Mental Age (Vocabulary Test) × 100. Mental age norms were established on 1,046 young subjects who had been given a group intelligence test. It was assumed that normal persons, regardless of native intelligence, would approach CQ's of 100. This assumption proved to be roughly true within normal limits. A CQ above 90 was considered normal; one between 76 and 89, suspicious; and a CQ below 75, pathological. The test was validated on 171 state hospital cases and 203 private hospital cases. Shipley and Burlingame (1941) claimed that the test would discriminate between normals, schizophrenics, and organics, and it is for this reason that the test is included here. They found that organics did worst, that neurotics and normals fell close together, and that the psychotics came in between.

This test may be criticized severely on many grounds. The standardization data were completely inadequate, only young intelligent normals being used in the construction of the scale. There was no control for age, sex, or intelligence, yet the factor of age is of particular importance in this test. Subsequent research has shown beyond doubt that the test does not discriminate between organic and other groups without considerable overlap.

Thus, Aita and his colleagues (1947) found that, of a control group of 61 normal subjects, 47 percent obtained a CQ that was suspicious or pathological, and 26 percent of these 61 subjects obtained a definitely pathological score. Of a brain-damaged group of 70 patients, 33 percent fell within the normal range of scores. Contrary to Shipley's assertion, they found that mild or moderate neurosis lowers the CQ, although they present no figures. Canter (1951) used the Shipley-Hartford scale on 47 cases of multiple sclerosis and obtained a mean CQ score of 85.8 ($SD = 14.31$). Despite the unfavorable difference in age between his group (mean age, 32) and the standardization group of Shipley, he found that 50 percent of his cases obtained CQ's greater than 76, and 40 percent obtained CQ's greater than 90, indicating considerable overlap with normals.

Magaret and Simpson (1948) gave the test to 50 patients consisting of psychotics and neurotics, aged 40-49, and found a mean CQ of 74 ($SD = 12.7$), with a range of scores from 55 to 105. Of the 50 cases, 29 obtained a CQ lower than 70. Here again, although age would be expected to work in favor of lower scores, the overlap with normals would still be considerable, while the overlap with organics would be even greater. Furthermore, correlations of the CQ with psychiatric ratings of deterioration and with the Wechsler deterioration index were not significantly greater than zero. These results are the more remarkable in that Garfield and Fey (1948) showed that, in fact, the CQ did decline steeply, solely as a function of age. Their results otherwise agree with those of Magaret and Simpson: using a group of 100 patients (58 psychotic, 37 neurotic, 13 unclassified), they found a mean CQ of 79.1 for the psychotics and 85.2 for the neurotics.

A further study by Manson and Grayson (1947) was even more disturbing. Of Shipley's standardization group, 26 percent obtained a CQ below 90. Of a group of 1,262 military prisoners examined by these authors, no less than 59.1 percent obtained a CQ less than 90; 34.6 percent a CQ less than 80; and 14.2 percent a CQ less than 70; the mean CQ for the group was only 88.8. They suggested that the reason for this discrepancy was a spuriously high vocabulary score, and showed that substitution of the Army General Classification Scores for the vocabulary scores produced figures very similar to those of Shipley. This confirms the previous findings that spuriously organic scores may be obtained on tests which use vocabulary level as a measure of previous intellectual functioning. Manson and Grayson also report that 45 percent of severe neurotics scored below 80 on this test. This was confirmed by the work of Kobler (1947), who reported that, of 500 neurotics at an army rehabilitation center for combat fatigue, 78 percent made CQ's below 90; 26 percent had CQ's below 70 and thus fell within the organic range.

Fleming reported that 20 depressives obtained a mean CQ of only 73.2. However, the mean age of his group was 57.6 years. Ross and McNaughton (1944) used 90 subjects with head injury and found that the results bore no relation to severity of the injury or to EEG or pneumoencephalographic evidence of cerebral damage except in cases of severe injury. No statistical data were given, however.

How far the original faulty standardization of the test and lack of care in its construction have been responsible for the failure of subsequent workers to establish the validity of the test is difficult to estimate. The findings quoted, however, certainly indicate that the test has not been adequately validated.

There have been a number of attempts to develop indices of deterioration by using the Wechsler subtests in various combinations. The rationale of these tests is well known. A ratio is calculated between those tests which are said to hold up with age, and those which do not hold up with age. The underlying assumption is the rather curious one that organic deterioration is similar to the deterioration accompanying age, differing only in its early onset. Wechsler (1944) found that the index discriminated between young normals and young brain-damaged patients, the percentage overlap, however, being high. Thus, there was a restriction on the usefulness of the test right from the start. Levi, Oppenheim, and Wechsler (1945) specifically claimed that the DI was useful, not only in confirming, but also in discovering, organic conditions. They claimed that it would assist in differentiating organic memory impairment from hysterical amnesia; in finding corroborative evidence of organic involvement where clinical and neurological data are not clear-cut; in distinguishing between mental deficiency and mental deterioration; and in differentiating between psychosis with and without organic deterioration. With the exception of the first, these claims have been tested and invariably have been found wanting; and it seems safe to say that the first has not been found wanting only because it has not been tested.

Two important modifications of the Wechsler DI are Reynell's index (1944), which makes use only of the verbal subtests, and Hewson's deviation ratios (1949), which are based on various combinations of the subtests. Reynell's index, however, has been incorrectly criticized by some workers—its intention was not to discriminate brain-damaged cases from others, but to discriminate those brain-damaged cases *with* deterioration from those without (and hence assumed initial knowledge of brain damage).

Many studies have now been published on the DI. This paper is concerned only with those investigating the validity of the tests as a measure of brain damage. At least six studies concur in reporting unfavorably on its use. Thus Gutman (1950), using 30 organics and 30 controls, found that the Wechsler DI correctly identified only 43 percent of organics, the Reynell index 50 percent, and the Hewson ratios 60 percent; whereas the DI misclassified 33 percent of the normal group, the Reynell index 30 percent, and the Hewson ratios 17 percent. The three measures agreed in the diagnosis of brain damage in only 33 percent of the cases. Five cases of clinically verified brain damage did not fall in the organic range on any of the tests. Allen (1947), using as his criterion of deficit a loss greater than 20 percent, found that the Wechsler DI definitely screened out only 54 percent of the total study group of 50 patients. Rogers (1950) evaluated the DI for seven groups (349 subjects) and found that, using a cutting score of 10 per cent, 75 percent of subjects will be correctly identified, provided that only the brain-damaged and normal groups are used; but that, when other clinical groups are included, the results are no better than chance. Andersen (1950), using 55 male soldiers with definite clinical evidence of brain damage, showed that, when a cutting score of 10 percent was used, nearly one-third of the total sample fell outside the organic range; yet when a cutting score of 20 percent was used, nearly two-thirds of the patients fell inside the normal range. He divided his group of patients into those suffering predominantly from injury to the dominant hemisphere and those suffering from injury to the nondominant hemisphere. This did not materially improve the results. Kass (1949) gave the test to 18 cases with known organic damage and 12 cases of dubious organic diagnosis, and concluded that the DI failed both in detecting and confirming the presence of organic conditions resulting largely from traumatic brain injury. As a percentage-loss method for expressing psychological deficit, it was found inapplicable in two-thirds of his cases. Diers and Brown (1950), using 25 cases of multiple sclerosis, concluded that the DI was not sensitive enough to be used clinically. Garfield and Fey (1948) found that an equal number of psychotic and non-psychotic patients obtained pathologically high DI's, suggesting that the overlap between organics and functionals would be quite high. Magaret and Simpson (1948) found that the DI rating did not correlate with the psychiatrist's ratings of degree of deterioration. The only study so far to produce reasonably favorable results with the DI was that by McFie and Piercy (1952). Using 56 brain-damaged patients and a cutting score of 10 percent, they were able to identify 43 (71 percent) of them; using a cutting score of 20 percent, they identified 37 (66 percent). No functional patients were tested. In view of the unfavorable results summarized above, it seems clear that indices of deterioration are of little clinical use in their present form.

Halstead (1947), using factorial analysis and various systems of weighting, developed a battery of tests which discriminated at a high level of confidence between normals and patients with lesions of the frontal lobes. The ten tests having the highest t value were selected as the basis of an impairment index. In this arrangement, an individual whose scores fell below the criterion scores on all ten of the key tests had an impairment index of 0.0; while, on a simple proportion basis, an individual who satisfied the criterion score on three of ten key tests had an impairment index of 0.3; or on all of the key tests, an index of 1.0. Using a cutting score of three, he was able to identify all 27 cases of frontal lobe injury and 29 out of 30 normals. The impairment index did not discriminate between normals and other cases of brain damage.

Of the ten tests, the Halstead Category Test (1943; 1947), involving the ability of the subject to "abstract" various organizing principles such as "size," shape," "color," etc. from a series of 336 stimulus figures presented visually and serially by means of a multiple-choice projection apparatus, proved particularly successful. Using a cutting score of 70, he correctly identified 27 out of 29 normals and 10 out of 11 cases with frontal lobe injuries.

When, therefore, the patient is known on other grounds to be neither psychotic nor neurotic, this battery of tests offers a very accurate indication of whether or not the lesion is situated in the frontal lobes. The impairment index was validated on a group different from the standardization group and was repeated on an independent group. The only obvious objection to the index is the inadequate representation of groups other than normals or brain-damaged.

PERCEPTUAL AND MOTOR TESTS OF BRAIN DAMAGE.   Many attempts have been made to use the Rorschach test for the diagnosis of brain damage. The approach has usually been made in terms of signs specific to brain damage. The approach is basically similar to that used in tests employing the concept of deterioration, for the signs are taken to indicate inadequate or lowered performance. One of the earliest approaches was made by Piotrowski (1937; 1938), who used 33 records, consisting of 18 brain-damaged cases, 10 cases with noncerebral disturbance of the central nervous system, and 5 cases of conversion hysteria. Ten signs were selected as differentiating between the three groups. These signs were very carefully defined by Piotrowski. The organic group produced a mean of 6.2 signs; the other groups, a mean of 1.5 signs; there was no overlap between the groups. Thus, it was considered that the presence of five or more of the Piotrowski signs was indicative of brain damage. In a later paper (1940), Piotrowski showed that the number of signs produced was a function, in part, of the severity of the personality changes produced by the disorder, and that the number of signs also increased with age. He also pointed out that some of his signs were produced by schizophrenics and neurotics. He claimed that, out of 56 patients producing five or more signs, 55 were in fact organic; of 25 patients originally considered, but later rejected as such by neurological tests, only one produced an organic record.

Ross (1941) tried to repeat the findings of Piotrowski. He used two groups which closely approximated those used by Piotrowski. He also tested several other groups and found that the signs occurred highly significantly more often in the group with cerebral lesions, and significantly more often in the epileptics, than in all the other groups together. However, although five or more of these signs were found most often in patients with disease of the cerebral cortex and subcortical tissue, they were not specific for these lesions. Thus, 55 percent of brain-damaged patients showed five or more signs, but so did 30 percent with noncortical lesions of the central nervous system, and also 20 percent of the psychotics and 14 percent of the neurotics. Furthermore, Ross showed that 50 percent of the cortical cases and 53 percent of the epileptic cases showed five or more of the Harrower-Erickson signs of neurosis.

In two later papers (Ross, 1944; Ross and Ross, 1944), Ross divided the signs into four groups: those common to neurotic and organic patients; the neurotic differential signs; the organic differential signs; and the organic excluding signs. Each sign was then weighted in rough proportion to its differential incidence in the groups of individuals being compared. The four sets of scores were then combined for each individual to give two ratings. These two ratings were called the "instability" and "disability" ratings, and were standardized on 50 neurotics, 24 organics, 50 superior, and 50 average normals. This represented an advance on Piotrowski's method, in that a patient could be given a rating on both the organic and the neurotic dimensions.

The next important contribution came from Hughes (1948; 1950), who derived 14 signs from a factor analysis of the 22 signs he found in the literature on brain damage. Different weights were assigned to these signs according to their discriminatory power. He used 218 subjects, including 50 with brain damage, 68 schizophrenics, 74 neurotics, 4 manic-depressives, and 22 normals. The point-biserial correlation between presence or absence of brain damage and score on the sign patern was +.79, which was highly significant. When a cutting score of seven or above was used, 82 percent of the organics were correctly identified, while only 1 percent of nonorganics were falsely identified as organic. Using Piotrowski's signs, Hughes could correctly identify only 20 percent of the organics without including many nonorganics.

However, these encouraging results were shown to have a serious flaw by the recent work of Diers and Brown (1951). They took a group of 25 multiple sclerotics and divided them into two groups, 15 with an IQ above 102, and 10 with an IQ below 102. This latter group was carefully matched with 11 nonorganic patients with IQ's below 102. The three groups were then tested and the results analyzed for Hughes's signs. The mean number of signs for the more intelligent organics was only 0.33, none obtaining a score above seven, and ten obtaining a zero or negative score. As opposed to this the organics of average or dull IQ obtained a mean of 5.2 signs, and the nonorganics of average or dull IQ obtained a mean of 4.18 signs. None of the patients in these groups obtained a negative score. Diers and Brown concluded that there is an inverse relationship between IQ measurement on the Wechsler and the weighted Hughes score, independent of the factor of intracranial pathology. The Hughes signs are, therefore, invalid, unless obtained with a patient of high intelligence—and the study showed that, in fact, none of the intelligent organics used by Diers and Brown fell within the organic range.

A new approach was made to the problem by Dörken and Kral (1952), who, instead of asking what signs the organic patient would show on the Rorschach, investigated what signs he would be likely *not* to show. Seven signs were determined, and each sign was weighted according to degree of occurrence in organic or nonorganic states. By this means, a total possible score of ten was determined. In terms of the frequency distribution, the cutting point was fixed between two and three; that is, scores from three to ten, inclusive, exclude a diagnosis of brain damage. Using this method, they claimed that 92.9 percent of organics were identified, and 83.3 percent of nonorganics were identified as such. If Piotrowski's signs were used however, only 50 percent of the organics would be identified; while use of the Ross "disability" ratio identified 75 percent of the organics.

One additional study may be mentioned here. Buhler, Buhler, and Lefever (1948), using 30 normals, 70 neurotics, 50 psychopaths, 27 schizophrenics, and 30 organics, developed a Basic Rorschach Score. They claimed that this score was capable of separating clinical groups in a statistically reliable manner. But they also stated that

the variability of scores within each clinical group indicates that the Basic Rorschach Score alone is not a sufficient basis for individual diagnosis. The placement of the individual case on a scale of adjustment or ego-integration does, however, appear to be a highly probable outcome of the use of the Basic Rorschach Score (p. 161).

In other words, the technique is designed, not to discriminate between organic and other groups as such, but rather to give an estimate of the degree of mental illness—a procedure which is based, apparently, on the theory that persons vary on a single dimension from normal through neurotic to psychotic, and which has been criticized by Eysenck (1952; 1953). A more recent monograph by Buhler, Lefever, Kallstedt, and Peak (1952) confirmed the results obtained in the initial study.

The major criticisms to be made of the Rorschach as a test of brain damage seem to be that in all the scoring systems, except that of Dörken and Kral, the greatest weighting is given to those factors that are the most difficult to score and that depend, therefore, to the highest extent on the subjective evaluation of the examiner. Second, although all authors using the sign approach seem to obtain adequate differentiation of groups for their particular study, the differentiating power invariably drops considerably when these methods are repeated by other workers. Thus, where Piotrowski claimed powerful discrimination for his signs, Dörken and Kral found that they identified only 50 percent of their organic group; and other groups of signs used by Ross declined to an efficiency of 75 percent. Third, most of the studies have ignored the influence of age and intelligence; the classic example of this is, of course, the work of Hughes, which at first sight seemed so promising. We must conclude, therefore, that, while most workers in this field report satisfactory discrimination, the constant "dog eat dog" method by which one set of signs is set aside as unusable and replaced by a new set by subsequent workers does not inspire confidence in the validity of the most recent method, that of Dörken and Kral. That the Rorschach offers distinct promise in this problem cannot be denied; that it has been shown to be a satisfactory test of brain damage is open to question.

Several tests have been recently constructed which are not very well known. Two of these are described in the monograph by Armitage (1946). In their original form, these tests are known as the Trail Making Test and the Patch Test. The Trail Making Test consists of two parts. Part A consists of a sheet of paper on which there is printed a series of circles. In the center of each of these is a number, with a range for the test proper of 1-25, and for the sample, which is on the opposite side of the page, of 1-7. These circles are spatially arranged in a random order. The patient is required to draw a line between the circles, starting at number 1 and finishing at number 25. He is asked to work as rapidly as possible and to erase errors.

Part B is very similar, but more complex, in that the numbered circles are mixed with circles lettered from A onwards. The task is to draw a line from circle one to circle A; then to go to circle two, then to circle B, and so on. Scoring is in terms of time and accuracy. If no errors are made, or if an error is corrected very quickly, the score obtained depends directly on the speed with which the test is completed. If the item is accomplished in less than 20 seconds, a maximum score of ten is given; however, if longer times are taken, partial credits are given. The Patch Test requires the duplication of nine colored circular patterns, one serving as a demonstration design. For every pattern, the materials provided consist of 19 paper circles of different colors. Some of these are solid, while others have different sections of the interior part removed so that, by placing them on top of one another, a pattern may be formed. The test materials are arranged in front of the patient in a standard order. The eight test designs are in graded order of difficulty, and the test is terminated after two failures. Each design, with one exception, can be duplicated only by putting together specific pieces out of the 19 provided. In the standardization of these tests, Armitage used as subjects 44 patients known to have sustained brain damage (9 focal, 17 focal-diffuse, 18 diffuse). The control group consisted of 45 normal subjects and 16 mild neurotics. The groups were considered roughly comparable as to age, level of education, and preinjury occupation.

It was found that Trail Making Test A, the simplest of the tests, discriminated the brain-damaged group best from the two control groups. With a cutting score of 10, the total misclassification was 16 out of 95, 32 of the 44 organics being positively identified. Trail Making Test B identified 39 out of 44 organics, but misclassified 15 out of 51 normals; and a combined score was not more effective. As a clinical instrument, the Patch Test identified 26 out of 43 organics, misclassifying 7 out of 51 controls. The tests would appear to be useful ones and merit further study. Unfortunately, no data are given on the performance of psychotic patients, and the study has not been repeated.

The genesis and construction of the Block Design Rotation Test has been described in three articles by Shapiro (1951; 1952; 1953). This test resulted from the observation that some patients, while doing the Goldstein block design test, left the completed design in a rotated position compared with the test figure. This rotation might be as great as 45°, but rarely exceeded it. Various hypotheses were examined and it was found that the rotation effect could be maximized when three factors were interrelated in a certain way—namely, the factors of figure shape, ground shape, and angle of the line of symmetry (the line of symmetry being defined as the line which divided a design into mirrored halves). Thus, rotation was found to be maximal when the figure and ground shapes were in a diamond orientation and the line of symmetry was at an angle.

From various theoretical and empirical considerations, it was deduced

that the rotation effect would be maximized under these conditions in brain-damaged patients. Accordingly, a special set of cards was devised, 40 in all. Each design could be reproduced by using four Kohs blocks. Two groups of subjects, 19 brain-damaged and 19 psychiatric patients (the latter without brain damage), were carefully matched for age and sex, and given the test under identical conditions. Results were according to prediction, the brain-damaged patients rotating an average of 8° per card, while the functional patients rotated an average of only about 2° per card. Considering the matched pairs together, every brain-damaged patient rotated more than the corresponding functional patient, with one exception—and this patient's diagnosis was later changed independently to one of compensation neurosis. With a cutting score of 6° rotation per card, the test identified 14 out of the 19 brain-damaged patients, but misclassified only 1 functional patient. Nearly all the functional patients rotated a total of less than 200° for the 40 cards, and only one rotated more than 250°. Many brain-damaged patients, on the other hand, rotated more than 400° or 500° for the 40 cards, and much higher totals have been encountered in clinical practice.

When a further group of 19 brain-damaged patients (this time consisting of patients who had actually been operated upon) was tested, a closely similar pattern of results was found. Data on several normal control groups showed that the test also discriminated between normals and brain-damaged patients, and revealed the curious and unexpected fact that, as a group, the controls rotated significantly more than the functionals (though this was significant at the .05 level only). The effects of age, sex, and intelligence have also been calculated and will be published shortly. Thus, the rotation test satisfies the criteria laid down in this paper in that it provides data on at least three groups of subjects, it takes into account factors such as intelligence, age, and sex, and its results have subsequently been confirmed on new, independent groups. It is also an entirely objectively scored test, the amount of rotation being recorded (in the later studies) photographically, with reference to a constant base line.

Using the original two groups of subjects, Shapiro (unpublished data) also found that the manual dexterity test and the finger dexterity test of the U. S. Employment Service battery of tests discriminated very significantly between brain-damaged and functional patients. The former test identified 14 out of the 19 brain-damaged patients and misclassified 3 out of the 19 functionals; the latter identified 12 out of the 19 brain-damaged patients and misclassified 5 out of the 19 functionals. Used together, the tests successfully identified 16 of the brain-damaged patients.

DISCUSSION

It is doubtful whether any aspect of psychological testing has been more inadequately treated than the diagnostic assessment of brain damage. From a wide range of possible criticisms, some of the most obvious will be cited.

(a) In many instances, validation studies have not used comparable groups. For example, the majority of cases in Hunt's (1943) brain-damaged group were paretics and others suffering from diffuse brain damage. In his validation study, Armitage (1946), on the other hand, included many patients suffering from traumatic head injury as the result of penetrating missiles. There is no reason to suppose that these two groups were at all comparable with regard to type, locus, or severity of brain damage. Armitage's procedure may be justified, however, in so far as Hunt described his tests as a measure of brain damage without further qualification.

(b) Few authors, when constructing their tests, choose their cases with sufficient care, in most instances considering brain damage as a unitary factor. That this is unsound from the point of view of diagnosis may be shown by evidence from many sources. Thus, if a random group of brain-damaged patients is given a test, the results nearly always fall into an abnormal distribution (i.e., are skewed). Many of the brain-damaged group behave on a given test like normal controls or functional patients, while others obtain very abnormal scores. Frequently, this sort of pattern accounts for the significance of differences between the groups. This kind of distribution was encountered in the Block Design Rotation Test and was recently seen in a study by Battersby, Teuber, and Bender (1953) on the behavior of brain-damaged patients in a problem-solving situation. From an anatomical and physiological standpoint, there is likewise no reason why all brain-damaged patients should belong together. As Penfield and Evans (1935) pointed out, there is a wealth of difference between the brain damage resulting from scar formation on the temporal lobe following an accident, and the scar formation resulting from a temporal lobectomy. Similarly, there is no reason to suppose that a leucotomy operation will have the same effect as diffuse brain damage.

(c) Many investigators neglect almost completely the elementary necessity for evaluating and controlling various relevant factors such as age, sex, and intelligence. The Shipley-Hartford Retreat Scale, the Rorschach, and the Goldstein test are noteworthy examples where failure to do this has led to ambiguity in the clinical use of the test. That factors such as these cannot be neglected without serious risk of error is apparent from an article by Hebb (1945). Using simple patterns that had to be reproduced with pieces of wood, Hebb found that "no pattern could be devised, which was so easy that all patients in the public wards of a general hospital could succeed with it in one minute, even though other tests showed that one was not dealing with a population of mental defectives" (1945, p. 16). Hebb concludes that, although this kind of material tends to be eliminated in tests which are adequately standardized, "in special tests which have not been standardized, there is a real danger of assuming that a variation from the norm, which is frequently obtained for the normal population, can be due only to the effects of cerebral injury" (p. 17). In addition, many authors fail

to state whether or not their subjects were tested for specific defects, even when this is clearly necessary. The Trail Making and Patch tests, for instance, might well be performed badly by normal persons with defective eyesight. These tests might be peculiarly successful in identifying soldiers suffering from penetrating wounds as brain-damaged, and be completely unsuccessful in cases of diffuse brain damage.

(d) Many tests employ very unreliable and subjective scoring systems. This applies particularly to the Rorschach, where most weight is given to factors such as impotence, perplexity, etc., but also to the Hunt-Minnesota Test, where, for example, more credit is given for a response within one-half of a second than for a response within one-half to one second.

(e) Occasionally, there is failure to realize that a test may discriminate between two groups statistically at a high level of significance, and yet still be unusable clinically because the misclassification would be very high.

(f) In many tests, there is failure to control relevant variables. Thus, in the Hunt-Minnesota test, it is claimed that immediate and long-term memory are being measured. Examination of the items, however, reveals failure to control for differential learning ability.

These criticisms are made on methodological grounds; there seems no reason why they should not be overcome. Assuming that they were overcome, would it be possible to develop adequate tests of brain damage? The answer would appear to be in the negative, *as long as a purely engineering approach is made.* Thus a most painstaking study by Lynn, Levine, and Hewson (1945) was concerned with the aftereffects of exposure to blast during the war. Such exposure might result in a closed head injury with accompanying residual symptomatology determined by the brain damage alone; or in a neurotic syndrome, identical clinically to that attributable to brain damage, but without any actual trauma to the brain: or (most commonly) in a combination of the two. Starting with over 4,000 patients, they reduced this group to 81 "pure" cases and attempted to differentiate these by means of a battery of tests. Elaborate precautions were taken to minimize unreliability of diagnosis and to control for age, sex, intelligence, etc., and a large number of independent validating groups were used. Nevertheless, for these "pure" groups the misclassification was still 12 percent. For the validation groups, it is arguable that the statistical techniques were inadequate, but the results are still disappointing.

The basic flaw in most of the tests discussed above lies, however, in the theoretical approach. Examination of the tests suggests that one major hypothesis concerning the psychological effects of brain damage permeates the work; this is, that brain damage results in deterioration of a relatively permanent nature. Such a theory is unlikely to provide a satisfactory basis for the construction of test of brain damage because it is not exclusive to brain damage. This criticism seems more important than the usual one that deterioration is an ill-defined concept—so much so that Hunt (1944) preferred the neutral term "psychological deficit." Similarly, provided the test is rigorously scored, the assumption that vocabulary level is resistant to the effects of mental illness has been shown to be false by the work of Yacorzynski (1941), Capps (1939), and Simmins (1933); while Crown (1949), using 4 cases of myxedema (which causes apparent intellectual deterioration) tested before and after treatment, found that the Shipley vocabulary MA of these patients rose by an average of 10.2 months following treatment by thyroxine, and on another vocabulary test, the mean vocabulary IQ rose by 6 and 14 points in two of the cases.

The first essential in the construction of tests of brain damage, therefore, is the development of a theory which is exclusive to brain damage. One possible theory has been presented by Shapiro (1951; 1952; 1953) in his articles, and may be stated as follows: *Brain damage results in the development of states of exaggerated inhibition.* Such a theory is more satisfactory than a theory of deterioration (in so far as it is supported by experimental evidence) because it would not be postulated to account for functional disorder or for the behavior of normals. Hence, it becomes possible to make deductions and set up experimental situations in which brain-damaged patients behave differently from others, and through which verification of the theory and development of tests of brain damage are feasible. Having done this and verified the theory in its broad outlines, it now becomes possible to consider alternative hypotheses and also to consider why some brain-damaged patients do not behave as predicted. One immediate possibility, of course, is location of the damage. Halstead (1947) and Rylander (1939; 1943) concur in demonstrating that it appears to be much easier to distinguish brain damage in the frontal lobes from that in other areas of the brain. Another possibility is the significance of previous personality. The interaction of personality structure and the effects of brain damage have been largely ignored by most investigators, although it is known that extensive brain damage may have little or no effect on functioning, and that a brain-damaged patient may be neurotic or psychotic. Now Eysenck (1952) has shown that there are tests which discriminate between psychotics and normals but not between neurotics and normals, and vice versa; he has argued, on this basis, that neuroticism and psychoticism are orthogonal (independent) factors. At this stage, therefore, it would be possible to construct a battery of tests which would give a particular patient a factor score on each of these three dimensions—psychoticism, neuroticism, and brain damage. The question to be answered would then become, not, is the patient psychotic or neurotic or brain-damaged, but what is his performance with respect to these three variables, and what is their interrelationship. At this point, the internal validity of the tests would become important since it would be necessary to show that those tests measuring the effects of brain damage have significantly positive intercorrelations among themselves, but not with the tests of psychoticism or neuroticism. It is clear, therefore, that the problem is much more complex than was suggested in the early part of this paper. In the view of the writer, a purely empirical approach is unlikely to yield satisfactory results, nor is an approach based on a theory which has not been adequately tested experimentally. A satisfactory test of brain damage should be based on a reasonable theory that has been experimentally tested, has been supported by adequate statistical treatment, and has taken into account all relevant variables. Such an approach would at least help to overcome the impasse which seems to have been reached with many of the tests reviewed above.

References

Aita, J. A., Armitage, S. G., Reitan, R. M., and Rabinowitz, A., The use of certain psychological tests in the evaluation of brain injury, *J. gen. Psychol.*, 1947, 37, 25-44.

Allen, R. M., The test performance of the brain-injured, *J. clin. Psychol.*, 1947, 3, 225-230.

Andersen, A. L., The effect of laterality of localization of brain damage on Wechsler-Bellevue indices of deterioration, *J. clin. Psychol.*, 1950, 6, 191-194.

Armitage, S. G., An analysis of certain psychological tests used for the evaluation of brain injury, *Psychol. Monogr.*, 1946, 60, No. 1 (Whole No. 277).

Ash, P., The reliability of psychiatric diagnoses, *J. abnorm. soc. Psychol.*, 1949, 44, 272-276.

Battersby, W. S., Teuber, H. L., and Bender, M. B., Problem solving behavior in men with frontal or occipital brain injuries, *J. Psychol.*, 1953, 35, 329-351.

Boyd, H. F., A provisional quantitative scoring with preliminary norms for the Goldstein-Scheerer Cube Test, *J. clin. Psychol.*, 1949, 5, 148-153.

Buhler, Charlotte, Buhler, K., and Lefever, D. W., *Development of the Basic Rorschach Score with manual of directions* (Los Angeles, California: Rorschach Standardization Studies, No. I, 1948).

Buhler, Charlotte, Lefever, D. W., Kallstedt, Frances E., and Peak, H. M., *Development of the Basic Rorschach Score. Supplementary monograph* (Los Angeles, California: Rorschach Standardization Studies, 1952).

Buros, O. K. (Editor), *The third mental measurements yearbook* (New Brunswick, New Jersey: Rutgers University Press, 1949).

Canter, A. H., Direct and indirect measures of psychological deficit in multiple sclerosis, Part II, *J. gen. Psychol.*, 1951, 44, 27-50.

Capps, H. M., Vocabulary changes in mental deterioration, *Arch. Psychol.*, 1939, 34, No. 242.

Corsini, R. J., and Fassett, Katherine K., The validity of Wechsler's mental deterioration index, *J. consult. Psychol.*, 1952, 16, 462-468.

Crown, S., Notes on an experimental study of intellectual deterioration, *Brit. med. J.*, 1949, 2, 684-685.

Dier, W. C., and Brown, C. C., Psychometric patterns associated with multiple sclerosis. I. Wechsler-Bellevue patterns, *Arch. Neurol. Psychiat.*, 1950, 63, 760-765.

Diers, W. C., and Brown, C. C., Rorschach "organic signs" and intelligence level, *J. consult. Psychol.*, 1951, *15*, 343-345.

Dörken, H., and Kral, V. A., The psychological differentiation of organic brain lesions and their localization by means of the Rorschach test, *Amer. J. Psychiat.*, 1952, *108*, 764-771.

Eysenck, H. J., *The scientific study of personality* (London: Routledge & Kegan Paul, 1952).

Eysenck, H. J., *The structure of human personality* (London: Methuen, 1953).

Fleming, G. W. T. R., The Shipley-Hartford Retreat Scale for measuring intellectual impairment. A preliminary communication, *J. ment. Sci.*, 1943, *89*, 64-68.

Garfield, S. L., and Fey, W. F., A comparison of the Wechsler-Bellevue and Shipley-Hartford scales as measures of mental impairment, *J. consult. Psychol.*, 1948, *12*, 259-264.

Goldstein, K., and Scheerer, M., Abstract and concrete behavior. An experimental study with special tests, *Psychol. Monogr.*, 1941, *53*, No. 2 (Whole No. 239).

Grassi, J. R., The Fairfield Block Substitution Test for measuring intellectual impairment, *Psychiat. Quart.*, 1947, *21*, 474-489.

Grassi, J. R., *The Grassi Block Substitution Test for measuring organic brain pathology* (Springfield, Illinois: Charles C Thomas, 1953).

Gutman, Brigette, The application of the Wechsler-Bellevue scale in the diagnosis of organic brain disorders, *J. clin. Psychol.*, 1950, *6*, 195-198.

Hall, K. R. L., The testing of abstraction with special reference to impairment in schizophrenia, *Brit. J. med. Psychol.*, 1951, *24*, 118-131.

Halstead, W. C., Preliminary analysis of grouping behavior in patients with cerebral injury by the method of equivalent and nonequivalent stimuli, *Amer. J. Psychiat.*, 1940, *96*, 1263-1294.

Halstead, W. C., *Brain and intelligence. A quantitative study of the frontal lobes* (Chicago: University of Chicago Press, 1947).

Halstead, W. C., and Settlage, P. H., Grouping behavior of normal persons and of persons with lesions of the brain. Further analysis, *Arch. Neurol. Psychiat., Chicago*, 1943, *49*, 489-506.

Hebb, D. O., Man's frontal lobes, *Arch. Neurol. Psychiat., Chicago*, 1945, *54*, 10-24.

Hewson, Louise, R., The Wechsler-Bellevue scale and the substitution test as aids in neuropsychiatric diagnosis, *J. nerv. ment. Dis.*, 1949, *109*, 158-183, 246-266.

Hughes, R. M., Rorschach signs for the diagnosis of organic pathology, *J. proj. Tech.*, 1948, *12*, 165-167.

Hughes, R. M., A factor analysis of Rorschach diagnostic signs, *J. gen. Psychol.*, 1950, *43*, 85-103.

Hunt, H. F., A practical clinical test for organic brain damage, *J. appl. Psychol.*, 1943, *27*, 375-386.

Hunt, J. McV. (Editor), *Personality and the behavior disorders.* Vol. 2 (New York: Ronald, 1944).

Hutton, E. L., The investigation of personality in patients treated by prefrontal leucotomy, *J. ment. Sci.*, 1942, *88*, 275-281.

Juckem, Harriet, J., and Wold, Jane A., A study of the Hunt-Minnesota test for organic brain damage at the upper levels of vocabulary, *J. consult. Psychol.*, 1948, *12*, 53-57.

Kass, W., Wechsler's mental deterioration index in the diagnosis of organic brain disease, *Trans. Kans. Acad. Sci.*, 1949, 52, 66-70.

Kobler, F. J., The measurement of improvement among neuropsychiatric patients in an army convalescent facility, *J. clin. Psychol.*, 1947, 3, 121-128.

Levi, J., Oppenheim, Sadie, and Wechsler, D., Clinical use of the mental deterioration index of the Bellevue-Wechsler scale, *J. abnorm. soc. Psychol.*, 1945, 40, 405-407.

Lidz, T., Gay, J. R., and Tietze, C., Intelligence in cerebral deficit states and schizophrenia measured by Kohs block test, *Arch. Neurol. Psychiat.*, Chicago, 1942, 48, 568-582.

Lynn, J. G., Levine, Kate N., and Hewson, Louise R., Psychologic tests for the clinical evaluation of late "diffuse organic," "neurotic," and "normal" reactions after closed head injury, *Proc. Ass. Res. nerv. ment. Dis.*, 1945, 24, 296-378.

McFie, J., and Piercy, M. F., Intellectual impairment with localized cerebral lesions, *Brain*, 1952, 75, 292-311.

Magaret, Ann, and Simpson, Mary M., A comparison of two measures of deterioration in psychotic patients, *J. consult. Psychol.*, 1948, 12, 265-269.

Malamud, Rachel F., Validity of the Hunt-Minnesota test for organic brain damage, *J. appl. Psychol.*, 1946, 30, 271-275.

Manson, M. P., and Grayson, H. M., The Shipley-Hartford Retreat Scale as a measure of intellectual impairment for military prisoners, *J. appl. Psychol.*, 1947, 31, 67-81.

Meehl, P. E., and Jeffery, Mary, The Hunt-Minnesota test for organic brain damage in cases of functional depression, *J. appl. Psychol.*, 1946, 30, 276-287.

Penfield, W., and Evans, J., The frontal lobe in man: A clinical study of maximum removals, *Brain*, 1935, 58, 115-133.

Piotrowski, Z., The Rorschach inkblot method in organic disturbance of the central nervous system, *J. nerv. ment. Dis.*, 1937, 86, 525-537.

Piotrowski, Z., Rorschach studies of cases with lesions of the frontal lobes, *Brit. J. med. Psychol.*, 1938, 17, 105-118.

Piotrowski, Z., Positive and negative Rorschach organic reactions, *Rorschach Res. Exch.*, 1940, 4, 147-151.

Reynell, W. R., A psychometric method of determining intellectual loss following head injury, *J. ment. Sci.*, 1944, 90, 710-719.

Rogers, L. S., A comparative evaluation of the Wechsler-Bellevue mental deterioration index for various adult groups, *J. clin. Psychol.*, 1950, 6, 199-202.

Ross, W. D., The contribution of the Rorschach method of clinical diagnosis, *J. ment. Sci.*, 1941, 87, 331-348.

Ross, W. D., A quantitative use of the Rorschach method. "Instability" and "disability" ratings which show clinical and psychometric correlations, *Amer. J. Psychiat.*, 1944, 101, 100-104.

Ross, W. D., and McNaughton, F. L., Head injury: A study of patients with chronic posttraumatic complaints, *Arch. Neurol. Psychiat.*, Chicago, 1944, 52, 255-269.

Ross, W. D., and Ross, Sally, Some Rorschach ratings of clinical value, *Rorschach Res. Exch.*, 1944, 8, 1-9.

Rylander, G., *Personality changes after operations on the frontal lobes* (London: Oxford University Press, 1939).

Rylander, G., Mental changes after excision of cerebral tissue. A clinical study of 16 cases of resections in the parietal, temporal and occipital lobes, *Acta Psychiat. Neurol.*, 1943, Suppl. 25.

Scheerer, M., An experiment in abstraction. Testing form-disparity tolerance, *Conf. neurol.*, 1949, 9, 232-254.

Shapiro, M. B., Experimental studies of a perceptual anomaly: I. Initial experiments, *J. ment. Sci.*, 1951, 97, 90-110.

Shapiro, M. B., Experimental studies of a perceptual anomaly: II. Confirmatory and explanatory experiments, *J. ment. Sci.*, 1952, 98, 605-617.

Shapiro, M. B., Experimental studies of a perceptual anomaly: III. The testing of an explanatory theory, *J. ment. Sci.*, 1953, 99, 394-409.

Shipley, W. C., A self-administering scale for measuring intellectual impairment and deterioration, *J. Psychol.*, 1940, 9, 371-377.

Shipley, W. C., and Burlingame, C. C., A convenient self-administering scale for measuring intellectual impairment in psychotics, *Amer. J. Psychiat*, 1941, 97, 1313-1325.

Simmins, C. A., Studies in experimental psychiatry: IV. Deterioration of g in psychotic patients, *J. ment. Sci.*, 1933, 79, 704-734.

Tooth, G., On the use of mental tests for the measurement of disability after head injury. With a comparison between the results of these tests in patients after head injury and psychoneurotics, *J. Neurol. Neurosurg. Psychiat.*, 1947, 10, 1-11.

Wechsler, D., *The measurement of adult intelligence* (Baltimore: Williams & Wilkins, 1944).

Yacorzynski, G. K., An evaluation of the postulates underlying the Babcock deterioration test, *Psychol. Rev.*, 1941, 48, 261-267.

SECTION B: Diagnostic Procedures

20 DIAGNOSTIC METHODS USED WITH LEARNING DISABILITY CASES

R. F. Capobianco ~

Perhaps the one irrefutable characteristic attributed to children with learning disabilities is their wide variability of behavior. Considerable time, effort, and money has been expended in attempts to describe, measure, diagnose, and remedy the learning problems which are commonly regarded as the aftereffects of brain injury. Efforts to group these children into categories variously termed neurologically impaired, exogenous, cerebrally dysfunctioned, and the like, have complicated the interpretation of research findings rather than providing a basis for operational definitions. With the intensity of effort to "pigeonhole" or classify these youngsters as one clinical entity, the behavioral descriptions which resulted have grown far out of proportion to functional diagnosis. Indeed, if the exhaustive list of behaviors attributed to neurologically impaired children were accepted at face value, then it would be difficult, if not impossible, to imagine a child who could not be labeled brain injured on the basis of one set of behaviors or another.

Modern educators and psychologists have attempted to skirt the problem of diagnostic difficulty by coining a new phrase for the old list of names —children with learning disorders (or disabilities). This new phrase provides for the inclusion of all youngsters with a syndrome of behaviors which interfere with the learning process and yet eliminates the inherent difficulty in establishing the existence of a brain injury. Hence, the modern special class for children with learning disabilities may be composed of youngsters who are brain injured, emotionally disturbed, visually impaired, auditorially handicapped, intellectually subnormal, or suffering from some motor imbalance—perhaps any one individual may be hampered by a combination

Reprinted from *Exceptional Children*, Vol. 31, No. 4 (December, 1964), pp. 187-193. By permission of the author and publisher.

of these handicaps. The apparent heterogeneity of these children according to the multiplicity of labels is deceiving. They are no less homogeneous than groups of students collected together merely because they have been categorized as brain injured. Nevertheless, it is suspected that for some time to come, classes for children with learning disabilities will still be composed predominantly of youngsters who meet the psychoeducational criteria established for the brain-injured—the only difference being that they will not be labeled brain injured.

Candidates for these special classes are selected primarily on the basis of the overt display of certain characteristics such as underachievement, hyperactivity, distractibility, poor motor coordination, impulsivity and short attention span and secondarily on their performance on selected psychological tests of perceptual processes. There is no intent here to argue for or against this approach; indeed, this author has suggested years ago that teachers should deal with symptomatology rather than etiology. Similar notes of caution have been voiced by Barnett, Ellis, and Pryer (1960), Gallagher (1957), Kirk and McCarthy (1961) and Newland (1963) among others. In the final analysis, the worth of the program will rest upon the adequacy with which specific methods tend to alleviate identifiable learning impairments without respect to causation.

Clinical-educational techniques have been devised which purport to lessen the difficulties in learning, characteristic of brain injured, or "Strauss syndrome" children. Varying degrees of success have been reported by psychologists and educators employing these methods. But who is to say that all children with learning disabilities need to be exposed to this intensive program of special education to insure learning? Certainly there would be less expenditure of time and effort and fewer demands for extensive professional training on the part of teachers if some of these children could learn without recourse to rigorous programs of education suggested by some professional educators. Hence, the importance of an exhaustive psycho-educational diagnosis to determine the need for specific clinical-educational techniques and devices which would eliminate or remedy certain behaviors detrimental to learning. Kirk and McCarthy (1961) have already differentiated between classification and diagnosis, as has Newland (1963) between testing and assessment. Mere classification and/or testing does not necessarily prescribe treatment—complete diagnosis or assessment implies a course of remediation with prognosis.

The diagnosis of brain injury is difficult to formulate. Even with identification, the problem is not so readily resolved; for the neurologically impaired do not follow any typical, preconceived set of behaviors. In fact, the behaviors exhibited, vary so greatly that the differences observed are as variable intragroup as between brain-injured and normal populations. To complicate the situation further, many of the neurologically impaired children do not present any specific learning problem in the classroom whereas non brain-injured children with supposedly organic behaviors do have difficulty.

One attempt to isolate and refine some subpopulations of brain-injured mental retardates according to behavior was described by Capobianco and Funk (1958). The Rorschach test was administered to exogenous and endogenous subjects representing both sexes. A pathology gradient was established, based upon electroencephalographic tracings, which isolated four groups: endogenous-normal, endogenous-convulsive, exogenous-convulsive and exogenous-focal. Omitting the first group, the remaining three may be considered brain injured. Although there may seem to be an apparent contradiction within the category, endogenous-convulsive, let it be known that the original endogenous-exogenous dichotomy was based upon the Riggs and Rain (1952) classification system before administration of the electroencephalogram (EEG). Thus, convulsive tracings were found in records of children who had originally been diagnosed as familial retardates (endogenous) without evidence of brain damage. Although the EEG is admittedly not a foolproof test, the proportion of abnormal tracings (58 percent) found the familial population far exceeded the expected error.

The emerging patterns on the selected Rorschach variables, followed closely the hypothesized gradient, reversals occurring occasionally between the endogenous-normal and endogenous-convulsive categories. Results were interpreted by the authors as follows: "If this function of pathology and etiology is 'real,' the exogenous-focal end of the distribution reflects more conceptualizing; more outward-directed affect; more interest in people; less immature, stereotyped thinking; more feelings of negative self-appraisal; less negativism; and more perceptual difficulty . . ." (Capobianco and Funk, 1958, p. 68). The authors caution that this pathology gradient is based upon the results of a very small sample of familial and brain-injured retardates but that it should promise to be a fertile area for research in the future.

Similar attempts to refine subpopulations of children according to specific kinds of brain damage and EEG tracings have been reported by Burns (1960) and Sievers and Rosenberg (1960).

DIAGNOSTIC PROCEDURES

The asserted preponderance of learning difficulties exhibited by organically impaired children has been the mainstay of the argument presented by those professionals who view the education of these children as a distinct and separate process. The fact that some of the neurologically impaired children do not experience difficulties in the learning process and that some nonimpaired children do, is not sufficient justification to eliminate special teaching methodology. Insofar as the teacher is concerned, the disturbing behaviors demonstrated by these children, brain-injured or not, must be eliminated or modified. The teacher will find no difficulty in recognizing that all is not well with a child who:

(1) Follows no logical pattern in his behavior.
(2) Never sticks with anything over a long period of time.
(3) Wanders aimlessly about the room apparently concerned with everyone else's business.
(4) Never sits still for a minute—always runs never walks.
(5) Acts before thinking—seldom considering the consequences of his behavior.
(6) Repeats, excessively, a task or movement.
(7) May be able to read but not comprehend the significance of what has been read.
(8) Experiences difficulties in arithmetic, performing at a level far below expectancy.
(9) Demonstrates visuomotor difficulties.
(10) Seems at times to be out of contact—does not hear you.
(11) Rapidly changes his mood or temperament.
(12) Performs inconsistently and with marked variability in the various school subjects.

These behaviors do not comprise a total list of indicators of potential organicity; however, they serve as specific examples of the many factors comprising the learning difficulty syndrome. It is not within the province of the school teacher's responsibility to make the diagnosis, but rather it is his duty to utilize techniques and methodologies which prove to alleviate the condition responsible for the inadequacy of the child's functioning. When the techniques at the teacher's disposal do not improve the situation, then it is time to request a diagnostic workup by the school psychologist.

It is a rare school system indeed which has available to its students the services of a neurologist. Hence, the problem of identification of the brain injury usually falls into the hands of the school psychologist. Working in collaboration with the classroom teacher and the school physician or nurse, a screening process is effected. If the evidence obtained is sufficient to warrant a referral to a neurological specialist, it is based upon the collective information gleaned from behavorial descriptions, medical evidence, and psychological assessment. Strauss and Lehtinen have established four criteria for a complete diagnosis of minor brain damage: (a) a history of trauma before, during or after birth, (b) neurological (or "soft") signs are present, (c) evidence that the child comes from normal familial stock, and (d) indicative evidence gleaned from psychological tests (1947). In recent years the trend in diagnosis of brain injury has been to rely more and more upon the results and interpretation of psychological tests. Complete neurological examinations, including the administration of the electroencephalographic test, often fail to discover positive evidence of injury, and, perhaps equally often, may discern an injury which is nonexistent. Positive identification through the utilization of multitudinous tests of perceptual and conceptual disturbances are equally questionable—but considerably less expensive and time consuming. Oftentimes, the behavior described by the classroom teacher may overtly appear to be an indicator of brain damage but may actually be the result of some emotional upheaval recently affecting the child. Other characteristic behaviors may be "read in" by the referring teacher, often in good faith, but without basis in fact. The failure of his particular teaching methods with the child in question may lead to a request for diagnostic information out of sheer desperation in not knowing what next to do. Whatever the reason for the request for further information on the child, the psychologist must serve as the first recourse for the teacher in the total assessment process.

The diagnostician is often forced to make a decision regarding the role he must play—to serve as an ancillary aide to the neurologist or to provide some practical suggestions for the teacher. Usually, the suspected degree of impairment serves to decide the course of action. Mild cases are groomed for the educator; more severe suspects are assessed for future referral to the neurologist. For education purposes, the psychologist is better equipped than the neurologist to offer recommendations regarding remedial techniques. Only for cases requiring medical treatment, such as post-encephalitis or tumors, would the referal to the neurologist be of subsequent help to the educator.

Armed with an array of information on the child which includes his cumulative record and the behavioral description prepared by the teacher, the psychologist then selects the particular instrument or battery of tests to administer in his search for diagnostic evidence. A multitude of tests are already available which purport to be of unique value toward the diagnostic evaluation of brain-injured behaviors. Many clinicians prefer to utilize various subtests from standardized instruments seeking to arrive at qualitative evidence in addition to quantitative scores. This type of assessment, a "cafeteria" approach has been described by Newland (1963) as an effective approach in the absence of individual devices suitable for use. This method of diagnosis is only as proficient as the clinician who employs it. In the hands of an inexperienced clinician or untrained personnel, the method would be relatively useless and perhaps dangerous.

Scatter patterns on some tests of intelligence have been investigated to determine characteristic performance of brain-damaged patients. Unfortunately, the results of research efforts in this area of diagnosis are often misleading and confusing—indeed, the results of one investigator may be directly contradictory to the conclusions formulated by another. Reitan (1955), in his very comprehensive work on Wechsler-Bellevue patterning, found that brain-damaged subjects generally exhibited characteristic patterns based upon the extent and localization of the brain insult. Verified left hemisphere damage usually resulted in lower Verbal than Performance IQ's while the reverse was true of right hemisphere lesions. Subjects with diffuse damage performed approximately equally well on both scales. Morrow and

Mark (1955) reported characteristically low performance by brain-injured subjects on Digit-Symbol, Digit-Span and Arithmetic in support of Reitan (1955) and Wechsler (1944). On the other hand, Beck and Lam (1955) found no characteristic subtest patterns for their brain-damaged subjects and Taterka and Katz (1955) reported that Coding, as a subtest, was affected adversely by brain damage. In an extensive comparative study of exogenous and endogenous subjects, Capobianco and Funk (1958) found similar patterns on the Wechsler Intelligence Scale for Children for both groups and both sexes. The differences between groups was in the predicted direction on the Arithmetic, Block Design, and Coding subtests; however, these differences were not statistically significant.

Many workers in the field have reported varying degrees of success in diagnosis of brain injury using perceptual organization tests such as the Rorschach, Bender-Gestalt, Graham-Kendall, Ellis Visual Design and a variety of cube, stick, marble, and mosaic tests. The results are inconclusive. Even though many of the studies demonstrated differences in performance between brain-damaged and nondamaged subjects, individual children who scored poorly on one of these tests did not necessarily score correspondingly on another. Many known cases of brain injury are not isolated by these instruments and the number of over referrals is overwhelming.

Even if the reader were willing to accept the diagnostic patterning of test scores and/or inferior performance on perceptual tests as truly characteristic of brain-injured functioning, he would still be at a loss to explain why these deficiencies apparently do not hamper educational progress. Research reports by Bensberg (1958), Capobianco (1956), Capobianco and Miller (1958), Capobianco and Funk (1958) and Gallagher (1957) among others, have failed to discern any significant differences in performance between brain-damaged and nondamaged subjects on a number of educational and psychological variables. In an exhaustive investigation of psychological and psychophysical abilities displayed by organic and familial retardates, Clausen found that of 51 variables measured, only one (critical flicker frequency) obtained significance at the .05 level (Personal communication, 1964). Although other investigators have reported poorer performance by brain-injured subjects on this test (but not consistently), this one significant difference out of 51 comparisons could easily have occurred on a chance basis. Barnett, Ellis, and Pryer (1960) suggest that the term "brain injury" be dropped since it has been demonstrated that all Ss so labeled do not exhibit distinct behaviors nor do they necessarily demand special modes of instruction.

The one significant finding pervading this research is the characteristic variability of performance by brain-damaged subjects, far in excess of the performance exhibited by the control subjects—mean performances, however, remained relatively consistent. Attempts to subgroup populations of brain-injured subjects along an ordered continuum [pathology gradient proposed by Capobianco and Funk (1958)], and new methods of differential diagnosis (Illinois Test of Psycholinguistic Abilities) recently developed by Kirk and McCarthy (1961) appear to offer keys to future success in the bothersome area of brain-injured functioning.

CLASSROOM BEHAVIOR

One cannot expect the teacher to be proficient in the administration and interpretation of projective techniques, intelligence tests, and tests of perceptual organization. The responsibility of the teacher in the total assessment process is far removed from the one to one clinical setting. First and foremost, the teacher is expected to keep complete records, including achievement tests, samples of school work, anecdotal reports and rating scales. One incidence of unpredictable behavior in the classroom is not sufficient reason to trot the child to the nearest psychologist. But periodic outbreaks of unexplainable behavior, short attention span and hyperactivity, coupled with poor scholastic performance, would warrant genuine concern on the part of the teacher. Unlike the consistently poor achievement characteristic of the mentally retarded child, the brain-injured child displays an irregular pattern of performance. He may be very proficient in reading and far below capacity in arithmetic. He may excel in verbal facility but experience considerable difficulty in reasoning. He may display superficial charm in initiating social acquaintances yet "wear off" with the passage of time. He may learn quickly some skills which emphasize rote but fail miserably in tasks which require independent thinking. These inconsistencies should be noted in the teacher's anecdotal records.

The periodic use of sociograms within the classroom often gives significant information to the teacher. The hyperactive, disinhibited youngster is seldom accepted by his classmates. The individual's own choices of peers on the sociogram give some clue as to the personality he himself may desire to be. Gross distortions in the child's art work serve to implement further the informal diagnosis within the classroom. The child at play exhibits behaviors which oftentimes yield more information regarding his problem than actual classroom performances. All too often the teacher does not take note of this particular fertile area for study. Obviously, the teacher cannot keep a complete, up to date, ongoing record on every child in his room but behaviors of note should be included in the anecdotal record. Trusting to memory, the teacher often fails to record significant behaviors which occur during the school day. The practice of attempting to record all pertinent information at the end of the school day should be abandoned in favor of immediate recording—not total descriptions of the incident but a word or two to identify the behavior, who was involved, and the time it occurred. Later, the more complete description may be recorded. With information as complete as described, the teacher not only systemizes his own interpretation of the youngster's behavior but also preserves diagnostic information which would be an invaluable asset to the psychologist who may ultimately be responsible for the complete assessment of the child.

Rating scales, such as described by Gallagher (1957), force an orderly account of the children's behavior. These instruments provide insurance against the tendency, on the part of many observers, to record only the negative aspects of behavior.

SUMMARY

The term brain injury has failed to serve any practical function. It is an etiological concept which offers little to the educator, psychologist, or other specialist who is interested in the behavioral symptomatology of the child with learning disabilities. The generic term adds more confusion to a field in which specialists are constantly seeking to differentiate subpopulations through newly formulated diagnostic systems. The term itself offers no help to the specialists engaged in the development of sound educational and therapeutic programs to ameliorate the problems demonstrated by children with special learning disabilities. Some investigators have proposed new titles for the general area of brain damage without essentially dismissing the criticisms leveled above. One of the effects of the newer terminology was to instill in the minds of the regular classroom teacher a greater fear of those youngsters labeled cerebral dysfunction, neurophrenia or organically impaired. In the eyes of the teacher these newer diagnoses quickly joined those originally labeled brain injured as youngsters "who cannot learn." Some attempts to isolate specific subgroups of brain-injured youngsters in accordance with differential characteristics are more rewarding. Differential diagnosis within this field, however, is still at the infancy stage of development.

Recently, parents of these children have established organizations which seek to collect and distribute information in an attempt to educate the layman regarding the disabilities of brain-injured children. This movement has been directly or indirectly responsible for the establishment of many public school special classes for these children. Psychologists and educators have collaborated with neurologists and pediatricians in helping the parent groups to present professional programs to their membership. Research and demonstration projects are currently on the upswing in this field. Specialists representing the allied areas of emotional disturbance, mental retardation, orthopedic handicaps, and remedial instruction have sought a reciprocal interrelationship with authorities in the field of neurological impairment to consolidate their respective gains made to date. State departments of education have included special classes for the brain-injured within their structure of reimbursement, special aids and transportation allowances. The growth within the field is constantly supplemented by new discoveries in the areas of neurology and psychology. Clinical educational techniques which have proven value in the training of brain-injured youngsters are periodically described in the literature. Hence, in spite of the large gaps which exist in our knowledge of this area, the infant field of brain injury is starting to grow up.

Diagnostic procedures, at this writing, are still somewhat spotty. It is difficult, at best, to expect the classroom teacher to succeed in the technical aspects of diagnosis when the instruments of the neurologists and psychologists are still subject to gross errors. Whereas one particular clinician may experience a high degree of success with one battery of tests, a similarly trained specialist may question its validity. The research literature compounds the confusion by presenting conflicting results often within the same issue of a specific journal.

The burden of action, nevertheless, remains with the teacher. Keeping complete records on learning disability cases is one of his major responsibilities. Armed with an organized series of reports, including tests results, rating scales, sociograms, anecdotal records, and personal impressions, the teacher is in an excellent position to discuss the particular problem with the school psychologist. Prescriptions for teacher reaction to the child's behavior are supplied by the psychologist. He may recommend firm control for the hyperactive, disinhibited child and more permissiveness for the withdrawn, apathetic youngster. Gallagher (1960) describes a system of tutoring which was successful with brain-injured, mentally retarded children. Perhaps the new movement to establish special classes for children with similar learning disabilities may reduce some of the frustrations suffered by the diagnostician who no longer will find it necessary to "prove" that a brain injury exists.

References

Barnett, C. D., Ellis, N. R., and Pryer, M. W., Learning in familial and brain-injured defectives, *Amer. J. ment. Def.*, 1960, 64, 894-901.

Beck, H. S., and Lam, R. L., Use of the WISC in predicting organicity, *J. clin. Psychol.*, 1955, 11, 154-158.

Bensberg, G. J., The relation of academic achievement of mental defectives to mental age, sex, institutionalization and etiology, *Amer. J. ment. Def.*, 1953, 58, 327-330.

Burns, R. C., Behavioral differences between brain-injured and brain-deficit children grouped according to neuropathological types, *Amer. J. ment. Def.*, 1960, 65, 326-334.

Capobianco, R. J., Quantitative and qualitative analyses of endogenous and exogenous boys on arithmetic achievement, *Monogr. Soc. Res. Child Develpm.*, 1956, 19, 101-141.

Capobianco, R. J., and Funk, Ruth A., *A comparative study of intellectual, neurological, and perceptual processes as related to reading achievement of exogenous and endogenous retarded children* (New York: Syracuse University Research Institute, 1958).

Capobianco, R. J., and Miller, D. Y., *Quantitative and qualitative analyses of exogenous and endogenous children in some reading processes* (New York: Syracuse University Research Institute, 1958).

Gallagher, J. J., A comparison of brain-injured and non-brain-injured mentally retarded children on several psychological variables, *Monogr. Soc. Res. Child Develpm.*, 1957, 22, (2).

Gallagher, J. J., *The tutoring of brain-injured mentally retarded children* (Springfield, Illinois: Charles C Thomas, 1960).

Kirk, S. A., and McCarthy, J. J., The Illinois test of psycholinguistic abilities—an approach to differential diagnosis, *Amer. J. ment. Def.*, 1961, 66, 399-412.

Morrow, R. S., and Mark, J. C., The correlation of intelligence and neurological findings on 22 patients autopsied for brain damage, *J. consult. Psychol.*, 1955, 19, 283-289.

Newland, T. E., Psychological assessment of exceptional children. In Cruickshank, W. (Editor), *Psychology of exceptional children and youth* (2nd Ed.) (Englewood Cliffs, New Jersey: Prentice-Hall, 1963).

Reitan, R. M., Certain differential effects of left and right cerebral lesions in human adults, *J. comp. physiol. Psychol.*, 1955, 48, 474-477.

Riggs, Margaret M., and Rain, Margaret E., A classification system for the mentally retarded, *Training School Bull.*, 1952, 49, 151-168.

Sievers, Dorothy L., and Rosenberg, C. C., The differential language facility test and electroencephalograms of brain-injured mentally retarded children, *Amer. J. ment. Def.*, 1960, 65, 46-50.

Strauss, A. A., and Lehtinen, Laura E., *Psychopathology and education of the brain-injured child* (New York: Grune & Stratton, 1947).

Taterka, J. H., and Katz, J., Study of correlations between electroencephalographic and psychological patterns in emotionally disturbed children, *Psychosom. Med.*, 1955, 22, 62-72.

Wechsler, D., *The measurement of adult intelligence* (3rd Ed.) (Baltimore: Williams & Wilkins, 1944).

21 DETECTING PSYCHOLOGICAL SYMPTOMS

OF BRAIN INJURY

Harry S. Beck

During the past ten or fifteen years educators have become increasingly aware of the existence of the brain-injured child, especially in association with remedial and special education programs. There has been a growing awareness, too, of the need for better program planning for these children in both academic and nonacademic areas, in and out of school.

Although a medical diagnosis of brain injury may not be of great importance, from a strictly pedagogical point of view, it is important from the standpoint of medical therapy which may make the child more accessible or amenable to learning, and in terms of prognosis for development.

As educators we are particularly interested in the psychological symptoms in terms of planning an educational program for these children. It should be pointed out that there are both psychological and physical symptoms associated with brain injury, and that traditionally the diagnosis has been based primarily upon the physical symptoms (i.e., neurological examinations, electroencephalograms, pneumoencephalograms, x-rays, etc.).

In effect, then, a medically diagnosed brain-injured child will usually display some psychological symptoms, but a child displaying these symptoms may not necessarily be brain injured from a medical viewpoint. This is certainly not the most desirable state of affairs, but it nevertheless represents the present situation. This point is brought up because it may well be that any correlation which exists between the so-called psychological symptoms of brain injury and medically or physically determined brain injury is an associative relationship, rather than a cause-effect relationship.

This article is primarily concerned with the effects of brain injury in

Reprinted from *Exceptional Children*, Vol. 28, No. 1 (September, 1961), pp. 57-62. By permission of the author and publisher.

children who show no gross muscular involvements such as some of the cerebral palsied. The emphasis is upon those cases that Strauss and Lehtinen (1950) refer to as exogenous, and Doll (1951b) classifies under neurophrenia. In these children the injury usually occurs before, during, or shortly after birth, and the children are more often than not considered to be problems of behavior or learning. According to Bender (1956) they usually are referred to clinics for some reason other than the brain injury itself.

The problem is, of course, to gain a better understanding of the particular symptoms which these children present and to determine whether there is a definite syndrome of symptoms characteristic of brain injury in children. Another aspect of the problem is concerned with the validity, in terms of medical agreement, of psychological tests for detecting this condition.

It was felt that the best approach would be to survey the literature and summarize the findings of some of the outstanding writers in this area. In this way it could be determined, to some extent, the amount of agreement among those writers concerning the symptoms of brain injury and their detection.

EXTENT OF PROBLEM

Although it is becoming more and more apparent that the brain-injured child exists in greater numbers than was suspected a few years back, the full extent of the problem is not known. Beck (1956) estimates that at least 60 to 70 percent of all educable mentally handicapped school children are brain injured, and Gesell and Amatruda (1954) estimate that the brain-injured comprise one-fifth of all cases of amentia and over one-third of the motor disabilities of crippled children. The number of cases having normal or better intelligence whose difficulties are manifested by personality problems, reading disabilities, and the like is unknown. Courville (1950) states that some degree of injury occurs during delivery in probably more cases than is commonly appreciated.

In reading literature describing the brain-injured child, it is not difficult to see that the various writers are talking about the same type of child. In other words, it can be readily seen that the child being described is one whom we know from experience to be brain injured. Yet when listing the actual symptoms described by these authors, no two lists are exactly alike. In all, 43 symptoms were found, with one writer listing 32, and another mentioning only six.

This, however, does not represent as great a diversity as it would appear on the surface. A great deal of the disparity results from the fact that some writers use very specific terms such as dysphasia and dysarthria, while another groups them together under language disorders. Another source of difficulty results from the fact that different authors are writing for different purposes. Strauss and Lehtinen (1950), for example, are quite definitive and describe a number of brain-injured children displaying different symptoms. Yacorzynski (1951), on the other hand, describes some specific disabilities such as those found in cases with frontal lobe involvements. As a consequence, it is almost impossible to compare these writings for the purpose of making a normative study. However, these different authors would probably be in agreement on any given case.

TABLE 21-1:   Symptoms Ascribed to Brain-Injured Children
                by Various Writers

distractibility	disparity in development
perseveration	hyperactivity
catastrophic reaction	difficulty in symbolization
temper tantrums	animistic thinking
disorganization	emotional instability
visual perceptual difficulties	insecurity
conceptual difficulties	daydreaming
detail consciousness	irritability
difficulty in spatial visualization	difficulty in forming associations
concrete thinking	confused laterality
difficulty in auditory perception	poor retention
dysarthria	convulsions
dysphasia	mental deficiency
agnosia	lack of insight
apraxia	fatigability
impulsiveness	rigidity
compulsions	abnormal stimulus boundness
disinhibition	poor body image and identification
poor motor coordination	anxiety
difficulty in visual imagery	clinging behavior
poor ability to anticipate	destructiveness
over-responsive to stimuli	

By grouping some of the more specific symptoms under more general headings, one finds that the majority of writers are fairly well agreed on 15 categories. Table 21-2 indicates the symptoms most commonly agreed upon by Strauss and Lehtinen (1950), Doll (1951b), Carmichael (1954), Tredgold (1952), Goldstein (1954), Bender (1956), Gesell and Amatruda (1954), and Yacorzynski (1951).

Doll (1951a) has summed up the situation rather well with his statement that it is not feasible at this time to delineate either the neurological antecedents or the behavior sequelae with definitive exactness, but rather, this must be left to further experience, observation, and research.

Although there is considerable agreement as far as the various symptoms are concerned, there is no indication that any given symptom must of necessity be present in any given case of brain injury. Kephart states, "In general the association of specific psychological symptoms with brain pathology has not been successful. It would appear that brain damage, except in specific motor and sensory areas, leads to a disturbance of the integration of behavior rather than to the development of isolated symptoms."[1]

TABLE 21-2:   Symptoms of Brain Injury Indicated by the
               Majority of Writers

perseveration	disparity in development
distractibility	hyperactivity
disorganization or lack	emotional instability
of integration	insecurity
perceptual difficulties	irritability
conceptual difficulties	convulsions
language disorders	mental deficiency
motor incoordination	poor retention

This is not too surprising, when one stops to consider that in most cases the injuries are minimal and diffused and that different areas and functions of the brain are affected to differing degrees in various individuals. Then, too, the inherent make up of the brain and its ability to resist, repair, or compensate damage varies from one child to another. Gesell and Amatruda (1954) indicate that the consequences of very slight injury are greatly aggravated by emotional sensitivity in the child and by faulty environment and care. They further state that in infants and young children the symptomatology of nervous disease tends to be diffuse rather than localized, and it is this diffuseness that accounts for the injury to intellect and to personality that so often accompanies affections of the nervous system in infancy and childhood.

This then brings us to Strauss and Lehtinen's (1950, p. 4) definition: "A brain-injured child is a child who before, during, or after birth has received an injury to or suffered an infection of the brain. As a result of such organic impairment, defects of the neuromotor system may be present or absent; however, such a child may show disturbances in perception, thinking, and emotional behavior, either separately or in combination." It seems to the writer that this definition is a good summary of the situation as it presently exists.

Since, as we have seen, the symptoms of brain injury can be quite varied, and as they do not necessarily fall into any given pattern, certain implications become apparent with regard to psychological testing. To begin with, we are faced with the problem of determining whether any of these symptoms exist, which means that an extremely large number of abilities and a wide range of behavior need to be sampled and evaluated. This would

[1] This statement was taken from a personal communication with Dr. N. D. Kephart.

imply that a shotgun type of approach be used in the beginning, followed up by more specific techniques in those areas which are suspected as pathological. If this be true, then it becomes necessary to evaluate both general tests or test batteries, and specific tests or tests of specific functions.

GENERAL VS. SPECIFIC TESTS

With regard to general tests, Strauss and Lehtinen (1950) have stated that, with few exceptions, there does not exist at this moment, a pattern or a type of response characteristic and specific for the brain-injured defective child on standardized tests of intelligence, academic achievement, and visuo-motor performance. Beck and Lam (1955), using a public school group of mentally handicapped children, found that the WISC Performance IQ's and WISC Full Scale IQ's of organics were significantly lower than those of nonorganics. In the organic group the Performance IQ's tended to be lower than the Verbal IQ's, whereas the nonorganics showed a reverse pattern. There was no characteristic patterning of subtest scores, however.

On the other hand, Newman and Loos (1955), using an institutional population, found that organics show no difference in WISC Verbal and Performance IQ's but that organics do have lower Performance IQ's than do familials and undifferentiated groups. Haines (1954) did a study using the Merrill-Palmer Scale of Mental Tests and concluded that it was not useful for the differential diagnosis of brain-injured children from problem or foster home children. Berko (1955) found that exogenous mentally handicapped children had a significantly larger scattering of misses on the Stanford-Binet items than endogenous mentally retarded children. On the basis of these studies, it would seem that disparities in the child's development are reflected in the child's performance on the WISC and Stanford-Binet, which may suggest, to the examiner, the possibility of brain injury.

On tests designed to evaluate more specific functions, there is also more doubt than certainty as to their validity in differentiating between brain-injured and non brain-injured. Most of them do not stand up under rigorous statistical analysis. Yates (1954) reviewed some of the more commonly used qualitative and quantitative tests and noted that most of them are subject to criticism. He found only two tests that seemed to differentiate organics consistently. One was the Block Design Rotation Test, and the other was the Manual and Finger Dexterity Tests of the U. S. Employment Service Battery. Unfortunately these tests are designed and/or standardized on adults and not children. Strauss and Kephart (1950) also studied some of the tests commonly used with children and concluded that the validation of tests of this sort was still incomplete. One of the main objections was that there had been no systematic attempt to differentiate brain-injured from emotionally disturbed children. Of all the tests studied, the two most promising were the Ellis Visual Designs and the "Method" or "Approach" score on the Marble Board Test. These two were far superior to the others.

Inasmuch as most tests are lacking in statistical validity as predictors or indicators of brain injury, it is interesting to note Goldstein's (1954, p. 114) comment on this situation: "In pathology, results of examinations can be evaluated only by analyzing the procedure by which the patient has arrived at his results. This precludes any statistical comparison with the results of normal subjects. Any quantitative rating, as to success and failure by use of the usual tests, constitutes an infinite source of error." It would seem then that diagnosis is, at its present stage of development, more of an art than a science, and consequently the diagnosis must necessarily be a function of the examiner and not the tests.

Yates (1954) feels that the basic flaw in most of the tests of brain damage lies in the theoretical approach. Instead of employing the theory that brain damage results in deterioration, he suggests that what is needed is a theory which is exclusive to brain damage. Strauss and Kephart (1950), on the other hand, seem to feel that what is needed is further development and refinement of some of the tests presently in use.

The big problem in differential diagnosis seems to lie in the ability, or lack of ability, of tests to distinguish between organic brain damage and emotional disturbances. This, however, assumes that the symptoms are the same, or can be the same, in both conditions. If this be so, then it would seem impossible to devise a test to distinguish between the two conditions, since the overt behavior which the test measures would be the same in either case.

FUNCTIONAL BRAIN IMPAIRMENT

At this point the writer would raise the question as to whether or not it is actually possible to get the same identical symptoms, or constellation of symptoms, in both conditions, or whether the apparent confusion is the result of our inability to make an adequate medical diagnosis. This also brings up the question of the possibility of functional brain impairment. If, for example, an individual developed an emotional disturbance, which resulted in some change in body chemistry, this might conceivably result in electrical changes in the brain, which in turn might affect its functioning.

In fact, Darrow (1950, p. 59) states, ". . . feedback effects which, when they act moderately, appear to provide regulation of the central nervous system, but which, when they become excessive in strong emotion, may produce relative functional decortication." Darrow (1950b, p. 248) also states, "Furthermore, if these mechanisms are operative during the child's early stages of rapid growth and development, it is easy to understand how chronic states of emotional perturbation not only may alter the normal activity of the brain but may even prevent its normal development." If this is possible, then final diagnosis may depend upon the determination of the reversibility of the condition.

It would seem that Yates (1954) has put his finger on the crux of the whole situation. If psychological tests are going to be employed to determine the etiology of malfunction, then it is necessary to determine functions which are characteristic of, and peculiar to, the precise etiological factor in question. This may prove to be a formidable problem in the light of present knowledge. This is particularly true, when even medical or physical diagnosis of brain disorder is based on inferences as the result of the neurologist's evaluation of the individual's functioning. Actually medicine is, to some extent, faced with the same problem as psychology, and until better means are found to make the medical determinations, it is doubtful how far psychological testing can be extended.

From a practical point of view, the outlook perhaps is not as dismal as the theoretical considerations would suggest. In the case of a child, we are concerned with several problems, all of which can be dealt with fairly well regardless of the theoretical problems. For example, neurological examination, plus E.E.G.'s, X-rays, pneumoencephalograms, etc., can determine fairly well whether or not there are any major injuries, tumors, convulsive disorders, etc., and, if so, the proper procedures can be instituted. If medical evaluation definitely reveals damage then, of course, there is no problem of diagnosis. The problem then becomes one of determining the desirability of medication or other therapy, and the prognosis for future development.

If, on the other hand, the medical diagnosis is uncertain or negative, then the problem is whether or not there is damage which is medically undetectable. This is the dilemma with which we are faced in trying to prescribe adequate emotional and educational procedures, therapy, rehabilitation, and the like. Actually this doesn't present too great a problem, since the same procedure can be used in either case. The greatest difficulties resulting from this sort of situation might be some loss of time, and injury to the ego of the psychologist, if after treatment, the diagnosis turned out to be different than he predicted.

If the child displayed emotional or behavior problems, they would be handled about the same in either case. If he displayed learning difficulties suggestive of brain injury, he would be taught with techniques designed to overcome these difficulties. If a child displayed difficulty in perception or concept formation, the teaching techniques would be the same whether he turned out to be brain injured or not. When one considers the practical aspects of the situation, it then becomes apparent that present psychological techniques, especially if they can be more fully developed and refined, can be of real value as far as treatment is concerned.

References

Baker, H. J., *Introduction to exceptional children* (New York: Macmillan, 1945).

Beck, H. S., The incidence of brain injury in public school special classes for the educable mentally handicapped, *J. ment. Def.*, 1956, *60*, 818-822.

Beck, H. S., and Lam, R. L., Use of the WISC in predicting organicity, *J. clin. Psychol.*, 1955, *11*, 154-158.

Benda, C. E., *Developmental disorders of mentation and cerebral palsies* (New York: Grune & Stratton, 1952).

Bender, Lauretta, *Psychopathology of children with organic brain disorders* (Springfield, Illinois: Charles C Thomas, 1956).

Berko, M. J., A note on "Psychometric Scatter" as a factor in the differentiation of exogenous and endogenous mental deficiency, *Cerebral Palsy Rev.*, 1955, *16*, (1).

Buros, O. K. (Editor), *The fourth mental measurements yearbook* (Highland Park: The Gryphon Press, 1953).

Carmichael, L., *Manual of child psychology* (New York: Wiley, 1954).

Courville, C. B., *Pathology of the central nervous system* (Mount View: Pacific Press, 1950).

Darrow, C. W., A mechanism for "functional" effects of emotion on the brain. In W. C. Halstead (Editor), Brain and behavior, *Comp. Psychol. Monogrs.*, 1950a, No. 2.

Darrow, C. W., A new frontier: Neurophysiological effects of emotion on the brain. In M. L. Reymert (Editor), *Feelings and emotions* (Mooseheart Symposium) (New York: McGraw-Hill, 1950b) Chapter 20.

Doll, E. A., Mental evaluation of children with expressive handicaps, *Amer. J. Orthopsychiat.*, 1951a, *21*, 148-154.

Doll, E. A., Neurophrenia, *Amer. J. Psychiat.*, 1951b, July, *108*, 50-53.

Doll, E. A., Varieties of slow learners, *Except. Child.*, 1953, *20*, 61-64.

Doll, E. A., Mental deficiency vs. neurophrenia, *Amer. J. ment. Def.*, 1953, *57*, 477-480.

Doll, E. A., and Walker, Mabelle S., Handedness in cerebral palsied children, *J. consult. Psychol.*, 1951, *15*, 9-17.

Gesell, A., and Amatruda, C. S., *Developmental diagnosis* (New York: Hoeber-Harper, 1954).

Goldstein, K., in H. Michal-Smith, *Pediatric problems in clinical practice* (New York: Grune & Stratton, 1954).

Grassi, J. R., *The Grassi Block Substitution Test for measuring organic brain pathology* (Springfield, Illinois: Charles C Thomas, 1953).

Haines, Miriam S., Test performance of preschool children with and without organic brain pathology, *J. consult. Psychol.*, 1954, *18*, 371-374.

Hunt, J. Mc. V., *Personality and the behavior disorders* (New York: Ronald, 1944).

Louttit, C. M., *Clinical psychology* (New York: Harper & Row, 1947).

Mikesell, W. H., *Modern abnormal psychology* (New York: Philosophical Library, 1950).

Newman, J. R., and Loos, F. M., Differences between verbal and performance I.Q.'s with mentally defective children on the Wechsler Intelligence Scale for Children, *J. consult. Psychol.*, 1955, *19*, 16.

Penfield, W., and Rassmussen, T., *The cerebral cortex of man* (New York: Macmillan, 1952).

Pennington, L. A., and Berg, I. A., *An introduction to clinical psychology* (New York: Ronald, 1954).

Penrose, L. S., *The biology of mental defect* (London: Sidgwick & Jackson, 1949).

Sarason, S. B., *Psychological problems in mental deficiency* (New York: Harper & Row, 1949).

Strauss, A. A., and Kephart, N. C., *Psychopathology and education of the brain-injured child*; Vol. 2, *Progress in theory and clinic* (New York: Grune & Stratton, 1950).

Strauss, A. A., and Lehtinen, Laura E., *Psychopathology and education of the brain-injured child* (New York: Grune & Stratton, 1950).

Tredgold, A. F., and Tredgold, R. F., *Mental deficiency* (Baltimore: Williams & Wilkins, 1952).

White, R. W., *The abnormal personality* (New York: Ronald, 1948).

Yacorzynski, G. K., *Medical psychology* (New York: Ronald, 1951).

Yates, A. J., The validity of some psychological tests of brain damage, *Psychol. Bul.*, 1954, 51, 359-377.

22 DIAGNOSIS OF CEREBRAL DYSFUNCTION IN CHILDREN

Leo J. Hanvik, Sherman E. Nelson,
Harold B. Hanson, Arnold S. Anderson,
William H. Dressler, and V. Richard Zarling

INTRODUCTION

Workers in the various fields of child behavior have long been aware that mental disturbances of different kinds result, in some patients, from some type and degree of organic defect causing either generalized or localized impairment of function of brain tissue. The pathological manifestations of cerebral damage are usually believed to be of two general types—first, those symptoms which result directly from the loss of or damage to cerebral tissue, and, second, symptoms not directly associated with tissue loss, but, rather, symptoms of indirect or "superimposed" psychological disturbances, e.g., the patient's reactions to or attitudes toward disability occasioned by brain damage. Evidence of cerebral dysfunction may show up in one or more areas, such as sensory or motor function, intellectual functioning, emotional control, manifestation of seizure phenomena, and others.

In medicine, the classical picture of the brain-injured child has traditionally included some motor defect as a primary condition. Beginning with the work in the early 1900's of Pierce Bailey, William Healey, and others, an extensive literature has grown up over the years dealing with the psychological consequences of concomitants of brain damage in children. Interest in brain dysfunction has become interdisciplinary and has been particularly high in the fields of psychology and education, in addition to medicine. At the present time, there are in this country private and public schools and classes for the education of "brain-injured" children. As a result of such great attention to this problem, a broadening diagnostic approach has evolved and there have been developed many diagnostic tools for use in

Reprinted from the American Journal of Diseases of Children, March 1961, Vol. 101, pp. 364-375. Copyright 1961, by American Medical Association.

diagnosing brain damage. Interest in the problem of brain damage and the differential diagnostic difficulties have grown apace. As the number of avenues for diagnostic analysis have multiplied, the problem of disagreement among the various diagnostic procedures has arisen. It has been this lack of agreement among various accepted procedures or criteria for the diagnosis of brain damage, as well as our needs and interests as practitioners in the child guidance field, which have prompted the present study.

A brief description of the clinic in which this study was done should be given. Washburn Memorial Clinic provides outpatient psychiatric treatment for children with emotional, behavioral, and personality problems. The clinic accepts children for psychiatric treatment, the latter being carried out along conventional child guidance lines, the "team approach" of psychiatrist, clinical psychologist, and psychiatric social worker being used. The clinic does not accept cases for diagnosis only. At the clinic we see a wide range of problems ranging from minor disciplinary problems to quite serious personality or adjustment disorders. Known mentally retarded children are excluded from clinic services.

The title of the present interdisciplinary research study, "Diagnosis of Cerebral Dysfunction in Children as Made in a Child Guidance Clinic," delineates the area of investigation only broadly. Our main aims in the present study can be summarized under the following three headings designated Aim 1, Aim 2, and Aim 3.

AIM 1. A study of the diagnostic agreement among clinicians using three separate diagnostic procedures for evaluating brain damage: (a) the medical history and general physical and neurological examination methods as employed by a pediatrician on the research team; (b) an electroencephalographic examination as employed by a neurologist on the research team; and (c) a clinical psychological examination. Under procedure (b) and still related to Aim 1 above, a side study was done in which a second electroencephalographer evaluated the electroencephalographic recordings independently, thus providing the investigators with a "reliability" or consistency rating of the electroencephalogram, that is, a measure of interexaminer agreement on the same individual records. Under Aim 1 we tried to answer the question, "How well do the pediatrician, electroencephalographer, and clinical psychologist agree on which children are to be called brain-injured children?" In addition, we tried to answer the question "How well do two electroencephalographers agree on what is an 'abnormal' electroencephalographic record?"

AIM 2. An evaluation of the electroencephalogram as a diagnostic test or criterion for brain damage in children. In attempting to get at this phase of the problem, the investigators made comparisons between a group of children with "normal" electroencephalograms and a group of children with "abnormal" electroencephalograms with respect to history and medical and psychological examination data, as will be described in detail below. Under

Aim 2 we tried to answer the question, "How do children with 'abnormal' EEG's differ from children with 'normal' EEG's?"

AIM 3. A final computation as to the "incidence" of brain damage in child guidance clinic patients, defining brain damage both in terms of the individual diagnostic tools used and in terms of a final diagnosis as made by a psychiatrist using any and all of the data mentioned above and using, in addition, the social work "intake" study of the child done at the time of admission to the clinic. Under Aim 3 we tried to answer the question, "How many children coming to this particular child guidance clinic during this period are called 'brain injured' by a pediatrician, electroencephalographers, clinical psychologists and a psychiatrist?"

The description of the methods used in the study, as well as a description of the patient samples studied, will be given in the next section, following which the results of the investigation will be summarized and discussed.

METHOD

The general method used was performance of routine electroencephalographic, pediatric, and clinical psychological examinations on all children of ages 7 through 14 years who were referred to the Washburn Memorial Clinic, a children's psychiatric clinic, in an 18-month period between September 15, 1955, and March 15, 1957. During this period of time, all of the above studies were completed on a total of 150 patients. All nonwhite children and all known cerebral palsied children were excluded from the study by provisions in the research design. Children with previously diagnosed convulsive disorders were not excluded, and a total number of 3 of these children came into the research sample. The total sample of children studied amounted to 90 percent of the entire total of children referred to the clinic during the period mentioned above. (Two cases out of the total of 150 were omitted from final data analyses owing to lack of complete details in all examination areas; hence, most tables given below relating to the total group show a total N of 148. All tables based on the matched group of cases show an N of 108.)

As indicated above, the electroencephalogram was obtained on all children in the study, and in this phase of the study the children were classified into 2 groups—those with normal EEG's and those with abnormal EEG's. No borderline categories were used for purposes of the study. "Normal" and "abnormal" evaluations were given according to standards for age in the "Atlas for Encephalography" (Gibbs and Gibbs, 1950). Electroencephalographic recordings were made on an eight-channel, Grass instrument, Model III D. The following technique was used: Disk-type electrodes were attached to the scalp, using Bentonite electrode compound. Ten recording electrodes were placed on the scalp on the frontal, parietal, temporal, and occipital areas on each side and on the ears. A ground electrode was also attached to the scalp. All of the children were given identical tests

—scalp to the respective ears, scalp to scalp, and scalp to the ears interconnected. Three minutes of hyperventilation were induced while recording scalp to ears interconnected. Two separate electroencephalographers read each EEG recording independently and arrived at independent conclusions as to normality or abnormality on each record. This procedure was followed to provide an opportunity for the investigators to get some data on the agreement of independent EEG readings as was referred to under Aim 1 of the study outlined in the Introduction. Another advantage of having two judges in the study was that an extra check for errors or other discrepancies in the classification of the electroencephalographic records was provided, inasmuch as each record which yielded a different rating by the two different readers was then reread by both judges together, so that the reading of the electroencephalographic record on those children in which there was initial disagreement was really a joint reading of both judges, reflecting the opinions of both as they reread the tracing together.

From the pool of cases collected by means of the above method, a group was obtained which consisted of a matched group of pairs of children, one member of the pair having an abnormal electroencephalogram and one member having a normal electroencephalogram. The matching of cases was done by the investigators with respect to the following features: (1) Age: within one year. (2) Sex. (3) Socioeconomic group: Census classification of labor force categories of fathers' occupations was used, according to 1955 census data. (Mother's occupation was used instead of father's in cases in which there was no father in the home.) (4) Race: all white. (5) Intelligence: within 15 IQ points of the full scale WISC IQ. (Matching within Wechsler's Intelligence Classification categories was achieved in most instances.) (6) Marital status of parents: married and living together, separated, divorced, or widowed. After all possible matching of cases was completed, the resultant study group consisted of 54 matched pairs, i.e., 108 cases of children aged 7 through 14 years. The general features of the study group were analyzed and deemed to be a representative sampling of the socioeconomic groupings of the community served by the clinic. About three-fourths of the sample of children were living with both natural parents. About four-fifths of the total sample of children studied were boys, a proportion which has remained quite constant over several years in this clinic.

The psychological test battery, which made up one of the main areas of evaluation of the children, was a standard battery which took about two hours average time to administer and which consisted of the following tests: (1) The Wechsler Intelligence Scale for Children (11 subtests); (2) Bender Gestalt Test; (3) Goodenough Draw-A-Man Test; (4) Seguin Formboard (from Arthur Point Scale, Revised, Form II, 1947); (5) Knox Cube Test (from Arthur Point Scale, Revised, Form II, 1947); (6) Porteus Mazes; (7) Memory for Designs Test (Stanford-Binet subtest); (8) Raven

Progressive Matrices (1947); (9) cerebral dominance test (simple test of eye, hand, and foot preference); (10) Jastak Wide Range Reading Test.

In addition to the formal test battery, the psychologist who did the examination also completed a behavior rating scale on the child. This scale, called "Rating Scale A," was designed by the clinic specifically for the present research study and should be described briefly here. This rating scale was the result of a study of the literature on rating scales and of a study of the clinic files, with particular attention to the kinds of descriptive adjectives which intake workers used in describing children's behavior disturbances as reported by the parents, particularly at the time of admission to the clinic. After preliminary work, a scale of ten items was developed and this 10-item behavior rating scale was used by the psychologist at the time of his study of the child. The items were selected for this rating scale on the basis of the feasibility of making a rating on the variable as the result of a relatively short contact, i.e., no items were included on this scale which were deemed not capable of being rated after a contact of about two hours with the child in the office. The behavior tapped by the rating scale included the following areas: activity or motility pattern which the child exhibited in the test and interview situations, expressions of fear, of anger, reactions to approval given by the psychologist to the child, coordination, insofar as it could be observed during the studies, verbal output of the child, any habit spasms or manipulations or mannerisms exhibited by the child, speech quality, attention span, and, finally, the degree to which the child showed insight into the reason for his referral to the clinic, that is, the degree to which he talked about his problems. The scale itself was a four-step rating scale and there was an attempt in designing the scale to organize the ratings from 1 to 4 in such a way that the child who answered to what the investigators considered the "stereotype" of the uninhibited, hyperactive child would be rated in the high direction, that is, the child would tend to obtain high scores on the 10 variables. The withdrawn and the generally placid, conforming type of child behavior would result in low scores on this rating scale. It was anticipated that the total score itself might be useful in differentiating the children with normal electroencephalograms from those with abnormal electroencephalograms, that is, to see whether these children behaved differently. It should be added that one of the reasons that the notion of rating scales was developed in the present study was that the investigators' preliminary study of the files and also of the literature revealed such variability among various intake workers in describing child behavior or interpreting the parents' descriptions of such behavior, that it was felt that some formalization of the behavioral descriptions was necessary if any structured comparisons were anticipated between the clinical groupings. The psychological examination setting was chosen as one logical place in which to have ratings obtained on the child since this was the first contact of the child at the clinic and, therefore, no "halo effect" from other data on the child could be operating. This was the first contact of the parents at the clinic, so that any ideas or interpretations which the parents obtained in their initial interview had no bearing on the child's behavior since the child was seen and rated simultaneously while the parent was having the initial interview with the social worker. The psychologist's ratings were uncontaminated by any data other than that coming out during his examination, since at the time he did the ratings he knew nothing of the child's problems from any prior source and was reacting purely to the child and to his behavior in the clinical situation at the moment.

Although not developed for use as a part of the psychological examination, another rating scale, "Rating Scale B," was developed through procedures similar to those used in developing Behavior Rating Scale A. As the former scale was finally used in the study in its completed form, it consisted of 30 items which tapped various areas of the child's behavior on which we felt the parents would be able to rate the child. The procedure for using the scale was to have each of the parents rate the child at the time of the initial contact with the clinic. These ratings were done independently by the parents without any assistance from anyone at the clinic. Each of the 30 items was distributed along a 6-step continuum and, as was the case in Behavior Rating Scale A, the scale was designed so that children who scored in the low direction would tend to be the less active children and those who scored in the high direction would tend to be, again, the hyperkinetic "behavior problem" type of child. Also, the idea of scoring the scale by using the total summation of the ratings was followed through on Scale B as well as in Scale A. In Scale B, therefore, the total possible score would be 180 if the child should be rated 6 on all 30 items— and the lowest possible score would be 30—if the child should be rated 1 on all items. The design of the scale is such that it resulted in a "forced choice" situation for the parents, inasmuch as no average ratings were allowed, although the scale was built around the concept of "the average child."

The general behavior areas covered by Rating Scale B were the following: quarrelsomeness, tendencies to anger, introversion-extroversion, bossiness, tendency to commit cruel acts, fearfulness, hyperactivity, sleeplessness, consideration for others, physical coordination, separation anxiety, jealousy, moodiness, sensitivity, tenseness, personal neatness, compulsiveness, daydreaminess, stubbornness, destructiveness, exhibitionism, ability to give and receive affection, and general negativism. The results of Rating Scale B were not available to the psychologist who did the psychological examination at the time of the examination, and his evaluation of the child as to the presence or absence of brain damage was based entirely on the results of his battery of tests and his own ratings of the child on Rating

Scale A. As in the case of Rating Scale A, it was hoped that this second rating scale would help us to determine if children with normal EEG's behaved differently from those with abnormal EEG's.

At the conclusion of his examination and rating of the child, the psychologist was required to enter into a notebook a final evaluative judgment as to the presence or absence of brain damage. This judgment was in the form of a rating system of positive or negative. A numerical system of degrees of confidence in the rating was appended; for example, a child might be rated $+3$, meaning that the psychologist thought the tests and his general examination of the child yielded a positive finding for brain damage and that in this finding the psychologist placed the strongest degree of confidence. The total range was from $+3$ to -3, with no indeterminate ratings.

The pediatrician's examination, like the electroencephalographic and psychological examinations, was done independently, and, like the other two examination procedures, was done as a part of the intake process at the time the family applied to the clinic and prior to any psychiatric treatment at the clinic. In accordance with the research design, the pediatrician, upon conclusion of his study of the child, formulated a diagnostic impression as to whether or not the child he examined was to be considered as showing evidence of organic brain damage. The pediatrician made use of either history or clinical findings or both and made a judgment assigning an unequivocal positive or negative final rating with respect to brain damage in each case. As a part of his examination procedure, the pediatrician completed an examination record checking individual abnormalities which he found, e.g., positive tests for adiadochokinesia, incoordination, abnormal tendon reflexes, abnormal postural righting reflexes, etc. The complete medical history which the pediatrician took as a part of his study of the child was supplemented by the intake worker's social history to which the pediatrician had access at the time of his study of the child.

RESULTS AND COMMENT

The results will be summarized under the three aims given in the Introduction.

For findings under Aim 1 as to the degree of agreement among the various diagnostic procedures the reader is referred to Table 22-1. From Table 22-1 it can be seen that, with the exception of the relationships between the EEG ratings and the medical examination ratings (the latter including both history and examination findings), the correlations show agreement of a degree which is significantly different statistically from chance findings, but which, nevertheless, is not of a very high order. In the case of the agreement between the EEG ratings and the psychologist's ratings, it can be seen that the degree of agreement increases if the "borderline" categories (plus 1 ratings and minus 1 ratings) are omitted from consideration. The coefficient of correlation between the EEG ratings and the psychological examination ratings is 0.40 if the +1's and —1's are included, but it goes up to 0.58 if these ratings are omitted. This finding would suggest that when the psychologists rating the children had more confidence in their rating of "brain damage" or "no brain damage," there was greater agreement between their rating and that obtained on the electroencephalogram. This type of comparison cannot be done in the other study diagnoses because no borderline types of ratings were available for either the medical examination results or the EEG findings.

Also under Aim 1, as to the agreement between the two electroencephalographers, it was found that the two independent interpretations of the same EEG record corresponded with each other to a statistically significant degree. From Table 22-1 it can be seen that the coefficient of correla-

TABLE 22-1: Correlations between diagnostic procedures ($N=148$).

Procedures	r	P
EEG and medical examination ratings	0.04	above 0.05
*EEG and psychological examination ratings	0.40	0.01
Medical examination and psychological examination	0.35	0.01
Two independent interpretations of same EEG record	0.64	0.001

° Coefficient of correlation (r) is 0.58 if "borderline" ratings on the psychological examination (i.e., number "1" ratings) are omitted and only strongly positive and strongly negative ratings are used in the comparisons with the EEG ratings. (No borderline type ratings were available on the EEG or medical examination.)

tion between the 2 independent EEG ratings was 0.64, which is significant at the 0.001 level of probability. That is, the two independent raters of the same EEG records agreed frequently enough that one probably could not account for their degree of agreement on the basis of chance. In terms of the actual number of records on which the two electroencephalographers agreed or disagreed, it was found that the two individuals rated 107 of the total number of 150 records in the same direction, while they disagreed on the remaining 43 records. Percentage-wise, they agreed on 71.33 percent of the records which they read independently and they disagreed on the remaining 28.67 percent. The percentage of agreement which would be expected on the basis of chance would be 52.04 percent agreement (i.e., chance is not 50 percent because abnormal-normal ratings were not split evenly in the study population). After reading the records independently to start with and after tabulation of the degree of independent agreement and disagreement, the two electroencephalographers took the 43 records on which they had disagreed and went over the tracings together, arriving at a final joint rating on these records. (The actual total of records reread turned out to be 41 records, rather than 43 records, because two of the records which were disagreed upon and which were to be reread were some-how lost and, therefore, were not reread and not included in the study from that point on. As has been indicated previously, this is the reason why several of the tables show the total number of cases to be 148, rather than 150.) Thus, using the final results where a single diagnostic conclusion had been reached on each record, it was found that 94 records, or 62.83 percent of the total number, were read as normal records, and the remaining 55 records, or 37.17 percent of the total, were reread as abnormal.

Our overall conclusion from the intercorrelations among the various diagnostic procedures is that evidently there is a common denominator in the various diagnostic procedures to which all of the clinicians react through their respective techniques, but that the resultant agreement is not very high, even though it is in all except one instance significantly different from chance. This aspect of the study has suggested that, at least within the limits of the present study, we perhaps cannot look upon any of the tests used singly as a definite or final test to be used alone in the diagnosis of brain damage. Evidently, we are defining brain damage differently, just as we are testing different aspects of cerebral functioning. It would appear that the only sound procedure is to look upon the problem of making a diagnosis of this sort as one requiring a variety of diagnostic tests, such as the electroencephalogram, clinical psychological examination, physical examinations, and perhaps other studies. A thorough social history on both child and family is invaluable. Through the use of these various techniques a clinician, or a team of clinicians, could arrive at a final diagnostic choice which in a practical situation probably would include not only the definitely abnormal and definitely normal cases, but also the borderline or suspicious group of patients. With respect to the samples studied in the present investigation, it also should be kept in mind that in terms of the overall continuum of patients showing evidence of brain damage, the Washburn Clinic sample would, in its entirety, be a sample which would be expected to exhibit relatively mild degrees of brain damage if present, for the more obvious and gross brain damage syndromes, e.g., cerebral palsied patients, have been eliminated or diagnosed previously. As will be discussed further on, the arrival at some sort of final or definitive single diagnostic label is also not always necessary in the clinical situation, although it is recognized that in some situations it is necessary because further diagnostic studies as well as treatment procedures might be dependent upon the diagnostic impression of the presence or absence of brain damage (Anderson, 1960).

It will be recalled from the Introduction that Aim 2 of this study was to evaluate the electroencephalogram as a "criterion" for brain damage in children by comparing a group of children with normal electroencephalograms with a matching group of children with abnormal electrocephalograms. The basis for matching and the data available for comparison have been given in the Introduction. The results of this phase of the study can be rather briefly summarized because the differences which showed up between the normal EEG group and the abnormal EEG group on either the psychometrics, the behavior rating scales, or the pediatric examination were rather small. On the pediatric examination, including history, there were no significant differences among the various findings when the normal EEG group was compared with the abnormal EEG group. On the neurological examination, there was an interesting tendency for the children with abnormal EEG's to be more frequently noted as having done poorly on the coordination tests, such as the finger-nose test, etc. However, these were only trends, and they were not statistically significant. On the rating scales, there were trends for children with abnormal EEG's to be rated higher, i.e., in the hyperactive and aggressive direction, but these trends were not significantly different when compared quantitatively. By the clinical psychological examination it was found that among the 11 Wechsler Intelligence Scale for Children subtests, there was only one significant difference between the normal EEG group and the abnormal EEG group, and this was on the Coding subtest of the Performance Scale. The patients with abnormal EEG's scored significantly lower on the Coding subtest. The difference between the mean Coding subtest scores of the two groups was significant at the two percent level. Out of all of the other clinical psychological examinations administered, the only other test showing a significant difference between the abnormal EEG group and the normal EEG group was the Bender Gestalt Test (Bender, 1938), where the subjective rating of the protocol by the examiner showed a significant agreement with the abnormal EEG's. This was the case in spite of the fact that the overall scores, according to the Pascal-Suttell System, did not show any significant difference between the abnormal and the normal EEG group. The correlation between the psychological examiner's subjective ratings as to normality or abnormality on the Bender and the EEG rating was 0.33, which is significant at the five percent level. An interesting finding in relation to Bender Gestalt Test differences between the normal and abnormal EEG groups was that, although the total score on the test did not differentiate the normal and abnormal EEG groups, nevertheless, the following three items in the scoring system did differentiate the two groups: (a) the number of dots on Figure 3; (b) asymmetry of the curved portion of Figure 4; and (c) distortion of Figure 8. There were no differences in frequency of rotation such as a previous study suggested might be present (Hanvik, 1954). All of the above differences were in the expected direction, i.e., the abnormal EEG group did significantly poorer than the normal EEG group on the above three items. Evidently the system of scoring the Bender is less predictive of EEG diagnosis than is a subjective system of Bender evaluation based on the psychologist's experience.

The results of Aim 3, the final aim of the study—to obtain a computation as to the "incidence" of brain damage in the children studied—can be seen in Tables 22-2, 22-3, 22-4A, and 22-4B. As has been stated above and can be seen from Table 22-2, of the total of 148 children examined in the study 37 percent had electroencephalograms which received a final rating of "abnormal." As Table 22-2 also shows, 49 percent of all of the

TABLE 22-2: Percentage of Abnormalities on Electroencephalograms and in Psychometric, and Medical Examinations.

Total Group $(N) = 148$		
	N	%
Abnormal electroencephalogram	55	37.16
Abnormal psychometric examination	73	49.33
Abnormal medical examination	49	33.10

children had clinical psychological examination findings which were rated as indicative of brain damage, and 33 percent of the children were rated as brain-damaged by the pediatrician as a result of his clinical *and* historical study of the child. Of the total of 148 children, 26 children, or 17.56 percent, were rated by the pediatrician as having a *history* which was significant for brain damage. In addition to the examinations completed and rated independently, the study plan called for one other rating, and this was the psychiatrist's overall diagnosis, arrived at by using data available on the children examined. Of the total of 148 children in the study, the psychiatrist diagnosed as brain-damaged a total of 88 patients, or 59 percent of the cases. Various other figures on base rates can be seen through a perusal of Tables 29-3, 29-4A, and 29-4B. It is plain from the tables that the answer to the question, "What is the incidence of brain damage in the Washburn Clinic study population of children?" will vary considerably, depending on which criterion or test for brain damage one uses. Taking the pediatric examination, EEG examination, and psychometric examination separately, the range of abnormality is from 33 percent to 49 percent. Taking a composite-type diagnosis, the psychiatrist's diagnosis, the percentage of children rated as brain-damaged goes to 59 percent. If one diagnoses as brain-damaged only those children whom the pediatrician designates as having a *history* of brain damage, the percentage goes down to 17.56 percent, and if we limit our criterion to positive clinical neurological findings, the abnormal percentage is 30 percent. If we should make our criterion of brain damage so rigorous as to require that all three of the above examination procedures agree in rating the child as brain-damaged, the percentage goes as low as 10.13 percent (cf. Table 22-3). On the other hand, using the "unanimous agreement" approach and being consistent, one also would have to say that, out of the total number of children studied, only 27.71 percent could be rated as being free from the possibility of a diagnosis of brain damage, inasmuch as this was the percentage of cases in which all three of the above diagnostic procedures were rated normal (cf. Table 22-3). In brief, the findings of the present in-

TABLE 22-3: Combinations of normal-abnormal ratings on electroencephalograms and in psychometric and medical examinations ($N=148$).

Combinations	N	%
Abnormal EEG, other 2 normal	15	10.14
Abnormal psychometric examination, other 2 normal	23	15.54
Abnormal medical examination, other 2 normal	14	9.45
Normal EEG, other 2 abnormal	15	10.14
Normal psychometric examination, other 2 abnormal	5	3.37
Normal medical examination, other 2 abnormal	20	13.52
All 3 procedures rated abnormal	15	10.13
All 3 procedures rated normal	41	27.71
Total	148	100%

vestigation under the third aim of the study, in which an attempt is made to assess "base rates," or incidence, of brain damage in a child guidance clinic, suggest that a simple answer to this question may not be feasible at the present time, in view of the variability of results among the various criteria used. Evidently, each of the different specialties is measuring different aspects of cerebral dysfunction, but all are using the term "brain damage" to label what each considers dysfunction in the area being measured. The reader is left to draw his own conclusions as to which of the diagnostic procedures should be given the heaviest weighting or as to the degree of unanimity which will be required among diagnostic tools for a final pathological diagnosis if more than one tool is used (Blau and Schaeffer, 1960).

In the practical clinical situation, the clinician is, of course, not interested solely in the degree to which a diagnostic conclusion of "brain damage" on the basis of one diagnostic tool, agrees with some other diagnostician who is using tools which might also result in the diagnosis "brain damage." One of the things which is also accomplished by the use of the various diagnostic procedures available in this area of central nervous system functioning is that the results of such diagnostic studies can be viewed in one sense as a tabulation of the child's abilities and disabilities. In a treatment plan, even if it should involve long-term psychotherapy, it is well for the therapist to know about the various assets and liabilities of the patient, both of a physical and psychological nature. Visual-motor dysfunction, such as is measured by the Bender Gestalt Test, is certainly an important item of information about a patient, particularly if the degree of incoordination is severe, and particularly if the patient in whom it appears is a child who is exhibiting a behavior problem or learning problem or any other problem. Looked at in this light, the findings of a psychological test, for example, are not merely bases for a diagnostic "reading" which may or may not agree with the reading of someone else using a different gauge, but are of value because of what they reveal about the patient and his capacities and abilities at the moment. Thus, the awareness by the clinician that he is assessing abilities and disabilities, as well as arriving at diagnostic labels, should temper any dismay which he might have when he finds that his diagnostic conclusion does not agree with that of someone else using some other diagnostic procedure. The clinician can still hope for the ideal in which there would be a high degree of agreement among various tests in common use for arriving at a diagnosis of brain damage and, to be sure, in many individual cases, especially those patients who have sustained a large amount of cortical damage, there will be a high degree of agreement among persons using the EEG, other medical tests, psychometric tests, etc. In the child guidance clinic setting, however, any brain-damaged children likely to be seen almost invariably have suffered a relatively mild degree of cortical damage and hence present difficult diagnostic problems.

As has been seen from Table 22-3, only approximately 10 percent of the children in the present research study received abnormal ratings on all three independent diagnostic procedures. However, as is exemplified by the psychiatrist's diagnostic figure of 59 percent brain-damaged based on all data available, a clinician would by no means be expected to rule out a diagnosis of brain damage in an individual child in the 90 percent of the group where several abnormal findings were present in at least one area studied. Thus, (cf. Table 22-4A and B) a final diagnostic hypothesis might

TABLE 22-4A: Number and percentage of abnormalities in the group of "brain-damaged" patients (per psychiatrist's diagnosis N=88).

TABLE 22-4B: Number and percentage of abnormalities in the group of "not brain-damaged" patients (per psychiatrist's diagnosis N=60).

	N	%		N	%
Abnormal EEG	53	60.22	Abnormal EEG	1	1.66
Abnormal psychometrics	61	69.31	Abnormal psychometrics	10	16.66
Abnormal medical findings	37	42.04	Abnormal medical findings	11	18.33

be expected to have to ignore either normal or abnormal findings in individual study areas for the purpose of arriving at a single diagnosis. Nevertheless, the individual area in which there is an abnormality might still possess great importance for a clinician charged with the responsibility of working with the patient in treatment or in making other plans for him. This formulation would agree with Bender's. In discussing the psychopathology of children with organic brain disorders, she stated, "The problem of the physician and the social worker and the teacher in all such cases will be to find out the proper level of performance on which emotional adaptation is still possible. Otherwise, the child will react as Pavlov's dogs which lost all their conditioned reflexes when too complicated differentiations between similar forms were demanded from them" (1956). Bender also emphasizes a point which we would echo, and that is that, although the child should be examined by various individual techniques which deliberately fragment his total unity, the child should be given also a final total evaluation which is arrived at through a synthesis of the various individual diagnostic pieces of data in an effort to understand and "organize" the individual as a whole in some compensatory fashion. This final organization in a child guidance clinic setting necessarily involves the integration of the child in his environment, which includes not only himself and his own strengths and weaknesses, but also his parents and other persons in his environment. Bender underscores this point by continuing, "Children that have come to the psychiatric division of Bellevue Hospital with a behavior problem associated with an organic brain disorder have always other emotional and social problems in their life situation severe enough to account for the behavior disorder on a reactive basis alone. Thus, the follow-up studies on children with virus and inflammatory encephalitis have led us to emphasize the inadequacies of early childhood emotional-social experiences as at least contributory factors in subsequent behavior disorders" (1956). From a practical standpoint, it needs to be emphasized that, in the cases of most behavior-problem children with a diagnosis of brain damage, the only real remedial treatment resources available are primarily environmental in character, since actual correction of structural defects in the central nervous system is usually not possible.

The results of the present study might be interpreted as suggesting that the chronic brain syndrome, at least in the behavior-problem children included in the present study, is a highly unspecific syndrome as to its pathological manifestations. Somewhat more speculatively, one might add that this syndrome is also unspecific as to its etiology, therapy, and prognosis. In speaking of brain damage as an entity, we are probably dealing with a mixed concept and with a continuum, just as we are when we speak of health as an entity. The fact that children exhibiting behavioral difficulties may frequently be suffering with some deficiency of central nervous system functioning seems clear to us. That the manifestations of this deficiency are varied also seems clear, as is our conclusion, tentative to be sure, that there is not and probably will not be any single definitive test of an entity of "brain damage." Certainly "normal" EEG or physical examination findings by themselves do not "rule out" the possibility that some type of cerebral dysfunction may be present.

Recent studies such as the one by Gibbs *et al.* (1959) are strongly indicative of the probability that many more children are suffering with central nervous system disorders than has in the past been thought to be the case. The Gibbs study would also suggest that childhood contagious diseases may be responsible for a considerable amount of central nervous system disorder since it was found that, of a total of 717 children hospitalized with measles, 381, or 53 percent, exhibited either clinical or electroencephalographic evidence of encephalitis during the acute or immediate postacute phase of their illness. Of five childhood diseases studied, measles was found the most likely to be accompanied by evidence of encephalitis. In the light of this and other evidence concerning the threat of encephalopathy to a child, the present study finding that 59 percent of child guidance clinic patients are given an overall diagnosis of brain damage does not seem unduly high.

SUMMARY AND CONCLUSIONS

Routine electroencephalographic, pediatric, and clinical psychological examinations were administered at time of intake to children of ages 7 through 14 who were referred to a child guidance clinic during a one-and-one-half year period. The results of the investigation, briefly summarized, are the following: (1) Children with abnormal electroencephalograms differed from a matched group of children with normal electroencephalograms on Bender Gestalt Test ratings and on Coding subtest scores of the Wechsler Intelligence Scale for Children, but on no other psychometric test scores out of a two-hour battery of tests. (2) Medical history and examination findings, including neurological examination findings, were not significantly different between the abnormal electroencephalogram group of children and the normal electroencephalogram group of children. (3) Behavior rating scales showed no significant differences in rated behavior between the abnormal EEG and normal EEG groups of children. (4) There were statistically significant coefficients of correlation between two independent readings of the same EEG record and between an abnormal EEG rating and an abnormal clinical psychological examination rating on the patients regarding brain damage. (5) There was a significant correlation between the pediatric examination rating and the psychological examination rating of the patients regarding brain damage. (6) There was not a statistically significant correlation between EEG and pediatric examination ratings on the patients regarding brain damage. (7) Out of a total of 148 electroencephalograms routinely administered to child guidance clinic patients of ages 7 through 14, 37 percent were rated "abnormal" by a team of two electroencephalographers. (8) Out of a total of 148 two-hour psychological examinations routinely administered to the same children by three different psychologists, 49 percent were rated "abnormal," i.e., as indicative of brain damage. (9) Out of a total of 148 routine pediatric examinations given by the same pediatrician during the study, 33 percent were rated as indicative of brain damage. Of the total number of 148 children, 17.5 percent were rated by the pediatrician as exhibiting a history of brain damage and 30 percent exhibited abnormal clinical neurological findings. (10) A final diagnosis of brain damage was given to 59 percent of the total of 148 children studied in the investigation. This diagnosis of brain damage was given by a psychiatrist who studied the examination records of each of the children and who made use of all history and examination data provided in the complete work-up by social workers, psychologists, pediatrician, and electroencephalographers. (11) A total of 27.7 percent of the children studied were rated as "not brain-damaged" by unanimous agreement of findings provided through the pediatrician, psychologists, and electroencephalographers' examinations. (12) A total of 10 percent of the children studied were rated as "brain-damaged" by unanimous agreement of findings provided through the examinations of pediatrician, the psychologists, and the electroencephalographers. (13) In approximately 62 percent of the children studied, mixed diagnoses were obtained among the three main diagnostic tools used in investigation; i.e., in approximately 62 percent of the cases, some of the findings indicated that the child was brain damaged and some of the findings indicated that the same child was not brain damaged.

The conclusion seems apparent that, at least in the sample of children studied with the diagnostic tools used in the study, the diagnosis of brain damage varies widely among the various diagnostic tools. Because of this variation and, also, because of the varying functions measured by different tools used for diagnosing brain damage, no one of the examination procedures investigated could evidently be considered a "good" or final test for brain damage when used singly. Presumably, the wisest procedure to follow in ruling out brain damage in the type of patients studied here would be to use several diagnostic tools and then have one clinician assume the responsibility of making the final diagnosis by using any and all of the findings available, according to his own judgment. Preferably, the clinician assuming this responsibility should be a physician, even though some of the data provided for his use might be obtained through nonmedical practitioners. When this procedure was followed in the present study, over one-half of the child guidance clinic patients studied were given a diagnosis of brain damage. The hypothesis was advanced that, on the basis of this and other recent evidence, the incidence of brain damage among children with behavior problems might be much higher than has often been suspected in the past. The investigators in the present study feel that there is a need for closer rapport among educators, practitioners in the so-called "behavior fields," and the various medical specialties, so that a multidiscipline diagnostic approach will become a routine procedure in all cases of children in whom there is a suspicion of some type of cerebral dysfunction.

References

Anderson, A. S., Behavior problems and brain injury in children, *The Bulletin*, St. Louis Park Medical Center, 4 (2).

Bender, L., Psychopathology of children with organic brain disorders (Springfield, Illinois: Charles C Thomas, 1956).

Bender, L., A Visual-Motor Gestalt Test and its clinical use (New York: American Orthopsychiatric Association, L. G. Lowrey, 1938).

Blau, T. H., and Schaeffer, R. E., The Spiral Aftereffect Test (SAET) as a predictor of normal and abnormal electroencephalographic records in children, *J. Consult. Psychol.*, 1960, 24, 35-42.

Gibbs, F. A., and Gibbs, E. L., Atlas of electroencephalography: Methodology and controls, (2nd Ed.) (Cambridge, Massachusetts: Addison-Wesley Press, 1950).

Gibbs, F. A., Gibbs, E. L., Carpenter, P. R., and Spies, H. W., Electroencephalographic abnormality in "uncomplicated" childhood diseases, *J.A.M.A.*, 1959, 171, 1050-1055.

Hanvik, L. J., A note on rotations in the Bender-Gestalt Test as predictors of EEG abnormalities in children, *J. Clin. Psychol.*, 1954, 9, 399.

23 THE PSYCHOLOGICAL APPRAISAL OF
CHILDREN WITH NEUROLOGICAL DEFECTS

Edith Meyer and Marianne Simmel

There seem to be two chief purposes in the psychological examination of children suffering from neurological defects. The first of these is to provide information to aid in the medical differential diagnosis. The second is to offer a detailed picture of the nature and extent of psychological impairment, together with the implications of this impairment for the subsequent development and education of the child. Prevailing methods, with their almost exclusive emphasis upon the end-products of psychological functioning and upon global scores and with their blindness to the critical distinction between evidence of present functioning level and evidence of past functioning levels, are too crude to supply optimal aid in the achievement of these purposes. It is not sufficient for the clinical psychologist merely to establish *that* a child has intellectual difficulties; nor is it sufficient to determine in *which areas* of functioning a child's difficulties lie. It is necessary also, through intensive study of the child's procedure in solving given tasks, to understand these difficulties in terms of underlying mental *processes*, normal as well as deviant.

Our aim in the present paper is to suggest how the purposes of the psychological examination of children with neurological disorders may be more completely achieved. To that end we shall (1) indicate a theoretical orientation which we have found useful, (2) describe some modifications of standard methods of examination as well as present some less well-known methods, (3) cite some case examples of the application of the methods, and (4) show how the application of these methods contributes to the differential diagnosis and supplies further information which provides a better basis for treatment.

Reprinted from *Journal of Abnormal and Social Psychology*, Vol. 42, No. 2 (April, 1947), pp. 193-205. By permission of the authors and publisher.

THEORETICAL AND GENERAL
METHODOLOGICAL ORIENTATION

With respect to theory of both mental development and functioning, the orientation we have adopted is that of Goldstein and of Piaget. The general theory of intellectual functioning derived by Goldstein from his work with brain-injured adults (Goldstein, 1942; Goldstein and Scheerer, 1941) is a theory to which, on the whole, the cases under discussion conform.[1] In brain-injured children certain volitional and abstracting functions are also impaired. But because we are concerned with children whose processes of abstraction are still in formation, genetic considerations and developmental norms must constantly be kept in mind. The fact that when we deal with brain-injured children we are dealing with individuals who are still developing complicates the problems of diagnosis and prognosis, and makes it necessary for the examiner to take both the pathological and the genetic points of view.

The most complete understanding of the developmental level attained, or of the changes resulting from brain injury, can be secured, as Piaget (1928; 1937) and Goldstein (Goldstein, 1942; Goldstein and Scheerer, 1941) have made clear, only when the examination methods yield information not merely about the product, i.e., what and how much has been achieved, but also about *how* it is achieved. Since the end-product in testing, a correct or incorrect response, may be an outcome of more than one type of process or level of functioning, it is often necessary to "go behind" the test response. Only an intensive study of the child's *procedure* in solving given tasks can, we believe, give us the information required for a better diagnosis and prognosis. With the available methods of investigation, we can observe the manifestations of the developmental level with especial clearness in the processes of *reasoning* and *attention*. Since these same two processes also are most sensitive to disturbance in cases of cerebral pathology they are singled out for special consideration in the examination.

We use "reason" here in the more extended sense, as does Piaget, to designate, both at the prelinguistic as well as at the linguistic levels, those objective, stable systems of reference or coordinations of relationships and of points of view which serve (a) progressively to deliver the individual from his intellectual egocentricity, (b) to create a stable world in spite of the flux of immediate experience, and (c) to make possible volitional behavior and those systemic mental operations which at their highest level of development are formal conceptual thought. Reason or understanding, in this sense, appears toward the end of the first year and develops by a gradual process of assimilation and adaptation in an orderly succession of stages (Piaget, 1936; 1937a; 1937b). Piaget's concept of reason, it should

[1] The factual material on which this discussion is based will be the object of future publications.

be observed, does not differ in principle from Binet's (1905) concept of judgment. It does differ profoundly, however, in the empirical elaboration and refinement offered in validation of the concept. The view of reasoning developed by Wertheimer (1946) is also congruent with Piaget's view.

A genetic progression can also be traced in the related phenomena of attention. Both in the genetic and in the clinical literature, a variety of terms—span of attention, sustained attention, lack of attention, distractibility, perseveration, concentration—are used to describe the duration and intensity of the subject's fixation of the task before him. Both from the genetic and from the pathologic points of view, two classes of phenomena are named by the one word "attention"; and these classes correspond to different stages of subject-object differentiation. In the early developmental stages the child is essentially "stimulus-bound," a term utilized by Goldstein to describe a similar lack of differentiation in his brain-injured adult patients (1942; 1944). At any one time the child in this early stage is attracted by the experienced stimulus completely and to the exclusion of everything else. Symptoms of this stimulus-boundedness are extreme lability, that is, instability of attention as well as extreme rigidity and perseveration. The latter phenomenon is primarily, though not exclusively, a pathological one, especially in its extreme degrees. The lability, on the other hand, may be a pathological sign, but it is also symptomatic of early developmental stages. We do not expect a baby to "pay attention," i.e., to remain fixated voluntarily on one and the same object, for any length of time. While in the earlier stages an object is no longer stimulating after it has disppeared, such an object is still a stimulus for an older child, who looks for it, goes after it, and tries to recover it. The second kind of attention, which evolves from beginning somewhere in the later preschool years, differs in important respects from the mere stimulus-boundedness discussed above. This second kind involves, on the one hand, the capacity to exert a voluntary effort to *persist* in a given activity despite the attraction of extraneous stimuli, and, on the other hand, the ability to make a voluntary *shift* to new activities if the task requires it, even though the activity in progress is still fascinating. Children in kindergarten or first grade who have not developed these capacities are often described as "immature" even if they seem "intelligent" enough in other ways. They are unable to exert this voluntary persistence and to shift as required in the school situation. The distinction between these two kinds of attention is essentially the genetic analogue of Goldstein's (Goldstein, 1944; Goldstein and Scheerer, 1941) distinction between the *concrete attitude* and the *abstract attitude*. From the fact that in both the immature child and the brain-injured adult we are dealing with phenomena of incomplete differentiation of the subject-object relationship, it might be inferred that the brain-injured adults are manifesting a regression phenomenon. In a later section we shall make clear why this is not the case.

METHODS

Systematic genetic studies concerned with the descriptive analysis and the interpretation of normal children's behavior-forms through the stages of development, such as have been carried out by Piaget and his group as well as by other investigators (Piaget, 1928; 1936; and 1937; Rey, 1934; Gesell and Amatruda, 1940; Bender, 1938), provide a system of reference and set of norms within which we may evaluate the performances of the child in the clinical examination. Such norms are largely descriptive and qualitative rather than quantitative. Since they are expressed in terms of observed processes rather than in terms of mere success or failure, they provide for greater descriptive accuracy, a fact which makes the results of the examination more meaningful.

The examination, like a well-conducted interview, is both rigid and flexible. It always canvasses certain areas of functioning, but its goal is not to obtain a global score or to perform a psychometric ritual. An initial general estimate of functioning in different areas is secured. The clues emerging from this early phase of the examination together with the presenting problems and symptoms dictate the further examination procedures. If new hypotheses emerge as the examination continues, appropriate procedures are introduced to verify them. The testing situation provides a controlled medium for observation and combines the advantages of the normative and the qualitative approaches.[2]

Essentially the same controlled flexibility characterizes the administration of the individual tests. Each item is first presented under standard conditions and then modifications are introduced to test the comprehension underlying success or failure. Such modifications take the form of demonstration, repetition, varied presentation, suggestions and others. For our purposes, it is more important to know whether and in what respects the child can profit from these than to know whether he can immediately solve a given task. Analysis of his trials and errors give us a better insight into the processes at work than can be provided by rapid and complete success. Arithmetical reasoning problems, for instance, are an excellent source of such information. We gain insight into the quality of the child's comprehension by asking the child to explain his procedure and by introducing certain systematic variations in the problems. The fact is that the same correct or incorrect result can be reached by means of different methods, some of them indicating a higher level of reasoning than others. Sentences with "verbal absurdities" are another example. Individuals with vivid visual imagery may solve these in terms of global syncretic visualization of the whole situation. Their procedure is based primarily on perceptual processes. Others achieve the same result by logical analysis and coordination of multiple factors (Piaget, 1928 and 1937b). The latter is a more abstract

[2] Cf. discussion by Rey (1936).

procedure. These two modes of comprehension can often be distinguished by the form in which the original result is given as well as by subsequent explanations.

Application of these considerations is to be shown in the following pages. A good many items from the standard scales[3] can be utilized, in addition to a series of less widely used or well-known tests[4] designed primarily for more qualitative study. The basic examination proceeds somewhat as follows. It starts with a nonverbal test, e.g., formboards, block-building, object assembly; introduces language gradually through tests activating short verbal responses and automatisms, e.g., identification of pictures and objects, counting of objects, repetition of digits; and proceeds to more complex language functions and to reasoning problems and learning processes. There follows usually a study of more or less specific visuomotor functions. In addition, any number of methods for specific problems may be introduced, including projective techniques for the evaluation of the general emotional situation.

The following cases not only illustrate the examination procedures but also illustrate two of the diagnostic categories which we shall present in the next section.

Case 1. Sybil R.

Aged $6\frac{1}{12}$. First-grade pupil. Normal development. Had one convulsion in infancy with high fever. Three weeks previous to admission fell on her head, apparently without immediate sequelae. Three days later had one severe seizure lasting three hours, requiring hospitalization and ether. Broke out with measles rash two days later. Admission to Neurological Ward with questionable diagnosis of: Recent Head Trauma; Recent Measles Encephalitis; Recurring Convulsions of Old Origin.

The first psychological examination was of necessity rather brief as the child was irritable and apprehensive, ready to refuse cooperation at any time.

Seguin Formboard Test: Has no difficulty with simpler forms—circles, squares, etc. Picks up hexagon, trying to fit it into diamond, puts it aside. Picks up star, brings it to correct place but has difficulty in placing it, gets impatient and puts it aside. Picks up cross, brings it to correct place, is unable to insert it, tries other openings. Continues to proceed in the same manner using both hands. Restless, unsteady movements. Evidently recognizes correct placements but is too impatient to fit the individual forms.

---

[3] Gesell; Merrill-Palmer; Minnesota Preschool; Pintner-Patterson; Stanford-Binet; Wechsler-Bellevue; etc.

[4] Goldstein-Scheerer Tests (1941); Rey's various Learning Tests (1934; 1942); Wood's Picture Completion Test (1940); Piaget's Reasoning Tests (1928); Ellis' Visual Design Test (1940); Goodenough's Drawing Test (1926); Bender Visual Motor Gestalt Test (1938); Porteus' Maze Test (1933).

Accepts help as a means of getting rid of the task rather than as an aid to solution.

Mare and Foal Test: Proceeds in essentially the same manner, seemingly recognizing shapes, fitting some accidentally but paying very little attention to details of color or meaning.

Block Construction Test: Builds spontaneously an unsteady tower out of seven blocks. Tower falls; patient immediately loses interest. Examiner demonstrates three-block bridge. Patient immediately copies model. Copies six-block bridge similarly without interest.

Counting Tests: Counts twelve blocks or thirteen pennies correctly. Knows ten fingers.

Picture Vocabulary Test (Stanford-Binet): Names pictures quickly and fluently.

Opposite Analogies (Stanford-Binet): Normal performance for six-year-old.

Picture Identification Test (Stanford-Binet): Points quickly to the correct pictures. The following modification is introduced: The examiner says, "You ask me now. I will guess." Patient, "Which bird sings in the tree?" Examiner points to the bird, saying, "But you told me." Patient, "What do you eat?" The form of the last question is essentially correct. However, it applies to several of the objects depicted and not exclusively to the apple which the child is clearly focusing on. Nevertheless the form of the second question is of better quality than that of the first one, in which the child could not dissociate herself from the intended object and therefore included verbally in her question the only possible solution which she was trying to obtain.[5]

Discrimination of Animal Pictures (Stanford-Binet): Starts out by matching two or three correctly, then matches squirrel with cat. Seems to lose interest and points haphazardly to subsequent pictures. Responds to encouragement and completes two or three further matchings correctly. Evidently she is capable of fulfilling the task but has difficulty in seeing it through to completion. The material quickly loses its attraction for her and the child depends on examiner for encouragement and constant restimulation.

Naming of animals: Names eight out of twelve animals correctly. Normal performance for a six-year-old is twelve out of twelve.

Mannikin Test: Attaches head to trunk. Places right arm and right leg loosely near shoulder. Same on left side. Examiner demonstrates. Adequate performance after demonstration.

Copying of Geometric Forms (Gesell): Copies square and triangle

---

[5] We have found this procedure extremely useful for differentiation of stages of reasoning. At the lowest stage, the child points to the object, saying, "Where is the apple?" It has been our experience in this test that children between five and six years of age usually are able to put their questions entirely correctly.

adequately. In her copies of the square cross the lines barely cross at right angles. She succeeds with the oblique cross. In her copy of the diamond she emphasizes the four corners in such a way that it resembles a star. Her copy of the rectangle divided by mid-lines and diagonals stresses a multitude of divergent lines, several roundish figures and the whole circumscribed by a long rectangle. The striking feature of these performances is the emphasis on rather primitive Gestalt-qualities, especially the marked angularity of the crosses and the diamond and the global qualities of the last figure.

Reading: Reads adequately at first-grade level. Prints her name.

PRELIMINARY CONCLUSIONS: The child has an adequate stock of information and vocabulary (picture identification, animal names, picture vocabulary). No speech defect. Reads at first-grade level. Has adequate number concepts (counting objects), and has acquired normal routine verbal automatisms (opposite analogies, picture identification, general conversation). Poor visuomotor control, inadequate perceptual functioning (formboards, mannikin, copying of forms). Essentially stimulus-bound behavior with very little voluntary control of attention, especially on prolonged tasks (formboards, block construction, discrimination of animal pictures). Unsteady hand movements (formboards, block construction, mannikin, drawing). Child is irritable, and sudden mood swings of crying and laughing were observed. Gross restlessness—child gets up from her chair continually.

Overall impression: Intelligent child with acute cerebral involvement. Recent encephalitis seems to be reasonable hypothesis.

Second examination. Two weeks later a second examination was undertaken; to follow up the above-described clues and impressions. Not much change of general attitude, though emotional lability was even more striking.

Seguin Formboard Test: Essentially the same processes and results observed. Does not seem to profit from aids and repetitions.

Five-Figure Formboard: Unsuccessful attempts under standard conditions, proceeding very much as in Seguin Formboad. If examiner places one half, child matches other half correctly but has difficulty in inserting it.

Goodenough Drawing Test: Child draws very fast and rather sloppily. Makes several corrections without attempting to eliminate original lines. Draws ears first. Then continues the same round stroke regularly around the circumference of the head and calls it all hair. According to Goodenough, performance is on a five-year-old level.

Naming of animals: This time child names seven out of twelve, failing some in which she succeeded before and vice versa.

Picture Description (Stanford-Binet): Adequate but not elaborate description.

Goldstein Stick Test: Model—diamond: In her reproduction after removal of model, patient uses six sticks and arranges them as a hexagon which is correctly oriented, standing on its point. Model—triangle: After removal of model, constructs a figure having a base and two vertical lines which do not meet. Model—house: With model remaining, constructs outlines, but has difficulty in keeping parts together. Accidentally upsets outline when trying to place window. Gets restless and stops.

Astereognosis Test, Head (12): (This test was done because of poor motor control observed in stick test.) Recognizes large wooden bead in either hand. Fails on block in either hand. Becomes restless and cannot keep eyes closed. Complete failure with next objects—key and nickel. Succeeds with nail in right hand and screw in left hand. Failure is apparently due to restlessness rather than inability to discriminate. Both hands are equal.

Additional Findings: At the present time the child obviously does not utilize fully her previous acquisitions. Her performance at any one time is haphazard (naming of animals, picture description, astereognosis test).

CONCLUSION: The first impressions are reinforced by the second examination. The child has adequate information and good comprehension in tasks which can be solved immediately. Her fleeting attention and inconsistent reasoning processes together with the again demonstrated difficulty in form comprehension and poor fine-motor-coordination fit into the picture of recent encephalitis.

Case 2.   Barbara M.

Aged 11%12. Sixth grade. Normal development. Considered bright. Three and a half years ago suffered serious frontal head injury. Chief complaint—serious behavior problem, stealing, truancy, etc. She has always done well in school until recently. Unstable family, father having had series of court appearances. Family is known to many social agencies. Question whether behavior disturbances should be accounted for primarily on basis of old head injury or family situation.

Superficially friendly and sociable yet actually remote and lacking genuine affective contact with people around her. On the ward she soon proved to be the instigator of considerable mischief into which she managed to lead the younger children without involving herself.

The child was examined psychologically on several occasions during her stay on the ward. She was always cooperative and interested in doing well.

Formboards: Five-figure, casuist, and two-figure boards. Child proceeded systematically, looking for specific parts to be inserted and completing each board rapidly.

Rey's Nonverbal Learning Test (21):[6] Systematic search, immediate learning and retention of standard position. Loses structure of positions as soon as boards are interchanged in spite of explicit demonstrations of inversions.

Digits: Eight digits forward without difficulty and also five digits backward. In both tasks the digits are responded to as a global unit rather than as discrete stimuli.

Similarities Test (Wechsler-Bellevue): Either good solution immediately or complete failure due to partial analysis and juxtaposition of factors, e.g., the wagon has wheels, and the bicycle we ride on; an egg is round and a seed is small.

General Comprehension Test (Wechsler-Bellevue): Basically good. Often very quick judgment without too much foresight, e.g., theater: "Tell everybody to get out." Process essentially that observed in similarities.

Arithmetic Reasoning Test (Wechsler-Bellevue): Has acquired a good stock of arithmetical facts and produces the correct solution of simple problems automatically, but arithmetical reasoning problems, involving a choice of operation, are attacked in a completely "hit-or-miss" fashion. The following example may illustrate this: If 7 lbs. of sugar cost 25¢, how many lbs. can you get for $1.00? Patient, "For one dollar you get 4 lbs." Examiner, "How do you get that?" Patient, "No, 21 lbs., because it's 4 and you have to subtract 4 from 25." Evidently the problem immediately suggests to her the figure "4" but she does not know how to deal with it and where to apply it.

Memory for Designs (Stanford-Binet, Form M): On nine-year-old level, the gross outlines are correct but there is a striking lack of analysis and integration of various features. At eleven-year-old level essentially the same; produces large and small diamond, the latter being embedded in a horizontal band.

Block Design Test (Goldstein, 1941): Succeeds well on early models, but has considerable difficulty with some of the later ones. A typical segment of her procedure is the following: Goldstein Design No. 10—(Kohs Design No. 9). Small undivided model: Child says immediately, "We need some more blocks." Large undivided model: "I had that before." Does not succeed. Large divided model: Child constructs correctly but does not

---

[6] This test is designed to study and measure a process of sensory-motor learning. It consists of a simple so-called "manual maze." The maze comprises four seven-by-seven-inch boards with nine pegs arranged in three rows protruding from each board. Eight of these pegs are loose while the ninth is fastened to the board and can be used to lift it. The position of the fixed pegs varies from board to board. The boards are presented piled one on top of the other. The S is required to learn how to lift the boards one after the other without errors, i.e., without touching any one of the loose pegs. A record is kept of the number and sequence of errors for each board and also of the number of repetitions required to meet the standard of three successive perfect performances. The observed and recorded learning process can not only be evaluated in terms of age levels, but is especially useful for the appraisal of pathological disorders of mental functioning.

realize her success and breaks it up again. On second successful attempt, asks whether this is correct and is not completely convinced. Small undivided model: Repeated with success. Next model successfully imitated. Then previous (small undivided) model again presented. Child says, "I forgot again." Eventually succeeds.

Vocabulary Test (Stanford-Binet): Credit at fourteen-year-old level. Definitions are of good quality.

PRELIMINARY CONCLUSIONS: Good immediate rote memory, particularly in auditory field (digits). Has assimilated a good repertoire of verbal information, factual material and automatisms (arithmetic, vocabulary, comprehension). Reasoning of poor quality, attracted immediately by one outstanding feature of problem with some perseverative tendency (similarities, comprehension, arithmetic reasoning). Visuomotor functions rather poor, lacking particularly in spatial orientation and integration of multiple factors (Rey's nonverbal Learning Test, memory for designs, block designs).

On reexamination, three days later.

Picture Learning Test:[7] Fifteen pictures of the Stanford-Binet picture vocabulary are presented in quick succession at three-second intervals, then removed and the child is asked to name all the pictures which can be remembered. This is repeated five to six times, with the examiner recording the results each time. Child reveals good immediate memory and quick learning ability. Monotonous recital. Tends to reiterate words previously given, showing a lack of working control.

Picture Arrangement Test (Wechsler-Bellevue): Good performance on Series 1 to 3; fair on 4. Her performance on the Series 5, "Fish," is described in some detail because it clearly illustrates the inability to coordinate multiple factors: Child arranges sequence in order of G,F,I,E,H,J. Comments: "He's fishing. (G) He gets a little fish (F) so he yells down. (I) He puts it down again (E). Up comes the big fish and something comes up." (H,J.) Examiner points out that in some pictures the basket is empty, in others it contains fish. Child then arranges sequence in order of F,E,H,G,I,J. Comments: "He's fishing. (F) Here he has the thing (line) in, he has no fish. (E) Here he has fish (H). Here he has more fish (G), and here he has some more fish (I). She evidently follows one train of thought at a time. In her first solution she considers the action of the line and ignores the fish in the basket. Through the examiner's suggestions she shifts her attention to the fish in the basket and now ignores the action of the line. She does not coordinate two trains of thought.

Piaget's Test of Logical Relationships. Test of Right and Left (1928): Points correctly to her own and examiner's left hand, right eye, etc. Presented with two objects, she indicates correctly "pencil to the left of the box and box to the right of the pencil." When a third object (scissors) is

[7] Adapted from Rey's Learning Tests (1942).

added and put between the two, she has difficulty in stating that the middle object is at the right of the pencil and, at the same time, at the left of the box. According to Piaget she has passed the stage in which left and right are considered from the child's own point of view and has reached the one in which they are also considered from that of the other person. She has not reached the stage (normally to be expected around the age of eleven) which marks the moment when right and left are also considered from the point of view of the things themselves.

Ellis Visual Designs Test (Wood and Shulman, 1940): Vague reproduction of the general structure with no appreciation for the particular characteristics of the Gestalt.

Wood Picture Completion Test (1940): In terms of the standard age norms her performance is roughly on an eight-year-old level. There are no absurd solutions. Each placement has some justification and some connection with the whole situation. However, in almost every picture the finer details are overlooked and the whole is only loosely integrated.

CONCLUSION: All of the child's mental functioning is characterized by her impulsive responsiveness to one outstanding feature and her neglect of other less prominent aspects of the problem. Her reasoning performance is of the "hit-or-miss" kind. She either solves a problem well and immediately or misses it entirely. She has an excellent memory which is particularly evident in the auditory field. By means of this ability she has gathered a good stock of information and a good vocabulary. Quantitatively she reaches her highest level in the vocabulary test (fourteen-year-old level) but achieves approximately an eight-year-old level on reasoning tests. In spite of a relatively high mental level, the child shows definite characteristics usually associated with organic brain damage.

DIFFERENTIAL DIAGNOSIS

The concepts, recovery, and restitution of mental functioning, on the one hand; and regression, arrest of development, and deterioration, on the other, have long been used in characterizing the psychological sequelae of diseases or injuries to the nervous system in adults (Goldstein, 1942 and 1944). It is important to bear in mind that these terms must be specially defined when applied to psychological sequelae in cases of diseases or injuries to the nervous system in children. Crothers and Lord (1938; 1942) have pointed out that recovery in an adult can be assumed if the patient after illness performs his previous activities with as much competence as before. A developing child, however, who is restored after illness merely to his previous level of functioning has lost ground. Full recovery in a child implies making up for lost time; and, more important still, it implies his continuing, subsequent to his illness, to develop at the same rate as before and continuing to display the same capacity for learning and the same quality of achievement. Recovery to a previous level without new elaborations thus becomes "arrested development" and progress at a slower rate with a poorer quality of functioning can become "deterioration."

Determination of the time when the cerebral insult occurred is important in the study of children, not only from the diagnostic point of view, but also with regard to prognosis and its emotional and educational implications. It is important to know as accurately as possible how, and how far, the child had developed at the time of onset and how he has been doing between the time of onset and the present examination. Any striking changes reported may supply important clues. A good developmental history is an invaluable aid to this end. On the other hand, we have found that the psychological study as described can provide fairly accurate information in the absence of other sources or in addition to these.

We distinguish grossly between three groups of patients: I. Children with prenatal or neonatal impairment. II. Children with impairment following acute insult after varying periods of normal development. III. Children with phasic disturbances of mental functioning.

I. In this group, there are two subgroups. The first comprises children with congenital defects of the central nervous system who show more or less severe retardation. On standard scales with predominantly verbal content, such as the Stanford-Binet, they have low IQ's without much "scatter." The typical psychometric picture is that of superiority of performance items over verbal items. In the performance field they are at their best with the simpler formboard problems. In the verbal field they perform best on tasks requiring only recall or recognition and those permitting ready translation into visual imagery. One notes also slowness in acquisition as well as in reproduction; the utilization of very simple, concrete, and poorly differentiated systems of reference; and subnormal as contrasted with abnormal rigidity (Werner, 1946).

A second subgroup comprises children whose normal development has been impaired in the neonatal period through some insult to the nervous system. Although these children may achieve normal IQ's, from the point of view of educability they must be considered defective. Their electroencephalograms are usually normal. The distinctive finding in the psychological examination is the large discrepancies in their achievements in different fields.[8] Superficially, these children often seem to have good verbal facility. Closer qualitative investigation, however, proves this to be based largely on a relatively inflexible repetition of things heard, immediate associations, and social imitation. These children show a deficiency in processes of abstraction which manifests itself in all spheres of activity. This defect usually is most conspicuous in visuomotor performances, form comprehension and

---

[8] Such discrepancies and their educational implications have been described systematically by E. Lord (Bender, 1938; Lord, 1937; Lord and Wood, 1942) and by Werner and his collaborators (Bijou and Werner, 1945; Strauss and Werner, 1942; Werner, 1946).

analysis, where compensation cannot be as easily effected as on the verbal plane. Special investigation will, however, reveal it in the latter area too. Such a child of six may be able to count, but will not be able to manipulate simple number concepts usually at the disposal of much younger children. Similarly, an older child in this group may have acquired simple number facts, yet cannot utilize them as tools in the solution of arithmetical problems. These patients may be able to "learn" but, since their acquisition of content is achieved through mechanical memorization rather than through actual comprehension, their progress is slow and laborious. Unfortunately, the basic defect of these children often goes unrecognized for a long period of time, the children being regarded as lazy and blamed for lack of effort. The very fact that they appear in many situations to be able to compete normally often leads to serious frustration and superimposed emotional problems.

Occasionally the above described features are accentuated. There is combined with a pronounced general defectiveness a singular channelization on this primitive memory capacity. Extreme cases have been described as "idiots savants" and "feeble-minded lightening calculators" (Scheerer, et al., 1945). Somewhat less spectacular is the following case:

A boy of twelve with some evidence of birth injury and with serious disability in all performance fields has never been able to follow the regular school curriculum. However, he displayed outstanding achievements in the area of "push-button" memory; he knew by heart every tool listed in the Sears-Roebuck catalogue and could carry on with great verbal fluency a conversation not transcending the boundaries of this inventory. Yet he could not use his knowledge to any constructive purpose. His inability to plan, his inconsistency and lack of concentration was obvious in all his activities and led also to complete failure of occupational therapy during his stay in the hospital.

II. The second group of children are those who have apparently developed normally up to the time when they suffered a sudden injury or disease. (a) Children with severe head injuries or rapidly developing neoplasms[9] and (b) encephalitic children are included here.

In subgroup (a) the main findings resemble the picture described in adult patients (Goldstein, 1942; Rey, 1942 and 1943). The psychological study reveals a stock of information acquired previous to the acute insult remaining almost completely intact and easily activated under certain conditions. In contrast to this are serious difficulties in reasoning and learning. Here again tests of visuomotor functions prove to be particularly sensitive to impairment of abstraction. Learning fatigues the child easily and becomes a laborious process for him. It seems to lack the fluent organization

[9] Also in some of the rare cases of rapid progressive deterioration of the central nervous system.

only by means of which the still recognizable original level could have been attained. This very discrepancy in quality of functioning helps to determine whether the intellectual difficulties of the patient can be directly related to the neurological insult or whether they are longer standing. This distinction becomes particularly important in cases in which the neurological evidence is not clear-cut. The psychologist is then called upon to try to decide whether certain learning difficulties can be explained on the basis of (1) acute insult to the brain, (2) old defect of the central nervous system, or (3) whether they are of nonneurological origin.

In children recovering from encephalitis, subgroup (b), the basic defects are essentially the same as those just described. But the distinguishing feature is the fleeting quality of their mental activity. Their ability to learn is impaired even more seriously than in the previous group because of their pronounced "attention difficulties." They cannot remain centered on a task for any length of time and thus are unable to acquire its structure. They have, at least temporarily, lost the capacity to exert a voluntary effort to persist in a given activity in the presence of extraneous stimulation. Usually there is a gradual improvement but sometimes for months or even years they appear hyperactive, irritable, emotionally labile, and altogether at the mercy of immediate stimuli. Again there is a striking contrast between their present functioning and their previously attained level. A problem common to all the children in this group is their difficulty in meeting their own standards. If tested they may still score a satisfactory mental age, which, however, may be considerably below their previous achievements. Having been discharged from medical care as physically recovered, both the child, his parents and teachers are puzzled by his ineffectiveness. Various reactions may result. We find the child who, previous to his illness, earned A's in school achievement with C's in "effort," who now receives C's in achievement and A's in "effort." Such a child becomes increasingly frustrated. Many of these children during this period develop serious behavior problems of all sorts.[10] Experience has shown that this picture of "post-encephalitic or post-traumatic" behavior can be effectively mitigated through understanding of the underlying difficulties and resulting protection of the child. This has been described by Crothers and Lord (1938; 1945).

III. The third group includes patients with recurring seizure-like states. These children suffer periodically loss of effective contact with the environment, ranging from severe *grand mal* seizures and prolonged *psychomotor attacks* to the various forms of clinical and subclinical *petit mal* attacks. The diagnostic study of the mental processes reveals quite strikingly the common psychological disabilities in all of these subgroups. The so-called subclinical group, it should be observed, is identifiable only by the electro-

---

[10] Systematic studies of recovery in cases of this type are in progress.

encephalogram and careful observation of the qualitative features of mental functioning.[11] The distinctive finding is the periodic fluctuation in the quality of the child's performance during a given examination or between examinations given at varying intervals. The child does poorly on tasks previously attacked successfully. Careful observation shows that the child's effort is still the same, that he seems to try just as hard as he did before and that he is not distracted. The intensity of his mental activity, itself, seems suddenly diminished. It is very important not to confuse this rather subtle syndrome with the very different attention difficulties caused by emotional factors of all kinds, including plain boredom and negativism. It is seen only in children with paroxysmal electroencephalograms. These fluctuations of quality seem to account for the results of psychometric studies on these patients. The only consistent finding is that of irregularity of successes and failures; there are no characteristic scatter patterns. This phenomenon is just as symptomatic as the frank seizure. Depending on the underlying physiological disturbance, it may appear in combination with other defects. Thus in cases of local lesions we may find this symptom accompanying the typical disturbances of mental functioning described in the preceding section (Group II), but it is not found frequently in the so-called "idiopathic" dysrhythmias.

Such continual disorganization of mental activity is bound to generate its own sequelae, irrespective of whether the disturbance takes the form of the frank seizure or of a subclinical attack described above and regardless of the duration of the "absence." A child with such attacks is constantly missing out on fragments of events in his environment which would normally contribute to his stock of experience. This fact must lead gradually to some impairment of his mental development.[12] The confusion resulting from events lost and the baffling experience of missing out on things continually create certain mechanisms of protection. We find that some of these patients resist changes and try to avoid whatever might prove to be an added complication. They often appear rigid, repetitive and one-track-minded, both intellectually and in their emotional attachments. These characteristics have been described as typical features of the epileptic patient. Still, the fact cannot be overlooked that many patients with frank seizures do not conform to this psychological picture, nor do they seem to show any other deviations from normal. The crucial factors determining such differences have yet to be established.

Finally, one might wonder if complete restitution of mental functioning should be expected with cessation of seizures. The problem remains of

[11] Our first observations along these lines were made on a group of patients referred as behavior problems to the Psychiatric Unit of the Pediatric Department of the New Haven Hospital. The psychological findings in these children were borne out by the psychiatric evaluations.

[12] This discussion disregards certain important physiological concomitants of seizures which may produce primary mental deterioration.

whether, once established, deviations of mental functioning in children are entirely reversible. This problem is, of course, not restricted to the cases discussed in this last group, it is an unsolved one for a wide range of conditions in which mental development has been disturbed.

SUMMARY

The psychological examination of children with various neurological disorders must be qualitative and descriptive in order to become meaningful for differential diagnosis as well as for prognosis and therapy. The prevailing quantitative test methods should be supplemented by an orientation and by procedures based on genetic studies of reasoning and attention. Two examples of examination are briefly outlined. Three distinct groups of patients are discussed: (1) children with impairment since birth who are predominantly characterized by a lag in the development of the processes of abstraction; (2) children with impairment following acute cerebral insult who are conspicuous because of the discrepancy between their present inadequate level of functioning and the level of achievement attained previous to the impairment; and (3) children with phasic disturbances of mental functioning who show the effects of periodical loss of contact with their environment. Detailed description of the evidence on which this discussion is based will be the object of other publications.

References

Bender, L., A *visual motor gestalt test and its clinical use* (New York: American Orthopsychiatric Association, 1938).

Bijou, S. W., and Werner, H., Language analysis in brain-injured and non brain-injured mentally deficient children, *J. genet. Psychol.*, 1945, 66, 239-254.

Binet, A., New methods for the diagnosis of the intellectual levels of subnormals, *Ann. Psychol.*, 1905, 11, 191-244.

Crothers, B., and Lord, E., The appraisal of intellectual and physical factors after cerebral damage in children, *Amer. J. Psychiat.*, 1938, 94, 1077-1088.

Crothers, B., Lord E., and McGinnis, M., Prognosis after encephalopathology in infancy, *J. Mt. Sinai Hosp.*, 1942, 9.

Gesell, A., and Amatruda, C., *Developmental diagnosis* (New York: Hoeber-Harper, 1940).

Goldstein, K., *Brain injuries in war* (New York: Grune & Stratton, 1942).

Goldstein, K., Mental changes due to frontal lobe damage, *J. Psychol.*, 1944a, 17, 187.

Goldstein, K., Physiological aspects of convalescence and rehabilitation following central nervous system injuries, *Federation Proceedings*, 1944b, No. 255.

Goldstein, K., and Scheerer, M., Abstract and concrete behavior, *Psychol. Monogr.*, 1941, 53, No. 2.

Goodenough, F., *The measurement of intelligence by drawing* (New York: Harcourt, Brace & World, 1926).

Head, H., *et al.*, *Studies in neurology*, Vol. 2 (London: Froude, Hodder & Stoughton, 1920).

Lord, E., *Children handicapped by cerebral palsy* (New York: Commonwealth Fund, 1937).

Lord, E., and Wood, L., Diagnostic values in a visuo-motor test, *Amer. J. Orthopsychiat.*, 1942, *12*, 414-428.

Penfield, W., and Erickson, T. C., *Epilepsy and cerebral localization* (Springfield, Illinois: Charles C Thomas, 1941).

Piaget, J., *Judgment and reasoning in the child* (New York: Harcourt, Brace & World, 1928).

Piaget, J., *La naissance de l'intelligence chez l'enfant* (Neuchâtel and Paris: Delachaux and Niestlé, 1936).

Piaget, J., *La construction du réel chez l'enfant* (Neuchâtel and Paris: Delachaux and Niestlé, 1937a).

Piaget, J., *Principal factors determining intellectual evolution from childhood to adult life* (Cambridge, Massachusetts: Harvard University Press, 1937).

Porteus, S. D., *The maze test and mental differences* (Vineland, N. J.: Smith, 1933).

Rey, A., D'un procédé pour évaluer l'éducabilité: Quelques applications en psychopathologie, *Arch. de Psychol.*, 1934, *24*, No. 96.

Rey, A., *Reflexions sur le diagnostique mental* (Geneva: University of Geneva, 1936).

Rey, A., L'examen psychologique dans les cas d'encephalopathie traumatique, *Arch. de Psychol.*, 1942, *28*.

Rey, A., L'examen psychologique dans les encephalopathies traumatique, *Arch. suisses Neur. Psychiat.*, 1943, *50*.

Scheerer, M., Rothmann, E., and Goldstein, K., A case of "idiot savant," *Psychol. Monogr.*, 1945, *58*, (4).

Strauss, A. A., and Werner, H., Disorders of conceptual thinking in the brain-injured child, *J. nerv. ment. Dis.*, 1942, *96*, 153-172.

Werner, H., *Comparative psychology of mental development* (New York: Harper & Row, 1940).

Werner, H., Abnormal and subnormal rigidity, *J. abnorm. soc. Psychol.*, 1946, *41*, 15-24.

Werner, H., The concept of rigidity: a critical evaluation, *Psychol. Rev.*, 1946, *53*, 43-52.

Wertheimer, M., *Productive thinking* (New York: Harper & Row, 1946).

Wood, L., A new picture completion test, *J. genet. Pychol.*, 1940, *56*, 383-409.

Wood, L., and Shulman, E., The Ellis visual design test, *J. educ. Psychol.*, 1940, *31*, 591-602.

SECTION C: Diagnosis of School Learning Disabilities

24 ESTIMATING DEVELOPMENTAL POTENTIAL OF PRESCHOOL CHILDREN WITH BRAIN LESIONS

Else Haeussermann

SCOPE OF THE PROJECT

This paper represents the second phase of a pursuit dating back to the late thirties concerned with the problem of testing children handicapped by cerebral palsy. The first phase was carried on empirically, tentatively and mainly to answer certain needs arising out of practical daily problems in the educational management of children handicapped by cerebral palsy.

While the earlier phase dealt primarily with the problem of circumventing the physical limitations of cerebral palsied children in the testing situation, this present study concerns itself with the problem of deviations in the mental, emotional, sensory and sensory-motor functioning of children with lesions of the brain.

In the earlier report, the procedure was mainly to shift the burden of proof from the cerebral palsied child, who had to react to the test items, to the items themselves. This was done by the use of a scale of progressively more difficult or more abstract situations, to which the child, however, could continue to respond with a sign of affirmation or negation within his physical capacity. The aim, and the result, was not to obtain a quantitative measure of the child's intelligence, although such a measure became evident during the procedure. The aim was to obtain an inventory of the development level of the child.

CONTENT OF THIS PAPER

The present report deals with the larger group of children, who have lesions of the brain and who, as a result, may have a motor handicap with or with-

Reprinted from *American Journal of Mental Deficiency*, Vol. 61, No. 1 (July, 1956), pp. 170-180. By permission of the author and publisher.

out associated changes in the organization of brain function, or who may have changes in this function without a gross motor handicap.

Some approaches used and some items employed to study the developmental potential of children so handicapped will be described.

As in the earlier study, the aim of the procedure is not a quantitative measurement of the child's level, although such a level becomes evident during the evaluation procedure. The aim is an inventory of the child's development potential and of the intactness or lack of intactness of his pattern of functioning.

The method used is a structured interview with parallel objective and subjective evaluation and conclusions. This method does not presume to take the place of standard testing but rather to supplement it.

In contrast with standard tests, this method represents an attempt to provide a scale of functions with items so arranged as to provide a basis for judging the level of functioning achieved by the individual child.

We want to demonstrate, whether or not the child is able to function in a particular area of functioning, which falls into a unit of functions.

What remains to be done in a third and last phase of the project is to describe in detail the items and approaches used; the expected reactions of the children in question to the items and approaches; finally, the interpretation of the observed and expected reactions.

INDIVIDUAL DIFFERENCES IN CHILDREN WITH CEREBRAL PALSY

In the work with cerebral palsied children, Dr. Winthrop M. Phelps, who followed Dr. Bronson Crothers, Elizabeth Lord and Mary Trainor as a pioneer in the rehabilitation of children with cerebral palsy, has cautioned generations of physicians, educators and therapists against the fallacy of generalization by his constant reminder that "no two of them are alike." The injury to the brain, causing cerebral palsy, is unpredictable, selective, and unpatterned. Even though a classification is possible, such as spasticity, athetosis, ataxia, rigidity and tremors, depending on whether the area impaired is in the motor cortex, the basal ganglia, or elsewhere, the classification alone does not suffice to describe the degree of impairment. The spastic child may be monoplegic, hemiplegic, paraplegic or tetraplegic. Similarly, the athetoid child may show severe athetosis of all limbs, the neck, the organs of speech and even the muscles controlling the movement of the eyes, or he may have a relatively mild degree of athetosis, evident only in mild involuntary motion of hands or arms. Or a child may have better control of shoulder and arm muscles on one upper extremity, with a poor grasp of the hand on that side, while the other hand may be less involved but subjected to constant involuntary motions of shoulder and elbow. Such a child may eventually learn to use the better hand by stabilizing it with the opposite, but better controlled, arm.

INDIVIDUAL DIFFERENCES IN CHILDREN
WITH BRAIN LESIONS

The consequence of a lesion of the brain is determined by the location, size, extent, time of developing or of acquiring the lesion. Not only do the nature and extent of the physical impairment depend on the kind of lesion present, but, depending on the location of the lesion, functions other than motor ability may be impaired. Altered functioning of mental organization, deviations in behavior, impairment of sensory intactness and/or disturbance of sensory-motor integration, impairment of recall of correctly perceived image and other manifestations may thus be present in addition to the motor handicap or may exist as a result of a lesion of the brain in the absence of a motor handicap. Isolated functions may be selectively impaired, with the child otherwise appearing and functioning entirely normal, or a combination of any two or more impaired functions may be found in the same child.

The fact that impairment of functioning patterns may be present in the absence of a motor handicap makes it possible to study patterns of behavior, deviations and difficulties without the additional obstacles frequently presented by the motor handicap. These obstacles are the obvious limitations in expression, which may be a complete disability or a partial difficulty of the child to express a reaction in the testing situation by either language or manipulation.

We would expect to find, by studying the nonmotor handicapped child with a brain lesion, some of the qualities which might operate also in the functioning pattern of some motor handicapped children.

APPROACHES LEADING TO DIFFERENTIAL
DESCRIPTION AND DIAGNOSIS

At the Morris J. Solomon Clinic, a clinic for the rehabilitation of retarded children of the Division of Pediatric Psychiatry at the Jewish Hospital of Brooklyn, the practice of team work makes possible an approach of constant and simultaneous observation of the child and his pattern of functioning. This is carried out by medical specialists, psychologists, speech therapists, and others. Examinations and evaluations result in a sum of facts about a child's functioning as a developing and learning organism. A psychologist or teacher or other nonmedical worker is not qualified to diagnose the basis for deviations in a child's functioning. He can explore, describe and ask questions. It will be the neurologist who will answer the questions, confirm the described pattern of deviate functioning and who will trace back the demonstrated pattern of behavior to the neurological basis, gross or subtle, substantiated or postulated. On neurological examination no gross neurological signs may be found, although on closer observation subtle neurological signs may be demonstrated. The continuous mutual compiling of observed facts, the pooling of findings, as well as the reciprocal confirmation of clinical impression and demonstrated findings make possible the study, identification, and description of certain patterns of functioning.

We aim to explore and define those areas of functioning, which we find to be vulnerable to impairment. At present we are permitting ourselves the use of a wide variety of materials and approaches, including those which in their present form might not be suitable for all children with cerebral palsy. Only by a careful survey of the total behavior can we hope to learn about the possible range of deviations in the child with cerebral palsy.

EXPECTED USEFULNESS OF THESE
APPROACHES AND FINDINGS

The third and last phase of the project, which will follow the completion of the present phase, will return to the study of approaches suitable for testing the child with any degree of motor involvement. It will then be possible to bring back to the task of estimating the developmental potential of cerebral palsied children a deepened recognition of the possible effects which lesions of the brain may produce in areas other than motor areas. Such effects, influencing learning and integration, have been pragmatically recognized by those teaching and rehabilitating children with cerebral palsy. It should be helpful to construct testing instruments, which will serve to probe such suspected findings. By making it possible to demonstrate the presence or absence of intactness of the various areas of mental functioning prior to educational placement and program planning, more suitable placement and grouping of the children and more appropriate accommodation of each child's needs can be accomplished without subjecting the child to a prolonged period of experimentation, possible failure, needless frustration and similar time consuming and destructive experiences.

It is possible that the approaches used and the estimates gained through their use may prove valuable in the educational planning and management of other children as well. In the distant future it seems feasible that more widespread use of refined testing methods in the routine testing of all children may bring to light children who are minimally neurologically impaired, but who in themselves have found resourceful means to compensate for impaired functioning. At present we only know that such children exist. They may have a history of difficulties during pregnancy, birth or in the neonatal period. The developmental data may give a clue to their initial difficulties. Mild unrationalized anxiety, possibly related to initial difficulties in language production or in manipulation, prolonging a child's dependence on his mother beyond the usual period, may be noted without suspecting the organic basis. Some of these children may function at a par with normal children, but might otherwise have had a superior endowment; it is this superiority, which enables them to function relatively adequately in a normal group. By identifying such children early, educational measures might be planned for them, which may help them avail themselves of their true potential.

AREAS OF FUNCTIONING STUDIED TO ARRIVE AT AN ESTIMATED POTENTIAL

The procedures used to estimate developmental potential of preschool children with lesions of the brain are planned to provide an opportunity to observe the physical behavior of the child as well as his intellectual, emotional and social functioning. The areas studied are:

> *Physical behavior:*
>> Balance and locomotion, including stair-climbing and descending; handedness and manipulative ability; eye-hand coordination; sensory intactness and sensory behavior, including eye motion, visual field, hearing and listening, tactile sensitivity; orientation of localization and the awareness of a body image.
>
> *Mental behavior:*
>> Language behavior, history of speech development, comprehension and communication, verbal or nonverbal; attention, interest, ability to follow suggestions; reactions to impressions; perceptual behavior; discrimination; concept formation; association; ability to abstract; memory; ability to imitate; capacity for adaptation and problem solving; reasoning and judgment; ability to make believe or role playing; ability to shift and ability to inhibit; orientation in space, time and in sequence.
>
> *Emotional and social behavior:*
>> This includes an observation of the child's attitude to his parents, to the interview situation and his reaction to clinic visits during the work-up period; stability, endurance, resourcefulness, adaptability, perseverance; sense of humor, frustration tolerance.

INTERRELATIONSHIP OF IMPAIRMENT AND FUNCTIONING

Even a gross observation of the child's reaction to the interview shows the interrelationship and influence of the lack of intactness in one area upon functions in other areas. Thus, a child with a severe strabismus of one eye may have learned to use mainly only the other eye; the result may be a lack of depth perception, which can be spotted when a child feels for the indentations on a form board instead of looking for them or when he becomes frightened in trying to descend stairs and when the parents reveal that he is afraid to step into the bath tub. A child, who has difficulty in spatial perception and orientation may have a corresponding difficulty in forming concepts of amounts. A disinhibited or a distractible child may not permit himself the chance to demonstrate what he actually may comprehend. A child handicapped by an expressive language difficulty may shun the company of children, thus hampering his social adaptation. These examples illustrate the type of consequence which may be found when functional linkage is interrupted.

PREMISE OF EXPLORATION AND EVALUATION

If then the aim of the interview is to estimate the potential which the child may have for development, in spite of the possibilities of impairment due to lesions of the brain, it becomes the task of the examiner to sample and probe the various faculties which are considered to constitute the prerequisites for learning and developing. It does not suffice to measure quantitatively a child's performance level against a yard-stick of criteria. It does not even suffice to chart the range of successes and failures, or to explore the nature of the items which a given child consistently fails or those which he consistently passes. What the examiner seeks to determine is the presence or absence, the intactness or defectiveness of the whole range of a child's capacity to receive impressions and to react to them appropriately.

The questions which the examiner seeks to answer are:
(1) How can we conclusively demonstrate the nature of the child's reaction to the stimulus we present?
(2) How can we modify the stimulus so that the child is motivated to react to it?

Although this is not the place to delineate the way in which this evaluation interview differs from a standard test, for the sake of clarity it may be helpful to describe briefly the concept behind this procedure of evaluation. Rather than being a comparative scale, which certainly has its place in the testing of children for purposes of grouping and perhaps classifying them, this procedure results in a description of the child. Most of us agree that current standard tests are often misleading and inaccurate and not a substitute for careful clinical observation. Perhaps this test represents a compromise; it is not a standard psychometric measuring standardized achievements nor is it a prolonged observation. It is an evaluation resulting in a description of the child and his way of functioning in certain specifically circumscribed areas. Rather than judging to which point in his development a given child can go, we try to observe how he manages to get there. When we do not just look for standardized abilities presumed to be characteristic for given developmental levels and count how many of such abilities a given child can demonstrate during the testing situation, we are able to more accurately observe and describe the "in between" abilities, the beginning awareness, the fragmentary glimpses of comprehension which foreshadow eventual adequate comprehension.

For the purpose of evaluating potential, such an individual exploration of the child is more appropriate than a psychometric test. The description of patterns of functioning frequently results quite clearly in indications for teaching and for special educational needs, as well as for levels of readiness in a given area.

MATERIALS AND APPROACHES USED IN THE INTERVIEW

In order to answer the posed questions the examiner utilizes a wide range of materials, with gradations in difficulties and gradations in appeal. The examiner also needs a whole arsenal, consisting of experience with normal child development and of sensitivity to and resourcefulness with children (and parents), as well as the courage to be unorthodox and ingenious in constantly adapting procedures to a given child and to his evident or suspected handicaps in functioning and reacting.

Since it is not the purpose of this paper to serve as a manual for estimating developmental potential and since space only permits a sampling of approaches, some procedures will be described to illustrate the principle of this method of painstaking exploration of the total child. The procedure of the structured interview, with flexibility within the structure, consists of a gradual retreating to an ever lower level of response, while yet conclusively demonstrating the faculty for which we test the child.

DEMONSTRATING A CHILD'S ABILITY
TO PERCEIVE FORMS

To demonstrate a child's ability to perceive similarities and differences in forms, a simple three-hole form board is presented. The child may show his inability to comprehend the task by piling the forms, chewing on them or by pushing the form board off the table. In the process of unorthodox adaptation we then go back one step, if a child does not comprehend what is expected of him. Sometimes a child may become interested if we place a round cookie in the round indentation and remove it again, leaving it within convenient reach of the child. The child may replace the cookie in the round hole, then eat the cookie, then look around for another round form to put in its place in the empty round hole. He then may go on and try to fit the square form and even the triangular one. If the child does not get the idea, we casually remove the board and line up some round and some square cookies before the child. A child who does accept a cookie, will reach for the round one. Children seem to prefer round forms. If he then reaches for a second round one, skipping a square one or pushing a square one out of the way, he demonstrates his ability to discriminate between these two forms. A child who refuses to be trapped by this procedure may respond to the lure of boxes. We place before him a square and a round pill box, with the covers placed in a vertical row between the boxes and the child. With a very concretely functioning child an object, such as a pellet, may have to be placed in the box, in order to make the task of closing the box meaningful. We observe if the child reaches immediately for the correct top to place on the box, or if he tries to force the wrong cover on a box, desisting either entirely when failing, or using trial and error until he has fitted both boxes. A negative child may resist the box situation, but may be tempted by doll cooking pots of various shapes. Again we observe the child's reaction and the wrong moves, if any, he has to make before succeeding. Some extremely retarded children will reveal a beginning awareness of form differences by consistently reaching for the round cover, regardless where it is placed in relation to the square one; such children may attempt to chew the cover, but selectively only the round one. While they may entirely disregard or fail to associate the bottom of the box belonging to the cover, they do demonstrate their ability to perceive the difference in form, although they may be unaware of the significance of such a differentiation.

As an aside to those who have wondered about the child who seems to play so inadequately and "emptily," by simply turning a toy car upside down or a doll carriage on its side, and then seemingly aimlessly spinning a wheel around and around, it is mentioned here that perhaps we deal in those instances with a child who does not have or not yet have imagination and abstracting power enough to perceive a miniature car as a car at all, and who never yet has quite figured out the nature and composition of the carriage in which he used to be wheeled around. Attracted by the roundness and mobility of a wheel, such a child demonstrates to us what, in his little vague world, makes some sense to him. His selective regard of the wheel gives us a hint of his emerging ability to discriminate forms.

The importance of the principle of testing by gradual retreating to the level, on which the child's reaction can be conclusively elicited, is self-evident. One of our unresolved dilemmas in testing children with brain lesions has always been the question: does the child reliably perceive what we present to him? Is his failure to react correctly due to perceptual disturbance or is it due to his intellectual inability to comprehend what reaction is expected of him in the presented task? If it is possible to demonstrate that a child can, for whatever primitive purpose, consistently select one form in a choice of two or more, the primary barrier to successful performance on a higher level of this item is not his inability to perceive what we present, but to comprehend at that specific level of abstraction what we wish him to demonstrate to us. The task, then, for such a child, does not investigate perception but intelligence. This element of uncertainty, when an item is failed, can be eliminated by the described probing for the faculty of perception, while carefully and measurably lowering the intellectual demand inherent in the form of the original presentation of the item.

DEMONSTRATING AWARENESS OF THE BODY IMAGE

In estimating a child's level of awareness of the body image, we attempt to let him draw a picture of a person, or we let him place cardboard cut-outs of body parts of the conventional man figure in the pattern in which he wishes to present a man. If a child is unable to comprehend either of these two procedures, or is too shy, negative, disinhibited or otherwise unable or unwilling to comply with the request, we again retreat gradually to lower levels of awareness. We present a doll and a doll nursing bottle. If the child brings the bottle to the doll's mouth spontaneously he demonstrates by his reaction that he perceives the doll as the replica or miniature image or make believe representation of a child. Sometimes an appeal to the child's emotion rather than to the intellect will give the desired clue to the child's ability or inability to see the doll as such; we may suggest that the child "kiss the baby" or "pat the baby" and observe whether this means anything to him in connection with the toy in front of him. If the child picks up the doll at random, carries it around by grasping it somewhere, or upside down, we gently replace the doll with a small pillow and observe whether the child accepts this substitution without any sign of protest, awareness or recognition. For him the doll may just be a bundle of soft material, pleasant to hold until he casts it away indifferently. The next step is to confront the child with a mirror and to observe his reaction. If his glance glides over the mirror image without apparent interest or recognition of a face reflected in it, we ask his mother to step behind him so that her face appears unexpectedly in the mirror. We observe if the child glances at her image or continues to regard the surface of the mirror without great interest, perhaps becoming interested in the frame or in licking the surface, or if he looks at her image, smiles at it, and finally turns from the image to his mother or tries to search for her in back of the mirror. If he fails to respond to the mirror image, we place a mask over the mother's face, after she has attempted to engage the child's attention. We observe his reaction to the mask. Does he become startled? Does he attempt to remove the mask? Does he look at his mother's skirt, lap and arms and only then try to dislodge the mask? Or does he continue to smile blandly at the mask, as he has smiled at his mother's face?

By his reaction it becomes possible to estimate the child's level of awareness and recognition of a person. Other items during the interview, such as his reaction to a shoe or spoon, tell us additional facts about his self-awareness or lack of it. The child who, on being shown a shoe, lifts his foot, or looks at his foot, or the adult's foot, indicates his degree of body awareness. Similarly, the child's reaction when shown a spoon, even if verbal instructions may not be received appropriately by him, may reveal a degree of body awareness.

SPOTTING, PINPOINTING, AND EXPLORING
SPECIFIC AREAS OF DEFICIT

Going now from the approach of a gradual retreating to lower levels of functioning to the approach of probing laterally, an illustration will serve to demonstrate the usefulness of this form of evaluation interview. This illustration is selected to show how difficulties in functioning and in learning may be spotted if our concern is with an observation of *how* the child performs a task, rather than simply with a decision of the child's success or failure on the task.

A hundred hole formboard is used to explore the child's ability to imitate a pattern from a sample and another pattern from memory. The nature of the child's performance, as well as the result of it, reveal much about the way in which he perceives, the way in which he translates into visual-motor performance, the way this performance may change if the demand is to reproduce a pattern from memory.

Suspected difficulties can be narrowed down by eliciting specific responses.

If we find that a child can reproduce a pattern involving two connected squares from the sample in a fairly well organized fashion, but reverses or rotates either parts of the pattern or the total configuration, when he tries to reproduce it from memory, we experiment with simpler figures. We further experiment with locating such figures in the three other corners of the pegboard. By such methods we can establish whether the child's difficulty is constant, whether practice has any effect on his performance or not, whether the pattern only becomes rotated for him when he tries to recall the after image. We can finally establish whether or not he is able to detect his errors, when he can compare his product with the original sample.

We observe whether a tendency to perseverate prevents the child from shifting from a once executed incorrect performance to the more correct pattern.

We observe his preferred hand, we try to determine the leading eye, if any, and the footedness as well.

We provide an opportunity to use resourcefulness, ingenuity and any ability at the child's disposal to solve this problem. We observe the way he mobilizes himself and maintains his attention. One child may finally succeed by counting, another by verbalizing, a third by comparing the total pattern or its components to some concretely visualized form or object. Another child may simply be unable to proceed or succeed.

The observation of the child's attempts to solve the problem, as well as of his attitude towards a problem solving situation, reveals much about his learning pattern and his difficulties, as well as his way to meet difficulties.

But we are equally careful not to jump to conclusions, since by young children, who are concrete, and who acquire academic skills in an intensely personal way, number symbols and letters are experienced as a sort of little people, who can be coming or going, who can tumble, stand on their heads, or walk straight along a line.

The accepted left to right progression of writing and reading is a habit, which has to be acquired and accepted just as artificially as other arbitrary agreements of the culture, in which a given child is being raised.

If by the described method we are able to spot and analyze specific difficulties in functioning, and to understand their relationship to learning difficulties, the total picture of a child's behavior sometimes becomes illuminated. Instead of coping with the resulting behavior problem we can then more properly help the child by coping with his underlying difficulties in a certain area of functioning, thereby effectively clearing up the behavior problem.

These few samples of testing procedures, while being only a small percentage of items and approaches used, illustrate the principle underlying the methods of estimating developmental potential. By applying such a careful individual exploration of all the above enumerated areas, we believe it is possible to spot areas which are not intact.

It then becomes possible to explore the nature and extent of deviation in functioning in such areas in the individual child.

STATING THE REASONS FOR THE DIGRESSION FROM OTHER PRACTICES

Since we accept the warning that "no two of them are alike," since we emphasize our conviction that there is not a clinical entity of either "the cerebral palsied child" or "the brain-injured child," we resist the premature temptation to find a formula, to develop a system of testing for isolated functions, which are presumed to be typical of deviations in functioning in "these children." There is a danger in looking for symptoms rather than looking at the child. There is a difference, whether one looks at the child as the sum total of his handicaps or whether one sees the child as a dynamic organism with the impetus to maximum development.

STATING THE DIFFICULT FINAL PHASE OF THE PROJECT, MAKING THIS MATERIAL ACCESSIBLE TO OTHER PROFESSIONAL WORKERS

The most difficult aspect of this project remains yet to be worked out. This is the task of conveying to qualified professional workers the validity of the use of unorthodox approaches. It is the task of pointing out the necessity to fathom a child's potential by using a plumbline or a sinker, rather than by using a yardstick to measure a child's visible performance and readily accessible achievement. Similarly, it remains a difficult final task to make accessible the description of the possible anticipated reactions of children to the items and approaches and to give a clear and extensive interpretation of the implications of the expected reactions.

CONCLUSIONS

This paper attempted to describe children with lesions of the brain with and without motor handicap.

The aim, method, and underlying principle of using a structured interview with parallel objective and subjective evaluation and conclusion was described.

Some illustrations of the approaches and materials used to study developmental potential in the child with a brain lesion were given.

The emphasis on an inventory of a child's total functioning and a description of the intactness or nonintactness of the areas of functioning was stated.

The remaining phase of this project was briefly stated.

25 TESTS DESIGNED TO DISCOVER
POTENTIAL READING DIFFICULTIES
AT THE SIX-YEAR-OLD LEVEL

Katrina de Hirsch

It is a well-known fact that our schools carry a fairly large percentage of educational and emotional casualties, bright children whose life at school is a burden because they suffer from a more or less severe reading disability. We have only to look at the intake of a pediatric-psychiatric clinic or at a sample of the youngsters referred to our child guidance centers to find a sizable number of intelligent children whose somatic complaints or behavioral disturbances developed only after they had been exposed to the experience of continued failure at school.

Since remedial facilities in our private and public educational institutions are few and far between, we shall have to find ways to prevent the occurrence of reading failure. In order to do this we need tools which enable us to predict with reasonable certainty which youngsters are liable to run into trouble in the first and second grades. Once we select these children we may find that some of them simply need more time in which to mature, but that others might do very well if given specific techniques right from the start. Careful selection and consistent planning on our part might easily prevent a great deal of heartache and frustration later on.

How then can we find out at the end of the kindergarten year, in the five- to six-year-old group—and I stress this time since it is crucial as far as certain maturational processes are concerned—which children are liable to find the going rough?

The remarks offered here are of an entirely tentative nature.

At the Pediatric Language Disorder Clinic, Columbia-Presbyterian Medical Center, we believe that we have evolved some procedures designed to predict future reading performance and we think that in a fair percent-

Reprinted from *The American Journal of Orthopsychiatry*, Vol. XXVII, No. 3 (July, 1957), pp. 566-576. By permission of the author and publisher.

age of cases our prediction has been correct. We have not as yet done a statistical evaluation, but having experimented along certain lines, we are now trying to find out where such experimentation will lead us.

We use the well-known intelligence tests as an over-all measurement of the child's basic intellectual endowment. Among them the Bellevue-Wechsler Scale for Children seems to be the most satisfactory. However, in a large percentage of cases these tests do not predict future success or failure in reading, spelling and writing. The better-known reading readiness tests, which we also use, do not seem to us to cover all the facets of behavior which we think are significant. The Metropolitan Readiness test is probably the best since it stresses comprehension not only of single words, but also of more complex verbal units. It does not, however, test ability to use verbal material and it fails to evaluate a variety of aspects which enter into reading performance. We agree with Gillingham's observation that children with a mental age under 6½ are not ready for the printed word (1949).

Reading readiness is a function of development. We look on development, emotional and neurophysiological, as a progressive increase in complexity of behavioral patterns. Studies on normal development show that psychological functioning and cerebral organization reveal a steady increase in differentiation and integration through adolescence. As the child grows older he has to cope with increasingly more differentiated and highly integrated organizations. Among these more complex skills is the ability to use verbal tools. At the age of six, children are supposed to have mastered oral symbols. We expect them to have organized an enormous number of arbitrary phonetic signs into the pattern of language, a formidable achievement which by no means all children have accomplished at this age, as evidenced by the numerous youngsters who still show infantile speech patterns.

Once a child reaches first grade he is expected to cope with a secondary symbolic system, with visual signs which have to be correlated with meaning. In order to read a little word like "hat," a sequence of letters seen, a sequence in space has to be translated into a sequence of sounds heard, a sequence in time. We feel that without a measure of maturation—perceptual, motor, conceptual and behavioral maturation—the child will be unable to cope with this task. The youngster whose neurophysical organization still is primitive, the one whose language equipment is inferior, is the one who will probably run into trouble in the first and second grades. It is this often very intelligent child whom we have to single out before he is exposed to reading failure.

Children between 5½ and 6½ usually make dramatic strides in overall maturation, strides so dramatic, in fact, that one occasionally feels one can literally see them blossoming forth. The best time to test them, therefore, is at the end of their year in kindergarten.

Since maturation and development involve the whole child, we observe the youngster's total behavior in order to determine reading readiness.

We usually direct our attention first to those who have trouble with integration of coordination. Movement, like perception, requires patterning. A certain level of motor skills is not only essential for learning to write and print, but it is also indicative of the child's over-all maturity.

The youngsters I refer to do not usually show the severe deviations in large muscular control which we find in cerebral palsied children, but they sometimes have trouble throwing a ball, riding a bicycle, skipping rope. We ask our children to throw darts, to walk on their heels, to hop on one foot. We do occasionally find some who not only have difficulty with the execution of these movements, but who also fail, as in ideomotor apraxia, to get the idea of the act itself. Their overall motility is often like that of younger children, and it is of interest that Bender and Yarnell (1941) have commented on motility disturbances in children suffering from various forms of language disabilities.

Some have not attained the neurological maturation which enables them to execute movements of specific muscle groups. They retain some of the characteristics of the global, total motor response which is typical for the very young child. For instance, they turn the whole head when asked to flex the tongue.

Lags in integration and patterning of finer muscular control and a degree of dyspraxia, as described by Orton (1937), are observed relatively frequently, though occasionally this dyspraxia is confined to graphic activities. Oseretsky's tests (1940) provide an extensive survey of muscular skills and have been standardized in terms of normal development. They are thus useful in determining in which areas a child's performance lags. Unfortunately, these tests are difficult to administer and for practical purposes we have to rely on our own observations. We give our children identical tasks to perform in order to get a basis for comparison. We watch for jerkiness and arhythmicity in the smaller muscles of the hand and tongue. The way in which a child handles construction toys will not only reveal his manual dexterity and the fluidity of his movements, but it also provides opportunities for observing many other facets of his behavior: his span of attention, his frustration threshold, his curiosity and his zest.

Research of the last ten years—especially Werner's work (1952)—has revealed the close relationship between perceptual and motor functioning. Basic to reading, of course, is the child's ability to cope with perceptual organization.

The very young child normally has difficulty in breaking up the totality of a pattern; his perceptual organization is somewhat diffuse; single parts are poorly differentiated. However, the differentiation of small details and the understanding of the essential relationship between the parts and the whole as a *sine qua non* in reading.

In the Metropolitan Readiness test we find a few items which require the child to discriminate between small visual details. In fact, much of the reading readiness work done in kindergarten and in the earlier part of the first grade is dedicated to the training of such discrimination, and any of the books used in this readiness work can be used for testing.

The Bender Gestalt test (1938), designed for evaluation of visuomotor functioning, is one of the most important in our battery. Visually perceived configurations are offered to children with the request that they be copied. Obviously the infant does not experience perception as the adult does. But the child who is expected to read and write must have visuomotor experiences similar to those of the adult.

Bender says the evolution of visuomotor gestalten is a maturational, not an educative process. It is true that the average 6-year-old does not usually copy all the figures correctly. Developmentally there is a progression in the performance of the copied patterns from a controlled scribble at age 3 to all figures clearly perceived and reproduced at age 11. However, as Silver (1950) points out, it is of interest that many of our highly intelligent dyslexic children are unable to cope with this task even at 12 or 13. They are unable to grasp or retain visual patterns made up of discrete elements. In our children we not only observe difficulty with the handling of the pencil and trouble with manual control, but we also see immature forms (loops, perhaps, instead of dots) which are characteristic for the ages of 4 and 5. We note verticalization of horizontally oriented figures. We find, in other words, inability to correctly perceive and reproduce given configurations—functions required in the reading process.

Many of our youngsters have great difficulty spacing these figures on paper. The ability to cope with spatial relationships is of primary importance since in reading and writing the child has to deal with a pattern laid out in space. A developmental lag in this area will thus show up in the youngster's reading performance.

Notions of space originally derive from the child's consciousness of his own body. We use the Goodenough Draw-a-Man test (1926) not as an intelligence measurement, nor as a way to evaluate the child's image of self in the emotional sense, though both are of interest. We use it primarily as a relatively reliable indicator of the child's body image, a concept which refers to his awareness of parts of his own body and their relationship to each other. This image is closely related to spatial concepts and is often strikingly immature and primitive in the type of child we are discussing here.

Awareness of left and right, of course, is a significant aspect of the child's notion of space. Since the ability to cope with the specific directional discipline of left to right progression is required for reading in our culture, this aspect deserves further discussion.

As described earlier, we carefully watch the child while we test his finer muscular coordination. Since most of the activities in which he is engaged are untrained and are not influenced by early conditioning, they are useful in determining the degree to which a youngster has established a functional superiority of one hand over the other. Failure to establish such superiority may be related to familial factors; it may also indicate physiological immaturity and thus tend to show up in reading. We take note of early attempts to switch handedness, as well as of the family history with regard to laterality. In testing we evaluate strength, precision and speed. We carefully note eye dominance since crossed laterality may adversely influence reading performance.

In the small child, awareness of concepts of right and left progresses slowly. The average child of six can demonstrate right and left on his own body—usually with the help of gestural (motor) responses—but not on anybody else's. That is why Head's finger-to-eye test (1926) (originally devised for brain-injured individuals and first used with children by Simon [1954]), which calls for mirror imitation of the examiner's movements, had to be discarded in this form. It seemed to us that the test requires a level of abstraction which the six-year-old has not yet attained. The child of six, however, should be able to imitate one's movements when sitting alongside one and watching one's gestures in a mirror. We have observed that a good many children who fail in this respect later develop reading difficulties.

The Horst's tests (1954), which we include in our battery, are useful because they give us a clue as to whether or not the youngster is able to discriminate between identical shapes when they are presented in correct and in reversed form.

Spatial and directional concepts are not the only ones which are pertinent in reading. Language, spoken or printed, is laid out in a time-space pattern. Thus we have to investigate not only spatial but also temporal organization.

It is of interest that a number of workers, like Stambak (1951) and Mottier (1951), have consistently found rhythmic difficulties in children suffering from reading disabilities, especially in those whose oral language is already somewhat insecure.

We ask our youngsters to imitate tapped-out patterns of varying difficulty and have observed that a goodly percentage of them fail in the repetition of even short and simple sequences. Rhythm is a configuration in time, and fundamentally our children have trouble with all types of configurations.

We further require that our children repeat a series of nonsense syllables, and find in the large majority of cases that they have strikingly short auditory memory spans. The correlation of this feature with language disability seems especially high. The child of six should be able to repeat at least four or five syllables, but most of our youngsters manage just three.

There is another area which has so far received little attention and which is closely related to perceptual organization. We know that brain injury, and in fact any lowering of integrative efficiency, brings about an impairment in figure-background relationships. Weaknesses in figure-ground relationships have not been systematically explored in children with severe reading disabilities. However, the indications are that these young-sters, though to a lesser degree than do brain-injured ones, have difficulties in this area.

In order to cope with spoken or printed language the child must be able to pick out the figure from the background. For one to interpret a sentence heard (the spoken configuration), the message (like the tapped-out pattern) must stand out clearly. For one to decipher a printed sentence, the configuration must be well defined and sharply delineated against the page. I have seen innumerable youngsters look at printed material as if it represented a meaningless design. Only if the figure does stand out will the sentence or the phrase have structure, or, in other words, meaning. Some of our children have trouble separating figure from background. They do not discover, for instance, the significant design in one of the puzzles when asked to find the lion in the jungle. If one gives them raised geometric figures to reproduce graphically from touch, one often finds that they are drawn to the background, to the roughness of the cloth, for instance. The Marble Board test, which was originally designed to evaluate figure back-ground relationships in brain-injured children, is difficult to administer. At the clinic we therefore use an adaptation of the Figure Background cards presented in Strauss and Lehtinen's book on brain-injured children (1947).

It has been established by Goldstein's work (1948) that a certain measure of abstract functioning is a requisite of language performance. The question then arises, What does abstract functioning mean at this early age?

We know that the formation of abstract relationships is a develop-mental process which starts with perceptual and configurational relation-ships and develops in the direction of conceptual classification. This applies to both nonverbal and verbal behavior.

The small child who tries to use the toy toilet for his own use while playing with it has not yet understood that a toy only represents the real thing. This experience, a nonverbal one, comes later. It is a tremendous step forward when the child first "pretends" to be a nurse or a pilot. Some children are relatively concrete at the age of six. Practically all brain-in-jured children are. But we find the group which has difficulties with various aspects of language function to be similarly concrete—if to a lesser degree —and this concreteness is by no means restricted to the verbal area.

In order to test abstract behavior on a nonverbal level, we give our youngsters block designs to copy, and watch whether they are able to ana-lyze wholes into parts and as the next step to synthesize these parts into wholes. Guided by the Goldstein-Scherer tests (1941), we give them a variety of objects to sort out, and observe whether they are able to isolate eating utensils, "things to eat with," so as to find out whether they have some form of categorical behavior, at least on a perceptual level.

The testing discussed up to this point has been confined to nonverbal tasks; we go from these to verbal ones. The ability to handle verbal tools is basic to reading. In order to cope with visual symbols the child must have mastered auditory ones, oral language. Careful testing in this area often reveals significant gaps which are frequently overlooked. Authors like Orton (1937), McCarthy (1954), and Borell-Maisonny (1951) have long stressed the close relationships between reading efficiency and oral language skills.

First of all we have to make sure that the youngster fully understands spoken material. Units like "in front of," "inside," "beneath," which are fairly abstract concepts, are by no means always as securely established as we are inclined to think. We place the child in front of the dollhouse and suggest he put the baby *next* to the bathtub and so on. Carrying out complex directions is not always easy for our children; many are unable to interpret a somewhat involved story; as a matter of fact, a few are not ready to listen at all. Some do not catch on when presented with an absurdity couched in verbal terms, although they are easily able to see the point if the absurd is presented in pictorial form.

Comprehension of language is one thing; use of language, another. We carefully check on articulatory patterns; we note length of units and listen for difficulties in word finding. There are children who have a relatively good use of the idiom on an auditory perceptual basis; they *sound* as though they have a large vocabulary, but some of them fail when asked to give a word on being presented with a picture.

We are interested in vocal patterns—an unusual degree of monotony may reflect a difficulty with structuralization, perhaps a figure-background problem.

The child's ability to form correct grammatical constructions is of importance. Grammar is an expression of structure, and the child who leaves out small connectives in the sentence may have difficulties with the temporal, spatial, and causal relationships expressed by these words.

We further want to know whether the youngster is able to tell a simple story and to bring out its salient features. Some children's organization of verbal material is so poor that they never get their point across; they get so involved in the intricacies of the "Three Little Pigs" that they ramble on indefinitely.

In the beginning the child's spoken language is on a very concrete level. A three-year-old who says "brush" does not refer to the category "brush," to the object whose essential qualities are unchanging from situation to situation. "Brush" to him might mean one time, "Brush my hair"; another time, "The brush is on the table." He does not use the word in a categorical sense.

In testing abstract functioning on a verbal level we look for the youngster's ability to classify and categorize. We ask him to name all dining-room furniture. If he includes the wallpaper or the silver dishes on the sideboard he shows thereby that he has not yet understood the category "furniture." Werner (1940) cites the example of the boy who includes bread and a pipe with the bench, the saw and the hammer when asked to list tools, explaining, "When you have finished working at the bench you want to eat and smoke a pipe." In other words, he grouped objects according to a concrete situation and not according to the more abstract category "tools." We use the Columbia Mental Maturity Scale to test categorical behavior. The intelligent boy who, when shown a picture of a hen, a stove, a pot and an egg, says that the egg and the pot belong together, "because you cook an egg in the pot," indicates that he is unable to free himself from the concrete and is not yet ready for classifications.

We test the child's ability to give definitions. At the age of six, children define objects in terms of function. A six-year-old who says, "You hold it up here," when asked what a violin is, behaves in a very concrete way, which, if persisting, is a poor prognosis in terms of academic functioning.

If one asks a number of six-year-old children what a policeman is, one is apt to receive a variety of answers from: "He wears a blue suit," or "He stands at the corner" (which are concrete responses), to "He directs traffic." In the last response the child tries to cope with function, while in the first ones he limits himself to description. It is usually the child with a language difficulty who is more concrete than others are.

Most children who later develop reading disabilities seem to have trouble with patterning the units of words and sentences in spoken speech. Orton (1937) has shown how frequently these youngsters tend to reverse both oral and printed symbols. The same boy who says "Crice Ripsies" for "Rice Crispies" is the one who later on reads "was" for "saw" and "now" for "won."

Reversal and confusion in the order of sequences—which are closely related to temporal organization in the sense in which it has been discussed —are usually not confined to syllables and words. The whole sentence is often jumbled, showing again that it is in the area of organization and structuralization of both short and long units that children with language deficits have outstanding difficulties.

Most of our tests are designed to measure the child's ability to pattern, structuralize, and adequately respond to the endless stream of stimuli to which he is exposed at every moment. However, organization of perceptual and motor patterns is not the only area which presents difficulties for our children. Many of them have trouble with integration of behavior. The result is hyperkinesis and lack of control. Most children suffering from developmental language lags are enormously hyperactive. Their trouble with inhibition and channeling of impulses seems to be but another aspect of their inability to organize stimuli (arising from inside as well as from outside) into behavioral configurations. Hence they find it difficult to sit still several hours a day. Such children (they may or may not be emotionally disturbed) are bound to have trouble concentrating. Since they are unable to exclude a variety of stimuli, they are incapable of focusing their attention on a specific gestalt, or an assigned task.

Children in kindergarten are usually given a good many motor outlets, but once they get into first grade they find it difficult to cope with a more structured framework, since their frustration tolerances is low and their need for large muscular activity considerable.

Among the children whom we have tested during the last few years we have found a fairly steady, though small, number of youngsters whose perceptual deviations, trouble with figure-background relationships, outstandingly poor motor performance and limitation in abstract behavior seem far more severe than is usual for the child who suffers from a developmental language disability. Careful investigation of these cases has sometimes revealed a positive history, for instance, of anoxia at birth. These youngsters do not necessarily show the usual positive signs on the classical neurological examination. However, more refined testing procedures show that they have difficulties at various levels of integration. Watching these children copy the Bender gestalt figures, one often finds a marked tendency to disinhibition, accompanied by compensatory rigidity. We find perseveration in various areas and a tendency to go to pieces when the number of stimuli becomes too great. Many of these relatively subtle signs go undiscovered until the time when these children are confronted with a task which is as complex as is the mastering of oral and printed symbols.

I do not want to give the impression that our testing takes a great deal of time. After some experimenting we have brought the time down to between 40 and 45 minutes. The tests are usually administered during one session or, preferably, two. Careful observation of the child as he functions in kindergarten, moreover, will eliminate many of the more formal procedures.

In conclusion I should like to sum up a few points: Maturation is largely a process of integration and differentiation. The child of six and older whose perceptual, motor, visuomotor, and conceptual performance is still relatively primitive, the child who has trouble with structuralization of behavioral patterns, is the one who is liable to run into difficulties when he is exposed to reading, which requires the smooth interplay of many facets of behavior.

Some of these children need more time in which to mature. Postponing formal training and discipline for 6 to 12 months may prevent future regrading with its attending experience of failure and humiliation which might easily spoil the youngster's entire learning pattern.

But our testing should do more than simply pick out the children who are not as yet ready for first grade. It should assist us in determining what type of help would be suitable for those youngsters who we feel are able to make the grade if given specific assistance and support.

The hyperactive child, for instance, needs a teacher who has some tolerance for the child's specific difficulty. He needs, if possible, a setting which allows him a good many motor outlets while at the same time providing a somewhat structured environment which protects him from an excess of environmental stimuli. Such a youngster would fare better if seated in the front of the room where he sees only the teacher and not his classmates.

The child with an oral language disability, on the other hand, whose lags are confined to specific areas, might do all right if he were referred to a speech therapist and helped to establish more adequate motor speech patterns and a more extensive vocabulary. Another youngster might need assistance with straightening out his confusion in cerebral dominance, and help in establishing left-to-right progression.

Most of these children, as Orton (1937) has pointed out, usually do better with a phonetic approach to reading than with the whole-word attack. There are good reasons for this fact and they lie precisely in the direction we have discussed. The child who has trouble with the organization of visual patterns is naturally bewildered and confused if he is confronted with what to him seem to be diffuse and undifferentiated configurations. He will benefit immensely if words are broken up into small phonetic units. This breaking-up process actually represents a transposal of spatial sequences into temporal ones. In this manner many youngsters are able to cope with single sounds, short auditory configurations which they slowly learn to fuse into larger entities. This procedure facilitates the structuralization of—for them—undifferentiated wholes and thus gives them a larger measure of security.

There are, of course, exceptions. There are children who fail to respond to the phonetic method. These particular children fall into three categories: The hyperactive child does not always possess the span of attention required for the laborious sounding out of words. The process is too slow for him and he tends to get discouraged and frustrated. Into the second category fall the youngsters who have trouble with abstract behavior. The process of analyzing a word into its parts and then synthesizing the parts requires a certain level of abstraction. Moreover, the very concept that a letter seen represents a speech sound heard is difficult for the brain-injured child (who is usually hyperactive as well) to grasp. In the third category falls the youngster who shows obsessive tendencies. He will stick compulsively to single sounds; he will be too anxious to blend them successfully into words or to integrate them into meaningful sentences.

Thus the tests for prediction of future reading disabilities are not only designed to discover the child who is liable to run into trouble with reading, but are also meant to indicate the areas in which a child's performance lags. The tests should actually do more: they should provide a lead as to what specific techniques could be used to advantage in future training.

Precious time is thus saved, and some children, at least, are spared the humiliating experience of failure in reading, writing and spelling (which are all important in the earlier grades), a failure which will often carry over into other learning experiences.

Not all children suffering from potential reading difficulties are primarily emotionally disturbed. However, their basic developmental lag in physiological-psychological functioning makes them especially susceptible to adverse educational experiences and as a result they often develop secondary emotional difficulties very early.

We hope to discover some of these youngsters before they become educational and emotional casualties.

References

Bender, L., A *visual motor gestalt test and its clinical use* (New York: American Orthopsychiatric Association, 1938).

Bender, L., and Yarnell, H., An observation nursery, *Amer. J. Psychiat.*, 1941, 97, 1158.

Borell-Maisonny, S., Les troubles du langage dans les dyslexies et les dysoriographies, *Enfance*, 1951, 5, 400.

Doll, E., *The Oseretsky Tests of motor proficiency* (Minneapolis: Educational Publishers, 1940).

Gillingham, A., Avoiding failure in reading and spelling, *Independent School Bull.*, Nov. 1949.

Goldstein, K., *Language and language disturbances* (New York: Grune & Stratton, 1948).

Goldstein, K., and Scherer, M., Abstract and concrete behavior, *Psychol. Monogr.*, 1941, 53, 1.

Goodenough, F., *Measurement of intelligence by drawing* (New York: Harcourt, Brace & World, 1926).

Head, H., *Aphasia and Kindred Disorders of Speech*, Vol. I (London: Cambridge University Press, 1926).

McCarthy, D., Chapter 9 in *Manual of child psychology*, Leonard Carmichael (Editor), 2nd Ed. (New York: Wiley, 1954).

Mottier, G., Über Untersuchung der Sprache lesegestörter Kinder, *Folio Phoniatrica*, 1951, 3, (3).

Orton, S. T., *Reading, writing and speech problems in children* (New York: Norton, 1937).

Silver, A., Diagnostic value of three drawing tests for children, *J. Pediat.*, 1950, 37, 1.

Simon, J., Contributions à la psychologie de la lecture, *Enfance*, 1954, 5, 438-447.

Stambak, M., Le Problème du rhythme dans le développement de l'enfant et dans les dyslexies d'évolution, *Enfance*, 1951, 5, 480-493.

Strauss, A., and Lehtinen, L., *Psychopathology and education in the brain-injured child* (New York: Grune & Stratton, 1947).

Werner, H., Towards a general theory of perception, *Psychol. Rev.*, 1952, 59, 5.

Werner, H., *Comparative psychology of mental development* (New York: Harper & Row, 1940).

26 SPECIFIC LEARNING DIFFICULTIES

IN CHILDHOOD

T. T. S. Ingram

Social changes since the turn of the century have been reflected in changes in the interests and attitudes of those concerned with child health. As child mortality has lessened, so the attention that can be given to handicapped children has increased. Initially, attention was concentrated on those handicaps which were most obvious and provision was made for children who suffered from the effects of poliomyelitis, gross orthopædic deformities, cerebral palsy, and blindness or deafness. The problems of the mentally handicapped child have also received increasing attention and are now treated in a positive rather than a negative way; so that the main aim of treatment is no longer to segregate the subnormal child in such a way that he will not be a nuisance to other people, but is to find ways in which he can best be helped to achieve the optimum social adjustment and educational level of which he is capable. Still more recently, enlightened local authorities have made special provision for very highly gifted children and for children who are emotionally maladjusted.

There is at least statutory provision for children who suffer from obvious handicaps today, though it is important to distinguish between what Acts of Parliament say should be provided and what Local Education Authorities do provide. The claims of many directors of education, that handicapped pupils in their areas are so wildly scattered that it is impractical to provide the special schools and classes, occupation centres and nurseries which are needed, should be treated with reserve. The implementation of the Education Act, certainly in Scotland, leaves a lot to be desired. A large number of children who need special educational facilities are being denied

Reprinted from *Public Health*, Vol. LXXIX, No. 2 (January, 1965), pp. 70-80. By permission of the author and publisher.

them because of the reluctance of statutory authorities to take a constructive view.

Other handicapped children with whom this discussion is predominantly concerned suffer because their handicaps are less obvious and may not be recognised. It is important to emphasise that such children are only a minority of those with school difficulties. The majority who fail to make normal progress at school are mentally dull, or emotionally too immature to withstand the vicissitudes of a class of forty other children of their own age and a teacher with a strap, or they may have lost a lot of schooling or have been subjected to frequent changes of teaching methods. Nevertheless, a minority of children fail to do well in school because they have special defects of attention or specific perceptual difficulties which impair their ability to learn as other children.

THE HYPERKINETIC SYNDROME. The hyperkinetic syndrome is the name given to that disorder which results from brain damage in young children and causes them to be extremely restless, distractible, overactive, uninhibited, and violent. The brain damage which is commonly situated in one or both temporal lobes may be sustained in the perinatal period, usually as a result of hypoxia or may be caused by encephalopathic illnesses, particularly acute parainfectious encephalopathies. Immediately after brain damage has been sustained, patients are commonly rather drowsy, unreactive and passive but after a period of weeks or months, they become progressively active and in those with congenital brain damage, overactivity is well marked by the time they begin to walk. The overactivity takes the form of motor restlessness. The patients cannot sit still for more than a second or two at a time and are always "on the go." They pay attention to no single object for very long but are highly distractible and move from stimulus to stimulus in their immediate environment with great rapidity. They have a tendency to explore their world by touch rather than by vision and have a habit of picking things up, feeling them, very often putting them to their mouths for further exploration and then rejecting them—the rejection being shown by their throwing them away or dropping them. Their behaviour is highly compulsive and any attempt to deviate them from their immediate aims is met by an aggressive response. They will hit, kick, bite and scratch even adults who try to modify their purpose, and parents often describe quite dramatically the way in which older siblings are dealt with—"He doesn't just hit his big brother" said one mother, "he tries to destroy him." Punishment has little effect except perhaps to increase resentment and aggressiveness.

Since brain damage is the underlying cause of this abnormality of behaviour and attention span it is hardly surprising that a relatively high proportion of patients suffer from epilepsy and cerebral palsy or less severe abnormalities of motor function. Many doctors attempt to treat them by giving phenobarbitone which commonly exacerbates the behaviour disorder whereas primidone, hydantoate, sulthiame, and amphetamine are all successful in modifying the overactivity in a proportion of cases. In some centers, unilateral or bilateral partial ablation of the temporal lobe has been recommended as a treatment but since a high proportion of patients show marked improvement between the ages of six and ten years and some may later show virtually normal behaviour, the indications for early operation must remain debatable.

It may be argued that patients suffering from the hyperkinetic syndrome do not show specific learning difficulties, but they do present as very difficult educational problems and in the classroom are restless, uninhibited, unpredictable and liable to be violent. Even when the full fury of the hyperkinetic syndrome is beginning to abate, there is persistent fidgetiness, clumsiness, and inability to concentrate. In addition, many patients have associated perceptual problems (Ounsted, 1955; Ingram, 1956).

Other specific neurological abnormalities may also produce difficulties at school, particularly in learning to read and write. A large number of neurological disorders have produced difficulties in learning to read and write for these are very complex processes. It is rewarding to look briefly at what is involved in reading and writing before considering what is meant by dyslexia and dysgraphia.

READING AND WRITING DIFFICULTIES

What he cleverly calls "the operational processes" involved in learning to read and write have recently been described by Professor Meredith of Leeds (Meredith, 1964). He points out that "apart from its meaning, which may be manifold, a word has four operational aspects:

"(a) it has a certain visual shape which must be identified
(b) it has a certain sound (sic) which must be pronounced
(c) it has a certain alphabetical structure which must be spelt
(d) it has a certain graphic structure which must be written."

He points out that "Those who can read and write can start from any one of these and produce the other three forms. This is the condition of literacy. . . . A child can be said to know fully any particular word if he can correctly and readily transpose one form to another."

This is but one of many analyses of what is involved in reading and writing, and it is in fact a somewhat simplified one. It is immediately apparent, however, that a large number of different abnormalities may produce difficulties in learning to read and write. A child with defective vision may fail to recognise the word's "certain visual shape." A child with hearing impairment may fail to recognise the word's "certain sound." A child who is clumsy may not be able to reproduce letters correctly. An unintelligent child is usually unable to undertake the various processes involved as readily as a child of average intelligence. A surprising number of neurological disorders impair the ability to read and write. Ataxia, for example, which is the most often missed type of cerebral palsy is often accompanied by serious difficulties in learning to read and write. Children with ataxia have incoordinate movements and tremor which are liable to make their writing clumsy and wobbly. In addition, many have difficulties of visual fixation which makes their eyes wander over a printed page rather than follow a line when they read. Their abilities to perceive and relate patterns are impaired and many of them confuse directions. Many have speech defects. In these circumstances it is hardly surprising that they fail to recognise letter spaces, confuse the order of letters in words, tend to read from back to front, are unable to reproduce letters or words correctly and that their attempts to write are often so ill-formed as a result of these difficulties and because of their incoordination that they are illegible.

SPECIFIC DYSLEXIA AND DYSGRAPHIA.   It was recognised as early as 1896 that there were children who appeared to be of average intelligence and without defects of vision, who could not learn to read or write (Morgan, 1896; Kerr, 1897). The condition was called "word blindness" and was considered analogous to the loss of ability to read in adults which occasionally followed head injury or cerebral vascular accidents. It was soon realised, however, that in many cases "word blindness" was familial and occurred in children who were otherwise normal (Thomas, 1905; Fisher, 1905). A family in which 6 cases occurred in two generations including 4 in one sibship of 11 children was described by Hinshelwood of Glasgow (1917). By this time, knowledge of "congenital word blindness" had increased substantially and Hinshelwood was able to define it as "a congenital defect occurring in children with otherwise normal and undamaged brains, characterised by disability in learning to read so great that it is manifestly due to a pathological condition, and where the attempts to teach the child by ordinary methods have completely failed."

He recognised that congenital word blindness affected boys more often than girls and that it was often familial. The blindness might be only for words or it might be for both words and letters and in some cases the patients were blind for figures also.

Children with word blindness could commonly copy written material quite well since this did not involve remembering word and letter shapes, but would be quite unable to write to dictation. Hinshelwood noted the tendency of affected children to guess at words which they could not identify from the context and particularly from accompanying pictures in their reading books. He felt that the prognosis for "congenital alexia" or "word blindness" was much less grave than had been previously stated to be the case in the literature.

In this description are to be found most of the important features of specific dyslexia, though Hinshelwood failed to comment on the frequent history of slow speech development given by patients and on the fact that they were frequently ambidextrous, which had in fact already been observed by the American McCreedy (1910) before Hinshelwood published his paper.

It is rather unrewarding to detail the work of later researchers. Orton (1925, 1937) greatly advanced knowledge of specific dyslexia in the United States, but overemphasised the importance of mirror writing and ambidexterity in the syndrome. In Denmark, Hermann (1956) and Hallgren (1950) contributed accurate descriptions of many patients and studied the causes of the condition. Until recently, however, specific dyslexia has become notorious as a subject of controversy, largely conducted by neurologists and educational psychologists, rather than as a suitable subject for scientific enquiry in Great Britain (Critchley, 1964). Many psychologists have regarded it as a mythological beast which does not exist (Daniels, 1962), others as something akin to the Loch Ness Monster which may or may not exist; only a few have accepted that it is a relatively common bird which requires more attention and study than it has received (Shankweiler, 1964). This attitude is very surprising to child psychiatrists and neurologists to whom are referred so many children whose specific difficulties in learning to read and write have caused severe educational backwardness and frequently great emotional distress. Fortunately the views of those who accept that there is a minority of school children who have special difficulties in learning to read and write are gaining ground.

THE NATURE OF THE DIFFICULTIES

The difficulties found are not different in kind from those encountered by normal healthy children. But whereas a high proportion of normal children reverse letters and small words or have difficulties correlating written with spoken sounds transiently at the age of five or six years, children with specific dyslexia commit these mistakes for much longer and sometimes even into adult life.

There are many different errors to be noted. These are listed in Table 26-1 in which an attempt has been made to follow the process of reading through from the stage of recognising the visual symbol on the printed page to the stage of comprehending the significance of the series of read and sounded words which the child has managed to derive from them.

Rather arbitrarily it is possible to classify these errors into three main categories (Table 26-2) but it must be emphasised that this suggested classification of reading and writing difficulties is arbitrary and many equally satisfactory or better classifications have been suggested for different purposes (Vernon, 1957, 1963). All children suffering from specific dyslexia appear to have correlating difficulties by which are understood difficulties in relating the written to the spoken symbol. But not all have

TABLE 26-1:   List of reading and writing errors.

Reading errors	Writing errors
Mistaking one letter for another especially for its mirror-image, *b* for *d*, *p* for *q* or *g*, leading to misreading of words.	Writing one letter for another, especially its mirror-image and writing distorted letters.
Altering the letter order in a word, or part of a word, often reading backwards, *pot* for *top*, *its* for *sit*.	Confusing the order of letters or groups of letters in a word especially tending to reverse them.
Repeating the first letters or group of letters at the end of the word, *gag* for *gas*.	Repeating the initial letter or group of letters at the end of the word.
Omitting small words and reversing word order when reading prose.	Omitting small words, especially prepositions.
Inability to take in the whole word pattern and guessing at the word from the first or last letters or from the context.	Inability to recall visual word patterns and tendency to resort to phonic spelling, *i.e.* guessing from analogies of sounds.
Confusing the sounds belonging to the written symbols, *e.g.* sounding *sit* as r-u-p. This may lead to neologisms.	Inability to connect the correctly analysed sounds of the word with the appropriate written symbol.
Inability to synthesize sound units into meaningful words or to synthesize the sounds in the correct order, though the units are correctly sounded. (The child spells out p-o-t but cannot produce the word *pot*—spells out s-i-t and says *its*.	Inability to analyse the word into its constituent sound units or to retain these in the correct order.
Inability to recognize the meaning of a word or a phrase, though it may be correctly sounded and synthesised.	Syntactical and other confusions in connected material indicative of inability to perceive the meaning of what is to be written.

both visuospatial and speech sound difficulties. Visuospatial difficulties are commoner and tend to persist for longer than word-sound difficulties and are often in children with poor directional sense or poor ability to deal with patterns, shapes and sizes (Fig. 26-1). Word-sound difficulties occur most often in children with a history of slow speech development (Fig. 26-2). In some children both visuospatial and word-sound difficulties occur (Fig. 26-3). Since it is possible to compensate for visuospatial difficulties to some

FIGURE 26-1   Dictation by an intelligent boy of 10 with predominantly visuospatial difficulties.

TABLE 26-2: Classification of difficulties in reading and writing.

Visuospatial difficulties	Correlating difficulties	Speech-sounding difficulties
Recognition of written symbols: (a) *Reading*: Mistaking individual letters and groups of letters. Tendency to guess words from shape rather than content.	Relating visual symbols and spoken speech sounds: (a) *Reading*: Being unable to find equivalent speech sounds for individual letters or groups of letters. (As a result of guessing the sound equivalent especially in monosyllabic words).	Synthesising words from component sounds: (a) *Reading*: Inability to construct words from correctly identified components. (Often guessing from first syllable in consequence).
(b) *Writing*: Difficulty in reproducing letters and groups of letters correctly.	(b) *Writing*: Being unable to find the written equivalents for individual syllables or words (especially monosyllabic words).	(b) *Writing*: Inability to break down words into syllables (sound components).
Orientation of written symbols: (a) *Reading*: Confusing and often reversing letters, the order of letters in syllables, syllables in words, and words in phrases. Reading backwards.		Relating words and meaning (word sense): (a) *Reading*: Inability to comprehend individual words or sentences correctly read.
(b) *Writing*: Reversing or confusing letters' shapes, the order of letters in syllables, syllables in words, and words in sentences, *e.g. god* for *dog, was* for *saw*.		(b) *Writing*: Inability to find words or sentence schemata with which to express meaning.

extent by skill in phonetic analysis and vice versa, such children are more gravely handicapped.

OTHER CLINICAL CHARACTERISTICS. Patients who suffer from specific dyslexia have other characteristics which are of importance in diagnosis and also of importance when one considers prognosis.

It is possible to define two groups of patients by apparent cause. Firstly, there are patients with evidence of malformation of the brain or brain damage. The damage may be the result of perinatal trauma or hypoxia but may follow encephalopathies in early life, particularly measles encephalitis or reactions to vaccination or immunisation. The learning difficulties of children who have sustained minimal brain damage at the time of birth have been well described recently by Prechtl, in Holland, and by Scott of Glasgow, in this country. In patients with neurological abnor-

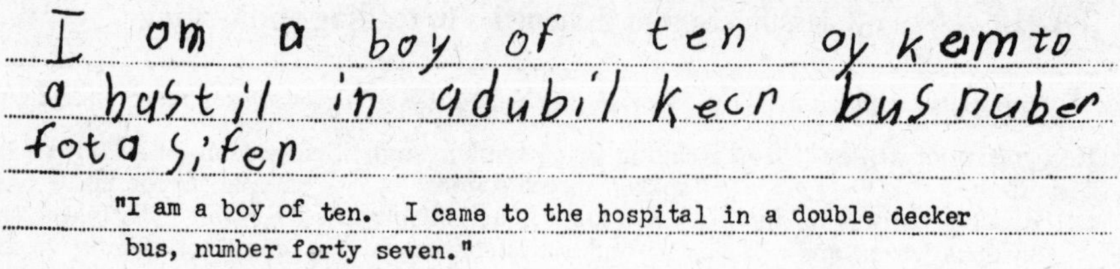
I om a boy of ten oy kemto
a hastil in adubil kecr bus nuber
fota sifen

"I am a boy of ten. I came to the hospital in a double decker bus, number forty seven."

FIGURE 26-2 Dictation by a boy of 10, of average intelligence with both visuospatial and word sound difficulties.

malities on examination it is usually possible to be fairly confident about the fact that brain damage has occurred, but in patients with a history only suggestive of possible brain damage, such as having been born blue after a prolonged labour, it is often very difficult to be sure whether damage has occurred, or not, in the individual case.

The second group of patients which can be defined by cause consists of those in whom specific dyslexia appears to be genetically determined, probably most often by a monohybrid autosomal recessive trait. In many of these patients, there is a family history of specific difficulties occurring in parents, brothers and sisters, uncles, aunts and cousins. There is a higher proportion of twins in these families than in the general population and a greater prevalence of left-handedness and ambidexterity. It is often interesting when reading the letters written by parents making appointments for their offspring to find how badly spelt they are.

In this second group there is a very marked male preponderance amongst clinic referrals, usually in the region of 5, or even 7 to 1. This difference by sex is greater than that in the birth injury group. Patients in the second group, like their relatives are also very often left handed or ambidextrous. In a study some years ago, using simple tests of eyedness and

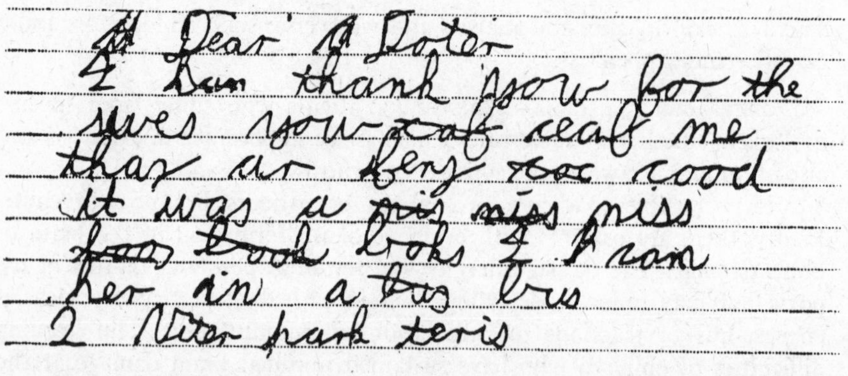
Dear Dotor
I thank yow for the
swes yow ceaf me
thay ar cood
it was a niss
broks I cam
her in a bus
2 Niter park teris

FIGURE 26-3 Letter written by a boy of 10, with visuospatial and word sound difficulties.

footedness we found that only 29 percent of patients studied were firmly right or left handed, 18 percent were virtually ambidextrous and just over half were weakly lateralised. In the general child population, only about 14 percent of patients would have been classified as ambidextrous or weakly lateralised.

Patients with specific dyslexia may also be divided into two groups according to whether their speech development has been normal or has been slow. In most child guidance clinics between a quarter and a half of patients with specific dyslexia are found to have been slow to talk (or to use the current ugly jargon, they suffer from developmental expressive dysphasia), by which I mean that they had no intelligible words of speech other than "ma," "da" and possibly "bye-bye," which do not count, by the age of two years and no intelligible phrases by the age of 3½ years. As I have indicated, these groups are rather important to distinguish, for patients with slow speech development are much more likely to suffer from word sound difficulties later with correlating difficulties and with or without visuospatial difficulties. A proportion of the children with slow speech development who are more severely affected will have associated difficulties in understanding speech, auditory imperception, or developmental receptive dysphasia.

THE SYMPTOMS OF PATIENTS SUFFERING FROM SPECIFIC DYSLEXIA. As the condition of specific dyslexia becomes more widely known, increasing numbers of children aged 7 or 8 years are being referred to clinics on account of reading and writing difficulties. The difficulties of a high proportion of patients, however, still come to light because of other symptoms, usually anxiety symptoms, only when the children have reached 10 or 11 years. The symptoms, other than educational backwardness, complained of by a series of patients referred to a department of child psychiatry were not found to be different from those of patients without specific dyslexia. The commonest were symptoms of withdrawal, such as day-dreaming, solitariness, clinging to parents, night terrors, aggression to other children, temper tantrums, enuresis and stealing (Ingram & Reid, 1956).

By the time children are referred for advice their attitudes to school are usually very changed from those they had when they first went there. There is a common course of events after their first careless rapture. To begin with, all is well, for unless the child attracts attention by having a speech defect it is likely to be some time before his overworked teacher finds he has special difficulties. He manages his early reading by memorising the text, with the aid of pictures and usually manages the early stages of writing quite well because it only involves copying. When reading becomes more difficult to memorise and there are fewer pictures, the dyslexic children begin to have difficulties and these are also found when spontaneous writing or writing to dictation as in spelling exercises is required. After about 18 months or two years, the teacher realises that the child has not learnt the basic processes required to enable him to read and write. Often, extra homework is first prescribed and then the child is sequentially accused of being lazy, stubborn, and of below average intelligence. At the same time, the child goes from being anxious to do what is asked of him to being frustrated by his inability to oblige and resentful that people do not understand his difficulties. By the time children are referred to clinics they are often what I call "educationally resistant." They hate their teachers, they resent any attempt to teach them and resist any effort to help them to learn. It is hardly surprising that so many have symptoms of emotional maladjustment.

THE MANAGEMENT OF CHILDREN SUFFERING FROM SPECIFIC DYSLEXIA

The early diagnosis of specific dyslexia depends largely upon the teacher. Unfortunately in present conditions, teachers are handicapped by the fact that specific dyslexia is hardly mentioned in standard textbooks which they read during training and primary classes are so large that to assess the reasons why some children are not making average progress is obviously difficult.

When a child seems to be failing, particularly in learning to read and write, he should be fully assessed by a doctor and psychologist, supported when necessary by social workers and other educational and medical specialists. Defects of vision and hearing must be excluded; intelligence must be measured and a careful investigation of the nature of the learning difficulty must be made.

There is no doubt that remedial teaching at an early stage can do a great deal for children suffering from specific dyslexia which may be impossible to achieve later. A skilled educational psychologist is essential so that the best form of remedial teaching may be advised and in supervising it or actually carrying it out if the teacher cannot manage to do so himself. Children with severe word sound difficulties, for example, may manage to achieve much higher reading standards by using look and say methods, which would be disastrous for those with predominantly visuospatial difficulties. There is a strong case to be made out for a central boarding school to serve the most severely dyslexic children throughout Scotland. These are not very numerous but they do present special problems which any one Education Authority is unlikely to provide for.

A residential centre of the type envisaged would provide facilities for research into teaching methods as well as providing the necessary schooling for the pupils attending which they would not get elsewhere. Surveys show between 10 and 20 percent of children have reading ages two or more years behind their chronological ages at the end of their primary education and may be described as functionally illiterate. In a recent survey of 897 Scottish secondary pupils with an average of 13 years 9 months, "in the lower half of the intelligence range" it was found that 40 percent were three or more years retarded compared to their chronological age, and that many had reading quotients 20 points or more below their intelligence quotients.

I have emphasised that specific dyslexia is the cause of serious reading difficulty in only a minority of patients, but these figures are frightening and indicate the need for much more research into the problems of teaching reading. An intensive study of patients suffering from specific dyslexia in whom reading difficulties are so clearly manifest could not fail to be rewarding for children whose difficulties are less severe.

References

Critchley, M., *Developmental dyslexia* (London: Heinemann, 1964).

Daniels, J. C., In *Word blindness of specific developmental dyslexia* (London: A. W. Franklin (Editor), 1962), p. 87.

Fisher, J. H., A case of congenital word blindness (inability to learn to read), *Ophthal Rev.*, 1905, 24, 315.

Hallgren, B., Specific dyslexia, *Acta psychiat. neurol. scand. Suppl.*, 1950, 65.

Hermann, K., Congenital word blindness, *Acta psychiat. neurol. scand. Suppl.*, 1956, *108*, 117-184.

Hinshelwood, J., *Congenital word blindness* (London: H. K. Lewis, 1917).

Ingram, T. T. S., A characteristic form of over-active behaviour in brain-damaged children, *J. menta. Science*, 1956.

Ingram, T. T. S., and Reid, J. F., Developmental aphasia observed in a Department of Child Psychiatry, *Arch. Dis. Childh.*, 1956, 31, 161.

Kerr, J., School hygiene in its mental, moral and physical aspects, *J. roy. statist. Soc.*, 1897, 60, 613.

McCreedy, E. B., Biological variations in the higher cerebral centers causing retardation, *Arch. Pediat.*, 1910, 27, 506.

Meredith, P., Word blindness: An operational approach, (Torquay: *Health Congress of the Royal Society of Health*, 1964).

Morgan, W. P., A case of congenital word blindness, *Brit. med. J.* 1896, 11, 378.

Orton, S. T., Word blindness in school children, *Arch. neurol. psychiat.*, 1925, 14, 581.

Orton, S. T., *Reading, writing and speech problems in children* (London: Chapman & Hall, 1937).

Ounsted, C., Hyperkinetic syndrome in epileptic children, *Lancet*, 1955, 2, 303.

Shankweiler, D., A study of developmental dyslexia, *Neuropsychologia*, 1964, 1, 267.

Thomas, C. J., Congenital word blindness and its treatment, *Ophthalmoscope*, 1905, 3, 380.

Vernon, M. D., *Backwardness in reading: A study of its nature and origin* (Cambridge: Cambridge University Press, 1957).

Vernon, M. D., *Brit. J. educ. Psychol.*, 1963, 33, 83.

27 NEUROLOGICAL AND PSYCHOLOGICAL
TRENDS IN READING DIAGNOSIS

E. Gillet Ketchum

Reading specialists, psychologists, psychiatrists, neurologists, and clinicians in general who deal with children's learning agree on a pragmatic definition of reading deficiency. They concur that it is a mild to severe retardation in learning to read which is disparate with the individual's general intelligence and with his cultural-linguistic and educational experience (Bryant, 1962). It is a functional anomaly which, within the limits of this definition, is easy to identify via current psychoeducational tests (Money, 1962). Such a relatively empirical approach constitutes the outer limits of agreement concerning reading deficiencies in the school-age population. Beyond this point differential diagnosis is imperative, and discord emerges as to the causative meaning of single and configurational findings.

A profusion of historical and current theory and evidence provides us with no neat and simple explanations for specific reading disorders. Certainly, this is not for lack of trying! The spotlight of hypotheses has paused to illumine first one theory, then another. When new concepts and their related remedial panaceas become untenable, the focus turns to new ideas. The last twenty-five years have seen reading disorders blamed at times on faulty educational methods. Then neurological (Money, 1962; Mountcastle, 1962; Orton, 1937), psychological (Bryant, 1962; Fernald, 1943; Fitt and Briskin, 1960), endocrine (Pasamanick and Knobloch, 1961; Smith and Carrigan, 1959), and psychodynamic constructs (Rabinovitch, 1959) have been sought, individually, as explanations for this most prominent learning dysfunction. These "specialties" have presented no single scientifically acceptable rationale to enlighten us as to "final answers." This shortcoming

Reprinted from *The Reading Teacher*, Vol. 17, No. 8 (May, 1964), pp. 589-593. By permission of the author and publisher.

has led to a joining of forces, and we now have the interdisciplinary team (Bryant, 1962; Rabinovitch, 1959) seeking ultimate etiologies and pertinent prevention and treatment methods. Despite fiercely enthusiastic devotion to certain hypotheses, and recent claims for a "universal" theorem demonstrably making all other rationales obsolete (Delacato, 1963), we still have vast areas of ignorance as to just what causes certain reading disorders in certain children. In the field of neurology this is particularly true.

At present much of our knowledge of how the human brain deals with listening, speaking, reading, spelling, writing, and the manipulation of thought is derived from studies of the adult brain (Penfield and Roberts, 1959). The pioneer specialists deduced from their observations of man's anomalous language function, following brain injuries and excisions of cortical material that these skills had their origins in definite anatomical locations in the cerebral cortex (Brain, 1961; Mountcastle, 1962). This concept of a direct function-to-location relationship has become outmoded. Modern surgical techniques, aided by electroencephalography, electrical stimulation, and new neurophysiological techniques, provide us with more valid insights into the exquisite complexities of the brain's cellular metabolism and the unending "pathways" which serve our language function. Science has at last become able to "look inside" the skull, however shallow may be the vistas. These new findings appall us with what we don't yet know, and should tend to quell indulgence in glib neurological sophistry about the brain's mechanism for speech, reading, and writing, especially in school age children (Penfield and Roberts, 1959).

As is known, the human cerebral cortex consists of a right and a left hemisphere. Research has demonstrated that the cellular and anatomical structure of these hemispheres is precisely similar except in their opposite orientation (Orton, 1937; Penfield and Roberts, 1959). In each hemisphere identical "motor areas" innervate and coordinate muscular activity on the side of the body opposite to their respective locations. Thus, the right hand and foot, and the motor act of right-eyed sighting originate in the "motor strip" in the left hemisphere. The exception to this is the speech musculature, which is served by both hemispheres simultaneously. It is this bilateral function, with its primary and secondary "energizing" areas, which permits recovery of speech *articulation* in adult and child following unilateral permanent injury, or excision, of these cortical areas (Penfield and Roberts, 1959).

The balance of the language functions in man does not appear to be bilaterally represented. Research reveals that in well over 90 percent of adult mankind, language is served unilaterally, and in the *left* hemisphere, *regardless* of whether the individual is left- or right-handed (Penfield and Roberts, 1959; Rabinovitch, 1959; Smith and Carrigan, 1959; Walter, 1953). We know that given normal acuities, the auditory and visual afferent pathways carry incoming impulses to *both* hemispheres simultaneously.

If monocular blindness or unilateral total deafness is present, nature has provided us with interhemispheric connections which still allow this simultaneous bilateral reception. It is now apparent, however, that each hemisphere actually deals with these stimuli differently (10). The central parts of the cerebral cortex, designated as the temporal-parietal regions, are currently assigned separate, yet not mutually opposing nor wholly independent, functions. The one, the left in the majority of cases, reacts to and utilizes those stimuli which refer to language, be it individual symbols, symbol-sound associations, whole words, or more complex material. The other, the right side, deals with and serves nonverbal purposes: body schema, time and spatial perceptions, and related sequential patterns, directional orientation.

The present data reveal that, in the adult, injury to those hemispheric cortical regions which serve the language function creates corresponding loss of efficiency in the related facets of our verbal functions: expression of ideas via speech, understanding of the spoken word, the various facets of reading, spelling, and writing (Money, 1962; Mountcastle, 1962; Penfield and Roberts, 1959). Damage to the opposite side, the nonverbal areas, leaves established language patterns intact, but deterioration is observed in the nonverbal functions. Loss of function on either side reduces the total efficiency of the intellect, and also results in differential effectiveness in the individual's dealings with language and the environment.

In young children the brain's gray matter is in a very plastic developmental stage. Science has not been able to study the young cerebral cortex along lines similar to adult research. Yet we may infer the obvious, that the young brain is developing towards the status of the adult. Through his first six or seven preschool years the child's cortex is busy evolving, synthesizing, and integrating for the sole purpose of becoming able to deal with "adult" nonverbal and verbal demands. To accept ideas and postulations contrary to this goal and what is known of the adult's cortical function is to be either credulous or unscientific.

It becomes clear, then, that our increasing knowledge of the cortex demands more careful and circumspect thinking from all of us about the etiology of reading disorders in school age children (Bryant, 1962; Fernald, 1943; Money, 1962; Rabinovitch, 1959). The hypothesis of "mixed dominance," based on the brilliant Samuel T. Orton's antitropic and engrammatic views of the cortex, seems no longer tenable (Delacato, 1963; Orton, 1937). Recent evidence does not support the view that mixed preferences for the use of hand, for eye-sighting, and for foot use are a clue, or a symptom of failure in children to establish one-sided cerebral dominance for the language functions. In fact, there arises the question as to whether such "mixed dominance," such difficulties in laterality, in directional stability, may not arise from inefficiencies within the nonverbal hemisphere *itself* (Penfield and Roberts, 1959). One is tempted to infer a failure to establish an efficient nonverbal hemisphere which could aid the child, through the interhemispheric connections, to develop stable directional and sequential skills and in turn help him keep his letters and associated sounds "in order."

The term "dominance" is altogether too loosely used these days by individuals, professional and otherwise, who hold a sadly oversimplified view of the intra- and interhemispheric complexities of man's cerebral cortex. When reading disorders in the young are not clearly assignable to primary emotional disturbances or discernible psychologic factors, there appears a too ready reference to the "organic," a too facile designation of "neurological," both of which often bear the connotation of "brain injury" (Rabinovitch, 1959). Psychologists may feel that certain patterns in their test results bespeak neurological dysfunction and refer the case for neurological study (Bryant, 1962). The neurologists, however, may return an evaluation of normalcy, and some mutter resentfully at the psychologist's broaching upon their field. Yet clinicians in the field of learning disorders who equate results with what *is* known of cortical functions do not claim to diagnose "disease," or "brain damage." Rather they are trying to differentiate a *dysfunction* which may, or may not, be the result of pre- or postnatal trauma, toxicity, or congenital factors (Bryant, 1962; Hutt and Briskin, 1960; Pasamanick and Knobloch, 1961; Rabinovitch, 1959). The ultimate diagnosis is important. It directly affects treatment techniques, prognosis, and intelligent educational planning.

As our knowledge expands, so does the need for eclectic, thorough evaluation. No worthy study can afford to omit a careful history of the child's family background, socioeconomic status, his medical and developmental record, his early school experience, and the initial teaching techniques. Psychologic evaluation must include appropriate individual psychometric inquiry, formal and informal study of the nature of the child's entire language function, and projective tests for information as to the contribution of his personality dynamics. Other "disciplines" should be called upon as needed for diagnostic study, opinion, and therapeutic recommendations to achieve as scientific and complete an evaluation as possible.

As you may know, reading disorders are presently considered to have three etiologic classifications: the psychologic, those associated with demonstrable brain damage, and those of constitutional, or congenital, origin. Careful, interdisciplinary differentiation in a spirit of mutual respect for knowledge and purpose is growing and can lead to further clarification. Dr. Rabinovitch and his co-workers at the Hawthorn Center in Michigan, Dr. William S. Langford and Katrina de Hirsch at the Pediatric Language Disorder Clinic of the Columbia-Presbyterian Medical Center, Dr. Dale Bryant of the Albany Center for Learning Disabilities are a few of the specialists who integrate neurology, psychiatry, and education in research and treatment (Bryant, 1962; Rabinovitch, 1959).

Casual attitudes towards identification and remediation of reading disorders and their related dysfunctions are still unfortunately prevalent in some schools today. Other flaws are insufficient diagnosis and insufficient, or inefficient, treatment. We must maintain a more cautious stance towards bandwagon enthusiasms and fads (Money, 1962). Various chemotherapies have proved capricious (Bryant, 1962; Smith and Carrigan, 1959). The stability and accuracy of electroencephalograms need refining. Physiotherapies and certain "motion" therapies need to be validated (Delacato, 1963). The reading specialists must continue to maintain a flexible view concerning the various kinesthetic, visual, auditory, and tactile remedial techniques. We still need to fit the treatment to the child and not vice versa. We have a duty to understand the emotionality of the crippled learner, and to be vigilant and insightful about our own emotions and attitudes towards these problems. Treatment should not be postponed or stopped too soon.

We need to refine and improve research design and technique to better our exchange of information. We are still greatly dissatisfied with our present situation, and this is good.

References

Brain, Sir Russell, *Speech disorders* (Washington: Butterworth, 1961).

Bryant, N. D., Reading disability: Part of a syndrome of neurological dysfunctioning. In J. Allen Figurel (Editor), *Challenge and experiment in reading* (New York: Scholastic Magazine Press, 1962).

Delacato, Carl H., *Diagnosis and treatment of speech and reading problems* (Springfield, Illinois: Charles C Thomas, 1963).

Fernald, G. M., *Remedial techniques in basic school subjects* (New York: McGraw-Hill, 1943).

Hutt, Max L., and Briskin, Gerald J., *The clinical use of the revised Bender-gestalt test* (New York: Grune & Stratton, 1960).

Money, John (Editor), *Reading disability—Progress and research needs in dyslexia* (Baltimore: Johns Hopkins Press, 1962).

Mountcastle, V. B. (Editor), *Interhemispheric relations and cerebral dominance* (Baltimore: Johns Hopkins Press, 1962).

Orton, Samuel T., *Reading, writing and speech problems in children* (New York: Norton, 1937).

Pasamanick, B., and Knobloch, H., Epidemiologic studies on the complications of pregnancy and the birth process. In G. Kaplan (Editor), *Prevention of Mental disorders in children* (New York: Basic Books, 1961).

Penfield, Wilder, and Roberts, Lamar, *Speech and brain mechanisms* (Princeton: Princeton University Press, 1959).

Rabinovitch, Ralph, Reading and learning disability, In Silvano Arieti (Editor), *American handbook of psychiatry* (New York: Basic Books, 1959).

Smith, Donald E. P., and Carrigan, Patricia M., *The nature of reading disability* (New York: Harcourt, Brace & World, 1959).

Walter, W. Grey, *The living brain* (New York: Norton, 1953).

~IV~

TEACHING THE CHILD WITH LEARNING DISORDERS

INTRODUCTION

T HE CLASSROOM TEACHER is the most important factor in the educational process. It is the teacher who plans, arranges and executes learning activities. Many teachers follow predetermined teaching patterns while others draw upon available resources as the situation requires them.

Children with learning disorders present special challenges to the teacher because whether or not these children are grouped for instruction, each has learning abilities which require individual planning and specially designed procedures. The teacher needs to know how theory, general procedures, and specific teaching tasks can be effectively combined in a program which helps each child learn in accordance with his potential. Norms cannot substitute for knowledge in dealing with learning disorders.

SELECTING AN EDUCATIONAL RATIONALE

A baseball manager may substitute a batter because he believes that left-handed batters hit best against right-handed pitchers. If the substitute gets a hit, the manager's strategy will be praised. The manager may insist that all team members adopt the general practice of hitting from the left when the opposing pitcher is right handed. A left-handed batting coach may be hired to promote left-handed hitting competence. Statistics may support the manager's belief and other teams may adopt the same strategy.

In a similar way, many educational practices become established because they seem to work. If statistical support is accumulated, the accuracy of the rationale is ignored. Thus, when a child fails to learn, it may be assumed that he is not trying hard enough, is immature, or is rebelling. Remedial procedures are then aimed toward motivation, developmental tasks, or psychotherapy.

Many practices are accepted before the underlying rationale is fully established and tested. Teachers use procedures with problem learners without knowing why the procedure is expected to work. As the baseball manager, the teacher is pleased if "everything works out" most of the time. Educators, too, become quite dogmatic when they achieve statistical success.

Suppose, for a moment, that the more suitable rationale in our baseball illustration were related to the position of the batter's dominant eye rather than the pitcher's handedness. In other words, batters whose dominant eye was closer to the pitcher hit better whether the pitcher is right or left handed. They probably were able to turn their heads less and follow the ball more closely. Appropriate training would thus now be established upon a sound rationale. (In this case, batters would be taught to bat from that side of the plate which placed the dominant eye nearest the pitcher.)

There are many confusing, but nonetheless dogmatic, explanations given in support of special training programs. Some argue that reading instruction should have a motor base (involve body movement), others argue that reading behavior can be "shaped" following operant principles (appropriate use of reward), while many others strongly support a stimulus-trace rationale arguing for drill, repetition, and overlearning techniques.

Since the rationale dictates the selection of materials and special procedures, it is important to understand the differences among those prevalent in education today. Many treatment concepts being applied in the area of learning disabilities conflict with one another. More often, however, the similarity among approaches is obscured by terminology differences rather than clear differences in practice.

RATIONALE AND TREATMENT

Among the many names, theories and research reports, several rationales have emerged which are influencing teaching procedures. These are summarized with descriptive labels as a means of emphasizing the differences which lie under the development of teaching procedures. While such differences underscore the divergent thinking abilities of man, they do not provide the simple cure-all point of view which some teachers seek.

(a) *Stimulus bombardment rationale* implies that some nerve centers are malfunctioning and must, therefore, be bypassed. If a child is not able to associate concepts with words presented visually then he must be bombarded simultaneously with auditory, tactual, kinesthetic, olfactory, gustatory, or other sensory stimuli appropriate to the concept in order to circumvent the inoperable nerve centers and establish the association.

(b) *Environmental control rationale* implies that the disabled learner is unable to select, screen, and reject environmental stimuli thus producing the symptoms of hyperactivity, distractibility, etc. Therefore, learning will occur only as these factors are controlled. Such a rationale eliminates movies and TV (they flicker), competitive games (they excite), and gaudy clothes (they distract) since these affect perceptual ability as well as behavior.

(c) *Brain-Computer rationale* implies that the brain can only select responses which have previously been "programmed" into it. This usually occurs through normal development as children move, crawl, explore, and mimic. When the child has not established a full repertoire of responses, he must be "patterned" to stimulate brain activity in those centers responsible for controlling a particular activity. The rationale further suggests that gaps in early programming (crawling, creeping) result in subsequent malfunction of later performance (reading, language). Procedures designed to reprogram the brain, would, by analogy, remove aberrant language abilities.

(d) *Behavior modification rationale* implies that human behavior is modified continuously as a result of interaction with the environment; further, this interaction can be manipulated for deliberate ends as interactions are designed to produce gratification for the operant. Behavior shaping activities are sought which require the disabled learner to behave in a manner that increasingly approximates the desired goal-behavior. For each new modification in the proper direction, learners are rewarded. Smiles, stars, M & M candies, or chips with monetary value may be used to reward behavior.

(e) *Modality isolation rationale* implies that learning requires integration of many kinds of sensory information. Pressure, temperature, sounds, odors, tastes, sights, and movements are "sensed" through the peripheral nervous system where they elicit responses following incredibly complex reactions with memory, emotion, and volition. Learning disabilities can thus be treated best by isolating the systems that are functioning from those that are disordered and through activities designed especially for the intact channel—visual, auditory, or kinesthetic—remediation can successfully progress from strengths to weaknesses.

(f) *Language deficit rationale* implies that language is an overlay accomplishment in human learners and thus can be impaired and inadequate even without an inherent deficit or pathology in the learning organism. The teacher must, therefore, understand language functions and analyze disabilities in terms of receptive associational and expressive deficits (for example, practice on sound discrimination will not improve spelling, if the deficit is an expressive rather than a receptive one). No single set of materials is necessary to remediate language problems using this rationale since the problem may arise from cultural deprivations, emotional disturbances, poor teaching, neurological impairment, sensory handicap, or other causes. The remediation is based upon educationally relevant behaviors regardless of etiology. Materials are chosen for the language function required rather than for the inferred cause of the language deficit.

(g) *Perceptual training rationale* implies that percepts are learned, they do not just happen. That is, the understanding and systematic use of the impressions which we see, hear, and feel differ among humans as do other characteristics. A more efficient use of information seen, heard or felt leads to higher levels of performance in reading, arithmetic and thinking. Thus, perceptual training may be necessary even though vision and hearing are excellent. Exercises are designed to establish an awareness of left-right directionality, differences between figures and background, relationships of objects in a spatial field and the feeling of rightness associated with coordinated eye-hand behaviors. Perception training techniques seek to establish secure bases for conceptual activities; thus, a systematic program of perceptual training that helps one develop the interpretive skills associated with seeing, hearing, and moving is thought by some to be the logical place to begin training when conceptual deficits are noted regardless of etiology.

(h) *Curriculum based rationale* implies that school tasks will have to be learned and, therefore, variations in presentation must be developed until the learner is able to master the task. (For example, when a child sees the letters C-A-T, he must learn to respond "cat" and must grasp the meaning.) Inability to read following training would, by this rationale, simply require adjustments in the approach used. If the child had failed to learn letter-sounds and rules for combining them into words, he might be taught to trace entire words until they become fixed in his memory and subsequently be shown how to analyze them into their component sounds. This rationale requires that the teacher understand the differences among curriculum materials and the activities suggested by the many published manuals available today.

LEARNING DISABILITIES IN THE PUBLIC SCHOOL

The school administrator must provide for the education of all children. When children fail to learn in the regular classroom, the administrator as well as the teacher has a serious problem. If the child has a known learning disorder, the administrator finds himself pressured to (1) create a special class, (2) provide special remedial services with liaison to the regular class, (3) give special training to the regular class teacher, (4) put the child in a traditional special education class for the retarded, (5) exclude the child and recommend institutional assistance, (6) begin a system-wide training program suggested by some national figure, or (7) ignore the child's problem and concentrate on less controversial matters.

Eventually the school must take the responsibility for teaching the child with a learning disorder and all children who exhibit school learning disabilities. Some trained adult will have to work with these children. What procedures will be used? Stuart has provided a partial answer in her recent book, *Neurophysiological Insights into Teaching* (1963). Earlier handbooks include Fernald's *Remedial Techniques in Basic School Subjects* (1943) and Gillingham's *Remedial Training for Children with Specific Disability in Reading, Spelling and Penmanship* (1960). Cruickshank (1961), Kephart (1960), Lewis (1960), Money (1962), and Strauss (1955) have authored other books whose contents are relevant to selecting procedures for the classroom.

References

Cruickshank, W. M., Bentzen, Frances A., Ratzeburg, F. H., and Tannhauser, Mirian, *A teaching method for brain-injured and hyperactive children* (Syracuse: Syracuse University Press, 1961).

Fernald, Grace M., *Remedial techniques in basic school subjects* (New York: McGraw-Hill, 1943).

Gillingham, Anna, and Stillman, Bessie, *Remedial training for children with specific disability in reading, spelling and penmanship,* distributed by Anna Gillingham, 25 Parkview Ave., Bronxville, N. Y., 1960.

Kephart, N. C., *The slow learner in the classroom* (Columbus, Ohio: Merrill, 1960).

Lewis, Richard S., Strauss, A. A., and Lehtinen, Laura E., *The other child, the brain-injured child; A book for parents and laymen* (New York: Grune & Stratton, 1960).

Money, J. (Editor), *Reading disability, progress and research needs in dyslexia* (Baltimore: Johns Hopkins Press, 1962).

Strauss, A. A., and Kephart, N. C., *Psychopathology and education of the brain-injured child,* Vol. II (New York: Grune & Stratton, 1955).

Stuart, Marion F., *Neurophysiological insights into teaching* (Palo Alto: Pacific Books, 1963).

SECTION A: Rationale for Education

28 A HIERARCHY OF EDUCATIONAL TASKS

FOR CHILDREN WITH LEARNING DISORDERS

Frank M. Hewett

The child who fails to learn in school is communicating vital information about himself. He may be revealing his general intellectual limitations or some specific sensory or perceptual-motor handicap. He may be apprising us of the inadequacy of his previous schooling due to poor teaching methods or sporadic attendance. He also may be communicating an inability to cope with social and emotional stress which is manifest through poor concentration, comprehension, and recall in the classroom.

Seldom is such a child's message clearly understood and seldom is the explanation for his learning problem a simple and specific one. Constitutional, environmental, and psychological factors usually overlap, making it difficult for the educator to properly program the child according to his most basic needs.

In the search for remedial and educational guidelines, teachers have looked to the clinical psychologist, the educational psychologist, and the child psychiatrist for assistance. While these child specialists offer relevant generalizations regarding learning and behavior, their contributions are not always practical in the classroom setting. The battle strategies laid down by the military advisors in the tactical planning room may need alteration and clarification before they are useful to the field general on the front lines.

It is this gap between theory and practice that the concept of a hierarchy of educational tasks for children with learning disorders attempts to narrow. The basic assumption underlying the hierarchy holds that an effective educational program for children with learning disorders depends on

Reprinted from *Exceptional Children*, Vol. 31, No. 4 (December, 1964), pp. 207-214. By permission of the author and publisher.

the establishment of a point of meaningful contact between the teacher and the child. Such a point of contact is only possible when the child is experiencing gratification in the learning situation and the teacher is in control.

There is a wide range of types of gratification which the child may experience while learning (from a candy reward for each correct response to recognition for academic efforts by a place on the honor roll), and there are many levels of teacher control (from permissiveness in structuring to careful setting of behavioral limits and academic expectations). It is establishing this point of contact while providing appropriate student gratification and teacher control that is a crucial consideration for the teacher of children with learning problems. The normal achiever may be motivated by grades, competition with other students, and a variety of other social and intellectual rewards, but the nonachiever may be deterred from entering into the learning situation by these same factors. While normal classroom procedures may dictate that all students be held for definite academic and behavior standards, the child with a learning problem may have to be viewed within a broader educational frame of reference.

The theoretical framework to be presented in this paper has grown out of three years experience teaching hospitalized emotionally handicapped children and adolescents with learning problems at the Neuropsychiatric Institute School (NPI) at the University of California, Los Angeles. It is the result of a felt need on the part of the staff teachers for a set of working hypotheses with which to formulate realistic goals for their complex and highly variable students.

Meaningful contact and varying degrees of student gratification and teacher control are possible on seven educational task levels. These will be discussed following a brief historical review of the concept of a hierarchy of human development and behavior.

REVIEW OF HIERARCHIES

Hierarchies of developmental tasks and human motives are basic to the writings of Freud (Munroe, 1955), Erickson, Havighurst, and Maslow.

Freud's psychosexual stages of development form such a hierarchy and presuppose mastery and gratification at each earlier level before an individual is free to devote his energies to succeeding stages. Thus, an individual who experiences a faulty oral stage of development may have to divert a disproportionate amount of his energies toward oral gratification during later years. In Freud's own metaphor, an army general is less likely to win a war if he must leave a number of his troops to deal with unfinished battles along the way.

Erickson (1950) and Havighurst (1952) have described developmental tasks of early and middle childhood, adolescence, and adult life. Learning a sense of trust in others, learning social and physical realities, building a

wholesome attitude toward one's self, and developing a clear sense of identity are a few of the tasks to be mastered for successful ascension up the
ladder of life.

Maslow (1954) has suggested that human motives arrange themselves
in a hierarchy from the most basic biological needs to self-actualization.
Beginning with body needs such as hunger and thirst and moving step by
step through safety needs for self-preservation, love needs for approval of
others, esteem needs for self-enhancement, and finally, at the top of the
scale, self-actualization needs for realization of one's utmost potential,
Maslow has constructed a hierarchy within which he attempts to explain
all human motivation. Maslow postulates that successful achievement and
satisfaction of higher level needs is dependent upon reasonable fulfillment
of needs at the lower levels.

The hierarchy of educational tasks which makes up the subject matter
of this paper represents an attempt to organize and formulate psychological
principles of development into practical terms for the educator. Each level
is concerned with the reciprocal tasks of student and teacher in the formation of a working educational relationship. In an ascending order, the hierarchy of educational tasks consists of primary, acceptance, order, exploratory, relationship, mastery, and achievement task levels.

PRIMARY TASK LEVEL

The most primitive level on which teacher and child may interact is the
primary task level. Here, the teacher's task is to provide maximum gratification and to establish contact on the student's own terms, thus laying the
groundwork for future interactions in which more control and direction
may be exercised. This level is generally only applicable in cases of severe
learning disability where the student is inaccessible to social controls or
totally resistant to learning. The child's task is minimal at the primary
level. The teacher may appeal to such basic needs as a desire for candy or
money rather than to more complex social needs. It is at this level that
operant conditioning work with severely regressed schizophrenics and autistic children is undertaken. Lindsley (1956), Ferster (1961), Isaacs (1960),
and Weiland (1961) have demonstrated that such inaccessible individuals
may take note of a teacher or therapist who has a piece of candy, gum or
the like, pay attention and begin to learn or relearn appropriate behaviors
in order to obtain the desired reward.

Related work starting at the primary level has been done by Slack, (in
a lecture to NPI Staff, 1963), who has shown how a desire for money may
be an effective motivator for getting a school drop out with serious motivation and learning problems to learn to read. Slack approached such individuals and asked them to help him evaluate a teaching machine reading
program. For their efforts these boys were given a penny for each frame of
the reading program. In the course of acquiring $30 and exposure to a

basic reading vocabulary, many of these boys actually learned to read. More important, many manifested a new interest in school and learning and continued their formal education. Similar methods have proven successful with inmates in state prisons.

In the NPI school, a two-year educational program was recently completed with a twelve-year-old autistic boy who had never developed speech (Hewett, 1964). The goal of the program was to teach this withdrawn and unsocialized boy to read and write and thus enable him to communicate more appropriately with the environment. Candy gumdrops established the first point of contact between teacher and student. The boy paid attention and engaged in simple reading activities such as picture-word matching in order to obtain an immediate candy reward. Once this contact was established, the boy was given higher level tasks. This is an important characteristic of the hierarchy; while the teacher may initiate contact with the child on the lowest appropriate level, the eventual goal is to engage him in higher level tasks.

ACCEPTANCE TASK LEVEL

The second task level consists of acceptance tasks for both teacher and child. At this level, the teacher communicates complete acceptance of the child and attempts to establish the beginning of a relationship with him, still primarily on the child's terms. While the child may have perceived the teacher as an undifferentiated means to immediate gratification at the primary level, he now has the task of relating to the teacher as a social object. The child acknowledges the teacher's presence and responds more attentively to verbal interaction. This is only the very early stage of a genuine interpersonal relationship between teacher and child which will be the focus of a later level. At the acceptance level the teacher sets few behavioral limits and usually works on a one-to-one basis with the child. The student competes only with his own record and no grades are given. In addition, academic demands are minimal and the teacher's main goal is to make the child secure and successful in the learning situation. Toward this end a variety of activities such as playing games and taking walks may be utilized.

The child who refuses to get out of his parents' car and come into the classroom may be joined in the back seat by the teacher who initiates contact through reassurance and gradual building of an accepting relationship. At the NPI school, teachers often go on the wards and into the bedrooms of frightened withdrawn children who refuse to get out of bed and come to school. The teacher may sit on the bed next to the child and use a small projector to show him colored slides on the ceiling, or read him stories, or play simple games with him. The teacher who hopes to be successful with children who have serious learning problems and who are threatened by the prospect of further failure should be prepared to settle for the minimal but significant tasks on the acceptance level.

ORDER TASK LEVEL

Once the child feels accepted and is secure enough to form a limited relationship with the teacher, he is ready to be held for order tasks on the next level of the hierarchy. The teacher's task at this level is to increase her control and gradually impose structure, routine, and definite limits in the learning situation. Although academic deficiencies are still completely accepted, the student is now held for more appropriate behavior. He no longer works on his own terms and must accept certain conditions for learning. The work of Cruickshank (1961), Haring and Phillips (1962) suggests that well structured classroom environments facilitate learning among hyperactive and distractible students with learning problems. The concept of order and routine is basic to an effective learning situation for all children but particularly important for children with learning disorders whose erratic patterns of functioning in the classroom have contributed to their failure to learn. At the order level the teacher carefully judges the child's capacity for choice, presents him with small realistically attainable units of work and removes extraneous stimuli which are distracting in an effort to promote maximum gratification and success in the classroom.

At the NPI school, a resistant, nonconforming child who has failed to learn is often brought into the classroom for periods of ten to fifteen minutes a day. During this short period, the child's task is to function at the order level as a "student"—sit at a desk, follow simple directions and routines, and control his behavior. Longer periods are introduced as the student is able to tolerate them. During this time the child may be given certain order tasks to do such as sorting objects on the basis of size and color, puzzle making, or map coloring and labeling.

Recently a seventeen-year-old boy with a severe physical disability who had never learned to read was provided with an elaborate experiential reading program based solely on his great interest in rockets. The teacher spared no amount of effort in providing the boy with stimulating and interesting material. The boy, however, came to school when he pleased, would only work as long as he wished, and in essence set his own limits in the learning situation. Despite the ingenuity and total dedication of the teacher, the reading program was a complete failure. It was only after a staff conference during which the lack of limits and teacher control in the program were examined that a change was made. The boy was later told that an instructional program in reading was available for him but only at certain specific times. If he wanted to learn to read, he had to participate exactly as the teacher directed, otherwise he did not have to come to school. The results were surprising. The boy showed up in class regularly and began to learn to read. He worked diligently and functioned on the teacher's terms. While for some students, an experiential or exploratory program, such as the one first tried with this boy, would be successful, it was necessary in this case to engage the student in tasks at the order level before learning could take place. Exploratory educational activities, to be discussed at the next level, are more likely to be successful once the student is functioning on the order-task level.

The task of maintaining order may be overlearned by the rigid and obsessive-compulsive child with a learning problem. It will be the teacher's task to direct such a child's energies from, rather than toward, more order and routine. This is another characteristic within all levels of the hierarchy. It is the teacher's task to help students who display extreme behavior to achieve a healthier balance.

EXPLORATORY TASK LEVEL

Exploratory tasks are found on the next level of the hierarchy. Once the teacher and child have formed a beginning working relationship, they may explore the environment together. Now it is the teacher's task to introduce learning by offering the child a rich variety of multisensory experiences. The child's task is to reach out and explore the real world around him with his eyes, ears, hands, nose, and even his taste buds. It is the appeal that exploratory activities have for the child, not their appropriateness for his chronological age or grade level, that is important.

The teacher assesses the sense of modalities by which the child learns best. Where sensory and perceptual motor problems exist, particular attention is paid to making the child's learning experience as reinforcing as possible. The work of Kephart (1961) and others has stressed the importance of readying a child for more complex educational tasks by special emphasis on the basic perceptual motor components of learning; these are undertaken at the exploratory level. Concrete experiences are utilized as a basis for instruction. The stimulus value and impact of all materials is enhanced and immediate feedback is provided the child following each exploratory experience. Exploratory activities such as music, simple games, imaginative play, story telling and arts and crafts, are often useful in reaching a child who is not ready for academic instruction.

The Fernald (1948) method of kinesthetic word tracing and experiential story writing as a means of teaching remedial reading and spelling is an example of an educational program organized at the exploratory level. The child is given a highly reinforcing means of word learning which provides him with visual, auditory, and kinesthetic cues. In addition he writes a daily story in class about anything of interest to him. This combination approach which reinforces reading and spelling offers an opportunity written expression and is a highly successful approach with children with learning disorders.

An eleven-year-old catatonic schizophrenic boy in the NPI school was carried to school in a rigidly immobilized state. After several weeks he interacted and cooperated with his teacher for the first time by pushing a lever which turned on a slide projector and exposed a series of colored pictures of prehistoric animal life in front of him. The boy was motivated by a strong personal interest in prehistoric animals. A teacher of sixth grade normal children observed this boy's daily lever pushing interaction with the teacher and remarked that it was "interesting" but expressed concern because no regular sixth grade science curriculum in her school included the study of prehistoric life. Needless to say, the concept of a hierarchy of educational tasks and the necessity for establishing a point of contact with a severely handicapped child was alien to her.

RELATIONSHIP TASK LEVEL

Relationship tasks are found on the next level of the hierarchy. The teacher has the task of increasing her value as a social reinforcer and forming a genuine interpersonal relationship with the child. This implies more than mutual acceptance which was the focus of the acceptance task level, for the interpersonal relationship now becomes an important source of motivation. The child is concerned with gaining the teacher's approval and recognition. The teacher expresses more personal interest in the child and uses social approval and disapproval more freely as a means of motivation and control. It is at this level that the child's peer relationships also are of greater concern to the teacher. Students with similar interests and needs may be paired and more group instruction may be utilized.

Since the child who has failed to learn in school has often been subjected to considerable social devaluation, the tasks at this level are of particular importance. The teacher who sets realistic academic goals for the nonachiever and who helps him achieve success resulting in deserved praise and recognition will be shaping positive academic and social attitudes which may have far-reaching implications. A relationship with an adult who objectively deals with one's shortcomings while communicating respect and acceptance may be highly significant to the child with a learning disorder who has had previous faulty relationships with rejecting parents and unreasonable teachers.

A bright thirteen-year-old boy in the NPI school who was deficient in all achievement areas, particularly long division, had adopted the position that he was far too intelligent to concern himself with mundane educational matters. He was going to design a computer that would solve all mathematical problems in order to prove his genius. This boy's fear of facing the reality of his educational needs was prompted by achievement-conscious parents who would not settle for anything but an all "A" report card. The teacher devoted almost an entire semester forming a relationship with this boy. The relationship was developed while working on science experiments at the exploratory level. The turning point occurred when the boy completed a simple electrical device with the teacher's help. He found he could diagram and explain its function mathematically. The boy explained to the teacher, "This is the first thing I ever made that worked and that I really understand." From this point on, the boy talked less and less of his grandiose and unrealistic aspirations and began to work on his existing school problems.

The five previously discussed levels are essentially readiness levels for formal academic work. They have been stressed more than will be the remaining two levels because their importance may be overlooked by the teacher who views the child with a learning disorder as primarily in need of remedial academic help. Not until the child has shown the capacity to handle the lower level tasks is he seen as really ready to undertake remedial work solely on the mastery level. While remedial work may be given on any level, the emphasis will not be on academic accomplishment but on more basic educational needs as implied by the hierarchy.

MASTERY TASK LEVEL

When the child is ready to deal with his academic deficiencies and concentrate on basic curriculum, mastery tasks on the next level of the hierarchy are undertaken.

The teacher's task at the mastery level is to help the student acquire essential information and understanding about the environment and to develop the intellectual and vocational skills necessary for social survival. The students learn reading, writing, and arithmetic since these skills are basic for all learning. The emphasis is on practical application of these skills to daily living. Intelligence and achievement testing are important at the mastery level. The teacher carefully assesses a given child's learning potential as well as his specific academic deficits before formulating a program on the mastery level. In addition, the use of progress tests and grading may be introduced.

Since the emotionally handicapped child with a learning disorder may have a marginal if not faulty reality orientation and limited resources for communication and social interaction, mastery skills are vitally important to him. One of the characteristics of emotionally handicapped children is that they often complete tasks on the hierarchy out of sequence. The schizophrenic child may learn to read, spell, and master number concepts while relating to the teacher on the primary level. Despite these academic gains, such a child may make no progress on the acceptance, order, exploratory, and relationship level. In the broadest sense, despite academic progress, the child is still suffering from a serious learning disorder and the teacher's goals should be set accordingly.

ACHIEVEMENT TASK LEVEL

Not a great deal needs to be said about achievement tasks which constitute the higher level on the hierarchy. The child who is consistently self-motivated, achieving up to his intellectual potentials, eager for new learning experiences, and socially well-integrated in the classroom, is functioning on the achievement level. All teachers know the joy of working with such children. These are the children who have successfully completed all the tasks described on the lower levels and who are in a position to devote their energies to learning.

DISCUSSION

The staff teachers of the NPI school have found it useful to describe and program all students within the framework of the educational task levels on the hierarchy. The student's observed functioning level is plotted for each task shortly after his enrollment and an educational program is formulated for him. In the charting of these plans, the following considerations are made:

(1) The most significant goals will be set on the lowest task levels where the student is either deficient or given to extremes. The chances that a student will be successful at a given task level are greatly increased if he is adequately functioning at all lower levels.

(2) The educational program may be best instituted on a task level where the student is functioning reasonably well. This initial level may be above or below the level viewed as most in need of emphasis. Therefore, the schizophrenic overachiever may be reached initially on a purely academic and intellectual level with the more important tasks of the relationship and exploratory levels emphasized as soon as possible.

(3) Once contact has been established with a student on a particular level, the teacher attempts to deal with unmet tasks on lower levels, and then to move up the hierarchy as quickly as possible.

(4) Several task levels may be worked on concurrently and seldom will a teacher restrict an educational program to only one level. However, lower, unmet task levels will receive greater emphasis.

(5) From time to time, students may regress in their functioning at a particular task level necessitating a reassessment of goals and a possible alteration of the educational program.

Figure 28-1 provides an example of the description and program of Steven, an eleven year old boy who had refused to go to school for more than a year prior to hospitalization. The teacher's initial observations appear in the left column and her suggestions for the educational program in the right column. In the case of Steven, the basic task for teacher and student was set at the acceptance level. The teacher was most concerned with communicating an attitude of acceptance and helping this boy feel secure in the classroom at the expense of higher level tasks. While this was her major concern, the boy was held for some level of functioning with higher tasks.

Most children with learning problems are given tasks at all levels with the possible exception of the primary and achievement levels which are not

Student: Steven

Description	Program
Achievement Not functioning at this level	
Mastery —Underachieving in all subjects. —Claims can't do basic addition and subtraction which he has previously demonstrated. —Will do some silent reading at approximately third grade level but has poor comprehension.	**Mastery** —De-emphasize academic accomplishments particularly in arithmetic and give easy third grade reading.
Relationship —Becomes very anxious when singled out by the teacher for praise. —Relates with other students only through provoking them to test classroom limits.	**Relationship** —Maintain distance both physically and interpersonally. —Respect his preference to be dealt with as member of group.
Exploratory —Demonstrates few interests. —Holds back in all activities and claims no interest in anything. —Has shown some interest in movie projector and how it works.	**Exploratory** —Arrange to have science teacher let him experiment with an old projector. —Start him on a simple electrical project when he seems ready.
Order —Overcontrolled, rigid in his behavior —Refuses to have haircut or remove his red jacket in the classroom.	—Arrange seating so he will not be next to volatile class members. —Encourage some freedom of movement. —Avoid discussion of jacket or haircut at present.
Acceptance —Suspicious, guarded in relation to teacher. —Withdraws when teacher approaches. —Asks to work in study booth alone.	INITIATE CONTACT HERE —Permit independent study in booth. —Give small units of work and request he bring to teacher's desk. —Approach initially in business-like but friendly manner. —Attempt to find some simple classroom chore he might do for teacher while other students working.
Primary Not functioning at this level.	

FIGURE 28-1   Hierarchy of educational tasks—Student program.

applicable in the majority of cases. Once establishing contact at the acceptance level, the teacher carefully weighed the factors of student gratification and her own control and initiated the program as described. Her educational plan was not a static one; it changed from day to day. The teacher increased her control step by step until after a six-month period, she had the student functioning effectively on the mastery level. He was able to tolerate interaction with teacher and peers, explore the classroom environment more freely, and display a consistent level of performance in his class work.

It is hoped that this concept of a hierarchy of educational tasks may make psychological principles of development more meaningful to teachers and provide them with a measure of educational economy in understanding and adequately programming for children with learning disorders.

References

Cruickshank, W., A teaching method for brain-injured and hyperactive children (Syracuse: Syracuse University Press, 1961).

Erickson, E., Childhood and Society (New York: Norton, 1950).

Fernald, G., Basic techniques in remedial school subjects (New York: McGraw-Hill, 1948).

Ferster, C., and De Meyer, M., The development of performances in autistic children in automatically controlled environments, J. Chron. Dis., 1961, 13, 312-345.

Haring, N., and Phillips, E., Educating emotionally disturbed children (New York: McGraw-Hill, 1962).

Havighurst, R., Developmental tasks and education (New York: Longmans, 1952).

Hewett, F., Teaching reading to an autistic boy through operant conditioning, The Reading Teacher, 1964, 17, 613-618.

Isaacs, W., Thomas, J., and Goldiamond, I., Application of operant conditioning to reinstating verbal behavior in psychotics, J. Speech and Hearing Disorders, 1960, 25, 8-12.

Kephart, N., The slow learner in the classroom (Columbus, Ohio: Merrill, 1961).

Lindsley, O., Operant conditioning methods applied to research in chronic schizophrenia, Psychiat. Res. Rep., 1956, 5, 118-139.

Maslow, A., Motivation and personality (New York: Harper & Row, 1954).

Munroe, R., Schools of psychoanalytic thought (New York: Holt, Rinehart and Winston, 1955).

Weiland, H., and Rudnick, R., Considerations of the development and treatment of autistic children. In Ruth S. Eissler et al. (Editors), The psychoanalytic study of the child, Vol. 16 (New York: International Universities Press, 1961).

29 THE PERCEPTUAL BASIS FOR LEARNING

Joseph M. Wepman

At the Berkeley Conference on Personality Development in 1960, Roger Williams made a cogent observation about the biological approach to the study of personality which seems most appropriate to the central theme of these proceedings—meeting individual differences in reading. Speaking of personality differences, he said, in part:

> Consider the fact that every individual person is endowed with a distinctive gastrointestinal tract, a distinctive circulatory system, a distinctive respiratory system, a distinctive endocrine system, a distinctive nervous system, and a morphologically distinctive brain; furthermore, that the differences involved in this distinctiveness are never trifling and often are enormous. Can it be that this fact is inconsequential in relation to the problem of personality differences? (Williams, 1960)

We might begin by asking a similar question with regard to the learning of reading. Can it be that this fact is inconsequential in relation to the problem of differences in learning to read? Literally all of the systems that Williams itemizes are involved in the development of learning in children—differences not only within the systems but between them which establish the individuality of the entity, the child, with which we are concerned.

If we grant that such differences exist, and much of this chapter is devoted to a demonstration that they do, the next and most important task is to isolate the differences of maximal importance to the act of learning to read, or stated otherwise, to identify the factors which are most likely to produce differences in children that will affect their ability to learn to read.

Reprinted from H. Alan Robinson, ed., *Meeting Individual Differences in Reading*, SEM, Vol. 26, No. 94 (Chicago: University of Chicago Press, 1964), pp. 25-33.

It is the argument in this chapter that major differences do exist in children at the perceptual level of learning which may materially affect their learning; that these differences are fundamental to learning; that they underlie the conceptual level and provide the basic percepts upon which concepts are built; and that they must be understood and clarified before the conceptual level is focused upon. Too much attention, it is held—to the extent of preoccupation—has already been given to the conceptual domain, which in fact is the final stage of the learning act, and too little to the lower levels in the hierarchy. All learning, according to this theoretical position, proceeds in a hierarchical fashion from the perceptual to the conceptual level, from the decoding of an input signal below the level of comprehension before a meaningful interpretation can be placed on it through association with previously received and memory-stored percepts and concepts. The key to this integration of present stimulus with past learning lies not only in the intactness of the input transmission pathways but in the capacity of each type of signal to arouse past learning received along other modalities.

Our concern, our immediate concern, is not with the partially sighted or the partially deafened but with the child who must learn with unimpaired organs and processes. That is not to say that we should not explore in each child the adequacy of his sense organs and their capability of transmitting the signals for which they are peculiarly endowed. But assuming that they function well and transmit the sensory messages, our major attention should be directed toward understanding the individual capacity for prelinguistic perceptualization. It is this level, between absolute reception and transmission of the signal, at the point where the transmutation from signal to sign occurs, where input signal becomes translated into the alphabet of letters and sounds to form the stimulus for comprehension, that seems to be so frequently overlooked as we study the learning act. Our concern, then, lies with the differences between children in their modes of perceptualization and the effect of these differences upon their ability to learn, which stage in learning may be the very core of the reading problem.

THE MODALITY CONCEPT

Approaches to reading have stressed the gaining of comprehension directly through whatever means rather than the explication of individual differences in learning ability or the underlying processes of reading. It seems to this writer, however, that the teacher's problem lies not in the prescribed approach that is to be used with all of the children to be taught but with the approached, that is, with the child who must learn to read. What is proposed here is that the teaching of reading should be child-centered rather than method-centered; that the differences in children need to be understood to determine which methods might be most useful for a particular child or group of children. Stated differently, the question should not be whether visual sight reading or phonics or any other method is the approach to use, but which children among all of those to be taught should be taught by which method. No method should be considered incorrect for any member of a group because it has not reached all of the children. Quite to the contrary, all that the modality concept holds is that we should predetermine which child can learn best by which method. The central focus should be on the child, not on the method.

It seems time to take stock, to explore in reading what has become so evident and accepted in other fields—that to understand the group one must first understand the individuals that make up the group, that learning is an individualized process in many ways for each child. Just as he is different in personality, in intelligence, and in language ability, so, too, is he different from others in how he learns.

For this writer, much of this viewpoint is meaningful in the present context only when it is translated into the perceptual differences between children. A child's learning type—his maximal modality or pathway of learning, his differential ability to learn by eye, or by ear, or even by touch —needs to be understood before a particular approach to reading can be determined for him. Only after we have studied each child for such propensities should we think of grouping him with others and then, to the degree possible, with those others who have like propensities. That is, before we explore whether a given child or group of children should be taught by sight-recognition methods or by phonic methods, we should determine which of the perceptual building blocks he can utilize best in the integrative, conceptualizing process of gaining meaning from the printed page. It is with these prelinguistic skills that the so-called modality concept of learning concerns itself. And it is with the belief that today this determination can be made with reasonable accuracy, that we can predetermine which of the sensory input pathways each child can function with best, that we recommend this approach.

Perhaps we should cast our questions in more specific terms to avoid misunderstanding. In a previous paper, the writer isolated three functions which, for all practical purposes, are what is meant by the auditory perceptual level, and postulated that these same three functions, namely, (1) discrimination, (2) memory (retention and recall), and (3) sequential behavior or patterning, are probably of equal importance in the visual perceptual act (Wepman, 1960). To these should be added a fourth which is presently receiving a considerable amount of attention in research—intermodal transfer, or the ability to shift from one modality to another, to stimulate a given modality in recall and association through its opposing modality.

To express these ideas in even more specific terms, we might ask of a given child whether he has difficulty in auditory discrimination, in visual recall, or in the sequential patterning of either, or whether he functions adequately with each of these individual processes but cannot utilize the stimulation received along one type of pathway to arouse the necessary integrative behavior previously received along the other type of pathway.

Let us illustrate some of these questions with actual cases. Consider the child who cannot discriminate between the sounds of the language. To him, the /p/ sound in "cap" sounds like /t/; the /th/ sound is indistinguishable from the /t/ sound in the word "thin"—as just two examples of a possible host of sound discriminaton confusions he may have. Such a child, it is held, should get his primary instruction in reading through the visual pathway. It has been the writer's lot to take care of many such children over the years, not initially because they were having difficulty learning to read, but because they were encountering problems in the acquisition of language and speech. One such boy comes to mind who perfectly illustrates the point.

This lad was first seen when his parents brought him to the Speech and Language Clinic at the University of Chicago when he was nearly four, with the complaint that he had not yet started to talk or that when he did try it was impossible to understand him. Examination revealed a child of adequate intelligence when assessed by nonverbal tests, without visual or auditory acuity problems. He was hyperactive, frustrated in every attempt to communicate with the adults in his environment, and said to be unusually "stubborn and mean." We found him to be relatively manageable when separated from his well-meaning but extremely anxious and demanding parents. His speech was largely jargon, but when studied, a predictable one. That is, he always substituted specific sounds for others, and when we could understand the substitution pattern, we could understand his speech. For our present purposes, let us pass over his early development of speech. With proper stimulation and understanding and especially with the passage of time and the normal course of auditory maturation, his articulation became relatively adequate. At kindergarten age, he was understandable enough, although still far from perfect in his articulation. The sounds which we know are invariably learned last by children were the sounds he produced with most difficulty. His auditory discrimination was extremely inadequate even at this time, but it continued to improve. Auditory training for discrimination seemed to help some, but without question, he acquired very little information along the auditory pathway. Since he gained most of his knowledge along the visual pathway and he was motorically adequate, he passed the usual reading readiness tests with ease. The difficult part of his schooling began in the first grade. In his school, every child was taught to read through a phonic approach. It took some time and considerable doing to convince the teachers that (1) he was not unintelligent because he couldn't learn phonics and (2) that he could learn to read if visual training methods were used.

For this child things worked out reasonably well. His school was willing to provide him with special tutoring in reading; even though the teachers continued to teach all of the other children through phonics, they permitted him to receive a sight-training program and he learned to read. We were, however, less successful in convincing the school that the other children in the first grade who were having difficulty learning to read might also need a different approach. The parents were pleased but also failed to learn from the experience. Although recognizing that the child was learning to read visually where he had failed when approached aurally, they failed to recognize that auditory imperception is not only a factor in learning to read but is, rather, a fact of life. Just recently the parents brought the child in for his yearly reevaluation, and they brought the following inexplicable behaviors to our attention. The father complained that often when the child came to him with a question and he took the trouble to explain it to him—orally, of course—the child might nod his head as though he understood and yet five minutes later would again ask for an answer to the same question. They also found it strange that the child, who is now eight, "invariably gets confused when told something over the telephone." Both of these examples, of course, point to the auditory imperception of the child. When told something, the answer is retained only momentarily; he has notably poor auditory recall. When he receives a message over the telephone, when all of the usual visual components and clues to meaning are missing and all of the message must be understood from the auditory stimuli, he gets confused. He has continuing, and probably will have life-long, difficulty with any purely auditory stimulus. He needs, more than most children, the reinforcement of visual, tactual, and kinesthetic clues.

Teachers of such children, especially when they are in the category of the child whose problems in learning we have just reviewed, children for whom the auditory pathway is simply not functional, have two courses open to them. They can either teach them through a very directed visual approach, using auditory clues only after the child has developed that modality sufficiently through the processes of maturation so that it can be used for reinforcement, or they can approach the child visually and attempt quite separately to improve his auditory skills. When the latter approach is used, it has been our experience that the two modalities should be trained quite independently, since combining the two approaches before the child is capable of utilizing them both leads more often than not to confusion. It has also been our experience that if a child below the age of eight shows many articulatory inaccuracies in speech or oral reading because of poor auditory discrimination auditory training does him little good. Only after full maturation have we been able to see much change in such children as the result of auditory training. On the other hand, if children show auditory imperception but do not have articulatory inaccuracies, they frequently respond quite well to auditory training, even before the age of eight. The present statement is based on long standing clinical experience on this point. However, there has as yet been no carefully controlled research—and it is sorely needed.

The approach through a single modality rather than through the combined modalities receives further confirmation from our work with adult language-impaired subjects, with whom, both in speech and in reading, it was found that the multiple approach method was often more confusing than helpful. In these adults it was also found that if the impaired pathway was separately trained, it frequently became useful for reinforcement of learning along the unimpaired pathway. It should be recognized, however, that reinforcement is only of value when it reinforces; when it confuses or takes more time than the single pathway, it may become a negative factor in learning. From this type of evidence it is argued that, in teaching reading, one should capitalize on the modality of preference, train the undeveloped or impaired pathway separately, and bring the two together when they each can add something to the other, but not before.

SHIFTS IN MODALITY

Our second question deals with the degree of limitation a given child may have along a specific pathway. Fortunately, most children have some capacity to function with both visual and auditory perception. The two abilities have their own rates of development and, when mature, most often show only approximately equal maturational levels. When a child shows his best ability to be visual and his lesser ability to be auditory, the visual approach in reading is suggested, with immediate auditory reinforcement and, in addition, auditory training to improve that capacity.

Naturally, the opposite approach would be best for the child with good auditory ability but only fair visual ability. Here it is suggested that the teacher should use a phonic approach, with strong, but secondary, sight training to bring the lesser developed pathway up to a level of major usefulness.

Parenthetically, it should be added that, although vision and audition are the major modalities discussed here, the other input sensory pathways should not be overlooked. Tactile and kinesthetic skills are for some children—fortunately very few—the best learning pathway. When they are the best approach, they should receive the same concentration of teaching attention suggested for vision and audition. They have not been stressed here in order to reduce the confusion that comes with a discussion of the multiplicity of sensory pathways and because, quite truthfully, we know much less about successful teaching of reading through other senses than vision and audition. Kinesthetic methods are available, however, and should be used. At this point, the writer must express as strongly as he can what he believes to be true—that it is the rare child of school age who needs a tactile-kinesthetic approach as the central core of his instruction.

It is as wrong in the present framework to begin the teaching of reading by such an approach with any group of children who have not been previously determined as "tactile" or "tactile-kinesthetic" as it is to adopt a "visual" or "phonic" approach for any unselected group. There is no magic in any method; there are just differences in children which must be taken into account.

Our third question relates to those processes of transfer and shift from one modality to another, which for lack of a better name we call "intermodal transfer ability." In gaining comprehension from any input signal, a child must use that signal to evoke previously learned symbols received along many input pathways to form the associations necessary for comprehension. This act of arousal and integration is seen as the probable final stage of perceptual behavior before comprehension is achieved. Thus, a child who sees the printed word "dog" must evoke not only previous visual stimuli of printed forms but life forms as well; he must shift from the visual input to previously received and stored auditory patterns making up the word "dog" and perhaps to the tactile sensations of petting a dog, of his small and even his frisky movements, before the printed word has full meaning for him. Without this shift to other modal learning, little integrative meaning may be attached to the printed word. Intermodal transfer, then, seems to be vital to the learning act. Katz and Deutsch, in an extensive study of good and poor readers on a variety of perceptual tasks, concluded in part that "poor reading is associated with difficulties in shifting from one sensory mode to another" (1963, p. 45).

When children are suspected of having inadequacies in this phase of learning, when each modality seems adequate when studied by itself but the capacity to shift from one to another seems affected, the teacher's task seems explicit. Experience and training at cross-modal interpretation, in using each input pathway as the originating stimulus carrier and striving for the appropriate associations, is necessary for these children.

At this point we might well turn to a brief discussion of some of the suspected causes for the differences observed in the perceptual behavior of children. Extreme cases of learning problems have been described in the literature and specific causes ascribed to them, which could be overcome, the investigators suggested, by utilizing compensatory modalities. Eisenberg pointed out very clearly in his discussion of the reading problem in brain-injured children that

the deficits in performance we observe may represent not at all the inherent handicap of his disease, but rather the most he has been able to accomplish in the absence of what he needed. We cannot conclude from the fact that he has not learned to read by the methods adequate for the ordinary child that he could not if attempts were made to bypass his deficiencies, by making use of other sensorimotor channels. (1964, p. 69).

In general, the evidence from the impaired child seems quite widely accepted. Recently, de Hirsch hypothesized a "neurophysiological immaturity" in many children with reading and language defects (1964). Katz and Deutsch have explored reading problems in the socially underprivileged, and in an as yet unpublished series of reports, they have noted the explicit modality deficiencies which seem to exist above and beyond the socioeconomic and environmental handicaps from which these children suffer. They hypothesize that the auditory deficiency may be a consequence of their environment.

Individual differences in perceptual transmission and conceptual learning can be demonstrated to be along modality lines; methods for teachers or the school system to determine a given child's maximal learning modality, if they are inclined to do so, remain to be discovered.

Perhaps this is the best reason for stressing individual differences in children at this time, for during the past decade there has been a tremendous burst of interest in identification of perceptual modalities directly related to reading. While time and space forbid a complete review of the evidence, a study of the references as well as the articles themselves concerned with this factor will well repay those who are interested. It will be recalled that even some twenty years ago Monroe in her Reading Aptitude Tests (Houghton Mifflin Co., 1935) differentiated between visual and auditory functioning. Auditory-discrimination testing has been going on for almost the same length of time, and this writer as well as many others has put forth the concept that auditory-discrimination inadequacy is related not only to speech development but also to learning type and to reading disability (Wepman, 1961). Visual memory and matching tests have been devised and are now being standardized that will point up explicit difficulties with that facet of learning. Visual-motor tests, which have been standardized on preschool children as well as early school-age children, point to difficulties in prelinguistic function along that combination of modalities (Frostig, Lefever, Wittlesey, 1961). McCarthy and Kirk, building on theories and models of brain function which Osgood and Wepman had independently proposed, developed a test assessing language and prelanguage levels of function along each modality; from its protocol, the language needs of children at both the perceptual and the conceptual levels can be identified (1963).

The reality of prediction is here. Its application to reading is being tried in a wide number of reading clinics and school systems throughout the country, although, unfortunately, almost solely in centers for remediation of severe learning problems. If, however, the approach seems valid for remedying reading problems, it should be equally useful for teaching those beginning to learn to read, for special reading problems are not seen as being outside the realm of the normal but as being at the extremes of the total population distribution.

The children who are easiest to identify, of course, are the so-called remedial reading problems, since they have tried and failed to achieve in the regular classrooms. How much better it would be if we were to study all children before they become problems and thus offset their lags in development—if that, indeed, is where their problems lie. Such children are, unfortunately, not the occasional child but, according to some widely quoted figures, amount to as many as 25 percent of all school children. And the remainder—the 75 percent who succeed—to what degree do they do so? How many of these children would learn more, be better able to read, find more enjoyment in reading, if they were taught by the right approach for them instead of having to learn despite the methods used?

CONCLUDING STATEMENT

It has been the writer's experience that education and educators are slow to move to new ideas, that they grudgingly adopt new approaches, but that when they do they apply them frequently without reason; whose school systems have adopted a particular new approach to reading as though a panacea had been discovered that would eradicate all the educational ills of their children. No method, no specific approach, no new text or cartoonist's illustration, no matter how apt, will solve the problems of children who are by nature as different in learning type as they are alike in anatomy. It is, for example, still not uncommon for reading readiness tests in which only visual skills are assessed to be given to whole school systems. It has also been called to the writer's attention that whole school systems have turned from vision and audition, as specific approaches to teaching reading, to kinesthetic tracing without determining which children could utilize kinesthetic skills and which could not.

It seems a wiser course to recognize that perceptual ability is the precursor to comprehension. It provides the underpinning for understanding and for generalization. It precedes and permits integration. Man has not evolved with separate visual, aural, and tactile sense receptors and a central process for integration without purpose. By determining the individual child's specific abilities and utilizing them in an organized way, reading, like all other language forms, can be acquired with a minimum of discomfort and a maximum of pleasure.

The modality approach to reading—by differentiating the perceptual levels of transmitting input signals and their ability, in the intermodal transfer, to arouse the associations necessary for integration and thus meaning—only nominates the directions of individualized training. It permits each child to function in the manner for which he is best equipped. It predicates the need for understanding each child as a total organism complete within himself. It is presented here as a challenge to every teacher—a means for assisting in the largely implausible task of making every child literate.

References

de Hirsch, Katrina, Jansky, Jeanette, and Langford, William S., The oral language performance of premature children and controls, *J. Speech and Hearing Disorders*, February, 1964, 29, 60-69.

Eisenberg, L., Behavioral manifestation of cerebral disorders in childhood. In *Brain damage in children: The biological and social aspects*, Herbert George Birch (Editor) (Baltimore: Williams & Wilkins, 1964).

Frostig, Marianne, Lefever, D. Welby, and Whittlesey, John R. B., A developmental test of visual perception for evaluating normal and neurologically handicapped children, *Percept. mot. Skills*, June, 1961, 12, 383-394.

Katz, Phyllis, and Deutsch, Martin, *Visual and auditory efficiency and its relationship to reading in children*, Cooperative Research Project No. 1099 (Washington, D.C.: Office of Education, U.S. Department of Health, Education and Welfare, 1963).

McCarthy, James J., and Kirk, Samuel, *Illinois test of psycholinguistic abilities* (Institute for Research on Exceptional Children, University of Illinois, 1963).

Osgood, Charles E., and Miron, Murray W., Approaches to the study of aphasia (Urbana: University of Illinois Press, 1963).

Wepman, Joseph M., A conceptual model for the processes involved in recovery from aphasia, *J. Speech and Hearing Disorders*, March, 1953, 18, 4-13.

Wepman, Joseph M., Auditory discrimination, speech and reading, *Elem. Sch. J.* 1960, 9, 325-333.

Wepman, Joseph M., The interrelationship of hearing, speech, and reading, *The Reading Teacher*, March, 1961, 14, 245-247.

Williams, Roger J., *The biological approach to the study of personality* (a paper delivered at the Berkeley Conference on Personality Development in Childhood, University of California, May 5, 1960 [offprint only]).

30 CHILDREN WITH SEVERE BRAIN INJURIES: NEUROLOGICAL ORGANIZATION IN TERMS OF MOBILITY

Robert J. Doman, Eugene B. Spitz,
Elizabeth Zucman, Carl H. Delacato,
and Glenn Doman

The large number of conferences, seminars, and publications regarding the brain-injured child indicates not so much the volume of new information available but rather the intensity of the search for new information.

We had long been dissatisfied with the results of our own methods of treatment and believed that the time requirements in treating children with severe brain injuries could scarcely be justified in light of the low percentage of marked successes as compared with children who were essentially without treatment.

During 1956 and 1957 we developed a new approach to such cases, the goal of which was to establish in brain-injured children the developmental stages observed in normal children. The program which aimed at both normal and damaged brain levels consisted of (a) permitting the child normal developmental opportunities in areas in which the responsible brain level was undamaged; (b) externally imposing the bodily patterns of activity which were the responsibility of damaged brain levels; and (c) utilizing additional factors to enhance neurological organization.

The team used consisted of a physiatrist, a neurosurgeon, an orthopedic surgeon, a nurse, a physical therapist, and a psychologist. In 1958, a two-year outpatient study was begun which used these developmental stages in the treatment of 76 brain-injured children. Each patient was seen bimonthly.

MATERIAL

SUBJECTS. This study of 76 children includes every child seen in the Children's Clinic during the study period who met the following criteria:

Reprinted from *Journal of the American Medical Association*, Vol. 174, No. 3 (September 17, 1960), pp. 119-124. By permission of the authors and publisher.

(1) The existence of brain injury. (For the purpose of this study, brain-injured children are defined as those children whose lesion lies in the brain. The definition includes both traumatic and nontraumatic lesions but excludes children who are genetically defective.) (2) A minimum of six months' treatment. (3) No child was eliminated because of the severity of his involvement.

DIAGNOSIS OF BRAIN PATHOLOGY. The diagnosis was made after neurological examination and, in most patients, after an EEG (36), air study (42), and subdural tap (22) had been done. The group of 76 was composed of children who had spasms, athetosis, ataxia, rigidities, tremors, and mixed symptoms; 24 of these children had clinical seizures.

CLASSIFICATION OF BRAIN PATHOLOGY. The brain pathology was classified as to type, location, and degree in the following manner.

TABLE 30-1.

Stage	Level	Mobility	No. of Children
	0	None	20
Movement	1	Rolling over	17
	2	Circling or going backward	2
	3	Moving forward flat on abdomen without pattern	5
Crawling	4	Homologously	4
	5	Homolaterally	3
	6	Cross-pattern	2
	7	Without pattern	1
	8	Homologously	2
Creeping	9	Homolaterally	0
	10	Cross-pattern	0
	11	Pulling up to erect position holding on to furniture & standing, holding onto furniture	0
Walking	12	Walking without help, without pattern	20
	13	Walking, cross-pattern	0

1. *Type:* (a) unilateral brain damage: This group contained 15 children with either subdural hematoma (all operated on), vascular malformation, or hemiatrophy of nonspecific causation. Of these 15 children, four had hemispherectomies performed by us. (b) bilateral brain damage: This group contained 61 children with conditions such as hydrocephalus, subdural hematoma (all operated on), kernicterus, postencephalitic damage, dysgenesis of corpus callosum, dysgenesis of cerebellum, dysgenesis of cortex, porencephaly, or diffuse cortical atrophy of nonspecific causation. We performed 14 ventriculojugular and two ventriculoperitoneal shunts on the 16 hydrocephalic patients. The therapeutic program was instituted no sooner than ten months after surgery.

2. *Location:* Upon air study, 30 children demonstrated dilatation of the lateral ventricles, and 12 demonstrated dilatation of the entire ventricular system, thus indicating the presence of subcortical as well as cortical damage. Locating these lesions in terms of the Phelps-Fay classification (Abbott, 1953), there were 61 cerebral lesions (spastic patients), 12 midbrain lesions (athetoid patients), three basal ganglion lesions (two patients with tremor, one with rigidity), and ten cerebellar lesions (ataxic patients).

3. *Degree:* Both clinical examination and neurosurgical diagnostic procedures indicated that the degree of brain damage ranged from mild to severe. No child was eliminated from this study due to severity of either clinical symptoms or degree of brain pathology.

AGE AT BEGINNING OF STUDY. The ages ranged from twelve months to nine years, with a median age of 26 months and a mean age of 30 months. The children were separated into three age groups of developmental significance: 0-18 months, 16 children; 18-36 months, 41 children; and over 36 months, 19 children.

LEVEL AND STAGES OF MOVEMENT AT BEGINNING OF THERAPY. The level of movement was defined according to a modification of the developmental patterns of Gesell and co-workers (Gesell and Amatruda, ·1947; Gesell, 1943) and Fay (Fay, 1948 and 1955), and these were numerically designated for reference purposes. The stages described are (a) moving arms and legs without forward movements, (b) crawling, (c) creeping, and (d) walking (Table 30-1). In our experience, each stage described was dependent on the successful completion of the previous stage.

IQ, AFFECT, AND SPEECH. No child was eliminated because of severity of deficiency in these areas.

DURATION OF TREATMENT. The duration of treatment ranged from six to 20 months, with a mean of 11 months.

METHOD

After thorough neurological studies, the children were evaluated to determine their disabilities in functional terms. An outpatient program of neurological organization was then prescribed and taught to the parents. The parents were required to carry out the program exactly as prescribed. The children's course was reviewed by the team on an average of every two months, and treatment changes were made to correspond to new developmental levels of accomplishment. The treatment consisted of two types.

TREATMENT TYPE I. All nonwalking children (56) were required to spend all day on the floor in the prone position and were encouraged to crawl (prone method) or creep (hand-knee method) when that level of accomplishment was possible. The only permissible exceptions were to feed, love, and treat the child. This increased the opportunity for the reproduction of the normal function-positional situation of a healthy child during the first 13 months of life.

TREATMENT TYPE II. In each case, at that level of accomplishment at which pathology precluded the child's advancement to the next developmental stage, a specific pattern of activity was prescribed which passively imposed on the central nervous system the functional activity which was normally the responsibility of that damaged brain level. Initially these patterns were in some cases partially, and in other cases completely, those which had been described by Fay (1948). As time passed, our team discontinued some of these, modified others, and added those which it believed to be useful. Each of these patterns had its counterpart in the normal developmental growth of a healthy child so well described by Gesell and Amatruda (1947). The children were patterned for five minutes, four times daily, seven days a week without exception. The patterns were administered by three adults. One adult turned the head, another moved the right arm and leg, and the third moved the left arm and leg. The patterns were to be performed smoothly and rhythmically at all levels.

Activity Pattern I (Homolateral): Children who could not crawl (44) and those who crawled below cross-pattern level (7) were patterned in the homolateral pattern, which was accomplished by one adult turning the head while the adult on the side to which the head was turned flexed the arm and leg. The adult on the opposite side extended both limbs. As the

TABLE 30-2.

Level	Children at Beginning of Study		Children at End of Study	
	No.	%	No.	%
0	20	26.3	0	0.0
1	17	22.4	0	0.0
2	2	2.6	6	7.9
3	5	6.6	9	11.8
4	4	5.3	4	5.3
5	3	3.9	5	6.6
6	2	2.6	5	6.6
7	1	1.4	3	3.9
8	2	2.6	0	0.0
9	0	0.0	1	1.3
10	0	0.0	8	10.5
11	0	0.0	4	5.3
12	20	26.3	7	9.2
13	0	0.0	24	31.6
Total	70	100.0	76	100.0

head was turned, the flexed limbs extended while the extended limbs flexed.

Activity Pattern II (Cross-Pattern): Children who could crawl in cross-pattern or who could creep (5) were patterned in cross-pattern, which was accomplished by one adult turning the head, while the adult on the side toward which the head was turned flexed the arm and extended the leg, the adult on the opposite side extended the arm and flexed the leg. When the head was turned, the position of the limbs was reversed.

Activity Pattern III (Cross-Pattern): Children who walked but poorly (20) were also patterned at the cross-pattern level.

TREATMENT FOR NEUROLOGICAL ORGANIZATION. To enhance neurological organization, the children were evaluated in the light of the functions described below, and a treatment program was devised. The program included the following stages: (1) When tests showed sensory losses or when results of tests were indefinite due to communication problems, the children were placed on a program of sensory stimulation which included application of heat and cold, brushing, pinching, and establishment of body image appreciation by letting the child experience the relationship between his hand and his face, his hand and his mother's face, and similar relationships. (2) As each child reached the point where laterality influenced neurological organization, a program to establish dominance was instituted. (3) A breathing program to improve vital capacity was prescribed. All other therapy and use of mechanical aids were discontinued, except for anticonvulsant medication when indicated.

RESULTS

The results were evaluated according to the following categories: (1) global results; (2) results in the light of chonological age; (3) results in the light of the individual disposition of each patient; and (4) results in the light of the functional level at the onset of the program.

GLOBAL RESULTS. The mean improvement of mobility was 4.2 levels. The mean level of mobility was 4.4 at the beginning of the program and 8.6 at the end of the program. The range of improvement was 0 to 12 levels. If we consider perfect walking the potential for every child, the group achieved 51 percent of this goal (Table 30-2 and figure 30-1).

The following findings are of interest: Of the 20 children unable to move and the 17 unable to walk, none remained at these stages. Twelve children were ready to walk at the end of the study. Eight were creeping cross-pattern (level 10), and four were holding onto objects (level 11).

Eight of the group who could walk initially improved significantly in their walking but did not become perfect and, therefore, could not be considered as having increased their functional competence by one level. All but two of the other children improved by one or more levels.

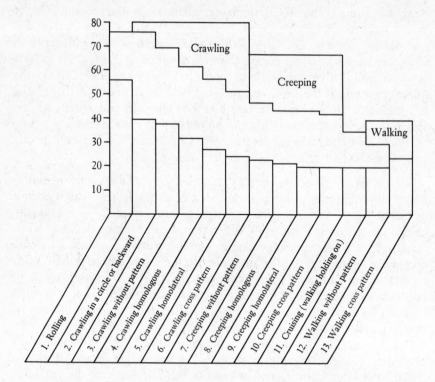

FIGURE 30-1   Graphic presentation of results, in terms of mobility levels, of treatment of children with severe brain injuries.

Eleven children learned to walk completely independently. All but two of these had begun treatment at, or before, two years of age, and all achieved completely independent walking in less than 12 months of treatment. The functional level of this group at the beginning of the study was virtually the same as the level of the other 65 children. The entire group mean level at the outset was 4.4, compared with a mean of 4.1 for this group of 11 who learned to walk independently.

Only six children were discharged, all of whom had learned to walk perfectly; three of these had been walking poorly and three had been unable to walk at the beginning of the program. The other eight who had learned to walk and the other 17 who had improved in walking were not discharged because of residual problems in speech or behavior.

RESULTS IN LIGHT OF CHRONOLOGICAL AGE.   The children were separated into three age groups of developmental significance for purposes of evaluation. There was no significant difference of mean improvement among the three different age groups (Table 30-3).

TABLE 30-3*.

No.	Age, Mo.	Improvement		
		In Stages, Mean	Maximum Possible	% of Potential Achieved
16	Under 18	5.0	10.8	46
41	18 to 36	4.1	8.2	50
19	Over 36	3.2	6.7	47

* Numerical representations correspond to 13 stages of development described above.

INDIVIDUAL RESULTS IN LIGHT OF FUNCTIONAL LEVEL AT BEGINNING OF STUDY. An analysis of the original level–ultimate level disposition of each case indicates an over-all improvement of 4.1 levels within the study. The improvement in individual patients is shown in Table 30-4.

TABLE 30-4.

Developmental Level		Level at End of Study													
No.	No. of Children in Each at Beginning	0	1	2	3	4	5	6	7	8	9	10	11	12	13
0	20	..	..	5	4	3	2	..	1	..	1	1	..	1	2
1	17	..	..	2	1	1	2	4	1	..	..	4	2	..	..
2	2	..	..	..	1	..	..	..	..	..	..	1	..	..	..
3	5	..	..	..	2	..	1	1	..	..	..	1	..	..	..
4	4	..	..	..	..	..	..	..	..	..	..	..	2	2	..
5	3	..	..	..	..	..	..	..	1	..	..	..	..	1	1
6	2	..	..	..	..	..	..	..	..	..	..	..	..	2	..
7	1	..	..	..	..	..	..	..	..	..	..	1	..	..	..
8	2	..	..	..	..	..	..	..	..	..	..	..	..	..	2
9		..	..	..	..	..	..	..	..	..	..	..	..	..	..
10		..	..	..	..	..	..	..	..	..	..	..	..	..	..
11		..	..	..	..	..	..	..	..	..	..	..	..	..	..
12	20	..	..	..	..	..	..	..	..	..	..	..	..	8	12
13		..	..	..	..	..	..	..	..	..	..	..	..	..	..
Totals	76	..	..	7	8	6	5	5	3	..	1	8	4	14	17

RATE OF IMPROVEMENT IN LIGHT OF FUNCTIONAL LEVEL AT BEGINNING OF STUDY. The levels of improvement were evaluated by analysis of 13 levels in terms of functional components (Table 30-5).

TABLE 30-5*.

| | Improvement | | |
Functional Level	In Levels, Mean	Maximum Possible	% of Potential Achievement
No mobility	5.8	13.0	43
Rolling	5.7	12.0	47
Circling	4.5	11.0	45
Moving straight without pattern	2.4	10.0	24
Crawling	6.5	8.0	80
Creeping	4.3	5.3	80
Walking	0.8	1.0	80

* Numerical representations correspond to 13 levels of development described above.

COMMENT

We found significant improvement when we compared the results of the classic procedures we had previously followed with the results of the procedures described above. It is our opinion that the significance of the difference tends to corroborate the validity of the hypothesis set up as the theoretical basis of the program.

These procedures are based on the premise that certain brain levels, that is, pons, midbrain, and cortex, have separate, consecutive responsibilities in terms of mobility. The goal of these procedures (neurological organization) is to create a climate in which a brain-injured child may develop and utilize those brain levels which are uninjured as they are developed in the normal child concurrent with myelinization during the first 18 months of life (Thomas and Dargassies, 1952).

We have observed that the opportunities to crawl and creep are rarely accorded to the brain-injured child. Great emphasis should be placed on permitting the brain-injured child to remain on the floor, which Gesell and coworkers have described as the normal child's "athletic field," thus giving the child an opportunity to utilize and exploit uninjured brain levels and achieve the functions for which such brain levels are responsible.

After neurological examination and testing had established the level of brain injury, we imposed on the child's central nervous system patterns of activity which have as their goal the reproduction of normal activities which would have been the product of the injured brain level had it not been injured. The pattern aspect of the procedure was achieved after a study and modification of Fay's work with the brain-injured child and Gesell's work with the normal child and was then integrated into the procedure developed by us.

It is our opinion that, to be successful in such a program, the procedure must be carried out "wholistically." While we placed varying emphasis upon the importance of different areas within the program, it was our experience that success could not be achieved by using the components of the program in isolation.

We believe that the program must include (a) the opportunity for the brain-injured child to spend prolonged periods on the floor in the prone or quadruped position, so that he may crawl or creep in order to utilize uninjured brain areas in physiological development. Given this opportunity, the brain-injured child may advance several developmental levels unaided; (b) the utilization of patterns of activity administered passively to a child which reproduce the mobility functions for which injured brain levels are responsible; (c) a program of sensory stimulation to make the child body-conscious in terms of position sense and proprioception. We believe that sensory reception is a prerequisite to motor expression; (d) a program of establishing cortical hemispheric dominance through the development of unilateral handedness, footedness, and "eyedness." This was instituted when a lack of neurological organization at this level so indicated (Delacato, 1959); and (e) the institution of a breathing program to achieve the maximal vital capacity, since, in our experience, we had observed the restricted vital capacity and the recurrence of respiratory difficulties in many brain-injured children.

While we think that this program resulted in benefits to the children studied in the areas of language and affect, we confined this report to results achieved in terms of mobility. A later report will deal with the results achieved in other areas by this program of neurological organization.

We wish to stress the fact that no child was eliminated from the study due to initial lack of affect or mobility. It can be observed from the facts presented that many of the children, when initially evaluated, showed little affect and no mobility, and that a large number of them made significant progress. It should also be stressed that during the study all other programs of therapy or habilitation were discontinued and that no mechanical aids, such as braces or crutches, were used.

We place emphasis upon the fact that the children studied were evaluated and treated with reference to the central neurological lesion rather than upon the symptomatic results of the central lesion.

It is our opinion that the results of this study, when compared with the results of our previous work, are sufficiently encouraging to warrant an expanded and continued study of these procedures.

We do not believe that all the techniques which would be useful in achieving neurological organization have been developed by this study. We think that many additional techniques may be developed which could speed the process of habilitation of children with severe brain injuries and perhaps increase the number of types of brain injuries which can be treated. Later reports will deal with the results of studies being conducted at the time of writing.

SUMMARY

A two-year study was conducted on 76 brain-injured children. Its goal was to determine whether a program aimed at neurological organization would be productive of greater results in terms of mobility than we had previously achieved by more classic therapy.

The children studied were both evaluated and treated in light of their central neurological lesions in a program which we had devised to utilize undamaged brain levels to achieve the physiological functions for which such levels are responsible and to assist children at damaged brain levels in achieving function, as far as possible, by means of a program designed to reproduce normal activity. The preliminary results of this study are encouraging. Further studies of these procedures will be undertaken.

References

Abbott, M., *Syllabus of cerebral palsy treatment techniques* (New York: College of Physicians and Surgeons, Columbia University, May, 1953), p. 10.
Delacato, C. H., *Treatment and prevention of reading problems: Neuro-psychological approach* (Springfield, Illinois: Charles C Thomas, 1959).
Fay, T., Neurophysical aspects of therapy in cerebral palsy, *Arch Phys. Med.*, 1948, 29, 327-334.
Fay, T., Origin of human movement, *Am. J. Psychiat.*, 1955, 111, 644-652.
Gesell, A. L., and Amatruda, C. S., *Developmental diagnosis: Normal and abnormal child development*, 2nd Ed. (New York: Harper & Row, 1947), chapter 11.
Gesell, A. L., et al., *Infant and child in culture of today: Guidance of development in home and nursery school* (New York: Harper & Row, 1943).
Thomas, A., and Dargassies, S. A., *Études neurologiques sur le nouveau-né et le jeune nourrisson* (Paris: Masson, 1952).

31 GENERAL PRINCIPLES IN THE
EDUCATION OF THE BRAIN-INJURED CHILD

Alfred A. Strauss and Laura E. Lehtinen ❧

The brain-injured child is a child who began his life with a normal brain potential but whose expected course of even development has been disturbed by accidental destructive events. The ensuing damage has reduced the original potential and has changed the manner and the means of the organism to achieve the new one. Thus we may find that an injury may have caused generalized destruction of nerve substance with conspicuous loss of intellectual ability and disturbances of behavioral control. Or intellectual development may be relatively normal, with an isolated disturbance in visuomotor integration, leading us to assume that the lesion is a circumscribed one. The motor areas may be damaged, with crippling effect, or they may be intact. Behavior and learning, it is now beginning to be recognized, may be affected by minimal brain injuries without apparent lowering of the intelligence level. In all these disturbances we are dealing with damage to the central nervous system above the level of the midbrain and, as explained in previous chapters, we can expect to find a basic similarity within apparent variability. This similarity, which can be clinically observed, is also apparent in the classroom.

We may deduce from the researches with brain-injured adults and the recognized benefits of physiotherapy for cerebral palsied children that the undamaged portions of the brain hold resources from which the organism may substitute, compensate for, or restitute the disabilities resulting from the injury. It is this intact reserve which we attempt to reach in education. The methods of educational treatment which will be described in the

Reprinted from *Psychopathology and Education of the Brain-Injured Child*, Chapter IX (New York: Grune & Stratton, 1947), pp. 128-145. By permission of the junior author and publisher.

following pages are based upon the clinical and psychological findings previously described,[1] the observed effect of the general disturbances upon attention, perception, and behavior, and the effect of specific disturbances of particular perceptual fields upon learning of special academic skills.

The general disturbances as they appear in various aspects of the school situation will be discussed first. The brain-damaged organism, as we know, is abnormally responsive to the stimuli of his environment, reacting unselectively, passively, and without conscious intent. When such a hyper-vigilant organism—one whose reactibility is beyond his own control—is placed in a situation of constant and widespread stimulation, he can only meet the situation with persistent undirected response. The brain-injured child is therefore the focus of the teacher's permanent reminders to "tend to his own work." He pivots in his seat to watch the activity of the children sitting near him. His attention is caught and held by any child who leaves his place. Any noise may cause him to attend; any motion seemingly insignificant may attract him. The teacher will repeatedly find him gazing at pictures and decorations while the lesson is neglected on his desk.

He presents a picture of a child who is extremely mobile in attention and activity, unduly attracted by the doings of others or by the presence of normally inconspicuous background stimuli, inconstant and variable in interests, lacking persistence and sustained effort.

While the distractibility of most brain-injured children is observable in their psychomotor behavior, there are a few children in whom this symptom is not obvious. Such a child is equally handicapped in a learning situation. He is the one who sits quietly at his desk, apparently absorbed in work; at the end of the period his lesson is uncompleted; he is adjudged lazy or a daydreamer. Close observation reveals that a brain-injured child of this type is constantly at the mercy of stimulus details provided by the pictures and page numbers in his book, by flaws and marks on the paper, or by any features of the material which are, for the normal person, additional or irrelevant; he wanders away from his intended goal under the influence of the shifting and uncontrolled associations of his own thoughts. This child is described as inattentive, and certainly with respect to the purposes of the teacher or other members of the class he is. From the child's point of view, however, his seeming inattentiveness is the expression of an abnormally attentive condition. The countless irrelevant stimuli which the normal child disregards the brain-injured child is unable to withstand.

If the brain-injured child is hyperactive and disinhibited in relation to other children, these reactions are likely to be interpreted as expressions of aggressive, antisocial tendencies and treated on this basis. In brain-injured children, however, disinhibition, hyperactivity, and distractibility should be regarded as manifestations of exaggerated responsiveness to stimuli and,

[1] See *Psychopathology and education of the brain-injured child* (New York: Grune & Stratton, 1947), Part I.

in young brain-injured children, as behavior reactions beyond the reach of effective cortical control. Such a child not only attends to the noise outside but is unable to inhibit the impulse to run to the window to find it. Classmates sitting near-by or passing his desk are a constant source of excitation to which he responds by reaching out to hit or punch or push. Class games designed to motivate and interest the normal or familial mentally retarded child are overstimulating for the brain-injured child, with the result that a child who is hyperactive and disinhibited is driven to boisterous talking, shouts, uncontrolled laughter, running about the room, etc. This is the child whom the teacher describes as unresponsive to correction. Scoldings or deprivations, reasoning, subtle approaches by precept or example are equally ineffectual, since the organic irritability and the situational irritating agents remain.

The reactions of children with gross neurological handicap are similar. Many observers have noted the presence of distractibility and hyperactivity in cerebral palsied children. A recent survey undertaken by the California State Departments of Public Health and Education included teachers' reports of typical problems in the education of these children. Included in the area designated in the survey as "Emotional Control" were the following statements: "Very emotional." "Hard to deal with; highly nervous." "Too nervous to attend regular classes." "Has given evidence of high temper in the past but seems to have achieved better control." "Cries easily." Reports listed under "Influence of the Group" were as follows: "Spasticity increases when child is in group and learning becomes slower." "Restless in a crowd and demands much personal attention." "Reacts with increased nervousness to group stimulation."

It is scarcely necessary to point out that a large measure of the educational and emotional problems of brain-injured children can be traced to their organic restlessness and distractibility. Primary disturbances of behavior impede group adjustment and learning; repeated experiences of failure and the unrelenting demands of school and home produce secondary emotional problems which further complicate readjustment.

What methods, then, can be developed to help the brain-injured child to control his vacillating attention and motor drive? Since the organic lesion is medically untreatable, our efforts may extend in two directions: in manipulating and controlling the external, overstimulating environment and in educating the child to the exercise of voluntary control. Can these therapeutic ends be achieved in the usual classroom situation, with individual adjustments and an understanding teacher? With a few notable exceptions, it is our experience that such a method of treatment is not feasible, that the brain-injured child requires an environment especially suited to his particular needs.

The therapeutic educational environment for the brain-injured child is planned initially to counteract as much as possible the general organic disturbances of behavior and attention. The class group is small—twelve children is the maximum number which we have found can be successfully taught. The classroom for these children is large enough to permit each child to be seated at a considerable distance from any other. There is only a minimum of pictures, murals, bulletin boards, and the usual stimulating visual materials of the average classroom. We would even recommend entire absence of these materials for the first half-year of a child's attendance in the special class. Since the never absent sights and sounds outside the classroom form another great source of distraction, the most suitable classroom is one on the second floor or one in which the windows face an infrequently used court. It is also possible to cover the lower quarter of the windows with light paint or paper which will admit light and at the same time screen the view.

The extent of the child's abnormal attraction to stimuli may be illustrated by the effect produced by the teacher's dress. She will soon discover the distracting influence of ornamentation such as bracelets, earrings, dangling necklaces, and flowers in the hair. For the brain-injured child she will be no less attractive and more effective as a teacher if these distractions are avoided.

Despite the extremely constricted range of stimuli provided by such a neutral environment, the group situation itself may be too disturbing for many children. In order to curtail further the number of distracting influences, the child may be removed to the periphery of the group by placing his work table in contact with the wall, so that his back is toward the other children.

The reason for the separation is explained to the child, making certain that he understands that its purpose is not punitive but constructive—to help him "work better where other children won't disturb him." For a very hyperactive and disinhibited child we have even resorted to the expedient of isolation behind a clinic screen.

The behavioral response of the children in the special classroom is immediate and can be taken to substantiate the adequacy of our therapeutic approach. Loud talking, running in the room, attacks on other children diminish and often disappear in a matter of days; the formerly unmanageable child becomes quite tractable. A first grade pupil whom the teacher finally refused to keep in her class ran about the room, sang, laughed out loud, removed shoes and stockings, and completely disrupted any organized group activity. After a week behind the screen in the special class, this behavior disappeared so completely that the screen was no longer necessary; the behavior described has recurred only in moods of exaltation or in situations of relatively unusual excitement. The children often recognize the transformation in themselves and verbalize their reactions to the change in environment. A brain-injured child who was transferred to the special class from a sight-saving classroom because of inability to control loud talking, laughing, and wandering about the room remarked after a brief period of adjustment, "I'm glad I'm not in that other room any more; there were just too many kids in there; I couldn't stand it." (In reality the number of children in the sight-saving classroom at one time was no greater than in the special methods class.) The response to facing the wall or sitting behind the screen is similar. The children recognize the purpose of the separation and become aware of the feeling of well-being it produces. On some days children will spontaneously request permission to sit away from other members of the group or behind the screen. It is not unusual for a child whose desk has been replaced within the group after a period of separation to request a return to the old arrangement, explaining that he "feels better" or he "gets more work done."

We must strongly emphasize that these arrangements do not produce withdrawal or autism or encourage mannerisms, since the brain-injured child, like any normal child, needs social contacts, enjoys group living, and wishes to return to his fellows as soon as he feels himself no longer disturbed by the presence of other children.

The learning handicap of the child who is not hyperactive or disinhibited but who is distracted by the multiplicity of detail he finds in his books can be similarly alleviated by applying our knowledge of the general control of distractibility. If the child's materials are divested of everything but the merest essentials—by actually cutting away borders or pictures or by enclosure within a cover which exposes only a small area at a time— the child is able to accomplish his task with relatively little distraction.

At this point it should be mentioned that brain-injured children are invariably attracted by moving stimuli; a hyperactive, distractible child will often be occupied for long intervals with playthings which can be moved or manipulated; a motion picture or automobile ride will successfully hold the attention of even the most distractible child. In the classroom, therefore, lessons should be planned to include motor activity— sorting, cutting, printing, manipulating counters or a gadget—even within the area of the child's desk.

It is in such an especially adjusted environment that many children for the first time experience adequacy in meeting intellectual requirements. With decreased interference from the general organic disturbances comes an increased responsiveness to the learning situation. As the child gains in knowledge and skills, his lessons are carried out with understanding, the area of successful performance is enlarged and the disturbances diminish proportionately. The action of these processes is reciprocal: control of behavior makes learning possible; knowledge gained makes possible more effective control of behavior. Lack of interest closely follows lack of understanding or ability to achieve; realization of goals and the satisfaction of accomplishment are awakeners of interest.

Direction of the child's behavior, however, should eventually be effected from within himself rather than from externally regulated conditions. As the organic disturbances are lessened, the protections are gradually removed; a child's desk is placed within the class group, pictures and bulletin boards make their appearance, and experiences in which a group participates become more numerous. After another period of adjustment with further reduction of the general disturbances as well as possession of the requisite skills and knowledges, the child can return to a regular class group which is suited to his needs.

The basic function of perception in human development has been discussed. Its relation to learning is no less fundamental. As the normal child matures and gains experiences, his perceptions develop also, partly in fulfillment of natural processes of growth and partly in response to new experiences. Thus he structuralizes perceptual patterns through differentiation of their details; he apprehends as wholes more complex and highly organized patterns. His behavior changes; the responses he makes are different. We say that he is learning. In place of the diffuse, undifferentiated, unstructuralized wholes of the young child are the more clearly structuralized, highly organized, infinitely related wholes of the maturer organism. We may even say that developing the process of perceiving is learning. A normally integrated, intact organism is so constituted that it will naturally respond to patterns of stimuli, perceive relationships, make generalizations, and find applications. Teaching is in part concerned with making available in suitable form and at the appropriate developmental level those areas of human knowledge which experience or tradition have judged essential. With guidance and positive motivation, learning progresses as naturally as physical growth.

The brain-injured organism must be seen from a different aspect. The organic damage produces disturbances of figure-ground perception, disintegration in the perception of visual form and space, disturbances of auditory perception, and disturbances of general integration which render the pathological organism unable to perceive stimuli in the same relationships as do most normal children or to respond to patterns of the expected complexity. The ambiguous figure of vase and profiles will serve to illustrate the necessarily different approach toward the education of brain-injured children. For the normal individual, the lability between figure and ground can be made to diminish and to disappear entirely if one or the other aspect of the picture is accentuated. The vase can be made the stable foreground figure by outlining it with a colored or a heavy black line, or the profiles will assume permanent foreground value if details of the faces are sketched in. In a similar way, insofar as comparisons are possible between a normal and an abnormal organism, structuralization of perceptual patterns with regard to the organization of figure and ground, space, or form, will direct or enforce the disintegrated organism to achieve a more or less organized perception. Without external ordering his perceptions are as vacillating as those of the normal person perceiving an ambiguous figure. Thus if the picture a child is to color is outlined with a heavy black crayon, the heavy line is a cue which enables the child to keep constant the relationship between the foreground of the picture and the background of the paper and to color successfully within the lines. Perceptual patterns can likewise be effectively organized by the addition of color. For example, if contours of letters of the alphabet are clearly delineated with color cues, a child with a disturbance in the perception of form can learn to recognize and distinguish the letters. In counting, the use of beads or dots of various colors will enable him to keep his place and proceed in an orderly fashion, combating the fluctuation of figure and ground and the resulting erratic procedure. Our emphasis on color for this purpose derives from observation of its usefulness; we have found that color perception and responsiveness to color remain intact in spite of the severest disturbance of perceptual or general integration.

The responses of brain-injured children can also be directed or organized through the use of instructional material or devices constructed in accordance with our knowledge of the particular disturbances of these children. It is a strong temptation to regard the material or devices as the method itself. Although it is true that the materials are used extensively, they are but one means of reaching the child and, as such, represent the externalization of the method. Without knowledge of the method as a whole, the materials are merely static devices. It is for this reason that no description of the materials can ever be complete. The materials described here are those which have been found helpful in practice; they are offered as illustrations of and guides to the type of analysis which must be made. Within limits the amount and kind of materials used will depend upon the teacher herself and the variety of children who require her help.

The materials are constructed to demonstrate, dramatize, or concretize a process. They present a process or skill clear of everything but the bare essentials. Thus they constitute an abstract presentation, since the process is explained not through the medium of a life situation but through laying bare the structure of the process itself. The basic principle of any of the materials with general or specific purposes—to aid in overcoming disturbances of perception, to bring about understanding by structuralizing a process of perception, to provide a crutch until skill and understanding are secure—is this presentation of only the essential elements.

We have mentioned earlier the desirability of providing, whenever possible, motor activity to engage the child directly in his task and to hold his attention on the process involved. It should be emphasized that while the materials provide manipulative activity, they are not games to increase motivation or to teach through play. Distractibility and disinhibition expressed motorically can often be reduced to a degree which imposes less of a handicap by indirect channeling of motor activity.

In beginning counting, for example, the child's disinhibition drives him through the activity at such a rate that objects to be counted are omitted or combined or counted as one; the child is spontaneously or voluntarily unable to impose a check on his drive. If he is given a device which requires that he fit blocks over screws or pegs as he counts, he can succeed. The counting process is unadorned by any other activity and the required "slowing down" is accomplished through the particular construction of the device.

In a similar way, numbers and dots on a wheel which must be rotated to make new combinations provide variety of stimuli and activity for the distractible child.

Other materials have been devised for the purpose of demonstrating a process, pointing out its rationale, and aiding to promote insight into its operation. For example, artithmetic problems may be solved with an abacus until the combining and analyzing of groups of numbers is so well structuralized that the child is able to attempt these processes independently. "Carrying" in addition is demonstrated by means of a device; "taking away" is concretely represented; addition of any number to a base of ten is shown, and so on. The child often uses these materials only once or at most a few times until he achieves some insight into the process in question. However, because of the handicap imposed by particular disturbances, such as a lack of integration in the organization of space and form, a long period of work with one of the crutch-like aids may be necessary before independent work on a particular level is possible. For example, carrying in addition is demonstrated with a device and then followed by problems which the child solves with his abacus.

The materials are all of such nature that they can be constructed by the teacher and to a large extent by the children. The latter feature is an especially important one. While he measures, cuts, pastes, or prints, the hyperactive, disinhibited child is occupied motorically. At the same time he acquires understanding of how the material is constructed and how it should be used.

Most of the materials are basic and are used at some time by all of the children. However, because of the variety of disturbances, adjustments or even specific devices must often be made in order to meet the needs of each individual child.

Because of this variability and because of the individual instruction necessitated by the general disturbances of behavior, the materials must also have the feature of being self tutoring. That is to say, their purpose is not to teach a child new processes (as a normal child might follow directions in learning how to cancel out nines) but they help the child to be independent of the teacher. Dependence upon adults for assistance and demands for constant attention are a characteristic of many brain-injured children. However, when the work is on the child's level of ability and adjustments have been made to decrease the interference from his disturbances, he is able, and can therefore be asked, to work without demanding the adult's undivided attention. This independence has the added practical advantage of freeing the teacher's time for another child.

We have mentioned before that commercially prepared materials which a normal child might use consistently, such as workbooks in reading and arithmetic, are generally unsuitable for the brain-injured child. Conspicuous faults are the distractions and the amount of study material: pages are large with many, often complex, activities; exercises are closely spaced; many pictures or notations are present. Since they are designed for normal children, the rate of progress is too rapid to insure mastery of processes for the brain-injured child. These published materials are valuable as source books and useful if they are presented as separate pages, with unessential details cut away, or cut up entirely and rearranged into simpler form.

It is necessary to ask about the child's response to a method of teaching and to materials which he never has encountered in a previous classroom. This is an especially important consideration in teaching the older child whose problem is a remedial one and who is usually particularly sensitive to teaching procedures which suggest simplification on his account. For most children the novelty of using concrete, manipulative materials for academic work is captivating and highly motivating; even those with remedial problems readily accept the devices or technics, realizing that they make the formerly obscure academic work easier and more understandable. With success often comes an eagerness to work which is astonishing. One teacher remarked about a 7-year-old boy who had been unusually lethargic and unresponsive, "K's idea of a good time now is to do arithmetic problems." The children soon appreciate individual differences and disabilities and recognize the need for adjustments. One child questioned, "Why does J. write with red and blue lines on his paper?" When it was explained that the colors were to help him to keep his letters on the lines and to make them the correct size, the boy remarked with admirable tolerance, "Isn't it funny, he can't write very well, and I can't read." The children are quick to offer assistance to each other and to wish to lend devices which they have enjoyed and found particularly helpful. Other children have invented materials for less capable classmates to use.

Teachers often ask with justifiable concern whether the use of devices or aids does not result in dependence upon these "crutches." Almost invariably when a child has understood the meaning of a process and feels secure in the method of work which he is using, he spontaneously discards the aid. A brain-injured girl, for example, with a severe disturbance of visuomotor integration had used a device to learn partial counting. On one day she announced to her teacher that she had worked all of her problems without "the machine." The teacher, wondering whether to be gratified with this success, asked for an explanation of the child's method of work.

"Oh," answered B. casually, "I just remembered the biggest number and counted the rest in my head." Occasionally, however, a perseverative child will feel so comfortable with a device that he cannot be induced to relinquish it. For such a child it may be necessary to supply a number of devices to demonstrate to him that he can do the work without his particular favorite and gradually to remove all of the devices entirely.

A discussion of academic learning would be incomplete without mention of the subject matter or curriculum. The instructional plan for brain-injured children, described here, has been limited to the basic school skills, since failure in these effectively blocks further school progress. For children with several years of previous school experience and retardation in one or more academic skills, the special methods class is a remedial situation. For the younger brain-injured children, it is similar to a primary classroom in which tool subjects receive the greatest amount of allotted time. Thus instruction in social studies, geography, history, science, etc., is incidental.

In the education of brain-injured children the use of projects or activities in the classroom, such as a store, a post office, or a bank, is unpropitious if one has in mind either teaching academic tools through realistic experiences, as recommended by the most progressive educators, or practicing them. The activity is replete with countless inherent distractions and exciting situations to divert attention from the skills which may be needed. For the brain-injured child a project may be used for other purposes: planning and carrying plans to successful completion or checking on the thoroughness with which academic skills have been established, i.e., if a brain-injured child, even in the excitement of playing store, can count or read correctly, the teacher has one indication of progress. We do not wish to give the impression that the educational principle of learning through "doing" does not apply to the brain-injured child. It applies for him perhaps even more than for the normal child, but it needs reinterpretation. The experience of "doing" in order to learn is for the brain-injured child also a matter of solving a problem and gaining insight; however, it need not be with an activity modeled after a life situation. These objectives can be more nearly accomplished by the brain-injured child if his range of activity is small and the possibilities of wandering away from the central issue are limited.

The therapeutic environment may appear restricting and narrow unless one is well aware of its purpose. Such an instructional program is not offered as a substitute for the varied experiences of a regular classroom; it is only an interim environment of remedial or therapeutic nature. That is, the brain-injured child enters the special methods class because of inability, resulting from organic damage, to meet the intellectual or social demands of a normal school environment. For him the therapeutic class is instituted for the purpose of overcoming or alleviating his manifold disturbances; it becomes unnecessary as soon as these adjustments are effected. The child is then transferred to a suitable group: for a child with normal or near-normal intelligence this will be a regular grade classroom, for a cerebral palsied child it will be a class for orthopedically handicapped children, and for a child whose major handicap is mental deficiency it will be a special class for retarded children.

Our description of the classroom for brain-injured children as a therapeutic environment implies by analogy that the teacher is the therapist, since her aim is one of rehabilitation. She must be skilled in the observation of behavior. She must be well acquainted with each child, not only from a personality standpoint but from the point of view of particular organic disturbances. She must have the ability to analyze a failure and to devise a correction for it. To this end, if a child fails a task given him, the teacher must ask herself: Why? Were too many elements presented at once? Was the material too distracting? Did the activity lack structure, so that foreground could be confused with background? Was the child's perception fragmented? Did he lose sight of the whole by fixation on details? Did he seem to understand but fail because of perseveration? Through such analysis the source of the failure can usually be discovered and a plan devised which will prevent it. In a similar way an analysis should be made of a child's behavior disturbances. Outbursts, explosions, refusals—deviations from established behavior—can usually be traced to injudicious handling or to demands in excess of the child's ability or emotional reserve.

Beyond the disturbances of behavior and perception are additional mental peculiarities which frequently manifest themselves and which become significant in the educational situation. The brain-injured child often possesses an excellent verbal memory. For this reason the teacher must be very critical of a child's performance to avoid being deceived into regarding repetition of an automatized verbal formula as understanding. The extremes to which such automatization may extend is illustrated by J. M., a mentally retarded brain-injured boy. J.'s method of work in solving several multiplication problems gave the impression that his analysis was derived from understanding of the process; for example, "6×4" was solved as "2 sixes are 12, and $12 + 12$ are 24." Close observation showed that the process of solution was an automatized act and that J. was unable to apply the implied thought process to derive other answers.

This characteristic excellent verbal memory and tendency to automatization has profound significance for the teaching method for brain-injured children. It is a common human feeling that if a child repeats a statement often enough and in varying contexts he must surely understand its meaning. The established way in which to achieve repetition is by drill. For the brain-injured child, drill on formulas, such as number combinations or words, encourages automatization and memorization without meaning. Habituation through drill should be the last step of the brain-injured child's learning of academic skills. Repetition in learning is necessary but it must come through frequent experiences on the child's part of insights and analyses.

A closely allied characteristic type of behavior is perseveration, already described as it appears in experimental situations. In academic learning it is often in evidence, particularly when a task offers difficulty. In reading, for example, a child may repeat a phrase several times before he is able to continue; in word study he may incorrectly name a well known word or incorrectly sound out letters which are known accurately as separate units. In writing, a word is incorrectly spelled, erased, and written again with the same error. In arithmetic, dots or blocks are counted several times; in mixed problems of addition and subtraction all the problems are solved by using either addition or subtraction. The approach we have found most successful when perseverations of this type occur is to quietly substitute another activity or suggest to the child that he omit the particular word or problem and return to it later. After a brief interval of slightly different activity, the perseveration disappears and the child can continue. Any repetitive activity, such as rote serial counting or practicing the writing of one letter a number of times, will encourage perseverations when the situation is modified even very slightly.

A further precaution should be added regarding motor acts which easily become automatized as perseverative repetitions. The following incident, not without its humorous element, was also very instructive. In attempting to teach R. partial counting, the teacher had explained to him to hold in mind one group as a unit and then to add the others. To emphasize further her words she indicated her forehead, telling R. to "think the number, than add the others." R. was impressed and learned the process but, to the teacher's dismay, only by touching his pencil to his forehead for each problem. At the end of the period mute evidence of how often he had thought was easily visible.

The "catastrophic reaction" is another characteristic response which, although it does not occur with great frequency, is important to recognize.

It is natural that the work habits of these children should be poor. Problems are scattered at random over a page, writing is careless and scarcely legible, with little regard for lines, and attention is constantly diverted from the lesson. Many of these faults are in truth the result of poor work habits; many, however, stem from the organic disturbances and should be treated from this aspect.

In striking contrast to the careless performance and poor work habits of many of these children is the exactitude and meticulosity shown by many others. Instead of an asset, it is a hindrance, since the slightest deviation from the child's standard of orderliness must be corrected by him. As a result, an unduly long time may be spent on one handwriting lesson with letter after letter erased and carefully made again. As much time is spent in arithmetic in carefully writing the answer as in arriving at the solutions; blocks are meticulously arranged before they can be counted, etc. With such a child, the teacher should be aware of the abnormally strong need for orderliness and should provide as much oral work as possible. Giving short assignments and stipulating a definite time when the work should be completed will also aid in counteracting extreme meticulosity.

The teacher will also be astonished at the variability of a child's performance. A skill or bit of knowledge apparently mastered on one day is as strange on the following day as though encountered for the first time. On some days a child will seem alert and bright and capable of many things; on other days he will be sluggish, inert, incapable, and extremely distractible. Children who are usually good humored will occasionally be irritable, destructive and unapproachable. The reasons for this variability will be found in two sources. In the first instance—the so-called "forgetting" from lesson to lesson—the lack of stability is usually the result of a lack of understanding. Learning accomplished with insight and understanding is retained; that which is repeated on the basis of automatization is soon lost. When true insight into a task has been achieved, the brain-injured child retains the knowledge remarkably well. Even with brain-injured children of low ability we have experienced excellent retention over as long a period as a two months' summer vacation. The second factor contributing to variability of performance is the child's extreme responsiveness or irritability to his environment. Disagreeable weather, exciting occurrences of a very minor order, sometimes a cut or bruise, at other times an unexplainable hypersensitivity are quickly reflected in school work. On these days, the teacher gains her best results by asking a minimum requirement of the child and avoiding the introduction of any new processes or skills.

We have presented here general principles of the educational method for brain-injured children. The method described obviously applies in many ways beyond the beginning steps of academic learning on the one hand and the academic subjects on the other hand. We can only touch briefly on these other fields.

(1) As soon as a child is ready to leave the special classroom he should do so. The therapeutic environment is then no longer necessary and the special teaching technics should be only supplementary. That is, for new developmental levels or stages of learning, such special adjustments may become necessary even in a regular classroom but they will be used only as additional aids to establish teaching procedures. The description of these additional procedures would consist of an accumulation of incidents, case histories, and detailed procedures.

(2) The teaching of rhythm by the classroom teacher or by a music teacher is a helpful and necessary aid especially in training auditory perception and control of motor functions. Rhythm exercises are known and

described in many books pertaining to the subject. It should be kept in mind that the exercises should be simple, definite and without too much playlike procedure. Considerations similar to those observed in our academic methods will prevent failures in teaching rhythm to brain-injured children.

(3) Speech training is a necessity for many brain-injured children and should be taken over by specialists in the field who are well aware of the problems and can offer specialized technics for correction.

(4) Manual training should not be overlooked if brain-injured children remain in the special methods class for more than remedial purposes. Although our observations of a handwork program for brain-injured children have not been extensive enough to warrant publication, we wish simply to emphasize that the training in woodwork, metal craft, cardboard, leather, etc., is based upon our psychopathological findings in clinical and experimental situations, the peculiar mental organization of brain-injured children in general, and their deficiencies in the perceptual fields in particular.

SECTION B: Educational Procedures

32 EDUCATION OF CHILDREN WITH LEARNING DIFFICULTIES

Marianne Frostig

The purpose of this paper is to outline some of the principles which underlie the training of children with learning difficulties, and to illustrate them with case histories. If we consider the types of facilities that are commonly available to children with learning difficulties, we can observe the usual categories into which they are divided. There are classes for the mentally retarded, emotionally disturbed, blind, deaf, speech handicapped, physically handicapped, and even neurologically handicapped. Either a diagnosis of the main symptom, as with a mentally retarded child, is used to classify him, or else a diagnosis of the basic cause (etiology) as with a neurologically handicapped child. Both types of classification seem to be inadequate.

The cause of a child's learning difficulty is frequently not known, and a child may have more symptoms than the one that is used to classify him. The danger in the first instance is that he may be regarded as an unknown quantity and receive no treatment at all; while in the second instance, he may receive only the treatment accorded to his classification while his other symptoms may not be considered. Such classification tends to place an emphasis on a defect of the child, so that he is often approached as if he were his label, a defect himself, *"the emotionally disturbed child"* or *"the retarded child"*, with many characteristics which will all interrelate to influence his future. It is the whole child that the educator must consider, not merely a part of him.

For administrative reasons, it is sometimes necessary to segregate children according to a single major symptom, or a given cause, but such a

Reprinted from *Distinguished Lectures in Special Education*, University of California, pp. 3-8. By permission of the author.

division can never form an adequate basis for planning an effective remedial program. It is proposed that this can best be done by considering the over-all developmental status of the child, evaluating his potential according to the results and planning his remedial program on this basis. In considering the various developmental areas of a child, one is regarding him as a dynamic organism, capable of change and progress, rather than as a static entity with an unalterable label.

It has been found practical to take into consideration six areas of development in a child's physical and mental growth. They are motor development, perceptual development, language, intellectual development, emotional and social development. A lag in any of these areas of development may lead to learning difficulties.

About 2 percent of our public school population show general learning difficulties, which may be attributable to retardation in *intellectual development*. But 10 to 15 percent of all children show specific learning difficulties of one kind or another (though most of these difficulties are in reading), without indicating a lack of intelligence. Since emotional disturbance accounts for but a small proportion of these learning failures, the necessity for probing other areas of development becomes apparent.

Inadequate *motor coordination*, for instance, is a common cause of learning disabilities. Children who lag behind their classmates in the lower grades have so often been found to have difficulties in motor development. Some leading modern educators, for example Kephart and his co-workers (Kephart, 1960; Radler and Kephart, 1960) have based their remedial and school readiness programs upon the development of motor coordination and eye movements. Without good motor coordination, a child is handicapped not only on the playground but may also be retarded in all his learning. Moreover, difficulties in motor coordination influence also the perceptual development, as discussed by Kephart and others.

Retarded *language development* is also a considerable handicap in school learning. Teachers become aware that there are some children in every class with communication disorders. These children cannot profit well from the classroom experience because they cannot understand their teacher's directions or ask questions, and they become isolated from the other children because they cannot engage in meaningful conversation with them.

The *social development* of a child also affects his ability to learn. Although it is closely related to *emotional development*, it is yet a distinct aspect of the growing personality. Some children who are well adjusted and happy at home are still socially immature; they cannot engage in the social give and take with peers which is expected of a child in kindergarten and primary grades. These children may then become isolated from their own groups, withdraw into a fantasy world, and as a result have difficulties with learning.

What is possibly the most frequent cause of learning difficulties is perhaps the least widely recognized of all. This is a disturbance of the child's *perceptual abilities*—either his visual perception, his auditory perception, or his kinesthetic perception (muscle sense). Perception means the recognition of the world around us. What we perceive by means of our senses is all we have to connect us with other human beings and with the inanimate objects in our daily lives. Without adequate perception a child is isolated from his environment.

Perceptual disturbances do not only occur when sense channels are defective—when a visual or auditory defect occurs in the end organ, the eye or the ear. Many children have perfect hearing and 20-20 vision yet still lack perceptual skills. The difficulty lies in the brain's faulty interpretation of the sense data.

The plight of children with this difficulty is a severe one. Children with difficulties in *auditory* perception may fail in academic learning because they are unable to differentiate between similar sounds such as *v* and *th*, and the short *e* and short *i*. It may be most difficult for them to learn phonics. Some children with auditory perceptual difficulties may have their fine auditory discrimination intact, yet be unable to perceive an auditory sequence of any length, such as a paragraph, or even a sentence.

Children with disabilities in *visual* perception are at an immense disadvantage. *At home* they have difficulty in performing the simplest tasks. Even dressing himself or handling a knife and fork at the meal table presents difficulties to a child who cannot perceive accurately the positions of objects in relation either to himself or to each other. *On the playground,* such a child cannot compete with his agemates in sports and games. And in the *classroom* his confusion when asked to learn to read or write symbols which appear to him distorted or jumbled can well be imagined. He will be unable to recognize words, pictures, or directions, or the shapes and sizes of objects. In addition, his recall of auditory or visual material may be disturbed. A child with these disabilities is likely to give the impression that he lacks intelligence, or is unwilling to work. He is likely to receive little sympathy from parents, teachers, and other children, who often do not understand the difficulty, and regard him simply as "stupid"; he may feel himself to be abnormal and incapable of succeeding in work or play as his agemates succeed. He may therefore become imbued with a deep sense of unworthiness and failure, and show the additional symptom of emotional disturbance.

The possible causes of a learning difficulty are therefore many. Moreover, the case histories will show, there is rarely a single cause, in a given child, but rather a combination of factors. This means that preventive and remedial measures in education must be based on a multi-factorial study of the child that takes into account his emotional, social, and psychological development. And, in evaluating a child and planning a program for him, his *assets* should be taken into consideration quite as much as his disabilities. They can be used as an indication of his potential ability in other areas, and their development can be of help to him both for their own sake and also as the means of giving him the experience of success which is so essential to the young child.

There are three aspects of the evaluation of a child's development status: measurement, prediction, and the planning of remedial procedures. The inclusion of the planning of remedial procedures in this operational definition of the term "evaluation" suggests an optimistic educational philosophy, for one does not attempt remedial procedures unless one hopes for positive changes. This optimism may seem unwarranted to some educators, who hold that as the individual disabilities in a child's development are an expression of maturational forces they are therefore beyond the realm of educational influence and intervention. This does not appear to be borne out by experience, which suggests that degrees of maturity in the various areas of an individual's development are not predetermined by inherent characteristics, but may be influenced by experience. J. McV. Hunt (1961) reports, for instance, that a group of very young white children who did not have an inherent potential greater than that of a similar group of Negro children, yet reached a higher stage of maturation in motor, language, emotional and social development because of the richer stimulation they received in their relatively privileged home and social environments. To give another example, it is a matter of common sense observation that a child's motor skills can be improved, for his ability to play a ball game, skate, swim, or ride a bicycle will undoubtedly improve with practice. It is a matter of general knowledge that many youngsters who have had a motor handicap were goaded by their failure in competition with their peers to practice until they excelled in such sports. The same achievement is possible with other than motor abilities, but the possibility is not so easily recognized because the handicaps in other areas are less evident and the child is unable to train them by himself without specialized help. Even the complicated forms of behavior we refer to as "intelligence" can be modified by experience; indeed, this fact is the *raison d'être* of any educational system (Hunt, 1961).

The attempt to train lagging function is often postponed because the educator wants to wait until the child reaches a certain maturational level.

Study of animal development has shown beyond doubt there are brief "critical periods" in the development of animals during which specific forms of behavior are learned, and after which the behavior which is learned cannot be unlearned. This kind of learning depends upon the reception of certain stimuli during the critical period, and is called "imprinting." A somewhat similar development process takes place in human beings during their early years, in that there seems to be "optimum periods" for the development of such abilities as motor skills, speech, perception and intelligence, but these periods last longer than the "critical periods" in animals. If a child is delayed in making progress in developing a specific functional skill he may still catch up, or at least make some advancement, especially if he receives skilled help. For example, speech development appears to be at its optimum between the ages of one or two and six or seven years of age. Although most children speak before three years of age a child who only begins to learn at the age of six, may still be successful in speaking, especially if he is helped by a skilled speech therapist. Similarly, perceptual development normally takes place between the ages of three and seven and a half, at which age the cognitive development becomes the child's primary task. A child with perceptual difficulties who receives perceptual training between these ages has a good chance of overcoming his difficulties, *especially if the training is commenced early in the period.*

This last point requires emphasis because educators have been so aware of the dangers of attempting to train an ability too soon, *before* the child's development was sufficiently advanced, that they have sometimes delayed too long and missed the developmental "tide" for the ability concerned altogether. In general, the earlier that educational procedures are introduced, the easier and more effective they will be. Dr. Cronbach (1962) supports this view. He exhorts educators to rather change teaching methods than to postpone educational efforts. He writes, "Sophisticated psychologists, such as Gates and Brownell, have long insisted that readiness is dependent upon teaching method as much as on subject matter." Therefore special teaching methods should be devised to help children at whatever point of development they may be. In this view, psychological tests are not a means simply for categorizing children, but for evaluating them so that the appropriate training methods may be put into effect.

As stated above, the three aspects of evaluation are measurement, prediction, and planning an educational program. The first two aspects, measurement and prediction, do not necessitate the same global approach. A single intelligence test can predict school achievement. Only if we want to know what specific teaching methods to use for the child who scores low on an intelligence test must we know more about his specific abilities and disabilities. Only with this aim in view is there reason to introduce a comprehensive program of appraisal which explores the various causes which may be a deterrent to the child's school progress.

Evaluation in the public school setting would therefore have to be a two-step procedure. First, it would consist of a general screening of all children; and secondly, of a careful individual appraisal of those children who have exhibited by the results of the screening tests or by their school behavior marked deviations from the norm in the direction of a deficit. But usually, too few resources are available for individual appraisals. But this difficulty is not insurmountable. I propose that both procedures, screening and individual testing should serve all three purposes of evaluation—measurement, prediction and outline of treatment procedures, including educational measures. The screening procedures themselves may be informal and observational, or formal group tests may be given. Informal appraisal by teacher is certainly a respectable method, and should not be discarded as unscientific. Research of others as well as of this author has shown that teachers' estimates are usually well founded although both group testing and teachers' judgments are prone to include errors. In the last instance, much of test validation has been effected by the subsequent judgment of teachers, including and since, the first Binet test. Thus final appraisal should include at least opinions of the psychologist, the teacher, principal, and whenever possible, the school nurse.

Parental judgment and opinion should be considered also. Parents have the most intimate knowledge of their child; and even when their observations are colored by their desires or their disappointment, they are an important source of information. Moreover, they disclose during interviews their attitudes, beliefs, and needs which have to be considered in any effective planning for the child. It has already been maintained that the time-honored method teacher observation and appraisal can and should be augmented in the classroom by group screening tests. Teacher observation throws further light on the child's development in the six areas discussed above.

Group intelligence tests are so well known and so widely in use that a further discussion here seems unnecessary. Motor development can be appraised by tests such as the Vineland adaptation of the Oseretski tests (Training School Bulletin) or the Kraus-Weber Test for minimal muscular fitness (University of California, Department of Physical Education).

If a formal test is to be used for the estimate of language, many of the verbal sections of group tests of intelligence can be used, although observation of the oral speech of the child in the classroom permits a more comprehensive appraisal.

Emotional and social adjustment most frequently is expressed in overt behavior, and therefore can be observed directly, but the child's self-expressive products obtained in group procedures, such as free drawing, drawings of people, paragraphs, and compositions are also most helpful. For a study of this topic, the book by Charlotte Buhler and associates is very useful (1952). Of the six behavioral aspects outlined, one, namely perceptual ability, is the least accessible to direct observations. Behavior typical of children with disabilities in visual perception frequently may be explained by other causes.

For instance, when a child cannot button his coat, his eye-motor coordination, his fine muscle coordination, or his visual perception of the form and position (spatial relationship) of button and hole may be at fault. When a child cannot find the sentence in the book which answers a question printed at the bottom of the page, inability to understand the question, inability to recall the story, inability to understand its content, or a disturbance in visual figure-ground perception may be at fault. In the latter case, we are dealing with one of those children whose mothers complain, "He can't find anything, even if it's in front of his nose."

The inability to locate something in the visual field, to discriminate the position of an object or symbol, to differentiate visually between forms, such as letters or auditorially between sounds, as well as other perceptual difficulties, seem to be very frequent, especially in the children in lower grades. The use of perceptual screening tests seems therefore to be of importance.

The growth curves for all known visual and auditory perceptual abilities are not yet established and even all the abilities are not defined. That there are separate abilities has been borne out by the work of Cruickshank (Cruickshank et al., 1957) and of Wedell (1960) and others.

Five different visual abilities seemed to have special implications for school learning. A test (Frostig et al., 1961) was developed during the last five years which attempts to sample a child's ability in these areas of visual perception. It is a paper and pencil test, which can be given either to individuals or to groups; the average testing time is 40 minutes.

In subtest I, eye-motor coordination, the child is asked to draw lines with no specific beginning and ending points between increasingly narrow boundaries, and also to join dots, which do provide precise beginning and end points. In subtest II, figure-ground perception is first sampled by having the child outline a particular figure among several intersecting figures and later by having him find hidden figures. In subtest III, form constancy is tested by the child's outlining of circles and squares on pages containing many different forms. In subtest IV, the child indicates his perception of position in space by marking either the same or a different figure in a sequence of reversed or rotated figures. In subtest V, which tests perception of spatial relationships, the child is required to copy patterns by linking dots.

Our data show that there is low correlation (.18 to .30) among the subtests (except for subtest IV and V, where the correlation is about .47). The test shows a clear-cut age progression from 3 to about 7½ years of age, with little development after 7½, a finding entirely in accord with the observations of Piaget (Piaget and Inhelder, 1956; Inhelder and Piaget, 1958) who found that at about 7½ years of age cognitive elements become predominant.

USING TEST FINDINGS FOR EDUCATIONAL PROCEDURE

EVALUATION AND THE REMEDIAL PLAN. The term "retardation" is usually applied to the child with low scores on intelligence tests. But many so-called retarded children are retarded in other areas of behavior also, as in social, emotional, or perceptual development, although this is not always the case.

Abe may serve as the example of a child whose intelligence was incorrectly estimated by an intelligence test, which did not disclose fully the source of his difficulties.

Abe was a nine-year-old, tall, fairhaired boy. He suffered from a prenatal damage which had affected his central nervous system and his hearing, as his mother had suffered a severe case of measles during the third month of pregnancy. Abe had been diagnosed as borderline mentally retarded: his scores on the WISC showed a verbal IQ of 72 and a performance IQ of 95. His hearing was poor and his ability to listen even poorer. He had been excluded first from a regular class and then from a class for the deaf. He had withdrawn into a world of fantasy to compensate for a difficult life situation. He felt excluded because of three reasons: first because of his deafness; then because his parents were divorced and neither of them really wanted him; and thirdly because he had no friends.

A survey of Abe's behavior showed that he was retarded in language ability, in emotional, and in social development. He was superior in motor development and in perceptual development, and adequate in problem solving when the verbal concepts needed for the solution to a problem were available to him. Psychotherapy helped him to direct his attention to an environment from which he had withdrawn, and training in language development and lip reading helped him to communicate more effectively. He was able to function so much more efficiently that he scored 20 points higher on an intelligence test one year later and 25 points higher two years later.

Abe's mother had suffered much anguish and her relationship with her son had deteriorated because she had thought that he was too retarded to be educated or to ever make a decent living. This probably could have been avoided by a more global and at the same time more cautious early diagnosis, appraising various behavioral aspects and including the boy's assets as well as his liabilities. Abe's excellent perceptual abilities and motor skills made the prognosis more hopeful than was disclosed at first. Despite his relatively poor verbal ability, there were many careers open to him, as a draftsman, X-ray technician, taxidermist, and so on.

As with mental retardation, emotional disturbance is often taken to be the sole reason for a child's learning difficulties. This may lead to a treatment of the emotional disturbance without consideration of other difficulties, which may even be in part responsible for the emotional involvement.

An example is Miro. Miro walked late (at 20 months) and talked late (first word at 27 months). Now, at 12 years of age, he still has somewhat slurred speech. Coordination is poor. He still sucks his thumb. He looks messy and unattractive. His hand are in perpetual motion, usually pulling at something. He had been toilet trained at three years, but began to wet and soil again in kindergarten, and his bowel control is still uncertain. He was kept back in first grade. He could never make friends, and the other children laughed at him because of his clumsiness, messiness, and nervous fidgeting.

Intelligence tests showed low average intelligence. The psychologist and psychiatrist who were consulted at various occasions diagnosed an emotional disturbance, and play therapy was administered between the ages of 5 and 7 with no appreciable results. At 12 years of age, Miro's testing showed the following scores:

WISC verbal scale IQ 100
WISC performance scale IQ 86

Miro's performance test showed little scatter. Behavioral observation and analysis of test results indicated that problem solving, memory, and planning ability were good.

It was most striking that Miro had very poor motor development. Retardation on the Frostig test of visual perception was five to six years in each of the five areas tested. Language was, with the exception of slurring, unimpaired. Oral and written communication were superior. Emotional development was poor. Miro was infantile, withdrawn, often complaining, and a passive boy. Social development was very poor. Miro could only get along with very much younger children. School achievement, as found in the Wide Range Achievement Test, was eighth grade in word reading skills, ninth grade in spelling, and fifth grade in arithmetic skills. Thus the most striking aspect of the test results were the previously unsuspected perceptual and perceptuomotor difficulties.

When taking the visual perception test, Miro could not draw a straight line between two small circles a few inches apart. He had difficulties in finding hidden figures which can usually be found by a seven-year-old. He could not differentiate between a trapezoid and a square. Although he is twelve years of age, his perceptual skills are at the level of a six- or seven-year-old child. His difficulties during his first years in elementary school must have been enormous, for his perceptuomotor skills must have been far too low both for many school tasks and for the exigencies of daily life. No wonder he became emotionally disturbed in kindergarten, when first required to color, cut or build, tasks far beyond him. No wonder he was retained in first grade. No wonder he still feels so inadequate that he dare not compete with children of his own age level.

Miro must have exerted superhuman effort to succeed in school as well as he did, expending far more energy in trying to master his books than he could afford. Nevertheless, because of his visuomotor difficulty, he is still unable to learn arithmetic, mainly because he places the numbers on his page incorrectly. He never knows for certain which numbers to add, subtract, multiply, or divide. Thus he feels rejected and inadequate even in the learning situation.

It was decided to embark with Miro on a program of educational therapy. This includes training in visual perceptual skills, disguised as simple geometry, topographical geography, and a bit of astronomy. Remedial math is taught also. But the most important feature of the program is probably that this youngster, who had had so many experiences of failure, now finds his difficulties understood and can finally experience success in learning. He, who had felt so inferior in the learning situation, now feels liked and appreciated by a teacher. No wonder that Miro now seems to shine, and that his passive and hopeless attitude is changing to one of self-reliance and self-assertion.

The global survey of a child's development status which has been proposed is only the first step in setting up an individualized teaching and training program for the child with learning difficulties.

Further evaluation revealed a perceptual quotient of only 65 of the Frostig test with severe disabilities in all areas of visual perception. Bill also had difficulty in planning and in grasping temporal and spatial sequences. He could not execute three commands in the correct sequences, retell a paragraph correctly, or put into the correct order pictures illustrating a temporal sequence.

Speech was adequate. In fact, Bill was so verbal that his mental retardation had not been recognized during his first three years in school.

The educational program developed on the basis of these findings included the following measures:

(1) Practicing the planning and reproduction of simple sequences. For this purpose the recognition of the position of an item in a sequence in space as well as in time was taught first. "Before," "after," "in front of," "in the back," were explained. Then the reproduction of line patterns arranged in sequences was practiced. Both pictures and sentences were arranged in a logical order, so as to form a story.

(2) To help Bill develop perceptual skills, training was introduced in all of the five areas of visual perception tested. Workbooks developed by the author and her staff were also used (1962). Special emphasis was placed on the recognition of position in space and spatial relationships.

Bill's specific difficulties were also taken into consideration in teaching him basic skills. In spelling and reading, for instance, he was helped to recognize the sequence of letters correctly by careful phonic analysis.

Arithmetic was introduced by first teaching the ordinal (sequential) function of numbers and by the use of visual and kinesthetic methods. For instance, number symbols and/or objects had to be placed in the correct space in a row. Only after he became proficient in using ordinal numbers was he introduced to the cardinal function of numbers—their "3ness," "4ness," and so on.

As Bill experienced success through these methods, his emotional and social difficulties diminished considerably. Although he is definitely mentally retarded, he now functions at a high third grade level in all school subjects, and holds his place in public school without difficulty.

Sen was referred to the clinical school at the age of eight and a half. He was a thin, whining youngster whose IQ could not be established because he was too severely emotionally disturbed to take the test. He screamed and cried when asked to do something which was difficult for him or which had a personal and threatening meaning for him.

He became upset when being told a story in which the mother *left* to go to the store. In arithmetic, the phrase *take away* made him panicky. He was worried about *"losing" the letter "y"* when a word ending in that letter was changed from singular to plural. For a time he carried a lock around which signified his being safely locked into his new school, which he experienced as a haven. All of the pieces of paper he used had to be collected carefully, because *throwing away* anything also signified loss, abandonment, or mutilation. At times his fears made him feel desperate, and on these occasions he exhibited violent temper tantrums.

During the first half year of remedial training, Sen was not able to work with a group, but had a tutor. He also needed psychotherapy, which he was given outside the school. At the same time the parents were given counselling to help them understand Sen's fears of destruction and realize that these were the basis of his behavior, not just "naughtiness."

The teacher had an important role in the treatment program. She encouraged as much self-expression as possible, and channeled Sen's expressions of anger into socially acceptable behavior. Sen learned to write down dictated short stories designed to help him understand and handle his anxieties, and later he was encouraged to write his own.

Sen himself introduced the subject of the caterpillar changing into a butterfly, and this process was discussed in full as a natural and pleasing transformation. He also discussed puppy dogs that were afraid of the dangers of the street and had to be fenced in, centipedes who lost an occasional leg but had 99 left, and so on. All of these stories Sen illustrated with drawings.

The teacher had to use carefully designed procedures to assuage anxiety aroused during the teaching of basic skills. Subtraction, a "loss" process, had to be checked immediately by addition, and Sen had to be reassured that what is taken away can be replaced, in life in general as well as in arithmetic.

Sen was eventually introduced into a small class under careful supervision, so that he could form relationships and learn to work in a group. He was also given physical education at a boy's club, where he gradually overcame deficits in motor ability, which had caused him to fear using gym equipment and participating in sports. An intelligence test given one year after enrollment showed superior mental abilities and age adequate perceptual abilities. It had been shown that deviations found in any aspect of development may lead to difficulties in school progress and adjustment and so require additional and new methods of evaluating and teaching. What could the public schools do for children like Abe, Miro, Bill, or Sen?

At the present time, teachers and school systems might not be in a position to appraise correctly Abe, extend lip-reading instructions to Abe, train Bill in sequential thinking and visual perception, or find a home teacher to work with Sen. Still I propose that such tasks should be the responsibility of public schools. Speech teachers who can teach lip reading, kindergarten teachers who understand perceptual training methods and can detect and train children with difficulties in visual perception, home teachers who can understand the overwhelming anxiety of a child like Sen, all can be trained in our higher educational institutions so that these professional educators will have these skills when needed.

If children like Abe, Bill, and Sen are correctly evaluated before they have suffered the trauma of continued failure, and if they receive skilled help from properly informed educators, they can be helped to lead happy and productive lives.

But all too often no such help is available. The result is that such children often drop out of school at an early age and fail to become self-supporting; or they may become delinquent; or they may enter institutions for the mentally retarded or the mentally ill, leading unhappy and unfulfilled lives and adding to the ever-increasing burden of the taxpayer.

References

Buhler, Charlotte, Smitther, Faith, and Richardson, Cyril, *Childhood problems and the teacher* (New York: Holt, Rinehart and Winston, 1952).

Cronbach, Lee, Psychological issues pertinent to recent American curriculum reforms. In Scard, A. G., and Husen, J. (Editors), *Child and education* (Copenhagen: Munksgaard, 1962).

Cruickshank, W. M., Bice, M. V., and Wallen, N. E., *Perception and Cerebral Palsy* (Syracuse: Syracuse University Press, 1957).

Frostig, Marianne, and Horne, David, *Resource Materials for Training Visual Perception*, pictures by Bea Mandell, Experimental Edition. Copyright 1962.

Frostig, Marianne, Lefever, D. Welty, and Whittlesey, John R. B., *Developmental test of visual perception*, 3rd Ed. (Los Angeles: Marianne Frostig School of Educational Therapy, 1961).

Hunt, J. McV., *Intelligence and experience* (New York: Ronald, 1961).

Inhelder B., and Piaget, J., *The growth of logical thinking from childhood to adolescence* (New York: Basic Books, 1958).

Kephart, Newell C., *The slow learner in the classroom* (Columbus, Ohio: Merrill, 1960).

Piaget, J. and Inhelder, B., *The child's conception of space* (New York, The Humanities Press, 1956).

Radler, D. H., and Kephart, N. C., *Success through play* (New York: Harper & Row, 1960).

Training School Bulletin, 46, (3-4), Vineland, N.J.

Kraus-Weber Test for minimal muscular fitness, University of California, Dept. of Physical Education.

Wedell, Karl, Variations in perceptual ability among types of cerebral palsy, *Cerebral Palsy Bull.*, 1960, 2 (3), 149-157.

33 EDUCATIONAL THERAPY FOR
BRAIN-INJURED RETARDED CHILDREN

Lotte Kaliski ❧

When we speak of educational therapy we mean measures designed to prevent or to remedy defective or deficient functioning in the educational area. Therapy is treatment of one or multiple disorders. In educational therapy we treat these disorders, we make the child receptive for retraining, for rehabilitation. Therefore our approach is therapeutic. We apply principles which are conducive to the child's mental health. We create a climate of warmth and of emotionally gratifying experiences, carefully calculating the level of the child's mental intake capacity. We mobilize strong motivational resources, in other words we set the stage for learning and growth—which is the objective of education, but we are using detours and special techniques to prepare and to support the child during his learning process; therefore the foundation of our work and our guiding principles are of therapeutic significance.

Brain-injured children have suffered from an injury to or infection of their brain before, during or after birth. I would just like to delineate our discussion of this group to comprise mainly those children who do not show gross motor involvement as a result of the brain injury, as we know it from the group of cerebral palsy children. We are to consider those children whose brain damage resulted in disturbances of mental functions.

However, working with these children over the years has taught me that there is no clinical entity, with a definite personality pattern displayed in all of these children. The personality development shows just as many variables as any group, and the disturbances are different in degree and kind.

Reprinted from *American Journal of Mental Deficiency*, Vol. 60, No. 1 (July, 1955), pp. 71-76. By permission of the author and publisher.

Nevertheless, there are certain specific symptoms which do recur in the educational area and which sometimes tempt us to reach conclusions in regard to diagnosis in cases when neurological diagnosis was inconclusive.

We have the characteristics of perceptual disturbances, disorders in conceptualization, and behavior difficulties. Applied to education we can easily see that the fundamentals of learning have to be reconstructed. The children have to be redirected, rehabilitated in space and time. Perceptual disturbances occur in the visual, auditory, and kinesthetic fields. Concept formation, reasoning, comprehension may be fluctuating, incoherent, not integrated, confused. Tolerance for emotional stress is very limited and once the threshold is transcended, an emotional state of high tension ensues. Excessive crying, which to the onlooker appears out of proportion to or without any cause, is often a characteristic feature of that state. Involuntary movements may occur as concomitants of excitement and tension.

In my work with these children (I am referring to chronological ages from 5 to 14) I found the perceptual disturbances outstanding and therefore challenging to the remedial worker. Because of the limited space I can only present a few selected techniques.

Training in focusing on objects in the room or on articles spread on the table or laid out in left to right sequence precede academic work. Recall from memory of displayed articles, picture description and recall with emphasis on location of parts are practiced. Differentiation of people as to sex, sizes, relationships, discrimination of animals and of objects are stressed. Perception is diffuse, and must not be confused with limited experiences of the children and/or language difficulties. I remember a boy of nine for whom every animal in a picture was a dog, regardless of whether it was a cow or a mouse, every object a table. In this connection it is nevertheless important to encourage the parents to offer their children selected but varied experiences with emphasis on differentiation. Sticker games (i.e. geometric pieces of gummed colored paper to be pasted in designated places—copied after a pattern—building up a picture from its parts) for concept formation and for training their sense of location are enjoyable and of remedial value.

Whatever copying is done, whether it concerns play material or writing, it is important to place the material that is to be copied directly above their working space—that is—in a vertical position rather than lateral. This procedure enhances the child's sense of direction.

Spatial relationships can be trained through form boards, puzzles, matching of forms with outlines on cards, blocks graded in size (to be piled up or to be arranged in a designated order). I find the Montessori kindergarten material, which originally was designed for retarded children, most stimulating and helpful. However, there are other educational toys which lend themselves to training in size and spatial relationships. I found it essential to present only one item at a time to these children in order to focus their attention on one outstanding object while a display of numerous articles, even if they are parts of a whole, leads to confusion and over-stimulation because of the diffuse nonstructured perception. Concepts of sizes and forms are to be reinforced by kinesthetic cues, i.e., I have the child put his fingers into the holes of the graded cylinder board and also feel the surface of the corresponding wooden cylinder in order to get the feel for the *largest* and *smallest* respectively. To be emphasized is the discrimination of the widest range at first. That means the *very largest* and the *very smallest* must be discriminated before intermediate size relationships are introduced.

In this connection I should like to stress that in working with these children much emphasis has to be placed on directed work and play, on copying from patterns—which may appear contrary to the accepted principles of progressive education—with the accent on creative and imaginative work. However, as an intermediate step, it is of indispensable necessity for the brain-injured child.

As a preparatory stage for perception of printed or written symbols it is also found most helpful to train and activate the children's tactile and kinesthetic sense. Metal geometric forms are used for outlines of circles, squares, etc. The child's finger tips of the dominant hand are guided along the contours to get the feel of the respective form. Later on, crayons are to be used and gradually the basic forms and directions underlying letter formation are perceived. From the point of view of the most effective rehabilitation devices, I have noticed the strong motivational force inherent in kinesthetic cues. The drive to move can be capitalized on by the educational therapist through guided movements of fingers. To still exaggerate the kinesthetic perception I have found it of great therapeutic value to use clay and sandpaper, especially for the introduction of letter and number symbols, to children who had no previous training and for remedial purposes with those who showed reversal tendencies or other confusions.

The mere presentation of printed material, even after sufficient preparation regarding contents, is meaningless to many children of our group and should be immediately discontinued if found ineffective. The "whole word" method, as applied in most schools over the past years, is frequently a hopeless attempt to teach our children how to read because of their fundamental deficiency in their perception of the "gestalt." The brain-injured child may focus on a detail of the word, he may become fixated on one part of or one particular letter—like he may focus his attention on some unessential detail of someone's clothing—and thereby be incapacitated to perceive the configuration of the word as a whole. It is therefore absolutely advisable to proceed analytically to synthetically build up the "gestalt" from its components. Visual, auditory and kinesthetic associations are formed in teaching sounds and letters. Sandpaper and clay letters and numerals are used to reinforce visual and auditory engrams and again the emphasis on tactile sense and movement is of therapeutic and motivational significance.

I remember a boy of 7 whose interest in letters was awakened by my presentation of the symbols in a playful way. We made a simple train (for the pleasurable association with movement) from construction paper, cut out windows which could be opened and closed and pasted two identical letters behind each window of each respective car. The corresponding sandpaper letters, in larger size, were spread on the table and also large letters, corresponding to the window letters, were printed on each car and associations between letters of different sizes were formed from games. In order to prevent association of letter form with one particular size of the letter this device worked out well and was later applied to printed and script symbols. Of course many other devices like letter puzzles work effectively too. Simultaneously, with sandpaper and clay, tracing of stencils (letters and numerals) and of printed forms is practiced.

In number work we often encounter a psychological mechanism which is descriptive in its term—called "disinhibition"—meaning the child's drive to rush through counting, naming numerals without being able to point at the one object or picture to be associated with the one particular number. The outcome is omissions or combinations. This drive can be encountered by structuralizing the numerical sequence, number combinations or whatever arithmetical fundamentals are to be taught. Here again motoric involvement is therapeutic, exerting an inhibiting effect. Therefore, placing sticks, toothpicks, beads or whatnot into different boxes, use of an abascus, are satisfactory devices for the beginning in numerical concepts as well as for the fundamentals of addition and subtraction. I found it helpful, besides, to simply place an article in a designated place and saying the number, to associate also the auditory perception of a knock with the auditory number symbol in order to prolong the act of naming the particular number—setting each count off as a distinct unit. The application of rhythm in counting and in spelling is of great therapeutic value. With young children the rhythmic singing of directions to be followed has been found to be soothing and effective.

Color cues also structuralize perception and are helpful as counting devices, one color is used for designating one dot, another color for two dots, etc. Another technique serving to offset the diffuse and undifferentiated perception of numbers and their sequence and to structure the foreground against the background is the frequent application of "boxes" at the stage when concrete material can gradually be eliminated and when pencil and paper are used. Numbers are written within boxes in sequence, in combinations like adding and subtracting with the result that numerical concepts and position of numbers become better established and more meaningful.

Space does not permit to elaborate nor even touch upon the teaching of number configurations, partial counting, application of number concepts in concrete situations, etc. There is one point in connection with arithmetic, however, which I would like to bring out because disregarding it might be detrimental. To apply drill and frequent repetition of arithmetical formulas is not indicated since as a rule the brain-injured child's rote memory is good and formulas could be retained without the child's acquiring basically an insight into the numerical processes involved. Besides frequent repetition would support the trend for perseveration which is marked in many of our children. The therapeutic aim is to help these children acquire cues which enable them to attack new tasks with numbers or words independently.

The brain-injured children's orientation in space and time is poor, caused by the disturbances of perception of spatial relationships. There is marked inability to point, to follow somebody else's pointing, to copy movements. The child has a distorted body image. Laterality is often not well established and the child's concept of laterality most times is confused also in cases when dominance seems definite. Therapy includes games like imitations of somebody's actions or to follow directions as to what bodily acts to perform. It is even confusing to many of these children to copy the most primitive movements. In connection with reading, we often act out words like "here," "there," "where," etc. and the child has to guess the meaning of our actions which, at the beginning, is found very difficult because of the defective body concept.

In the following I should like to mention an example of a specific language difficulty characterized also by defective orientation. One child of ten, whose language development was considerably delayed but who now has a perfectly adequate vocabulary, found it exceedingly difficult to ask questions of another child when he was expected to structure a question from the elements of a command, i.e., "Billy, ask Johnny what he did on Saturday!" This particular language difficulty in connection with a disturbed body image seems to indicate difficulty in self-identification.

Just a word about some behavior aspects of these children which, as I pointed out at the beginning, show many variables. I would like to cite one example to show you the confusions in thinking entering into the reactions of the child. A girl of 14, who exhibits great pride in her ideals of nondiscrimination and assumes an overprotective attitude toward the "weak" and toward minorities in a way, fell into hysterical crying when the children sang a spiritual, which she likes very much, with the words "I want to be ready," and adapted it in a very cheerful mood to the approaching lunch hour by singing "I want to be ready for lunch." When the girl was asked why she was crying she replied that the others were making fun of the Negroes. Now you can see what a far-fetched reasoning it was, how irrelevant her reaction was to the stimuli which simply were "spiritual," implying Negroes, and "laughing." All the connecting ideas were omitted, no integration attempted and the two ideas—"Negro" and "laughing"—taken out of context.

To what an extent we find here a layer of neurotic behavior is another question. But it is very important to us educators to evaluate a situation like this soberly and not to get impressed by the expression of superficial compassion. The same child may show surprising insight into relatedness of facts and situations on other occasions. The inconsistencies and often contradictory elements displayed in their behavior become apparent when they show sound reasoning and ability for abstraction in one situation and lack of it in another. The situation seems aggravated when the child is confronted with a demand, no matter how informal it might be, and focusing of attention is expected. Thinking becomes erratic, fluctuating, and diffuse, with the ensuing lack of comprehension and reasoning ability. Of course we again have to take into consideration possible psychological mechanisms developed as a result of deficient mental functioning. A very reassuring approach and breaking up the question into its components are therapeutic measures.

Just a word about parental attitudes. Often we come across a "could do better" philosophy with parents of brain-injured children. The reason is obvious. These children show an uneven mental development. They function comparatively satisfactorily in one area, are deficient in another, which, at the stages of early life may not be too apparent, or they may often be expected "to grow out of it," unless professional advice is sought for early. These children may be accepted, in a limited way, by a social circle of peers up to school age when their difficulties become outstanding in the academic areas. Then parents become puzzled and undecided in their approach to the child, often exerting too much pressure, which leads to more complications in terms of the child's emotional and social behavior. Parents of brain-injured children need guidance in order to be able to judge what to expect and how to evaluate their child's functioning and behavior.

In closing, I should like to emphasize that certain basic general principles, which more or less apply to all children with educational difficulties, have grown out of my work with them. The "total child" must be considered within the framework of his medical and family history and must be treated and taught on an individual basis, with the group as background for guided social experiences. Motivation for learning must be strong, undesirable stimuli must be reduced, incentives must be created. The transference of "learning" from school to home must be accepted as a very slow process.

The therapeutic approach sets an objective but no standards, as a set curriculum would. The child progresses at his own pace. Any special techniques applied over the maturing years serves as a crutch to be used temporarily until safer ground has been reached, at which point it can be abandoned.

However, no matter what methods and techniques have been found to be of remedial value, I consider the therapist's approach, intuition and resourcefulness as the prerequisites for the brain-injured child's rehabilitation.

34 PERCEPTUAL-MOTOR ASPECTS OF
LEARNING DISABILITIES

Newell C. Kephart

The following discussion outlines a portion of the rationale for dealing with the child with learning disabilities developed by the author over the past twenty-five years. It is based largely upon clinical observation of the behavior of many such children and forms the basis of the therapy program of the Achievement Center for Children, Purdue University.

Most of the learning experiences which the public school presents to the child are oriented toward symbolic materials. Visually, we present words, diagrams, and similar representations on a printed page. Verbally, we manipulate conceptual items and deal in intricate, logical sequences. Underlying such presentation is a fundamental assumption: that the child has established an adequate orientation to the basic realities of the universe—space and time. It is well known that ability to deal with symbolic and conceptual materials is based upon consistent and veridical perceptions of the environment. Numerous, normative studies have indicated that the child, under normal conditions, has established a stable world by the age of six years when he comes to us in the public schools. Therefore, our fundamental assumption is legitimate.

However, in a significant percentage of children, accidents occur during the developmental period. The accident may be any one of a large number of events. Its effect is to interfere with the establishment of a stable perceptual-motor world. As a result, many children come into our school system lacking the fundamental assumptions which underlie so much of the material which we present.

For the child who has been unable to establish the three dimensions of Euclidean space in his visual world, the words on a page of print may

Reprinted from *Exceptional Children*, Vol. 31, No. 4 (December, 1964), pp. 201-206. By permission of the author and publisher.

become an unintelligible mass of meaningless marks. They may not hold together into the compact groups, words and phrases, with which we deal. They may not hold still, but float about on the page. Worst of all, they may look different to him at different times and under different circumstances.

For the child who has been unable to establish a firm temporal dimension in his environment, the verbal discussions which we present may be no more than a meaningless jargon of sounds. Our intricate, step by step logical procedures may be difficult to organize without a temporal dimension along which to arrange them. Consider the difficulty which many children have in organizing the sequence of steps in long division.

For this significant percentage of children, the materials which we present in the classroom may cause difficulty, not because of the content or inability to deal with the content, but because of inability to deal with the mechanics of the presentation. Where the mechanics of the task break down, the content of necessity suffers. It may be that the child has not so much difficulty in learning to read as he has in seeing the words on the page. It may be that he has not so much trouble in understanding arithmetical reasoning as he does in organizing the steps of this reasoning in time.

ENVIRONMENTAL INTERACTIONS

The child's first interactions with his environment are motor. His first learnings are motor learnings. His first attempts to organize the environment are based upon these motor interactions. For a very large number of children, the learning difficulty begins at this early motor stage. He learned to use his motor responses to accomplish certain ends, but he failed to expand or generalize these motor responses so that they formed the basis of information gathering. He has learned a motor response for a specific end, but has not developed a motor interaction with his environment.

The difference here is that between a motor skill and a motor pattern. A motor skill is a motor act which may be performed with high degrees of precision. However, it is limited in extent; it is designed for a specific result, and only limited variation is possible. The motor pattern on the other hand involves lesser degrees of precision, but greater degrees of variability. Its purpose is much broader, and extensive variation is possible.

Consider the difference between walking as a motor skill and walking as a part of a locomotor pattern. The young child first develops a walking skill. He learns how to maintain an upright position while he puts one foot in front of the other. This process allows him to move from point A to point B. However, most of his attention must be devoted to the motor process itself—what part must move and how must it move. Very little attention can be devoted to the purpose of the movement. The skill is very limited and little variation is possible. Thus, if he encounters an obstacle in moving from point A to point B, he may well have to stop and give up the entire task. He cannot veer around the obstacle or step over it because these adjustments involve greater variation than his limited skill will permit.

Consider on the other hand the locomotor pattern of the older child. He can get from point A to point B by any one of a number of specific skills. He can walk; he can run; he can skip; he can jump, and so on. If an obstacle looms in his way, he can veer around or go over or under it as the problem demands. In all of these extensive variations, he does not need to expend attention on the motor act itself. This act has been generalized; it is no longer specific. As a result, he can shift directions or shift movement sequences without undue attention to the process itself.

With the walking skill the child is limited to rather specific purposes and ends. The process does not involve a continuous, changing, viable relationship with the environment. Only through a locomotor pattern can the child maintain a consistent, uninterrupted interaction with the environment surrounding him. The development of a stable body of information about this environment demands such a continuous, reliable interaction. Thus motor patterns become essential for information gathering at this basic early stage in the development of the world of the child.

There are four of these motor patterns which appear to be of particular significance to us in the field of education.

BALANCE AND MAINTENANCE OF POSTURE. All spatial relationships in the world about us are relative. Right and left, up and down, behind and before are relationships which are not given directly by perceptual data. They develop out of the observation and organization of relationships between objects. A well-organized system of such relationships will include the three Euclidean dimensions of space. All of these relationships, however, are relative. Each object is related to each other object, and there is no objective direction. The child must systematize this set of relationships through the learning resulting from his interaction with the objects in his environment.

The point of origin for all such relationships is the force of gravity. It, therefore, becomes important for the child to establish a relationship to the force of gravity and to be able to maintain this relationship and the awareness of the center of gravity throughout all of his activities. It is only through a constant and stable relationship to gravity that a point of origin for spatial relationships can be established. This stable relationship to gravity is achieved through the motor pattern of balance and posture. By maintaining the relationship of his body to the force of gravity, the child identifies the direction of the line of gravity and maintains this constant throughout his interactions with the environment.

The child should be able to maintain his balance and relationship to gravity under many conditions and with his body in a large number of different positions. He should not lose balance or lose his awareness of gravity when the position of his body changes or when its motion alters. On the other hand, his relationship to gravity should be variable so that he can maintain this relationship under a large number of conditions. His balance and posture should be dynamic and fluid rather than rigid. It is only through such a dynamic relationship to gravity that a continuous awareness of its direction can be maintained.

LOCOMOTION. The locomotor skills are those motor activities which move the body through space: walking, running, jumping, skipping, hopping, rolling, etc. It is with the pattern of locomotion that the child investigates the relationships within the space around him. By moving his body from one point to another, he learns to appreciate the properties of this surrounding space and the relationships between the objects in it. Out of such knowledge a space world with stable coordinates will develop. Locomotor skills should be variable. They should permit the child to divert his attention from the movement itself to the purpose of the movement. They should permit the child to adjust to changes in the environment and to obstacles which may lie in the path of his movement.

CONTACT. The contact skills are those motor activities with which the child manipulates objects. Involved are the skills of reach, grasp, and release. It is with the contact skills that the child investigates through manipulation the relationships within objects. In order to obtain this information, he must be able to reach out and make contact with the objects; he must be able to maintain this contact through grasp until he has obtained the necessary information, and he must be able to terminate this contact through release and move on to the next object. From the knowledge so gained, form perception and figure-ground relationships will develop.

The skills of reach, grasp, and release should be established well enough so that the child can divert his attention from the motor acts to the manipulation. They should also be sufficiently variable to permit him to make complex manipulations in search of information.

RECEIPT AND PROPULSION. With the skills of locomotion, the child has investigated the relationships in the space around him. With the skills of contact, he has investigated the relationships within an object. However, many of the problem situations with which he must deal involve the movement of objects in space. It is with the skills of receipt and propulsion that he investigates movements in space.

Receipt skills involve those activities by which the child makes contact with a moving object. Such skills include, not only the pursuit of the moving object, but also the interposition of the body or parts of the body in the path of the moving object, as in catching. The skills of propulsion involve those activities by which the child imparts movement to an object. Included are throwing and batting, and the like. Also included are the more continuous skills of pushing, pulling, and the like.

Through the use of these four motor patterns, the child investigates the vast array of relationships in the environment around him. Out of this investigation he puts together a system of these relationships. The initial information is motor. It comes from the interaction through movement of the child with his environment. To develop a system, however, these interactions must be extensive, and they must be consistent. If the interactions are not sufficiently extensive, the system will not be sufficiently inclusive. If the interactions are inconsistent so that the observed relationships are not stable, the development of a system is impossible. To develop such extensive and consistent investigations, motor patterns as opposed to motor skills are required. Therefore, we are not interested in whether or not the child can walk; we are interested in whether or not he can locomote in order to obtain information about objects in space. We are interested in a sort of motor generalization by which the repertory of movements, whatever they may be, available to the child are used for the purpose of gathering information about the environment around him.

Many children find the motor learning required for a learning pattern difficult. As a result, they stop with a motor skill. They require additional help and additional learning experiences to continue this motor learning until a level is reached which will permit the use of movement, not only for specific purposes, but for the more generalized purpose of information gathering. It becomes the responsibility of the public schools to offer this aid and to help the child expand his motor learning.

DIRECTIONAL RELATIONSHIPS

Out of these motor investigations of the environment comes a system of relationships. At this point the system is primarily a motor system. It exists within the child's own body. The directions of space are beginning to develop, but they are limited to the movement relationships which occur in his body. The vertical direction has developed and stabilized out of his use of balance and posture. Out of his more extensive motor activities he has developed a laterality among his own movements. He now knows when a movement is on the right side of the body, and when it is on the left; and he knows how far to the right, or how far to the left it may be. He has developed a sort of a right-left gradient within his own movement system.

For further progress, however, this system of directional relationships must be transferred to outside objects. Since he cannot investigate in a motor fashion all of the objects in his environment, he must learn to investigate them perceptually. These perceptual data, however, do not at this point possess the spatial relationships which his motor data possess. Perceptual data come to have such relationships by projecting motor information onto perceptual information.

It is through the perceptual-motor match that the child makes this projection. As he manipulates an object or relationship motorwise, he observes the perceptual data which he is receiving concurrently and particularly he observes changes in these perceptual data. Through a matching of the motor data and the perceptual data, these two areas come to give him the same information. Now perceived objects have a right and a left, just as manipulated objects have a right and left. Now he can *see* up and down, just as previously he learned to feel up and down. Through such a projection process, the perceptual world comes to be systematized and organized in the same fashion that the motor world was organized. It is only through such a projection that a veridical organization of the perceptual world is possible.

Important here is the control of the external sense organs. The sensory avenue which gives us the greatest amount of information, and which is most subject to control, is that of vision. The visual information is controlled by the direction in which the eye is pointed. The pointing of the eye in turn is controlled by the extraocular muscles. The child must learn to explore an object with his eye in the same way in which he previously explored it with his hand. It is important, however, that the exploration with the eyes duplicate the exploration with the hand, and that the resulting information match the earlier information.

Two problems arise at this point. First of all, the child must learn to manipulate his eye through the development of patterns of movement in the extraocular muscles. The second, and perhaps a more important problem, is that of learning to manipulate the eye in terms of the incoming information. The only way in which the child can know that his eye is under control is to evaluate its information. The criterion of ocular control is the visual information which results. However, the child is only now developing a stable visual world with which to evaluate the present perception. Therefore, the body of information which should provide the criterion for ocular control is not yet present. On the other hand, without ocular control the incoming contributions to the body of visual information are inconsistent and spotty. Thus the control of his eye is hampered by his lack of a stable visual world while at the same time the stability of his visual world is impaired by his lack of ocular control.

The solution to this dilemma is in motor manipulation. The child investigates motorwise. He then experiments with the movement of his eye until it gives him information which matches his motor information. Since the body of motor information is reasonably stable, he stabilizes the visual information when a match occurs. Through many such experiments, he develops a visual world which duplicates his motor world. He has established a perceptual-motor match. When this match is adequate, he can drop out the intervening motor manipulation and use his now stable visual information to control the eye and thus control new visual input. Now all information—motor or perceptual, sensory input or motor response—is a part of a stable overall system which gives consistent information wherever it is tapped. Control of perceptual information and of motor response are both possible and are both a part of one consistent system.

It is obvious that such learning will be difficult and will require extensive experimentation. Here again the learning process frequently breaks down with the result that an adequate match between perceptual information and motor information is not accomplished. For such children there is limited stability in the perceptual world. They cannot *see* the relationships of right-left, up-down, and so on. For them, the letters on our page do not present a stable directional relationship. If you cannot *see* a difference between right and left, it is very difficult to distinguish between a "b" and a "d." If you do not *see* a difference between up and down, it is easy to confuse a "b" and a "p." Thus, for such children the mechanics of the reading task become extremely difficult. To deal with our symbolic material, the child requires a stable spatial world. Such a stable spatial world can be established only through the development of a system of spatial relationships learned first in the motor activities of the child and later projected onto perceptual data. Such a system must be both generalized and extensive.

OTHER RELATIONSHIPS

The behavior of the child occurs not only in space but also in time. For this reason there is another dimension of behavior which must be generalized and systematized. This is the temporal dimension. There are three aspects of time which are important to us in education: synchrony, rhythm, and sequence.

The basis of temporal judgments arises through synchrony. The child must first be able to appreciate simultaneity in time before he can appreciate serial events in time. Synchrony is the point of origin of the temporal dimension.

Having developed a point of origin through synchrony, the child requires a temporal scale. This scale must be characterized by stable, equal intervals. Rhythm provides such a temporal scale. It is through rhythm that he can estimate and evaluate temporal intervals.

Sequencing is the ordering of events in time. It is obvious that such ordering is difficult or impossible unless there is a temporal scale upon which to superimpose this order. Unless the child can appreciate temporal intervals it is difficult to organize events in terms of their temporal relationships.

As with the relationships in space, relationships in time also developed first in the motor activities of the child. Synchrony is observed when muscles move in concert. Rhythm is developed when muscles move alternately or recurrently. Sequence is observed when movements occur in coordinated patterns. From the generalization of many such observations, a temporal system evolves, and a temporal dimension develops.

This motor-temporal system must then be projected onto outside events just as the motor-spatial system was projected onto the perception of outside objects. Now auditory rhythm develops and speech begins to be rhythmical. Now the eyes move rhythmically across a page of print preserving the temporal relationships of the material as well as the spatial relationships. Now the step by step procedures of logical reasoning can be organized in time.

When these two systems are adequate, the child can translate activities from one to another. Consider the task of drawing. The child first looks at the copy. His visual perception gives him a simultaneous spatial presentation of the material. As he begins to draw, however, he must translate this simultaneous spatial impression into a series of events in time which will preserve the continuity and relationships of the whole. If the copy is a square for example, he must translate the four simultaneously presented lines into a series of directional movements performed one at a time, but resulting in a square form.

As in the development of spatial relationships, so in the development of a temporal relationship, many children experience difficulty. As a result, they have difficulty organizing events in time, and they have particular difficulty with our educational materials in which temporal sequence is vital. We must be prepared to aid these children in the development of a temporal dimension of behavior.

CONCLUSION

Since the materials and activities which we present in the public school are so frequently highly symbolically oriented, we have a tendency to look primarily at the child's symbolic response and at the symbolic aspects of his performance. Perhaps our preoccupation with symbolic variables has blinded us to the more fundamental problems of many children. It is possible that their orientation to the physical universe which surrounds them is disturbed. It is possible that, as a result of this disturbance, their difficulties are not so much with the content of our activities as with the mechanics involved. Greater attention to the child's methods of handling the mechanics of our tasks might result in less frustration for us and more learning for the child.

References

Bartley, S. A., *Principles of perception* (New York: Harper & Row, 1958).
Gessell, A., Ilg, Frances L., and Bullis, G. E., *Vision—Its development in infant and child* (New York: Hoeber-Harper, 1941).

Jersild, A. T., *Child psychology* (Englewood Cliffs, New Jersey: Prentice-Hall, 1954).

Kephart, N. C., *The slow learner in the classroom* (Columbus, Ohio: Merrill, 1960).

Kephart, N. C., *The brain-injured child in the classroom* (Chicago: National Society for Crippled Children and Adults, 1963).

Kephart, N. C., Perceptual-motor correlates of education. In S. A. Kirk and W. Becker (Editors), *Conference on children with minimal brain impairments* (Urbana: University of Illinois. 1963), pp. 13-25.

Piaget, J., and Inhelder, B., *The child's conception of space* (London: Routledge, 1956).

Small, V. H., Ocular pursuit abilities and readiness for reading. Unpublished masters thesis, Purdue University, 1958.

Strauss, A. A., and Lehtinen, Laura E., *Psychopathology and education of the brain-injured child*, vol. I (New York: Grune & Stratton, 1947).

Strauss, A. A., and Kephart, N. C., *Psychopathology and education of the brain-injured child*, vol. II (New York: Grune & Stratton, 1955).

35 SOME PRINCIPLES OF REMEDIAL
INSTRUCTION FOR DYSLEXIA

N. Dale Bryant

Specific, severe disability in word recognition (dyslexia) is usually resistant
to standard remedial procedures. Many children with dyslexa remain vir-
tual nonreaders in spite of years of remedial work. Dyslexia cases can learn
to read, but only if the teacher recognizes the nature and extent of the
child's difficulties and uses procedures appropriate for dealing with those
difficulties. Teachers need a frame of reference for planning remediation of
these cases—some principles as well as techniques. The points outlined below represent an application of learning principles to the specific disabilities
found in working with several hundred reading disability cases. The principles are not inappropriate for teaching retarded readers other than those
with dyslexia. Characteristics of dyslexic children have been discussed by
many authors, notably Money (1962) and Bryant (1962). The relationship
of dyslexia to other reading problems has been discussed by Rabinovitch
(1954) and Bryant (1963). Bibliographies in these references provide a
more comprehensive introduction to this extensive literature.

The following principles are not a method of remediation but are, instead, a partial framework on which effective remediation can be built.
Several principles are common to all efficient learning. They are emphasized here because the learning difficulties of dyslexic children necessitate
close adherence to general learning principles.

PRINCIPLE 1. Remediation should initially focus on the simplest, most
basic perceptual-associational elements in reading: perception of details
within the Gestalt of words and association of sounds with the perceived
word elements.

A child with dyslexia does not readily abstract and make generaliza-

Reprinted from *The Reading Teacher*, Vol. 18, No. 7 (April 1965), pp. 567-572, with
permission of the author and the International Reading Association.

tions like those that allow the normal child to improve basic skills of reading on his own. If a child is reading second grade material, merely practicing at this level can benefit some retarded readers, but a child with dyslexia is likely to continue to be confused. The teacher should focus remediation upon the child's difficulties and simplify the work so that confusion is avoided and the basic perceptions and associations are learned so well that they will not be forgotten.

One of the major problems exhibited by dyslexia cases is the difficulty in perceiving and retaining a detailed image of a word. This is seen clinically when a child recognizes a word on one line and is unable to recognize it, or incorrectly identifies it, on the very next line. The child is operating on rather minimal cues (often the initial letter, the length and general shape of the word) and the context of the selection being read. *Calling attention to the details within a word is an important aspect of remedial teaching.* Writing or even tracing the word is useful not only because of possible kinesthetic-tactile facilitation of memory but, perhaps more important, because the child's attention is called to each letter within the word. Another effective technique consists of presenting the word with one or more letters left out. As the child fills in blanks and finds that he is right, he is forced to become aware of the missing details. Flash cards or tachistoscopic practice can insure the rapid recognition of the details within words that is necessary in actual reading. Practice in rapid discrimination of words from other words that differ only slightly insures that the perception of details is well established.

A second major problem for dyslexia cases is the difficulty in associating sounds with letters and perceived word parts. This is a basic element of all reading by children who have usable hearing, and it functions in recognizing "sight words" as well as in its more obvious role in sounding out new words. Until basic symbol-sound associations are established, learning new words and increasing reading level are likely to provide only inconsistent gains. To get around the inability of the dyslexia case to abstract these associations from words he learns, the remedial teacher should focus on a single association or, at most, a few associations until practice has firmly established the relationship.

To be effective in reading, when the letter is presented as a part of a word, the associated sound must be quickly blended with other sounds to produce the word. The child should, therefore, practice with words rather than individual letters. The words should be chosen so that the particular sound association is the only process requiring effort for the child. Every word that is written, every letter filled in, or word briefly seen should be pronounced aloud so that practice of symbol perception and sound association takes place. *Always the pronunciation should be correct, aloud (so you know it is correct), and immediate.* If the child ever falters, the word should be pronounced for him.

PRINCIPLE 2. Perceptual and associational responses should be over-learned until they are automatic.

An automatic response occurs when a response to a letter or word part becomes so well established that a person does not have to consciously try to select an appropriate response. For example, an immediate association of sound with a letter (or common combination of letters) is usually made by normal readers. All common associations should become automatic for good reading, including the modification of a sound because of another part of the word (as in the rule of silent e). In quickly recognizing a word, many component discriminations and associations are automatically made that otherwise would confuse or distract from other discriminations or associations.

To develop automatic responses for the basic discrimination of letters, and for the association of sounds, the child needs to overlearn these basic skills and to practice them in complex words. Flash cards, tachistoscopic practice to discriminate from similar words, or the rapid reading of sentences are useful in establishing automatic responses. *The teacher should not encourage laborious sounding out.* Simple enough tasks should be used in learning so that recognition is always quick. As learning progresses, the difficulty of the task can be increased until, even in difficult words, the association of sound responses to the word parts is relatively quick and automatic.

Typically, dyslexia cases cannot deal at any one time with many discriminations or associations that are not automatic, and this is probably a major reason for failure of remediation with these cases. Even three-letter words often cause confusion. Dyslexic children cannot single out the perceptual and associational elements basic to word recognition on their own, so the remedial teacher must present tasks which will cause the child to develop automatic responses in the basic elements of reading one at a time.

PRINCIPLE 3. The remedial teacher should plan the learning experience and modify the presentation of the task and material on the basis of the child's performance so that the child is correct in nearly all of his responses, regardless of whether they are made aloud or to himself.

Incorrect responses can produce negative learning and confusion, as well as damage the confidence and motivation of the student. Every teacher has seen a child make an error and then have other errors snowball, even for tasks the child was previously able to do. This is particularly characteristic of dyslexia cases. They seem unusually vulnerable to confusion, perhaps because they have less depth and stability in their previous learning. Learning is based primarily on increments of correct response with immediate knowledge that the response is correct. *Any remedial session in which the child is allowed to make predominantly incorrect responses, particularly when he thinks even for a minute that they may be correct, is damaging to the child.* He may lose what he has gained, and may handicap future learning. Any time a child, who is trying, makes several errors in a row, it is likely that the teacher has made an incorrect judgment in selecting materials or tasks. Long delay in a response that should be automatic is in itself an error. Many concepts and techniques for keeping tasks within the capability of the child are the same as those described in articles on programmed learning.

PRINCIPLE 4. When two discriminations or associations are mutually interfering, the following steps should be taken consecutively: (1) one of the discriminations or associations should be learned to an automatic level; (2) the second should then be learned to an automatic level; (3) the first should be briefly reviewed; (4) the two should be integrated, starting with tasks only the difference between the two need to be perceived; and, finally, (5) in graduated steps both should be made automatic when the task requires discriminations and associations in addition to the mutually interfering ones.

Mutually interfering discriminations or associations occur frequently and remain a source of confusion to the dyslexic learner. Probably the best example is the association of several sounds for a particular letter. Vowels look somewhat alike and are often used interchangeably by dyslexia cases. Complicating the situation is the fact that every vowel has more than one sound and that the sounds are very similar to those of other vowels. This is a major stumbling block for dyslexia cases because it is a basic perceptual-associational element of even simple reading (Principle 1). It is important to overlearn each symbol-sound association until it is automatic (Principle 2). Not only will this overlearning contribute to phonic skills in sounding out new words, but the association of the sound seems to give more definite structure to the visual image of a letter and facilitates its rapid recognition within a word. The problem facing the dyslexic child is that he has difficulty in abstracting the different letters and sounds in a normally complex situation, so *the remedial teacher must limit the discriminations and associations required* to the point that the child can successfully handle them (Principle 3). When presented visually with a particular vowel, the dyslexic child is likely to respond with any one of five short vowel sounds or with any other sound with which vowels are associated. These are mutually interfering discriminations and associations (Principle 4). Even his visual discrimination of vowels is often poor, perhaps because the vowels are not clearly differentiated in terms of sounds.

If the reading teacher can stabilize the discrimination of each letter and the correct association of a *short* vowel sound with the appropriate sound, most of the confusion can be eliminated. The child will then possess the stable skills which will allow him to go on and learn conditions under which vowels have long or other sounds. Following this principle, a teacher might work with simple words using a single vowel, such as short *a*, until the child correctly and automatically responds with a short *a* sound any time this vowel occurs in a word. Then a second vowel (e.g., *o*) would similarly be associated with its short sound until the perception and association became automatic. A review of the short *a* association would be made to insure that the later learning had not caused the forgetting of the earlier learning (retroactive inhibition). Then, since both of these associations would have been established, whenever the child knows that a word is going to contain a short *a* or that it is going to contain a short *o* sound, the remedial teacher would start with words which differ only in the medial vowel. All should be words that the child has previously perceived and sounded automatically.

The flash card presentation of pairs of words such as *cat* and *cot*, *hat* and *hot* would give the child practice in rapidly discriminating which vowel is present and also practice in giving the correct short sound associated with it. If the child has some trouble, the teacher should limit practice to a single pair of words (e.g., let the child know the word is going to be either *cat* or *cot*) so that little discrimination is required of him. If his recognition skills are somewhat more advanced, or after practice with simpler discrimination tasks, the child might know only that a card will be drawn from four specific pairs of words with which he has previously practiced.

Eventually, the task should be such that in a flash card presentation or in the reading of sentences the child can rapidly and correctly discriminate the vowel and give the correct short sound association at the same time that he is discriminating any other combination of consonants. At that point he would be able to recognize and immediately pronounce any three-letter word having as its medial vowel either short *a* or short *o*. In fact, he should be able to perform correctly with nonsense syllables in which the medial vowel is either short *a* or short *o*.

Once he is stable in his discrimination of short *a* and short *o*, the entire cycle can be repeated with his learning a third vowel. After the sound association of a short sound with this third vowel is well established, the short *a* and short *o* words should be briefly reviewed. Discrimination of words containing this third vowel (e.g., *cut*) from similar words containing either the short *a* or the short *o* (e.g., *cat* and *cot*) could be practiced in increasingly more demanding tasks until any three- or four-letter word containing one of the three vowels can be identified in less than a second. The same procedure would be repeated with the fourth short vowel and the fifth short vowel with integration and practice each time.

Rate of progress will depend upon the child's impairment. Some children can establish automatic association of short vowel sounds with their respective letters in a few sessions. Other children may require months to become stabilized in even a few short vowel associations.

Of course, the foregoing example is only one illustration of the application of the principles. Such procedures would have to be incorporated in a comprehensive program. A full discussion of the application of the principles would be too long for this paper. Nevertheless, some examples of other areas might include the following: As nonphonic words are needed, they can be taught as sight words, reminding the child not to sound them out. Sight words should be overlearned with attention given to discrimination of details within the word. Once a child can recognize any brief short vowel word, his perceptual and associational skills are likely to be well established. Polysyllabic words can be introduced by combining known words. (The child is likely to introduce them himself and with reasonable skill.) Long vowel sounds can be taught by starting with words the child knows and showing him how they change when, for example, silent *e* is added, or when the vowel ends the word. Once basic skills are stabilized at an automatic level, routine remedial procedures using small steps and lots of reading will take a dyslexic child the rest of the way to adequate reading achievement.

PRINCIPLE 5. There should be frequent reviews of basic perceptual, associational, and blending skills, and as rapidly as possible these reviews should involve actual reading.

Dyslexia cases are often thought to have poor memory, and, indeed, they do for reading material. This may be because their learning is not well established. It is essential that every skill that a child learns be frequently reviewed. This occurs normally in reading, but because of the low level of skill of most dyslexia cases and their avoidance of the reading situation, review must be planned within the remedial session itself. Review should always be slanted towards rapid perception, rapid discrimination, and rapid association—all need to be automatic skills. It is possible to obtain or to construct reading exercises which utilize only the skills the child has already learned, thus giving him practice in what he has learned and avoiding skills not yet established, thus avoiding confusion.

Remedial activities based upon the principles discussed above are not intended to be mechanically applied. Successful remedial instruction of dyslexia will be influenced by the extent to which the teacher can couple the richness of previous teaching experience with (1) skill in identifying the cause of the child's difficulty at any point in the lesson, and (2) ability to modify instruction so that only the most basic difficulty is worked on until it is solved and integrated. Within the scope of the principles outlined for work with dyslexic cases, many procedures can be used effectively —and finding new techniques should be a creative challenge to the teacher.

References

Bryant, N. D., Reading disability: Part of a syndrome of neurological dysfunctioning. In J. A. Figurel (Editor), *Challenge and experiment in reading* (New York: Scholastic Magazine Press, 1962).

Bryant, N. D., Learning disabilities in reading. In J. A. Figurel (Editor), *Reading as an Intellectual Activity* (New York: Scholastic Magazine Press, 1963).

Money, J., (Editor), *Reading disability: Progress and research needs in dyslexia* (Baltimore: Johns Hopkins Press, 1962).

Rabinovitch, R. D., Drew, A. L., DeJong, R. N., Ingram, W., and Withey, L., A research approach to reading retardation. In R. McIntosh and C. C. Hare (Editors), *Neurology and psychiatry in childhood* (Baltimore: Williams & Wilkins, 1954).

36 PIAGET'S THEORY OF PERCEPTION: INSIGHTS FOR EDUCATIONAL PRACTICES WITH CHILDREN WHO HAVE PERCEPTUAL DIFFICULTIES

Gloria F. Wolinsky

In a previous paper (Wolinsky, 1962) it was suggested that Jean Piaget's particular thoughts and approaches to the problem of perception could be of considerable assistance in understanding the child who is presenting a problem in emotional or intellectual behavior that is attributable to difficulties in perception. Beyond understanding the youngster, Piaget's theoretical constructs offer an approach to method and technique that may aid the youngster in making more meaningful responses to a complicated environment. This discussion, therefore, will concern itself with (1) Piaget's thinking on the phenomenon of perception, and (2) an attempt to derive some pragmatic approaches for instructional situations that are intrinsic to the learning process. It should be stated also that in no way is this paper to be viewed as exhaustive of Piaget's considerable theoretical and practical work on perception but rather conceived as a review in terms of the problems that face readers of this journal.

THE APPROACH TO THE STUDY OF PERCEPTION

In discussing Piaget's concept of perception, two important facts should be remembered. The first is that the major part of Piaget's endeavors, as well as those of his collaborators, has been guided by a philosophy of intellectual functioning that is developmental; the second is that much of his writing on perception is in direct response to, as well as a critique of, a viewpoint of preformation, most exemplified in the Gestalt approach to perceptual phenomena. In understanding his work, therefore, one is involved in a

Reprinted from *Training School Bulletin*, Vol. 62, No. 1 (May, 1965), pp. 12-26. By permission of the author and publisher.

genetic approach to the development of thought that attempts to comprehend the relationships that perception has to the ontogenesis of cognition.

The problem of perception and the role it plays in cognition have
always been studied, commented upon, and referred to in all observations
in the thirty-odd years of work that culminated in L'Epistemologie Genetique, the monumental investigations on cognitive development in children. Perception is viewed as an aspect of intelligence and was investigated
as an important part of the sensory-motor period or of sensory-motor development. The sensory-motor period is that time, roughly from birth to 24
months, when the infant proceeds from a neonatal reflex level of nondiffer-
entiation between the self and the world to a relatively more sophisticated
organization of his sensory-motor actions with his immediate environment.

Intelligence in human beings, according to Piaget, passes through various stages and, rather than being fixed in terms of actual age, continuities
are characterized by an order of succession. Intelligent behavior has two
poles (Piaget, 1960), a figurative and an operative; the figurative aspect
precedes the operative and is particularly functional at the preoperative or
sensory-motor stage. Figurative behavior is perceptual and is the clue to
understanding the sensory-motor stage. It serves as the basis for all operational or intelligent behavior. During the sensory-motor period, for example, there is considerable manipulation of objects in a trial-and-error pattern
and an attempt at the formation of the behavioral concepts of permanent
objects. Probably the most familiar of these observations on infantile perception is the apparent non-interest or non-pursuit of a vanished object.
Studying the phenomenon phase by phase to the moment of actual retrieval, he concluded that object concept is developed.

THE NATURE OF PERCEPTION

In studying perceptual phenomena, Piaget has contributed several interesting concepts that assume important theoretical foundations for his work.
A major one is the idea of perception as different from intelligence. Perception is the knowledge we have of objects, as of movement, by direct or
immediate contact (Piaget, 1960; 1947). During the sensory-motor period
the child responds in a direct motor fashion to the immediacies in the environment. Each situation has a perceptual organization or equilibrium of
its own that is distinct from the previous one. This phenomenon is illustrated by the Delboeuf's illusion where the illusion increases or diminishes
but does not conserve its own value (Piaget and Lambercier, et al., 1942).
What actually occurs is a displacement of equilibrium which, according to
the terminology of Piaget, obeys "Laws of Maxima." A particular relationship generates an illusion and produces an uncompensated charge. This
process is actually self-limiting, for the illusion diminishes when the limiting point is reached since the distortion then assumes the value of the new
relationship, hence "maxima." In actual operation, therefore, the child

reacts to the new value but does not incorporate the past knowledge. Incorporation of past experiences is a higher-level process which is not involved in perceptual activity.

Furthermore, when intelligence or intelligent thought compares two objects, neither the standard nor the compared entity, the measure nor what is being measured, is in effect distorted by the comparison (Piaget, 1960; 1947). However, in perceptual comparison and, specifically, when one constituent serves as a fixed standard for the judgment of variables, a systematic distortion occurs which is called "the error of the standard." In effect, concentration on a specific aspect of the experience distorts the perceptual phenomenon. Perceptual space, in view of this explanation, is not homogeneous. It is, in Piaget's terms, "centralized from moment to moment." In other words, the child moves with the activity of an unstructured field, and the object at hand becomes the absorbed focus of the moment.

CENTRATION AS A FACTOR IN PERCEPTUAL BEHAVIOR

The "Law of Relative Centralization or Centrations" is a further explication of the particularities that perception presents. Perceptual space, as has been stated, is "not homogeneous but is centralized from moment to moment." The area of centralization corresponds to a spatial expansion while the periphery of this area is progressively contracted as one proceeds outward from the center (Piaget, 1960, p. 72; 1947). Centrations or centralizations cause distortions; whereas, decentrations or decentralizations act as correcting factors since they actually coordinate different centrings. The "Law of Centrations" is independent of the absolute values of the effects of centring and expresses the distortions in perception as a function of the figure. Even when the elements to be compared are equally centered in vision, the objective difference is subjectively accentuated by perception (the error of the standard), a problem in perception which is peculiar unto itself. Perception, which proceeds step by step from the immediate but still in partial contact with the object, distorts the object because of centration.

PERCEPTION AS A STATISTICAL PROCESS

As for the initial aspects of perception, it is conceived as basically a process that is statistical in nature (Piaget, 1961). During the sensory-motor stage, the infant actually samples specific elements in his immediate awareness. This concept of sampling is stated in terms of probabilistic terms. Piaget assumes that perception is a brief period from a state where there is no perception to a relatively stable one. In effect, there are intervals in this schema of perception. The young child is involved in a series of encounters (*rencontres*)[1] set up by a stimulus. However, not all of the possible en-

[1] Terms in brackets are either the original terms as used by Piaget or early translations of terms to describe certain concepts.

counterable elements are engaged. A fraction or a random sampling is involved in the first encounter. What then follows is a second sampling, not of the entire possible area or stimulus, but rather of the remaining elements of the situation. This sampling procedure proceeds until the "sample" can be meaningfully utilized. It might be well to make a distinction here, too, between the perception of space, which is an aspect of early development and, according to Piaget, an aspect of perceptual behavior, and the representation of space, which is a later refinement and a part of cognitive or operational behavior (Piaget, 1955).

This probabilistic sampling (*rencontres*) in the early stages of development is incomplete because of previously stated inabilities to incorporate past experiences and complete absorption with the thing at hand. Therefore, error, particularly in early childhood, is caused by incomplete sampling (Piaget, 1961) which basically reflects time and space factors that are not fully realized. When the child is able to bring various sampling relationships into meaningful and more complex situations (*couplage*), error is corrected, for he is now able to utilize multiple encounters in time and space more effectively.

PERCEPTUAL BEHAVIOR AS SENSORY-MOTOR BEHAVIOR

Piaget has indicated that perceptual activity is an intimate part of the sensory-motor period and sensory-motor intelligence; but intelligence or cognitive thought does not come about until the child can free himself from the immediacies of perceptual and motor activity and then concentrate on activities of the higher mental processes or operational behavior.

There exists ". . . partial isomorphisms between logical and perceptual structures" (Piaget and Morf, 1958), for the phenomenon of perception does not meet the fundamental operations of logic (reversibility, additivity, transitivity, inversion) that, according to Piaget, is "intelligent" thought, except for an approximate and rather limited sense. For example, in figure-ground reversals the perceptual inversion does not satisfy the logical criterion of inversion since the boundary always remains part of the figure. Furthermore, in perception there are "pre-inferences" that are "partially isomorphic" to the mechanisms of inference in logical reasoning; for inference in the logical state is based upon the knowledge of the situation while the decision that is involved in perceptual response is in terms of pure sensory data.

Sensory-motor "thought" responds to perception and motor activity. As the child develops intellectually, aided by his interaction with the world of people and things, the process of decentring becomes more viable. The central processes of thought become more autonomous, and the properties inherent in intellective function, classification, ordering, and numbering, that are basic to logical groupings, take over.

THE LINK BETWEEN PERCEPTUAL AND INTELLECTUAL BEHAVIOR

If perceptual activity concerns the immediate and ultimately links up with intelligence as soon as it can free itself from the immediacy of the situation, what is the link that permits the higher intellectual process? The concept of "transportations" serves as the vehicle for understanding. When the child begins to respond to objects that are too distant to be included in the act of centring, perceptual activity is extended in the form of "transportation." What occurs is a reconciliation of "centrings" which leads the way to genuine comparisons. In effect, there is a decentralization that compensates for the distortion and, incidentally, also accounts for size and shape constancy. What actually happens in "transportations" is a coming to terms with spatial and temporal relationships that were difficult in the first stages of perceptual behavior. This is another aspect of *"couplage"* or more adequate sampling. This crucial step in the development of perceptual activity permits the individual to move towards an analysis of situations that is required for operational procedures.

What Piaget is saying, then, is that the complex of operations which have the characteristic of a Gestalt or *"structure d'ensemble"* are not preformed or innate in an individual. They actually evolve out of a history of a person's interaction with the environment, enabling him to use new experiences in terms of his past (assimilation) and to rearrange his response in terms of the demands of the environment (accommodation). Early in life the child acts without understanding or comprehension. It is the immediacies of his experience that fill his awareness. An example of this perceptual phenomenon is the young child's grasping of a geometric form and attempting to place it on a puzzle cutout that has no relationship to the size or shape of the form. The grasp response is perceptual and motor; whereas, the placement of the correct form in its proper spot is an aspect of the higher mental processes and comes later when the youngster is able to free himself from the preoccupation with the shape and notices similarities and makes generalizations concerning proper placement.

Piaget does not deny that these immediacies are "wholes" or "configurations," or that perceptual constancy does exist, or that in perceptual structure the whole is not reducible to the sum of its parts. Rather, he rejects that which the Gestaltists have considered to be there from the beginning, the laws of organization and the dismissal of the role of past experience.

There are indeed complex structures or "configurations" in the infant's sensory-motor intelligence but, far from being static and nonhistorical, they constitute "schemata" which grow out of one another by means of successive differentiations and integrations and which must, therefore, be ceaselessly accommodated to situations by trial and error and corrections at the same time as they are assimilating the situations to themselves (Piaget, 1960b, p. 66; 1947).

So it is with perceptual structures. While they differ from intelligence or operational structures, in that the latter is mobile and permanent and changes within the system do not modify it, perceptual structures also show a change that is the product of progressive construction arising from "adaptive differentiations and combinative assimilations."

EXPERIMENTS IN PERCEPTION

In order to illustrate and maintain his position about perception, Piaget has undertaken a series of almost classical experiments of a psychophysical nature and has been most concerned with the development of illusions as the underlying empirical evidence for his theory of perception as developmental. A system called the "concentric clinical method" (*methode concentrique clinique*) has been devised. It is modifiable for the individual child and derives its name (*concentrique*) from the presentation of extreme values that are presented first, and then smaller differences are introduced. Values are shown on an alternating basis, above and below the standard, to determine upper and lower thresholds (Lambercier, 1946, p. 141ff.). Piaget and his collaborators have used this method to illustrate that fractionation or ratio judgments, as seen in the overestimation of acute angles and underestimations of obtuse angles, are a function of age (Piaget, 1949). Average errors show a clear decrease with age.

In a project designed to study the perception of intersecting and incomplete forms (Piaget and von Albertini, 1954), it was found that after four years of age, with unswerving accuracy, children could recognize intersecting forms. The recognition of incomplete forms was much more difficult. At nine years of age, all incomplete forms could be recognized.

Constancy, according to Gestalt psychology, is organized within a boundary, and this boundary, with invariant relationships between particular aspects of stimulation, is the basis of constancy in perception. Piaget argues that constancy is a part of developmental learning (Lambercier, 1946; Piaget and Lambercier, 1951; 1956) and explains this phenomenon as part of his theory of transportation.

The results of his work and those of his associates on illusions have been reported systematically since 1942 in "Recherches sur le Developement des Perceptions," *Archives de Psychologie*, Geneva, and have recently been consolidated (Piaget, 1961). Flavel (1963) and Wohlwill (1960; 1962) have also made some valuable reviews of some of his work in this area. Basically, experiments on the developmental aspects of illusions are divided into three types: the ones that decrease with age, such as the Muller-Lyer

(Piaget and von Albertini, 1950; Piaget, Lambercier *et al.*, 1942; Piaget, Marie and Prevat, 1954); those which increase with age, such as the size-weight illusions; and the ones that increase to the age of ten years or so and then begin to decrease, as do certain aspects of the vertical-horizontal illusion. In making these differences concerning illusions, Piaget, as does Binet, distinguishes between the primary illusions (Binet's "innate") and secondary illusions (Binet's "acquired"). Primary illusions are examples of factors involved in centralization—the law of relative centrations—(Piaget, Lambercier, *et al.*, 1942; Piaget, Vingh-Bang, and Matalon, 1958). Illusions, such as Delboeuf, Muller-Lyer, diminish with age for they are caused by inadequate sampling. Secondary illusions are produced by the interaction between primary factors and perceptual activity and reflect more adequate samples. For perceptual activity has developed to the point where it becomes involved in decentralization and, therefore, is able to regulate any perceptual distortion. Secondary illusions involving acts of comparison and coordination are basic to intelligent thought and are formed differently than are primary illusions.

More recently there have been reports in the literature (Gaudreau *et al.*, 1963; Stein, 1964) indicating that the nature of the perception of certain optical illusions are being explored with the retarded. Furthermore, studies utilizing some of the concepts derived from his work have been and are in the process of completion (Elkind and Scott, 1962; Elkind, Koegler, and Go, 1962; Elkind, Koegler, and Go, 1964; Robinson, 1964). These studies tend to substantiate his major premises.

IMPLICATIONS FOR INSTRUCTIONAL SITUATIONS

THE EDUCATIONAL SCENE. It would be extremely difficult in the psychologically sophisticated times in which we live to avoid the word "perception" or words "perceptual processes" in discussing the problems of children who have difficulty in learning in the formal sense or who have difficulty in relating to the less formal but still demanding processes of daily living. Indeed, in view of the nature of man's intellectual organization, any discussion of adaptive behavior must imply a process of perception, even though not particularly specified at the time. In reading and listening to the current dialogue on malfunctioning of perceptual processes and the implication it has for the learning process, one cannot help but be aware at times of an intriguing naivete that reflects the innocent as he surveys a still virgin field. Though the first flush of the "discovery of perception" as a problem area with the exceptional has somewhat abated, the problem of comprehension and utilization in terms of the pragmatics of the child who has "perceptual difficulties" is still very much with us.

Admittedly, this sounds harsh. However, it is not meant as indictment but rather a comment on an inevitable consequence of the complexities that the seemingly simple word "perception" actually presents. The study of perception has been and still is a problem that is basic to philosophy and has deep roots in the scientific aspect of validation of theory (Hochberg, 1962). Furthermore, one man's theoretical approach to the problem is not another's, in either problem to be studied or aspect to be explored. And so studies on perception may vary from the physiological to the cultural, with gradients between. In terms of children with presupposed perceptual difficulties, for the most part our philosophical and psychological focus has followed "holistic" or "organismic" theory most exemplified in Gestalt approaches, such as Goldstein, Lewin, Kafka and Kohler, and Wertheimer. However, it would be wise to remember that the theoretical positions and confirmations of these suppositions have found major support within the functioning or nonfunctioning of perceptual processes in the adult. While the insights derived *ex post facto* have been creative and fruitful, basically, the question is the problem of possible perceptual difficulty arising in what is a primarily undifferentiated period of life.

What does the meaning of perception as developmental and of perception as different from intelligence but yet an important part of intellectual activity imply for educational research and practice? What can Piaget and his collaborators offer a situation that is complex, both in terms of intellectual approaches and intellectual breakdown? How can a theory of perception as described be put into use so that benefits can be reaped? Woodward's work (1959; 1961; 1962a) has shown us that there is some indication retarded children and adults proceed through the Piaget developmental schema, albeit more slowly, and reach a termination point prior to complete development. Other studies (Hood, 1962; Lovell *et al.*, 1960; 1962a; 1962b), utilizing retarded learners as part of their group of subjects, are presenting similar lines of evidence. Furthermore, Woodward (1962b) presents an interesting approach to the application of some of Piaget's work to the education of the retarded.

PERCEPTUAL LEARNING WITHIN A SCHEMA. What will be suggested here is that the position as presented: the interrelationship of the development of perceptual activity with the sensory-motor period, presents a schema for a possible sequence of learning experiences that will serve as an added dimension for corrected learning experiences. While Piaget's work is still to be quantified, no other psychologist offers us so detailed a description of different facets of development in the early years of life. While many of us have been successful in helping children who have difficulty in perception, most of our approaches have been intuitive—from the simple to the complex; however, the logical sequence, in terms of ontogenesis, has at times eluded us.

All human learning situations basically must be involved with a specified goal so that procedures and materials can be effectively utilized to achieve the goal. When there is no great pathology or obstructions, the goals may be broader or may assume a learning or an intellectual process that is in good use. However, with children who are presumed to have a basic deficit in the ability to organize themselves in relationship to the stimuli around them, the stated goals must always be specified in terms of the difficulties. A philosophical approach to curriculum planning, however comprehensive and/or specified in terms of methods and materials, is insufficient without a statement of suspected difficulties and a proper realization of how this particular approach is supposed to remedy the particular situation. When the diagnosis of perceptual difficulty is offered, this alone is not sufficient, for it must relate to the pragmatics of the effect of disturbance and then to the task of assistance. If learning experiences are to be built around the schema as presented by Piaget, we become involved with planning experiences on a developmental level that is quite specific in terms of ultimate intellectual or preintellectual goals. Furthermore, by planning in terms of specified sequence, a unique opportunity for analysis of nonleaning or stalemate is offered. While the dialogue concerning the ultimate meaning Piaget's work has for psychology will continue for some time, his preoccupation with the "why" and "how," the analysis of behavior, not simply "it is," may be crucial for those of us who are concerned with the education and care of exceptional children.

The sensory-motor stage, with its carefully analyzed stage sequences of development (Piaget, 1937; 1945; 1936), presents a unique opportunity for curriculum development. Earlier it was noted that perception is tied up with sensory-motor activity and as such is basically not an act of intelligence. It might be said that possibly what is seen in the behavioral activity of a brain-injured child is the activity of a child who has not completed the sensory-motor stage in certain areas and who is attempting to build acts of intelligence on a structure that is not yet free of the demands of the sensory-motor period. Since Piaget's work is detailed for these stages and since there exist at this time several fine analyses of this period (Flavell, 1963; Mc V. Hunt, 1961; Wolfe, 1960), a detailed account of this period is not presented here. However, a brief outline is presented in order that some of the preceding statements may be better realized.

During the sensory-motor period there are six stages that must be realized.

Stage 1 encompasses a period where the child is involved with inherent reflex activities, such as sucking, crying, and vocalization, movements of the head, arms, and trunk. (o-1 month)

Stage 2 is the period of the first acquired adaptations and the "primary circular reaction," i.e., when the child sucks his thumb as a result of hand-mouth coordination rather than the chance encounter between the two. With this stage the child is involved with substages during the development of the "primary circular reaction," what Piaget calls the "primary, secondary, and tertiary" aspect. Vision, phonation, hearing, and prehension develop here to a more purposeful use. Vision, itself, passes through three substages—passive, then a time of search and finally, a moment of recognition. Prehension involves five substages. (1-4 months)

Stage 3 is described by Piaget as the "secondary circular reactions" and the procedures destined to make interesting sights last. Primarily, this period involves activities that concern reproduction, recognition, and generalization. Vision and prehension having been coordinated, the infant can proceed to a level of intentional behavior. (4-8 months)

Stage 4 involves the coordination of the secondary schemata and their application to new situations. It is characterized by the appearance of certain behavior patterns which are superimposed on the preceding ones, and their essence is "the application of known means to new situations" (Piaget 1963//1936). (8-12 months)

Stage 5 is the time of the "tertiary circular reaction" and the "discovery of new means through active experimentation." Objects become permanent; and spatial, causal and temporal sequences are responded to. (12-18 months)

Stage 6 concerns the invention of new means through mental combinations. In other words, the child now has the capacity to represent certain activities rather than a simple performance; the child leaves behind him the sensory-motor period and is now in the preoperational stages. This is not to say that all sensory-motor activities are fully developed but rather the child is able to respond in a conceptual-symbolic manner rather than in pure sensory-motor behavior.

This extremely simplified version of the sensory-motor period, with its intricate subgrouping and substages, places our child with perceptual learning difficulties in a continuum that affords an analysis for the teacher-learner situation that I do not believe exists anywhere else. Nor, to my knowledge, is there a truly systematic hierarchy of the developmental aspects of perception and intellectual growth that we are presenting to teachers, in order to firmly base their classroom methods. Piaget's schema, coupled with experimental evidence of the perceptual development (Gibson and Olum, 1960; Vernon, 1962; Wohlwill, 1960) of young children, now affords us the rationale and the sequence of corrective and meaningful learning experiences.

THE DIMENSION OF PERCEPTION. In helping children with perceptual difficulties are we fully realizing all that is involved in what Allport (1955) calls the "six broad classes of perceptual phenomenon": sensory qualities, figural or configural aspects, constancy, dimensional frame of reference, concrete object, and effect of the prevailing set or state? And, granting that we can come to grips with the meaning of perceptual phenomenon, are we fully cognizant of each of the phenomenon's meaning, for example, on the development of space perception which, among other factors, involves visual size, depth and distance, tilt and tactual space? In methodology are we confusing the perception of space and the representation of space as Piaget feels experimenters are doing, because of our preoccupation with performance in terms of the normative demands of the school situation?

In so far as the confusion of the perception of space and the representation of space is concerned, is our methodology so bound up with the heritage of the early experimental work on the perception of form that we are not responding as we should to the interesting insights of Piaget's work on the development of space concepts (1963)? (These have been substantially confirmed in a number of experiments done in England.) For example, it is a rare teacher who does not present her "perceptual training" material, however simple, within the framework of Euclidian geometry or projective geometry. Piaget has shown, that, in terms of the perception of form, the process is from the topological or the concern with being connected or bounded to an appreciation of the Euclidian metric properties of space. What the child initially seeks in form are the proximity, separation, order, enclosure, and continuity of structural elements; then he responds to curves, angles, lines, and parallels. These factors are similar to Gestalt concepts, and workers with children who display perceptual difficulties try to plan for experiences incorporating these concerns. Nevertheless, the materials that the children are usually given are of the third order of difficulty, for the developmental order of form perception appears to be topological, projective, and then Euclidian. So, while recognizing a basic deficit, an attempt at remedy is made at a more sophisticated level of recognition of form; this is an unfortunate paradox and a basic error in logic of presentation.

What is suggested again is a rationale for experiences that is based upon a sequence that has built within it the time for analysis of behavior even as learned.

A rarely-quoted study of Meyer (1940), concerning the development of the comprehension of spatial relationships in preschool children utilizing the major developmental insights of Piaget, brings dramatic evidence as to how the analyses of stage can assist in providing instructional techniques for children with perceptual difficulties. While her study did not concern itself with technique for teaching, it did try to analyze the process within the development of a particular phenomenon. In its analysis it can serve as the rationale for remedial or corrective experiences.

We are never sure of the "perceptual sample" in either the "normal" and even more uncertain in the atypical. However, by analysis that is inherently part of an educational sequence, we can react to what is necessary, in either freeing the child from a "sample" that is being responded to out of proportion to its functional use or because the child does not know how to respond. Children, we must remember, respond to many stimuli because of an insufficient understanding of the field to which they are being exposed. However, an understanding of the demands of the field and the problems of the child as he relates to it must be understood. The difficulty in the extraction, for example, of the important factor in a particular learning experience may be more a problem of immaturity of space perception or poor visual motor coordination than the pathological inability to separate foreground and background. While the overt behavior may be the same, the methodology may not be.

Since the basic perceptual process develops according to this schema during the sensory-motor period, any training must involve the emerging sensory-motor patterns and areas. Specific techniques must involve the child in terms of the interaction of the particular phenomenon that is to emerge, i.e., prehension and vision. One cannot educate for a particular defect alone, for it belies the basic integration or assimilatory aspects that the child is groping towards. Furthermore, deficit in one area does not preclude the effects it may have on another. It may well be that in helping our youngsters to meet the demands of their environment we have to take them back to the relatively undifferentiated period of the neonate and build with them the schema that they were not able to build themselves.

THE CHALLENGE—AN ANALYSIS OF INTERACTION. Piaget's major contribution, aside from the obvious, is his addition of fuel to the always smoldering fire of thought that believes children are more than simply their biological heritage. His work extends further than classical developmental theory for, rather than waiting for this biological heritage to unfold, Piaget's work on perception, as well as most of his observations on cognitive development, leads us to the point where we can begin to examine the assistive aspects that an environment can afford to its children as they proceed through life. Though there will be replications of his studies, though his points of view will be debated and, indeed, there is much to understand and to debate, there is a liberating aspect in his work for teacher, student, and research worker. His whole approach to analysis, which is more than mere quantification of data, places this triad in a position where each one is involved in an intimate way with the process of how and why of the thought process. For research workers, if they follow this technique, must of necessity begin to explain why; the teacher must take this information and understand maladjustive thought processes and provide for a remediation in terms of an impairment of developmental function; and the child ultimately must come to terms with an environment that provides and involves thought and meaningful action.

The problem, then, is concerned not simply with an increased exposure to educational technique and academic content, but rather a correction or concern with a process that has not been completed or fully realized.

References

Allport, F., *Theories of perception and the concept of structure*, 2nd Ed. (New York: Wiley, 1955).

Elkind, D., Koegler, R. R., and Go, E., Studies in perceptual development: II, Part-whole perception, *Child Develpm.*, 1964, 35, 881-90.

Elkind, D., Koegler, R. R., and Go, E., Effects of perceptual training at three age levels, *Science*, 1962, 137, 3532, 755-756.

Elkind, D., and Scott, L., Studies in perceptual development: I, The decentering of perception, *Child Develpm.*, 1962, 33, 619-630.

Flavell, J., *The developmental psychology of Jean Piaget* (Princeton: Van Nostrand, 1963).

Gaudreau, J., Lavoie, G., and Delorme, A., La perception des Illusions de Muller-Lyer et D'Oppel-Kundt chez les deficients mentaux, *Canad. J. of Psych.*, 1963, 17(3), 259-263.

Gibson, E., and Olum, U., Experimental methods of studying perception in children. In P. H. Nussen, (Editor) *Handbook of research methods in child development* (New York: Wiley, 1960), pp. 311-373.

Hochberg, J., Nativism and Empiricism in Perception. In Leo Postman, *Psychology in the making* (New York: Knopf, 1962), pp. 255-330.

Hood, H., An experimental study of Piaget's theory of the development of number in children, *Brit. J. Psychol.*, 1962, 53, 273-78.

Hunt, McV., *Intelligence and experience* (New York: Ronald, 1961).

Lambercier, M., Recherches sur le developpement des perceptions, VI La constance des grandeurs en comparaison seriales, *Arch. de Psychol.*, Geneva, 1946, 31, 1-204.

Lovell, K., Healey, D., and Rowland, A., Growth of some geometrical concepts, *Child Develpm.*, 1962, 33, 751-767.

Lovell, K., Mitchel, B., and Everett, I., An experimental study of the growth of some logical structures, *Brit. J. Psych.*, 1962, 53, 175-188.

Lovell, K., and Slater, A., The growth of the concept of time: A comparative study, *J. Child Psychol. Psychia.*, 1960, 1, 179-190.

Meyer, E., Comprehension of spatial relations in preschool children, *J. Genet. Psych.*, 1940, 57, 119-151.

Peel, E., Experimental examination of some of Piaget's schemata concerning children's perception and thinking, and a discussion of their educational significance, *Brit. J. Educ. Psych.*, 1959, 29, 89-103.

Piaget, J., Les illusions relatives aux angles et a la longue de leurs cotes, *Arch. de Psychol.*, Geneva, 1949, 32, 281-307.

Piaget, J., *The construction of reality in the child* (New York: Barec Books, 1954) (La construction du Reel chez l'enfant, 1937).

Piaget, J., Essai d'une nouvelle interpretation probabilistic des effets de centrations de la loi Weber et celles des centrations relatives, *Arch. de Psychol.*, Geneva, 1955a, 35, 1-24.

Piaget, J., Perceptual and cognitive (or operational) structures in the development of the concept of space in the child, *Acta Psychol.*, 1955b, 41-46.

Piaget, J., Le developpement des mecanismes de la perception, *Bull. de Psychol.*, 1960a, Cours des 27 octobre et 17 novembre, 1960.

Piaget, J., *The psychology of intelligence* (Princeton: Littlefield, Adams and Company, 1960b) (La psychologie de l'intelligence, 1947).

Piaget, J., Les mecanismes perceptifs: modeles probabilistic, analyse genetique relation avec l'intelligence (Paris: Presses Universitarie de France, 1961).

Piaget, J., *Play dreams and imitation in childhood* (New York: Norton, 1962), (La formation du symbole, 1945).

Piaget, J., *The origins of intelligence in children* (New York: Norton, 1963) (La naissance de l'intelligence chez l'enfant, 1936).

Piaget, J., and Inhelder, B., *The child's conception of space* (London: Routledge, 1963) (La representation de l'espace chez l'enfant, 1948).

Piaget, J., and Lambercier, M., Recherches sur le developpement des perceptions, XII, le comparaison des grandeurs projectives chez l'enfant et chez l'adulte, *Arch. de Psychol.*, Geneva, 1951, 33, 31-130.

Piaget, J., and Lambercier, M., Recherches sur le developpement des perceptions, XXIX, grandeurs projectives et grandeurs reeles avec etalon eloigne, *Arch. de Psychol.*, Geneva, 1956, 35, 247-280.

Piaget, J., Lambercier, M., Bosch, E., and von Albertini, B., Recherches sur le developpement des perceptions, I. introduction a l'etude des perceptions chez l'enfant et analyse d'une illusion relative a la perception visuelle des cercles concentriques (Delboeuf), *Arch. de Psychol.*, Geneva, 1942, 29, 1-107.

Piaget, J., and Morf, A., Les isomorphismes partiels entre les structures logiques et les structures perceptives. In J. S. Bruner, F. Bresson, A. Morf and J. Piaget, *Logique et perception: Etudes d'epistemologie genetique*, Vol. 6 (Paris: Presses Universitaire de France, 1958), pp. 49-116.

Piaget, J., and von Albertini, B., Recherches sur le developpement des perceptions, XI, l'illusion de Muller-Lyer, *Arch. de Psychol.*, Geneva, 1950, 331-348.

Piaget, J., and von Albertini, B., Recherches sur le developpement des perceptions, XIX, observations sur la perception des bonnes formes chez l'enfant par actualization des lignes virtuelles, *Arch. de Psychol.*, Geneva, 1954, 34, 203-243.

Piaget, J., Vingh-Bang, and Matalon, B., Note on the law of the temporal maximum of some optico-geometric illusions, *Amer. J. Psychol.*, 1958, 71, 277-282.

Robinson, H. B., An experimental examination of the size-weight illusion in young children, *Child Develpm.*, 1964, 35(1), 91-107.

Stein, J., The growth of sensorimotor integration and behavior, as reported in *MR/Mental Retardation*, 2(5), 308.

Vernon, M., *The psychology of perception* (Baltimore: Penguin, 1962).

Vurpillot, E., Piaget's law of relative centration, *Acta Psychol.*, 1959, 16, 403-430.

Wohlwill, J., Developmental studies of perception, *Psychol. Bull.*, 1960, 57, 249-288.

Wohlwill, J., From perception to inference: A dimension of cognitive development. In W. Kessen and C. Kuhlman (Editors), "Thought in the Young Child," *Monogr. Soc. Res. Child Develpm.*, 1962, 27 (2), 87-104.

Wolff, Peter, The developmental psychologies of Jean Piaget and psychoanalysis, *Psychol. Issues*, 1960, 11(1), 1-181.

Wolinsky, G., Piaget and the psychology of thought: Some implications for teaching the retarded, *Amer. J. ment. Def.*, 1962, 67(2), 250-256.

Woodward, M., The behavior of idiots interpreted by Piaget's theory of sensory-motor development, *Brit. J. Educ. Psychol.*, 1959, 29, 60-71.

Woodward, M., Concepts of number in the mentally retarded studied by Piaget's method, *J. Child Psychol. Psychiat.*, 1961, 2, 249-259.

Woodward, M., Concepts of space in the mentally subnormal studied by Piaget's method, *Brit. J. soc. clin. Psychol.*, 1962a, 1, 25-37.

Woodward, M., The application of Piaget's theory to the training of the subnormal, *J. ment. Subnorm.*, June 1962b, 17-28 (reprint).

37 WHAT IS "STRUCTURED"?

Angie Nall

A cartoon in a newspaper depicted a doctor talking to a woman patient saying, "Madam, I refuse to accept the diagnosis as given by your bridge club." We can laugh over the absurdity of a group of women around a bridge table having the audacity to attempt to correctly diagnose a fellow-member's physical ills. It is surprising, however, how we can each relate many instances where a child's school or behavior difficulties are diagnosed and treatment is recommended by a group of parents, friends, or relatives over a cup of coffee or perhaps a bridge table. Many children have suffered educationally, emotionally, socially, or even physically because of these sincere but inept decisions.

One might think help to the parents concerning the educational difficulties of children would come from the schools. One must realize, however, that schools are teaching institutions, and the teachers are not trained diagnosticians. They can and do tell the parents why their children do not do their school work. They say that the child does not pay attention; that he is interested in watching his hands move or what other children are doing, instead of finishing his own work; that he is immature, that he is easily upset; that he can do the work one day but not the next; or that he cannot read (or write or spell). They might venture an opinion as to the cause of these difficulties; but, since they are not diagnosticians, they cannot know.

After talking with the school personnel, the next step usually on the part of the parents is to take their child to a doctor. This is the wisest thing to do. There should be a thorough, a very thorough, physical check-up to see if the child has difficulty in seeing or hearing or has any other physical malfunctions. For example, the child with a low metabolic rate performs at

Reprinted from unpublished manuscript, Beaumont Remedial Clinic, Beaumont, Texas. By permission of the author.

a much lower level than his intelligence would indicate, is tired, fussy, and disinterested in school work. Correction of this difficulty would make it easier for the child to concentrate, attack his work, apply himself without tiring so easily, and even to think more clearly. There are causes of reading disability, however, that do not come within the scope of the average physician.

The next step for those parents fortunate enough to have the facilities is a visit to the child psychologist. It is here that many other problems are diagnosed and corrected. The child is helped to make those necessary social and emotional adjustments for happy living in school and home, and the parents are helped to better understand and meet the needs of the child. There are some children, however, who seem to have personality difficulties but who do not respond positively to the therapy and recommendations of the psychologist. These children seem to feel rejected, insecure, jealous, inferior, negative, or rebellious. These feelings are often evidenced by inability to get along in the home or with large groups of children, and inability to do successful school work. Many hours of therapy with the psychologist, total cooperation on the part of the parents and school personnel, and desire on the part of the child to improve do not seem to be able to produce the desired results. Further diagnosis is then indicated to establish whether other disabilities might be the cause of these difficulties.

It has been estimated that one out of twenty school children has a severe educational problem. Many of these problems are correctable. Take a child with normal or superior intelligence, who is in this group because of a reading disability caused by a difficulty in the area of associative learning, visual or auditory perception, visual or auditory memory, concept formation or language development, and you will probably find a child who feels insecure, jealous, rejected, inferior, negative, or rebellious. Here is a child with a disability which has not been recognized, who tried hard until he gave up, who has been blamed and who blamed himself for acting in a way he could not help.

Remedial and Perceptual Development Clinics, as well as educators, doctors, and the general public, are now beginning to recognize these children with Brain Dysfunction Syndrome. This recognition makes it possible, but *only* with special training, for these children to function in those necessary areas of reading, writing, and spelling. This disability may be more understandable to most of us if we compare it with the inability to sing.

There are some people who can't carry a tune. This fact doesn't bother them or anyone else, unless there is a particular reason that singing in tune is mandatory. Few of these people sing in choirs, but they do not feel inferior because they don't. In fact, most people think it is funny that they "can't carry a tune in a bushel-basket." The minister from the pulpit often tells them jokingly to "make a joyful noise unto the Lord."

The reason they can't sing is because they cannot transfer messages from one particular area of the brain to another specific area. In other words, they have minimal brain dysfunction. Now suppose these people, who cannot carry a tune alone, had to stand up in front of their friends and acquaintances each day and sing a solo, knowing that a person, who was an excellent singer, was there to catch each mistake, correct them in front of the group, perhaps fuss at them and treat them as if they were "dumb," because they made the same errors over and over or didn't do what to them was an impossibility. What kind of personality difficulties would these people develop? Suppose these people, who can't sing had to sing on the twelfth grade level before they could graduate from High School. There would be many of them who would "fail" unless they had special training. They would no longer laugh at themselves nor would people laugh with them. They would feel different, inadequate, inferior, frustrated, rebellious, or perhaps would have given up trying to compete and would have found satisfaction in a fantasy world of their own.

The situation of the individual who cannot read, because of Brain Dysfunction Syndrome, is very much like that of the person described who cannot sing. One difference is in the common concept that some people cannot sing, but everyone can read if he has good intelligence and tries hard enough. How grossly in error this concept is! It is an established fact among authorities in the field that language functions, such as reading, writing, spelling and speech, are controlled by specific parts of the brain which are connected by association areas. Any difficulty in either a localized center or in the association areas can cause the person to have trouble. This difficulty can be overcome by specific training, comparable, somewhat, to the training given the post-polio patient in helping him to learn to walk again. It is a long and tedious job at times, and much patience needs to be used by all concerned. Understanding that pathways in the brain are being established or strengthened is imperative rather than thinking that the person is "just learning to read."

As one doctor described the situation, "If the telephone wires are down between towns A and B, and you wish to make a phone call between these two towns, you could phone from Town A to Town C and then to Town B." This procedure is analogous to the techniques employed in the training of the child who has lesions in the localized areas of the brain which cause severe difficulty in reading, writing, spelling and/or speech development. This is why the training must be individual, using special techniques, until the ability to make contact between the different areas of the brain is established. For example, the child needs to be able to perceive what is seen, to be able to describe what he sees, and to get meaning out of it. Some children need to hear what is said, get meaning from it, and remember it long enough to be able to follow the directions. It is understandable with the need for such special individualized training, many of our public schools cannot provide adequately for these children.

Difficulties of a neurological nature can be determined by testing. This is not a quick process but takes three or four days of intensive testing done in the neurological, psychological, physical, and educational fields. Many of us do not have such diagnostic facilities available, so we do the next best thing. We read all we can about the child with severe learning difficulties. We go to hear every speaker on the subject. We take notes. We discuss it with our spouses, our neighbors or anyone who will listen. And often we do not really understand what is said to the point that we can markedly improve the lot of our child.

Words get in our way, words that are easy to hear, to remember and even to repeat. To translate them into action is another problem. Take, for example, the term "structured." Every authority says in speeches or in writings that children with severe learning difficulty need to live in a structured environment, that they need structured tasks, that their lives should be structured. We'd be glad to give them all these structured things if only we really understood what "structured" means in terms of everyday living.

If you build a house, you end with a structure. It has limits. It is the same each time you see it. The kitchen never moves from where it is. The living room is in the same position in relation to the bedroom. It is permanent. You might remodel, but then your remodeled structure is always the same, never changing back to the way it was before remodeling. In order to remodel, you plan and permanently reconstruct. You don't do it in a wishy-washy way. It is well thought out and carried through as planned.

So it is with a structured life of a child. It is well-planned in advance and kept to the original plan unless actually remodeled. A case of remodeling would be the plan for life while school is in session compared to that for life when school is out for the summer. The structure planned, however, would stand, so that it can be depended upon. For example, the child would get up at a certain time, eat at a specified time, play at a certain hour, rest at certain hours and go to bed at a certain hour. This structure of his life can be written down and placed where he can consult it. It cannot be changed at anyone's whim any more than the walls of your home can.

Do not misunderstand and think that a child must do the same things every day of his life in exactly the same way. The structure could call for bedtime at eight o'clock on weekdays and nine o'clock on weekends, if so desired. The structure would not call, however, for spending the night at friends' homes or having company over at your house which would necessitate changing the regular routine. The structured life could call for free play after school during which time he has a choice *within specified limits* of what he would want to do. This structure does not mean, however, that all of a sudden something is thrown at him to do or not do. For example, the yard is littered with paper, twigs and the like. The parents are busy and the child has little to do, so there seems no harm in asking the child to clean the yard. It certainly is not a difficult or long task. It just happens to be given to him in his "free choice" time. His reaction could easily make him argue, become rebellious or frustrated, or could possibly make him retreat into a life of fantasy which is more pleasing than the one he has to face.

Often children do their own structuring. In fact, many times structuring is a bone of contention between parents and child. The child will do the same thing every day in the same way. Frankly, it is not the way we would do it. In fact, it is not always the logical way to do it.

Take, for example, a group of boys in a boarding situation who were fixing their lunches to take to school. On the table were arranged the sacks, bread, sandwich fillings, sandwich wrapping, candy, cookies, fruit and chips all in this order. The logical thing to do was for the first boy in line to start with the paper sack, fixing the sandwich to put in the sack, and then adding the "extras" as he wished. If the first day the fixing of lunches had been structured in that manner, all would have been well. Since it was not, the boys structured it themselves, fixing all the things they wished to take, putting them in a pile and then reaching for the paper sack to put it all in. This meant frequent reaching over the person to the right or left, and confusion often resulted. A housemother, trying to help and being absolutely logical from an adult point of view, tried to get these boys to fix their lunch in the logical order. But remember, these boys had already structured their task. To restructure it would take sitting down at an unrushed time, talking through the situation, getting them to see the value of changing and then getting their agreement to change. Merely explaining at the moment and telling them to "do it this way" only resulted in arguments and rebellion.

This same type of experience could be described by parent after parent. The child starts putting on his socks and shoes before he puts on his pants, and it is a major project to get him to change and put his pants on first. The child takes forever to get home from school, for he has to stop and browse through everyone's trash pile on the way. We correct him and correct him, but it seems to do no good. It just happens in both cases that the child has structured his own situation before we got around to helping him do it in a better way. To change something already structured to the child is a remodeling job. Remember to plan and then to rebuild. It isn't done in a day.

One of the most important items in a structured environment for the child is the parents. They should structure themselves. They must be dependable all of the time. If they say, "Don't slam the door," they mean it on Saturday as well as they did on Monday. If they don't, they should have said, "Don't slam the door *this time*." They should be dependable in all management and discipline. They must mean what they say, good or bad. They should be where they say they are going to be and be there when they say they will be. If not, the child should be notified by phone or neighbor. The parents are the child's Rock of Gibraltar. They should be "solid" for the child to be able to cling to. An undependable platform of dirt that crumbles at unexpected times and cannot be depended upon every time to give support would make anyone who stood upon it feel insecure. With the children who have learning difficulties, such insecurity is a catastrophe.

It is the dangling-in-the-air feeling that is so common to these children that makes them so hard to live with. They cannot make choices. Choices of too big a scope only frustrate them. Not knowing their limits frustrates them. This is the reason for the Structured Living. This goes into all areas of the child's life: structured tasks, structured discipline, structured play. Just remember the house you live in with its plan, its wall which makes its limits, and its dependability. So structure your child's life. The results are worth the effort.

SECTION C: Remediation of School Learning Disabilities

38   DIAGNOSIS AND TREATMENT
OF SPELLING DIFFICULTIES

Leo J. Brueckner and Guy L. Bond

CASE-STUDY DIAGNOSTIC PROCEDURES

When dealing with cases of serious spelling disability, procedures that are essentially clinical in nature must be utilized. They range from the use of systematic, standardized techniques to the application of informal observational analytical procedures.

THE ADMINISTRATION OF STANDARDIZED SPELLING DIAGNOSTIC TESTS. Standardized methods of studying spelling disabilities are utilized in certain diagnostic tests. The Gates-Russell Spelling Diagnostic Tests are the best-known standardized diagnostic tests available. They include the following series of nine tests:

(1) Spelling words orally (power test).
(2) Word pronunciation (reading and speech).
(3) Giving letters for sounds (oral).
(4) Spelling two syllables (oral).
(5) Spelling two syllables (oral).
(6) Word reversals (oral).
(7) Spelling attack (securing evidence as to usual methods of study).
(8) Auditory discrimination (hearing).
(9) Visual, auditory, kinesthetic, and combined study methods (comparison of effectiveness).

The nature of the contents of the first eight tests is identified by the titles. Standardized materials and procedures are provided in each case. Test 9 of the Gates-Russell Spelling Diagnostic Test series applies a simple

Reprinted from *The Diagnosis and Treatment of Learning Difficulties* (New York: Appleton-Century-Crofts, 1955), pp. 365-380. By permission of the publisher.

procedure for measuring the effectiveness of four different methods of studying words: the visual, the auditory, the kinesthetic, and a combined plan. The pupil studies four groups of three words of equal difficulty, one group by each method as carefully described by the teacher. The relative effectiveness of the four methods is determined by comparing the results of studying words by the four different methods. The visual method emphasizes "looking" at the word and studying it; the auditory method involves "hearing" the word and "spelling it letter by letter as the teacher spells it"; the kinesthetic method "writing" the word, getting the "feel" of it, writing it with eyes closed; the combined method involves elements of the visual, auditory, and kinesthetic methods. As the pupil studies the words, the teacher should note such factors as intelligence of approach, number of trials, effort made, hesitations, reading difficulties, attitude toward each method, and evidences of success in using the method. With the help of the teacher, the pupil in the remedial program should make subsequent use of these data to master an effective method of study.

Russell has shown that poor spellers are unable to make a varied or analytic approach to new words. Their methods are characterized by (1) incorrect syllabication and unsystematic division into word units, (2) spelling letter by letter, (3) spelling by small phonic elements, and (4) lack of syllabic analysis or syllabication. All of these deficiencies can be corrected by systematic instruction.

Performance on each of the nine diagnostic tests is evaluated in terms of grade scores and by recording brief descriptions of pupil reactions and responses. Details of scoring are given in the manual for the test.

The above data are supplemented by scores on standard tests of intelligence, spelling, silent and oral reading, vocabulary, memory of numbers and words, handwriting, vision, hearing loss, handedness, eyedness, and speech, as may be deemed necessary by the examiner. Figure 45-1 is an illustrative summary of the Gates-Russell test results.

The synthesis of the comprehensive information compiled by this many-sided testing program leads to the diagnosis of the nature of the spelling disability and to the identification of the causes most likely to be at the root of the difficulty. A remedial program can then be planned and undertaken.

AN ILLUSTRATIVE DIAGNOSIS IN SPELLING.   A summary of test results for a third-grade boy appears in figure 38-1. His grade scores on both written and oral spelling were more than a year below his actual grade level, 3.7. His reading scores, both silent and oral, were approximately one year below normal. According to test 6, he had serious deficiencies indicated by reversals and numerous spelling errors. His intelligence quotient of 119 indicated that he should be doing superior work.

He rated high on test 3, giving letters for letter sounds, and on test 8,

Name.. Age ..10.. I.Q. ..119.. Grade ..3.7..........

Examiner.. School .... Date....................

Language parents speak (a) to one another ...*English*............ (b) to children ..*English*.....................

To the Examiner:

This booklet contains tests fully described in Gates and Russell, *Diagnostic and Remedial Spelling Manual* (Bureau of Publications, Teachers College). The subject and the examiner must both be provided with booklets. They should exchange them for certain tests so that the written records of both subject and examiner may be contained in one booklet.

TEST	RAW SCORE	GRADE SCORE
1. Spelling Words Orally	7	2.4
2. Word Pronunciation	36	2.8
3. Giving Letters for Letter Sounds	9.7	5.5
4. Spelling One Syllable	6	3.0
5. Spelling Two Syllables	2	2.1
6. Word Reversals	17 errors	2.5
7. Spelling Attack		Poor
8. Auditory Discrimination		Excellent
9. Visual, Auditory, Kinaesthetic and Combined Study Methods		Poor

SUPPLEMENTARY DIAGNOSIS

Grade Score

1. Standard Test—Written Spelling ....2.2....

2. Standard Test—Silent Reading ....2.8....

3. Standard Test—Oral Reading ....2.7....

4. Vocabulary Test ....4.8....

5. Memory for Numbers ....*Ex*....

6. Memory for Words ....*Ex*....

7. Handwriting—Speed....*70*........letters per minute.

8. Handwriting—Quality....*40-50*....

9. Vision Test Comments: *Betts tests:*

   Failed on 6 tests; doubtful on 3;
   passed 6. Nearsighted; poor fusion; lateral imbalance

10. Hearing Loss. Left..*none*..%, Right..*none*..%.

11. Handedness. Comments: *Right*

12. Eyedness. Comments: *Right*

13. Speech. Comments: *Good*

14. Forming of Derivatives. Comments:

15. Use of Homonyms. Comments:

BUREAU OF PUBLICATIONS, TEACHERS COLLEGE
COLUMBIA UNIVERSITY, NEW YORK
Copyright, 1937, by Teachers College
4M-L-7-48
Printed in U.S.A.

FIGURE 38-1   Gates-Russell spelling diagnosis tests.

auditory discrimination. An examination of his written work showed that most of his misspellings were approximately correct phonetically. Evidently auditory abilities were not at the root of his spelling difficulties.

On the Betts telebinocular test he failed on six of the subtests and was rated doubtful on three others. He failed on both near-point and far-point fusion tests and on tests of refraction including nearsightedness and astigmatism for both eyes at 80 inches and at infinite distance; and was rated doubtful on lateral imbalance (tendency for eyes to deviate inward and outward from their normal position) and other ametropia tests. Clearly, this boy had definite visual difficulties that likely were causally related to his spelling problems and also his reading disability.

The first step in an improvement program in this case should be a medical examination and a fitting of glasses. Subsequent steps in improvement should be planned in light of the corrections of vision that prove to be possible and in light of his spelling needs as indicated by the spelling diagnosis. The mere correction of his visual difficulties will in no way correct the faulty approaches to spelling which he has established. The correction in vision will make success in improving his spelling more likely.

A SUGGESTED INFORMAL DIAGNOSTIC APPROACH. A less formal diagnostic program than the Gates-Russell tests was developed by Watson (1935). It can be utilized in diagnostic study by any interested teacher. The essential elements of Watson's procedure are as follows:

(1) Select a list of 30 to 50 words of average difficulty on some such basis as the frequency with which they are misspelled in written work, the kinds of errors usually made in spelling or pronouncing them, or the spelling rules that are applied in spelling them. The informal test described earlier[1] illustrates the approach.

(2) Administer the words as a list test to the class.

(3) Score the test papers. Select the four or five poorest papers for further analysis. Begin with the pupil whose score was lowest.

(4) Have the pupil define the words he misspelled. Discard all words he cannot define, indicating that he does not know their meaning.

(5) Then have the pupil spell the remaining words orally one at a time. Keep an exact written record of the spelling. Observe also spelling ryhthm, syllabication, and phonic quality of every syllable.

(6) Compare the original spelling with the oral spelling to see if the errors made are the same or if there are specific new or unique spellings.

(7) Have the pupil pronounce the words in the test. Note difficulties in speech, phonics, syllabication, etc.

(8) Make a quick analysis of the spelling errors made, classifying them

[1] See The diagnosis and treatment of learning difficulties (New York: Appleton-Century-Crofts, 1955), p. 363.

according to major categories such as those given earlier,[2] or according to the point of view from which the list of words was prepared; for instance, according to rules not known, or confusions of phonetic sounds. Note also lapses and slips.

(9) Draw conclusions as to the nature of the pupil's spelling difficulties. If possible, estimate the quality of his method of attack in studying new words in daily lessons.

On the basis of this and other available related information, steps to be taken to improve the pupil's spelling can be planned.

INFORMAL USES OF OTHER DIAGNOSTIC PROCEDURES BY TEACHERS. The teacher should not hesitate to apply informally, in the course of regular instruction, analytical diagnostic procedures similar to those applied systematically in the Gates-Russell Test.

Below are given illustrative uses of the various methods of case study and individual diagnosis[3] which the teacher can use to good advantage in the diagnosis of spelling difficulties.

A. Analysis of Written Work, Including Test Papers
    (1) Legibility of handwriting.
    (2) Defects in letter forms, spacing, alignment, size.
    (3) Classification of errors in written work, letters, tests, etc.
    (4) Range of vocabulary used.
    (5) Evidence of lack of knowledge of conventions and rules.

B. Analysis of Oral Responses
    (1) Comparison of errors in oral and written spelling.
    (2) Pronunciation of words spelled incorrectly.
    (3) Articulation and enunciation.
    (4) Slovenliness of speech.
    (5) Dialect and colloquial forms of speech.
    (6) Way of spelling words orally.
        (a) Spells words as units.
        (b) Spells letter by letter.
        (c) Spells by digraphs.
        (d) Spells by syllables.
    (7) Rhythmic pattern in oral spelling.
    (8) Blending ability.
    (9) Giving letters for sounds or sounds for letters.
  (10) Technics of word analysis used.
  (11) Quality and errors made in oral reading.
  (12) Oral responses on tests of word analysis.

[2] *Ibid.*, p. 358.
[3] *Ibid.*, chapter 4.

(13) Analysis of pupil comments as he states orally his thought processes while studying new words.

C. Interview with Pupil and Others
    (1) Questioning pupil about methods of study.
    (2) Questioning pupil about spelling rules.
    (3) Questioning pupil about errors in conventions.
    (4) Securing evidence as to attitude toward spelling.

D. Questionnaire
    (1) Applying check-list of methods of study.
    (2) Having pupil rank spelling according to interest.
    (3) Surveying use of written language.

E. Free Observation in Course of Daily Work
    (1) Securing evidence as to attitudes toward spelling.
    (2) Evidence of improvement in the study of new words.
    (3) Observing extent of use of dictionary.
    (4) Extent of error in regular written work.
    (5) Study habits and methods of work.
    (6) Social acceptability of learner.
    (7) Evidences of emotional and social maladjustment.
    (8) Evidences of possible physical handicaps.

F. Controlled Observation of Work on Set Tasks
    (1) Looking up the meanings of given words in dictionary.
    (2) Giving pronunciation of words in dictionary.
    (3) Writing plural forms and derivatives of given words.
    (4) Observing responses on informal tests.
    (5) Observing methods of studying selected words.
    (6) Estimating pupil success when using a variety of methods of studying selected words.

G. Analysis of Available Records
    (1) Records of scores on tests in reading, spelling, language, handwriting.
    (2) School history.
    (3) Health data; physiological deficiencies and defects, especially vision, loss of hearing, and motor coordination.
    (4) Sociological data.
    (5) Anecdotal records.

The brief descriptions below, based on informal observations of study habits used by six fifth-grade children when studying a list of 50 words, show how they varied and how unintelligent some of the learning procedures were:

Pupil 1   Copied the first word in the list and then rewrote it five times; then he did the same for the second word; and so on. He completed less than half of the words in the test during the study period. (Poor method.)

Pupil 2   Looked at the first word, closed his eyes and whispered the letters, and checked his spelling by looking at the word; then proceeded to the next word. (Fairly good method.)

Pupil 3   Looked at the first word, looked up, whispered the letters, and traced them in the air using large sweeping arm movements; then he wrote the word on his paper; he did this for all words studied. (Good method.)

Pupil 4   Dreams, looked at whole list in a random way; no whispering; no writing; no evidence that he had a systematic study procedure of any kind. (A poor speller and a typical complex disability case.)

Pupil 5   First skimmed the list of words, checking those about which she was uncertain; studied the words checked by using the "look, study, spell orally, check, write, check" method, a systematic study procedure. (Excellent speller.)

Pupil 6   Copied a word letter by letter, then with his pencil traced slowly the word he had written five or six times, whispering the letters as he traced them; no syllabication; he did the same for six other words he copied. (A low learning index.)

It obviously is necessary to attempt to appraise the effectiveness of the methods of study used by poor spellers and also to teach poor spellers how to study words. The teacher should first observe the pupil's methods of studying words either during the usual spelling lesson, or preferably under closer observation when he is studying a selected group of misspelled words. To evaluate the effectiveness of his study methods, the teacher then should test to see how many of the words he has learned to spell. On the basis of the observations and test results, the steps to bring about an improvement should then be planned.

THE TREATMENT OF SPELLING DIFFICULTIES

FACTORS ASSOCIATED WITH LOW SPELLING ACCOMPLISHMENT.   The major factors associated with low spelling accomplishment, which have been alluded to frequently in the preceding pages, may be summarized as follows:

(1) Poor study habits. Many pupils do not acquire effective methods of learning to spell, perhaps in large part due to inadequacies of instruction in spelling and written composition.

(2) Lack of interest and the presence of undesirable attitudes.

(3) Weakness in essential techniques, such as phonics, word analysis, and syllabication.

(4) Faulty speech habits, particularly in pronunciation.
(5) Slow, illegible handwriting.
(6) Visual defects and limitations.
(7) Inferior auditory discrimination.
(8) Low level of intelligence.

Some of these factors, vision, for example, can be corrected to a considerable extent. A skillful teacher can alleviate all of them by adapting the instructional program and methods of teaching to the needs and requirements of individual pupils. Usually a combination of several of these factors is contributory in a particular case. The approach to corrective treatment should therefore be multiple as well as directed to the correction of special disabilities.

The following references contain comprehensive discussions of factors associated with spelling disability. They should be consulted for details by anyone interested:

James A. Fitzgerald, *The teaching of spelling* (Milwaukee: Bruce, 1951).
A. I. Gates, *The psychology of reading and spelling with special reference to disability*, Contributions to Education No. 129 (New York: Bureau of Publications, Teachers College, Columbia University, 1922).
David H. Russell, *Characteristics of Good and Poor Spellers*, Contributions to Education No. 727 (New York: Bureau of Publications, Teachers College, Columbia University, 1937).
George Spache, Spelling disability correlates I—Factors probably causal in spelling disability, *J. Educ. Res.*, April, 1941, 34, 561-587.
George Spache, Spelling disability correlates II—Factors that may be related to spelling disability, *J. Educ. Res.*, October, 1941, 35, 119-137.
Alice E. Watson, *Experimental studies in the psychology and pedagogy of spelling*, Contributions to Education No. 638 (New York: Bureau of Publications, Teachers College, Columbia University, 1935).

The Gates-Russell Diagnostic and Remedial Spelling Manual contains a helpful discussion of the causes of spelling disability, case studies, and specific suggestions for remedial work in spelling.

In this section we shall deal primarily with general procedures for improving spelling rather than with specifics applied to special problems.

FACTORS RELATED TO THE EFFICIENCY OF METHODS OF STUDY. Evidence revealed by research about the methods that contribute to learning to spell may be summarized as follows:

(1) A pretest should reveal to the pupil the words he does not know how to spell.

(2) The pupil should focus his attention on the words or parts of words that he is unable to spell.

(3) In presenting words, visualization should be the predominant procedure. Correct pronunciation and syllabication of words should be emphasized. The writing of the word in all cases should be included in word study.

(4) Pupils should be encouraged to use any form or combination of types of imagery that will assist them to learn to spell, including visual, auditory, and kinesthetic imagery. It is very doubtful if there are dominant specific imagery types which can be the basis for deciding on methods of learning for all individuals.

(5) Sensory impression should be accompanied by attempts to recall the spelling of words as an aid to temporary retention at the time of initial learning. Overlearning also is desirable.

(6) Subsequently, distributed practice is necessary to insure retention of words learned, particularly in the case of slow learners. The amount and distribution of review needed will vary from learner to learner.

(7) Tests by which the pupil can measure his progress are essential, since awareness of improvement is a valuable method of motivation.

There is no evidence as to which of a variety of particular study procedures is the most effective. Undoubtedly, because of individual differences among learners, no one plan will be equally effective for them all. A general approach to learning to spell such as the following, suitable for grades above the primary level, incorporates to a considerable extent the essentials of the seven principles listed above:

Study Guide to Spelling (Grades 4-8)

(1) Look up in the dictionary the meaning, pronunciation, and syllabication of each unfamiliar word to be studied.

(2) Say the word as directed by the dictionary, first as a whole, then slowly several times syllable by syllable.

(3) Spell the word orally without looking at it; then check your oral spelling by referring to the printed word.

(4) Write the word, saying the syllables as you write. Do not say the letters. Check the written word.

(5) Repeat step 4 about three times for each new word.

(6) When reviewing difficult words, apply steps 1 to 4 as may be necessary.

With disability cases, the approach to the problem of improving study habits should be individual. In the early stages, close supervision of the pupil's work is necessary. The basis of the steps in the guide to study outlined above should be carefully explained to the learner. They should be demonstrated to him by the teacher. Under sympathetic guidance he should then try to apply them to the study of words he is learning to spell. The teacher should make every effort to secure the wholehearted cooperation of the individual. Evidence of success in applying the steps in the guide to learning is sure to arouse his interest and motivate his efforts to improve his spelling. It should not be expected that all learners will eventually use the same pattern of study habits. Intelligent adaptation within the general framework of the above principles should be permitted. Fernald (1943) has stressed the value of kinesthetic imagery in the treatment of spelling disability.

THE TEACHING OF SPELLING RULES. The teaching of a few important spelling rules should be done inductively, following a series of steps somewhat as follows:

(1) Select a particular rule to be taught. Teach a single rule at a time.
(2) Secure a list of words exemplifying the rule. Develop the rule through the study of words that it covers.
(3) Lead the pupils to discover the underlying generalization by discussing with them the characteristics of the words in the list. If possible, the pupils actually should formulate the rule. Help them to sharpen and clarify it.
(4) Have the pupils use and apply the rule immediately.
(5) If necessary, show how the rule in some cases does not apply, but stress its positive values.
(6) Review the rule systematically on succeeding days. Emphasize its use, and do not require the pupils to memorize a formalized statement.

The rules of capitalization, the writing of possessives and contractions, and other conventions should also be taught inductively in a similar manner.

LACK OF INTEREST AND THE PRESENCE OF UNFAVORABLE ATTITUDES. These undesirable types of behavior patterns are undoubtedly due in large part to an instructional program that is highly formal and that fails to take into consideration the interests and needs of the learners. Instruction in spelling in such cases is focused on the spelling of lists of words rather than on helping children to spell the words they need to use in their experiences. The words being studied also may be too difficult for the learner. Lacking success in spelling because of poor study habits, pupils often become discouraged and fail to make the effort necessary to learn to spell.

Three essential steps to bring about an improvement are:

(1) Provide a rich, vital series of learning experiences in which social pressure will make the learner increasingly aware of the necessity of being able to spell correctly.

(2) Make a study of the characteristics of individual learners to determine the possible factors that may have caused them to develop a bad attitude toward spelling.

(3) Make every effort to adjust the work of the pupil to his needs, requirements, and level of development. Especially try to help him to acquire efficient ways of learning to spell.

The reader should consult the many excellent books on the teaching of spelling for details as to curriculum and instruction.

OVERCOMING WEAKNESSES IN WORD ANALYSIS INCLUDING PHONICS AND SYLLABICATION. The procedures for improving knowledge, skills, and abilities in word analysis should be based on those that are used in reading, with the added stipulation that writing must be an integral part of the learning activity.

In some spelling cases, weakness in word analysis may be due to lack of knowledge of letter sounds, inability to blend sounds, and other faults revealed by reading diagnosis. Treatment should begin with procedures for overcoming these reading deficiencies, and then be carried over into the field of oral and written spelling.[4]

In other spelling cases, weakness in using word elements may not be associated with reading but more specifically with inability to recall what the word looks like, how it is pronounced, and how the elements are spelled. There is a vast difference between recognizing the elements within a written word in reading and recalling those elements for spelling. In such cases, a direct attack on the spelling difficulty, as shown by the diagnosis, is indicated.

For poor spellers, emphasis should be placed on the spelling of word elements rather than practice in reading them. First, the learner should learn to associate sounds of single letters and their written symbols, and then proceed to the study and writing of combinations of letters and phonograms. Each lesson should include the correction of the pupil's written work and a discussion of phonetic variants. Similar lessons should next deal with the spelling of common stems, prefixes, and suffixes. The learner thus gradually will become familiar with the spelling of a large number of useful word elements. Next he should study their use in selected groups of common words containing certain letters, phonograms, or other word elements, and practice writing the words. Every effort should be made to aid recall by using visual, auditory, and kinesthetic imagery to strengthen sensory impressions.

Games and devices similar to those commonly used to create interest

[4] *Ibid.*, pp. 375-376.

in remedial reading should be freely used in remedial work in spelling. Stress should be placed on correct spelling, not on reading correctly.

Spelling Games

(1) Anagrams. Pupils rearrange a disarranged group of letters as a word.

(2) Naming the words. The teacher says, "What is one word in the lesson?" A pupil names one, spells it, then pronounces another word. The next pupil spells it and so on until all of the words have been given and spelled.

(3) "Spelling and guessing." A pupil writes a word from the spelling lesson, for instance, *apple*, on a slip of paper and places it on the teacher's desk. Then he calls on some pupil to spell it. This child says, "Is it h-o-r-s-e?" "No, it is not horse." The next child called on says, "Is it a-p-p-l-e?" "Yes, it is apple." Then that child becomes "it," and the game continues.

(4) "Naming letters." Teacher writes a word from the spelling lesson on the blackboard. The children notice the order of the letters in the word carefully. Then they shut their eyes. The teacher passes about the room and touches children, who spell the word aloud with eyes closed.

(5) "Rhyming game." Children give and spell a word that rhymes with a word pronounced by the teacher or some pupil.

(6) "Picture game." Children spell names of objects in a picture.

(7) "Relays." Two teams are selected. A word family is chosen, such as *ate*. The children one by one from each team hurry to the blackboard and write a word in the family. The side with the most words and the fewest spelling errors wins.

Exercises such as the following, similar to some of those given for reading described elsewhere[5] and functional in nature, are especially useful in teaching word-analysis techniques required in spelling.

Special Exercises in Word Analysis

(1) Word study involving initial letter sounds
   (a) Write lists of words that begin with the same initial letter sounds, such as *boy, bird, big; cat, come, cow; hat, horse, house.*

(2) Word study involving vowel sounds
   (a) Writing words that contain long vowel sounds, such as long *ā* in *late, came, fail, plane.*
   (b) Similar exercise for the long sounds of *e, i, o, u.*
   (c) Writing words that contain the short sound of *a,* as in *cat, cap, nap, camel, plan.*

[5] *Ibid.,* chapter 7.

(*d*) Similar exercise for the short sounds of *e, i, o, u*.

(3) Word study involving initial blends and phonograms

    (*a*) Writing words that start like *blue; stop; play; street; thread;* etc.

    (*b*) Writing words that start with the initial sounds of the words chosen: *this; shed, what,* etc.

(4) Word study involving word endings

    (*a*) Writing other words rhyming with words ending with longer-sound elements, such as *day, skate, peck, like,* etc.

    (*b*) Writing words with their variant endings, such as

	ed	ing	s
walk	___	___	___
plan	___	___	___
like	___	___	___
suffer	___	___	___

    (*c*) Writing comparative forms of words, such as:

	er	est
small	___	___
fast	___	___
big	___	___
large	___	___

    (*d*) Special exercises on the spelling of plurals, contractions, and possessive forms of words.

(5) Word study involving structural analysis

    (*a*) Writing compound words made from two lists of words:

A	B	compound word
sand	road	_____
under	man	_____
rail	thing	_____
some	stand	_____

    (*b*) Locating and writing root words:

        (1) When suffixes are present:

wonderful	___	workable	___
likeness	___	bigger	___

        (2) When prefixes are present:

unkind	___	indoor	___
relive	___	improve	___

        (3) When affixed elements are present:

unlikely	___	important	___
reworked	___	unwrapping	___

    (*c*) Drawing lines between syllables heard in a word:

below	___	decide	___	natural	___
danger	___	ornament	___	declaration	___

ALLEVIATING FAULTY SPEECH HABITS, PARTICULARLY INCORRECT PRONUNCIATION. It is obvious that misspelling often is due to the mispronunciation of words. In some sections of the country, dialects and local ways of speaking may lead to misspelling. In the same way, slovenly speech often leads to misspelling.

It is necessary that special attention be given to both the meaning and the correct pronunciation of all spelling words being studied, as described in the guide for studying words.[6] Language instruction must pay particular attention to pronunciation, syllabication, and word analysis. In cases of serious speech difficulty or defective speech, the corrective speech teacher can make a valuable contribution to the improvement of spelling.

Speech faults are closely associated in spelling with an excessive proportion of errors of omissions of sounded letters and syllables, additions of syllables, and nonphonetic additions and substitutions. These errors can be identified by tests of oral reading, mispronunciation tests, and by having the pupil pronounce the words misspelled in written spelling tests. Correction of speech faults will gradually reduce the proportion of these spelling errors.

IMPROVING SLOW, ILLEGIBLE HANDWRITING. Russell (1937) reported a small but significant difference in the quality of handwriting of good and poor spellers. Information about illegibilities and malformation of letters, the rate and quality of usual writing, and the analysis of defects in slant, spacing, and alignment, are especially valuable in the diagnosis and treatment of low spelling performance. The letters that contribute most frequently to illegibility are *a, d, e, u, r*, and *t*. Writing inaccuracies such as failure to close and complete such letters as *a, d, q*, and *g*, and failure to dot the letter *i* or to cross the letter *t* often cause pupils to write words incorrectly. Calling the pupil's attention directly to such specific eccentricities and their effects on the correctness and legibility of written speech usually will suffice for correction with older pupils. For younger children, direct handwriting practice to correct deficiencies may be required. It must be recognized that poor spellers frequently write poorly in order to cover up spelling inadequacies. For example, in writing the word, *receive*, the poor speller may make the *e* and *i* look alike, since he isn't sure which one comes first.

Manuscript writing may be substituted for cursive writing in an effort to overcome handwriting difficulties in cases where they are due to motor incoordination or lack of training. Manuscript writing is of particular value in dealing with spelling cases where disability is due to poor handwriting, inferior motor control, or marked loss of vision.

CONSIDERATION OF VISUAL DEFECTS AND LIMITATIONS. Russell reports that there was no significant difference on the whole in visual acuity, verti-

[6] *Ibid.*, p. 372.

cal and lateral imbalance, and ametropia for good and poor spellers. However, he emphasized the importance of checking the vision of poor spellers because faulty visual imagery may be an important factor in specific cases.

Whenever it appears evident that a pupil may not be learning to spell or read because of visual defects and limitations, corrective measures should be taken under competent medical guidance. The teacher can also make such adjustments as seating the pupil with poor vision nearer the blackboard, using books with enlarged type, emphasizing auditory imagery, and the like.

As was indicated above, the substitution of manuscript writing for cursive script is regarded as desirable in spelling cases due to marked deterioration of vision.

Eye movements of good spellers have fewer regressions, shorter time of fixation, and more regular fixations than those of poor spellers. These points should be borne in mind when teaching poor spellers how to "look at" words when studying them, as required in the suggested guide for study.

INFERIOR AUDITORY DISCRIMINATION. Russell (1937) found that there is a significant difference in auditory discrimination between good and poor spellers. Inferior auditory discrimination may be due either to loss of hearing, which can be alleviated by hearing aids, or to lack of training in sound perception. Inability to give sounds for letters or letters for sounds, failure to discriminate letter sounds, blending difficulties, and weakness in phonics are symptoms of this deficiency.

A simple test of auditory discrimination of sounds of letters is the following:

(1) Give the pupil a paper on which are given the pairs of words shown below:
(2) Have the pupil mark the word (starred) in each pair that you pronounce. Speak in a normal tone. The pupil should be seated with his back to the examiner at a distance of 6 to 10 feet.

Test of Auditory Discrimination of Sounds

war was*	far fair*	sad sand*	noon*none
night* sight	mind find*	think*thank	these there*
say*hay	chip*ship	black*block	better butter*

This test would not be suitable for a poor speller who is also poor in reading. A better one for him would be to say a list of word pairs, such as *which* and *witch*; *bin* and *bin*; *pig* and *big*; and so on, and have him tell which pairs are the same and which are different.

When inferior auditory discrimination is owing to lack of ear training, exercises similar to those used in reading should be used to train pupils to discriminate sounds, to identify sounds, and to give sounds. These exercises should be closely integrated with phonic training, pronunciation, and improvement of speech.

LEVEL OF INTELLIGENCE. As indicated earlier in this chapter, there is a positive but rather low correlation between intelligence and spelling. It is known that pupils of low intelligence are very likely to be inferior in spelling. However, a high level of intelligence does not guarantee a high level of spelling ability. In planning remedial work in spelling, adaptations should be made in all cases to the pupil's level of intelligence and language development, including adjustments of the number of words to be studied, instructional procedures used, and the rate of progress to be expected. Individual progress goals should be set up by which each learner can measure the progress he is making.

References

Brueckner, L. J., and Melby, E. O., *Diagnostic and remedial teaching* (Boston: Ginn, 1931), Chapter 10.

Child development and the curriculum, Thirty-eighth Yearbook, Part I, National Society for the Study of Education (Chicago: University of Chicago Press, 1939), Chapter 12.

Fernald, Grace M., *Remedial techniques in basic skill subjects* (New York: McGraw-Hill, 1943), Chapter 13.

Gates, A. I., and Russell, D. H., *Diagnostic and remedial manual*, Revied edition (New York: Bureau of Publications, Teachers College, Columbia University, 1940).

Hildreth, Gertrude, *Learning the three R's* (Minneapolis: Educational Publishers, 1947), Chapter 18.

Kay, Marjorie E., Effect of errors in pronunciation in spelling, *Elem. Eng. Rev.*, Vol. 7 (March, 1930), pp. 64-66.

King, Luella, *Learning and applying spelling rules in grades 3 to 8* (New York: Bureau of Publications, Teachers College, Columbia University, 1932).

Russell, D. H., *Characteristics of good and poor spellers* (New York: Bureau of Publications, Teachers College, Columbia University, 1937).

Spache, G., Spelling disability correlates, *J. Educ. Res.*, October, 1941, 35, 119-138.

Watson, Alice E., *Experimental studies in the psychology and pedagogy of spelling*, Contributions to Education No. 638 (New York: Bureau of Publications, Teachers College, Columbia University, 1935), pp. 47-53.

39 ARITHMETIC AND THE BRAIN-INJURED CHILD

Lotte Kaliski ~

This paper is based on my experience in teaching "exceptional children" in my schools for children with learning difficulties. The majority of these children have been diagnosed as brain-injured, with varying degrees of educational retardation. The age range is from 7 to 17 years.

To quote Dr. Archie Silver (Silver and Hagin, 1960): "Approximately 70 percent of children with reading disabilities do not have 'organic' signs in the sense of structural damage, but they do have neurological and perceptual problems." Moreover, 22 percent of the reading cases in Dr. Silver's study did show evidence of more specific organic defects. These findings confirm the contention that the brain-injured child and his learning problems have a place among the children with specific language disabilities.

COMMON FACTORS

What are some of the factors interfering with the learning capacity of the brain-injured child? The following symptoms can be found singly, or in varying combinations and degrees, in brain-injured children in a classroom situation:

(1) Fluctuating attention
(2) Perceptual disturbances—visual and/or auditory or kinesthetic, related to
(3) Figure-background confusion, i.e., difficulty or inability in differentiating the foreground from the background, as in

Reprinted from *Bulletin of the Orton Society*, Vol. XI (May, 1961) and *The Arithmetic Teacher*, Vol. 9, No. 5 (May, 1962), pp. 245-251. By permission of the author and publishers.

    (a) Picture identification and discrimination, especially of outline pictures

    (b) Identification and discrimination of patterns of sounds in proper sequence

    (c) Identification and discrimination or reproduction of a sequential pattern by touch

  (4) Distortion of body image (the awareness of the parts of the body in relation to one's self, to others, and to space)

  (5) Visual and motor incoordination

  (6) Disturbed spatial, size, sequence, temporal relationships

  (7) Motor disinhibition—"drivenness"

  (8) Left-right confusion. Mixed lateral dominance

  (9) Perseveration (need to respond alike to different stimuli)

 (10) Language disabilities

 (11) Deficient conceptualization—difficulty in abstract thinking, and therefore

 (12) Need for concreteness. Difficulty in reasoning.

This list of components contributing to the dysfunctioning of the brain-injured child could be supplemented and extended but I feel that the above data are sufficiently significant for this discussion.

It is interesting to note that Dr. Silver (Silver and Hagin, 1960) found a number of the above-listed characteristics of brain-injured children in his group of reading disability cases: specifically, right-left confusion, visual-motor difficulty (Bender Gesalt), visual figure-background imperception (marble board), auditory imperception (matching sounds and particularly, blending), and body image distortion (Goodenough).

RELATION TO ARITHMETIC

What effect do these characteristics have on the learning needs of the brain-injured child, especially in regard to arithmetic? Although no scientific study has been undertaken, the majority of the parents whose children have struggled through the regular grades without the benefit of specialized training methods report that "his achievement in arithmetic is absolutely zero" or that "he has no number concepts." In contrast, some learning has been accomplished by the child in the language arts. It would be very helpful if the correlation between language and arithmetic disability in brain-injured children could be determined and diagnostic tools discovered to explain and predict failures in arithmetic. It seems to me that the predominance of certain of the above-listed characteristics over other characteristics may predetermine the specific difficulty in learning number concepts and processes.

We will not attempt to relate arithmetic difficulties to all of the symptoms mentioned above. However, if we consider certain ones, beginning with *spatial relationships*, we can see the tremendous obstacles which arise. Basic concepts usually acquired at the preschool level can be implanted only through specialized training. "Up," "down," "over," "under," "top," "bottom," "high," "low," "near," "far," "front," "back," "beginning," "end," etc., either can not be discriminated or are as confused as left-right orientation. These difficulties are distorting, in the language area, by producing the inversion-reversal tendencies in reading and writing. They show many similar effects in the numerical area, such as in acquiring the concept of quantities, perceiving configurations of number patterns, seeing relationships between numbers, and also in reading and writing number symbols. As Strauss and Lethinen (1947) point out: "Disturbed spatial perception leads to the inability to perceive the relative distances between numbers, e.g., is 3 closer to 4 or to 6?" Such difficulties interfere with the visualization of the entire number system.

SIZE RELATIONSHIPS, such as "big," "small," "long," "short," ("concrete"—geometric), "more," "less," ("abstract"—numerical), are not well established in the child's mind and basic concepts cannot be acquired, even if concrete material is used for teaching. If the child cannot differentiate and grade sizes, quantities, and measurements, we cannot expect him to get abstract number concepts. *Perception of sequences* (first—next—last) is essential for awareness, retention, and recall of the succession of numbers. *Temporal relationships*, which are related to spatial relationships (after, before, between, next, etc.), are fundamental links toward the acquisition of the basic processes of addition and subtraction, and, again, the structure of the number system with its relative position of numbers (units, tens, hundreds, etc.).

MOTOR DISINHIBITION—"drivenness"—interferes with the brain-injured child's ability to coordinate and integrate his visual, auditory, and motor activity. Such a child will not be able to count objects properly by pointing at the respective objects in the order in which they are arranged and, at the same time, say the respective number to be associated with the particular item. For example, if buttons are arranged in a row, it cannot be taken for granted that the child can determine the "beginning" of the row (spatial-temporal disorientation) and if he does point to one item at a time, he is apt to rush through the number names, or while he is saying, "one," "two," he may have arrived at the fourth item with his pointing finger. The child we have described has the verbal ability, however, to say the numbers in their proper sequence.

LEFT-RIGHT CONFUSION. The difficulty in left-right discrimination is frequently an essential factor underlying disorientation in regard to number sequences.

PERSEVERATION. The brain-injured child's difficulty in mentally shifting from one response to another according to different requirements in the learning situation, often results in what seems to be a purely mechanical performance, devoid of any thinking effort. However, this is not so. There is a mechanism at work which does produce the pseudo-robot response. However, if it is recognized for what it is, remedial measures can be most effective.

The perseverative trend is noticeable at many levels in learning the arithmetical processes, such as addition, subtraction, multiplication, and division. If one process alone is taught and practiced for any length of time, the transfer to another process is extremely difficult and constitutes a real mental hardship for the child. The same difficulty arises if objects are to be counted in one direction and numbers written in another, i.e., one horizontally and the other vertically. Similar difficulty is seen at a higher level if addition or subtraction or multiplication or division problems are presented in different directional ways or with different symbols, such as ÷ or ⌐ for division.

Although the processes themselves may be mastered by the child, they may not be recognized for what they are. We often encounter this problem in connection with counting coins of different denominations. The child may have mastered the skill of counting the dimes, nickels, pennies, or quarters in each respective unit group but the shift from counting one group of only dimes to another group of only nickels is a major problem, as is the task of counting a quantity of coins of mixed denominations. We will not go into a lengthy discussion of this problem relative to other arithmetical concepts and processes but many examples could be cited of the child's difficulty in all areas of mathematics.

DIFFICULTY WITH LANGUAGE SYMBOLS. Language disabilities may occur in the brain-injured child in the receptive or expressive area or in both. But even if we consider the child who has no particular language disturbance, we must admit that his mental apparatus must become geared and adapted to the special language of arithmetic, which is a symbolic, coded language with its own peculiar stenographic-like shortcuts, abbreviations, and telegraphic-like style. In the teaching of arithmetic to the nonhandicapped child, it is recognized that success or failure will depend to a large extent upon the wording used in teaching the numerical concepts and processes. How much more so does language constitute the foundation upon which comprehension and mastery of arithmetic skills are to be built by the brain-injured child! First of all, "casual" language must never be used because of the brain-injured child's deficient ability to focus visually and/or auditorily. Second, the child's receptive language capacity is often inadequate in regard to symbols. Third, the child's ability to express himself accurately and to the point, with "mathematically correct" answers, is limited.

Many brain-injured children have an excellent verbal memory which may be helpful in memorizing number facts by rote. However, this is not an index of the child's ability to comprehend or of his capacity for expressive language in relation to number concepts and processes. For those children who do not have a good verbal memory, however, or who may even be specifically handicapped in this respect, the need to recall the symbolic language of numbers presents great obstacles, especially in oral work. Even the most elementary mathematical vocabulary is a "foreign language" to these children. This is meant not only in the sense that the terms have foreign roots (plus, minus, etc.), but that the entire structure of the number system may present the child with his first encounter with the world of abstractions. This brings us to the next point in this discussion, difficulty in abstract thinking.

DIFFICULTY IN ABSTRACT THINKING. Many of the brain-injured children have perceptual difficulties, as we have seen. Since concepts normally grow out of percepts in the development of thinking processes, it is not surprising that we have to deal with difficulties in conceptualization in these children. Many of them show erratic features in thinking,—lack of continuity, farfetched reasoning, difficulty in seeing cause-effect relationships.

Numbers are of a much more abstract nature than most words. Common nouns and verbs ("basic words") can be immediately related to concrete presentations. Numbers cannot—without employing learned concepts related to spatial and sequential factors and to the process of counting. The often-prevalent difficulty in brain-injured children in abstract thinking and their lack of organizational ability lead to tremendous difficulties in problem solving in arithmetic. This difficulty is simultaneously related to language (reading and comprehension) and to reasoning, which is a function of abstract thinking.

SOME REMEDIAL MEASURES

Here again we do not propose to give illustrations of educationally therapeutic methods for all of the specific disabilities in arithmetic as outlined above, but rather a few of the techniques which we have found helpful in working with our brain-injured pupils. Moreover, we will not attempt to rigidly delineate the examples of remedial work as related to the specific arithmetical learning difficulties, since each child's special needs must be met with flexibility and fluidity while, at the same time, he must be provided with a well-rounded arithmetic program. Basically, I would like to state that it is of remedial value to mobilize, employ, and train *all avenues of mental functioning*. For the brain-injured child who has difficulty in focusing his attention and a deficiency in foreground-background differentiation, it is essential to find devices to overcome these barriers. Any cue is good which helps either to establish a concept or a skill or to provide reinforcement. *Concreteness* is necessary. *Color, tactile, visual, auditory* techniques are all helpful.

Form boards, pegboards, blocks in graded sizes, geometric forms—all are useful in establishing spatial, temporal and size relationships, sequences, left-right discrimination, and the writing of number symbols. Basic counting and even counting by two's, by five's, etc., become meaningful and enjoyable through rhythm, clapping and tapping (motor-auditory cues). Touching and circumscribing forms and sizes with a finger are helpful. Color is readily perceived by most brain-injured children and the use of crayons or chalk in different colors is an effective aid in teaching the differentiation of rows and such concepts as "beginning of the row," "end," "next row"; "first," "last," and "middle of the page." It is also helpful to have the children learn to "form a row" versus "walk in single file" for demonstration of lateral, vertical directions (first, last, before, after, next to, between, etc.). All of these concepts contribute to the child's perceiving the world around him in a more organized fashion.

Concepts of "uptown," "downtown," the rise and fall of temperature (comprehension of the directional factor inherent in subtraction by addition), are also some of the stumbling blocks which these children encounter. Here again, concreteness, color, emphasis upon making the child aware of the inter-relatedness and inter-changeability of certain concepts (e.g., up more $= =$ rise), are of value. "Concreteness" is brought about by presenting the child with the actual material (a thermometer), by drawings (streets, avenues), and by having the child perform with his own body ("Up," "Down," "Face uptown," "Face downtown," etc.), which relates to his body-image concepts. In connection with the body image, it is important to stress that many a brain-injured child has great difficulty in differentiating, perceiving the relationships in position, and making appropriate use of, his ten fingers. The *finger scheme* must be trained intensively. The use of the fingers for counting and computing must be encouraged. As a matter of fact, the finger scheme is, in a way, our native structure of the number system and one which the child can always rely upon. It embodies order, organization, unchanging position of its parts to each other and to the whole, reliability, concreteness,—all the elements from which the complex number system emerges later on.

Another point in regard to spatial-size relationships is interesting. Although disability in this area (longer—shorter, bigger—smaller, higher—lower, etc.) is frequently encountered, it seems to present less of a problem than the equivalent concepts of "more and less." However, if we compare these sets of concepts, we note that spatial and size concepts have more of a concrete quality than the purely numerical concepts of "more and less," specifically "less." Ascending to more advanced levels, it might be expected that geometry would be easier for these children than algebra. This is questionable, however, because the need for spatial perception becomes much more complex in geometry. However, at an intermediate level, it is our experience that graphic representations (lineal, bar graphs, scale drawings) are more meaningful and can be produced with greater facility by many brain-injured children than the corresponding tables of numerical values. By the same token, concepts of savings and deficits are more readily comprehended through graphic representation. Therefore, for remedial purposes, it is advisable to *express numerical values graphically* as far as possible.

DISINHIBITION—"DRIVENNESS"—with its resulting effects on the arithmetic process (omissions, combinations, etc.) can be overcome by structuralizing the number sequence, combinations, or whatever arithmetical fundamentals are being taught. *Motor involvement is therapeutic*; it exerts an inhibiting effect. Therefore placing sticks, beads, toothpicks, or what-have-you, into different boxes which have labels with the respective number symbols is a helpful device. Different boxes may also be used to make the fundamental processes of addition and subtraction more meaningful. Referring to our previous remarks on the use of all possible avenues for learning, we find it helpful to employ *auditory associative links* to form number concepts. This also serves to counteract the child's tendency to "rush through" and name numbers without pointing properly. If one or more knocks or taps are given with each item, the auditory perception will prolong the act of saying the respective numbers and will set each count off as a distinct unit. Rhythmic counting, "singing the number," also re-enforces sequences and concept development. The visual perception of number configurations can be greatly helped through color cues, and through concrete representation of configurational patterns by various items like coins, beads, etc., and by dominoes and other devices. Reproductions of these patterns by the child and *kinesthetic reenforcement* by touching the patterns with the eyes closed are also therapeutic.

PERSEVERATIVE TRENDS MUST BE RECOGNIZED. Preventive or remedial measures will be successful only if flexibility in approach and variations in materials and methods of presentation are maintained. Counting of coins of *different denominations in one group* must be stressed rather than counting of *different groups with like denominations*. The interrelationship and interchangeability of fundamental processes (addition—subtraction; multiplication—division) must continuously be demonstrated and examples presented in an unpredictable, irregular fashion. Even the writing or printing of the examples (laterally or vertically) must be changed frequently and different symbols used, such as, "divided by" ($\div$) and "into" ($\lceil$) in order to train the child's ability to shift mentally from one activity to another and to teach him to recognize fundamental likenesses as well as differences.

LANGUAGE AND REASONING. Perhaps the most fundamental educational therapy that is required in teaching arithmetic to the brain-injured child is in the area of language and reasoning. Stress must be laid on both *receptive and expressive oral language*. The instructor's language in teaching arithmetic must be simple, precise, and slowly graded from terms related to the child's every-day life and the world around him to the higher, more abstract, symbolic terminology of mathematics. We cannot take it for granted that brain-injured children understand us when we talk in the usual language patterns of mathematics. It is extremely difficult for many of these children to understand the verbal instructions, "Count these chairs," or "Draw five chairs," or such questions as, "How many chairs are in this room?" or "How many balls are in this picture?"

First of all, we must check ourselves frequently to make sure that our instructions or questions are clearly formulated and are not ambiguous. In order to answer "how many," the child must have acquired the knowledge that counting must be the first step, and have the ability to count objects with assuredness, and he must know that "the last number in his counting" will be the answer. Many children cannot carry out the simple instruction, "Draw five chairs," not because they cannot draw and not because they cannot count, but because one little word is missing. If we tell the child, "Draw *up* to five chairs," he has no problem. Why? Because, by the little word "up" we have broken down the instructions (regardless of whether they are given verbally or printed) into steps. He now knows that he must *count*, that he will get *up* to number five, and that once he gets there, he must *stop*. Without this device he would go on drawing chairs indefinitely. With this little crutch of one extra word, he will understand that *counting* and "*how many*" are related.

As previously stated, *more* and *less* present great obstacles. A young child is accustomed to the word and the concept of "more"—and it also has a gratifying emotional connotation—but he rarely hears or applies the word "less." It is often helpful at a certain stage to substitute "*not so many as*" for "less," as a step toward the goal. In this sense, "*fewer*" is also a difficult word and it can be conceived and properly applied only through a great deal of practice in relating all such words to the child's environment. The *concept of zero* is, as we know, one of the most difficult ones to comprehend in mathematics. Instead of adding or subtracting the meaningless, abstract, symbolic "o," we can make the process perfectly meaningful to these children by using the words, "nothing else."

Encouraging the child to "talk" in arithmetical terms is of great remedial value. We can ascertain if the child comprehends only by having him express in his own words the significance of a number concept or process. The less symbolic the language that the child employs, the more convincing it is that he understands the principle. If he can say that he wants to find out how many groups of nine jacks (in a row) *make* (not *"are"*) 18 jacks, rather than use the expression "9 into 18," we can be reasonably sure that the concept of division is understood. In order to work toward automatic responses, *reinforcement through auditory cues* is also desirable. In other words, verbal repetition of the example and answer is extremely important. Some children show a specific difficulty in auditory recall and will need special training in auditory perception.

As to *problem solving* in arithmetic, reading ability is required, of course, at a certain level but even before adequate reading skills are acquired and for those children who have specific reading difficulties, numerical problems in words must be presented. And no matter how elementary or how complex the problem may be, the child must be taught to analyze the problem and this requires reasoning ability. But by breaking the problem down into basic questions which are to be answered by the child, one by one, and by having him draw illustrations or graphically represent the problem, one can attain very satisfactory results.

REMEDIAL ARITHMETIC MATERIALS. Specific arithmetic material which is of tremendous remedial significance is the Montessori material and Catherine Stern's *Structural Arithmetic* (1949; 1954). Catherine Stern, who designed her material for normal healthy children has at the same time done a tremendous service to brain-injured children. Her nonconventional approach to number concepts by measuring rather than by counting has all the seeds for helping out children to grow up with a sound, sure, reliable foundation in number concepts and processes. The brain-injured child who is fortunate enough to take his first steps into the world of numbers with Catherine Stern's *Structural Arithmetic* enjoys and benefits from his work in arithmetic more than the child who is taught with the traditional material and technique.

References

Silver, A. A., and Hagin, R., Specific reading disability: Delineation of the syndrome and relationship to cerebral dominance, *Comprehen. Psychiat.*, 1960, 1(2), 126-134.

Strauss, A. A., and Lehtinen, L. E., *Psychopathology and education of the brain-injured child* (New York: Grune & Stratton, 1947).

Stern, Catherine, *Children discover arithmetic: An introduction to structural arithmetic* (New York: Harper & Row, 1949).

Stern, Catherine, *Structural arithmetic*. Course 1: *Experimenting with numbers and discovering arithmetic*; Course 2: *Discovering arithmetic*, Levels I, II, III, with kit of classroom materials, pupil's workbook, teacher's edition of pupil's workbook, and manuals (Boston: Houghton Mifflin, 1954).

40 METHODS AND MATERIALS FOR TEACHING WORD PERCEPTION IN CORRECTIVE AND REMEDIAL CLASSES

Lillian G. Fletcher～

Regardless of what one includes in the definition of "reading," the process must begin with the identification of words or the association of a printed symbol with an idea. Many individuals in remedial classes, especially in the elementary grades, have failed to acquire adequate skill in word perception and, therefore, cannot read efficiently.

Three basic methods have been developed for teaching words, and most instruction in this area utilizes some adaptations, variations, or combinations of these three techniques.

SIGHT METHODS

In the sight method the word to be taught is presented on a card and pronounced. The pupil then repeats the word while looking at it. He may close his eyes and try to visualize it or cover the word and write it from memory, then compare to see if he is right. When he thinks he knows it, the new word is placed with other familiar words and reviewed. As a follow-up, new words are used in teacher-made stories and sentences for the student to read aloud. The final test is the pupil's ability to recognize the words in new context.

When choosing words to be taught by a sight method, the tutor must keep in mind that the ultimate goal is to obtain meaning from the printed page. Many sets of word cards are available, but a child who is practically a nonreader will find these large sets extremely discouraging. Therefore, it is often better to make cards introducing only a few words at each lesson and choosing those which the pupil can put together to make sentences. His

Reprinted from H. M. Robinson, ed., *Sequential Development of Reading Abilities*, SEM, Vol. 22, No. 90 (Chicago: University of Chicago Press, 1960), pp. 46-50.

own dictated stories may help in determining which words to teach and will insure that they will be within his comprehension. As the fund of sight words increases the instructor may influence the choice of words to develop vocabulary necessary for reading some simple story. Careful selection will help keep the task within reasonable limits for the disabled reader and thus enable him to experience success.

The presentation of a printed set of word cards is less devastating for a pupil after he has acquired a fairly good sight vocabulary and had successful experiences with words. Some teachers have found it helpful to use a check list of the words in the set. After an initial test both teacher and pupil know how many words remain to be learned and can proceed with unfamiliar ones. In a few weeks (interval is dependent upon pupil's ability) a recheck will show gains made and words which need more attention. This definite evidence of progress is gratifying to the student and better than vague praise.

Although acquiring sight vocabulary is usually associated with beginning stages of reading, it is not limited to that period. As the student improves in reading he learns new ways of attacking unfamiliar words, but it is inefficient to sound out a word each time it appears or to resort to use of context. Therefore, those words which are missed frequently or which must be sounded repeatedly should be noted and taught as sight words. Word cards, often made by the student himself, should include the meaning, an illustrative sentence, and the pronunciation on the reverse side. Review may be provided in sentences and stories composed by the teacher.

At every step in teaching reading it is necessary to stress meaning. We cannot assume that a child understands a word just because he can recognize and pronounce it. In beginning reading the words used are those common in the speaking vocabulary of the average six-year-old child. But, as he advances, concepts arise which may be foreign to his experience. This is especially true of the person needing remedial work. He may confuse words which are similar in sound, or may know one meaning but not the one which fits the context. It is imperative to ask repeatedly, "What does it mean?" "Does the word have a different meaning in this sentence?" and the like. As students become sensitive to variations in meaning they are less likely to skip over the words which are not clear to them.

KINESTHETIC METHOD

Another method for teaching word recognition is kinesthetic tracing. The word to be taught is presented to the child in blackboard-size script and is pronounced for him. The pupil then pronounces the word slowly as he traces it with his first or second two fingers. He does not say the letter names, nor does he sound out letters individually. When he thinks he knows the word, the copy is removed and he writes the word from memory saying it slowly as he writes. The entire word is obliterated if he makes a mistake and he returns to the original copy to retrace. He never patches up a portion of the word; he learns it as a whole. When a word has been learned, the child uses it in his story and the large copy is filed in an alphabetical file box. If he should need it again, it can be brought out for review. As the individual improves he will need to trace less often and gradually will reach the point where he can learn the word by watching the teacher write it while pronouncing it slowly. Still later he will remember a word presented in printed form and pronounced for him. There is no clear-cut division between these stages, but growth in ability is gradual. Even after he has generally given up tracing, he may need to revert to it for an especially difficult word. Eventually he will also gain the ability to recognize new words from similarity to words which he had already learned.

When Fernald's (1943) method is followed, there is little difficulty with comprehension, for the words learned are those chosen by the student for stories which he is writing. Therefore, the words are those which are already in his speaking vocabulary. Attention must then be given to enlarging the speaking vocabulary and knowledge of words heard. When the pupil begins reading from books, more emphasis will be needed on word meanings.

PHONETIC APPROACH

Although English is not a strictly phonetic language, it is possible to work out a large proportion of the words by using sounds. Therefore, this is one of the important remedial techniques for teaching word recognition. It would be impossible in a report of this length to describe all the systems for teaching phonics, so this section is limited to some of the general principles and techniques which have been helpful in remedial work.

Some authorities recommend that phonics should not be introduced until the child has acquired a small sight vocabulary so that he can develop the sounds of the letters from words which he knows. While this is generally true, there are some children who have such extreme difficulty in learning words by other methods that they could never accumulate the number of words necessary to begin a study of sounds. In such cases instruction may begin with the slow development of individual consonant sounds through ear training, and pictures, until a few letters are mastered. A short vowel is then introduced and combined with the consonants to form simple words. Learning to blend sounds is likely to be extremely difficult and may necessitate repeated demonstration of the technique by the teacher before the process is grasped. In order to provide practice in reading the words in meaningful context, the teacher will probably have to make up his own sentences and very simple stories using the words the pupil can sound from the elements he has learned and the few nonphonetic sight words which have been taught. Reading will be slow by this method but is preferable to no reading at all. Such a pupil may eventually be able to recognize some words at sight after sounding them repeatedly, but he relies upon knowledge of sounds to prompt his memory.

Fortunately most of the retarded readers are not as handicapped as those just mentioned. They learn phonics to work out new words independently but combine this with other methods almost immediately. For example, as soon as some consonant sounds have been learned most pupils can be taught to substitute these in familiar words to make new words. In this way they can make *book, cook, hook, took,* and *shook* from *look* as soon as they have learned the necessary consonants. Such a method greatly increases a pupil's sight vocabulary. This may appear to be the old "family" method but differs from it in that substitutions are made at the beginning, end, or middle of the word. It requires the development of ear training so that the learner can discriminate between words which are quite similar in sound such as *bad* and *bat, set* and *sat, bet* and *pet.*

Use of sounds can also assist in the discrimination between words which are so similar in form that they cause confusion. For example, knowing the sound of the letter *s* may help to eliminate errors on *was* and *saw.* If the word begins with the *s,* it must begin with the *s* sound. If the child is confused regarding *house* and *horse,* he can remember that *horse* has the *r* letter and sound. In a similar manner he can learn to differentiate between *now* and *how, house* and *home, these* and *those,* and others.

Combining phonetic and contextual clues can also be started as soon as a few sounds have been taught. The pupil may know that the word refers to the father in the story but not know whether it is *father* or *daddy.* The initial sound will help him to decide. The carry-over of phonics to the practical reading situation cannot be left to chance. The teacher must help the student to use sounds whenever possible until the application of the principles he has learned becomes habitual.

When skill has been acquired in using the easier word-attack techniques, instruction is necessary in identifying prefixes, suffixes, root words, compound words, and syllables. Too many teachers rely entirely upon having children look up words in the dictionary. But this is hardly practical as those who are having difficulty will seldom take the time to do it when they are reading independently. Therefore, it is necessary to provide them with a few simple rules which they can remember easily and apply when necessary.

Publishers have made available an excellent supply of material for teaching word-attack skills. Most basic reading series include a built-in system of phonics in the texts and accompanying workbooks. These are suitable for remedial work if the child has not already used them. In addition there are numerous workbooks especially for phonics which may be used to supplement the usual texts. In remedial work we frequently use several different workbooks selecting appropriate lessons from each. Results will be most effective if the instructor is thoroughly familiar with the entire process for developing competence in word attack. This enables him to determine a student's specific area of weakness and choose suitable materials for correcting it.

COMBINING THE METHODS

Although the methods for teaching word recognition have been described separately an efficient teacher seldom uses one to the exclusion of all others. It is desirable that the disabled reader have the experience of reading something independently as soon as possible. Therefore, if he can learn by a sight method, he begins with it. But in order to achieve mature reading habits he must be able to unlock unfamiliar words without assistance, so he is gradually helped to improve auditory discrimination and perception and knowledge of phonics. Soon he learns to apply phonic principles to help him remember the sight words. When words are particularly difficult, he may resort to tracing. The instructor helps the student build on his strengths for rapid success but at the same time slowly builds up the weak aptitudes in order to establish a firm foundation in reading skill. Teaching is most effective when the best of all methods are used in combinations suited to the particular needs of the individual being taught.

References

Fernald, Grace, *Remedial techniques in the basic school subjects*, Part II (New York: McGraw-Hill, 1943).

41 NEUROLOGICAL APPROACH TO
READING PROBLEMS

Sister St. Francis Campbell, S.N.D. de N.

In the history of medicine, many heresies later become accepted doctrines. One can find volumes written on the educational methodology and evaluation programs for the seemingly ever increasing number of children with mental retardation due to brain injuries at birth or a lack of neurological functioning afterwards. A new approach, not so much of analysis but of therapy has been made by a team of men, whose theory is based in part on a theory of rehabilitation set down a generation ago by the late Philadelphia neurosurgeon Dr. Temple Fay. It is highly controversial and extends to all areas of human skill controlled by the brain. Let us begin with the unique and provocative book, *The Treatment and Prevention of Reading Problems*, by Carl Delacato in which he stresses a wholistic approach to the problems of language (1959). The whole human organism operates as a single unit physiologically, psychologically, and intellectually. Peripheral activity or peripheral modalities such as vision, dexterity, phonetics, and various reading techniques are meaningless in remediation if the total neurological organization is defective.

The prerequisite to peripheral therapy is central neurological organization. Previous studies dating from Rutherford in 1909, who felt that reading disability was the result of a differentiation within the germ plasm and was genetic in nature; and Rauschburg, who felt that it was a lack of a constant blood supply to the language area of the brain; to Orton in 1928, who felt that the answer lay not in structure but in function, indicate clearly a long recognition of the neurological implications in language difficulties. Dr. Delacato discusses as important factors in retarded reading such sub-

Reprinted from *The Catholic Educational Review*, Vol. 43, No. 1 (January, 1965), pp. 28-34. By permission of the author and publisher.

jects as sleep patterns, tonality, handedness, visual control, musical ability, footedness, dominance, carbon dioxide retention, fluid levels, and reflex serialization. Before defining the definite scope of this paper, it may be well to note that the theories and practices of Carl Delacato and his associates, Robert Doman, Edward Le Winn, and Glenn Doman of the Institute for the Achievement of Human Potential, located near Philadelphia, are not only not accepted but are regarded with outright skepticism by their colleagues in the field of rehabilitation. This was brought before the general public when Joseph P. Kennedy, father of the late President John F. Kennedy, entered the Institute where ten other in-patients, victims of stroke, were also receiving treatment (Clark, 1964). The Institute treats all manner of brain injuries from strokes, damages at birth, to complex or simple lack of neurological development.

The area of this paper of necessity will need to be limited. We will attempt to discuss the basis of the Institute for the Achievement of Human Potential's theory, together with related key concepts of sleep patterns, handedness, eye dominance and control, and crawling patterns as they relate to the whole and are used in therapy for both severely brain-injured children or adults, and in treating normal children who have reading problems. The rationale is the same, but the procedure easier to put into effect for the latter.

THEORY OF NEUROLOGICAL REEDUCATION

Neurological organization may be defined as that physiological optimum condition which exists uniquely and most completely in man and is the result of a total and uninterrupted ontogenetic neural development. Man's neurological organization and development recapitulates the phylogenetic development of the nervous system. The basic cortical difference between man and slightly lower forms of animals is not a difference in cellular acquisition or cellular quantity, but is in a great part a difference in cellular organization and function. The newest cells phylogenetically are those which, in part, give man the difference, with which this article is concerned, which he has from lower forms of animals, that is, language. These cells are in instances of trauma the most vulnerable cells that man has acquired. These same cells therefore, being the newest and the most complex, are also the most vulnerable to developmental interference. Trauma usually results in aphasia, that is, communication distortion.

The evaluation of slight cortical dysfunction or trauma is very difficult, and the evaluation of neurological disorganization even more so. Data indicate that language is controlled at a cortical level with the dominant side controlling the skill facets, and the subdominant hemisphere the tonal facets of language. In neurological studies we have always found that for the most part, disturbances of the language function result from lesions in the major or dominant hemisphere of the cerebrum, that is, the left hemisphere of right-handed persons, and the right hemisphere of left-handed persons (Grinker and Bucy, 1951). Occasionally, an extensive lesion of the proper area of the left hemisphere of an apparently right-handed person will not result in aphasia. In such cases, detailed examinations and careful inquiry into the patient's history and that of his family will elicit that one in reality is dealing with a left-handed person who, through early training, has changed handedness. In any case, the hemisphere which controls handedness, expression, and comprehension is known as the dominant hemisphere. Unilaterality is considered as a key factor and the most dynamic aspect of neurological development.

Human beings develop neurologically in a vertical pattern through the spinal cord. Man's physical abilities, the theory holds, proceed through four main stages of development governed at four levels of the brain. The infant's simplest movements in the short period following birth are governed at the level of the medulla and the spinal cord; the ability to crawl comes later, along with the development of the next higher brain center, the pons. At approximately nine months neurological development extends to the level of the midbrain. In terms of mobility this is typified by "cross-pattern" creeping. This orderly progression of mylenization moves on the cortex at about one year of age when walking begins. The walking pattern is gradually refined until about the age of three or four, it too becomes "cross-patterned." The final lateral progression, called cortical hemispheric dominance, takes place at the level of the cortex and is the process of making one cortical hemisphere dominant over the other. When the dominant-subdominant relationship is achieved the organism is complete and the problems of communication theoretically overcome. According to this theory then, a brain injury at the midbrain level would block the development between this level and the cortical level, and with the human skills involved. To circumvent such blocks, certain patterns are advocated such as creeping in cross-pattern form. Beginning with the lowest levels of organization to the highest let us examine briefly the rehabilitation therapy used in severe cases, or what is termed neurological re-education in retarded readers.

SLEEPING, CREEPING, AND READING

The lowest level is that of a sleep pattern. Theories concerning sleep are without number, especially in the area of childhood sleep. Historically, mothers have put their babies to sleep with the tops of their heads gently pushed into a pillow because they tend to seek this position and it seemingly enables them to sleep better and longer. Close observations have revealed that infants tend to assume amphibian level serialized postural reflexes prenatally, and postnatally for both rest and reaction. The aspect of this pattern that particularly interests us is that of the tonic neck reflex which is the asymmetrical attitude underlying most of his postural behavior in the early weeks of life. The tonic neck reflex is a combination of averted head, extended arm, and reflexed arm which dominates the waking life of the infant for some twelve weeks. This tonic neck reflex position serves to channelize the pathways of visual attention during the waking hours of the child. Now it is believed that the tonic neck reflex is still present and operative in the person who sleeps prone, and is considered a vital factor in neurological organization.

In analyzing neurological organization, one can readily understand the relationship of body position in sleep to total neurological organization. Even at its most superficial level, the cutaneous innervation, particularly in a quadruped position, displays a magnificent order. It is felt that only with a proper posturalization basis can the organism achieve the more complex neuromuscular unity and organization required by cortical control. This unity is prerequisite to skilled cortically controlled sensory motor functions which operate in a serialized pattern and affect the whole person, particularly his development of efficiency of communication. Proper posturalization in the prone position, and also the supine position but reversed, is as follows: (1) the eyes looking toward the subdominant hand, (2) the arm and leg flexed on the side which the person is facing, (3) the opposite (dominant) arm and leg extended, (4) the hand near the mouth (subdominant) palm down with the thumb pointing to the mouth, (5) the extended hand (dominant) palm up and near the hip. A group of forty-five retarded readers showed universally either a total lack of posturalization during sleep, or had a faulty sleep pattern, while good readers, beyond the area of chance, sleep with a definite pattern to favor total laterality.

The next level is that characterized by cross-pattern creeping. Retarded readers do cross-pattern creeping in a smooth serialized pattern both at home and as a part of the physical education program at school. Seriously brain-injured patients lie prone while one therapist turns his head, another flexes the arm and leg on one side, and a third extends the limbs on the opposite side to reinforce a crawling pattern. A routine such as this might be carried out for five-minute periods about four times a day until the patient is ready for the next higher stage of movement, that of creeping.

UNILATERALITY AND READING

The early acquisition of a dominant hand inclines the rest of the organism towards the establishment of proper visual dominance. Investigations have proven that when the dominant or controlling eye is on the side opposite that of the handedness, the motor initiation is poor, and difficulties in speech, reading, and writing ensue. Furthermore, these difficulties can be relieved by shifting the control of the binocular pattern to the side of the handedness. Five hundred patients with and without symptoms of reading difficulty, defects of speech, and allied visual-motor disorganization were investigated to prove this hypothesis beyond the operation of chance. Other

studies carried through by experimentalists in the field of reading retardation have also found more ambidexterity among retarded readers than
among good readers, more than could be ascribed to chance (Smith, 1950).
Neither left- nor right-handedness is preferable; the objective is to establish
unilaterality, be it left or right. Through training children may be taught to
be unilateral, by not being allowed to use the subdominant hand except as
an assistive measure. Children in an experimental program, ranging in age
from three to five with speech problems, made significant progress by literally putting their subdominant arm in a sling for several weeks. Problems
may be prevented early in life by helping the child to find and develop his
proper dominance. Both sides should be given equal chance to become
dominant until some preference for one side is evidenced naturally. When
a choice does appear naturally, every effort should be made to help the
child to keep that side as exclusively unilateral as possible. The preferred
hand may and should be encouraged in early toys, games, and skills as
crayoning and puzzle play.

The eye which controls the visual pattern is known as the predominant eye. It is ascertained first by sighting, both near and far; secondly, eye
control is determined through the telebinocular; and, lastly, the determining function is ascertained by finding which eye reads better, and the way
the head tilts and rotates when writing. The purpose in evaluating the
child's vision is to learn more about the eye-brain relationship which will
give us more data as to which cortical hemisphere is dominant. The sighting eye, the controlling eye, and the most efficient eye in reading, both in
terms of time and errors, should fall on the dominant side. Therapeutic
measures to establish this laterality if it is not present consists in occluding
the eye which should be subdominant, so that the other one which should
be dominant may become more efficient. This is not so much to be considered as a change over of vision, but as a peripheral activity designed and
aimed to unify the visual pattern with the rest of the scheme of neurological functions. The most recent and effective tool in developing the
predominant eye is the Stereo-Reader.[1] It is a small and inexpensive instrument that may be used both for home or school training.

When neurological organization is complete through all levels to total
unilaterality the problems of retarded readers begin to vanish. Once neurological organization has been achieved, reading methods are secondary.
Through basically the same program, severe brain-damaged patients may
be helped through training the healthy brain areas to assume control over
such motor and sensory skills as walking and speaking when the cells normally in control have been destroyed by strokes or other injuries.

The Archdiocese of Chicago School System has adapted the theories
of Delacato, Doman, and associates for its corrective reading program. The

---

[1] This instrument is manufactured and distributed by the Keystone View Company,
Meadville, Pennsylvania.

neurological organization and laterality of children in remedial groups is determined by simple methods designed for use by classroom teachers and parents. Instructions are given parents on a child's proper sleeping position as well as on how to carry out exercises in cross-pattern creeping and walking.

CONCLUSION

From what has been reported above, it is hoped that readers may have acquired some information on the neurological theory for helping retarded readers. If neurological reeducation can improve poor readers, is it not likely that used with good readers it may make them better readers? If through preventive activity with the very young and reeducative activity with those whose patterns are wrongly set children and adults alike can be taught neurological unity, good students may become even better ones, good language pupils more fluent, good spellers better, and facile speakers even more facile by the same methods and techniques.

The human organism is a unique and complex unit. Perfection of its operation may be achieved through many means. It seems that the only truly effective approach to the full realization of the potential bestowed on humans by Almighty God must be interdisciplinary. Educators should be alert to the contributions being made to the solutions of their problems by the medical profession and sincerely appreciative of them.

References

Clark, Matthew, Pattern of recovery? *Newsweek*, May 4, 1964.
Delacato, Carl H., *The treatment and prevention of reading problems* (Springfield, Illinois: Charles C Thomas, 1959).
Grinker, Roy R., and Bucy, Paul C., *Neurology* (Springfield, Illinois: Charles C Thomas, 1951).
Smith, Linda, A study of laterality characteristics of retarded readers and reading achievers, *J. exp. Educ.*, June, 1950, *18*, 321-9.

42 CLINICAL EDUCATION PROCEDURES
IN THE TREATMENT OF LEARNING
DISABILITIES

Edward C. Frierson~

Many children have learning disabilities which seem to prevent their acquiring the skills, knowledge and understandings normally being taught at school. The disabilities may be primarily affective, cognitive, sensory, or experiential. However, disabilities are never exclusive, affecting one dimension of the child and no other. An often forgotten fact is that dimensions of the human personality have been arbitrarily imagined, differentiated, labeled, researched, and described. To consider emotion, cognition, and sensory stimulation as separate facets of a compartmentalized organism is useful, but not necessarily truthful.

Schools can relieve much of the frustration created by children who do not learn well but many schools may not. Homes can relieve a great deal of the frustration associated with learning problems, but unfortunately, many homes may compound existing frustrations. Clinical education programs may relieve many of the frustrations of parents, educators, and specialists, but clinical programs do not yet exist in sufficient numbers.

The purpose of this paper is (1) to analyze the unique role of clinical education procedures; (2) to describe certain clinical education procedures in the teaching of reading; and (3) to suggest guidelines for increasing the effectiveness of clinical education programs. The area of reading is emphasized because reading continues to be the cornerstone skill upon which academic survival is based.

THE UNIQUE ROLE OF CLINICAL EDUCATION

The term "clinical education" is used to convey the notion of educational procedures which are based upon a thorough clinical evaluation of the

Distinguished Lecture, Midwest Orthoptic Conference, University of Missouri, May 2, 1966. By permission of the author.

child. Such education may or may not be conducted in a traditional clinic setting. Clinical education rests upon the availability of diverse diagnostic information. Sometimes this information can be accumulated in a center which actually houses representatives of many disciplines. On the other hand, a loose confederation of disciplines, housed in separate facilities, may effectively supply the information needed if systematic coordination is practiced.

The role of clinical education is that of service and leadership. By providing service to regular education programs in an exemplary way, the clinical education program provides leadership in developing, testing, and demonstrating new teaching procedures. The clinical approach is particularly suited for innovation, specificity, and individualization. New ideas for specific problems in particular individuals must be developed continually if the clinical approach is to have a maximum impact upon the regular program.

Clinical education must differ from regular education if the investment in an interdisciplinary approach is to be justified. The uniqueness of clinical education rests in its capacity to carry out educational treatments not always feasible in the regular program. However, the sound clinical approach provides models and patterns of teacher-student interactions which, if appropriately modified, would strengthen the regular program.

The difference between clinical education procedures and traditional procedures is that the former develops curricular experiences based upon clinical evidence from several disciplines. The traditional school program is determined by normative data, achievement test data, group ability test data, and local custom. That is, the children in the typical fourth grade are taught from fourth-grade readers, are expected to exceed grade level on achievement tests, are grouped by ability test scores which sample approximately thirty minutes of restricted behavior, and are kept with age group peers as is the custom.

The clinical approach finds children striving to accomplish tasks slightly more difficult than those already mastered regardless of level. The clinical approach measures growth in terms of individual gain on measures of specific skills. Students are grouped for instruction in terms of clinically measured abilities and are removed from chronological age groupings whenever such groups lead to distorted or unhealthy self concepts.

SELECTING MATERIALS FOR CLINICAL EDUCATION

In many cases, the materials used in the clinical approach are similar to those available to the regular classroom teacher. Material selection for clinical teaching, however, is based upon a thorough familiarity with those differences in materials which are directly related to strengths and weaknesses in individual learners. The traditional classroom generally uses materials which are thought to be best suited for the majority of the class members. It is no surprise that some reading disability can be traced directly to early training experiences which were good for the majority of the class but inappropriate for a particular individual.

The clinical educator must know the differences that make a difference in reading approaches. It is altogether likely that the clinical approach will selectively incorporate a combination of reading experiences drawn from several approaches. The combination will vary with each individual based upon a complete differential diagnosis. If a clinic approach is "packaged," it ceases to be a clinical approach!

A review of contemporary reading approaches will clarify the argument that no single approach is adequate for clinical teaching. Twelve identifiable approaches are presented in order to contrast the difference in the initial word recognition tasks involved and the general sequence which each suggests for progressing to the more complex skills of reading.

APPROACHES TO TEACHING READING

1. BASAL READERS. The basal reader is the backbone of American reading instruction, yet the basal series are not all the same. The vocabulary content is different, the rate of new word introduction is different, the amount of repetition is different, the stories are different, the linguistic patterns are different, the teacher guides are different, the supplementary exercises are different, the workbooks are different, the print is different, and in contrasting series, the rationale supporting the series is different. For the great majority of children, the differences are negligible. For the child with learning disabilities, the differences in print alone could be decisive.

The basal reader materials are excellent for teaching many skills. However, the clinical educator will be concerned about the conceptual as well as the perceptual characteristics of the series. The number of abstract words as well as the print and the illustrations will be matters of concern. The sequence and structuring of skills introduced will be as important as the cultural validity of the content. The basic vocabulary load will require varying degrees of visual memory ability, and must be considered against the phonic skills introduced which will require varying degrees of auditory integration ability.

Knowing that two children have been in basal reader programs will not assure the clinician that the children's experiences have been the same. The clinical educator must be aware of the differences between basal series.

2. LANGUAGE EXPERIENCE. The language experience approach to reading instruction has distinct advantages for the child with learning disabilities. The child begins the formal reading program with material having a high degree of interest and relevance. Daily lessons are developed in accord with the vocabulary and expressive patterns of the child. For the child who needs a high degree of structure and carefully sequenced skills presentation, the language experience approach is less appropriate.

The language experience approach is similar to the basal reader approach in that both attempt to provide the child with a sight vocabulary upon which to build other skills. Both approaches are initially more analytic than some other approaches. The clinical educator is aware of the inability which some children have in analyzing or seeing components. Thus the clinical educator does not endorse a language experience approach for all learning disability cases. It is more likely that the language experience approach would be employed with conceptually disabled children than with perceptually disabled children.

3. KINESTHETIC APPROACHES. A variation of the language experience approach is the reading by writing technique. Although popularized by Grace Fernald in the past thirty years, the method of tracing, copying and writing new words from memory must surely have been a part of many primary teachers' bag of tricks much earlier. Requiring a child to trace a new word until it seems that he "remembers" the way it is written adds a significant dimension to the teaching of reading. Most children do not have to write a word in order to recognize it when it is presented visually. Many children do not master the spelling of a word until they have written the word several times, however. The child with learning disabilities often benefits from a multimodality approach in which he speaks, writes, and hears as well as sees each new word to be learned.

There are several variations of the writing approach to reading. One process involves the steps of tracing, copying, writing from memory, and writing with eyes averted. Another procedure requires that the child trace each new word over and over until he thinks he can write the word accurately. Only when the word is written perfectly may another word be attempted. The writing approach may be used with a controlled vocabulary or with a language experience vacabulary.

The clinical educator adds other dimensions to the writing approach by employing tactile stimulation, temperature changes, and body exercise. Students might use sandpaper letters, draw letters in wet sand which is warmed or cooled and may trace letter forms with their feet or walk on balance boards having letter shapes.

4. ALPHABETIC METHOD. Rigid structure characterizes certain approaches to teaching reading. However, the structured approaches do not always emphasize the same aspect of reading. Among the most popular remedial approaches is the highly structured alphabetic method.

The alphabetic approach stresses the importance of visual-auditory, visual-kinesthetic, and auditory-kinesthetic association. The emphasis initially, however, is upon the two kinds of letters in the English alphabet—vowels and consonants. Children learn that consonants are sounded by blocking the flow of breath while vowels are sounded by shaping unobstructed air flowing through the throat and mouth. Consonants are presented on white cards while vowels are on salmon colored cards. Each letter has a key word associated with it.

Initially each letter of the alphabet is assigned only one sound. No exceptions are presented until mastery of many words is assured. Monosyllable words are presented as they can be built from letters which have been mastered. Silent *e* words, digraphs, *c* and *g* exceptions are not introduced until a secure foundation is established.

The difference between naming the letters in a word (spelling) and sounding the letters in a word (reading) is stressed from the beginning. The spelling-reading problem is overlooked by many other approaches. Breakdowns in reading and spelling are thought to be the result of irregular and conglomerate teaching. Although many children survive the inconsistency of much advice (look at the shape of the word . . . sound it out . . . what does the picture tell us? . . . etc.), the learning disability child is often confused.

5. PHONICS APPROACHES. The phonics approaches are relatively rigid in structure. Phonics training (learning to make sound-letter associations) is not to be confused with phonetics (the science of speech sounds). The most thorough organization of phonics involves the identification of the forty-four sounds common to the English language. These sounds range from the short *a* sound as in *apple* to the humming sound which occurs in the middle of the word *vision*.

A true phonics approach presents the English sounds systematically. Key words and regular examples are initially introduced with drill and supplementary exercises designed to reinforce the recognition of the sound being learned. Irregular spelling patterns are presented along with common spelling patterns so that inconsistencies are a part of the mastery process. For example, the letter combination *ough* as it appears in *tough* is introduced along with the letter combination *uff* as in *puff*. The *ph* sound as in *Phil* is included when the *f* sound is taught.

A phonics system can be presented in a primarily auditory fashion through records, tapes, or talking filmstrips. However, the teacher may establish a very supportive teaching environment using records and other materials only for independent drill.

A rigid phonics program has been suggested by some as the ultimate cure for all reading problems. Clinical teachers who deal with perceptual problems are aware of the high degree of cognitive integration which such an approach demands. Therefore, they know that some youngsters learn best in programs which deemphasize phonics.

6. PROGRAMMED READING—LINGUISTICS. Programmed reading approaches are also highly structured. Characteristically, programmed instruction is based upon the presentation of sequential tasks which have been broken down into logical units called frames. The student responds to each

frame and receives immediate feedback concerning his success. Good programs evoke practically no wrong responses because success in each frame is built upon previous correct responses.

The programmer of reading skills makes theoretical decisions which affect the content of the frames presented. One popular program proceeds from letter recognition to upper elementary grade reading difficulty in tasks which adhere to linguistic principles supplemented by story books, filmstrips, and programmed tests. The program is the same for all children. Only the rate varies as each child works independently. The learning disability child who has organizational problems but adequate perceptual skills may be helped significantly by such an approach.

7. PROGRAMMED READING—VISUAL DISCRIMINATION. Another programmed approach is based upon successive discrimination tasks. The frames in this program stimulate proficiency in several prereading skills requiring visual perception, discrimination, and integration. When one considers the slight difference between the words *there* and *these*, and the subtle discrimination which differentiates C from G, *dog* from *bog*, *mine* from *nine*, the value of a programmed discrimination approach is more clearly seen.

Most children have little difficulty identifying *b* and *h*, *P* and *R*, or *m* and *w*, whether they are presented singly or together. But the child with learning disabilities may confuse letters, reverse letters, substitute sounds or make other errors that discrimination training and visual tracking exercises might correct. For some, the successive discrimination approach would be boring, tedious, and needlessly extended. The clinical educator would use such an approach in selected cases based upon pertinent diagnostic information.

8. INITIAL TEACHING ALPHABET (I.T.A.). The use of an initial teaching alphabet is gaining wide approval as an aid to early reading instruction. The I.T.A. introduces one symbol for each sound in the English language. All of the traditional letters are used plus eighteen additional sound symbols. Once the child masters the I.T.A., he is able to pronounce accurately any word spelled with the symbols.

Two major obstructions to independent reading are removed. First, multiple spellings of the same sound are avoided. (The sound $\bar{a}$ is spelled over fifteen ways in traditional orthography including *eigh* as in *sleigh*.) Second, the word patterns are always the same since each symbol has only one form. (Many letters in traditional orthography have completely different capital forms which are unrelated to the lower case form.) Further, in traditional orthography, the same letter combination can have several pronunciations (*done, gone, one, bone*) while the I.T.A. spellings always correspond to the appropriate sounds which, if blended, will create the word.

The elimination of exceptions, "spelling demons," elaborate rules and confusing alternate letter forms makes the I.T.A. an unusually helpful addition to the clinical educator's resource pool. However, the child with auditory closure problems, auditory integration and auditory memory deficiencies will find the I.T.A. just as troublesome as traditional orthography in spite of its sound-symbol honesty.

9. RESPONSIVE ENVIRONMENT. A powerful new influence in all areas of learning is the operant conditioning approach, or, as it is described by some, the behavior shaping approach. There are many methods by which the operant or learner may be reinforced and thus have his behavior shaped. A rat or pigeon may learn if rewarded with food pellets. A child might modify his behavior for a gold star, a smile or a piece of bubble gum. Sometimes just knowing he is correct is rewarding enough to cause the learner to continue responding.

Computerized typewriters have enabled researchers to develop the responsive environment approach to reading. The learner in this approach "plays" with an electric typewriter. When he strikes a key, he sees the letter on a screen and a voice pronounces the letter. When combinations of letters are struck which make syllables or words, the computer can be programmed to say the word.

As the child becomes increasingly aware of the letter word combinations, he begins to store combinations in his memory. He begins to make approximations which are closer and closer to the ultimate goal of typing specific words upon command, reading specific words upon presentation, and spontaneously expressing ideas in written language.

The clinical educator incorporates mechanical devices and reward strategies in some learning disability cases. The regular class teacher cannot be as responsive to one child in a large class as the clinical educator whose response in a tutorial situation can be as immediate or as selective as the computer response. Knowing what to reinforce and how to reinforce is crucial. Haphazard responses can cause great confusion and retard progress toward reading.

The "talking typewriter" is a forerunner to techniques for teaching reading that are as yet not imagined. In some schools, computerized libraries, classroom and study centers have changed completely the process of acquiring information. Home stimulation through computerized instructional panels may bring individualized, clinically based teaching into every child's life.

10. LINGUISTICS. Linguists and psycholinguists, those who study language scientifically, have been concerned with the reading process for many years. In the true sense of the phrase, there is no linguistic approach. However, the clinical educator has much to learn from the findings and suggestions of the linguists.

Reading is merely substituting visual signs for the auditory signals associated with language signals, according to linguistic study. Therefore, reading is not to be conceived as a body of knowledge but rather as a process which requires ample opportunity for practice. Children who have already acquired language must simply practice using visual signs where they have automatically been using auditory signs.

The linguist is conscious of the patterns of language which must be mastered. Much of the typical reading instruction is disorganized linguistically. The structure of the language is unknown to many teachers who merely follow the isolated skills approach as outlined in the particular teaching manual the school has adopted.

An example from the teaching of spelling would illustrate the contrast between the structural and nonstructural approach. Nonstructural approaches to spelling (and reading) do not emphasize the patterns of language, but rather present new words selected for their appearance in a story, their supposed level of difficulty, or other functional purpose. Thus, rules and exceptions are learned quite apart from natural awareness of structural signals. Spelling lists often have no overall goal other than to introduce some words to be memorized. Twenty words per week becomes a magic number.

From a structural point of view, a spelling lesson emphasizing the patterns common to our written language might include the following:

man	mane	mean
ban	bane	bean
Dan	Dane	Dean

An upper elementary grade reading lesson might include a nonsense paragraph whose structure would reinforce the students' awareness of the common signals which our written language contains. Improved reading ensues as such signals key automatic responses.

11. WORDS IN COLOR. A very new weapon in the reading arsenal is color. Presenting words in color has the potential for changing completely the nature of the initial discrimination required for word recognition and for fluent reading. Letter combinations are relatively unimportant in a word color or color phonics approach. (One must insure, of course, that the learner is not color-blind!)

Essentially, the words in color materials assign a key color to each of the forty-four English language sounds. Charts are developed which present hundreds of words which are colored according to the way the word is pronounced rather than the way it is spelled. (E.g., the *ay* in *say* would be colored *red* since the long *a* sound is always red; also the *eigh* in *weigh* would be colored *red* for the same reason.)

Initially, children read and spell by color. A three letter word which also has three sounds such as *C A T* would be "spelled" orange-white-blue if these were the colors assigned to hard *c*, short *a*, and the consonant *t*. With the addition of the color clue, children identify words without having to memorize elaborate rules or having to depend upon visual memory or having to discriminate among confusing letters such as *n* and *h* or *t* and *f*.

There are real problems of word analysis and comprehension that are not resolved by adopting a color word approach. The clinical educator may find that a student has a color recognition threshold beyond which the introduction of new colors confuses rather than supports reading progress. Using color does not eliminate the problem of sequential skills introduction, nor does color automatically resolve problems of visual and auditory integration. Children who learn color sounds in isolation may have as much difficulty making words as do children who learn letter sounds in isolation.

Clearly the use of color in a systematic approach makes it possible for the clinical educator to treat selected learning disability cases in an experimental way. For some children, color may unlock the world of reading which were previously unavailable. It is equally clear from experimental find ings that the color word approach will prove confusing and unnecessarily cumbersome to many learners. The diagnostic findings are extremely important to the educator considering the use of such a system as part of the clinical education treatment.

12. THE REBUS—PICTURE SYMBOLS. The last approach to be considered is completely new. The approach is being experimentally tested in Chicago, Detroit and Nashville. Educators who deal with learning disability cases are particularly interested because nonreaders have responded remarkably well to the system. The approach is called a rebus or picture-word approach.

The rebus approach assigns a picture symbol to each word rather than to each sound as do other symbol systems. Nouns are relatively easy to depict and most youngsters know hundreds of these symbols on sight. Abstract words are the most difficult while verbs and adjectives pose problems peculiar to their usage. Families of symbols are readily learned: *in* = ▣; *on* = ▢; and *under* = ▢.

An important value of the rebus system is that written communication is possible upon one's first exposure to the symbols. No elaborate readiness seems necessary. In fact, the value of rebus as preparation for the typical reading program for all children is an important area to be explored.

In a recent test, trainable retardates were able to recognize enough symbols to make meaningful sentences after only ten minutes of training. A group of immature six-year-old children were able to read from a story book after a few weeks of training with the rebus followed by a transition to letter words. Present work with learning disability cases indicates that the advantage of experiencing success with rebus may outweigh the disadvantages of an approach which introduces a new symbol system. The relationship between rebus reading and the perceptual-conceptual abilities of children is being investigated.

INCREASING THE EFFECTIVENESS OF CLINICAL EDUCATION

The effectiveness of clinical education is directly related to diagnostic accuracy, thoroughness and significance. In the past, diagnostic workups often emphasized findings which had little educational relevance. As a result, educators tended to view clinical diagnoses with limited enthusiasm. Teachers complained that psychological reports did not tell them what to do with the child in the classroom.

The diagnostic information being sought today by the clinical educator may come from the neurologist, pediatrician, opthamologist, psychiatrist, psychologist or other specialist. Increasingly, however, these specialists will be asked to indicate the relevance of their findings along with the implications which these findings have for teaching the child. The educator must become more sophisticated in his grasp of the technical terminology of these disciplines which support his work.

The effectiveness of clinical education is also directly related to the teacher's selection of procedures which "fit" the diagnostic information available for each individual. No single remedial approach to learning disabilities can be best for all children.

The American public has an unenviable history of following "prophets" and climbing on bandwagons. In some cases, this has led to the creation of false hope and subsequent family disorganization when the method did not work for a particular individual. The most effective clinical education program must maintain an open, but objective, mind toward the prophets and the bandwagons in education.

Finally, the effectiveness of clinical education ultimately depends upon the empirical validity of the procedures adopted. Too often diagnosis and recommendations are divorced from treatment. The diagnostician seldom learns whether his suggested treatment produced the anticipated changes. The value of suggested treatments is not always demonstrated empirically. Changes in performance are assumed to be related to the educational procedures used with little recognition given to the influence of maturation, parental attitudes, measurement errors and social-emotional factors.

The clinical education approach will become more effective as evidence is accumulated which demonstrates the particular teaching procedures that are most appropriate for children having specific learning disabilities. Such evidence must be gathered by educators who are willing to subject their procedures to objective evaluation while not treating children as "subjects."

Behavioral scientists and educators must continuously view education as applied science rather than as a wholly intuitive art. Yet clinical education will be strongest if the children being served are considered first to be children having distinctly human needs and not merely broken-down learning machines whose needs can be met by following a service manual.

Each lesson presented to a child is an opportunity to test the null hypothesis that no significant differences in learning will occur. When the null hypothesis cannot be rejected after extended use of certain procedures, new methods must be used.

SUMMARY

Clinical education is viewed as an approach to curriculum which is based upon a thorough diagnostic evaluation of a child's specific learning abilities and disabilities. The question of what a child can do is as important as what he cannot do. Further, clinical education is based upon a thorough understanding of the differences in procedures and materials used to teach basic skills such as reading. Therefore, it is essential that clinical educators be familiar with many reading approaches, twelve of which are described in this paper.

The effectiveness of the clinical education approach to learning disabilities rests upon (1) thorough diagnosis; (2) sound selection of teaching procedures; and (3) objective measurement of success. It is imperative that many disciplines contribute to the fulfillment of the goal that each child be helped to realize his full potential.

GLOSSARY: TERMS ASSOCIATED WITH LEARNING DISABILITIES

Patricia M. Staffen and Edward C. Frierson

acalculia: loss of ability to perform mathematical functions
   dyscalculia: disturbance or impairment in the ability to do simple arithmetic
agitographia: a writing disability characterized by very rapid writing movements and the omission or distortion of letters, words, or parts of words
agnosia: cannot identify familiar objects through a particular sense organ
   auditory agnosia (nonverbal): cannot recognize the ring of the telephone
   auditory-verbal agnosia: can hear what is said, but cannot comprehend the meaning
   color agnosia: cannot name and sort colors
   geometric-form agnosia: cannot make correct-form discrimination
   picture agnosia: cannot perceive pictures correctly
   tactile agnosia: cannot recognize objects by touch
   tactile-verbal agnosia: cannot trace a word or read braille
   visual or optic agnosia: cannot recognize objects, persons, or places by sight
agrammalogia: inability to recall the structure of sentences. Same as *agrammatism*
agraphia: inability to recall the kinesthetic patterns that go into writing, i.e., cannot relate the mental images of words to the motor movements necessary for writing them.
alexia: loss of ability to receive, associate and understand visual language symbols as referents to real objects and experiences, i.e., a severe reading disability usually considered the byproduct of brain dysfunction
amnesia: lack or loss of memory. With some individuals the deficiency may be intermittent and person will remember things at one time but not another (amnesic reaction)
amusia: loss of ability to produce or to comprehend musical sounds
anarthria: loss of ability to form words accurately due to brain lesion or damage to peripheral nerves which carry impulses to the articulatory muscles
   dysarthria: partial impairment in the above
angular gyrus: area of the brain (left hemisphere) which governs some speech functions

anoxia: deficiency or lack of oxygen

aphasia: loss of ability to comprehend, manipulate or express words in speech, writing or signs. Usually associated with injury or disease in brain centers controlling such processes

> *auditory aphasia:* cannot comprehend spoken words. Same as word deafness and receptive aphasia

> *expressive aphasia:* cannot remember the pattern of movements required to speak words even though one knows what he wants to say

> *formulation aphasis:* cannot properly formulate sentences. Confusion occurs in relationships and tenses rather than in words themselves (e.g., Betty give I flowers)

> *nominal aphasia:* cannot recall the names of objects

> *paraphasia:* substitution of inappropriate words which maintain a structural relationship to words replaced. When parts of words are substituted the result is garbled speech. Severe paraphasia is sometimes called jargon aphasia

apraxia: loss of ability to perform purposeful movements

astereognosis: a form of agnosia. Cannot recognize objects or conceive of their forms by touching or feeling them

asymbolia: loss of ability to use or understand symbols, such as those used in mathematics, chemistry, music, etc.

auding: listening, recognizing, and interpreting spoken language. Not merely hearing and responding to sounds

auditory discrimination: ability to identify and accurately choose between sounds of different frequency (pitch), intensity (volume) and pattern. Includes the ability to distinguish one speech sound from another

auditory imperception: failure to understand oral verbal communication and failure to understand the significance of familiar sounds

auditory perception: ability to receive and understand sounds and their meaning

body image: awareness of ones' own body (conscious mental picture or subconscious knowledge of one's position in space and time). Includes the impressions one receives from internal signals as well as feedback resulting from contact with others. How one thinks he looks is referred to as *body concept*

brain damage: any structural injury or insult to the brain, whether by surgery, accident, or disease

central nervous system: the brain and the spinal cord. Referred to as C.N.S. by some authors

choreiform movements: spasmodic or jerky movements which occur quite irregularly and arhythmically in different muscles. Characteristically these movements are sudden and of short duration distinguishing them clearly from slow tonic athetoid movements

closure: the process of achieving completion in behavior or mental act. The tendency to stabilize, close, or complete a situation

cognitive style: an individual's characteristic approach to problem solving and cognitive tasks (e.g., Some persons tend to be analytical, seeing parts, while others tend to be wholistic, seeing things in their entirety with little awareness of components)

compulsiveness: insistance on performing or doing things in habitual ways

concretism: an approach to thinking and behavior in which a person tends to approach each situation as a unique one and is situation bound. Such a person does not see essential similarities between situations which normal persons would accept as similar or even identical

discrimination: the process of detecting differences

auditory discrimination: sometimes referred to as ear training, involves identifying sounds with respect to their likelinesses and differences

visual discrimination: discriminating between different objects, forms, and/or letter symbols

disinhibition: the removal of a conditioned inhibition. (In classical studies an animal might be inhibited from making normal responses to food. Retraining would remove the inhibition.) Educators link the term closely with impulsivity. Many use the term to mean lack of ability to restrain oneself from responding to distracting stimuli. Thus, a child may pursue his impulse to look out the window, go to another child, vocalize, run to the door, and many others, in spite of the situation or circumstances. In other words, he would not inhibit these responses from within

dissociation: the inability to see things as a whole, as a unity, or as a gestalt. The tendency to respond to a stimulus in terms of parts or segments; also difficulty in bringing two or more parts together into a relationship to complete a whole

distractibility: the tendency for one's attention to be easily drawn to extraneous stimuli or to focus on minor details with a lack of attention to major aspects. Often used synonomously with short attention span although the latter suggests an inability to concentrate on one thing for very long even without distractors

dysdiadochokinesis: inability to perform repetitive movements such as tapping with the finger

dysgraphia: partial inability to express ideas by means of writing or written symbols. Usually associated with brain dysfunction

dyskinesia: partial impairment of voluntary movement abilities, resulting in incomplete movements, poor coordination and apparently clumsy behavior

dyslalia: refers to speech impairment due to defects in the organs of speech. Not the same as slovenly speech

dyslexia: partial inability to read, or to understand what one reads silently or aloud. Condition is usually, but not always, associated with brain impairment. (Some authors refer to genetic dyslexia, affective dyslexia, experiential dyslexia, congenital dyslexia, etc.)

dysnomia: the condition when an individual knows the word he is trying to recall, recognizes it when said for him, but cannot recall it at will

echolalia or echophrasia: apparently uncontrollable response characterized by repeating a word or sentence just spoken by another person

electroencephalograph: an instrument for graphically recording electrical currents developed in the cerebral cortex during brain functioning; often abbreviated EEG

emotional blocking: inability to think or make satisfactory responses due to excessive emotion, usually related to fear

emotional lability: the tendency toward cyclic emotional behavior characterized by sudden unexplainable shifts from one emotion to another

etiology: the study of causes and origins, especially of a disease

Gerstmann's Syndrome: a combination of disabilities including finger agnosia, right-left disorientation, acalculia and agraphia

gestalt: term used to express any unified whole whose properties cannot be derived by adding the parts and their relationships. The something which is more than the sum of its parts (e.g. wheelbarrow is more than just a wheel + handles + basket)

hemianopia: the condition where one has only one half of the field of vision in one or both eyes

hemispherical dominance: refers to the fact that one cerebral hemisphere generally leads the other in control of body movement, resulting in the preferred use of left or right (laterality)

hyperactivity: excessive activity—the individual seems to have a surplus of energy

hyperkinesis: excessive mobility or motor restlessness sometimes referred to as driveness

hypoactivity: pronounced absence of physical activity

hypokinesis: diminished motor function or activity often appearing as listlessness

idioglossia: the phenomenon of "invented language" caused by the omission, substitution, distortion, and transposition of speech sounds. Same as *idiolalia*

imperception: lack of ability to interpret sensory information correctly. A cognitive impairment rather than a sensory impairment

impulsiveness: the tendency to act on impulse. Responding without thinking which is often explosive behavior where disorders exist

inhibitions: The restriction of specific activity usually related to mental condition although the restraint appears to exist in the environment

kinesthesis: the sense that informs one of movements of the body or of its several members

kinesthetic: pertaining to the sense by which muscular motion, position, or weight are perceived

kinesthetic method: a method of treating reading disability by having pupils trace the outline of words or in other ways systemically incorporate muscle movement to supplement visual and auditory stimuli

laterality: sidedness; the tendency to use either the right or left side of the body, especially in tasks requiring only one hand, one eye, or one foot

maturational lag: the concept of differential development of areas of the brain and of personality which mature according to recognized patterns longitudinally. A lag signifies irregularity in this pattern without a structural defect, deficiency, or loss

memory span: the number of related or unrelated items that can be recalled immediately after presentation

mixed cerebral dominance: the theory that language disorders may be due wholly or partly to the fact that one cerebral hemisphere does not consistently lead the other in the control of bodily movement (i.e., hemispheric dominence has not been adequately established)

negativism: extreme opposition and resistance to suggestions or advice. Normally observed in late infancy

neurological examination: an examination of sensory or motor responses, especially of the reflexes, to determine whether there are localized impairments of the nervous system

neurology: the discipline which studies the structure and function of the nervous system

organicity: refers to central nervous system impairment

perception: the interpretation of sensory information. The mechanism by which the intellect recognizes and makes sense out of sensory stimulation. The accurate mental association of present stimuli with memories of past experiences

> *perception of position in space:* the accurate interpretation of an object as being behind, before, above, below, or to the side
>
> *perception of spatial relationships:* comprehending the position of two or more objects in relation to oneself and in relation to each other
>
> *perceptual constancy:* the accurate interpretation of objects as being the same in spite of their being sensed in various ways (i.e., being turned, partially concealed etc.)
>
> *figure-ground perception:* the accurate selection from the mass of incoming stimuli, which should be the center of attention. These selected stimuli form the figure in the person's perceptual field, while the majority of stimuli form a dimly perceived ground. The figure is that part of the field of perception that is the center of the observer's attention. A disturbance in figure-ground may result because the individual confuses figure and background, reverses them, or is unable to see any difference between figure and ground

perseveration: continuing to behave or respond in a certain way when it is no longer appropriate (e.g. repetition of a word several times before going on, continuing a movement such as letter writing even at the end of a line, bringing up an idea over and over)

pneumoencephalogram: a medical diagnostic procedure which involves taking an electroencephalogram after injecting air or gas into the ventricular spaces of the brain

proprioceptor: an organ which is sensitive to the position and movement of the body and its members; such organs are found in the vestibule of the inner ear, the nearby semicircular canals, and in the muscles, tendons, and joints

psychoneurology: a term suggested to designate the area of study that concerns itself with the behavioral disorders associated with brain dysfunctions in human beings

reauditorization: the ability to recall the name or sounds of visual symbols (letters). Some individuals remember what letters look like but not which sound they make

rigidity: maintaining an attitude or behavioral set when such a set is no longer appropriate

specific language disability: usually the term is applied to those who have found it very difficult to learn to read and spell, but who are otherwise intelligent, and usually learn arithmetic more readily. More recently any language deficit, oral, visual or auditory is referred to with this term

strephosymbolia: twisted symbols—a reversal of symbols observed in the reading and writing performance of children with learning disabilities (e.g., was for saw)

AUTHOR INDEX

495